Nomads as Agents of Cultural Change

Perspectives on the Global Past

Jerry H. Bentley and Anand A. Yang
SERIES EDITORS

Interactions: Transregional Perspectives on World History
Edited by Jerry H. Bentley, Renate Bridenthal, and Anand A. Yang

Contact and Exchange in the Ancient World
Edited by Victor H. Mair

Seascapes: Maritime Histories, Littoral Cultures, and Transoceanic Exchanges
Edited by Jerry H. Bentley, Renate Bridenthal, and Kären Wigen

Anthropology's Global Histories: The Ethnographic Frontier in German New Guinea, 1870–1935
Rainer F. Buschmann

Creating the New Man: From Enlightenment Ideals to Socialist Realities
Yinghong Cheng

Glamour in the Pacific: Cultural Internationalism and Race Politics in the Women's Pan-Pacific
Fiona Paisley

The Qing Opening to the Ocean: Chinese Maritime Policies, 1684–1757
Gang Zhao

Nomads as Agents of Cultural Change: The Mongols and Their Eurasian Predecessors
Edited by Reuven Amitai and Michal Biran

Nomads as Agents of Cultural Change

The Mongols and Their Eurasian Predecessors

Edited by Reuven Amitai and Michal Biran

University of Hawai'i Press
Honolulu

Printed in the United States of America

20 19 18 17 16 15   6 5 4 3 2 1

Library of Congress Cataloging-in-Publication Data

Nomads as agents of cultural change : the Mongols and their Eurasian predecessors / edited by Reuven Amitai and Michal Biran.
pages cm — (Perspectives on the global past)
Includes bibliographical references and index.
ISBN 978-0-8248-3978-9 (cloth : alk. paper) 1. Mongols—History. 2. Nomads—Eurasia—History. 3. Eurasia—History. I. Amitai, Reuven, editor of compilation. II. Biran, Michal, editor of compilation. III. Series: Perspectives on the global past.
DS19. N653 2015
305.9'06918095—dc23

2014012570

University of Hawai'i Press books are printed on acid-free paper and meet the guidelines for permanence and durability of the Council on Library Resources.

Composition by Westchester Publishing Services.
Printed by Sheridan Books, Inc.

Contents

Acknowledgments

The present volume has benefited enormously from the support of the Institute of Advanced Studies at the Hebrew University in Jerusalem, which hosted the 2006 conference on Eurasian nomads that underpins this volume and provided a variety of technical and financial assistance to us in its preparation. We are also grateful to the Israel Science Foundation for helping to fund the conference and for providing us with significant support for our work over the past few years, including the writing of our chapters and other tasks involved in editing the volume.

Our colleague Professor Gideon Shelach-Lavi has been a key collaborator throughout and helped us with the editing of certain chapters, for which we are very grateful. It is a pleasant task to express our appreciation and thanks to Dr. Leigh Chipman and Mr. Avi Aronsky, who assisted with language editing, and to our students Or Amir, Ishayah Landa, and Yang Qiao, who helped with technical matters, not least in preparing the bibliography. We are grateful to all of our contributors for their goodwill, forbearance, and cooperation throughout the preparation of this volume.

Notes on Dates and Transliterations

1. Dates are generally given according to the Gregorian calendar. *Hijrī* and Chinese dates are given only when they have a special relevance in a particular article. When both *hijrī* and Gregorian dates are given, the *hijrī* comes first, followed by a slash and the Gregorian date. In Persian books, occasionally the *shamsī* year is given: if so, this is marked before the Gregorian date, and followed by the abbreviation S. and a slash.
2. Chinese names and terms have been transliterated according to the Pinyin system.
3. Arabic words, titles, and names have been transliterated according to the system used in the *International Journal of Middle Eastern Studies.* Words and names of Persian origin have usually been transliterated as if they were Arabic (e.g., Juwaynī, not Juvaynī; nāmah, not nāme). Common words and place-names, such as sultan, mamluk, Bukhara, Baghdad, are written without diacritical points. Well-known place-names are given in their accepted English forms (e.g., Jerusalem, Damascus).
4. Russian has been transliterated according to the system of the Library of Congress.
5. Names and terms of Mongolian origin have been transliterated according to Antoine Mostaert's scheme as modified by F. W. Cleaves, except for these deviations: č is rendered as ch; š as sh; γ as gh; and ǰ as j.

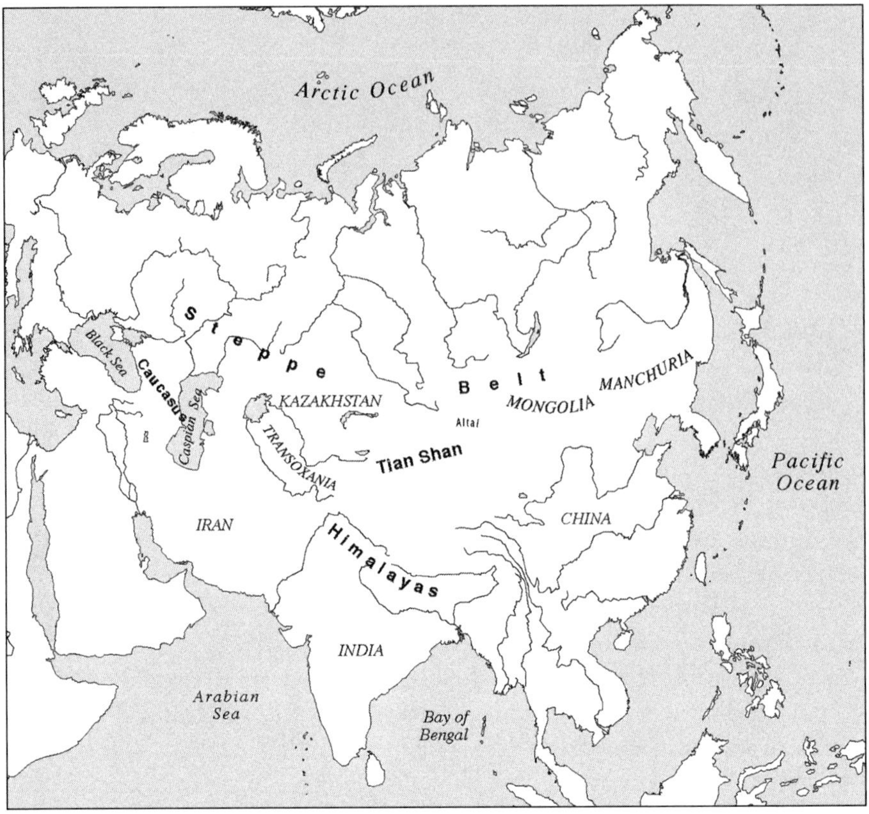

Figure 1.1. Eurasia. Adapted from R. Amitai and M. Biran (eds.), *Mongols, Turks and Others: Eurasian Nomads and the Outside World* (Leiden, 2005).

ONE

Introduction
Nomadic Culture

Michal Biran

When looking at the global past, one of the reoccurring phenomena from the late second millennium BCE and up to the eighteenth century CE is the political and military power of pastoral nomads on the fringes of the Eurasian civilizations, and—notably under the Mongol empire (thirteenth–fourteenth centuries)—at their hearts as well. The nomads' impact in the cultural field, however, is much less apparent. Representatives of the sedentary civilizations bordering the steppe—whether Chinese, ancient Iranian, Muslim, medieval Slavs, or other Europeans—often portrayed them either as a violent force that left no mark on their culture or as a source of negative influence that was responsible for "all that went wrong" with their civilizations.[1] If the nomads received some credit, it was for the *pax* that was created when they ruled over vast lands, allegedly enabling the sedentary civilizations to exchange goods, ideas, and technologies from one end of Eurasia to the other.[2] Some of these approaches arose as early as the mid-nineteenth century, after the final demise of the nomads' political power, and coincided with the rise of colonialism and nationalism, which often portrayed the nomads as either an empire's primitive subjects or as the past enemies of a certain nation-state.[3]

Recent research, first and foremost due to the works of our colleague and contributor Tom Allsen, has presented a much more complex picture of the relations between nomads and the societies over which they ruled or to which they were contemporaries. Concentrating on the Mongols, the largest and most documented nomadic empire—with which a large part of the chapters included in this volume also deals—Allsen showed that the nomads significantly contributed to cross-cultural exchange, not only as a passive medium who transferred elements from one sedentary civilization to another, but as active participants, who initiated much of the intercultural exchange and whose norms and priorities had been the filter and catalyst that determined which cultural elements would be transmitted along Eurasia. Moreover, Allsen demonstrated that the nomads played a dominant role not only with regard to practical domains, such as trade and military technology, but also in spheres connected with high culture (e.g., science, art, historiography).[4] This argument is the point of departure for this volume.

Despite the barbarian image often created by sedentary peoples, and the almost total lack of nomadic literary production, it can be argued that a sophisticated nomadic culture exists, which has had an impressive continuity over both time and space.[5] This culture was mainly political, since political interests (sometimes backed by real or mostly fictitious kinship and ethnic ties) had been the main glue that held the nomads together, whether in the framework of tribes or in larger political units.[6] Nomadic political culture had both religious-ideological components and practical organizational means. Its main aim was to win the subjects' acceptance of a single legitimate political authority. This was especially required for legitimizing the formation and the continued existence of a supratribal unit such as a nomadic empire. Overall, the tribal level sufficed for conducting most aspects of the nomads' everyday life, including small-scale raiding into their neighbors' realms. A supratribal unit, therefore, usually developed as a result of a crisis—ecological, natural, or political (among the nomads or their sedentary neighbors)—and was thus temporary in nature. Its utility was therefore questioned on nearly a daily basis, and for its successful maintenance its ruler had to be able to assure his followers that it was worthwhile for them to stay with him, especially since they could easily decamp to greener pastures.[7]

The salient components of this Inner Asian political culture from the time of the Scythians and the Xiongnu onward included both religious-ideological aspects and practical means for governing an empire: the notion of the divine mandate to rule bestowed upon a chosen clan by the sky-heaven, or even of the divine origin of the clan; the notion of charisma—the Iranian *farnah,* the Turkic *qut,* and the Mongolian *suu,* the heavenly ordained good fortune and the aura connected with this fortune; a highly developed system of royal and administrative titles; royal symbolism, including color; elaborate status and rank distinctions and practices associated with dressing and decoration; special investiture and funeral ceremonies; sacred territories and cult centers; the notion of collective or joint sovereignty, according to which a state and its populace belong not to an individual ruler but to all members of a ruling clan, or an extended family, as their corporate property; and convocations composed of members of the ruling clan and other nobles and worthies. On the administrative side, nomadic political culture included a patrimonial mode of governance that implied the practice of redistribution; that is, the sharing out of the booty, tribute, and cultural wares extracted from subject populations, which was both a means of rewarding followers and, at the same time, a mechanism of cultural exchange; a partial overlapping of the administrative system with the military organization; the importance of the aristocracy as a political system; and the significance of laws.[8]

Such political culture supported different political entities established by people with similar economies, from the centralistic Yeke Monggol Ulus under Chinggis Khan and his immediate successors (1206–1260), through more decentralized empires such as the Turks (sixth–eighth centuries CE) or the Xiongnu (third century BCE–third century CE) and up to the much looser framework of several tribal confederations or "headless states" typical to Mongolia in the sixteenth and seventeenth centuries or to the Qipchaq tribes in the pre-Chinggisid period.[9]

This political culture had a significant religious component, since Heaven (the Turkic and Mongol "Tenggeri"), the supreme sky god of the steppe, was the one conferring the right to rule on earth on a single clan, and thereby became the focus of steppe ideology and the primary source of supratribal unity in the steppe world. Unlike the Chinese case, Tenggeri did not bestow his mandate on every generation; that is, the steppe world was often left without a unifying ruler, but even during the periods of disunion the notion of the mandate remained as "an ideology in reserve," ready to be revived if the creation of a supratribal empire were to be attempted again.[10]

The possession of the mandate from Tenggeri was confirmed by the ruler's success in battle on the one hand and by shamanic ceremonies on the other, and was reinforced by the ruler's control of the sacred territory (in the case of the Turks, Uighurs, and Mongols the Otüken Mountains near the Orkhon River in central Mongolia). The rulers, many of whom also enjoyed prestige due to an animal ancestor (wolf, deer, etc.) or even the virginal conception of an ancestor,[11] also had certain shamanic functions of their own, which enabled them to dismiss or eliminate shamans whenever they threatened their authority, though more often they used their services. The shamans' ability to foretell the future, cure illness, and chart the power of nature, using various kinds of divination and spiritual journeys, was highly important for nomadic rulers and commoners alike. The nomads' attitude toward religion, however, was inclusive; that is, practicing shamanism did not prevent them from adopting other religions (mainly Islam and Buddhism, but there were cases of Manichaeism, Judaism, and Christianity). Nomadic conversion was initiated either for spiritual reasons—especially since shamanism was mainly directed to specific goals and was not concerned with the afterlife—or for a variety of practical, largely political, ones, mainly as a unifying force or as a source for legitimation. These new religions did not necessarily replace shamanism (at least not in the short run), but merely supplemented it.[12]

The nomads also had a distinctive material culture, comprised especially of small, light, and precious artifacts that could be worn or carried along by themselves or on their horses. Gold, the color of the sun that stands for durability and authority, played a major role in this material culture, and golden objects, such as belt plaques, daggers, knives, horse equipment, often decorated with zoomorphic designs (known as the "animal style"), were among its most typical artifacts throughout history. Textile was another major component of the nomads' material culture. In the Mongol period gold-embroidered silk, used for prestigious clothes and royal tents and known in Europe as "Tatar cloth," gained in popularity from the Adriatic to the Pacific.[13] Certain artifacts characteristic of nomadic taste displayed an impressive continuity—thus we find gilded burial masks among the Scythians in eastern Europe in the fifth century BCE, among the Wusun in fifth-century CE Xinjiang, and among the Liao emperors in tenth–twelfth century CE Manchuria; and a cup made of a killed enemy's skull appears in the Scythian world, among the Xiongnu in Mongolia; the medieval Turkic-speaking nomads such as the Pechenegs; the imperial and postimperial Mongols; and even the Safawids in sixteenth-century Iran.[14]

Nomadic culture also had its own set of organizational tools, the most typical and long-lived among them being decimal military organization, first attested under the Xiongnu. The army was organized in decimal units of ten, one hundred, one thousand, and ten thousand. Since every nomad was a soldier, the military organization was actually an important means of social organization. Although up to the time of Chinggis Khan the decimal units were arranged along roughly tribal lines, their existence was an important mechanism of control that enabled the ruler to bypass and neutralize tribal cohesion and authority. The decimal organization was also useful for incorporating additional nomads (and even nonnomads) into the empire's army. The establishment of a royal guard, also attested from the Xiongnu onward, served the same functions and enabled the ruler to create a new elite, personally loyal to him.[15]

Nomadic culture included also a set of social norms and usages, such as the important role of warfare in everyday life, the high position of women, and the practice of hunting as a royal sport. On a more general level, while in the steppe most nomads were generalists, that is, every nomad was versed in variety of skills that allowed him to survive in the steppe, they shared a respect for knowledge and expertise in many different fields (from military technology to religious practice, trade, administration, wrestling, astronomy, or cooking). They were thus ready to employ such experts and willing to learn from them when the need arose. Their interest in gathering "second opinions" of such experts often advanced cross-cultural encounters.[16] Moreover, nomads' ability to adjust themselves to changing circumstances, whether due to the natural forces in the steppe or to the changing political circumstances, meant that they were ready to learn from various outsiders and borrow from other cultures, as long as these borrowings were useful for achieving their goals, which were mainly assuring their rule. This often resulted in an amalgamation of different methods of administration, legitimation concepts, religions, and languages, especially while nomads were ruling also over sedentary populations. Such appropriation is often described as "barbarian" assimilation into more elaborated sedentary culture or as a proof of the nonautarkic character of nomadic culture. Instead, this amalgamation could better be described as part and parcel of the Inner Asian mode of governance and is consistent with the multicultural outlook of Inner Asian nomads. They acknowledged the practical political gains of such selective appropriation of cultural elements to the consolidation and legitimation of their rule in their new environments, and it often resulted in institutional changes. Yet the nomads did not necessarily see such appropriation as a threat to their indigenous identity.[17]

Indeed, nomadic culture was hardly isolated—the nomads' inherent mobility and the fragility of the nomadic economy resulted in continuous contacts with contemporary sedentary neighbors or subjects. The nomads, especially when they became rulers of certain sedentary population and territories, often borrowed from their subjects' administrative means, technologies, and ideas, thereby creating a unique state culture that combined elements of their own culture and that of their sedentary subjects. In the case of the Mongol empire, the evolving imperial culture included not only Mongol and local components, but also elements from other regions that came under Mongol rule (i.e., Chinese, Muslim, and Mongol elements in both China and Iran). The Mongols' own norms, however, were the main filter that determined which elements of the other cultures would be appropriated. Thus, for example, medicine, astronomy, geography, and cartography were enthusiastically encouraged by Mongol rulers due to their compatibility with Mongol shamanism.[18] As the chapters of Allsen, Lane, and Rossabi in this volume demonstrate, nomadic rule encouraged cross-cultural encounters, and was often accompanied by cultural efflorescence, caused by the nomads and not despite their presence. At the same time, nomadic rule also meant the actual physical movement and mobilization of individuals and groups, and in their aftermath the movement of ideas, texts, and artifacts. Such movements, as seen in the chapters of Allsen, Biran, Amitai, Vásáry, and Honeychurch, were also major channels of cross-cultural ties and influence, even resulting at times in significant identity changes.[19] Embedded with political and social content, cultural differences or their fading often resulted in noteworthy ethnic changes, as shown by Biran and Allsen.

The impact of nomadic culture on other cultures was proportional to the nomads' political power and was especially apparent when nomads ruled considerable sedentary territories. Their influence on global history, however, went far beyond these periods of nomadic rule, because elements of nomadic culture were preserved not only in nomadic states but also in postnomadic states, of which there are two types. First, states established by nomads or seminomads who gave up nomadism as part of their empire-building project and yet retained many aspects of nomadic political culture (e.g., the Seljuks, Qing China, the Ottomans, Mughal India, Uzbek Central Asia, and—in a way—Mamluk Egypt and Syria). The second type includes states that were once ruled by nomads and retained part of their political culture or administrative devices even though their rulers were those who vanquished the nomads and often saw them as their bitter enemies (e.g., Ming China and Muscovite Russia). These postnomadic polities assured that nomadic forms remained influential in wide swaths of Eurasia up to the nineteenth century, and therefore had an important impact on world history. Since what the nomads transmitted was not their ethnic culture but their imperial one, which was originally composed of different cultural elements (as described above), it was easy for the adopting empires to ignore their debt to the nomads.[20]

Borrowing from the nomads included both practical and ideological components. Thus, for example, the Mongols' successors were quick to acknowledge the usefulness of certain Mongolian institutions, and the Mongol postal system was retained in China, Russia, and the Muslim world long after the Chinggisids lost their political force. As for ideological borrowing, the main example is the Chinggisid principle, according to which only descendants of the Great Khan were eligible for bearing the titles khan or qaghan/khaqan/qa'an, which denote the highest political office. Although manipulations of this principle began quite early, it remained valid in Inner Asia up to the eighteenth century, long after the dissolution of the Mongol empire. It was also adapted in Qing China, where it became one of the many facets of legitimation of the Manchu dynasty, and had certain influence even in Ming China, Muscovy, and among the non-Chinggisid Ottomans.[21] In fact, while preparing this book for publication, the editors decided that a comparative analysis of postnomadic empires would be a worthy endeavor for a future volume. Such comparison will be another important step for evaluating the nomadic contribution to world history.

The chapters in this volume discuss different cases and facets in which the nomads played a significant role as cultural brokers, namely individuals who live in a cultural environment that is in some aspects different from their own as well as those who actively or deliberately transfer or cause to transfer cultural contents to a different environment.[22] The first three chapters deal with nomads of the ancient world on both sides of the steppe. Shelach-Lavi stresses that nomad–sedentary interaction in the northern zone of China during the second and early first millennia BCE was only one of many complex interregional contacts that influenced both what later came to be known as China and the nomadic polities to its north. Honeychurch, based on recent archaeological findings, highlights the active role of the Xiongnu in the shaping of the famous Silk Road, often described as connecting China and Rome, while ignoring the nomadic middlemen. Khazanov reviews the formative period of nomadic political culture throughout his discussion of the Scythians and their neighbors in the Mediterranean and East European zones. Togan's chapter treats the early medieval Turks, and how they were named in Chinese sources, showing the impact of the Turks on the development of Chinese historiography and terminology.

All the other chapters deal with the Mongols as agents of cultural change. The first five concentrate on the Mongol empire, the age in which the nomads reached their height in terms of their influence on world history. Allsen reviews the Mongol policy of population movements and concludes that Mongol programs of deployment, displacement, and replacement generated substantial changes in population distributions and the primary identities of communities, settled and nomadic, across Eurasia—some intended and others, like the notable expansion of Islam under Mongol rule, completely unintended. Biran's chapter follows this line and analyzes the fate of the Kitans in China in the wake of the Mongol conquest. She shows how, due to Mongol policies, most of the Kitans lost their ethnic identity and were either assimilated in China or reduced into tribal units in the new nomadic polities that rose from the ashes of the Mongol empire, thereby highlighting Mongol influence not only on the sedentary world but also on that of the steppe. Rossabi shows that the arts flourished in Yuan China due to the Mongols' active encouragement and not despite their presence. Lane's intriguing contribution gives an impressive example of how the Mongol *ordu* (camp, mobile court) in Iran became the rearing ground for both Mongols and Persians who were brought up on Mongol imperial culture. Not all will fully agree with this chapter, but it will certainly be a touchstone for future discussion on Mongol–Iranian relations. Amitai treats the Mongol impact—cultural and otherwise—on Mamluk Syria, a region that was not conquered for long by the Mongols, but that bordered the Ilkhanate and was deeply influenced by the ongoing Mongol presence in the region. Vásáry depicts the long-term legacy of Mongol rule on the political culture of Muscovite

Russia, a region ruled by the Mongols for nearly three hundred years, stressing both practical and ideological borrowing. Morgan's contribution wraps up the book by summarizing the rise of cultural history in the historiography of the Mongol empire (and other nomadic groups) in the last decades, with emphasis on the important role that the Mongols played as patrons of the arts in Iran. The chapter highlights the enormous strides that the study of Inner Asian nomads in general and the Mongol empire in particular has made in the last two decades, which is the basis for the studies in this volume. Building on such solid base, it is hoped that this book will shed more light on the nomads' role as cultural brokers and highlight the impact of nomadic culture on Eurasian history.

Notes

1. e.g., C. Halperin, "Russia in the Mongol Empire in Comparative Perspective," *Harvard Journal of Asiatic Studies,* 43 (1983), p. 239; B. Lewis, "The Mongols, the Turks and Muslim Polity," in his *Islam in History* (2nd ed., Chicago, 1993), pp. 189–190; also A. Lewis, *Nomads and Crusades 1000–1368* (Bloomington, IN, 1988), pp. 166–193, who asserts that the rise of Europe was made possible because it had been spared the Mongol conquest.

2. e.g., D. Christian, "Inner Eurasia as a Unit of World History," *Journal of World History,* 5 (1994), pp. 182–183; A. Gunder Frank, *The Centrality of Central Asia* (Amsterdam, 1992), pp. 25–40; W. H. McNeill, *The Rise of the West* (Chicago, 1963), pp. 322–326; R. Tignor et al., *Worlds Together, World Apart: A History of the World from the Beginning of Humankind to the Present* (3rd ed., New York, 2011), pp. 401–407.

3. David Sneath, *The Headless State* (New York, 2007), pp. 65–92.

4. T. T. Allsen, *Culture and Conquest in Mongol Eurasia* (Cambridge, 2001), esp. pp. 189–211; T. T. Allsen, "'Ever Closer Encounters': The Appropriation of Culture and the Apportionment of Peoples in the Mongol Empire," *Journal of Early Modern History,* 1 (1997), pp. 2–23; T. T. Allsen, "Mongols as Vectors for Cultural Transmission," in *The Cambridge History of Inner Asia,* vol. 2: *The Chinggsid Age,* ed. N. Di Cosmo, A. J. Frank, and P. B. Golden (Cambridge, 2009), pp. 135–154.

5. See especially Khazanov's chapter in this volume.

6. For political interests as the main bond in tribal society (as opposed to kinship) see R. P. Lindner, "What Was a Nomadic Tribe," *Comparative Studies in Society and History,* 24 (1982), pp. 689–711; Sneath, *The Headless State,* passim.

7. J. Fletcher, "The Mongols: Ecological and Social Perspectives," *Harvard Journal of Asiatic Studies*, 46/1 (1986), pp. 11–50; N. Di Cosmo, *Ancient China and Its Enemies* (Cambridge, 2002), p. 169ff.; R. Amitai and M. Biran, "Introduction," in *Mongols, Turks and Others: Eurasian Nomads and the Sedentary World,* ed. R. Amitai and M. Biran (Leiden, 2005), p. 4.

8. See Khazanov's chapter in this volume; Sneath, *The Headless State,* esp. pp. 176–179, 181–204; P. B. Golden, "Imperial Ideology and the Sources of Political Unity amongst the Pre-Chinggisid Nomads of Western Eurasia," *Archivum Eurasiae Medii Aevi,* 2 (1982), pp. 37–77; T. T. Allsen, "Spiritual Geography and Political Legitimacy in the Eastern Steppe," in *Ideology and the Early State,* ed. H. Claessen and J. Oosten (Leiden, 1996), pp. 116–135. Also, e.g., T. T. Allsen, *Commodity and Exchange in the Mongol Empire: A Cultural*

History of Islamic Textiles (Cambridge, 1997); Di Cosmo, *Ancient China,* p. 189ff.; R. Sela, *Ritual and Authority in Central Asia: The Khan's Inauguration Ceremony* (Papers on Inner Asia, no. 37) (Bloomington, IN, 2003), pp. 1–65.

9. Sneath, *The Headless State,* pp. 179–180, 188ff.

10. N. Di Cosmo, "State Formation and Periodization in Inner Asian History," *Journal of World History,* 10 (1999), p. 20; M. Biran, *Chinggis Khan* (Oxford, 2007), p. 13.

11. C. I. Beckwith, *Empires of the Silk Road* (Princeton, 2009), pp. 2–12; M. R. Drompp, "The Lone Wolf in Inner Asia," *Journal of the American Oriental Society,* 131 (2011), pp. 515–526.

12. e.g., W. Heissig, *The Religions of Mongolia* (Berkeley and Los Angeles, 1980), esp. p. 11; A. Khazanov, "The Spread of World Religions in the Medieval Nomadic Societies of the Eurasian Steppes," in *Nomadic Diplomacy, Destruction and Religion from the Pacific to the Adriatic,* ed. M. Gervers and W. Schlepp, "Toronto Studies in Central and Inner Asia," 1 (Toronto, 1994), pp. 11–33.

13. e.g., Allsen, *Commodity and Exchange,* passim; idem, "Mongols as Vectors," p. 140; Di Cosmo, *Ancient China,* pp. 44–90; and see Shelach-Lavi's chapter in this volume.

14. e.g., D. O. Morgan, *Medieval Persia* (London, 1988), p. 115; for more examples and references see Khazanov's chapter in this volume.

15. Fletcher, "The Mongols," pp. 29–30; Biran, *Chinggis Khan,* p. 13; Beckwith, *Empires of the Silk Road,* pp. 12–28.

16. Allsen, "Ever Closer Encounters," pp. 4–6, 9; Allsen, *Mongol Imperialism,* pp. 116–143; Allsen, *Culture and Conquest,* pp. 83–176; M. Biran, "The Mongol Transformation: From the Steppe to Eurasian Empire," *Medieval Encounters,* 10/1–3 (2004), pp. 338–361; M. Biran, *The Empire of the Qara Khitai in Eurasian History: Between China and the Islamic World* (Cambridge, 2005), pp. 132–170; R. Amitai, "Hülegü and His Wise Men: Topos or Reality?" in *Politics, Patronage, and the Transmission of Knowledge in 13th–15th Century Tabriz,* ed. J. Pfeiffer, (Leiden, 2014), pp. 15–34.

17. See, e.g., M. Biran, "Kitan Migrations in Inner Asia 10th–14th Centuries," *Journal of Central Eurasian Studies,* 3 (2012), pp. 85–108.

18. Allsen, *Culture and Conquest,* pp. 203–204, 208.

19. See also M. Biran, "The Mongols and the Inter-Civilizational Exchange," in *The Cambridge History of the World,* vol. 5, ed. B. Z. Kedar and M. Wiesner-Hanks, forthcoming.

20. Allsen, *Culture and Conquest,* pp. 199–202; Biran, *Chinggis Khan,* pp. 26, 74–75.

21. Biran, *Chinggis Khan,* pp. 104–105; for a general evaluation of the legacy of Mongol statecraft see Biran, "The Mongol Transformation," pp. 358–361; and see e.g., R. D. McChesney, *Central Asia: Foundations of Change* (Princeton, 1996); D. Ostrowski, *Muscovy and the Mongols* (Cambridge, 1998); P. K. Crossley, *A Translucent Mirror: History and Identity in Qing Imperial Ideology* (Berkeley, 1999); B. F. Manz, "Mongol History Rewritten and Relived," *Revue des mondes musulmans et de la méditerranée* (2000), pp. 89–90; D. Robinson (ed.), *Culture, Courtiers and Competition: The Ming Court (1368–1644)* (Cambridge, MA, 2008); L. Balabanillar, *Imperial Identity in the Mughal Empire: Memory and Dynastic Politics in Early Modern South and Central Asia* (London, 2012).

22. For various definitions of cultural brokers see M. von der Höh, N. Jaspert, and J. Oesterle, "Court, Brokers and Brokerages in the Medieval Mediterranean," in *Cultural Brokers at Mediterranean Courts in the Middle Ages,* ed. M. von der Höh, N. Jaspert, and J. Oesterle (Paderborn, 2012), pp. 9–10.

Two

Steppe Land Interactions and Their Effects on Chinese Cultures during the Second and Early First Millennia BCE

Gideon Shelach-Lavi

Addressing the subject matter of this book, *Nomads as Agents of Cultural Change,* in the context of Chinese society of the second and early first millennia BCE is a tricky undertaking. In the first place, China was not yet in existence. Instead, the territories of present-day China were inhabited by various sedentary societies possessing or developing cultural attributes that would eventually become associated with Chinese culture.[1] Their counterparts on the steppe and semisteppe areas in north and northwest China were hardly "nomadic." Some of these peoples, especially during the later phases of the period under review, may have been fully nomadic, but most were in different stages of adopting a pastoral economy—though in many cases, they simultaneously continued to engage in agriculture—and were heading toward a more mobile lifestyle.[2] While easier said than done, I will attempt to refrain from projecting either anachronistic views of contact between China and its nomadic neighbors or emotionally charged opinions on the nature and effects of such interaction.

Despite these difficulties, intersocietal interactions and their consequences are a worthwhile research subject that has yet to merit sufficient academic attention. The title of this anthology notwithstanding, my contribution examines the place of steppe societies, most of which were not yet fully nomadic, in the culture (in the broader sense of the word) of societies in China. In a paper presented at an earlier conference organized by Amitai and Biran, I suggested that the steppe was a principal venue and transit route for substantial contacts between the Eurasian continent's western and eastern parts during the late second and early first millennia BCE.[3] Over the course of the ensuing discussion, I plan to strengthen this hypothesis with new evidence. More specifically, I will home in on the following research questions: What were the routes of interaction and who were the likely bearers of influence? And how did these intercontinental reciprocities affect societies living in what are now the lands of China? Finally, I will explore whether these interactions were unique, or merely part of lively networks that encompassed "intra-Chinese" contacts as well as similar relations between "Chinese" societies and others to the north, west, and south.

Intellectual Background

Over the last century, research on the history of Chinese contacts with external societies and the ramifications thereof on Chinese societies has undergone marked changes. The roots of quite a few modern controversies can be traced back to traditional Chinese views about their neighbors and the latter's interaction with Chinese culture. For example, the "Wang zhi" chapter of the early Han-period *Liji* reads as follows:

> The people on the East were called Yi. They had their hair unbound, and tattooed their bodies. Some of them ate their food without it being cooked with fire . . . Those on the west were called Rong. They had their hair unbound, and wore skins. Some of them did not eat grain-food. Those on the north were called Di. They wore skins of animals and birds, and dwelt in caves. Some of them did not eat grain-food.[4]

While it stands to reason that attitudes toward foreigners, their culture, and ties with China varied throughout the imperial era, this passage from the *Liji* does represent the predominant view.[5] According to this outlook, China possessed advanced technologies, a developed economy, and a refined culture, whereas its neighboring societies were underdeveloped and uncultured. In addition, Chinese culture is depicted as a homogeneous and relatively stable entity with no place for local diversity and nonelite traits, much less external influences. Although this traditional model has been severely challenged by modern scholarship, it continues to be felt in research on Bronze Age societies.

The first half of the twentieth century was informed by polarized discourses about the origins and development of Chinese civilization. Some non-Chinese scholars applied the diffussionist models that were then current in Western scholarship to China.[6] A notorious champion of this school of thought is the Swedish geologist/archaeologist Johan Gunnar Andersson, who is credited with discovering northern China's Neolithic cultures, but also suggested that these cultures descended from earlier European prototypes.[7] At the other end of the spectrum was a group of Chinese scholars at the beginning of the 1900s; even the modernists among them, who disputed the traditional historiography of China, could not avoid reading the archaeological record through an age-old Sinocentric lens. In so doing, they labeled the central Yellow River basin "the cradle of Chinese civilization" and discussed how its culture gradually spread from this region to other areas of modern-day China.[8] These Chinese intellectuals, many of whom had strong nationalistic sentiments, averred that external origin theories, such as the ones put forth by Andersson, imposed an imperialistic view on the past.[9]

As it turns out, the wholesale criticism of models that ascribed external origins for many important cultural traits in China was not without basis. Over the last fifty years, Chinese archaeologists have demonstrated the indigenous origins of agriculture, pottery, and village life in China. Additionally, they have managed to push back the dates proposed by Andersson for the inception of these traits by at least 4,000 years. However, this kind of emotional reaction has also precluded any systematic research on intercultural and interregional contacts both within "China" and with societies in areas beyond its present-day borders.

It is probably no coincidence that the first cracks in the indigenous paradigm of Chinese archaeology appeared during the 1980s, just when Deng Xiaoping's reforms started to take effect. Among the first challenges to the prevailing "out of the Yellow River" model was the Chinese Interaction Sphere, an influential model developed by Chang Kwang-chi. According to this theory, the primary catalyst behind the development of Chinese civilization was interactions between regional Neolithic cultures, rather than the spread of culture from the so-called core area.[10] Initially viewed as heterodox by many archaeologists, this paradigm has since merited nearly unanimous acceptance in the Sinology and archaeology communities. These developments should also be viewed in the context of the tremendous upswing in archaeological discoveries over the past three decades in China—a spike that is partially explained by the Chinese government's affinity for salvage archaeology and the waves of construction projects sweeping through the country, including quite a few areas that were hitherto considered marginal by Chinese archaeologists. Many of these finds have shed light on the unique features of local cultures. As such, they have been used to create local tourist attractions and boost local pride. What is more, these discoveries have undergirded what some researchers deem to be a new "regionalist paradigm" of Chinese archaeology.[11]

Despite the new findings and the success of Chang's interaction model, the application of this or similar models was limited by their propensity for focusing on the eastern part of China during the Neolithic period. Interactions between many of China's outermost regions as well as their contacts with the core area were usually ignored, and the same can be said for interactions that were pivotal to the creation of state-level societies in China. Though recognized, long-distance contacts with "non-Chinese" areas were often seen as having a trifling effect from a political, cultural, and social standpoint.

Following in the footsteps of the newfound appreciation for the crucial role played by intersocietal interactions, there has been a mild renewal of interest in long-distance contacts between areas in present-day China and areas to its west. The most prominent example, in my estimation, is the attention—both academic and general—that is showered on the "mummies" that were unearthed in the Tarim basin, some of which have been identified as Caucasian and associated with Indo-European people.[12] Another case in point is *Ouya xuekan* (Eurasian Studies); published in China since 1999, this journal is devoted entirely to the history of interactions with the Eurasian continent. Needless to say, this interest has generated more data about these contacts. While not all the material is original, when placed in the context of renewed awareness even old data is capable of acquiring new meaning.

Unfortunately, discussions on these issues tend to be emotionally charged and to concentrate on issues of origins and primacy. For instance, the Russian archaeologist Elena E. Kuzmina claims that "a tremendous flowering of Chinese culture during the rule of the Yin dynasty was conditioned by three major innovations: wheeled transport, horse riding, and metallurgy propagated under the impact of the West."[13] While this is an extreme case of reverting back to the "diffussionist discourse," numerous other studies on the genesis of specific objects or styles are also frequently tinged with nationalistic ardor.[14] More importantly, the preoccupation with provenance has overshadowed questions that I consider much more intriguing: What were the modes of cross-cultural interaction? What were the ramifications of these developments on the societies that were exposed to them? How were external traits either accepted or rejected by a local culture?

This chapter can hardly hope to resolve or even address every single issue that pertains to interregional contacts during the second and early first millennia. Consequently, my objective is to illustrate how focusing on the geographic distribution of specific artifacts and styles, while eschewing overambitious generalizations, is conducive to more sophisticated reconstructions.

Historical and Geographic Background

Starting with the early development of agriculture and sedentary lifestyles at around 6500 BCE, societies in many areas of present-day China experienced a gradual transition to craft specialization, division of labor, socioeconomic stratification, and political hierarchy. The archaeological record for most of these regions—not only the middle and lower ridges of the Yellow and Yangzi Rivers, but also north and west of these waterways—suggests the rise of complex societies that were equivalent in scale to what anthropologists generally refer to as chiefdoms by the late third millennium BCE. More specifically, advanced ceramic, stone (including semiprecious), and bone industries; the nascent production of bronze and lacquer; and indirect evidence of religious specialists indeed attest to craft specialization and division of labor. Similarly, mounting differences in the size and opulence of graves are indicative of growing economic and social gaps, while hierarchical settlement patterns hint to political stratification. In many instances, the central nodes of the chiefdom's political hierarchy were significant fortified sites.[15] However, the size of each polity was still rather modest.

The heated debate over the Xia dynasty and the beginning of state society in China is beyond the scope of this chapter. That said, it bears noting that the centuries spanning the late third millennium and the first half of the second millennium BCE were crucial to the development of state-level society in China. The written records and archaeological findings suggest that by the end of this period a centralized and exceedingly hierarchical state-level society was established in the middle Yellow River area. Although the precise geographical reach of the Shang and Western Zhou control is under dispute,[16] they were clearly much larger than anything previously known in China. Likewise, the power concentrated in the hands of these polities' kings and elite far exceeded that of their late Neolithic and incipient Bronze Age counterparts. Monuments like the towering city walls at Zhengzhou, the royal graves at Xibeigang, and the Shang and Western Zhou's extensive and highly sophisticated bronze industry leave no doubt that the said rulers had considerable manpower and natural resources at their disposal. However, we must also bear in mind that the Shang and Western Zhou were by no means the only state-level societies in the region. By roughly 1500 BCE, complex large-scale societies already dotted the lower and middle ridges of the Yangzi River; by the late Shang and Western Zhou period most of China's core areas—including almost the entire length of the Yangzi River basin, the Yellow and Wei River basins, and areas to their north—were under the dominion of what may be referred to as the Zhou (or "Chinese") states. Although Chinese culture was far from homogenous at this point in time, the various states, especially their elites, were quite similar with respect to their material culture and apparently their fundamental beliefs, ideologies, and social norms. Conversely, to the south, west, and north of these states were societies that, for the most part, were probably less complex[17] and vastly different from a cultural standpoint.

In the next section, the stress will be on evidence of contacts between the Shang and Western Zhou states and their contemporaries to the north and west: areas of present-day northeast and northwest China and the south Siberian and Central Asian steppe lands. While there is no indication of state-level entities in these regions during the period at hand, this does not mean that they were simple egalitarian societies. Evidence of an advanced bronze industry suggests the existence of highly skilled artisans.[18] Furthermore, the discovery of graves that are ten times larger and richer than the average local grave points to an economic and social hierarchy.[19] As noted above, we should not presume that these were fully developed pastoral-nomadic societies. While some groups did fit this mold (particularly during the first millennium BCE), others were more sedentary and even agricultural.

Evidence for Interaction between the Chinese States and Steppe Societies during the Late Second and Early First Millennia BCE

The long-distance contacts between societies in the Yellow River regions and those beyond the northern and western frontiers of present-day China go way back. For instance, by dint of carbonized grains found at sites in western Gansu, it is estimated that wheat domesticated in western Asia entered China via the northwest at around the fourth or early third millennium BCE, before reaching the Central Plains at around the second millennium BCE.[20]

From the available archaeological evidence, it seems as though the rate and intensity of long-distance contacts picked up during the latter half of the second millennium BCE. The introduction of chariots into China is probably the best-known example of this phenomenon. There is no sign of any kind of wheeled conveyance whatsoever in the Yellow River basin prior to the outburst of chariots in the sacrificial pits of Yinxu, the late Shang-period center, where they are dated to approximately 1250 BCE. Since chariots are known to have existed in Central Asia from as early as ca. 2000–1800 BCE (in the Sintashta-Petrovka culture of what is now modern Kazakhstan), and given the close stylistic and technological similarities between the chariots of Central Asia and those found at Yinxu, there is a general consensus that the latter attest to the transmission of a new technology to the Yellow River basin from the west.[21]

The arrival of chariots to China indeed constitutes a long-distance transfer of a very complex product that involved many challenging aspects (e.g., the construction of light yet sturdy wheels and the harnessing of horses so as to channel their power efficaciously) and the synthesis of various industries (foremost among them carpentry, bronze casting, and ornamentation). It also entailed the mastery of new and diverse realms of knowledge, like charioteering and horse grooming (including specialized breeding and veterinary knowledge). The manner in which such a sophisticated range of interrelated technologies and expertise was conveyed over thousands of kilometers of rugged terrain is still unclear (one possible route is discussed below). No less importantly, the introduction of chariots should not be viewed as an isolated case, but rather a part of a considerably wider range of heightening contacts involving societies in modern-day China—the Yellow River basin included—as well as regions to the north and west, Mongolia and Central Asia, and as far as Eastern Europe.

The most prevalent type of evidence for this sort of interaction is metal artifacts, especially bronze. While most of these items are from the period under review, some even predate the Shang dynasty. Among the earlier metal objects were earrings and hairpins, usually of gold and bronze, which turned up in the early second-millennium BCE sites of numerous cultures north of the Yellow River. These discoveries are indicative of Chinese contacts with north China and with the Andronovo culture—notwithstanding the host of regional variations—which was scattered across a large portion of the eastern Eurasian steppe, from southern Siberia to Kazakhstan.[22] The Andronovo are also credited with other items, such as curved bronze knives and bronze daggers with leaf-shaped and pierced blades, spearheads, and socketed axes.[23] Most of the "Andronovo artifacts" that have thus far surfaced in China originate from Xinjiang and the western areas of north China.[24] However, some of the items, like two axes, a socketed axe, and a knife found at the Wanliu in northern Liaoning, derive from the northeast.[25]

That said, the identification of all these artifacts with the Andronovo culture, rather than the Karasuk, which dates between the latter half of the second millennium BCE and the early first millennium BCE, is highly controversial, even among those who support the western origins of such objects.[26] Appreciably more evidence can be confidently dated to around 1500 BCE and onward. For example, artifacts that were found by and large in northeast China (the modern-day provinces of Liaoning and Hebei and the eastern part of Inner Mongolia), a group that is occasionally referred to

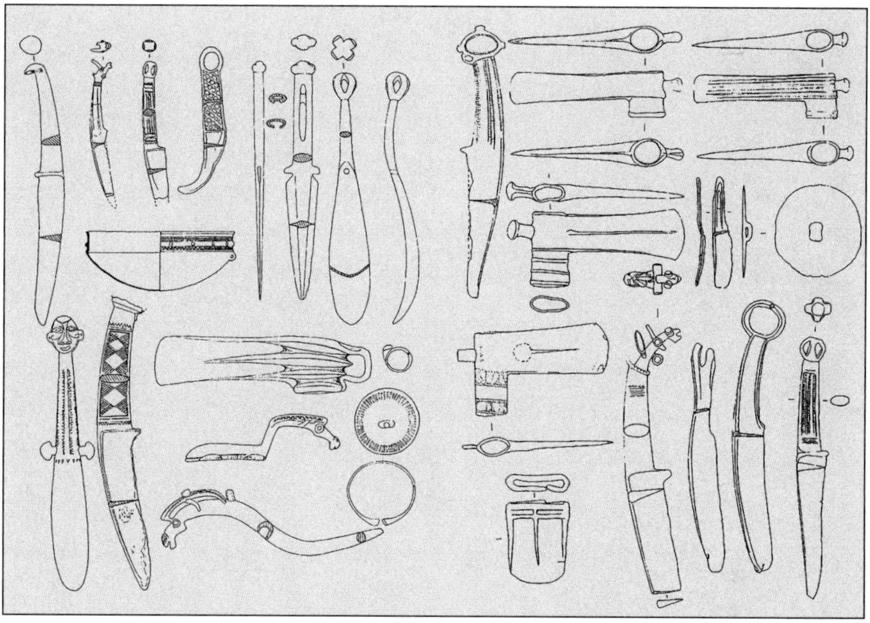

Figure 2.1. Artifacts of the so-called Northern Bronze Complex.

as the "Northern Bronze Complex" (Figure 2.1),[27] closely resemble bronze artifacts from the Karasuk culture in southern Siberia (ca. 1400–1000 BCE) and the Seima-Turbino complex farther to the west (ca. 1600–1300 BCE).[28] As shown elsewhere,[29] these sorts of resemblances are quite evident when comparing bronze knives that are embellished with animal heads, animal figures, or jingles attached to the tip of their hilt (Figure 2.2). The fact that such artifacts turned up not only in the Eurasian steppe and the northern zones of China, but in Shang elite graves at the Yellow River basin (Figure 2.3) suggests that Shang and Zhou societies were also linked to this sphere of interaction, either directly or indirectly.

Another interesting example, which has not been discussed in previous studies, is the bronze artifacts that are shaped like the Greek letter *pi* (π). These objects are relatively small, and despite certain variations in shape, they all have a central stem with a loop attached to each side. Some specimens feature jingles or other decorations (Figure 2.4). For the most part, these artifacts come from the Chifeng region, where they have been found in, among other places, Xiaoshiheigou grave no. 8061,[30] Chifeng City,[31] and other locations in northeast China.[32] The function of these contrivances is unknown, but some researchers believe that they are akin to the so-called

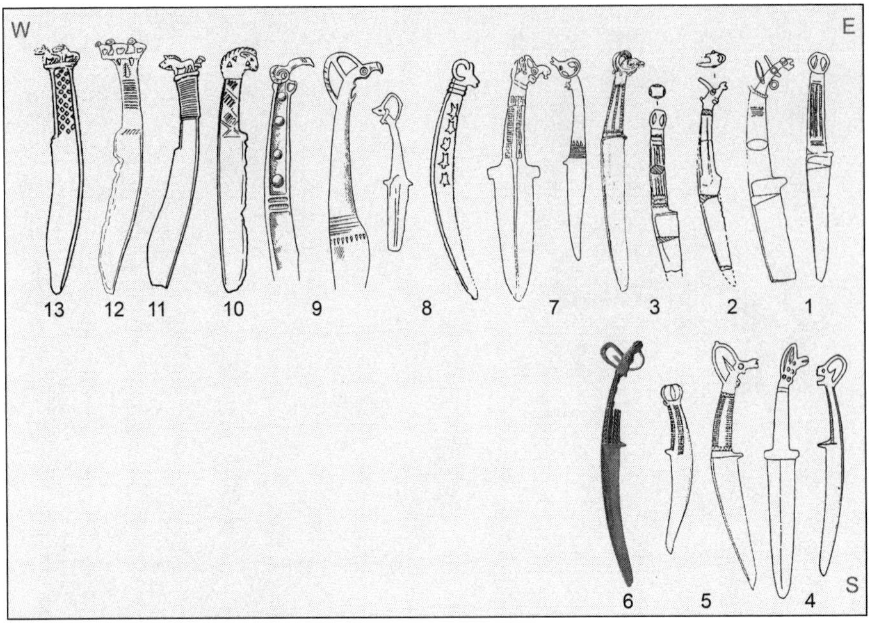

Figure 2.2. Knives with animal heads from different sites in the Northern Zone, North China, and the Eurasian steppes.

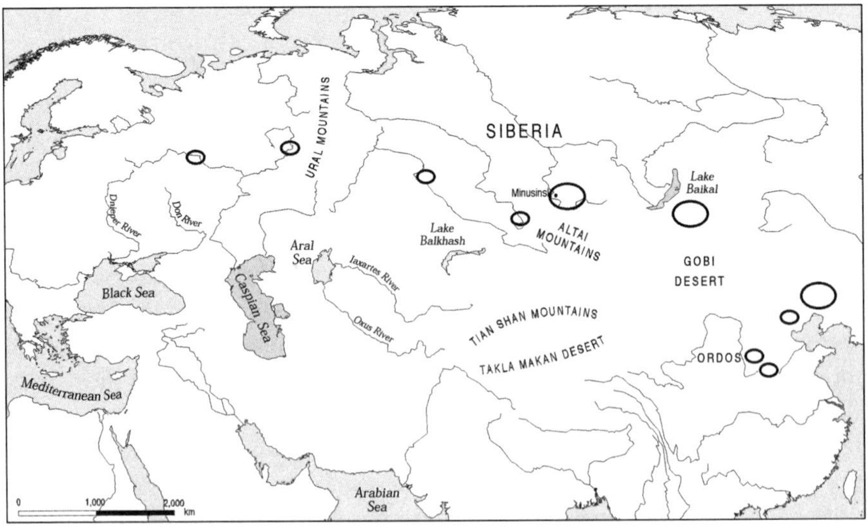

Figure 2.3. Map of the distribution of knives with animal heads.

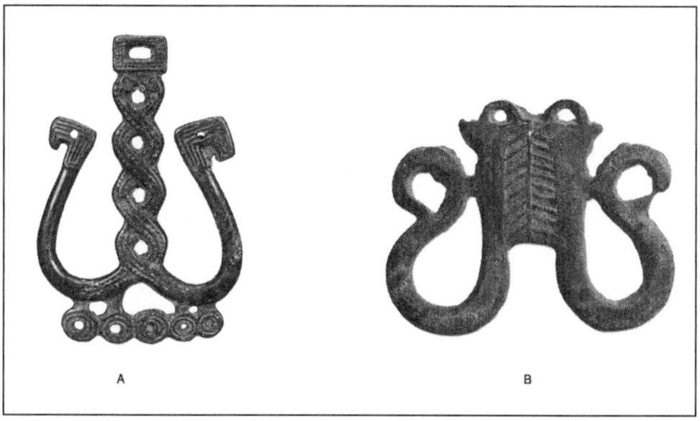

Figure 2.4. *Pi*(π)-shaped bronze objects from northeast China.

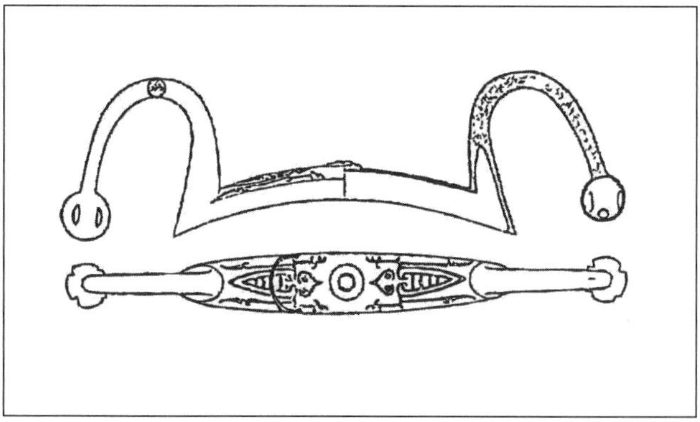

Figure 2.5. A bow-shaped bronze object. Adapted from Zhongguo shehui kexueyuan kaogu yanjiusuo, *Anyang Yinxu Huanyuanzhuang dongdi Shangdai muzhang* (Beijing, 2002), p. 159.

bow-shaped artifacts (Figure 2.5) and have suggested that they were used for charioteering.[33]

Some clues as to the function of these artifacts along with a clear indication of their link to Central Asia can be gleaned from the motifs that are engraved on monoliths known as "deer stones" (*olenniye kamni*). These monumental stone stelae, some up to 2.5 meters high, are primarily found in northern Mongolia and the Transbaikal region.[34] The most common prevalent motifs on these stones are deer with long antlers. Other themes are typical northern bronzes, such as daggers with animal heads and artifacts closely resembling the *pi*-shaped objects (Figure 2.6a). Like many of the other depictions of bronze objects on these monoliths, the object in Figure 2.6b was rendered as hanging from a belt.[35] This suggests that the artifact was not necessarily related to chariots; in fact, there is a greater likelihood that it was used by nomadic or seminomadic people. Although scholars have not been able to conclusively reconstruct any of its functions, one hypothesis is that the contraption helped attach rope.[36]

Contact with Central Asia or even western Asia during the Shang and early Zhou period was not limited to technology (such as chariots) or the shape of bronze artifacts. Rawson recently suggested that carnelian beads further testify to these sorts of interactions.[37] Unlike chariots and bronzes, which were locally produced in accordance to foreign styles and with the assistance of foreign techniques, carnelian was evidently transported from its natural sources in western Asia. Testimony of carnelian imports was uncovered in graves from as early as the beginning of the second millennium BCE, like those at the Dadianzi cemetery in the Chifeng region.[38] However, the majority of finds turned up in Western Zhou graves along the Wei and Yellow River basins. Some of the beads, like the sizable biconical variety (some 3.5 centimeters in length) were apparently imported as finished products from Mesopotamia, where such artifacts are indeed well documented.[39] In other

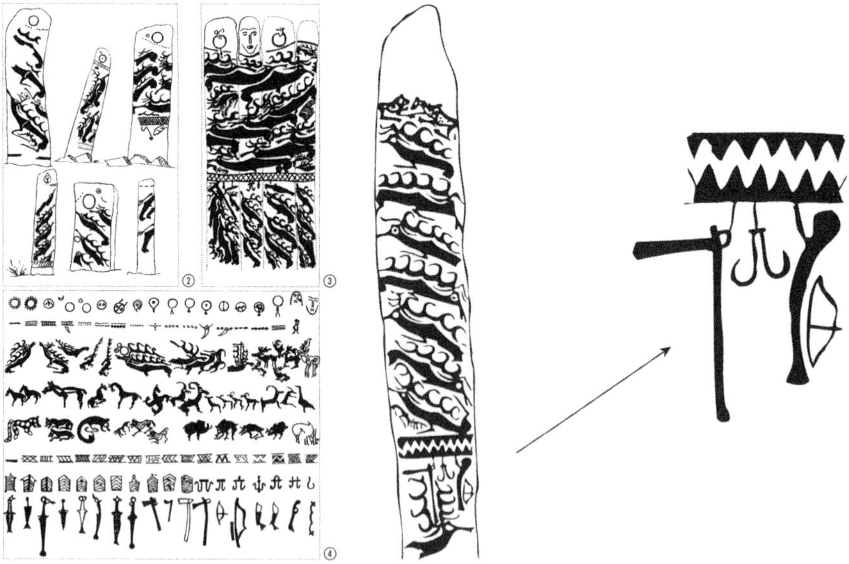

Figure 2.6. Depictions of *pi*-shaped bronze objects engraved on deer stones from northern Mongolia. (a) Collection of motifs on deer stones, bronze daggers and the *pi*-shaped objects are on the lower row (no. 4); (b) Depiction of the objects hanging on a belt. Adapted from N. A. Bokovenko, "Scythians in Siberia, " in *Nomads of the Euroasian Steppe in the Early Iron Age*, ed. J. Davis-Kimbal et al. (Berkeley, 1995), p. 32.

cases, the raw materials may have been imported, but the beads themselves were produced locally.

Routes and Modes of Interaction

As shown in Figure 2.3, what scholars currently believe to be the distribution network for the typical artifacts of the Northern Bronze Complex connected the Eurasian steppe with northeast China via a northern route running along the borders between the steppe and the forest zones of Central Asia. These artifacts have surfaced in the following places: cemeteries of the Seima-Turbino complex, west of the Ural mountains; Karasuk sites in the Minusinsk basin, east of the Ural Mountains and in northern Mongolia; and as far as the Chifeng region in eastern Inner Mongolia and the western and central parts of Liaoning (see Figure 2.3).[40] None of these objects have turned up in areas farther to the west, like Gansu or Qinghai. However, they were found in late Shang-period graves, such as the famous Fuhao tomb at Yinxu, and other late Shang and Western Zhou contexts.[41] All told, this suggests that interactions took place along a northern route connecting the Yellow River basin through the northeast to the steppe lands.

In the Shang context, there is a clear link between chariots and Northern Bronze Complex artifacts, such as knifes with animal heads or bow-shaped artifacts (Figure 2.7). Therefore, it stands to reason that chariots were introduced into China via the eastern part of the Northern Zone and not, as is commonly assumed, via its western side.[42]

These conclusions do not preclude the existence of more southern and western routes of interaction, which connected societies in the Yellow and Wei River basins with their counterparts in Central Asia through the Gansu corridor. In fact, socketed weapons and other bronze artifacts that are associated with the Karasuk culture have also surfaced in Xinjiang and northwest China.[43] However, we may infer from the discussion above that interactions along the two main routes—the "northern steppe route" flowing into the Yellow River region from the northeast and the "desert route" connecting to that same area from the west—differed in terms of the content that was transmitted and perhaps the nature of the interactions as well. These two main routes can be viewed as filters that determined the cultural content transmitted between east and west. This filtering was determined by the lifestyle of the people of the steppe and the dessert oases. In other words, materials, objects, and technologies that were unsuited for these regions' inhabitants were essentially kept out, while those that the populace could adopt for its own needs had a better chance of being transmitted onward.

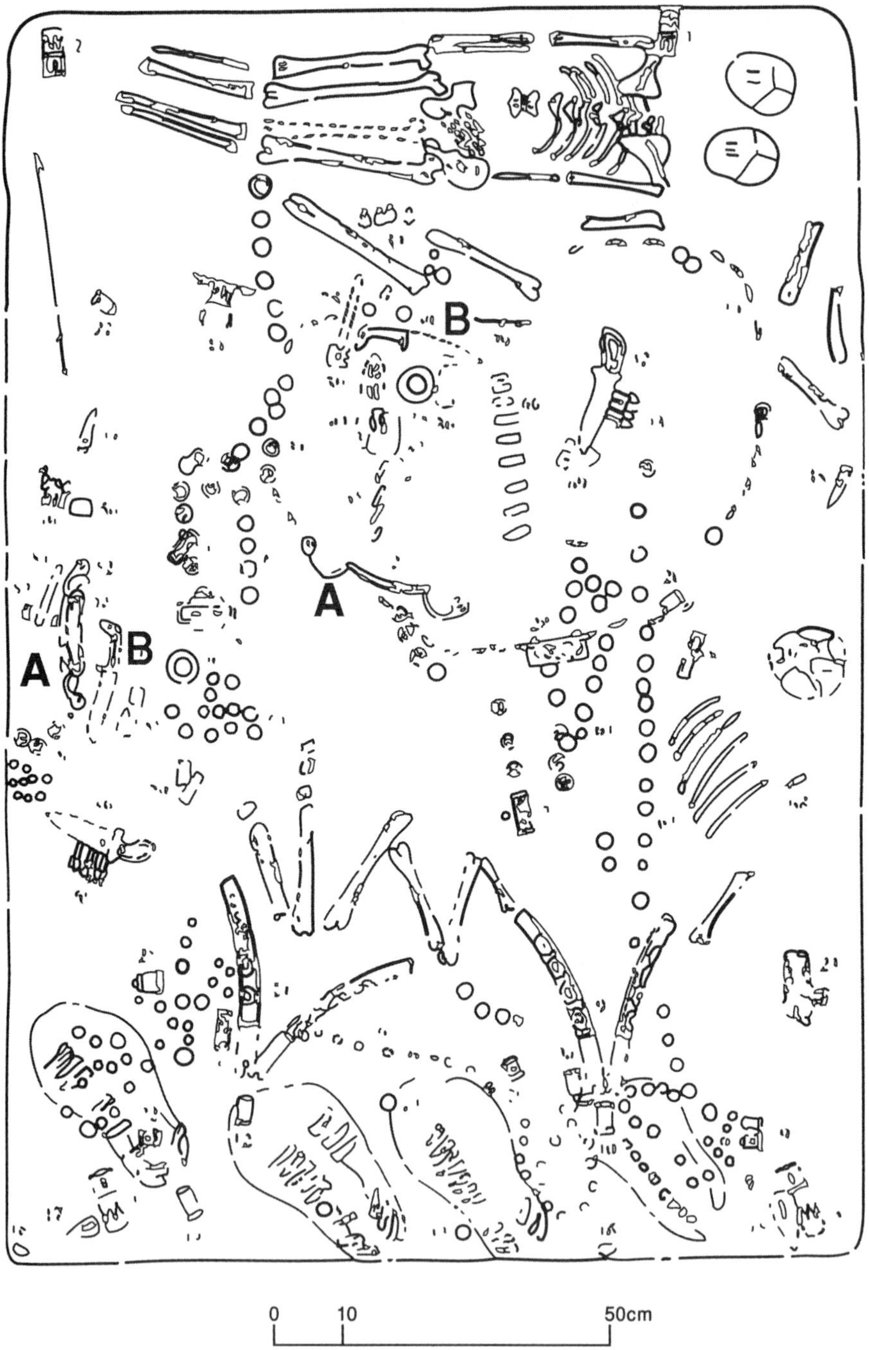

Figure 2.7. Chariot pit no. 20 from Xiaotun. A) bow-shaped objects; B) knives with animal heads. Adapted from Guo Baojun, *Yinzhou cheqi yanjiu* (Beijing, 1998), p. 45.

What, then, can be deduced from these observations as to the nature of the interactions and their consequences? The fact that at least some of these exchanges were conducted along the northern steppe land route, rather than the oases of the Tarim basin, suggests the involvement of seminomadic people, be they pastoralists, semipastoralists, or perhaps hunters. Some of the products and know-how that were transmitted thanks to these sorts of contacts, such as chariots and bronze items (either the goods themselves or the attendant production and design methods), originated among the people of the steppe. Other items, like the carnelian beads, were manufactured in regions with more sedentary populations, but were conveyed by the mobile people of the steppe.[44] Although the exchange of information between societies was facilitated by the above-mentioned commodities, it is worth remembering that artifacts do not travel on their own. In my estimation, there is sufficient evidence to contend that the people of the steppe were not merely carriers, but played a much more vital role in the exchange of information and cultural cross-pollination. While most of the participants probably did not traverse the entire route from west to east and from east to west, we should not underestimate the role of the steppe peoples in the transmission of cultural influences to the "Chinese" societies.

Inside many of the Yinxu chariot pits, human bodies are interred alongside horses, chariots, and other paraphernalia. While these people were indeed victims, their status appears to be higher than those buried in the sacrificial pits of Xibeigang. Whereas the latter were buried en masse without any burial gifts and most were decapitated, the skeletons in the Yinxu pits are intact and the deceased were graced with burial gifts.[45] Some of these burial objects may indeed be related to the chariots, but others appear to be associated with the individuals themselves. Among the more "personal" artifacts are bronze knives with animal heads in the Northern Bronze Complex style (see Figure 2.7). This suggests that non-Shang people from one of the regions to the north were present in the Shang center, where they perhaps served as chariot drivers and horse grooms, inter alia. Although the possibility exists that they were involved in chariot construction, there is no way to test this hypothesis. Under the assumption that not only the chariots themselves but the requisite riding, breeding, and maintenance skills were previously unknown in China, it stands to reason that "foreigners" provided crucial services and training, at least during the period in which chariots were still being assimilated into the local culture.

Against this backdrop, what were the ramifications of these long-distance contacts? Their immediate impact on the Shang and Zhou societies along the main river basins was probably in the realms of display and prestige. As Shaughnessy has demonstrated, chariots were only used for display and hunting during the Shang era, not warfare.[46] More specifically, these conveyances helped enhance the legitimacy of the Shang kings, though without directly contributing to their military prowess. In all likelihood, it took hundreds of years (i.e., until the second part of the Western Zhou era) for these polities to realize the military potential of this innovation. However, by the so-called Spring-and-Autumn Period (770–453 BCE), chariots were considered the Zhou states' most advanced military technology, to the point where a state's might was expressed by the number of battle chariots at its disposal. What is more, other types of vehicles, such as chariots and carts for traveling and transporting goods, were apparently modeled after the Shang and Zhou battle chariots. In light of the above, the introduction of chariots and other foreign technologies should not be viewed as a one-sided development, in which one party merely imported a finished product from another, but as an ongoing process of selection and modification on the part of the receiving societies. Carnelian and other prestigious materials that arrived at the Shang and Zhou centers by dint of long-range interactions were also largely used to showcase the prestige of the elite, but as Rawson argues, the broader context of these kinds of ties may be related to the introduction of new ideas that prompted ritualistic reforms in Zhou society.[47] Lastly, there is reason to believe that close and peaceful relations with people of the steppe (some of whom probably lived in the heart of the late Shang and Western Zhou lands) infused new ideas into Chinese society.

The consequences of these interactions on societies outside the Shang and Zhou's orbit might be more complex than on those within. For instance, the archaeological record from northeast China's Upper Xiajiadian society (ca. 1200–600 BCE) suggests that Zhou artifacts, such as bronze vessels, were used exclusively to boost the prestige of local leaders. Conversely, references to contact with societies west and north of northeast China, as expressed through the style and shape of local bronze artifacts, were used in a much more egalitarian way by all segments of that society. Interestingly enough, the majority of these items were personal possessions that individuals fastened to their clothing and/or adorned themselves with. Even weapons, such as the abovementioned daggers, were usually equipped with hooks for attaching them to a belt. Such a display of symbols by a large segment of the northeast's population suggests that people were intentionally using these artifacts to construct an explicitly non-Zhou identity.[48] In other words, rather than being manipulated or controlled by the more complex societies of the Shang and Zhou, these people used interregional and long-range exchanges to preserve the local hierarchy and attain or hold on to sociopolitical power. Last but not least, these interactions also helped them express their local and personal identities.

Concluding Remarks: The Broader Context of Long-Range Interactions during the Late Second and Early First Millennia BCE

The intensified contact between the Chinese societies of the late Shang and Western Zhou era and their counterparts in the steppe lands is not an isolated case, as there is evidence suggesting that relations with other areas were also ratcheted up. While this sort of interaction is known to have existed earlier, the relevant archaeological data suggests that the frequency and intensity of intersocietal contacts, especially the long-distance variety, rose dramatically across the regions of present-day China and further afield throughout the periods in question.

A case in point is the trade in cowry shells between "Chinese" societies and those to the south and southwest. There is quite a bit of evidence indicating that this trade was already underway by the late third or early second millennium BCE. For instance, 659 cowry shells were found in 43 graves in northeast China's Dadianzi cemetery, which dates to the beginning of the second millennium BCE.[49] Comparable findings also turned up in Erlitou and northwest China.[50] The exact source of these shells is under dispute; however, given the fact that cowries naturally flourish in warm sea waters, these goods must have been imported from the south coast of China or even the Indian Ocean, a minimum distance of at least 1,000 kilometers, and probably much more.[51] The amount of cowry shells in areas far from their natural habitat rose exponentially during the late second millennium BCE, thus attesting to the formation of an extensive network for the circulation of raw materials and finished goods. For example, 6,820 cowry shells were unearthed in the Fuhao grave, and similar finds, though rarely of such large quantities, have been made in practically every Shang and Western Zhou site.[52] At any rate, the distribution of cowry shells was not limited to "Chinese" societies. In northeast China, they have turned up even in relatively small and poor graves, so that the circulation network was apparently not limited to Shang and Zhou polities or only to the elite.[53] A similar inventory was discovered in the two Sanxingdui pits on the Chengdu plain of Sichuan. Dated to approximately 1100 BCE, the pits stand out for the elaborate and sizable bronze artifacts found therein. Although the scale of production suggested by these findings is on par with that of the Shang, the style and function of these objects—the majority of which are statues, not vessels—is reflective of an independent local culture. The pits also contained, among other things, gold and bronze items, jade artifacts, 80 whole elephant tusks, curved ivory objects, and over 4,500 cowry shells.[54] The shells connect the Sanxingdui culture to the Chinese network of exchange, thereby suggesting that the former was a key player on the Indian Ocean–China cowry trade route.

Further evidence suggests the heightening of mid- and long-range contacts during the late second and early first millennia BCE. This included the ample distribution of not only raw goods (e.g., turtle plastrons, tin, turquoise, and jade) and finished goods (e.g., Western Zhou bronze vessels found in Lingnan) but cultural norms as well.[55] A quintessential example of this is the spread of oracle bone divination (pyromancy), which is predicting the future by heating bones and diagnosing the resultant cracks. In all likelihood, this practice originated in the northeast and subsequently spread to many societies in north China by the fourth or third millennium BCE, reaching immense proportions in the areas under review by the second half of the third millennium BCE.[56] Numerous sites from the Lower Xiajiadian period (northeast China), Zhukaigou contexts (the Ordos region in northwest China), Qijia and related cultures (the Gansu region), and Longshan and Erlitou cultures (lower and central Yellow River) indeed attest to this phenomenon.[57] By Shang times, pyromancy was not only embraced by people throughout China, including the entire Yangzi basin, but constituted intersociety efforts aimed at elaborating on and standardizing this discipline.[58] Against this backdrop, it stands to reason that the rise of pyromancy can be ascribed to repeated intercultural and interregional interactions.

In sum, the spatial patterns charting the distribution of materials, artifacts, cultural traits, and styles bolster the hypothesis that the latter half of the second millennium and the first half of the first millennium BCE was a period of intensive mid- and long-range interactions between societies in different regions of present-day China and beyond. Contact with the Eurasian steppe's pastoral or semipastoral societies was but one dimension of these robust networks that linked up an assortment of cultures and ecological zones. This perspective sheds light on the ostensibly seamless integration of steppe cultural attributes into the culture of the Shang and Western Zhou states and the rapid acculturation of these foreign elements into what was eventually to become Chinese civilization. Needless to say, the receiving societies did not accept every last facet of steppe culture or all the innovations that its people had to offer. Instead, they selectively endorsed those features that suited the elites as well as the "Chinese" societies' sedentary way of life. Some of these elements, like the chariot, underwent a protracted transformation in China before assuming an integral role in the local culture. However, due to the social openness to new materials, artifacts, and cultural traits from the outside world, there was no principled objection to this process. In any event, this state of affairs was on the brink of change, as the dichotomy between Chinese and non-Chinese became more rigid during the second half of the first millennium BCE.[59] The famous anecdote from King Wuling of Zhao's court (r. 325–299 BCE) concerning the debate over whether or not to adopt "barbarian" clothes more fit for riding horses is symbolic of this new era.[60]

NOTES

1. Throughout this chapter, the term "China" refers to the territories of the modern Chinese state. The term renders no judgment as to the "Chineseness" of the ancient societies labeled thus.

2. G. Shelach, *Prehistoric Societies on the Northern Frontiers of China: Archaeological Perspectives on Identity Formation and Economic Change during the First Millennium BCE* (London, 2009).

3. G. Shelach, "Early Pastoral Societies in Northeast China: Local Change and Interregional Interaction during c. 1100–600 BC," in *Mongol, Turks and Others: Eurasia and the Outside World,* ed. R. Amitai and M. Biran (Leiden, 2005), pp. 15–58; also see E. N. Chernykh, *Ancient Metallurgy in the USSR: The Early Metal Age* (Cambridge, 1992), pp. 215–233; E. N. Chernykh et al., "Ancient Metallurgy of Northeast Asia from the Urals to the Saiano-Altai," in *Metallurgy in Ancient Eastern Eurasia from the Urals to the Yellow River,* ed. K. M. Linduff (Lewiston, NY, 2004), pp. 15–36; S. Legrand, "Karasuk Metallurgy: Technological Development and Regional Influence," in *Metallurgy in Ancient Eastern Eurasia from the Urals to the Yellow River,* pp. 139–156; Shelach, *Prehistoric Societies,* pp. 114–145; Wu En, "Ouya dalu caoyuan zaoqi youmu wenhua de jidian sikao," *Kaogu Xuebao,* 4 (2002), pp. 437–470.

4. *Liji* 12/26–27; translated in Mu-chou Poo, *Enemies of Civilization: Attitudes toward Foreigners in Ancient Mesopotamia, Egypt and China* (Albany, NY, 2005), p. 65.

5. For a detailed analysis of how the Chinese attitude toward their neighbors evolved over the course of the preimperial and early imperial period see N. Di Cosmo, *Ancient China and Its Enemies: The Rise of Nomadic Power in East Asian History* (Cambridge, 2002); Y. Pines, "Beasts or Humans: Pre-Imperial Origins of the 'Sino-Barbarian' Dichotomy," in *Mongols, Turks and Others: Eurasian Nomads and the Outside World,* ed. R. Amitai and M. Biran (Leiden, 2005), pp. 59–102; Poo, *Enemies of Civilization.*

6. E. M. Schortman and P. A. Urban, "The Place of Interaction Studies in Archaeological Thought," in *Resources, Power and Interaction,* ed. E. M. Schortman and P. A. Urban (New York, 1992), pp. 3–15.

7. M. Fiskesjö and Chen Xingcan, *China before China: Johan Gunnar Andersson, Ding Wenjiang and the Discovery of China's Prehistory* (Stockholm, 2004).

8. e.g., Te-k'un Cheng, "Some New Discoveries in Prehistoric and Shang China," in *Ancient China: Studies in Early Civilization,* ed. D. T. Roy and Tsuen-hsuin Tsien (Hong Kong, 1978), p. 7.

9. Yung-ti Li, "On the Function of Cowries in Shang and Western Zhou China," *Journal of East Asian Archaeology,* 5 (2003), p. 5.

10. Kwang-chih Chang, *The Archaeology of Ancient China* (4th ed., New Haven, CT, 1986), pp. 234–242.

11. L. Von Falkenhausen, "The Regionalist Paradigm in Chinese Archaeology," in *Nationalism, Politics, and the Practice of Archaeology,* ed. Philip L. Kohl and C. Fawcett (Cambridge, 1995).

12. Cf. J. P. Mallory and V. H. Mair, *The Tarim Mummies: Ancient China and the Mystery of the Earliest Peoples from the West* (New York, 2000).

13. E. E. Kuzmina, "Cultural Connections of the Tarim Basin People and Pastoralists of the Asian Steppes in the Bronze Age," in *The Bronze Age and Early Iron Age Peoples of Eastern Central Asia,* ed. V. H. Mair (Philadelphia, 1998), p. 65.

14. Among the profusion of examples are Wu En's attempts to show that most of the artifacts and art falling under the rubric of the so-called Scythian style (or animal style) derived from the East (i.e., present-day China). See Wu En, "Ouya dalu caoyuan"; Wu En, "Lüelun Ouya caoyuan zaoqi youmu yishu zhong de juanqu dongwu xingiang," *Kaogu,* 11 (2002), pp. 60–68; Wu En, "Lun Zhongguo beifang zaoqi youmu ren qingong daishi de qiyuan," *Wenwu,* 6 (2002), pp. 68–77. Alternatively, Chinese and Vietnamese archaeologists have jostled over whether bronze drums that surfaced in south China first appeared in the Dian culture of Yunnan (China) or the Dongson culture of Vietnam. See F. Allard, "The Archaeology of Dian: Trends and Tradition," *Antiquity,* 73/279 (1999), pp. 82–84; C. Higham, *The Bronze Age of Southeast Asia* (Cambridge, 1996), pp. 110–182.

15. For an in-depth account of these fortifications see L. Liu, *The Chinese Neolithic: Trajectories to Early States* (Cambridge, 2004), pp. 159–191; Ren Shinan, "Zhongguo shiqian chengzhi kaocha," *Kaogu,* 1 (1998), pp. 1–16; Shao Wangping, "The Formation of Civilization: The Interaction Sphere of the Longshan Period," in *The Formation of Chinese Civilization: An Archaeological Perspective,* ed. S. Allan (New Haven, CT, 2005), pp. 85–123; G. Shelach, *Leadership Strategies, Economic Activity and Interregional Interaction: Social Complexity in Northeast China* (New York, 1999), pp. 89–142; A. P. Underhill, *Craft Production and Social Change in Northern China* (New York, 2002).

16. e.g., E. L. Shaughnessy, "Historical Geography and the Extent of the Earliest Chinese Kingdoms," *Asia Major,* 2 (1989), pp. 1–22.

17. An example of a more complex society is the so-called Sanxingdui polity. Located in the Sichuan basin, it was probably a state-level society that was culturally quite distinct from contemporaneous Shang and Shang-like polities, with which it was nevertheless in contact. See R. W. Bagley, "Shang Archaeology," in *The Cambridge History of Ancient China,* ed. M. Loewe and E. L. Shaughnessy (Cambridge, 1999), pp. 212–219; L. Von Falkenhausen, "Some Reflections on Sanxingdui," in *Regional Culture, Religion and Arts before the Seventh Century: Papers from the Third International Conference on Sinology* (Taipei, 2002), pp. 59–97; L. Von Falkenhausen, "The External Connections of Sanxingdui," *Journal of East Asian Archaeology,* 5 (2003), pp. 191–245.

18. E. Chernykh et al., "Ancient Metallurgy of Northeast Asia," pp. 15–36; Legrand, "Karasuk Metallurgy"; Shelach, *Prehistoric Societies,* pp. 23–32.

19. S. Legrand, "Sorting Out Men and Women in the Karasuk Culture," in *Are All Warriors Male?: Gender Roles in the Euroasian Steppe,* ed. K. M. Linduff and K. S. Rubinson (Lanham, MD, 2008), p. 157; Shelach, *Prehistoric Societies,* pp. 16–47.

20. G. W. Crawford, "East Asian Plant Domestication," in *Archaeology of Asia,* ed. M. T. Stark (Malden, MA, 2006), pp. 78–80; S. Li, "The Interaction between Northwest China and Central Asia during the 2nd Millennium BC: An Archaeological Perspective," in *Ancient Interactions: East and West in Eurasia,* ed. K. Boyle et al. (Cambridge, 2002), p. 180; S. Li, "Ancient Interactions in Eurasia and Northwest China: Revisiting J. G. Andersson's Legacy," *Bulletin of the Museum of Far Eastern Antiquities,* 75 (2003), pp. 14–15. That said, some scholars, like Zhao Zhijun (personal communication), have recently stated that wheat was introduced to the Central Plains from the northeast.

21. D. W. Anthony, and N. B. Vinogradov, "Birth of the Chariot," *Archaeology*, 48 (1995), pp. 36–41; A. J. Barbieri-Low, "Wheeled Vehicles in the Chinese Bronze Age (c. 2000–741 B.C.)," *Sino-Platonic Papers*, 99 (2000), pp. 1–99; E. L. Shaughnessy, "Historical Perspectives on the Introduction of the Chariot into China," *Harvard Journal of Asiatic Studies*, 48 (1988), pp. 189–237.

22. K. M. Linduff, "An Archaeological Overview," in *Ancient Bronzes of the Eastern Eurasian Steppes from the Arthur M. Sackler Collections*, ed. E. C. Bunker (New York, 1997), p. 20.

23. K. M. Linduff, "The Emergence and Demise of Bronze-Producing Cultures outside the Central Plain of China," in *The Bronze Age and Early Iron Age Peoples of Eastern Central Asia*, ed. V. H. Mair (Philadelphia, 1998), p. 627; also see Chernykh, *Ancient Metallurgy*, p. 219.

24. J. Mei and C. Shell, "Copper and Bronze Metallurgy in Late Prehistoric Xinjiang," in *The Bronze Age and Early Iron Age Peoples of Eastern Central Asia*, ed. V. H. Mair (Philadelphia, 1998), p. 587; K. Peng, "The Andronovo Bronze Artifacts Discovered in Toquztara County in Ili, Xinjiang," in *The Bronze Age and Early Iron Age Peoples of Eastern Central Asia*, ed. V. H. Mair (Philadelphia, 1998), pp. 573–580.

25. "Liaonning daxue lishixi kaogu yanjiushi and Tieling shi bowuguan," *Liaoning faku xian wanliu yizhi fajue, Kaogu*, 12 (1989), pp. 1076–1086.

26. Cf. L. Fitzgerald-Huber, "Qijia and Erlitou: The Question of Contacts with Distant Cultures," *Early China*, 20 (1995), pp. 17–68; J. Mei, "Qijia and Seima-Turbino: The Question of Early Contacts between Northwest China and the Eurasian Steppe," *Bulletin of the Museum of Far Eastern Antiquities*, 75 (2003), pp. 31–54; Peng, "The Andronovo Bronze Artifacts."

27. Y. Lin, "A Reexamination of the Relationship between Bronzes of the Shang Culture and of the Northern Zone," in *Studies of Shang Archaeology*, ed. Kwang-chih Chang (New Haven, CT, 1986), pp. 237–273; D. Guo, "Northern Type Bronze Artifacts Unearthed in the Liaoning Region, and Related Issues," in *The Archaeology of Northeast China*, ed. S. M. Nelson (London, 1995), pp. 182–205; Wu En, "Yin zhi Zhouchu de beifang qingtongqi," *Kaogu Xuebao*, 2 (1985), pp. 135–156; Yang Jianhua, "Yanshan nan bei Shang Zhou zhi ji qingtongqi yicun de fenqun yanjiu," *Kaogu Xuebao*, 2 (2002), pp. 157–174.

28. Chernykh, *Ancient Metallurgy*, pp. 215–233; Chernykh et al., "Ancient Metallurgy"; Legrand, "Karasuk Metallurgy"; Lin, "A Reexamination"; Linduff, "An Archaeological Overview," pp. 29–32; Shelach, "Early Pastoral Societies"; Wu, "Yin zhi Zhouchu de beifang qingtongqi."

29. Shelach, "Early Pastoral Societies."

30. Ningcheng xian wenhuaguan, "Ningcheng Xian xin faxian de Xiajiadian shangceng wenhua muzang ji qi xiangguan yiwu de yanjiu," *Wenwu ziliao congkan*, 9 (1985), p. 28.

31. Liu Bing, *Chifeng bowuguan wenwu dianzang* (Hohhot, 2007), p. 46.

32. Cf. Liaoning bowuguan, *Liaohe Wengmin Zhan: Wenwu Jicui* (Shenyang, 2006), p. 84.

33. The bow-shaped objects also attest to close similarities between artifacts in Shang graves from the Yellow River basin (see Zhongguo shehui kexueyuan kaogu yanjiusuo, *Yinxu Fuhao mu* [Beijing, 1980], plate 75) and those from the Karasuk graves in the Minusinsk basin (see Legrand, "Sorting Out Men and Women," p. 169, fig. 8.7). Lin Yun, "Zai lun guajiang gou," in *Lin Yun xueshu wenji*, ed. Lin Yun (Beijing, 1998), pp. 302–310; Wu En, *Beifang caoyuan kaoguxue wenhua bijiao yanjiu* (Beijing, 2008), pp. 49–52.

34. N. A. Bokovenko, "Scythians in Siberia," in *Nomads of the Eurasian Steppe in the Early Iron Age,* ed. J. Davis-Kimbal et al. (Berkeley, 1995), p. 272; V. V. Volkov, "Early Nomads of Mongolia," in *Nomads of the Eurasian Steppe in the Early Iron Age,* pp. 325–332. Apart from a few in Xinjiang, no other "deer stones" have surfaced in China. We may thus deduce that this cultural phenomenon did not extend all the way east or west along the steppe.

35. Cf. Volkov, "Early Nomads of Mongolia," pp. 328–329.

36. Barbieri-Low claims that the bow-shaped bronze artifacts were also attached to the human body and not to the chariot and served as a "waist yoke," namely "a reins-holder which would have been strapped to the chariot driver's waist, allowing him to guide the reins with his body" (Barbieri-Low, "Wheeled Vehicles," p. 41).

37. J. Rawson, "Carnelian Beads, Animal Figures and Exotic Vessels: Traces of Contacts between the Chinese States and Inner Asia, ca. 1000–650 BC," *Eurasia Antiqua,* 14 (2008), pp. 1–43.

38. Zhongguo shehui kexueyuan kaogu yanjiusuo, *Dadianzi: Xiajiadian xiaceng wenhua yizhi yu mudi fajue baogao* (Beijing, 1996), pp. 168–169 and color plate 19.

39. Rawson, "Carnelian Beads."

40. Chernykh, *Ancient Metallurgy,* p. 219, figs. 74, 75, 77; Chernykh et al., "Ancient Metallurgy," p. 27, figs. 1.10 and 1.11; Legrand, "Karasuk Metallurgy," p. 148, fig. 5.4; Linduff, "An Archaeological Overview," p. 29; Lin, "A Reexamination"; Guo, "Northern Type Bronze Artifacts."

41. Zhongguo shehui kexueyuan, *Yinxu Fuhao mu,* photo 66.

42. Cf. Barbieri-Low, "Wheeled Vehicles," pp. 45–47.

43. J. Mei, *Copper and Bronze Metallurgy in Late Prehistoric Xinjiang: Its Cultural Context and Relationship with Neighboring Regions* (Oxford, 2000), pp. 28–29 and fig. 3.8.

44. Other commodities that may have been transported and exchanged, such as hide, wool, and other animal products, have not been preserved in the archaeological record, so that there is no material evidence of them.

45. G. Shelach, "The Qiang and the Question of Human Sacrifice in the Late Shang Period," *Asian Perspectives,* 35 (1995), pp. 1–26.

46. Shaughnessy, "Historical Perspectives." See also K. M. Lunduff, "A Walk on the Wild Side: Late Shang Appropriation of Horses in China," in *Prehistoric Steppe Adaptation and the Horse,* ed. M. Levine et al. (Oxford, 2003), pp. 139–162.

47. Rawson, "Carnelian Beads."

48. Shelach, *Prehistoric Societies,* pp. 143–145.

49. Zhongguo shehui kexueyuan kaogu yanjiusuo, *Dadianzi,* pp. 183–187.

50. Liu, Li, *The Chinese Neolithic: Trajectories to Early States* (Cambridge, 2004), p. 234; Li Shuicheng, "Ancient Interactions in Eurasia and Northwest China: Revisiting J. G. Andersson's Legacy," *Bulletin of the Museum of Far Eastern Antiquities,* 75 (2003), pp. 9–30.

51. Liu, *Chinese Neolithic,* p. 3.

52. Zhongguo shehui kexueyuan, *Yinxu Fuhao mu,* p. 15; K. Peng and Y. Zhu, "New Research on the Origins of Cowries Used in Ancient China," *Sino-Platonic Papers,* 68 (1995), pp. 9–10.

53. e.g., G. Shelach, *Leadership Strategies,* pp. 166–167; Zhangjiakou shi wenwu shiye guanlisuo, "Hebei Xuanhua Xiang Xiaobaiyang mudi fajue baogao," *Wenwu,* 5 (1987), pp. 41–51.

54. A few scholars contend that there were still elephants in the Sichuan basin during the late second millennium. Hence, according to this view, the tusks and ivory from the Sanxingdui pits are of local origin. In my estimation, however, the large number of tusks suggests that all or, at least, some of the items were brought to the area from India, where apparently even then elephants were much more commonplace. See also Von Falkenhausen, "Some Reflections on Sanxingdui," pp. 90–92.

55. Cf. R. Ciarla, "Rethinking Yuanlongpo: The Case for Technological Links between the Lingnan (PRC) and Central Thailand in the Bronze Age," *East and West,* 57 (2007), p. 311.

56. Shelach, *Leadership Strategies,* p. 109.

57. R. K. Flad, "Divination and Power: A Multiregional View of the Development of Oracle Bone Divination in Early China," *Current Anthropology,* 49 (2008), pp. 403–437.

58. Ibid., pp. 411–414.

59. Shelach, *Leadership Strategies,* pp. 146–152.

60. For a survey of this debate see Di Cosmo, *Ancient China and Its Enemies,* pp. 134–138.

THREE

The Scythians and Their Neighbors

Anatoly M. Khazanov

Ancient authors and some contemporary scholars have used the name "Scythians" in two different meanings: a generic name for the ancient nomads of the Eurasian steppes, semideserts and deserts, especially the Iranian-speaking ones; and for a particular ethnic group or several groups that, in the first millennium BCE, inhabited the East European steppes, which stretch from the lower Danube to the lower Don Rivers for roughly 620 miles, and from the area to the north from the Black Sea to the forest-steppe zone for over 310 miles. Although this chapter is devoted to the latter, there will also be a few cases where they will be discussed in the broader context of the ancient nomads.

At the beginning of the first millennium BCE, very important changes connected with the transition to pastoral nomadism had taken place in the great belt of the Eurasian steppes, semideserts, and deserts. These were accompanied by a drastic reconfiguration of the ethnopolitical map and the emergence of new archaeological cultures, which had but little semblance with those of the Late Bronze period. In all probability, these changes were somewhat connected to the temporary desiccation that modified the natural environment. This development negatively affected the agriculturally based sedentary life in the steppes,[1] and triggered the final transition to pastoral nomadism.[2] This transition was facilitated by a favorable external sociopolitical environment. By the first millennium BCE, pastoral nomads lived on the periphery of the sedentary states, emerging and expanding on the southern borders of the steppe zone.

Archaeological excavations and accounts in literary sources reveal that the cultures of the ancient Eurasian steppe nomads shared many striking similarities in the first millennium BCE. Many traits, artifacts, customs, and ideas were spread across the entire steppe zone and influenced the cultures of many sedentary peoples.

Especially significant in this regard was the so-called Scythian triad: weapons, horse equipment, and the artistic animal style. Local and other differences notwithstanding, the triad was shared by most ancient nomadic cultures in the Eurasian steppes, thus demonstrating their remarkable principle unity.[3] To a lesser degree, these cultures had other traits in common: sacrificed horses accompanying the dead in burials; bronze cauldrons; and the so-called *olennye kamni* (literally "deer stones"), namely stone stelae, bearing a set of certain engraved animals. Still, it is hardly accidental that the Scythian triad stood out from among the rest among the ancient nomads, as the first two reflect the same nomadic mobile and militaristic way of life and the animal style (discussed below) testifies to similar ideological-cum-religious beliefs and a shared political culture.

The sources of the earliest nomadic cultures are far from completely understood, and the search for them constitutes an intriguing problem. Likewise, the exact region(s) of origin of any particular element of the material culture that was common to the ancient nomads is still under debate. At the moment, the archaeological data seem to indicate that many of those elements first appeared in Inner Asia (Tuva), South Siberia (the Sayano-Altai region), and the borderlands of China. However, according to the Chinese sources, the earliest dating of mounted nomads on China's frontiers is the mid-fifth and, more conspicuously, the late fourth centuries BCE. In addition, the existing archaeological materials prevent us from categorically dating their provenance before the sixth century. Finally, there is no convincing evidence that pastoral nomadism emerged in that region earlier than in the western parts of the steppe.[4] In all likelihood, the similarities between the ancient nomadic cultures derive not so much from a shared place of origin but from a common lifestyle and, all the more so, intensive contacts among different nomadic groups that expedited the outspread of innovation and cultural miscegenation. Last but not least, this affinity can also be ascribed to numerous nomadic migrations—mainly westward, but also to the south, and perhaps also to the east—particularly during the earliest period.

Among the migrations—probably not the first of them—was the Scythians' movement to the East European steppes, under pressure from their eastern neighbors. Before heading west, their ancestors had lived near the Araxes River, either the Volga or the Amu-Darya.[5] Herodotus notes that the Scythians' predecessors in the East European steppes were Cimmerians.[6] However, numerous attempts to discriminate between archaeological materials dating from the ninth or eighth century to the first half of the seventh century BCE and even later that might belong to those peoples have come up short. Although they belonged to different polities, a wide range of scholars agree that Cimmerians and Scythians were, in all likelihood, closely related groups from an ethnic, linguistic, and cultural standpoint.[7] In any event, some Cimmerian groups were expelled from the South Russian (Ukrainian) steppes no later than the final quarter of the eighth century, while others were apparently subjugated and incorporated into the Scythian polity.

In the eighth and early seventh centuries BCE, the Scythian polity was predominantly nomadic. The sedentary life had indeed been almost completely abandoned in the East European steppes by the ninth century. Cultivation continued to exist only in the forest-steppe zone, which extends from the south Bug River to the middle Dnepr reaches, and to the middle Don River, but to a lesser extent than in the previous period. One possible reason for this development was the raids and other pressures that were exerted on the region by the nomads.[8] However, various contacts with the agricultural and urban world were indispensable for the normal functioning of pastoral nomadic societies. Contrary to the opinion of some scholars, there is no clear-cut evidence that large-scale horseback riding had been mastered before the latter half of the second millennium BCE. Mounted archery and, in all probability, the use of riding for military purposes emerged even later—in the beginning of the first millennium BCE.[9] After all, in order to mobilize and maintain mass cavalries, one should have adversaries against whom they could be efficiently deployed. Only since that time did the steppe nomads obtain long-term military advantage in confrontations with sedentary societies in the context of mounted warfare.[10]

It is hardly a coincidence then that the most energetic Scythians followed the example of the Cimmerians and no later than the 670s BCE invaded the Near East, where they would play an important role in the political life of the region for quite some time.

It is there, somewhere in Transcaucasia, possibly on the territory of contemporary Azerbaijan and/or adjacent areas, that the First Scythian Kingdom emerged and existed in the second half of the seventh century and in the beginning of the sixth century BCE. The opinion that it was located in the North Caucasus or even in the East European steppes seems very dubious, although it is quite possible that some Scythians remained there and maintained contacts with their brethren in Transcaucasia and the Near East.

Cimmerians and Scythians indeed wreaked havoc in the Near East. However, they also brought some important military innovations to the region: cavalry; mounted archery; a sigmoid composite bow, which the Greeks called "Scythian" and the Babylonians "Cimmerian"; and bilobate and trilobate arrowheads. The second millennium was the age of military chariots in the Near East. The last Assyrian kings hurriedly sought to form a cavalry, but their efforts produced tepid results.[11] Ninth-century Assyrian soldiers were only capable of riding in pairs, so that one rider controlled both horses and the other was free to use his bow. Individual riders appeared by the eighth century; however, the sole weapon at their disposal was the spear. The technique of controlling both horse and bow was mastered only in the seventh century BCE.[12] Compared to the Assyrians, the Medians and subsequently the Persians had more success adopting Scythian arms and archery techniques.[13]

In the end, the Scythians were defeated. According to Herodotus, at around 614 BCE, the Median king Cyaxares invited the Scythian chiefs to a feast; upon their arrival, the king got his guests drunk and murdered them.[14] The Scythians were driven back and had to conquer or retake the territories to the east and north of the Black Sea. First, they settled, or rather resettled, in the plains of the North Caucasus. In all likelihood, they had held on to this region even during their invasions of the Near East.[15] Their rich burial mounds (*kurgans*)—Kostromskaia, Kelermess, Ul'skii, Krasnoe Znamia, and others—were excavated in the western (Kuban River valley) and other regions of the North Caucasus.[16]

Some of these kurgans are dated from the mid-seventh to the first half of the sixth century and contained a number of objects of West Asian origin; others are dated to a later period, from the second half of the sixth to the early fifth century.[17]

According to classical authors, this area was inhabited by the Maeotae and other agricultural tribes, who apparently became the Scythians' vassals. However, the relatively small dimensions of the North Caucasus, with its limited economic potential and pasture lands, was insufficient for the nomads who were used to exploiting the rich countries of the Near East. The North Pontic steppes, which Herodotus characterized as "level, well-watered, and abounding in pasture," looked much more promising to the Scythians, and they soon moved their center to this area.[18]

Very little is known about the North Pontic steppes' population in the seventh and the early sixth centuries. Archaeological materials from this period are not numerous,[19] and I doubt that future excavations will drastically alter the situation. It appears that the East European steppes were depopulated at that time, partly because many nomads had moved to the Near East. It is also possible that the climate in the steppes was drier in the opening centuries of the first millennium BCE and thus less favorable to pastoral nomadism than in Herodotus's time. Nevertheless, some Scythian and

Cimmerian populations apparently remained there. The legend of the uprising of the Scythians' slaves, related by Herodotus, which probably goes back to Scythian folklore, may indicate that the Scythians had to reconquer the North Pontic steppes, an endeavor they successfully accomplished by no later than in the first half of the sixth century.[20] From the end of that century onward, the number and richness of Scythian burials in this region significantly increased.

At almost the same time, perhaps as early as the seventh century, the nomads increased pressure on cultivators in the forest-steppe zone to the north of the Pontic steppes. In consequence, the latter began to erect fortified sites. Traces of fire on many sites there probably stem from attacks launched by the nomads. Some of these sites were rebuilt after having been burnt down; some perished forever in the fires; and still others were abandoned by their inhabitants, who had decided not to wait for actual assaults. By the end of the sixth century, most of the region was brought to submission and began to be noticeably influenced by Scythian culture. Some of the Scythian groups may have even settled in the forest-steppe zone or roamed there for most of the year, returning to the steppe only in the winter. This might partially explain the comparatively small number of Scythian burials in the steppe zone throughout the seventh and the first half of the sixth centuries. Besides, one should keep in mind the fact that in the beginning of the first millennium BCE the border between the steppe and forest-steppe zones apparently shifted to the north, a development that may have indeed facilitated the nomads' utilization of the latter.

The sixth century was undoubtedly a period of Scythian expansion. Their devastating raids extended all the way to Central Europe. The earliest incursions can be dated to the beginning of the sixth century and perhaps even earlier, while the latest raids were launched in the late 500s or even at the outset of the ensuing century. The remains of fortified sites in the region (Smolenice, Kamieniec, and Wicina) leave traces of violent destruction and human loss; some of them were never used again. Arrowheads and other arms of the Scythian types, along with the timeframe of these events, testify to the Scythian origin of the invaders.[21]

The argument that there were previous Cimmerian raids to Central Europe seems less likely, although they cannot be excluded altogether.[22] In any case, the influence of the Pontic steppe cultures on those of the Carpathian Basin was evident no later than the close of the 700s.[23]

The Scythians' presence in the forest-steppe zone is confirmed by many and manifold archaeological finds. Some early graves contained artifacts of Near Eastern and, above all, Caucasian origin, thereby suggesting that the deceased Scythians had arrived from the North Caucasus. The Scythian migrations to the forest-steppe lasted for several centuries.[24] However, according to the archaeological data, the area's agricultural tribes retained their own aristocratic stratum. From the late seventh and early sixth centuries onward, these people sought to imitate the lifestyle and some practices, such as horsemanship, of their nomadic neighbors, who would later become their overlords. The general Scythization of local cultures in the forest-steppe zone notwithstanding, over the next hundred years or so, most of the nomads' weapons and other metal objects were produced by craftsmen in forest-steppe sites, where the main iron mining and processing centers were to be found.

As the result of all these events, a new Scythian state emerged in the sixth century that was to last for about three hundred years—a rather protracted longevity for a nomadic state. At the height of its power, this state occupied the vast areas between the lower Danube and Don Rivers. In order to distinguish this state from its predecessor in the Near East, I have named it the Second Scythian Kingdom.[25] Unfortunately, all too little reliable information exists about this state's political history; as is always the case in these circumstances, there is a surfeit of hypotheses. At any rate, by the end of the sixth century, the Scythian Kingdom was adequately powerful and consolidated enough to withstand the challenge of war with Darius, the king of Persia (514 or 512 BCE).

The sociopolitical organization of the Scythian state was based on the same patterns that characterized nomadic statehood in the Eurasian steppes for long historical periods.[26] Peter Golden has convincingly argued that a common nomadic political culture existed in the Eurasian steppes during the early medieval period.[27] In fact, there are many reasons to believe that it had already taken shape in the first millennium BCE.[28]

This quite original polyethnic political culture was represented by different synchronic and diachronic variants, which reflect temporal, spatial, and ethnic differences, inter alia, as well as foreign influences. Nonetheless, the culture was by no means confined to individual nomadic polities and states, as many of its characteristics were shared across the entire region. Despite numerous modifications, this political culture also demonstrated remarkable stability. This should come as no surprise, for the main features of the nomads' sociopolitical and economic organization were also quite similar and stable.

In fact, their political culture underwent substantial changes only after the cultural space in the Eurasian steppes was fragmented by the dissemination of various world religions, especially once most of the nomads had embraced Islam and the Mongols in the east had converted to Buddhism. Nevertheless, some of its age-old traits were still noticeable much later.

The Scythian state was indeed one of, if not the first in, a long line of nomadic states and polities that, to a greater or lesser degree, shared the same political culture. To prove my point I can refer to a sampling of Scythian political traditions that also existed in later nomadic polities: the notion of the divine origin of a chosen clan[29] and its equally divine mandate to rule;[30] the notion of charisma, the Iranian *farnah* (cf. the Turkic *qut*), namely heavenly ordained good fortune and its attendant aura;[31] a developed system of royal and administrative titles;[32] color symbolism, which in the steppe was used to make social distinctions and define political status;[33] and elaborate status and rank distinctions and practices that were associated with vestment and decoration;[34] special investiture and funeral ceremonies;[35] sacred territories and cult centers;[36] the idea of collective or joint sovereignty according to which a state and its populace belong not to an individual ruler but to all the members of a ruling clan or extended family, as their corporate property;[37] diets or convocations attended by members of the ruling clan and other nobles;[38] a partial overlap between the administrative system and military organization;[39] and a patrimonial mode of governance.[40]

The similarities with other nomadic polities and states may be traced even to minor cultural traits and customs. To provide some examples, I can refer to the Scythian custom of making cups from the skulls of killed enemies that was also documented among the Xiongnu, and some early medieval Turkic-speaking nomads, for example, the Pechenegs. Arrowheads as a symbol of war declaration were used not only by Scythians, but also by the Xiongnu and Kitans. Zoomorphic primogenitors, or totems, were characteristic not only of Iranian, but also of Turkic and Mongol nomads. Peculiarities of funerals of the Scythian kings resemble descriptions of the funerals of Attila, the Khazar kings, or Chinggis Khan. The number of such examples can easily be increased.

Still, in one very important respect the Scythian kingdom differed from other nomadic states. This difference was directly connected with the very peculiar historical situation created by the Greek colonization of the Pont and its consequences. Contrary to other nomadic states, the main partners of the Scythians were not traditional states and empires but Greek *poleis*, foci of the unique classic civilization.[41]

Due to ancient Greece's early urbanization and barren soils, the import of agricultural products, raw materials, and slaves played a key role in its economy. Along with several other reasons, like overpopulation and occasional social strife, Greek colonization was aimed at meeting the abovementioned demands. It is little wonder, then, that the Greek *poleis* on the northern seaboard of the Pontus were evolving into both agricultural and trading colonies. The founding of the earliest of these colonies basically coincided with the Scythians' return from the Near East. Olbia, a *polis* on the coast of the Bug River estuary, was established at the turn of the sixth century BCE although the preceding emporium and settlement on the island of Berezan (located opposite the *polis*) already existed from as early as the mid-seventh century. Panticapaeum, Nymphaeum, Tiritaka, Phanagoria, Pheodosia, and several other *poleis* were founded in the first half of the sixth century or a little later in the same century; only Chersonesus was founded later, in the second half of the fifth century. However, these *poleis* alone were unable to meet the growing demand on their own and had to rely on trade with indigenous populations. Already in the sixth century, a trilateral system of economic relations began to be established, connecting the Greek and barbarian worlds: Mediterranean Hellas—Greek *poleis* to the north of the Black Sea—and Scythia (in the broader sense of the word). The crux of the matter was that with regard to Scythia, the Greek *poleis* in the Northern Pontus played an economic role somewhat similar to that which their metropolises and other Greek centers played toward them. These *poleis* exported or reexported luxury items, wine, and other goods that were in high demand in the Scythian hinterland. In fact, to a large extent, the Greeks had indeed created this demand on their own. In return, they received raw materials and slaves.[42] It took some time for the system to evolve, and it far from always functioned smoothly. But its peculiarities at certain historical periods may explain a number of seemingly isolated and puzzling sociopolitical events both in the history of Scythians and of Greek *poleis* in the northern Pontic area.

At the outset, the Greeks had tried to trade directly with cultivators in the forest-steppe zone, especially along the Dnepr and Bug Rivers. This trade started no later than the second half of the sixth century BCE, perhaps even a few decades earlier.[43] However, in one way or another, the nomads were also involved in contacts with the Greeks. Nomad burials in the steppe region dated to that period contain Greek pottery vessels and excellent bronzes of the Ionian type.[44] Remarkably, approximately at that time Scythian slaves (actually, slaves sold by Scythians via the north Pontic *poleis*) first appeared in Greece. Still, the scale of early trade between Greeks and forest-steppe zone cultivators should not be overestimated.[45] During the sixth century, even Olbia—the most active player in this trade—apparently concentrated on the first link of the trilateral system: its own metropolis

The situation underwent drastic changes in the fifth and especially the fourth centuries BCE. In many regions of the forest-steppe, Greek imports dropped off significantly and the quality of life declined. The *kurgans* of that time are poorer than those dated to the earlier period, while many fortified settlements deteriorated and their total number decreased.[46] These developments may be explained by the growing subordination of the forest-steppe population to the Scythians, accompanied by a new wave of nomads who arrived on both banks of the middle Dnepr.

The Scythian nomadic aristocracy managed to bring the Greek trade with various regions of Scythia under its control. It realized tribute in kind paid by the dependent cultivators of the forest-steppe zone on the north Pontic Greek markets. The extremely rich black earth (*chernozem*) soils there allowed production of a surplus of grain and other products. According to Herodotus,[47] the "ploughmen Scythians"—one of the ethnic or administrative subdivisions of Scythia—grew cereals especially for sale. In return, Scythians received luxury items—jewelry, metalwork, and pottery of the finest quality—along with their much-loved wine. At the same time, they began to exert pressure on the Greek *poleis* in the North Pontic region. Some of the colonies were drawn into the sphere of Scythian political influence and, at times, were even forced to pay tribute; Olbia became directly dependent on the Scythian kings.[48]

Herodotus claimed that Scythians had "neither cities nor forts."[49] However, by the end of the fifth century, urbanization had commenced on the Scythian steppe. The best-known fortified urban site there is Kamenskoe gorodishche, on the lower Dnepr River. Apparently, it was the kingdom's main trading, handicraft, and administrative center. Remarkably, aristocrats and possibly governmental officials lived in an additionally fortified part of the town. There are striking functional similarities between the Scythian capital and the capitals of medieval nomadic states. It is hardly accidental that many burials of the Scythian kings and aristocracy are located in proximity to the Kamenskoe site.

The Scythian influence extended well beyond their territory, both to the west and to the east. Their weapons and equestrian gear were in great demand among Geto-Thracian tribes of the Carpathians and Balkans. Herodotus noted that Scythian merchants traded with the tribes to the east, conducting their business in seven languages with the assistance of seven interpreters.[50] Unfortunately, aside from the discovery of Olbian-made mirrors in the Urals, there is sparse concrete knowledge about the routes of this trade.[51]

The wealth and power of the Scythian ruling strata between the fifth and early third centuries BCE are evidenced by their burial mounds, especially by the so-called royal Scythian tombs. Actually, some of these mounds may belong not only to the royalty, but also to the Scythian aristocracy, and attempts to identify them with individual Scythian kings[52] are not particularly convincing. These burials contain numerous objects made of precious metals, including highly refined artworks, attesting to the striking differences between the lifestyle and status of the aristocracy and of ordinary Scythians. In spite of the continuous plundering of these burial mounds since ancient times, over twenty thousand gold objects were found therein, about a half of which were made by Greek jewelers. Those interested in ancient Greek jewelry and toreutics should visit the museums of St. Petersburg and Kiev before going to Greece. Some of the masterpieces in these institutions are of such outstanding quality that even nineteenth-century jewelers—with all their technologically advanced equipment—could not produce exact replicas of these treasures. Since the second half of the fifth century BCE onward, Greek influence over Scythian art steadily grew. However, relatively few of the objects from the Scythian tombs were designed in the pure Greek artistic tradition; even those were often made to meet the tastes and specifications of Scythian aristocrats. Some of them reflect themes from the Scythian myths and epos, while others were made for the Scythians in accordance with their indigenous tradition; the basic artistic inspiration for them was Scythian. The designs of many Greek-made objects form a unique, remarkably vital genre of decorative art, which is usually called "the Scythian animal style" with regard to European nomads and "the Scythian-Siberian animal style" with regard to the ancient nomads of the Eurasian steppes in general. This style portrays wild (mainly predatory and ungulate) or fantastic animals and birds in several canonical poses, sometimes on their own and other times locked in combat. In some of the artifacts, only parts of the animals are depicted; in others, one creature grows out of the body of another. Works in animal style are often small and portable; most of them decorated weapons or horse equipment.

These items had deep symbolic meaning for their owners, although we can only hazard conjectures as to what it was. In all likelihood, animal images had some sort of connection to religion and/or magic, and at the same time symbolized a high social status. Very little is known about the earliest history of the animal style in the Eurasian steppes, and the debate as to whether its origins are polycentric or monocentric has yet to be settled.[53] At the moment, some scholars tend to give priority to the Inner and Central Asian nomads, but a final conclusion would be premature. The animal style appeared almost simultaneously, and in a rather developed state, in various parts of the steppe somewhere around the mid-seventh century BCE and perhaps even earlier. Although some of its variants reflected Near Eastern, Chinese, and later Greek influences as well as some Late Bronze Age traditions, the animal style was quite original from its inception. The animal style was based on indigenous nomadic ideological, political, and cultural concepts, which were manifested in different forms and materials. Perhaps, originally the primary materials may have been wood and wool. In a new situation, when the Scythians and other nomads became acquainted with the art of various sedentary peoples, some of these concepts were translated into new forms and materials, originally with the assistance of foreign artists or under their influence. However, they always corresponded to the ideological and artistic criteria of the nomads, in the case of Greeks—with the Scythian ones. In my opinion, from a semiotic standpoint, the animal style can be characterized as a style of codes and quotations. Animals are but illustrations for, or citations from, a text. In addition, they may have also functioned as symbols and ideograms. Unfortunately, the whole text remains unknown to us, and I am afraid will remain unknown forever, which indeed opens a wide door to all manner of speculation.

Intensive contacts with the Greeks were instrumental not only to the growing stratification of Scythian society, but to its cultural segmentation as well. Whereas some members of the royal clan and the aristocracy were Hellenized to various degrees, the nomadic Scythian commoners derived few benefits from commerce with Greece. Only a handful of Greek objects have been found in their burials. Even the relatively inexpensive black-varnish vessels sometimes carry the traces of repair work, thus indicating that they were a major purchase for their owners and sparingly used. Even amphorae had a secondary use as jars for storing milk.[54]

At the same time, the growing contacts with the Greeks had one negative consequence for the Scythians. By the sixth century, their hard drinking and contempt for the Greek practice of diluting wine with water had become proverbial throughout Greece.[55] In the fourth century, amphorae used for storing wine were found across the entire Scythian steppe in much larger numbers than ever before.[56] Furthermore, it bears noting that most wine was transported into the Scythian hinterland in wineskins. It would thus be not a great exaggeration to say that the Greeks were encouraging the Scythians' propensity for intemperance, just as later European and Russian traders would do to North American Indians and Siberian aborigines. The trade and other contacts between Greeks and Scythians intensified and became even more advantageous to the latter during the fourth century BCE, when the Scythian Kingdom reached its zenith. Following the Peloponnesian War, Athens became more dependent on grain from the Pontus than ever before, and the Bosporus emerged as its main supplier.[57] In turn, the Pontic *poleis,* including the Bosporus ones, increased their purchases from the local populations. This situation apparently stimulated the sedentarization process, which became evident even in the steppe zone. As the Scythians, however, became more involved in the trade with Mediterranean Greece, they became less inclined to share profits with intermediaries. In the fourth century BCE, they increased their pressure on the Greek cities on northern shores of the Pontus, while simultaneously penetrating into the Balkans. The most famous Scythian king, Ateas, at the age of ninety, personally led his troops into a battle with Philip, a father of Alexander the Great, but was defeated and perished in 339 BCE in a battle that attracted great interest from ancient authors.[58] The recently excavated tomb that is thought to belong to Philip[59] not only stirred up a ridiculous conflict between the modern states of Macedonia and Greece over ancient Macedonia's symbolic heritage, to which both countries have an indirect tie at best. It contained several objects that are characteristic of Scythian art or that were made to Scythian order. One of them, a golden quiver, is identical to those found in the Scythian royal tombs and, apparently, was made by an Olbian artist. One can only conjecture as to how Philip obtained these treasures.

The defeat and death of Ateas was not yet the end of the Scythian kingdom. In 331 BCE, when Zopyrion, governor-general of Alexander the Great, besieged Olbia, his army suffered a shattering defeat at the hands of the Scythians.[60] The fall of the Scythian Kingdom came later, somewhere in the first half or middle of the third century BCE for reasons that have yet to be fully comprehended. Although other factors cannot be excluded, the Scythians may have succumbed to the pressure of Celts and Getae from the west and especially the Sarmatians from the east. What is more, in the third century BCE the Greek cities to the north of the Pontus entered a protracted economic crisis that negatively affected the Scythian economy. Regardless of the cause, during that same century, the *kurgans* of the Scythian aristocracy and even burials of ordinary nomads disappeared from the steppe, while cultures of the forest-steppe zone rapidly lost their Scythian traits. The later history of Scythia was accompanied by intensified processes of sedentarization and even urbanization. After somewhat recovering from their defeats, Scythians managed to establish two new but separate states, which Strabo dubbed Scythae Minores (Little Scythias),[61] as opposed to the previous Scythia Magna. One of them was located in Dobruja, in the Balkans, whereas the other in the foothills and steppes of Crimea and the lower Dnepr.[62] In Dobruja, the Scythian aristocracy retained their power over the agricultural Geto-Thracian population but had to abandon their nomadic way of life. In any case, this polity was short-lived and ceased to exist by the beginning of the first century BCE. Another Little Scythia, which I call the Third Scythian Kingdom, survived for several more centuries, yet during this time, the Scythian way of life and culture underwent serious changes. The pastoral nomadic economy requires vast pasture territories. In the absence of such lands, some Scythians were compelled to sedentarize along the banks of the lower Dnepr, where they built fortified settlements.

Likewise, in the Crimea, Scythians had no other option but to gradually sedentarize, although their kings and aristocracy might continue to maintain the nomadic way of life. Their political relations with the Greeks rapidly deteriorated. Having begun to grow cereals themselves, the Scythians preferred to sell it on the Mediterranean markets without middlemen. Moreover, they considered the Greeks in the Crimea to be competitors and strove to seize their cultivated territories and ports, but did so only with mixed results.

At the same time, the Scythians became much more susceptible to the Greek cultural influence. Their kings founded a new capital in the Crimea, Neapolis,[63] which was enclosed by a massive stone wall; it had Greek-style columns and marble statuary. The Scythian kings and aristocracy lived there in palaces and private houses that were built by Greek architects and adorned by Greek painters. They often used the Greek language and even began to worship the Greek gods. Even ordinary Scythians now preferred Greek pottery to their own.

The late Scythian culture became very syncretic, borrowing a great deal not only from Greek culture, but from the Sarmatian culture as well. Only a few cultural traits, such as pottery and burial tombs, retained the old Scythian traditions. In the third century CE, the last Scythian Kingdom was destroyed by some of the groups that were involved in the beginning of the Great Migration of Peoples, and with its fall, the Scythians departed forever from the historical arena.

In conclusion, I would like to return to the problem of continuity in the nomadic societies of the Eurasian steppes. I have already mentioned the remarkable similarity of the political culture, the main organizational principles, and many specific institutions of Scythians and other ancient nomads, on the one hand, and of medieval Turkic and Mongol nomads, on the other. These similarities need to be not only explored, but also explained. One may wonder if they were the result of similar but parallel indigenous developments and independent borrowings from sedentary peoples, or of mutual influences in the steppe zone. One explanation should not exclude another; still, I am inclined to think that with regard to the political culture certain steppe traditions were, at least, as important and long-lasting as influences from the outside world. Somewhere between the third or fourth and the sixth to seventh centuries CE, the Turkic-speaking nomads replaced the Iranian-speaking ones in the Eurasian steppes. This development still lacks a satisfactory explanation, especially since in the beginning of this process the latter should have been much more numerous than the former. Be that as it may, the ancestors and predecessors of the Turkic nomads had come under the Iranian nomads' influence already in the first millennium

BCE. Of course, the Xiongnu should also be taken into account, but their state emerged about three centuries after the Scythian one. In any case, the first millennium BCE may be considered the formative period for the political culture of the Eurasian nomads, and the Iranian nomads—that is, the Scythians, in the broader sense of the name—played a very important role in its creation. A study of the various mechanisms of its transmission in different historical, linguistic, and ethnic milieux is still a task for exciting future research.

Notes

1. For example, the number of sites and burials in the steppes between the Don and Danube Rivers decreased tenfold from the twelfth to tenth centuries BCE vis-à-vis the previous period, a trend that would continue over the next few centuries. See S. B. Makhortykh, *Kul'turnye kontakty naseleniia Severnogo Prichernomor'ia i Tsentral'noi Evropy v kimmeriiskuiu epokhu* (Kiev, 2003), p. 55.

2. A. M. Khazanov, *Nomads and the Outside World* (Madison, WI, 1994), pp. 94–95.

3. V. S. Ol'khovskii, *Skifskaia triada. Materially i issledovaniia po arkheologii Rossii, No. 1* (Moscow, 1997).

4. N. Di Cosmo, *Ancient China and Its Enemies: The Rise of Nomadic Power in East Asian History* (Cambridge, 2002), pp. 57, 75ff., 128.

5. Herodotus, IV, 11. Considering some Central and Inner Asian elements in the ninth- and eighth-century archaeological cultures, which can be identified rather tentatively as proto-Scythian, the second hypothesis seems more plausible at the moment. See A. Yu. Alekseev, *Khronografiia evropeiskoi Skifii* (St. Petersburg, 2003), p. 38ff.

6. Herodotus, IV, 11. The literature on the Cimmerians is rapidly growing, e.g., I. M. Diakonoff, "Cimmerians," *Acta Iranica,* 21 (1981), pp. 103–140; G. B. Lanfranchi, *I Cimmeri. Emergenza delle élites militari iraniche nel Vicino Oriento (VIII-VII sec. a.C.)* (Padua, 1990); A. Yu. Alekseev et al., *Kimmeriitsy: etnokul'turnaia prinadlezhnost'* (St. Petersburg, 1993); E. A. Grantovskii et al., "Kimmeriitsy na Blizhnem Vostoke," *Vestnik drevnei istorii,* 4 (1996), pp. 69–85; S. Tokhtas'ev, "Die Kimmerier in den antiken Überlieferung," *Hyperboreus,* 2/1 (1996), pp. 1–46; A. I. Ivantchik, *Kimmeriitsy* (Moscow, 1996); A. I. Ivantchik, "The Current State of the Cimmerian Problem," *Ancient Civilizations,* 7/3–4 (2001), pp. 307–339; A. I. Ivantchik, "Early Eurasian Nomads and the Civilizations of the Ancient Near East (Eighth–Seventh Centuries BCE)," in *Mongols Turks and Others: Eurasian Nomads and the Outside World,* ed. R. Amitai and M. Biran (Leiden, 2005), pp. 103–127; Makhortykh, *Kul'tyrnye kontakty.*

7. See e.g., A. M. Khazanov, *Sotsial'naia istoriia skifov* (Moscow, 1975), pp. 209–212; Diakonoff, "Cimmerians," pp. 132–133; Ivantchik, "Current State of the Cimmerian Problem," pp. 324–325, 338–339.

8. A. I. Terenozhkin, *Kimmeriitsy* (Kiev, 1976), p. 214; Makhortykh, *Kul'tyrnye kontakty,* p. 56.

9. Khazanov, *Nomads and the Outside World,* p. 94; N. A. Bokovenko, "The Origins of Horse Riding and the Development of Ancient Central Asian Nomadic Harness," in *Kurgans, Ritual Sites, and Settlements: Eurasian Bronze and Iron Age,* ed. J. Davis-Kimbal et al.

(Oxford, 2000), p. 304; E. E. Kuzmina, "The Eurasian Steppes: The Transition from Early Urbanism to Nomadism," in *Kurgans, Ritual, Sites, and Settlements*, pp. 118–119; U. L. Dietz, "Horseback Riding: Man's Access to Speed?" in *Prehistoric Steppe Adaptation and the Horse*, ed. M. Levine et al. (Cambridge, 2003), p. 197.

10. A. Sherratt, "The Horse and the Wheel: The Dialectics of Change in the Circum-Pontic Regions and Adjacent Areas, 4500–1500 BC," in *Prehistoric Steppe Adaptation and the Horse*, p. 247.

11. Y. Yadin, *The Art of Warfare in Biblical Lands: In the Light of Archaeological Study* (Jerusalem, 1963), pp. 286–287; A. M. Khazanov, *Ocherki voennogo dela sarmatov* (Moscow, 1971), p. 56.

12. J. Oates, "A Note on the Early Evidence for Horse and the Riding of Equids in Western Asia," in *Prehistoric Steppe Adaptation and the Horse*, p. 123.

13. Herodotus, I, 73; also see I. M. Diakonoff, "Kimmeriitsy i skify na Blizhnem Vostoke," *Rossiiskaia Arkheologiia*, 1 (1994), pp. 112–113.

14. Herodotus, I, 73, 74, 106.

15. V. G. Petrenko, "K voprosu o khronologii ranneskifskikh kurganov Tsentral'nogo Predkavkaz'ia," in *Problemy skifo-sarmatskoi arkheologii*, ed. A. I. Melyukova (Moscow, 1990), p. 75.

16. V. Yu. Murzin, *Proiskhozhdenie skifov: osnovnye etapy formirovaniia skifskogo etnosa* (Kiev, 1990), pp. 47–50.

17. V. G. Petrenko, "Scythian Culture in North Caucasus," in *Nomads of the Eurasian Steppes in the Early Iron Age*, ed. J. Davis-Kimball et al. (Berkeley, 1995), p. 5ff.

18. Herodotus, IV, 47.

19. A. I. Melyukova, "Scythians of Southeastern Europe," in *Nomads of the Eurasian Steppes in the Early Iron Age*, p. 32.

20. Herodotus, IV, 1, 3, 4.

21. J. Chochorowski, "Die Frage der Skythischen Expansion auf das Gebiet des Karpatenbeckens," *Acta Archaeologica Carpathica*, 15 (1975), pp. 5–30; J. Chochorowski, "Die Rolle der Vekeryug-Kultur (VK) im skythische Einflüsse," *Mitteleuropa. Praehistorische Zeitschrift*, 60 (1985), pp. 230–271; J. Chochorowski, "Skifskie nabegi na territoriu Srednei Evropy," *Rossiiskaia Arkheologiia*, 4 (1994), pp. 49–64. This rather widespread opinion about Scythian raids on Central Europe has been challenged by Partsinger (G. Partsinger, "Stepnye kochevniki na vostoke Tsentral'noi Evropy. Nakhodki—i pamiatniki v svete sravnitel'noi arkheologii," *Vestnik drevnei istorii*, 2 [1998], pp. 104–115). He argues that Scythian-type artifacts have surfaced in Central Europe because the eastern groups of the Hallstatt and Lausitzer cultures came into close contact with the nomadic population of the Pontic steppes in the eighth century BCE, borrowing some of the nomads' arms and elements of the horse harness. However, there are strong doubts as to whether these relations were always peaceful. In any event, the nomadic influence on the population of Central Europe is indisputable.

22. J. Chochorowskii, *Ekspansja Kimmeryjska na Tereny Evropy Srodkowej* (Krakow, 1993); Makhortykh, *Kul'tyrnye kontakty.*

23. C. Metzner-Nebelsick, "Early Iron Age Pastoral Nomadism in the Great Hungarian Plain—Migration or Assimilation? The Thraco-Cimmerian Problem Revisited," in *Kurgans, Ritual Sites, and Settlements: Eurasian Bronze and Iron Age*, pp. 160–184.

24. V. S. Ol'khovskii, *Pogrebal'no-pominal'naia obriadnost' naseleniia stepnoi Skifii (VII-III vv. do n.e.)* (Moscow, 1991), p. 166.

25. Khazanov, *Sotsial'naia istoriia skifov*, p. 229.

26. Ibid., p. 203ff.; A. M. Khazanov, "The Early State among the Scythians," in *The Early State,* ed. H. J. M. Claessen and P. Skalnik (The Hague, 1978), pp. 77–92.

27. P. B. Golden, "Imperial Ideology and the Sources of Political Unity amongst the Pre-Cinggisid Nomads of Western Eurasia," *Archivum Eurasiae Medii Aevi,* 2 (1982), pp. 37–76.

28. A. M. Khazanov, "Nomads of the Eurasian Steppes in Historical Retrospective," in *Nomadic Pathways in Social Evolution,* ed. N. N. Kradin et al. (Moscow, 2003), pp. 25–49.

29. Scythians claimed that their kings were direct descendants of Papaeus (a god identified with Zeus) and a daughter of the River Borysthenes (i.e., Dnepr) (Herodotus, IV, 5–7). In accordance with the version popular among the Pontic Greeks, the Scythian kings were descendants of Heracles (apparently Targitaus, the Scythian primogenitor) and Echidna, a local deity—half woman, half serpent—who was a daughter of the Borysthenes (Herodotus, IV, 8–10). Yet another version, which was conveyed by Diodorus (II, 43, 3, 4) relates that the Scythian kings were descendants of Zeus and Echidna. For an analysis of the Scythian ethnogenic legends see Khazanov, *Sotsial'naia istoriia skifov,* p. 36ff.; A. M. Khazanov, "Legenda o proiskhozdenii skifov (Herodotus, IV, 5–6)," in *Skifskii mir* (Kiev, 1975), pp. 74–93.

30. The aforementioned Scythian legend also relates that certain golden objects fell from the Heavens when Targitaus's three sons ruled Scythia. Only the youngest son, Coloxais, managed to take possession of them. The other brothers took this to be a sign of a divine mandate to rule and thus ceded all sovereignty to the younger sibling (Herodotus, IV, 5). The notion of a divine mandate also figures in the Greek version of the legend, albeit in a different form (Herodotus, IV, 9–10).

31. The golden objects that fell from the sky were not only proof of the heavenly mandate bestowed upon Scythian kings, but symbolized their charisma as well. Herodotus (IV, 7) claimed that the sacred gold was kept in the domain of supreme Scythian kings, who guarded it with the utmost care. In addition, they offered great sacrifices to these objects on an annual basis in order to propitiate the gods. They believed that whoever had the sacred gold with him at the festival and fell asleep in the open air would not live the year out.

32. For an analysis of Scythian aristocratic terminology see Khazanov, *Sotsial'naia istoriia skifov,* p. 179ff.

33. T. T. Allsen, *Commodity and Exchange in the Mongol Empire: A Cultural History of Islamic Textiles* (Cambridge, 1997), pp. 58, 65.

34. In this respect, gold associated with the sun and fire was especially prominent. It was not only a symbol of sacred royal power, but of high rank in general. Furthermore, it played an important role in the funerary rituals and practices of the Scythians (V. I. Guliaev and E. N. Savchenko, "K voprosu o roli zolota v pogrebal'nom rituale skifov," in *Evraziiskie drevnosti,* ed. A. I. Melyukova et al. [Moscow, 1999], pp. 151–157) and other Iranian nomads (B. A. Litvinskii, "Zolotye liudi" v drevnikh pogrebeniiakh Tsentral'noi Azii [opyt istolkovaniia v svete istorii religii]," *Sovetskaia etnografiia,* 4 [1982], pp. 34–43). Similar notions and practices existed in later nomadic cultures (see e.g., H. Serruys, "Mongol *Altan* 'Gold' = 'Imperial,'" *Monumenta Serica,* 21 [1962], pp. 357–378; and Allsen, *Commodity and Exchange,* p. 60ff.).

35. See A. M. Khazanov, *Sotsial'naia istoriia skifov,* p. 191ff., among many other publications.

36. Such sacred territory in Scythia was located in the country of the Gerhi; it was a place of burial of Scythian kings (Herodotus, IV, 71, 127).

37. Herodotus (IV, 7, 120) claimed that Coloxais divided his country into three "kingdoms" for his sons and that the tripartite division of Scythia was still in existence at

the time of the war with Darius at the end of the sixth century BCE. A few smaller subdivisions of Scythia (Herodotus, IV, 62, 64) might have also been ruled by members of the royal clan (Khazanov, *Sotsial'naia istoriia skifov,* p. 197ff.). On the existence of this notion during the subsequent, Crimean period of Scythian history see Strabo, IV, 4. 3.

38. The fact that these gatherings were held may be deduced from some hints in the literary sources. Coordinated actions by the Scythian kings during the war with Darius were drawn up at some preliminary meetings (Herodotus, IV, 120). It is also possible that governors of lower ranks also participated in decision making, at any rate in critical situations (cf. Herodotus, IV, 80, 120).

39. The division of Scythia into three "kingdoms" with their own troops (Herodotus, IV, 120) fully corresponds with nomadic military-political models. In all likelihood, the lower political subdivisions of the Scythian kingdom were simultaneously subdivisions of their military organization (Herodotus, IV, 120).

40. Every Scythian who killed an enemy had a right to a share in the military loot (Herodotus, IV, 64). In addition, district governors gave annual feasts in honor of distinguished warriors (Herodotus, IV, 66).

41. A. M. Khazanov. "Les scythes et la civilization antique: problèmes des contacts," *Dialogues d'histoire ancienne,* 7 (1982), pp. 7, 51.

42. Some scholars (e.g., T. S. Noonan, "The Grain Trade of the Northern Black Sea in Antiquity," *American Journal of Philology,* 94/3 [1973], pp. 231–242; V. D. Kuznetsov, "Nekotorye problemy torgovli v Severnom Prichernomor'e v arkhaicheskii period," *Vestnik drevnei istorii,* 1 [2000], pp. 26–27, 38) deny the importance of the grain trade during the Archaic period. However, by the early fifth century BCE, *sitodeia* ("grain shortage") had become a permanent fixture in most of Greece (I. Hahn, "Foreign Trade and Foreign Policy in Archaic Greece," in *Trade and Famine in Classical Antiquity,* ed. P. Garnsey and C. R. Whittaker [Cambridge, 1983], p. 33).

43. N. A. Onaiko, *Antichnyi import v Podneprov'e i Pobuzh'e v VII-V vv. do n.e.* (Moscow, 1966).

44. V. A. Il'inskaia and A. I. Terenozhkin, *Skifiia VII-III vv* (Kiev, 1983), pp. 90–113.

45. V. D. Kuznetsov, "Nekotorye problemy torgovli v Severnom Prichernomor'e v arkhaicheskii period," *Vestnik drevnei istorii,* 1 (2000), pp. 25.

46. Melyukova, "Scythians of Southeastern Europe," p. 55.

47. Herodotus, IV, 17.

48. Yu. G. Vinogradov, *Politicheskaia istoriia ol'viiskogo polisa VII-I do n.e.* (Moscow, 1989), p. 89ff.

49. Herodotus, IV, 46.

50. Herodotus, IV, 24.

51. T. M. Kuznetsova, *Etiudy po skifskoi istorii* (Moscow, 1991), p. 77.

52. See e.g., A. Yu. Alekseev, *Khronografiia evropeiskoi Skifii* (St. Petersburg, 2003), p. 218ff.

53. See Khazanov, *Zoloto skifov* (Moscow, 1975); G. Kossak, "Von den Anfängen des Skytho-Iranischen Tierstiels," in *Bayerische Akademie der Wissenschaften. Philosophisch-Historishe Klasse Abhandlungen,* Neue Folge, Heft 98 (Munich, 1987), pp. 24–86; Y. A. Sher, "On the Sources of the Scythic Animal Style," *Arctic Anthropology,* 25/2 (1988), pp. 47–60; E. V. Perevodchikova, *Iazyk zverinykh obrazov. Ocherki iskusstva evraziiskikh stepei skifkoi epokhi* (Moscow, 1994), p. 58ff.; M. E. Hall, "Towards an Absolute Chronology of the Iron Age of Inner Asia," *Antiquity,* 71 (1997), pp. 863–874; among many others.

54. B. M. Mozolevskii, *Tovsta Mogila* (Kiev, 1979), p. 65.

55. Anacr: fr.45a Bergk; on the later period see Herodotus, IV, 84; Ael., Var. hist., II, 41.

56. I. B. Brashinskii, *Grecheskii keramicheskii import na Nizhnem Donuv V-III vv. do n.e.* (Leningrad, 1981), pp. 89–93.

57. See e.g., Demosth., adv. Lept., 32.

58. Trog., Prol., IX; Just., IX, 1, 9; IX, 2, 1–16; IX, 3, 1–3; Aesch., In Ctesyph., 128; Strabo, VII, 3, 18; Plut., Reg. et imp. apophth. Ateas; Luc., Macrob., 10; Oros., III, 13, 4–7.

59. M. Andronicos, "The Royal Tombs of Philip II," *Archaeology,* 31/4 (1978), pp. 33–41.

60. Just., XII, I, 4.

61. Strabo, IV, 4, 5; VII, 4, 5.

62. S. V. Polin, *Ot Skifii k Sarmatii* (Kiev, 1992), p. 101.

63. T. N. Vysotskaia, *Neapol'—stolitsa gosudarstva pozdnikh skifov* (Kiev, 1979); Y. P. Zaitsev, "Skilur and His Kingdom (New Discoveries and New Questions)," *Ancient Civilizations,* 7/3–4 (2001), pp. 239–271.

Four

From Steppe Roads to Silk Roads
Inner Asian Nomads and Early Interregional Exchange

William Honeychurch

The concept of the trans-Eurasian Silk Roads has gradually become familiar to peoples around the world. This concept refers to a broad network of exchange relations that were practiced on and off across Eurasia from around the first century BCE to the fifteenth century CE. Although the emphasis is often on silk, a wide array of goods, animals, technologies, styles, ideas, religions, and even diseases and genes were transported and shared along these networks. Today, the name "Silk Roads" graces popular publications, exhibits, institutions, marketing campaigns, and even musical venues, courtesy of the cellist Yo-Yo Ma. It has become a common metaphor for interaction between different societies and for the benefits of cultural sharing.

As a historical concept for helping us understand the past, the "Silk Roads" label nevertheless has as much potential to obscure important actors and processes as it has to reveal others. This is partially because of the various sources of information used to document, describe, and analyze this early network. It is also due to a tendency to see the Silk Roads as an object or system that is isolated from local contexts and thus divorced from the complex relations, agendas, and actors that propelled intercultural contact.[1] As a result, this phenomenon of long-distance exchange and interaction is often imagined as a simple "road" (singular) stretching between urban centers in Europe and Asia along which products and ideas were in continuous transit.[2] In fact, as many researchers have stressed, "Silk Roads" is plural for a very good reason—the network consisted of many routes with intricate cultural dynamics that linked up diverse cultural zones both east to west as well as north to south.[3]

From a historical perspective, there were three major exchange corridors linking East Asia to western locales by way of eastern Central Asia.

The first was between India and Xinjiang via the Pamirs and Bactria; another between Xinjiang and Parthia via Ferghana and Sogdia; and the last one existed between Dzungaria and the Pontic region via the Sir Darya and around the Caspian Sea.[4] These areas are best understood as complex spheres of multidirectional and intercultural interaction, rather than simply routes for the movement of trade goods (Figure 4.1). The manner in which trade

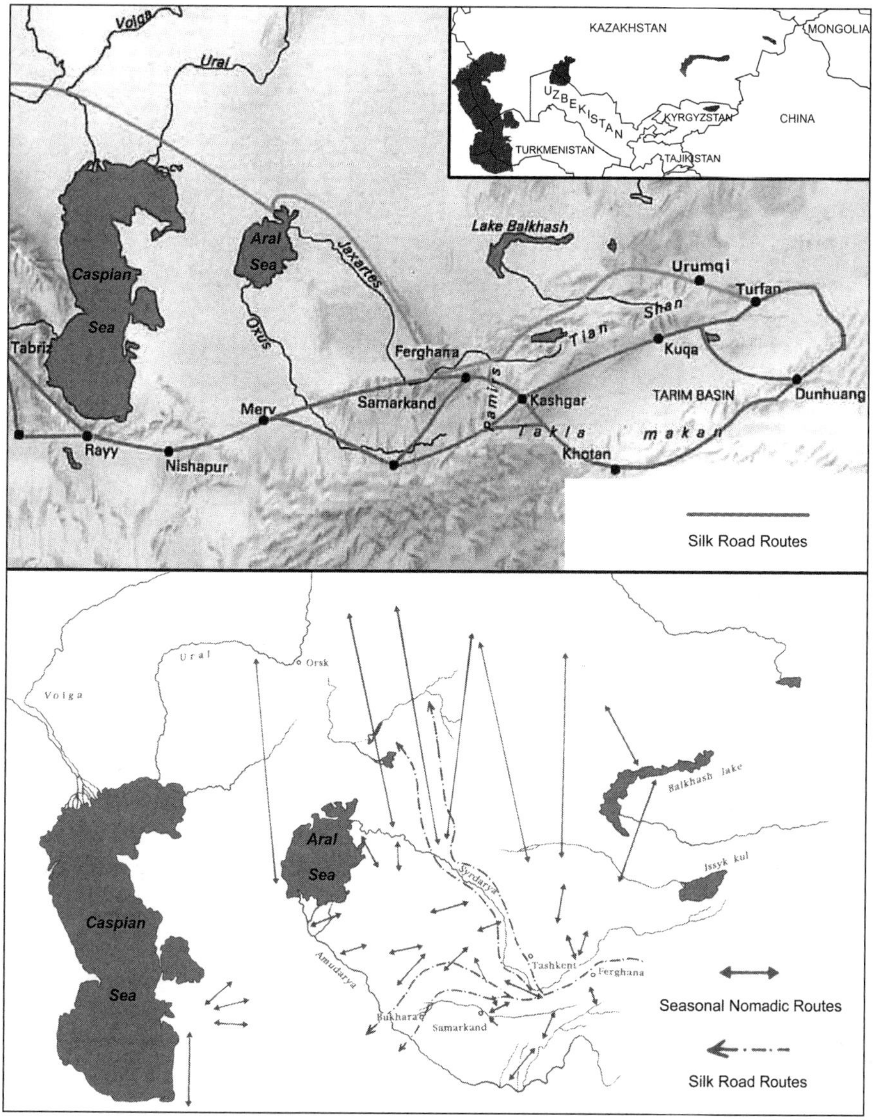

Figure 4.1. Mapping two different conceptions of early Central Asian exchange networks.

was conducted along these networks varied extensively and, for the most part, did not involve the grandiose caravan trade of stereotype. Instead, the most prevalent users were probably small groups moving on foot or with a few transport animals. What is more, these networks always tapped into more piecemeal, down-the-line exchanges with groups in the hinterlands.[5] The manner in which diverse peoples living within these zones participated in Silk Roads activity and the impact of their investments are the least highlighted yet provide the most interesting questions concerning this historic enterprise.

In this study, I continue a line of inquiry begun by the Eurasianist David Christian, who has provided both a title for this chapter and incentive to venture beyond two-dimensional line drawings of the Silk Roads.[6] Christian's article examines the input of transecological, usually north–south oriented, and largely prehistoric exchange in the making of east–west trade. His perspective accentuates the role of nomadic and forest groups that by and large have been forgotten in the standard historiography of the Silk Roads, forgotten because these peoples often had no histories of their own. In spite of this oversight, Christian's work aptly demonstrates that close and contextualized attention to the roles of nomadic actors in interregional collaborations has the potential to solve enduring problems in the study of Inner Asian history. In the ensuing pages, I supplement Christian's ideas with new archaeological data and elaborate on his hypothesis as to how nomadic political economies during the third to first centuries BCE may have functioned as predecessors to Silk Roads trade.

Inner Asian Lands, Nomads, and Politics

The eastern Eurasian steppe zone can be divided in numerous ways from a geographical standpoint but is probably most widely referred to as "Inner Asia," drawing on Owen Lattimore's famous ecological and historical study.[7] Although my focus is on the eastern steppe core (i.e., contemporary Mongolia), this study also will draw on ideas and data that have been generated by archaeological work in Inner Mongolia, Siberia, eastern Kazakhstan, Xinjiang, and northern China. These regions of Inner Asia have diverse kinds of environments including dense coniferous forest, a range of steppe grasslands, pebble and sand deserts, and high mountain ranges, such as the Altai and Tian Shan.

A major subsistence adaptation to this region has been and continues to be mobile pastoralism supplemented by horticulture, hunting, gathering, and fishing. Herd animals include horses, goats, sheep, cattle, camels, yaks, and in some areas reindeer. This subsistence system is "mobility-enabled";

namely its cultural practices, knowledge, and relationships facilitate movement when needed, though the degree to which groups actually move depends on productive, social, and political factors on both the local and regional scales. Household subsistence is best understood as a flexible and modulating system of productive inputs that can be recombined and adjusted to meet changing conditions and future outlook.[8]

The diverse peoples who inhabited Inner Asia over two thousand years ago are known to us through historical references from China, as well as through archaeological discoveries. The historical and archaeological records provide distinct bodies of information with different strengths and weaknesses and when compared and contrasted these records are particularly effective for exploring the Inner Asian past.[9] This is especially true when studying early nomads of the eastern steppe who entered textual history quite late but had a rich and influential prehistory. Inner Asian prehistory is important for understanding the development of Silk Roads trade prior to and overlapping the period of involvement of the Han dynasty in Central Asia from ca. 130 BCE. During this same period, the northern steppe peoples had formed a sizable polity known by the historical name "Xiongnu" (historically dated 209 BCE–120/150 CE).

Though Chinese texts provide information about the Xiongnu polity and its populace, these accounts often reflect the imminent threat that nomadic groups posed to the Han rather than providing an objective account of their society.[10] Sima Qian, the Han dynasty's first historian, described the Xiongnu state in chapter 110 of his *Shiji* history.[11] According to his account, the polity was geographically extensive, militarily powerful, and socially stratified with many levels of regional and local political leadership. He also provided a narrative of the Xiongnu state's expansion which began in a centrally controlled region followed by military conquests further east, west, and north.[12] The military prowess of the Xiongnu state's mounted archers continually threatened Han dynasty frontiers. As a result, Han emperors were compelled to pay tribute to the Xiongnu elite in return for peace along their borders.[13]

The Xiongnu polity was first in a long line of Inner Asian states and empires that eventually culminated in the rise of the medieval Mongol empire.[14] That said, surprisingly little is known of the indigenous political traditions in which these organizations were steeped. A number of historians, anthropologists, and archaeologists have proposed models explaining how and why nomadic people organized states among a nomadic citizenry. Whereas leaders in sedentary agricultural states might secure and control food surpluses which then could be reinvested in state infrastructure, leaders of mainly pastoral polities did not have such voluminous stocks at their disposal. Furthermore, mobile and well-armed nomadic populations were capable of resisting subjugation by political authorities. Based on these observations, the majority of anthropological and historical works on early steppe polities echo a common theme: due to mobility, lack of surplus, and fierce independence, pastoral nomads organized politically at either small scales or at larger scales only on a temporary basis.[15]

From this vantage point, the large and relatively stable Xiongnu state seems anomalous. Therefore, scholars commonly attribute its formation to the influence of Chinese neighbors.[16] Some of these explanations emphasize Sinicization processes whereby steppe peoples are thought to have adopted cultural and political models directly from Chinese states.[17] Other theories claim that the unstable pastoral economy required agricultural supplements from China. As a result, steppe nomads organized at levels comparable to early Chinese states in order to coercively secure such resources.[18] Finally, many anthropologists and historians simply doubt the complexity of nomadic organization and argue that centralization was in fact sporadic and consensual,[19] or stemmed largely from ideological incentives.[20] As we shall see, these explanations have been challenged by archaeological findings as well as by recent historical scholarship on Chinese textual accounts.[21]

Resurrected Ideas on Nomadic Political Economy

Drawing on historical reports of nomadic raiding along the frontier, researchers have long assumed that nomads of the steppe had little of value to offer neighboring civilizations but rather took every opportunity to obtain resources from these sedentary societies. In the texts mentioning early Eurasian states and empires, nomadic peoples were commonly portrayed as greedy, parasitic, and covetous of their neighbor's wealth.[22] Lattimore was among the first scholars to recognize that this wealth-seeking dynamic was linked to the internal reinforcement of political position, privilege, and rank within nomadic societies.[23] This strategy for bolstering a political system by using exotic and luxury items to mark distinction—sometimes referred to as "prestige good economies" or "wealth-based political finance"—was a common practice in many parts of the world among both nomadic and sedentary groups.[24]

In fact, the pursuit of such politically significant prestige items was important to Xiongnu and Han dynasty rulers alike.[25] In the case of the Xiongnu polity, Raschke, Christian, and Barfield have made independent arguments for taking this idea of a wealth-based political economy one step further.[26] They suggest that the Xiongnu rulership not only redistributed

Chinese luxury goods internally, but also disseminated them beyond their territory within a framework of elite exchange and alliance-building measures. In doing so, products and materials central to later commercial exchanges became known, valued, and desired among peoples far to the west of the Xiongnu. Centuries after the Xiongnu polity's collapse, Turkic empires in Mongolia managed lucrative exchange opportunities with Sogdian partners in Central Asia and, like their Xiongnu forbearers, this was also a part of political efforts to strengthen the Turkic elite.[27] During these later periods, exchange grew in volume and organization and became more like the classic commercial network of specialized traders that epitomizes the "Silk Roads."[28]

Against this historical backdrop, the following questions arise: Wherein lie the roots of this wealth-seeking approach to nomadic political economy? Did earlier forms of politics-based exchange prefigure and configure the later commercial Silk Roads of the first millennium CE? What was the Xiongnu nomadic state's role in the west and why were those regions eventually recognized by Han advisers as a critical juncture for attacking and weakening the Xiongnu polity? There is so far no definitive answer to these questions. In fact, different disciplines produce different answers on the basis of their own source records, be they textual, material, genetic, or linguistic. However, recent archaeological research on the Xiongnu polity is beginning to build a material foundation for assessing Barfield and Raschke's political economy model as well as the transecological exchange that Christian considers a significant part of the Silk Roads phenomenon. In the next sections, I discuss recent archaeological evidence for these early long-distance interactions and offer a revised explanation for Xiongnu investment in the far west.

Historical Texts on the Xiongnu and the Western Regions: A Brief Overview

Xiongnu activities in the western regions, which are referred to indirectly in the Han dynasty texts, are central to scholarly debates over Han exploration and expansion into Central Asia.[29] The regions in question include modern-day Gansu and Xinjiang provinces, along with areas of Kazakhstan, Kyrgyzstan, Uzbekistan, and Afghanistan. The relevant Chinese texts are the *Shiji* (ca. 100 BCE), the *Hanshu* (ca. 36–116 CE), and the *Hou Hanshu* (ca. 435 CE). In addition to the Sinocentric bias of the early Chinese historical project, several other historiographic problems arise regarding the credibility of these texts as information sources for Inner Asian societies and their cultural interactions. These include authenticity, later redaction, the reliability of informants and received reports, and the political agendas that shaped both the conveyance of information and the ultimate textual product.[30] In discussing the rise and westward expansion of the Xiongnu state, there is also the problem of roughly one hundred years that elapsed between the unfolding of events and their textual documentation. Although Sima Qian took over the job of recording state history from his father, the earliest phases of Xiongnu state emergence had certainly passed out of living memory by that time. In all likelihood, sources on early Xiongnu activites included a handful of official reports and commentaries supplemented by stories and legends from Han citizens, frontier dwellers, and steppe peoples living within Han territory.[31]

On the basis of these sources, Sima Qian relates a series of narrative passages about the rise to prominence of the leader Maodun (also known as Modun or Modu) as the primary architect of Xiongnu statehood in 209 BCE.[32] The defeat of the Han armies and the consequent tribute paid to the Xiongnu court can be dated to 198 BCE, at which time a major supply of silk and other luxury goods would have been under the direct control of the Xiongnu elite, though they probably had some access to such products beforehand.[33] The initial Xiongnu expansion began with conquests to the east, possibly as far as eastern Inner Mongolia or Manchuria. As per Di Cosmo's assessment of the *Shiji* text, the Xiongnu state's western extremity between 209 and 180 BCE appears to have been near the western bend of the Ordos loop. However, he goes on to say that "we do not know exactly how far west it extended north of the Yellow river, into present-day Inner and Outer Mongolia."[34]

Sima Qian provides additional information about Xiongnu interactions in the west by means of a letter that Maodun reportedly sent to the Han court. In this letter, Maodun mentions several wars launched by his westernmost forces against groups such as the Yuezhi and Wusun during the 170s/160s BCE. The text clearly indicates the defeat or capitulation of many of these peoples, as well as their flight from or integration into the Xiongnu political structure, and the expansion of both the victors' state and their sphere of influence.[35] According to Di Cosmo, these early wars allowed the Xiongnu polity to establish lasting political and economic influence in the Xinjiang region and Central Asia.[36]

While the goals of this expansion are shrouded in historical rhetoric, some scholars view the control of exchange to be a major factor behind the Xiongnu wars, especially those campaigns against the Yuezhi, who, according to some accounts, were key players in the western trade networks.[37] Unfortunately, we have little information about the precise nature of the Xiongnu polity's sway over Xinjiang and Central Asia. In the region of Xinjiang, the influence may have entailed taxation, corvée labor, and perhaps access to agricultural supplies and finished goods, but the extent of Xiongnu direct control was probably limited and sporadic.[38] The existing historical sources are similarly vague with respect to the Xiongnu state's interaction farther southwest, west, and northwest of Xinjiang. However, it stands to reason that Xiongnu ties with western peoples were as varied and complex as their relations with other foreign peoples, including the Chinese.

In any event, there is no doubt that, prior to the initial Han exploration of the west by Zhang Qian from 138 to 125 BCE, the Xiongnu polity was a major presence in the region and was involved in relationships with both sedentary and nomadic groups.[39] The objective behind Zhang Qian's mission was to forge a military alliance between the Han and the western Yuezhi in hope of defeating the Xiongnu. While the Han's offer was rejected by the Yuezhi, who occupied Bactria at that time, the information about the western regions that Zhang Qian brought back to the Han court turned out to be the most valuable part of his journey.[40] His expedition constituted the first Han exploration of genuinely unknown lands and attests to the dynasty's growing interest in geographies, peoples, and politics beyond its own territory.

Moreover, Zhan Qian's journey bears witness to a growing desire to confront the political challenge put forth by the Xiongnu.[41] It is worth noting that Han knowledge of external lands grew as a function of political and military expedience, whereas exchange was a secondary concern at best.[42] Looking at this process from the opposite direction, namely the perspective of western states and their knowledge of the eastern regions, we are presented with a strikingly different trajectory of knowledge. Early Sogdian peoples in the middle Zarafshan Valley (presently the Samargand region of Uzbekistan) knew of China and its products as early as the late third or early second century BCE. Westerners acquired this information most likely as a result of direct or indirect contact with the Xiongnu and their expanding political economy.[43]

To sum up this brief historical overview, I return to the logic implicit in Raschke, Christian, and Barfield's hypothesis for interregional Xiongnu exchange.[44] The Xiongnu had access to substantial amounts of Chinese goods by 198 BCE and probably earlier.[45] Based on textual accounts, the Xiongnu were in all likelihood engaged with the western regions by no later than 175 BCE. While their intervention in the west certainly included military action, subsequent alliances with groups such as the Wusun probably depended on political gift giving and elite exchange. It thus stands to reason that Xiongnu representatives understood that Chinese products, like silks, lacquerware, and bronze mirrors, had immense conversion value in the west, while western goods, and especially forest products, fetched high returns from Chinese frontier traders.[46] In fact, contrary to the notion that steppe nomads had little of value to exchange or to support internal political relationships, these nomads may very well have recognized opportunities early on for wealth conversion between these distant regions.

In my estimation, the Xiongnu political economy not only bridged different systems of value, but thanks to their political example and use of certain materials to represent leadership and political status, they probably helped create and define these systems as well. In other words, the western desire for eastern materials and goods was originally cultivated through a Xiongnu model of political prestige symbolized by these very products. This explanation, however, does not preclude the small-scale, down-the-line movement of Chinese goods via Gansu and the Xinjiang region, which certainly dates back to an even earlier period. However, the above model does enhance our historical understanding of the northern steppe nomads' unflagging desire for Chinese luxury items as well as the commensurate frontier trade that was pursued by Chinese of all social classes in search of "barbarian wealth" from the north and west.[47]

Unfortunately, there is one problem with this otherwise promising explanation. In his quest for the origins of Sogdian commerce in Central Asia, Étienne de la Vaissière observes the following:

> one could imagine a Sogdian commerce already partially oriented towards the steppe, perhaps in the direction of the Xiongnu so well supplied with Chinese silk. But given the total absence of commercial documents concerning these areas, this possibility remains only an hypothesis.[48]

Likewise, the historical sources in our own case of the Xiongnu are indeed extremely suggestive, but provide no direct evidence for such an interregional dynamic. While every so often new historical documents surface from the sands of the Tarim Basin in Xinjiang and similar locales, the argument concerning the roots of Silk Roads exchange must be evaluated primarily by archaeological means.[49]

Xiongnu Archaeology and the Proto–Silk Roads

The archaeology charting the emergence of the Silk Roads has developed in rather unexpected ways. Numerous studies have shown that the intercultural ties that linked up eastern Eurasia—east to west and north to south—date back thousands of years before the rise of the more commercial manifestation of the Silk Roads.[50] While there is evidence for increasing contact and higher volumes of exchange during the first century BCE, it is not until the first century CE that we can begin to refer to the kinds of specialized activities and trade volume that characterized the Silk Roads proper.[51] Clearly, nomadic precedents must be taken into account in order to fully understand these later economic processes.[52]

Turning from the historical to the material record of the proto–Silk Roads has advantages as well as drawbacks. With respect to the benefits, archaeological data from Siberia, Kazakhstan, Xinjiang, Mongolia, and Inner Mongolia create an appreciably wider geography for analysis. While historical documents tend to link any discussion of the western regions to a relatively narrow area—primarily Gansu and Xinjiang—archaeological research extends our perspective to the Central Asian steppe and northern forest zones. On the other hand, the Xiongnu archaeological record still leaves much to be desired. Considerable research is necessary if we are to understand the basic chronology and organizational development during this period, as well as the connections between archaeology and historical accounts.

To be clear, the Xiongnu archaeological record denotes a particular material culture argued to be related to the historical Xiongnu polity.[53] What links the histories to the material culture are clear references to long-term, regional-scale complex organization in areas north of the Han frontier; these same characteristics are exhibited by material patterns best known from present-day Mongolia. Xiongnu material culture consists of pottery styles, artifact types, mortuary remains, a wide variety of settlements, landscape arrangements, and patterns of association between these elements. From a geographic standpoint, it is distributed in Mongolia, parts of South Siberia—particularly in the Selenge River catchment—and some areas of Inner Mongolia and Ningxia. Elsewhere, I have provided multiple lines of evidence in support of this textual–material relationship.[54] Inherent to "defining" Xiongnu archaeological culture is the question of variation, of which there is plenty. Simply put, archaeologists must improve their understanding of temporal and geographic variability when associating material cultures with polities and peoples.[55] While recent work has been devoted to this problem, much more research is still required.[56]

The archaeological data on Xiongnu contexts in Mongolia and Buriatiia have expanded dramatically over the past five years, thanks to the efforts of Mongolian archaeologists and a number of international collaborations studying both mortuary and settlement patterns. The research on habitations has yielded some of the most informative and novel perspectives regarding Xiongnu-period lifeways. However, despite marked progress in the identification of seasonal campsites and recent excavations at larger settlements, the Xiongnu habitation record from Mongolia is still obscure. In addition, the settlement record presently lacks the capacity to address long-distance exchange and interaction to the same extent as the mortuary record.[57] For this reason, the present study focuses primarily on the results of burial excavations and artifact analyses.

Xiongnu Burials and Interregional Interaction

The nonlocal artifacts, materials, and styles revealed in burial contexts can provide a wealth of information on interregional ties. In contrast, it is much more difficult to understand the social chain of events that moved such goods over long distances or to assess their significance in funerary rituals. This overview of select Xiongnu burial inventories documents material evidence of contacts with the western regions. I do not provide the kind of detailed subregional study that explains how local areas engaged with sources of external goods, though such research will be crucial for the later testing of ideas on Xiongnu political economy.[58] Instead, as in the historical overview above, the focus of my archaeological analysis is on the interregional scale. This includes Xiongnu-period burial contexts and artifacts from the territory of Mongolia as well as the westward distribution of Xiongnu-style material culture. Throughout the discussion I refer to archaeological sites in Mongolia and Siberia, of which the most important are located on the reference map in Figure 4.2.

Cultural ties between central Mongolia and the far west have been a theme of Xiongnu material studies from almost the genesis of the discipline. Recovery of extremely well-preserved remains from large platform burials at Noyon Uul (also known as Noin Ula) in north central Mongolia demonstrated the polity's far-flung interactions. Numerous burials at this site have been excavated by Russian and later by Mongolian-led teams, starting with the famous Kozlov excavations in 1924–1925 and, most recently, a Mongol-Russian joint expedition.[59] The waterlogged and frozen conditions inside some of the deep burial chambers preserved organic materials—among them textiles, wood, lacquerware, plant remains, and even human hair—to an extraordinary degree. Many of the artifacts recovered in the 1920s show indications of western origins, as I describe in more detail below.

Generally speaking, two basic types of burials have been documented at Noyon Uul over the course of nearly a century of research. One type has a ring-shaped surface feature made of stone and soil, and the other, a large platform-like mound with several levels of deeply interred construction.[60] While there are similarities between these two sets of mortuary practices,

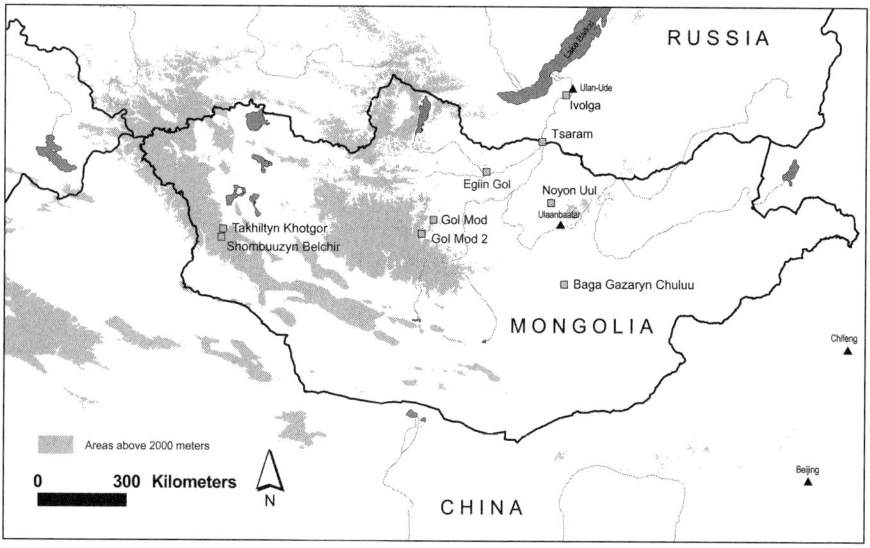

Figure 4.2. The locations of some major Mongolian and South Siberian Xiongnu-period archaeological sites referred to in the text.

they differ with respect to chronology, distribution, and association. Both forms have been identified at sites across Mongolia and Buriatiia, and ring burials are known from some cemeteries in Inner Mongolia as well.[61] Together, these two burial types have come to define the Xiongnu mortuary record. However, additional mortuary practices will almost certainly be discovered as archaeologists increasingly combine systematic surveys with exploratory excavations.[62]

Of the two, the smaller and more widespread site type is the Xiongnu-period "ring tombs." These burials have surface features measuring up to 65 feet in diameter and pit interments ranging in depth from 5 to 10 feet (Figure 4.3). The deceased were placed in a supine position oriented north, northeast, and northwest; there are also rare cases in which individuals were oriented to the east or south. The internal construction of these burial chambers generally comprise a simple earthen pit, a pit with stone slab siding, a wooden coffin, or an elaborate coffin in a timber-frame enclosure. Finds include the remains of domestic herd animals and wild fauna, ceramic vessels and bone tools, iron, bronze, silver, and gold artifacts, and various standard types of distant "imports," the most numerous of which are Chinese products (e.g., lacquerware, mirrors, silk, and coins). Cemetery sites vary from only a single interment to groups of over 350 burials.

Ring tombs are also commonly associated with the second type of Xiongnu-period burial: the so-called platform or terrace tombs. These

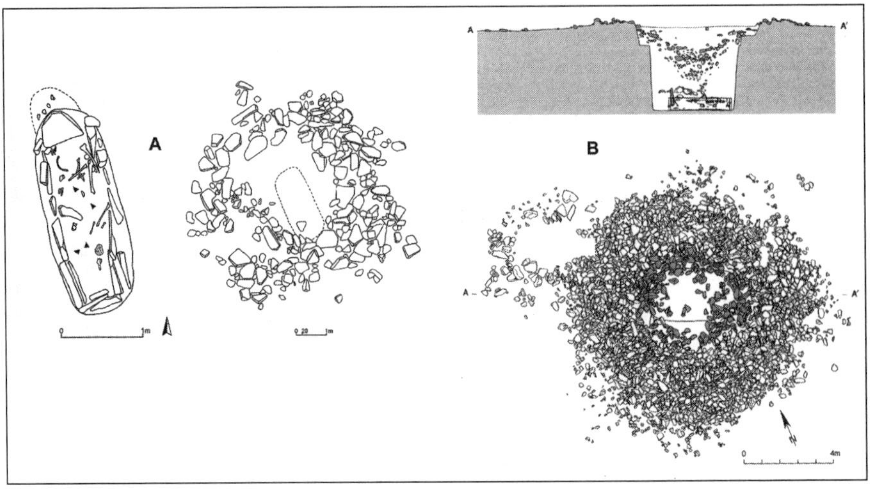

Figure 4.3. Examples of Xiongnu-period ring burials.

platform-like constructions have the same orientation as the ring tombs and consist of a low rectangular or slightly trapezoidal earth-and-stone mound ranging from 52 to 95 feet in length with a height of up to 6.5 feet above the modern-day surface (Figure 4.4). Platform tombs are often surrounded by ring burials in patterned spatial arrangements, which suggest intentional placement in relation to the central platform feature.[63] On the south side, there is a sloping entryway as much as 72 to 115 feet long that leads to a burial pit descending 33 to 65 feet into the ground. The pit consists of multiple soil, stone, and wooden layers overlying an impressive burial chamber made up of an inner and outer wooden framework from hewn logs and wooden planks of larch or pine. While some of the innermost chambers still house wooden coffins bearing the interred individual, many of the internal contexts of these sites have been destroyed by pillagers. Platform tombs were often furnished with precious metals and stones, large ceramic vessels, felt and woven carpets, silks, jade items, bronze mirrors, and lacquerware as well as entire horse-drawn carriages.[64] A wide range of horse-related equipment is also commonly found at these sites, as are the remains of horses, cattle, sheep and goats, wild animals, and quantities of domestic grain.

At it now stands, archaeologists can only provide a bare outline of the chronology, geographic distribution, and meanings of these two types of mortuary treatment. Although most work has been conducted on the smaller ring burials, several multiyear projects are currently underway at cemetery sites containing platform tombs. Some researchers suggest that the large

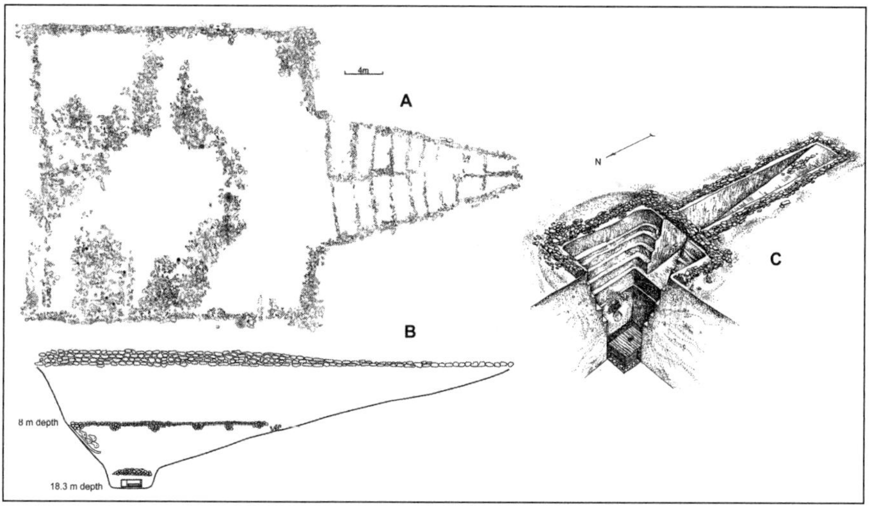

Figure 4.4. Examples of Xiongnu-period platform burials.

burial format might be connected to the ruling houses of the Xiongnu polity.[65] The smaller ring burials may have been reserved for different ranks of local elite. While only a few of either site type have been dated by laboratory methods, the chronology of the platform burials so far ranges from the first century BCE to the first century CE.[66] Radiocarbon dates from ring burials range from as early as the fourth/third century BCE to the third century CE.[67]

Western Products and Burials of the Uppermost Elite

The initial material evidence for Xiongnu relations with Central Asia was found at the above-mentioned Noyon Uul site. Because of the remarkable preservation within the burials many organic items were recovered intact and quite a few of these showed ties to cultures of the west as well as to China. Contexts of this sort remind archaeologists—who are generally accustomed to working with very minimal inventories—how much valuable information is permanently lost from the average, poorly preserved burial context. The cemetery at Noyon Uul contained many products that were manufactured in a wide range of Chinese workshops, from the imperial court variety to less distinguished commercial workshops.[68] Artifacts thought to be associated with western regions fall mostly under the category of textiles such as rugs and tapestries, felts, woolens, and cloth. The recovery of these objects has allowed archaeologists and art historians to discern artistic motifs and styles that are identified with the artwork of Greco-Bactria, Sogdia, Ferghana, and Parthia.[69]

First and foremost, scholars claim that tapestry depictions of the human countenance, clothing and headgear, animals, and images of vegetation represent western styles and themes with a strong Hellenistic component.[70] While appraisals of style can be subjective, the Noyon Uul textiles also have been studied using material and manufacturing analyses to provide information on weaving methods, raw fibers, and dyes. These tests further strengthen the case that some of the textiles, especially several woolen pieces, were produced in western regions, while others are of local or Chinese manufacture.[71] Although these technical studies were carried out in the early twentieth century, experts on Asian textiles have referred to them extensively within the framework of ongoing discussions regarding the origins and technology of steppe fabrics.[72]

In 2006, systematic excavations by Mongolian and Russian archaeologists at the Noyon Uul site revealed a great deal more about the construction of elite platform tombs and their inventories.[73] A relatively well-preserved assemblage of over 200 artifacts was recovered 59 feet below the surface of burial No. 20 in the Sujigt valley section of Noyon Uul. The findings include ceramics, silk, wool, and linen clothing fragments; remains of felt coverings; lacquerware; items made of bronze, gold, silver, and jade; bronze mirrors; equestrian equipment; and pieces of a lacquered coffin that was destroyed by early pillaging. While results from these latest excavations are still preliminary, the technology used to make woolen textiles from the burial chamber has Parthian origins and suggests either exchange or local manufacture by artisans who had migrated from the west.[74]

One decorative item from burial No. 20 offers striking testimony for some kind of interaction with the Greco-Bactrian or Parthian regions and supports the above-mentioned stylistic and technological analysis of textiles. A circular silver plaque that was recovered from the burial chamber is unmistakably of Hellenistic style and depicts what is quite possibly a satyr and maenad or some other scene from Greek mythology (Figure 4.5).[75] The Hellenistic tradition was introduced to Central Asia through the conquests of Alexander in the fourth century BCE. This was followed by extensive Greek settlement and the establishment of the Seleucid empire, which subsequently gave rise to the Greco-Bactrian kingdom of the mid-third century BCE.[76] Notwithstanding the decline of the Greco-Bactrians (late second century BCE), artwork using the Hellenistic vocabulary and incorporating non-Greek idioms persisted. In addition, manufactured goods from the Mediterranean world continued to enter Central Asia by way of Roman, Indian, and Parthian trade.[77] As indicated by the well-known discoveries of Hellenistic-style textiles, artwork, and coins from contemporaneous burials in Xinjiang, it stands to reason that such products were available in areas directly accessible to the Xiongnu.[78] Laboratory analyses of objects from the Noyon Uul excavations are still underway and should reveal more information on the chronology and origins of the exotic materials furnishing Xiongnu elite platform burials.

Other artifacts that bear witness to a relationship between Mongolia's eastern steppe zone and the western cultures of Central Asia were recently recovered from elite platform burials in other parts of the Xiongnu world. Archaeologists from the Russian Academy of Sciences have recovered an artifact inventory from burial No. 7 at the site of Tsaram in Buriatiia that, while similar to the inventories from Noyon Uul tombs, also attests to some interesting differences in mortuary ritual.[79] This context has been dated by multiple methods to the early first century CE. Like Noyon Uul's burial No. 20, the Tsaram excavations uncovered an artifact depicting what the excavators deem to be a satyr from Greek mythology, though it is not rendered in a Hellenistic style. The artifact is a gold-gilded iron buckle with turquoise and black stone inlay. The satyr depiction probably incorporates local styles,

Figure 4.5. Silver plaque recovered from the recent excavation of Noyon Uul burial 20.

perhaps from nomadic traditions, to express what was originally a Mediterranean theme (Figure 4.6). Scholars have yet to identify analogous objects with which to accurately assess the provenance of this buckle. That said, two buckles featuring a somewhat similar design and technology have recently been unearthed in Siberia's western Altai Mountains at the Xiongnu-period cemetery of Ialoman 2.[80]

Southwest of Tsaram, in Mongolia's west central Arkhangai province, the two neighboring platform burial sites of Gol Mod and Gol Mod 2 have been excavated by international teams over the past decade.[81] These digs have yielded more artifacts that are associated with Central Asia, mostly in the form of beads and jewelry.[82] The Gol Mod 2 site boasts one of the largest known platform tombs, which is surrounded by thirty ring burials, most of which are arranged in an arc formation to the east of the platform.[83] While the majority of these burials have been excavated and examined by a Mongolian–American collaborative project, a Mongolian team continues to explore the site under the direction of the archaeologist Diimaajav Erdenebaatar.[84]

Excavations at burial No. 30, one of the surrounding burial features at Gol Mod 2, uncovered an 11-foot-deep interment consisting of a wooden coffin and a wooden enclosure that contained an impressive assemblage of exotic artifacts.[85] Aside from more typical long-distance artifacts, such as lacquerware, silk, and bronze mirrors from Han dynasty China, Erdenebaatar reports amber beads, probably from the west, and a glass bowl which, on the basis of its style and make, originated in the Mediterranean workshops of Rome (Figure 4.7).[86] The glass bowl was found intact and has been

Figure 4.6. An iron and gold overlay belt buckle plaque in the form of a satyr, excavated from the cemetery of Tsaram, burial 7.

Figure 4.7. A blue-and-white ribbed glass bowl recently discovered from burial 30 at the Gol Mod 2 platform burial complex.

identified as a Roman ribbed bowl (Zarte Rippenschale). Its shape, size, and manufacture bear a strong resemblance to the blue-and-white ribbed bowl of the Roman Glass Collection at the Corning Museum of Glass.[87] The museum piece dates between the early and mid-first millennium CE, which is consistent with current assessments of platform burial site chronology. However, scholars have yet to publish the results of compositional analysis on the glass artifact or provide absolute dating for the burial context.

From Macro-region to Local Area: Silk Roads Evidence in the Gobi Desert

While the above-noted artifacts have been discovered at burials and cemeteries that are thought to contain the top echelon of the Xiongnu state, recent excavations at Baga Gazaryn Chuluu (BGC) in the Gobi Desert have demonstrated that western artifacts, namely, beads and pendants, were also circulated among the local or intermediate level elite. These artifacts are comprised of assorted materials: carnelian, agate, turquoise, amber, rock crystal, nephrite, river shell, and glass and faience. While the carnelian, amber, and turquoise probably derived from western sources, it is the glass and faience beads that strongly suggest origins as distant as the Mediterranean.[88]

BGC, in Mongolia's Middle Gobi province, is defined by a central granite-ridge system with several high peaks rising dramatically from a plain of arid grasslands. The granite ridges have eroded leaving deep valleys with natural springs, a water table accessible via shallow wells, and seasonal pasture for livestock. The region has been systematically surveyed and a bioarchaeology program was carried out from 2007 to 2008, mainly to investigate Xiongnu-period mortuary remains.[89] Excavations of two ring burial cemeteries at Alag Tolgoi (northeast BGC) and Ikheriin Am (west BGC) produced a large number of beads from nine different contexts, all of which are dated from between the fourth/third century BCE and the first century CE. The finds were visually inspected and compared to Lankton's Bead Timeline reference publication.[90] The information below derives from Lankton's initial assessment of the BGC glass and faience beads.

Beads that have been identified as arriving at BGC through western exchange, contact, or influence are threefold: triangular ribbon mosaic pendants, gold glass beads, and faience amulets. Triangular mosaic pendants (Figure 4.8) were recovered from two burials at the cemetery of Alag Tolgoi and from a surface site on the western side of the BGC ridge system. The two excavated burial contexts, EX08.25 and EX08.03, were both disrupted in antiquity and each held an adult female who died between the ages of thirty-five and forty-five.[91] Triangular pendants were discovered along with a variety of other beads, but the design and technique of these particular artifacts are unique enough to be matched with triangular pendants that have surfaced in Roman-period sites along the Mediterranean basin as well as major sites in South Asia, like Taxila.[92]

While the precise technique of manufacture is still uncertain, in all likelihood these pendants were constructed by heating and fusing together different strips of colored glass into a mosaic ribbon block. Once cooled,

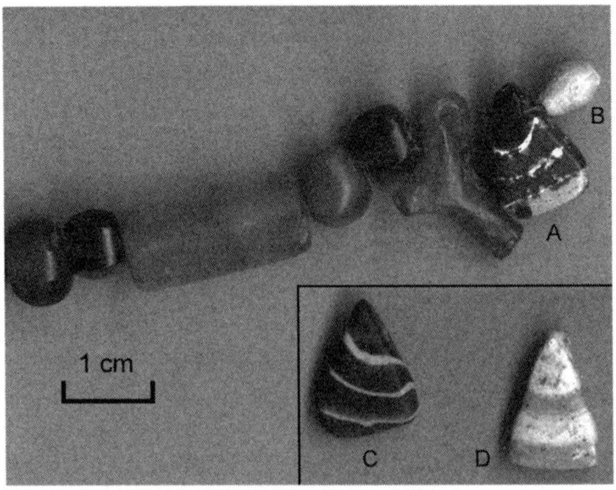

Figure 4.8. Beads and pendants excavated at the Baga Gazaryn Chuluu cemetery of Alag Tolgoi.

these pieces were cut into small triangular shapes and then reheated to smooth the edges, before being polished and drilled. The end result was a triangular design featuring undulating bands of color. Another possibility is that the triangular pieces were cut from a layered mosaic cane. In either case, the process likely involved a multistep, hot- and cold-working process. Production of these sorts of pendants in the west reached its zenith between the second century BCE and the first century CE, a period that roughly corresponds to the calibrated radiocarbon date 364 to 163 BCE, for the EX08.25 context at 94.3 percent probability. Similar pendants have also been found at a number of western burial sites with Xiongnu mortuary patterns and material culture.[93]

Gold glass beads (Figure 4.8) were more numerous in the Alag Tolgoi burial assemblage. Female adults between the ages of thirty-five and fifty occupied three burials in the cemetery (EX08.02, EX08.03, and EX08.06) and interred with them were several examples of gold glass beads.[94] Such beads have also turned up in other elite Xiongnu-period contexts in Mongolia and are associated with workshops in the Mediterranean as well as in parts of South Asia, such as the Bara site near Peshawar in northern Pakistan.[95] As with the ribbon mosaic pendants, the gold glass manufacturing process is still unclear, but there are at least two hypotheses. As the name implies, gold glass beads are embedded with gold. This might be accomplished by drawing out a miniscule tube of glass upon which gold foil is applied using an adhesive. The composite is subsequently inserted into a slightly larger glass tube, thereby sealing the gold inside. A second possibility is predicated on contemporary gold glass making on the island of Java in which the beadmaker applies gold foil to a glass tube and then seals the composite within a thin layer of glass casing by means of a hot-process technique.[96] Though weathered, all the gold glass beads from Alag Tolgoi were readily identifiable. Calibrated radiocarbon dates for these contexts are 180 to 10 BCE (EX08.02) and 170 BCE to 130 CE (EX08.06), at 95 percent probability.

Finally, the Ikheriin Am cemetery in the western section of BGC has fifteen Xiongnu ring burials and a very large ring feature with no evidence for additional interments below. One of the burials selected for excavation was that of a thirty to thirty-five-year-old woman (EX05.02). Her burial contained a decorated coffin and a number of beads including pendant amulets that were manufactured in the Mediterranean region, most likely Egypt, but were probably obtained by way of Central Asia.[97] In addition, the excavators recovered fragmentary evidence of ceramics, bone and iron items, a lacquerware cup, and faunal remains, especially of horses. Grave robbers pillaged the entire context in antiquity via a small shaft leading directly into the burial's chest and head section.[98]

The Egyptian artifacts (Figure 4.9) are known to be fertility and/or prosperity amulets well represented throughout the Mediterranean. More specifically, the anthropomorphic figurine is a faience image of Bes, an Egyptian god, and the blue faience amulet features a hand gesture known in Latin as the "manus ficus" (mano fica) symbol.[99] Egyptian faience was produced by a variety of methods. The most prevalent technique was to either mold or sculpt a figure and then apply a glaze compound, which vitrified upon firing.[100] The Ikheriin Am burial has been dated by radiocarbon analysis on human and animal bone samples as well as pine wood from the coffin. Combining these results into a pooled mean provides a calibrated range of 170 to 20 BCE at 95 percent probability.

Both of these faience artifacts have long histories in Egypt, Rome, and the Northern Pontic region. However, they are also recovered from cemetery and settlement sites in Tajikistan, Kyrgyzstan, and southeastern Kazakhstan.[101] The chronology of these finds overlaps the Greco-Bactrian and Kushan periods—from the second century BCE to the second/third century CE—and some forms of the Bes figure in these areas date as late as the sixth century CE. Sherkova discusses the Central Asian occurrence of these amulets and compares them with multiple analogs from the Mediterranean world.[102] She concludes that the Central Asian artifacts were probably manufactured in Egypt and then transported via the major trade routes.

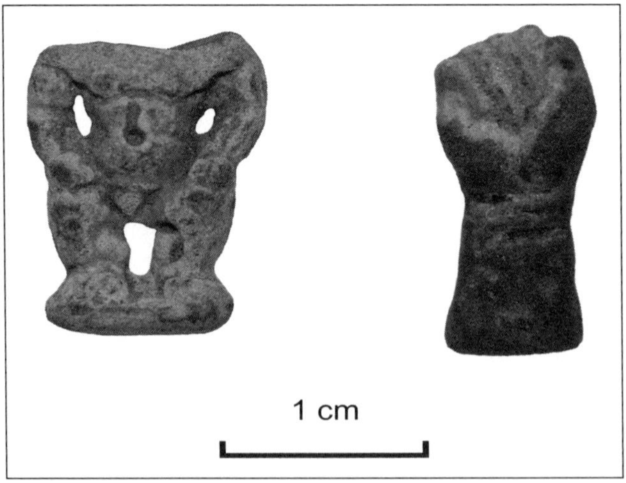

Figure 4.9. Two faience amulet pendants excavated from burial EX05.02 at the Ikheriin Am cemetery of Baga Gazaryn Chuluu.

While such finds are fairly well known from both Central Asia and the Black Sea region, they have only recently begun to turn up in Mongolia and adjacent areas. The nearest analogous artifacts to those in the Ikheriin Am site were discovered in the western Altai Mountains. These include the faience bead recently unearthed from the Xiongnu cemetery at Shombuuzyn Belchir and additional beads from the Kuraika cemetery on the Siberian side of the Altai Mountains.[103] Our assessment of the provenance of these BGC beads is currently being tested by compositional sourcing analysis using LA-ICP-MS.[104] These laboratory results will add significantly to earlier sourcing studies of Xiongnu-period glass artifacts from the Ivolga site in Buriatiia and the Gol Mod cemetery.[105]

Western products such as these from BGC were lightweight, portable, and clearly fit nomadic cultural tastes. Long-distance goods also appear in the burials of earlier periods, but the pervasiveness of these items in elite Xiongnu burials and the geographic distances involved in their procurement are entirely unique to the Xiongnu period.[106] A comparison of nonlocal mortuary artifacts over time within a single region (e.g., the Egiin Gol Valley, Mongolia) demonstrates a quantitative leap in the use of external goods in mortuary practices during the Xiongnu period.[107] This dramatic increase and the positive correlation of these goods with higher-ranking elite contexts suggest that nonlocal prestige goods facilitated social distinctions and indigenous politics among the Xiongnu.[108] The importance of these materials stemmed from their function in a society where political leadership was characterized by social stratification, hereditary transfers of status, and conspicuous displays of prestigious items. Xiongnu leadership roles were complex and not easily sustained and therefore display of impressive foreign objects likely represented an investment on the part of the Xiongnu elite in the maintenance of their own privileged positions vis-à-vis commoners.

The Western Interaction Sphere of the Late First Millennium BC

The archaeological evidence from Mongolia argues in favor of the political use of long-distance western exchange goods within the Xiongnu polity. This raises the question of what social and interactive processes brought these items into Xiongnu possession in the first place. Conceivable answers are many, among which simple frontier commerce, or gradual down-the-line exchange, or tribute exaction, are all potential candidates. There is also the possibility that some of these items were made within the Xiongnu polity by foreign craft specialists. If the above-noted ideas about prestige objects and political relationships are valid, then these goods were probably too significant to be obtained through casual exchange or border markets. Instead, they would have involved critical long-distance relationships that were managed by elite factions with a vested interest in political stability and control.[109] What is more, we might expect that such interaction along the Xiongnu polity's frontiers was a two-way process in which western items entered and Xiongnu material culture, ideas, and technologies were furnished to external groups. Such material patterns would have been especially prevalent in the case of Xiongnu alliance building, which would hypothetically involve co-option of western elites and, in turn, their use of Xiongnu material symbols to bolster their own legitimacy at home.

Spatial distributions of Xiongnu material culture in the western parts of Mongolia and beyond offer insight to the possibility of such long-distance dynamics. A series of survey, reconnaissance, and burial excavation projects in the western Mongolian provinces of Khovd, Uvs, and Bayan Olgii have considerably enhanced our understanding of the western periphery of the Xiongnu state.[110] One of the most comprehensive statements on this issue is a recent study by Miller on Xiongnu burial practices, cemetery organization, and mortuary landscapes at different western sites in Khovd province.[111] The objective of this research was to compare material patterns on the political fringes with those in central Mongolia. Miller argues that a group of sites surrounding the platform burial cemetery of Takhiltyn Khotgor demonstrates patterns that are indicative of political integration within the Xiongnu polity proper.[112] The western political frontier was therefore probably even farther to the west and comprised groups that inhabited present-day Xinjiang, Kazakhstan, and central South Siberia.

Though historical sources point to extensive Xiongnu activities in the Xinjiang region, the material evidence there is surprisingly limited. Drawing on a handful of artifact or burial similarities, archaeological studies suggest the possibility of some form of contact, although, in comparison to the Siberian record, the Xinjiang evidence is quite sparse. Archaeologists have cited possible evidence from the cemetery sites of Subashi/Subeixi, Aidinghu, Chaohugou, and most recently Dongheigou.[113] In Kazakhstan, to the west and northwest of Xinjiang, archaeology likewise provides little testimony of Xiongnu-period interaction.[114] However, in eastern Kazakhstan, the cemetery sites of Kula Zhurga and Slavianka (third century BCE–first century CE), north of Lake Zaisan, have some material-cultural similarities with the Gorno-Altai record and the people of that region likely had indirect contact with Xiongnu groups via the Altai interaction sphere.[115]

The Gorno-Altai region of South Siberia does possess substantial material evidence for Xiongnu polity interaction and supports the idea of significant forest-steppe and mountain frontier contacts during early Xiongnu state development. Based on a stylistic and comparative assessment of artifacts, this sphere of interaction is traceable across much of South Siberia, especially during the Shibe phase of Pazyryk culture, the late Tagar Tes phase in the Minusinsk Basin, and the Ulug-Khem culture of Tuva, all beginning in the second to first centuries BCE.[116] A series of initial radiocarbon analyses for burials that are associated with these cultures in both the Siberian Altai and Tuva provide some support for this chronology.[117]

Evidence for Xiongnu-related material patterns in Gorno-Altai include the following: Xiongnu ceramics were discovered in the fill of Pazyryk-period burial mounds at Uzuntal and Ulandryk; direct analogies to Xiongnu-period burial architecture and inventories are reported from the Ukok Plateau; and a substantial Xiongnu ceramics workshop has been well documented along the Iustyd River near Lake Zhalgizuirokkol'.[118] In Tuva, the late first millennium BCE phases of the Bai-Dag 2 and Aimyrlyg 31 cemeteries share construction techniques, tools/weapons, clothing accessories, ceramics, and bronze cauldrons with the Xiongnu record of Mongolia and Buriatiia.[119] In the Minusinsk Basin of the middle Yenisei River, Tes-period sites, like Bol'shoi Tesinskii, Kosogol'skii klad, Kamenka V, and Tepsee VII, contain numerous objects that are analogous to Xiongnu assemblages, among them weapon types, open-work rectangular belt plaques, a number of bronze or iron buckles, fasteners, buttons, and numerous items of personal adornment such as stone pendants.[120]

In each of these regional cases from Siberia, there is strong diachronic evidence for long-term and indigenous cultural sequences that incorporated materials from the heartland of the Xiongnu polity toward the end of the first millennium BCE.[121] The resultant cultural amalgam in these areas differed from preceding indigenous cultures and from mainstream Xiongnu culture. Moreover, this dynamic was not just one-way. There is good evidence for the transport of ceramics from sites in the western Altai to prominent Xiongnu cemeteries in the east as well as movements of people from the western Yenisei region of South Siberia eastward to Buriatiia.[122] It is also well substantiated that wherever Xiongnu material culture appeared in western sites, there likewise appeared the products of Han dynasty workshops and always in status-related contexts. The Han dynasty artifacts—especially bronze mirrors, silk fabrics, and lacquerware items—were the same goods used to mark status in Xiongnu burials and these were commonly accompanied by Xiongnu-made prestige goods like bronze belt plaques.[123]

This pattern of Xiongnu political contact and cultural interaction extends beyond the forest steppe of central South Siberia and is documented in West Siberia's forest-steppe region at a substantial distance from the center of Xiongnu power. By the late third and second centuries BCE, the mature Sargat culture, located between the Ural Mountains to the west and the middle Irtysh River in the east, apparently shared in these long-distance interactions. The Sargat record is well known for its mortuary sites, open settlements, and fortified enclosures corresponding to territorial enclaves spaced at 20- to 25-mile intervals along rivers and lakes.[124] Beginning in the mid-first millennium BCE, Sargat peoples interacted with pastoral nomadic groups to the south, in present-day north central and western Kazakhstan, thereby giving rise to a local cultural synthesis. Subsistence was based on mixed economies that featured various degrees of mobility and integrated horse, cattle, and small-stock pastoralism with agriculture and hunting and fishing. These changes are also evident in styles of Sargat ceramic production, increasingly sophisticated iron metallurgy, and the adoption of specialized weapon sets as well as the presence of many more nonlocal items due to participation in emerging networks of exchange.[125]

The extent of these external contacts is well attested in the Sargat mortuary tradition. Archaeologists have found evidence for clear social ranks marked primarily by external prestige goods.[126] While imported materials came from a number of regions, the second most represented class of nonlocal artifacts in Sargat burials are from the Xiongnu interaction sphere far to the east. Among these prestige items are lacquerware, silk, and impressive bronze and gold belt plaques, that archaeologists relate to networks of alliances involving the Xiongnu polity.[127] Similar to the Sayan-Altai region, other aspects of Xiongnu culture were also adopted by western Sargat groups, most notably the heavy Xiongnu composite bow and iron arrowheads. Unlike the smaller "Scythian" bow, these new armaments are described as being ideally designed for highly accurate, long-distance mounted warfare.[128]

Based on the early appearance of bone components from these distinctive bows in burial contexts, Sargat groups seem to have been the first users of this technology west of the Altai region. In all likelihood, Sarmatian nomadic groups southwest of the western Siberian forest steppe adopted this technology from their Sargat neighbors.[129] Archaeologists attribute these long-distance and likely indirect contacts between the Xiongnu and the Sargat groups to the rise of interaction networks along a "northern" route of the Silk Roads. This development significantly increased the availability of valuable forest products to societies to the south and southeast of the Sargat regions, though such interactions, prior to the first century CE, were more political in nature than they were economic.[130] The above material patterns strongly suggest that by way of alliance building, elite gift giving, and tribute extraction, valued goods made their way from west to east into the hands of Xiongnu emissaries and Xiongnu and Han prestige products went westward to the Ural Mountains and probably beyond.

Steppe Roads: A Reorientation of Perspective

Two independent records, one textual and the other material, testify to early interaction networks in the west that involved the Xiongnu state. An overview and comparison of these records show different conceptions of the geographical extent and orientation of interregional contacts during the late first millennium BCE. The original Raschke hypothesis attributed early Silk Roads activity to the Xiongnu in order to explain silk arriving in the Mediterranean prior to Han dynasty involvement in western exchange.[131] The dates for early silk in the Mediterranean range from the fifth to the second centuries BCE.[132] However, subsequent historical and archaeological studies have shown that these early silk fabrics were probably not from China, but produced from indigenous wild silks or domesticated silks from India.[133] It bears noting that, according to the latest archaeological research on Indus Valley sites in Pakistan, sericulture dates as far back as 4,000 years in South Asia.[134]

That said, Raschke's hypothesis is still valid and intriguing, especially when integrated with other theories for Inner Asian politics. Lattimore argued that Han dynasty and Xiongnu frontier relations were not based on economics per se, but on a system of elite gifting which had important political implications on both sides of the frontier.[135] According to Lattimore, this was the main reason for the occurrence of Han luxury goods far to the north and west. Barfield and Christian build on this conception of the frontier political economy by linking it to a proposed Xiongnu framework of long-distance exchange that foreshadowed the commercial Silk Roads.[136] Christian's analysis also demonstrates the essential role played by transecological north–south contacts especially involving groups of the Eurasian forest and forest-steppe zone. Though predating the advent of the fabled Eurasian trade route, the above researchers propose that this political exchange considerably shaped the later Silk Roads.

In the pages above, I have examined these hypotheses within the context of the rise and expansion of the Xiongnu polity. The historical sources suggest that the western regions provided critical support to the Xiongnu and that both knowledge of Chinese products and a system of value linking these goods to high status and authority was in place before Han involvement there. Archaeology provides material evidence for the two-way interaction between Xiongnu political centers and the western regions. Xiongnu elites had ample access to Chinese goods and to western products that had great value in China—notably, the same products destined to become major imports and exports along the later commercial Silk Roads. The appearance of these items in status-related contexts suggests that elites managed the flow of these goods as well as the interregional relationships facilitating their exchange. Archaeological sites in the forest-steppe zone of Sayan-Altai and Western Siberia attest to significant interaction with Xiongnu groups who introduced both Xiongnu and Han prestige items to these lands. Such objects have been recovered by researchers in contextual patterns akin to those found in the Xiongnu heartland. In Xinjiang and Central Asia, Xiongnu material culture was not as widespread; however, early examples of Han prestige items are indeed present and could have been supplied through Xiongnu alliances in conjunction with down-the-line exchange prior to the Han military buildup in the region.

This difference in Xiongnu material patterns between Xinjiang/Central Asia and the northern forest steppe may stem from the contrasting political traditions in these two regions during the mid-to-late first millennium BCE. Xinjiang and Central Asia had a long tradition of kingdoms or petty state societies, a few of which were integrated into successive empires. For this reason, they probably already had stable investments in existing traditions of political order and the expression of that order by means of a particular symbolic and material culture. In contrast, the forest-steppe zone, especially that of West Siberia, was organized into multiple small-scale polities probably competing for followers, such that its leaders were greatly reliant on exotic goods and gifts to legitimize their standing.[137] Consequently, the forest-zone leadership would have been inclined to embrace new and politically significant prestige goods in order to gain an edge in cultivating local political relationships.

These regional differences would certainly have been understood by Xiongnu representatives as they expanded their political influence into the west and encountered varying peoples, traditions, and cultures during the second and first centuries BCE. Furthermore, Xiongnu leaders probably tailored their interactions with different groups to fit their own political needs. Archaeological data show that the basis for interaction along the Xiongnu polity's many frontiers was diverse and probably ranged from military coercion to inter-elite alliances and from co-option to migration and intermarriage.[138] On most of these frontiers, the use of Chinese prestige goods marked the influence of a Xiongnu political agenda rather than trade with China.

Explanations for the Xiongnu's acquisition of Chinese-manufactured goods have stressed the urgent need to sustain internal political relationships and the loyalty of followers through the bestowal of gifts and wealth.[139] If this was indeed the case, the purposeful outlay of what were valuable internal political goods in external regions suggests that some political return warranted this investment. One possible reason for such an investment might have been wealth conversion and accrual through recirculation. By means of interregional relationships, the Xiongnu elite exchanged rather accessible luxury items from China for northern and western goods, which had greater conversion value within their own political sphere. Thereafter, these same northern and western products may have been re-exchanged on the Xiongnu state's southern and eastern frontiers where maximum value could be realized. As one of many strategies to buttress their own positions, Xiongnu rulers may have managed an extensive geography, transport capability, and military advantage to create an interregional political economy not dissimilar to that of many sizable premodern imperial states.[140]

Although this proposed model requires additional testing, especially through the excavation and dating of Xiongnu-period sites in western Mongolia, it does help to clarify the social and historical processes that gave rise to trans-Eurasian Silk Roads exchange. Historians have examined the sudden increase in trade during the first phase of the commercial Silk Roads (ca. first to fourth centuries CE) and have contrasted it with the smaller-scale exchange up to that point.[141] This sudden flourishing of Silk Roads activity might be attributed to a system of cultural value that was created in the west through the Xiongnu's use of Chinese goods. These goods were connected with high-status leadership; they were rare and used primarily in support of political authority and alliance. Furthermore, this system of value connected with Han material culture would probably have had relevance across a broad swath of Central Eurasia, judging from the example of the Sargat groups.

This sort of politically based prestige goods economy is premised on restricting access to highly significant materials in order to maintain exclusivity, symbolism, and value. By the first century BCE, these same goods were being brought to Central Asia by Chinese envoys and informal traders who were eager to trade them for gold or silver coins, carpets, horses, or exotic stones. In purely economic terms, it stands to reason that the trade boom that followed in the wake of the sudden increased availability of such coveted products fueled trade volumes on a commercial scale. Though it was hardly the intention of Xiongnu leadership, their political economy, interregional interaction, and systems of nomadic value may have indeed triggered one of the great eras of economic networking and ancient globalization.

Acknowledgments

I would like to thank the organizers of the original conference for inviting me to participate and also for their great patience in seeing this study through to its final publication. The comments, edits, shared ideas, and appeals to finish the text were most helpful and greatly appreciated. This research is due to the efforts and assistance of many generous organizations, including the Wenner-Gren Foundation, the National Geographic Society, the National Science Foundation, the National Endowment for the Humanities, the Center for the Study of Eurasian Nomads, the Smithsonian National Museum of Natural History, and Yale University. My research in Mongolia would not have been possible without the kind encouragement of Professor D. Tseveendorj, director of the Mongolian Academy of Sciences' Institute of Archaeology. Thanks are also due to the people of Baga Gazaryn Chuluu and Egiin Gol who were extremely generous and hospitable throughout our work. This research was greatly assisted by Joshua Wright, Russell Nelson, Z. Batsaikhan, D. Erdenebaatar, Daniel Rogers, William Fitzhugh, and Bruno Frohlich. Special thanks are extended to our research staff members Michelle Machicek, J. Gerelbadrakh, J. Burentogtokh, P. Khatanbaatar, Erik Johannesson, Emma Hite, Jeremy Beach, and D. Molor. James Lankton has been critical in revealing the world of beads and glass analysis. I am greatly indebted to him and his colleagues for their interest in our materials and in Mongolia.

Notes

1. E. de la Vaissière, *Sogdian Traders: A History* (Boston, 2005).

2. C. I. Beckwith, *Empires of the Silk Road: A History of Central Asia from the Bronze Age to the Present* (Princeton, 2009), p. 343.

3. H. Parzinger, "The 'Silk Roads' Concept Reconsidered: About Transfers, Transportation and Transcontinental Interactions in Prehistory," *The Silk Road*, 5/2 (2008), p. 7.

4. de la Vaissière, *Sogdian Traders*, p. 41; D. Christian, "Silk Roads or Steppe Roads? The Silk Roads in World History," *Journal of World History*, 11/1 (2000), pp. 5–6.

5. e.g., de la Vaissière, *Sogdian Traders*, pp. 186–190; N. G. Gorbunova, "Traditional Movements of Nomadic Pastoralists and the Role of Seasonal Migrations in the Formation of Ancient Trade Routes in Central Asia," *Silk Road Art and Archaeology*, 3 (1993/1994), p. 7.

6. Christian, "Silk Roads or Steppe Roads?"

7. O. Lattimore, *Inner Asian Frontiers of China* (Oxford, 1940).

8. W. Honeychurch and C. Amartuvshin, "Hinterlands, Urban Centers, and Mobile Settings: The 'New' Old World Archaeology from the Eurasian Steppe," *Asian Perspectives,* 46/1 (2007), pp. 36–64.

9. N. Di Cosmo, *Ancient China and Its Enemies: The Rise of Nomadic Power in East Asian History* (Cambridge, 2002).

10. Mu-chou Poo, *Enemies of Civilization: Attitudes toward Foreigners in Ancient Mesopotamia, Egypt and China* (Albany, NY, 2005); O. Lattimore, *Studies in Frontier History* (Paris, 1962), p. 251.

11. B. Watson, *Records of the Grand Historian of China: Han Dynasty II* (New York, 1993), pp. 136–137.

12. Di Cosmo, *Ancient China and Its Enemies,* pp. 188–189.

13. Watson, *Records of the Grand Historian of China,* p. 139.

14. D. Sneath, "Introduction—Imperial Statecraft: Arts of Power on the Steppe," in *Imperial Statecraft: Political Forms and Techniques of Governance in Inner Asia, Sixth-Twentieth Centuries,* ed. D. Sneath (Bellingham, WA, 2006), pp. 1–22.

15. P. Salzman, *Pastoralists: Equality, Hierarchy, and the State* (Boulder, CO, 2004).

16. e.g., Yü Ying-shih, *Trade and Expansion in Han China: A Study in the Structure of Sino-Barbarian Economic Relations* (Berkeley, 1967), pp. 40–41.

17. D. Honey, *Stripping Off Felt and Fur: An Essay on Nomadic Sinification.* Papers on Inner Asia, no. 21 (Bloomington, IN, 1992); Yü, *Trade and Expansion in Han China,* p. 208.

18. J. Fletcher, "The Mongols: Ecological and Social Perspectives," *Harvard Journal of Asiatic Studies,* 46 (1986), pp. 11–50; S. Jagchid, and V. J. Symons, *Peace, War, and Trade along the Great Wall* (Bloomington, IN, 1989).

19. N. Yamada, "The Formation of the Hsiung-nu Nomadic State," *Acta Orientalia,* 36 (1982), pp. 575–582.

20. E. Kürsat-Ahlers, "The Role and Contents of Ideology in the Early Nomadic Empires of the Eurasian Steppes," in *Ideology and the Formation of Early States,* ed. H. Claessen and J. Osten (Leiden, 1996), pp. 137–152.

21. N. Di Cosmo, "Ancient Inner Asian Nomads: Their Economic Basis and Its Significance in Chinese History," *Journal of Asian Studies,* 53/4 (1994), pp. 1092–1126; Di Cosmo, *Ancient China and Its Enemies;* Sneath, "Introduction—Imperial Statecraft"; W. Honeychurch and C. Amartuvshin, "States on Horseback: The Rise of Inner Asian Confederations and Empires," in *Archaeology of Asia,* ed. M. T. Stark (Malden, MA, 2006), pp. 255–278; J. D. Rogers, "The Contingencies of State Formation in Eastern Inner Asia," *Asian Perspectives,* 46/2 (2007), pp. 249–274; J. D. Rogers, "Inner Asian States and Empires: Theories, Data, and Synthesis," *Journal of Archaeological Research,* 20 (2012), pp. 205–256.

22. Poo, *Enemies of Civilization.*

23. Lattimore, *Studies in Frontier History,* pp. 481–483; O. Lattimore, "Herdsmen, Farmers, and Urban Culture," in *Pastoral Production and Society,* ed. L'Equipe écologie et anthropologie des sociétés pastorales (Cambridge, 1979), pp. 479–490.

24. E. Brumfield and T. Earle (eds.), *Specialization, Exchange, and Complex Societies* (Cambridge, 1987); R. Blanton et al., "A Dual-Processual Theory for the Evolution of Mesoamerican Civilization," *Current Anthropology,* 37/1 (1996), pp. 1–14; N. N. Kradin, "Structure of Power in Nomadic Empires of Inner Asia: An Anthropological Approach," in *Hierarchy and Power in the History of Civilizations: Ancient and Medieval Cultures,* ed. L. Grinin et al. (Moscow, 2008), pp. 98–124.

25. Yü, *Trade and Expansion in Han China,* p. 194; T. Barfield, "The Xiongnu Imperial Confederacy: Organization and Foreign Policy," *Journal of Asian Studies,* 41 (1981), pp. 30–36.

26. Christian, "Silk Roads or Steppe Roads?"; Barfield, "Steppe Empires, China, and the Silk Route: Nomads as a Force in International Trade and Politics," in *Nomads in the Sedentary World,* ed. A. M. Khazanov and A. Wink (London, 2001), pp. 234–249; M. Raschke, "New Studies in Roman Commerce with the East," in *Aufstieg und Niedergang der römischen Welt im Spiegel der neueren Forschung II,* 9/2 (1978), pp. 606–622.

27. M. Drompp, "Imperial State Formation in Inner Asia: The Early Turkic Empires (6th to 9th Centuries)," *Acta Orientalia Academiae Scientiarum Hungaricae,* 58/1 (2005), pp. 101–111; de la Vaissière, *Sogdian Traders,* p. 206.

28. T. Höllmann, *Die Seidenstraße* (Munich, 2004), p. 37.

29. While the use of "western regions" in Chinese historical sources (i.e., *xiyu*) specifies areas of Xinjiang and some parts of eastern Central Asia, throughout this chapter I will use this term in a more general sense that encompasses present-day Central Asia and areas further west.

30. A. Hulsewè, "The Problem of the Authenticity of Shi-chi ch. 123, the Memoir on Ta-Yiian," *T'oung Pao,* 61/1–3 (1975), pp. 83–132; D. D. Leslie and K. H. J. Gardiner, "Chinese Knowledge of Western Asia during the Han," *T'oung Pao,* 68 (1982), pp. 254–307; K. Enoki, "On the Relationship between the Shih-chi, Bk. 123 and the Han-shu, Bks. 61 and 96," *Memoirs of the Research Department of Toyo Bunko,* 41 (1983), pp. 1–31.

31. Di Cosmo, *Ancient China and Its Enemies,* pp. 268–271.

32. Sima Qian (ch. 110); Watson, *Records of the Grand Historian of China,* pp. 134–139.

33. Di Cosmo, *Ancient China and Its Enemies,* pp. 190–196.

34. Ibid., p. 189.

35. Watson, *Records of the Grand Historian of China,* pp. 140–141.

36. Di Cosmo, *Ancient China and Its Enemies,* p. 197.

37. e.g., N. Odani, "Nomadic Tribes on the Silk Road: Da Yuezhi and Xiongnu," in *Opening Up the Silk Road: The Han and the Eurasian World, Silk Roads Nara International Symposium (2005 Nara-shi, Japan)* (Nara, 2007), p. 52. See Xinru Liu, "Migration and Settlement of the Yuezhi-Kushan: Interaction and Interdependence of Nomadic and Sedentary Societies," *Journal of World History,* 12/2 (2001), p. 265.

38. Di Cosmo, *Ancient China and Its Enemies,* p. 250; Ying-shih Yü, "The Hsiung-nu," in *The Cambridge History of Early Inner Asia,* ed. D. Sinor (Cambridge, 1990), pp. 127–128.

39. F. Kidd, "The Ferghana Valley and Its Neighbours during the Han Period (206 BC–223 AD)," in *Social Orders and Social Landscapes,* ed. L. M. Popova et al. (Newcastle, UK, 2007), pp. 359–360.

40. Yü, "The Hsiung-nu," p. 131.

41. C. Benjamin, "Hungry for Han Goods: Zhang Qian and the Origins of the Silk Roads," in *History and Society in Central and Inner Asia,* ed. M Gervers et al. (Toronto, 2007), pp. 4–7.

42. Di Cosmo, *Ancient China and Its Enemies,* pp. 282–283; Chun-shu Chang, *The Rise of the Chinese Empire: Nation, State, and Imperialism in Early China, ca. 1600 B.C.–A.D. 8* (Ann Arbor, MI, 2007), pp. 135–159.

43. de la Vaissière, *Sogdian Traders,* pp. 22–24. Knowledge of the eastern regions may have also reached western peoples through the "Southwest Silk Roads," which might have linked regions of present-day Sichuan and Yunnan to Southeast and South Asia (Bing Yang, "Horses, Silver, and Cowries: Yunnan in Global Perspective," *Journal of World History,* 15/3 [2004], pp. 281–322).

44. Raschke, "New Studies," pp. 606–622; Christian, "Silk Roads or Steppe Roads?"; T. Barfield, "Steppe Empires, China, and the Silk Route: Nomads as a Force in International Trade and Politics," in *Nomads in the Sedentary World,* pp. 234–249.

45. W. Honeychurch, "Thinking Political Communities: Social Stratification among Ancient Nomads of Mongolia," in *The Anthropological Study of Class and Consciousness,* ed. P. Durrenberger (Boulder, CO, 2012), pp. 29–63.

46. K. Rubinson, "A Reconsideration of Pazyryk," in *Foundations of Empire: Archaeology and Art of the Eurasian Steppes,* ed. G. Seaman (Los Angeles, 1992), pp. 71–72; Christian, "Silk Roads or Steppe Roads?" p. 18.

47. Yü, *Trade and Expansion in Han China,* pp. 200–201.

48. de la Vaissière, *Sogdian Traders,* p. 206.

49. E. Giele, "Evidence for the Xiongnu in Chinese Wooden Documents from the Han Period," in *Xiongnu Archaeology: Multidisciplinary Perspectives of the First Steppe Empire in Inner Asia,* ed. U. Brosseder and B. Miller (Bonn, 2011), pp. 49–76.

50. D. Anthony, "The Opening of the Eurasian Steppes at 2000 BC," in *The Bronze Age and Early Iron Age Peoples of Eastern Central Asia,* ed. V. Mair (Philadelphia, 1998), pp. 94–113; M. Frachetti, *Pastoralist Landscapes and Social Interaction in Bronze Age Eurasia* (Berkeley, 2008); E. E. Kuzmina, *The Prehistory of the Silk Road* (Philadelphia, 2008).

51. U. Brosseder, "Belt Plaques as an Indicator of East-West Relations in the Eurasian Steppe at the Turn of the Millennia," in *Xiongnu Archaeology: Multidisciplinary Perspectives of the First Steppe Empire in Inner Asia,* ed. U. Brosseder and B. Miller (Bonn, 2011), p. 414.

52. Parzinger, "The 'Silk Roads' Concept Reconsidered"; Beckwith, *Empires of the Silk Road.*

53. Iu. D. Tal'ko-Gryntsevich, *Materialy k paleoetnologii Zabaikal'ia* (St. Petersburg, 1999); Ts. Dorjsuren, *Umard Khunnu* (Ulaanbaatar, 1961); S. I. Rudenko, *Kul'tura khunnov i Noinulinskie kurgany* (Moscow, 1962); P. B. Konovalov, *Khunnu v Zabaikal'e* (Ulan-Ude, 1976); D. Tseveendorj, "Novye dannye po arkheologii khunnu," in *Drevnie kultury Mongolii,* ed. R. S. Vasil'evskii (Novosibirsk, 1985), pp. 51–87; S. Miniaev, "K probleme proiskhozhdeniia siunnu," *Information Bulletin of the Association for the Study of the Cultures of Central Asia,* 9 (1985), pp. 70–78; Z. Batsaikhan, *Khunnu: arkheologi, ugsaatny zui, tuukh* (Ulaanbaatar, 2003); T. Torbat, *Khunnugiin jiriin irgediin bulsh* (Ulaanbaatar, 2004); J. Holotová-Szinek, "Preliminary Research on the Spatial Organization of the Xiongnu Territories in Mongolia," in *Xiongnu Archaeology,* pp. 425–440.

54. W. Honeychurch, "Inner Asian Warriors and Khans: A Regional Spatial Analysis of Nomadic Political Organization and Interaction" (PhD dissertation, University of Michigan, 2004), pp. 102–104; W. Honeychurch, "The Nomad as State Builder: Historical Theory and Material Evidence from Mongolia," *Journal of World Prehistory,* 26 (2013), pp. 283–321.

55. K. M. Linduff, "The Gender of Luxury and Power among the Xiongnu in Eastern Eurasia," in *Are All Warriors Male? Gender Roles on the Ancient Eurasian Steppe,* ed.

K. M. Linduff and K. S. Rubinson (Lanham, MD, 2008), p. 194; G. Indrisano, "Subsistence, Environmental Fluctuation and Social Change: A Case Study in South Central Inner Mongolia" (PhD dissertation, University of Pittsburgh, 2006).

56. A. Nelson et al., "A Gobi Mortuary Site through Time: Bioarchaeology at Baga Mongol, Baga Gazaryn Chuluu," in *The Archaeology of Mongolia: Proceedings of the August 2007 Archaeological Symposium in Ulaanbaatar, Mongolia,* ed. E. Pohl (Bonn, 2009); B. Miller et al., "Xiongnu Elite Tomb Complexes in the Mongolian Altai: Results of the Mongol-American Hovd Archaeology Project, 2007," *The Silk Road,* 5/2 (2008), pp. 27–35.

57. S. V. Danilov and N. V. Tsydenova, "Ceramic Roof Tiles from Terelzhiin Dorvolzhin," in *Xiongnu Archaeology,* pp. 341–348; N. Pousaz et al., "Mission archéologique helvético-mongole à Boroo Gol, Mongolie: campagne de fouilles," *SLSA Jahresbericht,* 2007, pp. 219–232; D. Purcell and K. Spurr, "Archaeological Investigations of Xiongnu Sites in the Tamir River Valley: Results of the 2005 Joint American-Mongolian Expedition to Tamiryn Ulaan Khoshuu, Ogii nuur, Arkhangai aimag, Mongolia," *The Silk Road,* 4/1 (2006), pp. 20–32.

58. W. Honeychurch et al., "Death and Social Process among the Ancient Xiongnu of Mongolia," in *Xiongnu: The First Empire of the Steppes,* ed. Eunjeong Chang (Seoul, 2007), pp. 134–153.

59. Dorjsuren, *Umard Khunnu;* Rudenko, *Kul'tura khunnov i Noinulinskie kurgany;* N. V. Polos'mak et al., "The Burial Construction of Noin Ula Mound 20, Mongolia," *Archaeology, Ethnology, and Anthropology of Eurasia,* 34/2 (2008), pp. 77–87.

60. Ts. Dorjsuren, "Kharaagiin Noyon Uuland 1954 ond arkheologiin shinjilgee khiisen tukhai," *Shinjlekh ukhaan setguul,* 4 (1954), pp. 33–42; Miniaev, "K probleme proiskhozhdeniia siunnu."

61. N. V. Polos'mak, "Nekotorye analogii pogrebeniiam v mogil'nike u derevni Daodunzhei i problema proiskhozhdeniia siunnuskoi kul'tury," in *Kitai v epokhu drevnosti,* ed. V. E. Larichev (Novosibirsk, 1990), pp. 101–107; E. Bunker et al. (eds.), *Ancient Bronzes of the Eastern Eurasian Steppes from the Arthur M. Sackler Collections* (New York, 1997), pp. 76–98; Linduff, "The Gender of Luxury and Power."

62. A. Nelson et al., "A Gobi Mortuary Site through Time: Bioarchaeology at Baga Mongol, Baga Gazaryn Chuluu," in *The Archaeology of Mongolia: Proceedings of the August 2007 Archaeological Symposium in Ulaanbaatar, Mongolia,* ed. J. Bemmann et al. (Bonn, 2009), pp. 565–578.

63. S. Miniaev, and L. Sakharovskaia, "Soprovoditel'nye zakhoroneniia 'tsarskogo' kompleksa No. 7v mogil'nike Tsaram," *Arkheologicheskie Vesti,* 9 (2002), pp. 86–118.

64. Ch. Yerool-Erdene, "Khunnugiin yazguurtny orshuulgyn dursgalyn sudalgaa" (PhD dissertation, National University of Mongolia, 2010).

65. S. Miniaev and L. Sakharovskaia, "Elitnyi kompleks zakhoronenii Siunnu v padi Tsaram," *Rossiiskaia Arkheologiia,* 1 (2007), p. 201; N. Polos'mak et al., "The Burial Construction of Noin Ula Mound 20, Mongolia," *Archaeology, Ethnology, and Anthropology of Eurasia,* 34/2 (2008), pp. 85–87.

66. K. C. Trever, *Excavations in Northern Mongolia* (Leningrad, 1932), p. 15; W. André, *Al-Hind: The Making of the Indo-Islamic World,* vol. 2 (Leiden, 2002); S. Miniaev and L. Sakharovskaia, "Investigation of a Xiongnu Royal Complex in the Tsaram Valley: The Inventory of Barrow No. 7 and the Chronology of the Site," *The Silk Road,* 4/1 (2007), pp. 54–55; E. Chang et al., "Archaeological Research on Xiognu Tombs of Duurlig Nars, Mongolia," in *Xiongnu,* pp. 214–231; U. Brosseder, "Xiongnu Terrace Tombs and Their

Interpretation as Elite Burials," in *Current Archaeological Research in Mongolia: Proceedings of the August 2007 Archaeological Symposium in Ulaanbaatar, Mongolia,* ed. J. Bemmann et al. (Bonn, 2009), pp. 268–269.

67. Mongolian National Museum of History and National Museum of Korea, *Mongolyn Morin Tolgoi khunnu ueiin bulsh* (Ulaanbaatar, 2001), pp. 218–224; T. Torbat et al., *Egiin Golyn sav nutag dakh' arkheologiin dursgaluud* (Ulaanbaatar, 2003), pp. 136–137; Honeychurch, "The Nomad as State Builder."

68. F. Louis, "Han Lacquerware and the Wine Cups of Noin Ula," *The Silk Road,* 4/2 (2006/2007), pp. 48–53; Rudenko, *Kul'tura khunnov,* p. 36.

69. Trever, *Excavations in Northern Mongolia,* p. 13.

70. N. Ishjamts, "Nomads in Eastern Central Asia," in *History of Civilization of Central Asia: The Development of Sedentary and Nomadic Civilizations. 700 B.C. to A.D. 250,* ed. J. Harmatta (Paris, 1994), pp. 167–168; Rudenko, *Kul'tura khunnov,* pp. 105–108; Y. Lubo-Lesnichenko, "External Relations of Central Asia according to Material from Pazyryk and Noin-ula," in *The Chinese and Their Northern Neighbors (ca. 1000 BC–ca. 2nd Century AD),* ed. K. M. Linduff (Pittsburgh, 1991), vol. 2, pp. 1–33.

71. A. A. Voskresensky and N. P. Tikhonov, "Technical Study of Textiles from the Burial Mounds of Noin-Ula," *The Bulletin of the Needle and Bobbin Club,* 20, 1/2 (1936), pp. 3–73; A. Salmony, "Archaeological Background of Textile Production in the Soviet Russian Territory," *The Bulletin of the Needle and Bobbin Club,* 26/2 (1942), pp. 3–14.

72. Rudenko, *Kul'tura khunnov,* p. 97; K. Riboud, "A Comparative Study of Two Similar Han Documents: Polychrome Figured Silks from Lou-lan and Ilmovaja Pad," *Bulletin de Liaison du Centre international d'etude des textiles anciens (Lyon),* 28 (1968), pp. 26–61; I. Good, "On the Question of Silk in Pre-Han Eurasia," *Antiquity,* 69/266 (1995), pp. 959–968.

73. Polos'mak et al., "The Burial Construction."

74. T. A. Chikisheva et al., "Dental Remains from Mound 20 at Noin Ula, Mongolia," *Archaeology Ethnology & Anthropology of Eurasia,* 37 (2009), pp. 145–151.

75. See Figure 4.5; D. Tseveendorj et al., "Noyon Uuliin Khunnugiin yazguurtnii 20-r bulsh sudalgaa," *Arkheologiin Sudlal,* 4/24 (2007), pp. 288–304; D. Tseveendorj et al., "Noyon Uulyn Khunnugiin yazguurtny bulshny 2006, 2009 ony arkeologiin maltlaga sudalgaany ur dungees," *Arkheologiin Sudlal,* 29 (2010), pp. 255–273.

76. P. Bernard, "The Greek Kingdoms of Central Asia," in *History of Civilization of Central Asia*, pp. 117–119.

77. G. A. Koshelenko and V. N. Pilipko, "Parthia," in *History of Civilization of Central Asia*, pp. 137–139.

78. A. Sheng, "Textiles from the Silk Road: Intercultural Exchanges among Nomads, Traders, and Agriculturalists," *Expedition,* 52 (2010), pp. 38–40; E. Laong, "Recent Finds of Western-Related Glassware, Textiles, and Metalwork in Central Asia and China," *Bulletin of the Asia Institute,* 9 (1995), pp. 1–18.

79. Miniaev and Sakharovskaia, "Soprovoditel'nye zakhoroheniia"; Miniaev and Sakharovskaia, "Investigation of a Xiongnu Royal Complex."

80. S. V. Tishkin, "Characteristic Burials of the Xiongnu Period at Ialoman-II in the Altai," in *Xiongnu Archaeology*, p. 554.

81. Mission archéologique française en Mongolie, *Mongolie: le premier empire des steppes* (Arles, 2003); Allard et al., "A Xiongnu Cemetery Found in Mongolia," *Antiquity,* 76 (2002), pp. 637–638; Erdenebaatar et al., "Umard Khunnugiin yazguurtny bulshny sudalgaa," *Tuukhiin Sudlal,* 33 (2002), pp. 20–28.

82. U. Brosseder, "Khunnugiin ueiinkhen, tednii gadaad khariltsaa," in *Mongolie, les Xiongnu de l'Arkhangai,* ed. J.-P. Desroches and G. André (Ulaanbaatar, 2007), pp. 85–87.

83. D. Erdenebaatar et al., "Excavations of Satellite Burial 30, Tomb 1 Complex, Gol Mod 2 Necropolis," in *Xiongnu Archaeology*, pp. 303–304.

84. B. F. Miller et al., "A Xiongnu Tomb Complex: Excavations at Gol Mod 2 Cemetery, Mongolia," *Mongolian Journal of Anthropology, Archaeology, and Ethnology,* 2 (2006), pp. 1–21.

85. D. Erdenebaatar et al., "Excavations of Satellite Burial 30," pp. 311–313.

86. Ibid., p. 311; see Figure 4.7.

87. D. Whitehouse, *Roman Glass in the Corning Museum of Glass* (Corning, NY, 2001), vol. 2, p. 203.

88. J. Rawson, "Carnelian Beads, Animal Figures and Exotic Vessels: Traces of Contact between the Chinese States and Inner Asia, c. 1000–650 BC," in *Archäologie in China,* vol. 1: *Bridging Eurasia,* ed. M. Wagner and W. Wei (Mainz, 2010), pp. 1–42; A. V. Davydova, *Ivolginskii arkheologicheskii kompleks: Ivolginskoe gorodishche* (St. Petersburg, 1995), pp. 39–40; A. V. Davydova, *Ivolginskii arkheologicheskii kompleks: Ivolginskii mogil'nik* (St. Petersburg, 1996), pp. 22–23.

89. Ch. Amartuvshin and W. Honeychurch, *Dundgobi aimagt hiisen arkheologiin sudalgaa: Baga Gazaryn Chuluu* (Ulaanbaatar, 2010); Nelson et al., "A Gobi Mortuary Site through Time"; A. Nelson et al., "Caught in the Act: Understanding Xiongnu Site Formation Processes at Baga Gazaryn Chuluu, Mongolia," in *Xiongnu Archaeology*, pp. 213–228.

90. J. Lankton, *A Bead Timeline, Volume I: Prehistory to 1200 CE* (Washington, DC, 2003).

91. Ch. Amartuvshin and P. Khatanbaatar, "Khunnu bulshny sudalgaa," in *Dundgobi aimagt hiisen arkheologiin sudalgaa: Baga Gazryn Chuluu,* ed. C. Amartuvshin and W. Honeychurch (Ulaanbaatar, 2010), pp. 233–234, 240–241.

92. L. Dubin, *The History of Beads from 30,000 BC to the Present* (London, 2009), pp. 53, plate 42 upper left, 368, nos. 367a, b, c; H. Beck, *The Beads from Taxila* (Delhi, 1941), p. 30 and plate ix, no. 27.

93. P. M. Leus, "New Finds from the Xiongnu Period in Central Tuva: Preliminary Communication," in *Xiongnu Archaeology*, p. 520.

94. Amartuvshin and Khatanbaatar, "Khunnu bulshny sudalgaa," pp. 236–237, 241–242.

95. Brosseder, "Belt Plaques," p. 413; L. Dussubieux and B. Gratuze, "Nature et origine des objets en verre retrouvés à Begram (Afghanistan) et à Bara (Pakistan)," in *De l'Indus à l'Oxus. Archeologie de l'Asie Centrale,* ed. O. Bopearachchi et al. (Lattes, 2003), pp. 315–323.

96. J. Lankton, "Gold-Glass Beads in Hellenistic Rhodes and Contemporary Java: Technological Challenges and Choices," *The 18th Congress of AIHV on the History of Glass* (Thessaloniki, Greece, 2009).

97. Khatanbaatar et al., "Khunnugiin bulshnaas ilersen khar' garaltai oldvoruud," *Arkheologiin Sudlal,* 4/24 (2007), pp. 305–322.

98. Amartuvshin and Khatanbaatar, "Khunnu bulshny sudalgaa," p. 248.

99. Khatanbaatar et al., "Khunnugiin bulshnaas ilersen khar'garaltai oldvoruud," pp. 307–310; Lankton, *A Bead Timeline,* p. 85.

100. E. S. Bogdanov and I. Y. Sljusarenko, "Egyptian Faience Amulets from Gorny Altai," *Archaeology, Ethnology and Anthropology of Eurasia,* 32/4 (2007), pp. 78–79.

101. B. J. Staviskij, "Central Asian Mesopotamia and the Roman World: Evidence of Contacts," in *In the Land of the Gryphons: Papers on Central Asian Archaeology in Antiquity*, ed. A. Invernizzi (Florence, 1995), pp. 195–200.

102. T. A. Sherkova, *Egipet i Kushanskoe tsarstvo* (Moscow, 1991), pp. 74–75, 77–86.

103. B. K. Miller, "Permutations of Peripheries in the Xiongnu Empire," in *Xiongnu Archaeology*, pp. 572–573; Bogdanov and Sljusarenko, "Egyptian Faience Amulets."

104. Laser ablation inductively coupled plasma-mass spectrometry. J. Lankton and Ber. Gratuze, "Glass and Faience Beads and Pendants from Xiongnu Sites in Mongolia: Chemical Analysis and Preliminary Interpretation," LA-ICP-MS Analysis report for submission to Yale University, forthcoming.

105. See Figure 4.2; V. A. Galibin, "Osobennosti sostava stekliannykh bus ivolginskogo mogil'nika khunnu," in *Drevnee Zabaikal'e i ego kul'turnye sviazi* (Novosibirsk, 1985); Mission archéologique française en Mongolie, *Mongolie*, p. 122.

106. e.g., K. Chugunov et al., "Arzhan 2: la tombe d'un prince scythe en Sibérie du Sud. Rapport préliminaire des fouilles russo-allemandes de 2000–2002," *Arts Asiatiques*, 59 (2004), pp. 5–29.

107. Honeychurch et al., "Death and Social Process."

108. Kradin, "Structure of Power"; Barfield, "Steppe Empires, China, and the Silk Route."

109. Kradin, "Structure of Power," pp. 105–107; N. Di Cosmo, "State Formation and Periodization in Inner Asian History," *Journal of World History*, 10 (1999), pp. 23–25.

110. D. Navaan, *Khunnugiin ov soyol: arkheologiin sudalgaany material* (Ulaanbaatar, 1999); Miller et al., "Xiongnu Elite Tomb Complexes"; T. Torbat et al., *Mongol Altain Arkheologiin Dursgaluud—I Bayan Oglii Aimag* (Ulaanbaatar, 2009); E. Jacobson-Tepfer et al., *Archaeology and Landscape in the Mongolian Altai: An Atlas* (Redlands, 2010); Leus, "New Finds from the Xiongnu Period"; Tishkin, "Characteristic Burials."

111. Miller, "Permutations of Peripheries in the Xiongnu Empire."

112. Ibid., p. 578.

113. Enguo Lu, "The Podboy Burials found in Xinjiang and the Remains of the Yuezhi," *Circle of Inner Asian Art Newsletter*, 15 (2002), p. 22; C. Debaine-Francfort, "Archéologie du Xinjiang des origines aux Han: IIème partie," *Paleorient*, 15/1 (1989), p. 192; V. I. Molodin and Kang In-Uk, "The Yarhoto Site (Turfan Depression, China) in the Context of the Hunnu Problem," *Archaeology, Ethnology, and Anthropology of Eurasia*, 3 (2000), pp. 89–99; Xinjiang Institute of Cultural Relics and Archaeology and the Research Center of Cultural Heritage and Archaeology, Northwest China, "The 2006–2007 Excavation on the Dongheigou Site in Barkol County, Xinjiang," *Kaogu*, 1 (2009), pp. 3–27.

114. Iu. A. Zadneprovskii, "Rannie kochevniki Semirech'ia i Tian'-Shania," in *Stepnaia polosa Aziatskoi chasti SSSR v skifo-sarmatskoe vremia*, ed. N. G. Gorbunova (Moscow, 1992), pp. 73–87; N. A. Bokovenko and Iu. A. Zadneprovskii, "Rannie Kochevniki Vostochnogo Kazakhstana," in *Stepnaia polosa Aziatskoi chasti SSSR v skifo-sarmatskoe vremia*, pp. 140–148.

115. Ibid., p. 145; Yu. S. Khudyakov, "Problems of the Genesis of Culture of the Hunnic Period in the Altai Mountains," *Ancient Civilizations from Scythia to Siberia*, 3/2–3 (1996), p. 337.

116. M. N. Pshenitsyna, "Tesinskii etap," in *Stepnaia polosa Aziatskoi chasti SSSR v skifo-sarmatskoe vremia*, p. 225; A. M. Mandel'shtam, "Rannie kochevniki skifskogo perioda na territorii Tuvy," in *Stepnaia polosa Aziatskoi chasti SSSR v skifo-sarmatskoe vremia*,

p. 179; Khudyakov, "Problems of the Genesis of Culture," p. 345; N. Yu. Kuzmin, "Prospects for Correlating Radiocarbon and Archaeological Chronologies of the Scythian and Hunno-Sarmatian Age Burials in the Sayan-Altai Region," *Archaeology, Ethnology and Anthropology of Eurasia,* 35/3 (2008), pp. 79–80, 84–85.

117. Leus, "New Finds from the Xiongnu Period," p. 520; Tishkin, "Characteristic Burials," p. 557.

118. Khudyakov, "Problems of the Genesis of Culture," p. 345; Yu. S. Khudyakov, "Vliianie Khunnskoi kul'tury na drevnikh kochevnikov yujnoi Sibiri," *Arkheologiin Sudlal,* 31 (2011), pp. 148–160; D. G. Savinov, "Gunno-sarmatskoye vremya," in *Drevnie kul'tury Bertekskoi doliny,* ed. V. I. Molodin (Novosibirsk, 1994), pp. 144–146; T. A. Chikisheva and D. V. Pozdnyakov, "Physical Anthropology of the Gorny Altai Populations in the Hunno-Sarmatian Period," *Archaeology, Ethnology and Anthropology of Eurasia,* 3/3 (2000), p. 117; Khudyakov, "Problems of the Genesis of Culture," p. 345; Khudyakov, "Vliianie Khunnskoi kul'tury."

119. A. M. Mandel'shtam and E. U. Stambul'nik, "Gunno-sarmatskii period na territorii Tuvy," in *Stepnaia polosa Aziatskoi chasti SSSR v skifo-sarmatskoe vremia,* pp. 197–199.

120. Pshenitsyna, "Tesinskii etap," pp. 231–232.

121. Khudyakov, "Vliianie Khunnskoi kul'tury."

122. M. Hall and S. Minyaev, "Chemical Analyses of Xiongnu Pottery: A Preliminary Study of Exchange and Trade on the Inner Asian Steppes," *Journal of Archaeological Science,* 29 (2002), pp. 135–144; U. Brosseder, "Fremde Frauen in Ivolga?" in *Scripta Praehistorica in Honorem Biba Teržan,* ed. M. Blečić (Ljubljana, 2007), pp. 883–893.

123. Khudyakov, "Problems of the Genesis of Culture," p. 342; Mandel'shtam and Stambul'nik, "Gunno-sarmatskii period na territorii Tuvy," pp. 198–200; E. B. Vadetskaya, *Tashtykskaia epokha v drevnei istorii Sibiri* (St. Peterburg, 1999), pp. 65–71.

124. L. Koryakova and A. Epimakhov, *The Urals and Western Siberia in the Bronze and Iron Ages* (Cambridge, 2007), p. 299.

125. Ibid., pp. 298–299.

126. Ibid., pp. 307–308.

127. Ibid., pp. 310–311.

128. Yu. S. Khudyakov, "Armaments of Nomads of the Altai Mountains (First Half of the 1st Millennium AD)," *Acta Orientalia,* 58/2 (2005), p. 119.

129. Koryakova and Epimakhov, *The Urals and Western Siberia,* p. 309.

130. Ibid., pp. 333–336.

131. Raschke, "New Studies."

132. F. Wood, *The Silk Road: Two Thousand Years in the Heart of Asia* (Berkeley, 2002), p. 29; G. Richter, "Silk in Greece," *American Journal of Archaeology,* 33/1 (1929), pp. 27–33.

133. Good, "On the Question of Silk."

134. I. Good et al., "New Evidence for Early Silk in the Indus Civilization," *Archaeometry,* 50/3 (2009), pp. 457–466.

135. Lattimore, *Studies in Frontier History,* pp. 481–483.

136. Barfield, "Steppe Empires, China, and the Silk Route"; Christian, "Silk Roads or Steppe Roads?" pp. 16–17.

137. e.g., C. Renfrew and J. Cherry (eds.), *Peer Polity Interactions and Socio-Political Change* (Cambridge, 1986).

138. Brosseder, "Belt Plaques."

139. Di Cosmo, "State Formation," pp. 23–25.

140. W. Honeychurch and Ch. Amartuvshin, "Timescapes from the Past: An Archaeogeography of Mongolia," in *Mapping Mongolia: Situating Mongolia in the World from Geologic Time to the Present,* ed. P. Sabloff (Philadelphia, 2011), pp. 211–213.

141. Di Cosmo, *Ancient China and Its Enemies,* p. 248; Christian, "Silk Roads or Steppe Roads?" pp. 5–6.

FIVE

The Use of Sociopolitical Terminology for Nomads

An Excursion into the Term *Buluo* in Tang China

İsenbike Togan

The development of Chinese historiography from a literary genre to the Tang dynasty's Office of Historiography took many centuries. The process was expedited in 629–630 when Tang Taizong (唐太宗) commissioned historians and advisers to write the annals of earlier dynasties. One of the terms that these historical accounts used in referring to nomadic groups was *buluo* (部落). This term had actually been coined earlier in the *Weishu* (魏書), the history of the Northern Wei dynasty (386–534), whose rulers themselves were of nomadic origin, and Tang historians adopted it to elucidate their account. Thereafter, *buluo* continued to be used and acquired a number of nuances. The present study, which deals with the historical evolution of this term, reveals that changes in its meaning occurred when nomads ruled China. In this sense, they were agents of change in Chinese historiography.

State formation in Inner Asia has drawn the attention of many scholars. In attempting to shed light on the rise and fall of Inner Asian states, historians and anthropologists have disseminated an array of views. Discussions have largely centered on the nature and identification of kinship groups. However, Hilda Ecsedy, Lev Gumilev, and Halil İnalcık have emphasized the role of nonkinship groups in state building. According to these scholars, non-kinship groups served as intermediaries between kinship groups and the state. Although they share a common approach, these three scholars do not use exactly the same terminology. While Ecsedy used the term "tribe," Gumilev preferred *ordo*, a Turco-Mongolian term.[1] In his study on the emergence of the Ottoman state, İnalcık drew attention to groups that are referred to as *bölük* in the sources.[2] The present study draws inspiration from all three of these scholars. While preparing the annotated translation of the chapter on the early Türk in *Jiu Tangshu* (舊唐書, the *Old History of the Tang* [618–742]), my colleagues and I found rendering the sociopolitical terminology into Turkish posed a challenge.[3] Liu Mau-tsai's translation of this same source into German—in which certain distinctions were made between kinship groups (*Stämme*) and non-kinship groups (*Horden*)—paved the way for the present study.

In *The Headless State,* David Sneath has recently taken up this issue from an anthropological perspective, without addressing the works of the above-mentioned scholars.[4] Predicating his argument on the post-seventeenth-century history of the Khalkha Mongols, he states that kinship was not the organizing principle among this group. Sneath then claims that kinship only pertained to the aristocracy, whose followers consisted of non-kinship groups. What is more, he argues that this phenomenon can be seen throughout history by giving examples from the Xiongnu to Khalkha. At times, his cases extend over a large geographical area that even encompasses Turkey. Sneath's hypothesis that there were non-kinship groups in Inner Asia needs to be understood with some limitations. However, the idea that these groups surfaced throughout Inner Asian history, as well as the assertion that they were a product of the state and were thus a poststate phenomenon, cannot be substantiated by the historical record.

There are always problems in making generalizations, especially with respect to Inner Asian history. First, unlike European history, not all sources of Inner Asian history have critical editions. Frequently, all we have are translations of selected works by diverse authors. As a result, there are often several translations for the same term. Alternatively, different terms are translated into the same word in English or other European languages. Put differently, there is no standardization of the terminology, particularly in all that concerns the translations of Chinese sources. Therefore, it is difficult to make generalizations over a long period, especially on the basis of readable translations or secondary literature. While critical editions of historical dictionaries exist, they are mostly used by scholars who are familiar with primary sources. Furthermore, monolithic interpretations of Inner Asia overshadow the great vicissitudes that inform times of rupture. For instance, although the same words are used in different periods, they frequently take on divergent meanings according to the changing historical context. Hence it is important to take into account the changes that were wrought by Chinggis Khan in the thirteenth century and later by regional rulers in the sixteenth century.

With these considerations in mind, this chapter focuses on the eastern part of Inner Asia between the fifth and eighth centuries, a period of two hundred years that roughly corresponds to the reigns of the Northern Zhou

(*Beizhou* 北周), the Northern Qi (*Beiqi* 北齊), and the Sui (隋) until the mid-Tang period in China and the early Türk period on the steppe. Moreover, this chapter is not grounded on a particular theoretical approach, but on the examination of Chinese textual sources. On the basis of these texts, it is evident that non-kinship groups existed among the early Türk. It is also clear that, while these groups predated state formations in some cases, in others they were created by the state structure itself. However, within the state structure they did not exist solely by themselves but coexisted with kinship collectives. As we shall see, a distinct terminology composed of words like *zu* (族), *xing* (姓), *bu* (部), and *buluo* was used for both kinship and non-kinship groups.

The Chinese term for these non-kinship groups was *buluo,* one of the new terms that were incorporated into Chinese historiography. The Northern Wei (*Beiwei* 北魏, 386–532 BCE) introduced this term to refer to new developments on the steppe. The term *buluo,* which we do not encounter regarding the Xiongnu (third century BCE to third century CE), first appears in the *Weishu,* where it connotes tribe segments that are usually leaderless groups. At the same time, however, the Northern Wei used it to refer to non-kinship groups that were organized around leaders. During the Tang era, the term was used to describe the entourage and followers of rulers or high dignitaries. The *buluo* predated the establishment of the early Türk state. They were created by the Türk ruling family and state also, upon assigning contingents to princes and notables.

During the Yuan, the term's use was limited. There are only fourteen instances in the *Yuanshi* (元史), where it refers to nomadic communities in general. In the post-Yuan era, the composition and mobility of the steppe's population underwent some changes. One of the most visible was that leadership became more pronounced among these groups. If a ruler did not arise from within the community, the members sought to recruit one from the outside. That said, there were regional differences in the internal makeup of the steppe's communities. At any rate, in the post-Yuan Chinese sources, the term *buluo* continued to refer to all nomadic groups and became translated into European languages as "tribe." In retrospect, it seems as though this later understanding was projected onto earlier meanings. At present, the term's use is reinforced when works in English are translated into Chinese. Consequently, we can clearly see that the term *buluo* came to mean "tribe" in the aftermath of the Yuan.[5]

The Problem at Hand

Two related terms surface in the Turkic inscriptions: *bod,* namely tribe; and *bodun* (as a plural of *bod*), which is believed to mean "people." However, in the Chinese texts there are no equivalents to these words. Instead, these sources employ *buluo,* which is translated as "tribe" in European languages. Another term, *xing,* is sometimes translated as "clan," "tribe," or even as "surname." Two other terms, *shi* (氏) and *bu,* are also rendered as "tribe."[6] Moreover, *zu* and *zhong* (種) occasionally merit the same treatment. "As far as Chinese terminology is concerned," M. Dobrovits notes, "we can see many expressions such as *buluo, zhong, luo* (落), *bu* and *xing.* It is however, next to impossible to define their exact meanings."[7] This is precisely the problem. Does collapsing the meaning of various Chinese terms into a single word, or using the terms tribe, clan, and lineage interchangeably help us understand history?[8] "As both H. Ecsedy and B. Csongor pointed out," states Dobrovits, "only the term *buluo* can be translated in an exact way as tribe."

However, this is not the consensus view. In fact, the terms *bu* and *buluo* are both translated into English as tribe.[9] Additionally, modern Chinese scholars make no distinction between these two terms when interpreting historical texts, even though only *buluo* carries this meaning in modern Chinese. While such a generalization may seem beneficial from our sedentary viewpoint, it actually limits our comprehension of the past.[10] It is precisely this difficulty, which arose during our translation of the *Jiu Tangshu,* that has propelled us to examine these Chinese terms closely in both (1) their Chinese context and (2) when referring to nomads. An examination of these terms in historical and textual contexts indicates that *bu* and *buluo* had divergent meanings in these contexts. Sometimes the same term expressed a different meaning when it referred to the nomads. At other times, the sources revived an ancient term that denoted the steppe peoples. What is more, in other cases, historians introduced distinct terms in order to integrate nomads into the official historiography, especially when the nomads were ruling in China.

A closer look at the Chinese sources provides certain clues. Within the purview of this study, sources on the Türk are examined within the timeframe of the Türk themselves, namely between 552 and 742. Upon examining the sources for this two-hundred-year period in terms of the Türk's historiographical traditions, we become aware of the following two aspects:

a. Most of the sources derive from a similar period, either from 636 to 646 or 730 to the 740s.[11] In other words, these works were penned in a pre-Uighur timeframe.[12]
b. Chinese sources that were contemporaneous with the early Türk did not employ contemporaneous terminology.

To further clarify the second issue, Chinese sources of that time do not use a counterpart for the Turkic term *bodun* in the Türk inscriptions.

This ancient Turkic term symbolized a new development of great significance in the life of the steppe peoples. Nonetheless, it was not represented by either transcription or translation. Instead, the early Tang sources used a terminology that had entered Chinese sources through the Tuoba (拓跋 Tabghach) nomads who established the Northern Wei dynasty.[13]

Dating the Sources: Creating and Compiling

Getting back to the problem of the sources, historians often use documents in relation to the period they cover, rather than taking into account their date of creation and compilation. A case in point is the source material on a group that is widely known as Toquz Oguz.[14] The names of the clans in the Nine Clans/Toquz Oghuz/Jiu Xing (九姓) confederacy are explicitly noted in Chinese sources. In the Turkic inscriptions from the 730s, the Toquz Oghuz (Nine Oghuz) constitutes a general term that offers no information as to the clans that comprised the confederation. Moreover, they are sometimes referred to merely as the Oghuz. We know the names of the member clans thanks to the *Tang Huiyao* (唐會要), which was completed in 961; that is, it was compiled after the fall of the Uighur empire (744–840).[15]

According to the *Tang Huiyao,* the Uighurs were one of the Nine Clans, and this piece of information is confirmed by other sources from the tenth and eleventh centuries. However, in Du You's (杜佑) *Tongdian* (通典 *TD*)—a work that was completed in 801, but relied on a work from the 730s or 740s—there is no mention of the "Nine Clan" confederacy.[16] Furthermore, this work lacks an account of the Oghuz or Jiu Xing/Toquz Oghuz. While numerous small and at times insignificant tribes or people garner at least one or two lines in this work, the fact that the Oghuz—who were apparently crucial to the survival of the second Türk state—are omitted demands further explanation. While Du You does mention some of the clans that belonged to the later Toquz Oghuz confederacy, they are listed separately rather than as part of any union. For example, the Bugut, Bayïrqu, and Tongra appear in chapter 199 and the Uighurs (*huihe,* 回紇) merit a very short account in chapter 200.[17] In other words, these clans were not only listed separately, but turn up in different chapters.[18] Additionally, they are not referred to as clans (*xing*), but as separated tribes (*biebu,* 別部) of the Tiele (鐵勒).[19] A similar reasoning can be applied to the information in the *Jiu Tangshu*. In the chapter on the early Türk (ch. 194a), individual tribes like the Uighur and Bayïrqu also come up on their own and the Toquz Oghuz is used as a general term. On the other hand, the Toquz Oghuz tribes are enumerated in the Uighur chapter (ch. 195) of the *Jiu Tangshu*. As we know, the pre-An Lushan (安祿山) information in the Türk chapter derives from

Wu Jing's (吳兢) work from the late 720s, which covers the years 617 to 726.[20] Both of these early sources—Wu Jing (737) and Du You's source, *Zhengdian* (政典, 730–740)—illustrate the situation before the An Lushan rebellion (756), and before the establishment of the Uighur state in 744. Thus, while the chapter on the Türk (194a) in the *Jiu Tangshu* reflects a pre-An Lushan context, its Uighur chapter (195) reflects the situation after the downfall of the Uighurs in 840.

This review undoubtedly shows that the information on the Toquz Oghuz clans is dated no earlier than the mid-tenth century—the date of the Uighur chapter of the *Jiu Tangshu* being 945 and that of the *Tang Huiyao* 961. Moreover, the fact that only four or five of these groups appear by themselves and are even located in separate chapters in the *Tongdian* from 801 adds another dimension to the question of whether the information from 961 reflects an "after-the-fact" reality: Were the Uighurs considered a part of the Nine Clans after they assumed power?[21] Or is the missing information an oversight? The fact that this work covers very small groups but not the Nine Clans increases the importance of this problem. Why did Du You leave out this information? Was he ignorant of their existence or did they simply not exist at the time? We know of the Nine Clans from the Turkic inscriptions from 681 onward. In these stelae, they are sometimes referred to as Oghuz (i.e., clans) and are occasionally prefaced by numbers denoting their composition, such as Toquz Oghuz (Nine Clans) or Üch Oghuz (Three Clans).

This leads us to yet another problem. At that time, in Chinese the number nine had the connotation "many."[22] There are references to "Nine Sogdians (*jiuhu*, 九胡)," "Nine Türks (*jiu tujue*, 九突厥)," and to our Nine Clans (*Jiu Xing*) as well. Yet there is no evidence as to what the number nine may have signified in the language of the early Türk.[23] Additionally, while the *Tang Huiyao* (961) and *Jiu Tangshu* (945) speak of the Nine Clans from the outset, they initially enumerate only seven, before adding the final two. Could this mean that in the tenth century, nine denoted exactly nine, whereas earlier it meant "many"?

With these considerations in mind, we shall examine the sociopolitical terminology of contemporaneous sources that originated between 552 and 742. Texts like the *Weishu* originating in 554, before the Tang, serve to define the origins of the terminology. Sources stemming from the time of the Uighurs and later are used with reference to contemporaneous sources.

A close look at the sources of this period shows that the term *xing* means clans; that is, kinship groups, and *jiu xing* ("nine" or "many clans") refers to the Toquz Oghuz.[24] Tang sources call the On Oq (Ten Arrows) *shixing* (十姓). This was originally an intraclan organization, but was split up into decimal groups by Dielishi (咥利失) Khagan in 635.[25] In other words, as in the case of the Chinese use of *buluo* for the Turkic *bodun*, the Tang sources and Turkic inscriptions use different terms for the same phenomenon. However, as elucidated below, Tang sources continued to use the earlier historical terms, rather than defining the new developments.

In the ensuing sections, we will discuss sources and the use of terminology within the context of the time of compilation, with a focus on non-contemporaneous terminology in Tang sources. This point is taken up from the perspective of the developmental history of the term *buluo* and, to a lesser extent, other related words. The contemporaneous term in the Turkic inscriptions, *bodun*, does not appear in Tang sources. Instead, they avail themselves of the more familiar term *buluo*. To begin with, we will examine the use of the term *buluo* in the Chinese sources and its connotation in historical contexts, whereupon the discussion will turn to the *buluo* in the sixth to eighth centuries. The previous section on the origins of the term shows that it originated during the Tuoba Northern Wei period. *Buluo* remained in use even after the Turkic term *bodun* was introduced. However, the former took on a completely different connotation. The last part of the chapter is devoted to a contextual study of another term, *bu*. In so doing, we underscore the distinctions between *bu*, which is translated as "tribe," and *buluo*, which is translated as "tribe segments" or *bölük* in Turkish.[26]

A General Assessment of the *Buluo*

At the time of the formation of the first (sixth–seventh century) and second (seventh–eighth century) Türk state, there is no mention of large tribal groups or tribal leaders in either Turkic or Chinese sources. Those tribes that were distinguished by name were the ones brought under the suzerainty of the Türk state. Most of the documented personal names relate to the supreme leadership, the royal Ashina (阿史那) lineage, which was surrounded or followed by groups of people called *buluo* in the Tang sources.[27] These people are reminiscent of the *bölük* that are mentioned in the Turkish sources from the 1300s.[28] More specifically, the *bölük* were mercenaries who after finishing their "careers," much of which involved accumulating booty, became personages with movable property who were active in politics. Their leaders were military commanders who had embarked on successful campaigns and thus could bring back booty.

Focusing on individuals rather than groups, modern historians have drawn attention to the role of the *comitatus* or *Gefolge* (follower) in the aftermath of the Roman empire, and the *nökör* (companion) in Chinggis Khan's state and empire.[29] C. Beckwith considers this relationship a kind of social bondage system that is typical of sacral kingship.[30] In his estimation, the warriors' strong personal loyalty to their leader was due to the Central Asian Turkic state's political system, in which the former were paid handsomely to serve in a lord's guard corps.[31] In the case of the sixth and seventh centuries we do not encounter individuals, but groups. These collectives are referred to as *buluo* in the Tang sources.

During the Tang and the beginning of the Yuan era, the nomadic people who contributed to state formation were not organized as kinship-based tribes, but rather as composite groups. In *The Secret History of the Mongols,* they are referred to as *irgen* (people) or *bölök irgen,* who needed a leader like "a garment needs a collar."[32] The term *buluo* is used both in the sense of *irgen* and *qariyatu* (subjects).

While the "many people" in the sixth to eighth centuries are termed *buluo* in Tang sources, the Turkic inscriptions do not refer to any equivalent of the *buluo.* Instead, they speak of *bodun* as the basis of their organization. These same *bodun* are endowed with a semblance of legitimacy as subjects of the state. In contrast, the Chinese term *buluo* does not harbor any cachet of legitimacy and is descriptive. The word itself is comprised of two elements: *bu,* which is pronounced [pəwʽ], [pɦəwʽ], or [bəw'], meant "a section, a part" in the Tang period; and *luo,* which is pronounced [lawʽ] or [lak], in Tang times meant "to settle down, to settle as birds, to fall as leaves."[33] In sedentary contexts, it can also connote a "settlement." Together, the word was articulated [bəwlak] at the time. The term is rendered as "tribe" in western languages.[34] However, the character *bu* is also translated as "tribe." There is also no difference between *bu* and *buluo* in modern-day Chinese, as both continue to mean "tribe." Likewise, K. Wittfogel and Feng Chia-sheng see no distinction between the two and maintain that "tribe" is the most suitable rendering of *buluo.*[35] In addition, they state that the term *bu* is an equivalent of *buluo.*[36]

However, much later we see that the Yuan terminology exhibits differences from the Liao terminology, as analyzed by Wittfogel and Feng. In the *Yuanshi,* all references to the tribes in the pre-Chinggisid era—the names of whom are known—are called *bu* (tribe).[37] Generally speaking, though, these references pertain to the period of Chinggis's conquests.[38] In accounts of later periods, persons belonging to the same tribes are said to come from extended families or sublineages (*shi,* 氏).[39] This term *shi* is translated as "clan" when used in the Han Chinese context that deals with earlier periods.[40] Other contexts, however, were already devoid of tribal structures or lineages, and people merely used their tribal affiliation as a surname.[41] The use of the tribal name as a family or even clan name signifies that these denominations had no political meaning. In the Chinese context, *shi* (clan) also refers to localized lineages because of the landed property that they controlled. However, when used in relation to tribal people, the reader should not attribute any landed property to the subject. When the same term was used for people coming from tribal backgrounds, it was deprived of its economic connotation and did not possess any political reality. The tribal people who had been dispersed into units of the army of conquest were now "people of tribal background," and this background was denoted by the term *shi*. In sum, the same Chinese term possesses different meanings in Han and non-Han contexts. Since tribes no longer existed, the term *buluo* seldom comes up in the *Yuanshi*, where its most common meaning is "steppe people."[42] In a few instances, it denotes the followers of a person. Only with respect to the members of the encampment of the Qonggirad, a consort clan, is the term *buluo* used together with a tribal name, which dates back to at least the early thirteenth century. The term *buluo* indicates that the Qonggirad were a privileged consort clan, for unlike ordinary army units, the Qonggirad continued to have their own following—a tradition that they managed to preserve from before the Chinggisid age.[43]

Seeing that the terms differ in Yuan times, the Liao terminology should probably also be reconsidered.[44] The blurring of the distinctions between *bu* and *buluo* is a post-Mongol development; it is a manifestation of a period in which the tribal structures were more or less curbed by central governments throughout the Asian continent.[45] Correspondingly, the tribes themselves had stabilized, as migrations, conquests, and the blending of populations had by and large tailed off after the sixteenth century.[46]

When examining *The Secret History of the Mongols* in terms of how the Mongolian glosses are rendered in Chinese, we see that *buluo* is annotated as *qari*—a Mongolian term that has warranted a handful of English translations: "separate domain, principality," "country," and "tribes."[47] In an illustrative passage where Önggür of the Ba'arin asks Chinggis Khan's permission to gather in his Baya'ud brethren who had been scattered and dispersed in each of the diverse *qarin* (the plural of *qari*), this term is glossed with *buluo*. Both F. W. Cleaves and I. de Rachewiltz have translated *qarin* as "tribe." However, by that time, tribes no longer existed. Many had been defeated and their men had been distributed among the victors.[48] Favored persons like Önggür of Ba'arin knew that they were asking for special treatment by requesting that their tribesmen, who had been dispersed among many *qarin*, namely mixed composite groups, be united anew.[49] Large tribal groups consisting of numerous lineages are also referred to as *buluo* in the *Secret History* (§9, I:5a); in one instance, *qarin* is rendered as *buluomei* (部落每), a plural of *buluo*. These references indicate that the *Secret History* echoes an earlier use of the term, when there was still a distinction between composite groups and clans. Moreover, it refers to kinship groups, such as clans and subclans, which are called *omogh, obogh* in Mongolian, as *xing,* a Chinese term. While the *Secret History* uses *xing* as an equivalent of clan (*omogh*), the *Yuanshi* uses this term exclusively in the Chinese context. More specifically, it refers to common people as *baixing* (百姓), or is used together with *ming* (名, name), in the sense of a name and surname. The old use of *xing,* as in the case of the Toquz Oghuz, was apparently a thing of the past.

The *Buluo* in the Sixth to Eighth Centuries

In charting the use of *buluo* between the sixth and eighth centuries, it must be remembered that this was a pre-Mongol situation. Moreover, the circumstances on the steppe and the structure of the tribes and clans differed from the post-Mongol period. Therefore, the present author surmises that during this timeframe there was a difference between the terms *bu* and *buluo.* For our purposes, the term *bu* will be translated as "tribe," whereas *buluo* will either be translated as "tribe segments" or left in transcription as *buluo. Buluo,* which is pronounced [*bəwlak*] according to E. G. Pulleyblank and [*bulak*] according to Wang Li (王力), literally means "a section, a small group, a segment" without kinship ties.[50] Although she was aware of the lack of this sort of affinity, Ecsedy preferred to translate it as tribe:

> Both because of the obviously nominal and by nature mobile integrity of the Turk Empire and because of the evidences of *e.g.* the Chinese sources, we may rightly seek for a smaller, but constant and naturally integrated unit of the Turk society, taking a position between the empire and kinship groups, able to oppose the clan-system in order to found a basis for the political power of an empire, and strong enough to disturb the authority of an empire-sized political power too, as happened several times. For this biggest unit of the Turk society in the Chinese records *we find the consistently used term* pu-lo, *showing no kinship concern, or at least no basic connection with the kinship structure;* that is why, when analyzing the content of this term from the poor and indirect information given, we may seek in it for the diagnostic markers of the largest naturally functioning social unit of the Turks and other nomads, a potential society itself, say: "tribe."[51] (emphasis added)

If there is such a distinguishing characteristic, then it is advisable to use distinct terms in English as well. The use of a single term "tribe" only blurs the aforementioned differences.[52] Therefore, in order to understand what was going on, rather than bringing various concepts under a single rubric, we need to fathom the dissonance between the various existing terms and draw synchronic and diachronic distinctions between them.

The *buluo* sometimes appear in dispersed form; at other times, they are followers gathered around a leader. As Ecsedy also observed,[53]

> although independent and viable communities (societies) seem—as a rule—to have a name of their own, a nomadic tribe's name used to belong exclusively to the tribe in question only till the moment of its expansion, when the name could and might be used by the subjects too.

Sources like the *Jiu Tangshu* speak of, say, the *buluo* of Elig (Xieli 頡利) Qaghan, of Ishbara, or Ashina Simo (阿史那思摩).[54] In another passage a hundred thousand persons from the masses (*zhong* 衆) of Ashina Simo's *buluo* crossed the Yellow River.[55] In 689, certain Türks went to Xiazhou (夏州) and brought Ashina Funian (阿史那伏念) to the north, where he was made qaghan; the *buluo* were pleased with this development.[56] Likewise, in the *Suishu* (隋書), the qaghan tells the Sui emperor that "I, your subject, leading my *buluo* . . ."[57] In the light of Ecsedy's above-mentioned statement, if these leading personalities were from the Ashina clan, then in cases where *buluo* is translated as tribe, then the members must be Ashina too.[58] However, we see that this was not the case. In addition, there is an unusual passage in the *Jiu Tangshu* noting that the earlier or former *buluo* of Elig Qaghan were designated for settlement south of the Yellow River.[59] The *Jiu Tangshu* also contains the following reference to the Xie Yantuo (薛延陀):[60] "When they heard that Taizong had moved Simo to the north of the Yellow River, they feared that upon receiving this information their own *buluo* would change sides. As a result they brought together their horsemen and attacked Simo."[61] Here again we have a case where it is impossible to translate the term *buluo* as "tribe." Otherwise, we have people whose leaders were afraid that their tribal people would change sides and become another tribe. In another passage in the *Suishu*, it is stated that one of Shibi (始畢) Qaghan's trusted men, a Sogdian named Shishu Huxi (史蜀胡悉), arrived with his *buluo* in tow.[62] It is evident in this passage that the Sogdian dignitary was not leading a Sogdian tribe.

Furthermore, the Ten Arrows of the Western Türk are described in our sources as having come into existence as a result of a series of reorganizations and divisions of the earlier structures. According to *Jiu Tangshu*, each of the resultant "arrow" units was called a *buluo*.[63] In these sorts of passages, one would be hard-pressed to speak of the formation of a new tribe.[64] Instead, they are best understood as a new encampment with followers (*buluo*). As a result, in this pre-Mongol setting, it is inappropriate to use the

Mongol term *ordo, ordos* (royal encampment), as Gumilev has done, for in the setting the emphasis is on followers.[65] In the Mongol setting, however, *ordo* denoted a royal encampment that had a center.[66] More specifically, the *ordo* consisted of the retainers—their families included—who were tied to the dignitary who personified the center. Deprived of their right of volition, these retainers could not leave whenever they so desired. However, the *buluo* were free to join or leave at their own discretion. This sort of rights or the lack thereof is another way to understand what we commonly refer as chaos and order.

The Evolution of the *Buluo*

The term *buluo* does not appear in the earlier sources that pertain to the Xiongnu. In other words, it does not turn up in the *Shiji* (史記) and the *Hanshu* (漢書), which only employ the term *bu* (tribe).[67] The historical sources that follow these works in terms of the period they cover are *Jinshu* (晉書, 265–419 CE) and the *Weishu* (covering 386–550 CE). However, the *Weishu* was written earlier (554), under the Northern Qi, even though the *Jinshu* (646) deals with earlier periods. The same could be said for scores of other texts that were penned under the rule of Tang Taizong (627–649).[68] Therefore, *Weishu*'s usage of *buluo* provides clues as to the evolution of the term.

That said, it is a passage from the *Jinshu* that sheds light on the genesis of the practice that lent its name to the term. According to this passage in the chapter on the *Siyi* (四夷, Four Foreigners), when the southern Xiongnu submitted to China, they consisted of more than five thousand small encampments (*luo*), among the sedentary Chinese.[69] However, after the fall of the Han, during the Three Kingdoms under the Wei (220–265) and under Wudi (武帝) of the Jin (晉) Dynasty (265–419), these Xiongnu remnants were divided into five sections or groups (*bu*).[70] Their notables became their *shuai* (帥, leaders), and Han Chinese were appointed as *sima* (司馬, "minister of war") to oversee the former.[71] After the collapse of the Wei, the *shuai* were turned into *duwei* (都尉, commanders in chief).[72] The *duwei* of the group on the left (east) administered over eleven thousand small encampments in the Zishi (茲氏) county of Taiyuan (太原). The *duwei* of the group on the right (west) administered more than six thousand small encampments in Qi (祁) county. The *duwei* of the southern group administered more than three thousand small encampments; they were living in Puzi (蒲子) county. The *duwei* of the northern group administered more than four thousand small encampments in Xinxing (新興) county. The *duwei* of the central group administered more than six thousand small encampments in Daling (大陵) county. In sum, these thirty thousand small encampments were spread over an area between 34.5 and 37 degrees latitude and 104 and 112 degrees longitude, stretching over the northern half of the Ordos region.

This passage demonstrates that the Xiongnu who had been settled in China were divided into groups (*bu*) which were administered jointly by both their own leaders and Han Chinese officials. These groups consisted of a number of small encampments (*luo*); in this case there were more than thirty thousand small encampments. Gradually these small encampments came to be known as *buluo,* as can be seen from the references in the *Weishu* in which similar numbers (for instance, thirteen thousand small encampments) are given for a leading personality's *buluo.*[73] During the Northern Wei, many such *buluo* seem to have had hereditary leaders.[74]

In this context, most of the references in the *Weishu* are to persons who appear to be leading their *buluo* somewhere, coming to submit their *buluo,* or moving their *buluo* to some place.[75] Unlike tribes, these groups do not have their own names; they either appear under a general term or constitute somebody's following.[76] Ecsedy consistently refers to these groups in the sources of the Sui and Tang with the phrase ". . . 's tribe," which seems to be inappropriate, as "independent and viable communities (societies) seem—as a rule—to have a name of their own."[77] Yet with respect to the *buluo,* which she translates as "tribe," Ecsedy claims that "The separate *pu-los* had no name of their own, but were named only after their heads, and thus we read about *Apa qaγan*'s tribe, *Ch'i-min* khagan's tribe or about 'the tribe led by *Išpara,*' etc."[78]

As the earliest source that uses the term *buluo,* the *Weishu* offers some clues as to the evolution of this process.[79] We hear of a *xing* that separated itself into sections and became a *buluo.*[80] Another passage notes that, after defeating a certain people, Ruru Shilun organized the *buluo* and moved them to the north of the Gobi (*mo,* 漠). In consequence, they ended up entering the Gaoche (高車) country.[81] Afterward, Wei Taizu (魏太祖) broke them up (*fen,* 分) and dispersed (*san,* 散) many of the *bu* (tribes).[82] The extremely fierce and uncivilized Gaoche were the only ones that prevented anyone from using them as servants. For this reason, the Gaoche were allowed to separate themselves as a *buluo.* During this early period, those *buluo* that were dispersed could not retain this collective form.

In the chapter on how the different Tuoba groups changed their names, all the tribes in the four directions presented an annual tribute.[83] At the beginning of the Dengguo (登國) period (386–395), Wei Taizu dispersed all the *buluo,* thereby initiating a process by which they started to assimilate into the registered people (*bian ming,* 編名).

The original definition of *buluo* in *Zhongwen Da Cidian* (中文大辭典), a modern dictionary of Chinese, attests to these dispersals:[84] "During the

Southern and Northern period the foreign groups were broken up and settled in different places according [to] the equal field system and as a result they were called *buluo*." This explanation overlaps with the notice in the *Jinshu* according to which Xiongnu remnants in the third century had been divided up into groups or sections (*bu*) and that each of them consisted of numerous settlements (*luo*).[85]

These structures of small groups of people, rather than individuals, from diverse backgrounds are described in our sources as constantly shifting allegiance in pursuit of their own interests. Descriptions of the Türk also fall into this category.[86] In the *Suishu* we are told that "the followers of these *buluo* [of the Türk] are all people—they consist of thousand categories and ten thousand kinds—whose [hearts] are anything but pure."[87] In another passage, "The Türk *buluo* are disaffected in heart and harbor feelings of opposition."[88]

Although nomads are traditionally described as searching for grass and water, in the *Jiu Tangshu* they appear to be following their own interests and changing sides. Given the severe limitations of the institutions on the steppe (due, inter alia, to a lack of a large surplus), personal relationships were indeed more important. As a result, one would expect that loyalty would be more emphasized in the steppe than in the sown. However, as we can see from the *Jiu Tangshu*'s chapter on the early Türk, feelings of loyalty were not expected from the people and followers either. It was accepted that situations and relations were subject to change. In that chapter the author intermittently complains about the lack of loyalty among the early Türk.[89] However, this trait should be understood as a survival technique. For this reason, the early Türk inscriptions from the eighth century (located in the Orkhon Basin) never rail against disloyalty when speaking of the people (*bodun*). It seems as though this sort of behavior was to be expected. However, they do rail against the shifting alliances among the leadership. The inscriptions and the *Jiu Tangshu* express similar views in this regard, and neither reprimanded the common folk for their subversive ways.

On the other hand, Tonyuquq, the renowned statesman of the early Türk, imputes more initiative to the *bodun:* they separated themselves and then collaborated "with the khan," only to then desert the khan and become subjects of China.[90] In other words, it is not just the khan who is calling the shots; the *bod* and the *bodun* also promote their own interests. In fact, Tonyuquq reinforces this point by noting that "Heaven" holds the *bodun* responsible for the search for independence as well as their submission to outside powers (T1 W3).[91]

The French Turkologist R. Giraud also saw in the use of the term *bod,* which appears but twice in Tonyuquq's inscription and the prevalence of the word *bodun* in all the stelae, a manifestation of the dismantlement of the old tribal or clan structure.[92] However, this phenomenon also marked the end of kinship as a political unit.

According to Chinese sources, the Second Türk Qaghanate was established around 680; that is, half a century after Elig Qaghan's submission to Tang China. As mentioned earlier, the *Jiu Tangshu* notes that the early Türk who had submitted to China were first settled in the interior, to the south of the Yellow River. After a coup by a member of the Türk royal family (639) who was serving as a guard, these "submitted *buluo*" were retransferred to the north. However, dissatisfied with their ruler and the new circumstances, the *buluo* packed up and returned to China in 643.[93] This, then, is what Tonyuquq had in mind when he wrote that the people forsook their khan and became subjects of China.[94] The remnants of the early Türk who were living in the northwest under the leadership of Chäbish, a member of the royal family, were defeated in 650. Consequently, they all became subjects of Tang China and were divided up into two general protectorates. As per Chinese principles, they were settled in the new prefectures that were established especially for them.[95] In all likelihood, it was during this period that the curtain fell on the last traces, if any still endured, of the earlier tribal structure (*bu*). Moreover, the people who were settled in these protectorates were mostly members of *buluo* rather than tribes (*bu*), so that the distinction between the two started to blur. This assimilation process is barely expressed in the *Jiu Tangshu*'s chapter on the early Türk as it ends with the downfall of the second Türk state in 734, concentrating on the state of affairs before the An Lushan rebellion (756). The distinction between *buluo* and *bu* is even slighter in Song sources. However, those sources that were constructed on the basis of information provided by nomadic dynasties, like the Liao and the Yuan, do reflect this distinction.

Bu (Tribes) vs. *Buluo* (Tribe Segments)

As mentioned above, the Early Türk inscriptions refer to the common folk as *bodun*. It is generally accepted that *bod* is "clan" and *bodun* "clans, or an organized tribal community," as G. Clauson puts it, "a people in the sense of a community ruled by a particular ruler."[96] *Bodun* is understood to be the plural form of *bod,* which is assumed to signify a clan or sometimes a tribe. However, the term is translated into English as "people" and "tribes."[97]

The historical usage among the Oghuz, as well as the present-day usage in Turkey as *boy,* seem to play a role in this interpretation of *bod*.[98] That said, historical sources in Turkic usually call tribes by their name, that is, as "tribe A" or "tribe B." On the other hand, throughout history Turkic peoples living over a large geographical area have used various terms to denote the term "tribe." Although glosses for concrete objects in Turkic languages were stable over the ages, abstract terms such as concepts seem to vary. For instance, over the centuries, different Turkic peoples used *at* for the horse or *yurt* for the homeland, whereas the word for tribe differed both synchronically and diachronically.[99] Sometimes there are shifts in the meanings, as in the case of *apa* (elders). There are shifts in the gender and kinship relations that *apa* expresses among different Turkic peoples. In one community it might mean a male clan elder; other alternatives that surface are a woman who is respected in the clan and an elder sister. In parallel, sometimes different words were used to denote the same concept. The term for tribe is *ru* among the Kazakh and the Kyrghyz, but they occasionally used *aymak* or *oymak*, *boy*, and the Arabic words *qabila* and *qawm*. These examples perhaps attest to the "flux" of the term tribe across different geographical locations and over historical times. In consequence, scholars must think twice before identifying the *bod* of the eighth century with that of the eleventh or with *boy* of later periods. It is important to emphasize that we are dealing with a fluid term rather than a static one. In other words, the term *bod* may have continued to refer to kinship groups while its precise meaning changed.

In the inscriptions *bod* appears twice. However, in each case, it is used in the general sense of the word. More specifically, a tribal name is not affixed to the term and it does not denote a specific tribe. The first passage in which the term *bod* occurs reads as follows:[100]

> *(W1) bilgä toń uquq bän özüm tabγač iliñä qïlintim. türk bodun tabγačqa körür erti*
>
> *(W2) türk bodun qanīn bulmayin, tabγačda adrïltï, qanlantï. qanīn qodup tabγačqa yana ičikdi täñri anča temis ärinč: qan bertim;*
>
> *(W3) qanïñin qodup ičikdiñ. Ičikdük üčün täñri ölütmis ärinč. Türk bodın ölti, alqïntï, yoq boltï. Türk sir bodun yerıntä*
>
> *(W4) bod qalmadï.*

Talat Tekin interprets this passage as follows:[101]

> (W1) I myself, Bilgä Tonyuquq, was born in China. The Turkish people were subject to China (at that time).
>
> (W2) Without having found their khan, the Turkish people were parted from the Chinese, and got themselves a khan. They (soon, however) abandoned their khan and submitted to China again. Heaven, then, must have spoken as follows: "I had given you a khan;

> (W3) but you abandoned your khan and submitted again." As a punishment for this submission, Heaven caused the Turkish people to be killed. The Turkish people were killed, ruined, and extinguished. In the land of the Turkish Sir people
> (W4) there was no longer any ordered group of people left.

Another, slightly different possibility for the passage's second line (W2) is:

> As they did not find [a personality suitable][102] to be their khan, they separated themselves from the Tabgach (meaning Northern China). Then they acquired a khan. [But although they had now a khan], they abandoned their khan and became subjects of the Tabghach, China.

There are also problems with Tekin's understanding of *bod* as an "ordered group of people" (W4), which he also renders as "tribes." From this passage one can discern that *bod* existed earlier and that they left North China on their own, despite the absence of a qaghan, which Tonyukuk calls *qan*. The *bodun* subsequently acquired a khan. However, they were dissatisfied with him and resubmitted to China. Consequently, there were no more *bod* left. In this instance, then, *bod* can mean "tribe."

The second passage where *bod* occurs is of a more general nature:

> *(N1) il-teris qaɣan qazɣanmasar, yoq ärti ärsär, bän özüm bilgä toń uquq qazɣanmasar, bän yoq ärtim ärsär,*
> *(N2) qapɣan qaɣan türük sir bodun yerīntä bod yämä bodun yämä kisī yämä idi yoq ärtäči ärti.*[103]
> (N1) If İlteriš Kagan had not won, or if he had never existed, and if I myself, Bilgä Tonyuquq, had not won, or if I had never existed,
> (N2) in the land of Qapɣan Kagan and of Turkish Sir people, there would have been neither tribes, nor people, nor human people at all.[104]

Osman Sertkaya translates the latter half of the passage thus:[105]

> Oooh! Kapgan Kagan![106] There would have been neither tribes (bod), nor people (bodun), nor human beings in the land of the Türk Sir people.[107]

The person who makes these remarks about *bod* is the aforementioned Tonyuquq, the famous statesman of the early Türk in the eighth century. According to Tonyuquq's own testimony, he was born and raised in North China. In referring to the Chinese suzerainty over the Türk at the time of his birth, the statesman seems to be alluding to a period between 631 and

680. Toward the end of the last section, we set the historical context for these events, namely the defeat of Chäbish in 650. Let us take a closer look at these developments. After the defeat (630) and death (636) of Elig Qaghan, he was succeeded by his close associate Ashina Simo. This is indeed how the *buluo* acquired a khan. Under Simo's command, the *buluo*—numbering hundreds of thousands of members, among them forty thousand armed soldiers—crossed the Yellow River in 639 and headed north. However, they ran into resistance from the Xie Yantuo. It also appears as though a significant portion of the *buluo* revolted against Ashina Simo and returned to the south. At this stage, they asked the Tang authorities to be settled in the Sheng (勝) and Xia (夏) prefectures. The former was located along the belt of the Yellow River and the latter further southeast.[108] They were then ensconced in what is presently the Shaanxi (陕西) region of northern China. About ten years later (650s), the remnants of the Türk in the northwest who had remained with Chäbish were, as mentioned above, defeated and resettled in two protectorates of Tang China. In sum, the system consisting of *bu* and *buluo* did not dissolve in one fell swoop. It expired in piecemeal fashion over a few waves of settlement. Needless to say, their way of life underwent change and the Türk organization of the qaghans became a thing of the past. For instance, Tonyuquq himself became an administrator for the submitted *buluo* in the Chanyu protectorate.[109] The ancestors of Iltärish Qaghan, the founder of the second state, were in the service of the commander in chief of the Yunzhong (雲中) protectorate.[110] All of these Türk found themselves within the framework of a Chinese-style organization. Therefore, it is not surprising that there were no more *bod* left. Of all the pertinent sources, it is Tonyuquq who underscores the termination of the *bod*, whereas Chinese sources did not make an issue of this development at this point. However, the various alternatives for settling the Türk in 630 did come up in Chinese sources.[111] In that sense, Tonyuquq's statement and the information in the *Jiu Tangshu* complement each other. Furthermore, it is interesting to note that both sources do not only dwell on the leadership, but also broach the dynamic role of the people who are termed *buluo* and *bodun*, respectively.

Let us now turn our sights on the tribes that fell under the rubric of *bu*. In Tang times, the term *bu* was pronounced [*bəw*]. In the *Jiu Tangshu*, it surfaces in the context of groups with specific names, like Tatabi, Xi (奚), Bugut, Uygur Bayïrqu, and Basmil.[112] The Karluk and the Kyrghyz also seem to have belonged to this category, as did the Xie Yantuo.[113] Liu Mau-tsai refers to all these groups as *Stämme*. These are tribes consisting of kinship groups such as *xing*. For instance, there are examples such as the Three Clan (*xing*) Karluk.[114] As a result, one can say that during this period *bu* meant "tribe." Given the fact that kinship functioned in both the political and economic sphere, the argument can be made that the Karluk were something akin to what Sharon Baştuğ calls "segmentary lineage."[115]

The Turkic equivalent of the term of *bu* (pronounced [*bəw*]) was *bod*. While *bu* denotes a section in Chinese, it is difficult to explain the Turkic *bod>boy*. Differences in pronunciation rule out the hypothesis that the term was borrowed by either the Chinese or Türk. While there is no evidence as to the etymology of the term *bod* in Turkic, the information in Chinese sources sheds light on the system's inner workings. First of all, the *bu* could consist of clans or lineages called *xing*. In addition, they were tribes that had been subjugated by the Türk administration.[116] Therefore, they were either ruled by their own leaders or by *eltäber*, who were either members of the royal family or appointees of the Türk state. The regime also sent *tuduns* to collect taxes. It seems as though these were not regular levies but imposts. On the matter of taxation, there was indeed a major difference between *bu* (tribe) and *buluo* (tribe segments, people). Tribes occasionally rose up in revolt because of heavy taxes, whereas the *buluo* would simply disperse. For this reason, they are described in *Jiu Tangshu* as always seeking profit and exhibiting no feelings of loyalty. In all likelihood, the *buluo* were exempt from taxes and their ostensible greed pertained to their desire for booty.

While the *buluo* did not have names of their own, the *bu* possessed both distinct names and their own soldiers. We also know that part of the career path of members of the royal family had their training by administering the *bu* (tribes). At the beginning of the Türk chapter, the *Jiu Tangshu* notes that "those princes who administered other tribes (*bu*) with soldiers under their command were called *shad*."[117] We know that Elig Qaghan's nephew, Tuli (突利) Qaghan, exacted such heavy imposts from northeastern tribes (*bu*) like the Tatabi and the Xi that the latter submitted to China.[118] At other times, tribes revolted due to excessive imposts.[119]

References to the composition of the *bu* and the *buluo* reveal further distinctions between these two terms. The *buluo* were followers of a certain leader, so that they dispersed if something happened to the leader, and there was no way of reuniting them henceforth. However, the reverse was true for the tribes (*bu*). On two occasions, we hear of the "former tribes" of certain persons. Conversely, it is clear that this sort of scenario was impossible in a *buluo* context. The first instance concerns a repatriation toward the north. In 639, those Türk and Hu (胡 Sogdians) who had been settled in various prefectures were ordered to cross the Yellow River and rejoin their old tribes (*bu*).[120] These people were followers (*buluo*) of Elig Qaghan and others. They had been settled to the south of the Yellow River. They were even permitted to raise their livestock in these regions.[121] They were not coming from one specific tribe, but were the *buluo* of Elig Qaghan, as can be seen by the fact that when these people were repatriated they numbered several hundred thousand.[122] Elig Qaghan was a member of the Ashina clan (*zu*) and had followers who were called *buluo* in Chinese and *bodun* in Turkic, but he was not accompanied by a tribe. On the other hand, there were tribes (*bu*) like the Uighurs and Bayïrqu that recognized Türk suzerainty only to later rise up in revolt. In the other passage dealing with "former tribes," Kül Tegin, Bilge Qaghan's younger brother, gathered the tribes (*bu*) that had previously been under his administration and attacked the relatives of the deceased qaghan, his uncle.[123] It is known that princes were appointed to administer other tribes. For example, Bilge Qaghan was given twenty thousand soldiers upon becoming *shad* in 699.[124] Moreover, there was a special relationship between princes and other tribes under their purview: "Those princes who administered other tribes (*bu*) with soldiers under their command were called *shad*."[125] Apparently the princes who became *shad* had a coercive power of their own. However, they also needed the support of tribes that had their own soldiers. As we know, these tribes were sometimes subjugated; on other occasions, they joined the Türk at their own initiative, thus becoming allies-cum-subjects. Since subjects could revolt or depart and team up with others, the princes in this fluid world were best advised to proceed with caution.

Conclusion

From all these examples, it is obvious that the historians of the Tang period were very careful in their choice of terminology. If this is indeed the case, then why did they eschew the new terminology that reflected the changes in the steppe's social organization? Likewise, why was there no attempt on the part of the Tang sources to provide a Chinese equivalent of the Turkic term *bodun?*

One could say that the anachronistic use of the term *buluo* for *bodun* is analogous to references to Han-era Xiongnu, instead of the early Türk of the Tang period. But there must also be other reasons. For instance, Bilge Qaghan, the Bijia Kehan (毗伽可汗) of the *Jiu Tangshu,* is always referred to as *xiaosha* (小殺)—"the little *shad*." This was his title when he was young. As we have seen, the title *shad* was used by princes who had a military force under their command, while ordinary princes were called *teqin* (特勤), reflecting the Turkish *tegin.* In addition, the early Türk are mostly known to us by their titles, rather than their names. It was apparently more convenient to refer to one person with the same title throughout the entire text. The first usage was continued, as switching to the person's new title would have created confusion. Against this backdrop, can we say that the continued use of the old Northern Wei term *buluo* reflects similar considerations?

When dealing with familiar Chinese personalities, the sources generally recorded changes in their status. As already noted, the *Jiu Tangshu* referred to the Tang emperor Li Shimin (李世民) as Taizong even in contexts where he was just a prince, not even a crown prince. In other words, the historical sources availed themselves of his highest rank, even in the absence of the faintest textual hint that he was going to be the next emperor.

As Ecsedy observes, "When name-less, chief-less small groups of the Turks arrived in China, they shortly disappeared from the Chinese historiographer's view and probably from history too."[126] It is incumbent upon us to understand when and why they dispersed and sought a leader. The beginning of the sixth century seems to have been when they were in need of a ruler. Under this desired leader the *buluo* did not pay taxes; on the contrary, they took or were given a share of the booty. Thus they would not rise in revolt due to heavy taxation. Instead, the *buluo* would vote with their feet, walk away, and disperse. It is these *buluo* that are referred to as *bodun* in the Turkic inscriptions, and whom Bilge Qaghan beseeches not to disperse. The Inner Asian political formation was indeed vulnerable to these tribe segments that controlled their own destiny, rather than clans or tribes.

Recognizing that this element of volition was endangering his system, Chinggis Khan forbade the soldiers of his conquering army to leave their units. The resulting groups were thus neither tribes nor *buluo* (tribe segments), but *ordo:* encampments or units of the army whose members were tied to the leadership by the bonds of loyalty.

The term *buluo* was introduced into Chinese historiography by the Tuoba Wei who themselves were of nomadic origin. In Yuan historiography, the term shed the element of volition. In both cases, we see nomads ruling over China who acted as agents of change in Chinese historiography. Deprived of its dynamics of volition and its political content, the term *buluo* was used for all nomadic groups. By the fifteenth century these nomadic groups had assumed their present-day form—homogenous and uniform "nomadic tribes."

Notes

Over the years, I have discussed different aspects of this topic with various scholars. I would like to express my appreciation for the comments of the following colleagues (in alphabetical order): Peter Finke, Peter Golden, Anwar Mokeev, Wang Xiaofu, Wu Yugui, and Luo Xin. Of course, all shortcomings are mine. This paper has been prepared with the partial support of TUBA, the Turkish Academy of Sciences.

1. H. Ecsedy, "Tribe and Tribal Society in the 6th Century Turk Empire," *Acta Orientalia Hungaricae,* 25 (1972), pp. 254–255; L. N. Gumilev, *Drevnie tiurki* (Moskva, 1967), p. 63; L. N. Gumilev, *Eski Türkler* (Istanbul, 1999), p. 97.

2. H. İnalcık, "The Question of the Emergence of the Ottoman State," *International Journal of Turkish Studies,* 1 (1981–1982), pp. 75–77. İnalcık used the term *bölük* as a deverbal noun from *böl*—"to divide." Also see G. Clauson, *An Etymological Dictionary of Pre-Thirteenth-Century Turkish* (London, 1972), p. 332a.

3. I. Togan et al., *Eski Tang Tarihi (Chiu T'ang-shu) 194a Türkler Bölümü* (Ankara, 2006).

4. D. Sneath, *The Headless State: Aristocratic Orders, Kinship Society, and the Misrepresentation of Nomadic Inner Asia* (New York, 2007).

5. Following in the footsteps of, among others, Rashīd al-Dīn and Doerfer's studies, one can raise a similar argument for cases in Iran.

6. The use of *shi* for "tribe" is not frequent, as will be seen further below.

7. M. Dobrovits, "The Thirty Tribes of the Turks," *Acta Orientalia Hungaricae,* 57 (2004), p. 257.

8. Sneath, *The Headless State,* expounds upon the term "tribe" and different understandings thereof. His view whereby "tribe" is inadequate is well taken.

9. Liu Mau-tsai consistently translates the term as *Horde.* See Liu Mau-Tsai, *Die Chinesischen Nachrichten zur Geschichte der Ost-Türken (Tu-Küe)* (Wiesbaden, 1958), vol. 1, pp. 132, 144, 147, 149, 152, 153, 154, 155, 157, 158, 160, 161, 169, 171, and 180. Also see Togan et al. for a table charting the occurrence of these terms and their translations (Togan et al., *Eski Tang Tarihi,* pp. 331–336).

10. In modern Turkish, there are also many different terms with similar meanings, such as *boy, soy, kabile, aşiret, oymak,* and *yörük.* In general, these words are used interchangeably, yet there are still small distinctions between them that we unconsciously observe when speaking or writing. For instance, we say the Aegean *yörük,* but never the Aegean *aşiret.* The same can be said for the Central Asian Turkic terminology. A case in point is the slight differences between *tir, ara, taifa, baw,* and *nesil.*

11. I. Togan, "Court Historiography in T'ang China: Assigning a Place to History and Historians at the Palace," in *Royal Courts in Dynastic States and Empires: A Global Perspective,* ed. T. Artan et al. (Leiden, 2011), pp. 171–198.

12. I. Togan, *7. ve 8. Yüzyıllarda Çin ve Türk Resmi Tarih Anlayışına Farklı Yaklaşımlar,* Akademi Forumu 54 (Ankara, 2008).

13. C. Beckwith, "The Chinese Names of the Tibetans, Tabghach, and Turks," *Archivum Eurasiae Medii Aevi,* 14 (2005), pp. 5–20.

14. E. G. Pulleyblank, "Some Remarks on the Toquzoghuz Problem," *Ural-Altaische Jahrbücher,* 28 (1956), pp. 35–42; P. B. Golden, "The Migrations of the Oguz," *Archivum Ottomanicum,* 4 (1972), pp. 45–84.

15. See Wang Pu, comp. *Tang Huiyao* (Beijing, 1981); hereafter cited as *Tang Huiyao.*

16. Actually Du You, the author of *Tongdian* (Du You, *Tongdian* (Beijing, 1988), based his work on Liu Zhi's *Zhengdian,* which was completed in the late 730s or the 740s. See D. Twitchett, *The Writing of Official History under the Tang* (Cambridge, 1992), pp. 103–104.

17. See Du You, *Tong Dian,* vol. 5, p. 5466, for the Bugut; vol. 5, p. 5468, for the Bayïrqu; and vol. 5, p. 5467, for the Tongra.

18. The confusion that is created by the Nine Clans (Nine Oghuz) and by the Nine Uighurs was taken up in T. Senga, "The Toquz Oghuz Problem and the Origins of the Khazars," *Journal of Asian History,* 24/1 (1990), pp. 57–69.

19. According to Du You, the Bugut had soldiers and an *eltäbär.* They were first under the suzerainty of the Türk and then the Xie Yantuo, before ultimately submitting to China (Du You, *Tongdian,* vol. 5, p. 5466). The Tongra consisted of 15,000 families and had a *chor* as their leader. In the end, they were defeated by the Uighurs (Du You, *Tong Dian,* vol. 5, p. 5467). The Bayïrqu possessed 10,000 soldiers and were under the leadership of an *eltäbär.* They recognized China's overlordship by 649 (Du You, *Tongdian,* vol. 5, p. 5468).

20. Twitchett, *Writing of Official History,* pp. 198–236; Togan et al., *Eski Tang Tarihi,* p. xxvii.

21. See P. Golden, "The Migrations of the Oguz," p. 48, who recommends caution regarding these issues.

22. According to Pulleyblank (E. G. Pulleyblank, *The Background of the Rebellion of An Lu-shan* [London, 1955], p. 8 and p. 106, n. 8), the "nine" in the expression "nine barbarians" is not to be taken as having any numerical sense, at least in T'ang. The word for nine is listed as meaning "many" in present dictionaries. See e.g., Xia Zhengnong (ed.), *Cihai* (Shanghai, 1999), vol. 1, p. 104.

23. There are also references to "otuz oghuz" in Giraud's reading (R. Giraud, *Göktürk İmparatorluğu. İlteriş, Kapgan ve Bilge Hükümdarlıklan (680–734)* [Istanbul, 1999], p. 265). To the Chinese ear, these two numbers sound similar, even today. In the steppe terminology *otuz* (thirty) signified the limitations of an organization. See I. Togan, "Altınordu Çözülürken Kırım'a Giden Yol," *Türk-Rus İlişkilerinde Dün Bugün Sempozyumu. Ankara 12–14 Aralılk 1992* (Ankara, 1999), pp. 39–64.

24. Hence, the Toquz Oghuz are "nine clans," but *on oq* means "ten arrows."

25. The epithet of Qaghan Dielishi, the Western Türk who carried out the new reorganization of 635, is the "organizer" (*derish< terish* like *il terish*). These events are surveyed in Liu Xu (ed.), *Jiu Tangshu* (Beijing, 1995), ch. 194b, p. 5183 (hereafter cited as *Jiu Tangshu*); also see E. Chavannes, *Documents sur les Tou-Kiue (Turcs) Occidentaux* (Paris, 1903–1941), pp. 27–28; and C. Beckwith, *The Tibetan Empire in Central Asia* (Princeton, 1987), p. 209. For a recent disquisition on the evolution of the On Oq see S. Stark, *Die Alttürkenzeit in Mittel-und Zentralasien* (Wiesbaden, 2008), p. 61. He states that the designation On Oq (Ten Arrows) did not stand for ethnos or tribal organization. He dates the decimal (military) organization to the beginning of Western Türk rule (mid-sixth century). Moreover, he avers that what started out as a military subdivision gradually turned into tribal groups (S. Stark, "On Oq Bodun, the Western Türk Qağanate and the Ashina Clan," *Archivum Eurasiae Medii Aevi,* 15 [2006–2007], pp. 163, 170). In building this argument, Stark seems to have overlooked the policies carried out by Dielishi (Derish) Qaghan in 635.

26. For a separate study on translating the Chinese *buluo* into Turkish as *bölük,* see I. Togan, "Boy Devlet İlişkileri ve '*Buluo*' (*Bölük*) Meselesi," in *Halil İnalcık Armağanı,* ed. Taşkın Takış and Sunay Aksoy (Ankara, 2009), vol. 1, pp. 43–86.

27. Some of them are introduced below. For historical sources of the Tang in general see D. Twitchett, "Introduction," in *The Cambridge History of China,* vol. 3: *Sui and Tang China, 589–906,* part I (Cambridge, 1979), pp. 38–47, and for particular issues of historiography see Twitchett, *The Writing of Official History.*

28. One could say that the picture more or less looked like the one described by İnalcık for Anatolia at the end of the thirteenth century. In this epoch-making article, İnalcık shows explicitly that the emergence of the Ottoman state cannot be ascribed to tribes. The state was established due to the contributions of the mercenary groups of tribal background called *bölük* at that time (İnalcık, "The Question of the Emergence of the Ottoman State," pp. 75–77). In fact, sources for the period concerned speak of *bölük* in the following terms:

az zamanın arasında ol bölük
yoksul iken oldılar cümle mülük
Within a short time all those *bölük*
became rulers when earlier they had been poor.

29. İnalcık also discusses *yoldaş* and *alp* as counterparts of *nökör* (H. İnalcık, "Osmanlı Beyliğinin Kurucusu Osman Bey," *Belleten,* 71 [2007], pp. 479–537). There are also groups in the *küren* of Chinggis Khan's time. See I. Togan, *Flexibility and Limitation in Steppe Formations* (Leiden, 1998), pp. 133–134.

30. In his study on Central Asian guard corps, Beckwith draws our attention to similarities between the German *comitatus* and the Central Asian *châkar.* He sees the "Inner-Asian *comitatus*-type guard corps" as a manifestation of the "sacral kingship" that Turks and Germans were committed to (C. Beckwith, "Aspects of the Early History of the Central Asian Guard Corps in Islam," *Archivum Eurasiae Medii Aevi,* 4 [1984], p. 40). However there is no consensus on the prevalence of "sacral kingship" among all Turkic peoples. In fact, a recent study by Peter Golden states that it is only characteristic of Khazars, whereas others, like the early Türk, "had sacral, perhaps even sacerdotal qualities, but they were not sacralized" (P. Golden, "Irano-Turcica: The Khazar Sacral Kingship Revisited," *Acta Orientalia Hungaricae,* 60 [2007], p. 177; see also p. 172).

31. Beckwith, "Aspects of the Early History," p. 39.

32. See I. de Rachewiltz (tr. and ed.), *The Secret History of the Mongols: A Mongolian Epic Chronicle of the Thirteenth Century* (Leiden, 2004), §5, §33, 153, 162, 177, 279. In the *Secret History, irge(n)* is glossed with *baixing* (people). E. Haenisch, *Wörterbuch zu Manghol un Niuca Tobca'an* (*Yuan-ch'ao Pi-shi*). *Geheime Geschichte der Mongolen* (Wiesbaden, 1962), p. 83.

33. For these pronunciations see E. G. Pulleyblank, *Lexicon of Reconstructed Pronunciation in Early Middle Chinese Late Middle and Early Mandarin* (Vancouver, 1991), pp. 43 and 204. Wang Li, *Hanyu yuyin shi* (Beijing, 1985), similarly gives the readings as *bu* (p. 26, line 3, and p. 175, line 1) and *lak* (p. 8, line 9, and p. 117, line 10) respectively. Definition of *luo:* H. A. Giles, *A Chinese-English Dictionary,* 2nd ed. (New York, 1964), vol. 2, no. 7329.

34. K. Wittfogel and Feng Chia-sheng, *History of Chinese Society: Liao (907–1125)* (Philadelphia, 1949), p. 509, n. 49, mention that Chavannes (Chavannes, *Documents sur Les Tou-Kiue [Turcs] Occidentaux,* pp. 44 and 46) had used the word "horde" for both *buluo* and *zhong* (眾). But this was not always the case. Earlier, Bichurin intermittently rendered *buluo* as "tribe" (*rod*) and "settled tribes" (*aymak*) (see Togan et al., *Eski Tang Tarihi,* pp. 331–335). Liu Mau-tsai's German rendering of the term, *Horde,* was mentioned above. Wittfogel and Feng opine that "tribe" is the most satisfactory translation for *buluo;* and others like Ecsedy evidently concur.

35. Wittfogel and Feng, *History of Chinese Society,* p. 509, n. 49.

36. Ibid., p. 47.

37. See e.g., Song Lian (ed.), *Yuanshi* in the collected edition of the Twenty-Four Histories (*Erhshisi shi*, vol. 18 (Beijing, 1997), ch. 122, pp. 3013–3015.

38. In fact, an examination of a digital version of the *Yuanshi* revealed only nineteen references to the compound *buren* (部人) bearing the sense of "from the tribe." The other two instances of the term are related to the ministries, as the character *bu* also stood for the *liu bu* (六部), the six ministries known as "the Six Boards."

39. The following sentence is a case in point: "槊直腯魯華蒙古克烈氏 。初, 以其部人二百, 從太祖征乃蠻、西夏有功" "Jöchin Darughachi was of the Mongol Kereyi[d] family. Following Chinggis Khan (Taizu), he took part in the campaign against the Naiman and the Xixia with two hundred fellow tribesmen (*buren*). He was victorious." (*Yuanshi*, ch. 122, pp. 3013–3015.)

40. See e.g., Teng Ssu-yü, *Family Instructions for the Yen Clan: Yen-shih chia-hsün* (Leiden, 1968).

41. P. Ratchnevsky, "Zum Ausdruck 'T'ouhsia' in der Mongolenzeit," in *Collectana Mongolica: Festschrift für Professor Dr. Rintchen zum 60. Geburtstag*, ed. W. Heissig (Wiesbaden, 1966), pp. 173–191.

42. In the digital version of the *Yuanshi* there are only fourteen occurrences. See e.g., http://hanchi.ihp.sinica.edu.tw/ihp/hanji.htm (accessed October 8, 2012).

43. It should be noted that there is no specific term in Mongolian for the followers of the Qonggirad. In Mongolian they are described as serving a Qonggirad (F. W. Cleaves, "The Sino-Mongolian Inscription of 1335 in Memory of Chang Ying-rui," *Harvard Journal of Asiatic Studies*, 13 [1950], p. 76, line 41), whereas in the parallel Chinese text they are called *pei chen* (陪臣) "*doublement sujets*," denoting their status as servants of the Princes of Lu, who according to the Chinese view were also subjects of the Yuan emperor (ibid., p. 58, n. 217).

44. See Tuotuo, *Liao shi* (Beijing, 1974), ch. 32.

45. I. Togan, "Cycles of Retribalization and the Role of the State." A research proposal submitted to the Fairbank Center for East Asian Research, Harvard University (unpublished, 1987).

46. I. Togan, "Alternative Passageways to Modern Nationhood: Patterns of Power-sharing and Concentration of Power in Central Asia and the Near East," in *Beijing Forum. Evolution of Civilizations: Historical Experiences in the Modern Times of the East and the West. Collection of Papers and Abstracts* (Beijing, 2006), vol. 2, pp. 516–545.

47. See F. W. Cleaves, *The Secret History of the Mongols* (Cambridge, MA, 1982): realm (§255); tribes of realms and peoples (§262); and tribes (§213, 218); de Rachewiltz, *The Secret History of the Mongols:* separate domain, principality (§255); country (§262); and tribes (§213, 218).

48. P. B. Golden, "'I Will Give the People unto Thee': The Chinggisid Conquests and Their Aftermath in the Turkic World," *Journal of the Royal Asiatic Society*, 3rd ser., 10 (2000), pp. 21–41; Togan, *Flexibility and Limitation*, pp. 139–150.

49. For occurrences of *qari* in the *Secret History* as listed by de Rachewiltz in his index see, §51 (III:43a:3217); §51 (III:43b:3221); §197 (VII:48a:7228); §201 (VII:18a:7606); §213 (IX:8b:8318); §255 (30a:10429); §218 (IX:21b8521).

50. For the Tang pronunciations see Pulleyblank, *Lexicon of Reconstructed Pronunciation*, pp. 43 and 204; and for Wang Li's reconstruction (in *Hanyu yuyin shi*) see Togan et al., *Eski Tang Tarihi*, p. 363. This reconstruction of the Chinese as [*bəwlak*] reminds one of the Turkic terms *bölek* (*böleg*) and *bölük* (*böleg*). Deriving from the verb *böl* (to cut), they mean "a section" or "segment." In modern Turkish, there is a great difference between a kinship-based tribe, namely a *boy, kabile,* and a segment of people—*bölük*. Incidentally, *bölük* is used

more often for a military unit that is akin to a squadron. The difference between *boy* and *bölük* is evident from historical documents. The Chinese term sometimes appears as "Person A divided [*bu*] the people into a small encampment [*luo*, 落]." Although the Chinese and the Turkic terms sound similar and refer to the same phenomenon, they have independent origins and evolutions.

51. Ecsedy, "Tribe and Tribal Society," pp. 254–255.

52. See n. 34 above.

53. Ecsedy, "Tribe and Tribal Society," p. 245.

54. Xieli Kohan in *Jiu Tangshu*, p. 5162. Ishbara is Shabenluo (*Jiu Tangshu*, p. 5159; Liu Mau-tsai, *Die Chinesischen Nachrichten zur Geschichte der Ost-Türken (Tu-Küe)* [Wiesbaden, 1958], vol. 1, p. 140; Togan et al., *Eski Tang Tarihi*, entry 5159:10). For more on Ashina Simo see *Jiu Tangshu*, p. 5164; Liu Mau-tsai, *Die Chinesischen Nachrichten*, vol. 1, p. 153; Togan et al., *Eski Tang Tarihi*, entry 5164:10.

55. *Jiu Tangshu*, p. 5164.

56. For more about Ashina Funian see *Jiu Tangshu*, p. 5166; Liu Mau-tsai, *Die Chinesischen Nachrichten*, vol. 1, p. 157; Togan et al., *Eski Tang Tarihi*, entry 5166:9.

57. Wei Zheng (ed.), *Suishu*, in the collected edition of the Twenty-Four Histories (*Erhshisi Shi*), vol. 7 (Beijing, 1997), ch. 84, p. 1874 (hereafter cited as *Suishu*); Liu Mau-tsai, *Die Chinesischen Nachrichten*, vol. 2, p. 62.

58. There are some instances of this sort in which *zhong*, the term for masses or crowds, is used instead of *buluo* (*Suishu*, ch. 84, p. 1875). Liu Mau-tsai translated both (the *buluo* in *Suishu*, ch. 84, p. 1874 and *cong* in *Suishu*, ch. 84, p. 1875) as *Horde* (Liu Mau-tsai, *Die Chinesischen Nachrichten*, vol. 1, pp. 62–63).

59. *Jiu Tangshu*, p. 5163:11.

60. The modern pronunciation of the first character in this name is *xue*. However during the Tang, it was pronounced [sjɛˇ]/[siat]/[siat] (Pulleyblank, *Lexicon of Reconstructed Pronunciation*, p. 351).

61. *Jiu Tangshu*, p. 5164:13.

62. See *Suishu*, ch. 67, p. 1582.

63. *Jiu Tangshu*, p. 5183; Chavannes, *Documents sur Les Tou-Kiue (Turcs) Occidentaux*, p. 27. See also Beckwith, *The Tibetan Empire in Central Asia*, p. 209.

64. Ecsedy, "Tribe and Tribal Society," p. 257.

65. Gumilev, *Drevnie tiurki*, p. 63; Gumilev, *Eski Türkler*, p. 97.

66. For the Ordo (*woertuo*) in Kitan and Mongol contexts see also Wittfogel and Feng, *History of Chinese Society*, p. 732.

67. The *Hou Hanshu* states that 100,000 *luo* (settlement or household) made up a *bu* (邑洛各有小帥數百千落自為一部 (Fan Ye [ed.], *Hou Hanshu*, in the collected edition of the Twenty-Four Histories [*Ershisi Shi*], vol. 3 [Beijing, 1997], ch. 90, p. 2979). Were it penned at a later date, the passage would probably have referred to *buluo*.

68. These works were completed at about the same time: the *Jinshu* in 646, *Liangshu* in 636, *Bei Qishu* in 636, *Zhoushu* in 636, and the *Suishu* in 636. On the other hand, the *Jiu Tangshu* was finished in 945 (E. Wilkinson, *Chinese History: A Manual Revised and Enlarged* [Cambridge, MA, 2000], pp. 503–504). However the sections on the Türk date back to a work written by Wu Jing in the late 720s. This work was supplemented by Wei Shu in the early 750s. (Twitchett, *The Writing of Official History*, pp. 165, 175–178.)

69. "前漢末, 匈奴大亂, 五單于爭立, 而呼韓邪單于失其國, 攜率部落, 入臣於漢。漢嘉其意, 割并州北界以安之。於是匈奴五千餘落入居朔方諸郡, 與漢人雜處。呼韓邪感漢恩, 來朝, 漢因留之, 賜其邸舍, 猶因本號, 聽稱單于, 歲給綿絹錢穀, 有如列侯。子孫傳襲, 歷代不絕。其部落隨所居郡縣, 使宰牧之, 與編戶大同, 而不輸貢賦。多歷年所, 戶口漸滋, 彌漫北朔, 轉難禁制。後漢末, 天下騷動, 群臣競言胡人猥多, 懼必為寇, 宜先為其防。建安中, 魏武帝始分其眾為五部, 部立其中貴者為帥, 選漢人為司馬以監督之。魏末, 復改帥為都尉。其左部都尉所統可萬餘落, 居於太原故茲氏縣; 右部都尉可六千餘落, 居祁縣; 南部都尉可三千餘落, 居蒲子縣; 北部都尉可四千餘落, 居新興縣; 中部都尉可六千餘落, 居大陵縣" (Fang Xuanking [ed.], *Jinshu,* in the collected edition of the Twenty-Four Histories [*Ershisi shi*], vol. 4 [Beijing, 1997], ch. 97, p. 2548 [hereafter cited as *Jinshu*]). The term *luo* ("perching like birds in small groups") was mentioned above. However, there is no agreement as to how to interpret *luo* in this particular instance. The Russian scholar L. I. Duman ("Rasseleniie nekitaiskikh plemen vo vnutrennikh rajonakh Kitaiia i ikh sotsial'noe ustrojstvo v III-IV vv. n.e," in *Kitai: Istoriia, kultura i istoriografiia,* ed. N. Z. Munkuev [Moscow, 1977], pp. 40–61) thinks that *i-luo* (邑落) is a small encampment (*stoibitche*), whereas on its own *luo* refers to households or tents. As cited by Duman, N. V. Kyuner avers that *luo* is an encampment itself (*kochevie*). Since these settlements were inhabited by Xiongnu, the term "small encampment" seems to be more appropriate. Moreover, the definition "perching like birds in small groups" speaks of groups, not individual members. Lastly, the fact that it is inconceivable from both a security and economic standpoint for nomads to camp in units of one household casts doubt on Duman's hypothesis. Therefore, the present author has rendered *luo* as a "small encampment."

70. The *Zhonghua* edition includes Wei Wudi; as there were no Wudi under the Wei, it has to refer to Jin Wudi. In a related reference, Wei Zheng, the Tang minister, emphasizes the fact that, although they were being split into smaller groups upon resettlement, they still presented a danger to the state. He also accuses Jin Wudi of ignoring these warnings (see *Jiu Tangshu,* p. 5162; Liu Mau-tsai, *Die Chinesischen Nachrichten,* vol. 1, p. 150; Togan et al., *Eski Tang Tarihi,* entry 5162:17). Here the term *bu* does definitely mean groups, not tribes.

71. C. O. Hucker, *A Dictionary of Official Titles in Imperial China* (Taipei, 1985), §5713.

72. Ibid., §7326.

73. This passage from the *Jinshu* (ch. 97, p. 2548) refers to the Xiongnu Chanyu Huhanye's follower as *buluo.* However the original reference in the *Hanshu* (ed. Ban Gu, in the collected edition of the Twenty-Four Histories [*Ershisi shi*], vol. 2 [Beijing, 1997], p. 9:3797) uses *zhong* to connote masses or followers. Ayşe Onat has translated this phrase as "people" (A. Onat et al., *Han Hanedanlığı Tarihi. Hsiung-nu [Hun] Monografisi* [Ankara, 2004], p. 56). The occurrence in the *Jinshu* stems from the fact that, by the time the text was written in 646, *buluo* was the accepted term for composite groups of nomadic people. Wei Shou, ed., *Weishu,* in the collected edition of the Twenty-Four Histories (*Ershisi shu*) (Beijing, 1997), vol. 5, p 3:98.

74. *Weishu,* ch. 28, p. 681; ch. 30, p. 717; ch. 40, p. 901; ch. 42, p. 941; ch. 44, pp. 987, 991; ch. 73, p. 1629; ch. 74, p. 1643; ch. 89, p. 1919; ch. 95, pp. 2047, 2054, 2055; ch. 95, p. 2073.

75. Ibid., ch. 1, p. 9.

76. Ibid., ch. 4b, p. 108; ch. 74, p. 1644; ch. 95, p. 2055; ch. 101, p. 2244; ch. 103, p. 2308.

77. Ecsedy, "Tribe and Tribal Society," pp. 256–257; ibid., p. 245.

78. Ibid., p. 255.

79. The dictionary for literary Chinese, *Zhongwen Da Cidian* (Zhang Qiyun et al. [eds.], vol. 9, p. 14615 [hereafter cited *Zhongwen Da Cidian*]), ostensibly cites an example of the term *buluo* from the *Shiji.* However, on closer review, this remark is an annotation by a scholar, Cui Hao, who lived during the Northern Wei, at around 450.

80. *Weishu,* ch. 101, p. 2241. A similar development comes up later on (635) in relation to the "Ten Arrows." In this passage on the "Ten Arrows," Chavannes (*Documents sur les Tou-Kiue [Turcs] Occidentaux,* pp. 27–28) translates *xing* as "nom de famille" and *buluo* as "tribu." Alternatively, Beckwith (*The Tibetan Empire in Central Asia,* p. 209) renders *xing* as "clan" and *buluo* as "tribe."

81. "蠕蠕社崙破敗之後, 收拾部落, 轉徙廣漠之北, 侵入高車之地 [. . .] 太祖時, 分散諸部, 唯高車以類粗獷, 不任使役, 故得別為部落" (*Weishu*, ch. 103, p. 2309).

82. Here we can see that the *bu* have names like Yuanhe, a *bu* of the High Carts (Gaoche).

83. *Weishu,* ch. 113, p. 3014.

84. *Zhongwen Da Cidian,* vol. 9, p. 14615.

85. See n. 69 above.

86. *Jiu Tangshu,* pp. 5158, 5162, 5164, 5175, 5176; Liu Mau-tsai, *Die Chinesischen Nachrichten,* vol. 1, pp. 140–141, 149, 150, 154, 175, 177; Togan et al., *Eski Tang Tarihi,* entries 5158:3; 5162:11; 5162:18; 5164:17; 5175:12; 5176:9.

87. "部落之下, 盡異純民, 千種萬類, 仇敵怨偶, 泣血拊心, 銜悲積恨。圓首方足, 皆人類也, 有一於此, 更切朕懷。" (*Suishu,* ch. 84, p. 1867, line 4). See also the translation in Liu Mau-tsai, *Die Chinesischen Nachrichten,* vol. 1, p.47: "Die Menschen ihrer Horden stellen kein treues Volk dar; sie bestehen aus tausenderlei, ja zehntausenderlei Stämmen, sie betrachten sich gegenseitig als Feinde und bringen sich gegenseitig um, . . . /" As can be seen, he translated *zhong* (category) and *lei* (類, kind) as *Stämme,* i.e., "tribes."

88. *Jiu Tangshu,* p. 5173; Liu Mau-tsai, *Die Chinesischen Nachrichten,* vol. 1, p. 17; Togan et al., *Eski Tang Tarihi,* entry 5173:9.

89. *Jiu Tangshu,* ch. 194a.

90. Tonyuquq uses the term *khan* rather than *qaghan* for the developments before the establishment of the Second Türk Qaghanate.

91. T. Tekin. *A Grammar of Orkhon Turkic* (Bloomington, IN, 1968), p. 283 [Tonyukuk Stele I, West, line 4].

92. R. Giraud, *L'empire des Turc Celestes* (Paris, 1960), pp. 67–68; and Giraud, *Göktürk İmparatorluğu,* p. 104.

93. *Jiu Tangshu,* p. 5164; Liu Mau-tsai, *Die Chinesischen Nachrichten,* vol. 1, p. 154; Togan et al., *Eske Tang Tarihi,* entry 5164:20.

94. See below.

95. *Jiu Tangshu,* p. 5166; Liu Mau-tsai, *Die Chinesischen Nachrichten,* vol. 1, p. 156; Togan et al., *Eski Tang Tarihi,* entry 5166:2–3; and Wu Yugui, *Tujue Hanguo yu Sui Tang Guanxi Shi Yanjiu,* in the Tang Yanjiu Jijinhui Congshu Series (Beijing, 1998), pp. 227–272.

96. Clauson, *An Etymological Dictionary,* pp. 296b, 306a. Also see P. Golden, *Ethnicity and State Formation in Pre-Činggisid Turkic Eurasia* (Bloomington, IN, 2001), p. 21.

97. Some scholars prefer "nation," but this is an exaggerated notion for that early period.

98. R. Dankoff and James Kelly (tr.), *Mahmūd al-Kaşġarī: Compendium of Turkic Dialects* (Cambridge, MA, 1982), vol. 3, p. 75; and B. Atalay, *Divanü Lugat-it-turk Dizini. Endeks* (Ankara, 1943), p. 98.

99. The titles of the second-in-command, such as *atabeg, ulusbegi,* and *apa,* evolved in a similar fashion. This calls to mind Sinor's remark that the Turkic state was neither ethnically nor culturally homogenous (D. Sinor, "The Establishment and the Dissolution of the Türk Empire," in *The Cambridge History of Inner Asia,* ed. D. Sinor [Cambridge, 1990], p. 288).

100. Tekin, *A Grammar of Orkhon Turkic,* p. 249; and T. Tekin, *Orhon Yazıtları* (Istanbul, 1995), p. 82.

101. Tekin, *A Grammar of Orkhon Turkic,* p. 283; and Tekin, *Orhon Yazıtları,* p. 83. On the other hand, Rybatzki uses "Klan" for *bod* and "Türk-Klane" for *bodun* (V. Rybatzki, *Die Toñuquq-Inschrift* [Szeged, 1997], pp. 43–44 and 75–79).

102. Wang Xiaofu expressed this opinion in 2005 during a seminar at Peking University.

103. Tekin, *A Grammar of Orkhon Turkic,* p. 253; and Tekin, *Orhon Yazıtları,* p. 94.

104. Tekin, *A Grammar of Orkhon Turkic,* p. 290; and Tekin, *Orhon Yazıtları,* p. 95. In this passage, Rybatzki renders *bod* as *Klan* and *bodun* as *Gemeinschaft* (Rybatzki, *Die Toñuquq-Inschrift,* pp. 74, 123).

105. O. F. Sertkaya, *Göktürk Tarihinin Meseleleri* (Ankara, 1995), pp. 43, 122.

106. This correction is from ibid., pp. 43 and 122.

107. Sertkaya (ibid.) is inclined to understand *bod* as tribe (*boy* or *kabile*) and *bodun* as nation (*millet*).

108. *Jiu Tangshu,* p. 6420; Liu Mau-tsai, *Die Chinesischen Nachrichten,* vol. 1, p. 154; Togan et al., *Eski Tang Tarihi,* entry 5164:20.

109. *Jiu Tangshu,* p. 5167; Liu Mau-tsai, *Die Chinesischen Nachrichten,* vol. 1, p 158; Togan et al., *Eski Tang Tarihi,* entry 5167:5.

110. *Jiu Tangshu,* p. 5167:2; Liu Mau-tsai, *Die Chinesischen Nachrichten,* vol. 1, p. 158; Togan et al., *Eski Tang Tarihi,* entry 5167:2.

111. *Jiu Tangshu,* pp. 5162–5163; Liu Mau-tsai, *Die Chinesischen Nachrichten,* vol. 1, pp. 148–151; Togan et al., *Eski Tang Tarihi,* entries 5162:2–5163:3.

112. *Jiu Tangshu,* pp. 5160, 5165; Liu Mau-tsai, *Die Chinesischen Nachrichten,* vol. 1, p. 146, 155; Togan et al., *Eski Tang Tarihi,* entries 5160:11, 5165:11.

113. *Jiu Tangshu,* pp. 5158, 5165; Liu Mau-tsai, *Die Chinesischen Nachrichten,* vol. 1, p. 155; Togan et al., *Eski Tang Tarihi,* entry 5165:8; Liu Mau-tsai *Die Chinesischen Nachrichten,* vol. 1, p. 141; Togan et al., *Eski Tang Tarihi,* entry 5158:10.

114. H. Ecsedy, "A Contribution to the History of Karluks in the T'ang Period," *Acta Orientalia Hungaricae,* 34 (1980), pp. 23–37; *Tang Huiyao,* ch. 100, p. 2124; and Beckwith, *The Tibetan Empire in Central Asia,* p. 88.

115. S. Baştuğ, "Tribe, Confederation and State among Altaic Nomads of the Asian Steppes," in *Rethinking Central Asia,* ed. Korkut Erturk (Reading, UK, 1999), pp. 80–84.

116. We do not have the names of any original Türk tribes. All we know is that they were living in groups called *buluo.*

117. *Jiu Tangshu,* p. 5153; Liu Mau-tsai, *Die Chinesischen Nachrichten,* vol. 1, p. 132; Togan et al., *Eski Tang Tarihi,* entry 5153:6. We also know that Ashina Simo remained a *tegin,* as he was not promoted to *shad. Jiu Tangshu,* p. 5163; Liu Mau-tsai, *Die Chinesischen Nachrichten,* vol. 1, p. 152; Togan et al., *Eski Tang Tarihi,* entry 5163:8.

118. *Jiu Tangshu,* p. 5160; Liu Mau-tsai, *Die Chinesischen Nachrichten,* vol. 1, p. 145; Togan et al., *Eski Tang Tarihi,* entry 5160:11–12; *Jiu Tangshu,* p. 5163; Liu Mau-tsai, *Die Chinesischen Nachrichten,* vol. 1, p. 146.

119. *Jiu Tangshu,* pp. 5158, 5159; Liu Mau-tsai, *Die Chinesischen Nachrichten,* vol. 1, pp. 141, 153; Togan et al., *Eski Tang Tarihi,* entries 5158:10, 5159:3.

120. *Jiu Tangshu,* p. 5164; Liu Mau-tsai, *Die Chinesischen Nachrichten,* vol. 1, p. 153; Togan et al., *Eski Tang Tarihi,* entry 5164:11. The Hu (Sogdians) were living together, as

illustrated by E. G. Pulleyblank, "A Sogdian Colony in Inner Mongolia," *T'oung Pao*, 41 (1952), pp. 317–356.

121. *Jiu Tangshu,* p. 5164; Liu Mau-tsai, *Die Chinesischen Nachrichten,* vol. 1, p. 153; Togan et al., *Eski Tang Tarihi,* entry 5164:4–5.

122. *Jiu Tangshu,* p. 5164; Liu Mau-tsai, *Die Chinesischen Nachrichten,* vol. 1, pp. 153, 154; Togan et al., *Eski Tang Tarihi,* entries. 5164:4, 5164:20. In a similar situation, Rudi Lindner refers to the *bölük* of İnalcık as "Osman's tribe" (see R. P. Lindner, *Nomads and Ottomans in Medieval Anatolia* [Bloomington, IN, 1983]).

123. *Jiu Tangshu,* p. 5173; Liu Mau-tsai, *Die Chinesischen Nachrichten,* vol. 1, p. 171; Togan et al., *Eski Tang Tarihi,* entry 5173:6. This is the only instance that Liu Mau-tsai translates *bu* with *die alten Horden,* rather than *Stämme.* However, Kül Tegin always had his followers, i.e., his *buluo.* Hence, it stands to reason that the intention here is not ex-follower (*buluo*), but tribes that were previously under his administration.

124. *Jiu Tangshu,* p. 5169; Liu Mau-tsai, *Die Chinesischen Nachrichten,* vol. 1, p. 163; Togan et al., *Eski Tang Tarihi,* entry 5169:14.

125. *Jiu Tangshu,* p. 5153:6; Togan et al., *Eski Tang Tarihi,* entry 5153:6.

126. Ecsedy, "Tribe and Tribal Society," p. 255.

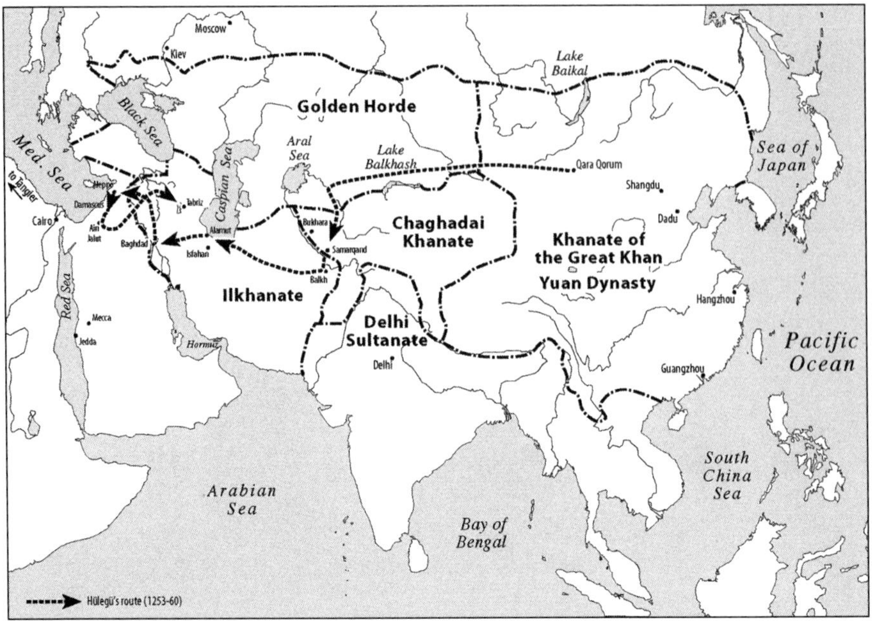

Figure 6.1. The Four Mongol Khanates 1290. Adapted from M. Biran, *Chinggis Khan* (Oxford, 2007).

Six

Population Movements in Mongol Eurasia

Thomas T. Allsen

Introduction

Pastoral nomads are, of course, synonymous with population movements; in normal conditions they pursue pasture and water in regular rounds and in periods of political or environmental crises launch far-reaching military conquests or long-distance migrations to find new homes, phenomena well exemplified by the history of the Alans in late antiquity and the Oirats/Qalmaqs in the early modern age. But such movements were hardly restricted to the nomads, for when they were in an expansive mode, neighboring sedentary communities were also set in motion.

Not unexpectedly, the Mongol explosion of the thirteenth century produced numerous population movements, a kind of *Volkerwanderung* of the Middle Ages. The issue of displacement, if treated at all, has been approached regionally, when in fact it was continental in scope. This, however, is only one facet of the problem, for such population dislocations were always preceded by nomadic military deployments that were themselves migrations entailing movements of entire communities—soldiers, their families, and dependents—over great distances. Furthermore, in many instances the Mongols replaced dispersed populations with peoples forcibly relocated from other parts of the empire. There are, then, intimate linkages between the different types of population movements, and these suggest the following sequence of presentation: we start with military deployment, turn to the displacement of defeated peoples, and end with the conquerors' efforts at repopulation.

But before entering into the body of the chapter, a few cautionary remarks are in order. First, the coverage is not intended to be exhaustive, but is, I believe, representative, drawing on examples from across the continent. Second, there is the perennial problem of numbers: firm figures are rare and claims, like that of Bar Hebraeus, that "all the inhabitants of Syria . . . fled to Aleppo" in the face of the Mongol attack of 1260–1261 cannot be taken at face value.[1] Nevertheless, such statements, which turn up repeatedly in the era's sources, disclose something useful about the frequency and magnitude of population flights and, on occasion, yield reasonable approximations.

Deployment

In their search for military manpower, the Mongols were systematic and demanding; all subject peoples, no matter their numbers, location, or subsistence patterns, were obliged to serve. Consequently, their polyethnic armies included formations that were recruited from the steppe, the agricultural lands to its south, and the forest zone to its north. Moreover, since the empire regularly used foreigners as security and garrison troops, conscripts were often posted far from home.

To the north, the Kyrgyz, who were subdued in 1207 and again in 1218–1219, were later drafted and deployed well beyond their Yenisei homeland. In the 1280s and 1290s, there are references in the *Yuanshi* to Kyrgyz troops stationed at Qaraqorum and to the transfer of a garrison from Zhili (the metropolitan province) to Shandong; the same work also notes that in 1308 a levy of Kyrgyz was destined for duty in the imperial guards, which were based around the capital of Dadu (i.e., Beijing).[2]

The Kyrgyz's near neighbors, the Mongolian-speaking Oirats, were also called up in substantial numbers and sent far greater distances. In the early 1250s, one of the contingents accompanying Hülegü to the West was an "army [*lashkar*]" raised from among the Oirat. Led by Temür Buqa, an imperial in-law, this unit campaigned in Iran, Iraq, and later in Syria.[3] Their numbers are hard to determine, and estimates are further confused by the fact that some military formations, the *Ja'un-i qurban*, reputedly 20,000 strong, are mistakenly identified as "Oirat" units due to their famous Oirat commander, Arghun Aqa.[4] These uncertainties notwithstanding, West Asian sources consistently view the Oirats as a prominent grouping among the Mongols and, as we will see, a political force to be reckoned with.[5]

Peoples farther to the west attracted the Mongols' attention as well. The Jochid rulers conscripted many Eastern Slavs following their subjugation, some of whom served much further east.[6] Bayan, who ruled the Golden Horde's eastern wing (i.e., modern-day Kazakhstan) at the beginning of the fourteenth century, had a number of "Rus" in his armies, and the same can be said for the Yuan rulers, whose Russian (Wolosi 斡羅思) troops can be tracked in the Chinese records.[7]

The first mention of Russian troops in China, dating from January 1329, is made in connection with the establishment of a new unit, the Imperial Assisting Guard (*Lungyi shiwei* 龍翊侍衛). They were recruited from a pool of nine thousand households belonging to Tangkish (Tangjishi 唐吉失), a Qipchaq officer, and were previously under the jurisdiction of the Left Qipchaq Guard (*Zuo Qincha wei* 左欽察衛). The resulting formation was ethnically diverse, consisting of Mongols, Jurchens, Koreans, and a contingent called the Proclaiming Loyalty Russian Imperial Guard (*Xuanzong wolosi huwei* 宣忠斡羅思扈衛).[8] During the next year, the Russian Guard came under the control of a Supreme Myarchy Office (*duwanhufu* 都萬戶府), which was directly subordinate to the Bureau of Military Affairs (*shumi yuan* 樞密院). Their new base was located north of Dadu on 130 *qing* of land (about 2,100 acres), which were purchased from local peasants.[9] By imperial command on January 1331, the guard was expanded to *tümen* strength; this unusually explicit decree orders the Myarchy Office "to gather and collect Russians until they reach ten thousand." To accommodate this expansion, the unit was given another hundred *qing* of land on which to establish a military colony (*tuntian* 屯田).[10] On this and other occasions, the Russian colony was supplied with oxen, seeds, clothing, food, agricultural implements, and hunting-fishing grounds.[11]

By the summer of 1331, the Russian Guard, having completed its transformation into a myarchy, was granted a silver seal and a new status, that of a commandery (*zhihui shisi* 指揮使司).[12] Little is known of this unit in later years but in 1334 Bayan, the powerful Mongol minister at court, was made honorary commander of the Russian Guard, and in 1346 this title fell to a Tangut, Irinjinbal.[13]

Since *tümen* were always below their nominal strength, we cannot mechanically assert that there were ten thousand Russians serving in China during the 1330s. Yet there are equally compelling reasons to refrain from minimizing their numbers. First, even after the Russian myarchy was established, Russians were still in great demand and the Yuan court encouraged "recruits" with generous rewards of silver and cash, a policy that yielded results: in January 1332, 16 Russians were presented to court; 170 the next month; 2,500 in early summer; and another 30 by the end of the season—all plausible figures.[14] Second, besides the personnel of the guard's myarchy, in 1331 there was a composite Alan-Russian (Asu-Wolosi 阿速—斡羅思) Border Guard stationed in Manchuria that drew supplies from the Liaoyang provincial authorities.[15] Therefore, regardless of how the strength of these units is calculated, there were tens of thousands of Russians in North China during the fourteenth century.

No less importantly, it is clear that the Russian myarchy was recruited from a population that was already in China and not, as sometimes assumed, from recent arrivals sent east from the Golden Horde. Indeed, all the Russians initially mobilized or subsequently presented to the court came from Yuan servitors who were longtime residents of the east, either Mongol families married into the royal house or powerful Qipchaq officials, like El Temür whose sons Tangkish and *Sadun were, statistically speaking, the primary "donors."[16] These ties and the fact that the Russians were always closely associated with Qipchaqs and Alans lead us to the suspicion that they came to China at a much earlier date. We can seek clarification on this issue, as well as the matter of the unit's numbers, by briefly comparing the histories of guard units formed in Yuan China from peoples of the western steppe and the Caucasus.

The best-documented case is the Alans. The imposition of Mongol rule in North Caucasia immediately resulted in the impressment of the Alans (Mongolian: Asud) for military duty. Starting in the late 1230s, the Chinggisids deported around ten thousand to China, where they first served in the Asud Army (*Asu jun* 阿速軍) and then in the Right and Left Asud Guard (*You Zuo Asu wei* 右左阿速衛), formed between 1309 and 1310.[17] At the very end of the dynasty, the Yuan court could still mobilize an army of six thousand Alans, whose military reputation remained high.[18] In 1368, many Alans accompanied the last Yuan emperor back to the steppe and subsequently assimilated, while others remained in China and served the Ming as military and police auxiliaries.[19] The history of the Qipchaqs in China is no less instructive. In 1286, they were formed into a single guard, before being divided into the Right and Left Qipchaq Guard in 1322. Its initial strength consisted of nineteen chiliarchs (*qianhu* 千戶) and three military colonies.[20] Even assuming that all components were only at half strength, there were at least ten thousand Qipchaq troopers serving Qubilai. When, though, did they come east? The Qipchaqs first appear in Mongolia in 1223, when Sübedei returned from the western steppe and obtained Chinggis Khan's permission to form the submitted Merkids, Naimans, Kereyids, Qipchaqs, and Qanglis into a composite unit. Thereafter, there is mention of Qipchaq participation in the final campaign against the Jin and in the opening attacks on the Song.[21] The experience of the Qangli—the Qipchaqs' eastern cousins—is also revealing. They also fought in China, under Güyüg (1246–1248) and Möngke (1251–1259). What is more, the exact method that was used in 1310 to form the pool of recruits for the guard is carefully spelled out: a register (*ji* 籍) of all Qangli troops serving in other Yuan units was instituted to verify the ethnic identity of everyone entering the new unit.[22]

Taken together, these findings prompt a number of conclusions: 1) the Alan, Qipchaq, and Qangli recruits came east in force in the course of the initial Mongol conquest of western Eurasia and, in all likelihood, so did the Russians; 2) with the exception of the Alans, these troops served in ethnically mixed units until segregated out in the late thirteenth and early fourteenth centuries and posted to homogenous guards units; 3) their numbers were substantial, some ten thousand or more in each case; 4) despite being away from their homelands for extended periods, all these groups maintained their identities across five or more generations; and 5) their success in doing so implies that they traveled east as communities of men, women, and children.

The empire mobilized other ethnic units, which were recruited in East Asia, for special service in West Asia. The Bekrin, or Mekrin, constitute a good example of the Mongols' discerning eye for the skills and military potential of subject populations, however small or isolated. Although their ethnic affinity is unknown, the Bekrin lived in the mountains of Uighuristan and were famed as cragsmen (*qayachi*).[23] Upon submitting to Chinggis Khan, they were organized into a chiliarch. Some came west with Hülegü in the 1250s and served in the Ilkhanid realm as "mountain couriers (*kuhrawī*)."[24] We next hear of the Bekrin during the reign of Abaqa (1265–1281), when a contingent of *qaya[c]hīyān*—still valued for their mountaineering skills—were posted to Irbil, in the hill country east of Mosul, to secure the region from Kurdish marauders.[25] In 1290, Mongol forces accompanied by two hundred auxiliaries, who the Syriac sources call *qayajye* and Bar Hebraeus refers to as Christians, clashed with the Kurds around the city.[26] Subsequently, when general violence broke out between the Christians and Muslims at Irbil in 1297, the Bekrin were centrally involved. Tensions between these communities continued up until 1310, when the Muslims gained the upper hand; most of the mountaineers were killed and their womenfolk were shared out.[27] This, however, did not spell the end of the Bekrin in the west for at the end of the fourteenth century Temür's forces encountered another group of these cragsmen during operations in the mountains of Georgia.[28]

Yet another specialist unit of note in Hülegü's train was composed of Chinese artillerymen whose strength, according to the Persian accounts, was "one thousand households [*hazār khānah*]." These troops were raised from North Chinese artisan households that were identified and registered in the census of 1251.[29] As was normally the case, these postings were permanent assignments from which few returned.

On the basis of this brief survey, it is evident that long-distance deployment of non-Mongol troops was an integral part of the Chinggisid military strategy and mode of expansion. More explicitly, it can be argued that the Chinggisids seized Central and West Asia with the human resources of East Asia and then expanded and secured their holdings in the east with personnel transported from western Eurasia, many of whom later formed ethnic-based guard units.

Displacement

The Mongols' expansion sparked numerous, at times massive, refugee movements, the comparative study of which promises an array of benefits. For one thing, it offers a new perspective on the Chinggisids' imperial venture. Most commonly, the scale of this enterprise is measured in terms of conquered territory, which was at least four times greater than that of any predecessor. However, the unique qualities of the empire's expansion might just as meaningfully be gauged by the unprecedented numbers of people who fled their advance.

A sense of the size and character of these displacements can be conveyed by examining the Hungarian reaction to the Mongol inroads into Central Europe in 1241. The invaders induced great panic and soon the Hungarian king, his court, and many of his subjects were on the move seeking safety to the west. No figures are given, but the refugees assuredly numbered in the tens of thousands, for when they arrived in Dalmatia, the difficulties of succoring them completely overwhelmed the local authorities and resources.[30] This, moreover, was merely one act in a larger drama of flight throughout western Eurasia.

The Qipchaqs, the last inhabitants of the steppe zone to be brought under Chinggisid authority, were widely and permanently dispersed—a movement that was initiated by the Mongol assault on Turkestan between 1219 and 1223.[31] Some Qipchaqs, allied with the collapsing Khwārazmian state, fled into Daghestan—a traditional safe haven—where fifteen thousand tents were still to be found in the vicinity of Darband in the mid-1220s.[32] Others made their way farther south, requesting sanctuary in Transcaucasia. The locals' reaction to these migrations ranged from offers of shelter and alliance to fierce resistance, which in one case ended with the destruction of "a large army" of Qipchaqs at Ganjak in 1223.[33]

A second, more extensive round of Qipchaq migration occurred a decade later, as Batu's campaign of 1236 against the western steppe gained momentum. On this occasion many Qipchaqs from the region of the Don and Donets escaped toward Hungary, arriving there just before the Mongols. After some delay, owing to the Hungarian court's period of exile, they were given sanctuary in the central regions of the realm and were granted a collective legal status under direct royal protection. Although the number of Qipchaqs that were accommodated is the subject of considerable dispute, estimates range from forty to eighty thousand.[34]

This, however, represents only one stream of migration. At about the same time, there was a separate and massive flow of Qipchaqs, wives and children included, into Bulgaria and thence into Thrace and Macedonia. Here, they took service as mercenaries with both the Latin empire and its Greek rivals.[35] Far less fortunate were those who escaped toward the Crimea; according to Rubruck's informants, these "Comans" (Cumans/Qipchaqs) entered the peninsula in such large numbers that many were reduced to cannibalism and starvation.[36]

The series of Mongol campaigns against the Qipchaqs coincided with their assaults on the Alans in the central part of the Caucasus Range. As elsewhere, some resisted and some submitted, while others fled. It seems likely that a contingent of Alans accompanied the Qipchaqs to the west in the late 1230s. However, there is no clear mention of them in Hungary until the fourteenth century. In any event, these may have been a remnant of the nomadic Alans still in the steppe. More certainly, many highland Alans found refuge within the kingdom of Georgia, a client state of the Mongols, where they soon found themselves in conflict with the local inhabitants. Later on, they were mobilized for military service by the Ilkhans; when Öljeitü invaded Gilan in 1307, his forces included a formation of "Alans residing in Gori," the future hometown of one Joseph Stalin.[37]

The Mongols' smashing defeat of the Khwārazmian state, which impelled so many Qipchaqs westward, also sent others streaming south. This episode is closely tied to the adventures of the last Khwārazm-shāh, Jalāl al-Dīn. His epic struggle with the Mongols, his daring escape across the Indus in 1221, the establishment of a short-lived state in northwest India, his move into Iran in 1223, and his efforts to found a new empire in Iraq and Transcaucasia can all be viewed as the retreat of a defeated army. But it was much more than this: a substantial number of Khwārazmian courtiers, military personnel, townsmen, and religious leaders departed their homeland, seeking safety in Khurasan and India. At every stage of his desperate odyssey, Jalāl al-Dīn strove to rally, ransom, and reassemble his subjects, who were in flux themselves.[38] In essence, then, his "retreat" was a large-scale and extremely chaotic relocation of peoples—nomadic and sedentary—throughout the eastern Islamic world.

The strength of Jalāl al-Dīn's forces varies greatly in the sources—four thousand, ten thousand, thirty thousand, and sixty thousand—partly due to inaccuracies in reporting, but also because the size of his following fluctuated continually.[39] Whatever the actual figures, when Jalāl al-Dīn arrived in

Transcaucasia in 1225 and defeated a combined Georgian-Armenian army, local chronicles depicted the invading Khwārazmians, their troops, families, and camp followers as a mass of humanity on the move, which the authors numbered at between 140,000 and 200,000.[40]

In turn, this wave of migration set in train various secondary population shifts. To begin with, after their above-mentioned triumph, the Khwārazmian forces began ravaging the rural districts of Armenia and Georgia, thereby encouraging, perhaps consciously so, the flight of the hard-pressed Christian peasantry. Secondly, since the victorious army was largely composed of Qipchaqs and Qanglis, there was a substantial influx of nomads into the region. Some argue that these developments altered both the ethnic and subsistence patterns of many regions in West Asia, changes that were accelerated and consolidated when the Mongols and their allies took up permanent station across Iran, Mesopotamia, Transcaucasia, and Asia Minor a few decades later.[41] As the last act of this drama, following the death of Jalāl al-Dīn in 1231, his commanders and their followers abandoned Transcaucasia, many settling in Syria and Egypt.[42] This too established a precedent of sorts, for a short while later, many Iranian elites fleeing the Mongol advance sought and found refuge in the Mamluk kingdom.[43]

Because of their mobility, nomads and ex-nomads often decamped as communities. This was not generally the case with sedentary peoples whose ability to move was largely determined by social class and economic resources. For the peasantry, whose wealth was largely immobile, flight was difficult—a choice of last resort. In contrast, elites and urban middle classes had a wider set of options. First of all, as was frequently the case in the eastern Islamic world, they were the strata of society most inclined to accommodate the Mongols, that is, to exchange their wealth or services for security.[44] But if this strategy proved too costly or impossible, they also had the means and connections to escape impending disaster, which they tended to do individually or in small groups. The steady stream of thirteenth-century immigration into northern India—long recognized as a force that did much to shape the Delhi Sultanate—is a case in point.[45]

Systematically encouraged by Sultan Iltütmish (r. 1211–1236), the pace of Muslim migration to India increased dramatically following the Mongols' invasion of Turkestan and Iran. In its wake, the subcontinent became a major haven for those Muslims able to flee—scribes, administrators, artisans, merchants, scholars, religious leaders, and soldiers. Among the last category, some arrived in India as military slaves (*mamlūks*), but many were freeborn Muslims—remnants of defeated armies who formed themselves into *condottieri* in search of a prince to serve. Those who made the journey thus formed a large pool of talent—both "men of the sword" and "men of the pen"—that was eagerly drawn upon to strengthen the Sultanate and encourage the spread of Islam on the subcontinent.[46] This led Jūzjānī, himself a recent immigrant from Khurasan, to proclaim that Hindustan was the final bastion in the defense of the faith against the ravages of the pagan Mongols and the last seat of an independent, functioning Islamic government.[47]

Population movements on an even more massive scale are documented in the Chinese sources. These flows began immediately after the initial Mongol invasion of the Jin between 1214 and 1216, when a reported one million military households (*junhu* 軍戶) from Hebei fled south into Henan.[48] Wholesale flight also occurred in Sichuan, which became a permanent theater of operations in the Mongol assault on the Song from 1231 to 1282. By all accounts, the Mongols' campaigns in this populous region were especially devastating. Most telling are the census figures: according to the Song registration of 1223, Sichuan numbered 2,500,000 households, but in 1282—in the immediate aftermath of the region's final pacification—the Yuan authorities counted a maximum of 500,000 households.[49] Although there is no way to determine what portion of the missing two million escaped death by taking flight, the magnitude of this displacement was obviously great, affecting all the province's inhabitants.

To this point, the chapter has concentrated on population movements that are directly tied to military expansion. However, we should not forget that, even after empires are formed, their policies and politics continue to generate refugees. In the Mongol case, the terms of surrender always stipulated a census and the resultant fiscal and service obligations stimulated the growth of unregistered floating populations, some of whom tried to elude the empire's authority permanently. For example, as "Tatar" census takers began circulating in the Rus principalities in the mid-1250s, a host of young people and artisans fled to Kholm in Galicia, which was not yet under the direct control of the Golden Horde.[50]

Domestic political struggles within individual khanates triggered other hurried departures. In the Ilkhanid realm, there was a steady outflow of military personnel to Egypt. Such defections were so common that they became institutionalized; whenever Mongol and Turkish troopers fled Iran, they were welcomed as *wāfidiyya,* "new arrivals," and quickly enrolled in the Mamluk army as cavalrymen.[51] The largest of these defections—that of the Oirats—was an immediate byproduct of their persistent involvement in high politics. This began in 1284 with their support of Arghun in a disputed succession.[52] In this instance, the Oirats backed a winner, but in the next contest they supported a loser, Baidu, who was toppled by Ghazan after a short reign. Fearing reprisals, in 1296, 10,000 Oirat soldiers hastily decamped, with their families and belongings, from their peacetime stations in the north Mesopotamian region of Diyār Bakr, led by the grandson of their original commander, Temür Buqa.[53] Despite attempts to stop them, they successfully reached Syria, where they were well received and initially settled in the coastlands near Qāqūn on the Palestinian coast.[54] In this way, Oirats of the older generation who began life near the banks of Lake Baikal end it near the shores of the Mediterranean, approximately 3,500 air miles (5,400 kilometers) away.

Out-migration that was induced by internal political and dynastic strife was more or less continuous throughout the Ilkhanid period. Fittingly, the regime's final collapse into chaos engendered one last round of flight. In the mid-1340s, incessant fighting around Tabriz between the last Ilkhanid pretenders caused the area's desperate inhabitants to depart in numbers to Transcaucasia, the Qipchaq steppe, Asia Minor, Syria, and Iraq.[55]

Factional conflicts within the Golden Horde had similar consequences. In the 1290s, the Jochid prince Noghai acquired an extensive following, which he used to influence and sometimes control the succession to the throne. When open war erupted between the sitting khan, Toqta (r. 1291–1312), and this kingmaker, many Alans joined the latter's cause.[56] With the disintegration of Noghai's power in 1299, his followers, including the Alans, fled toward the lower Danube. Two years later, eight thousand Alan warriors with a similar number of dependents passed through Bulgaria into Byzantine territory, where they served as mercenaries until defeated and decimated by the Catalan Company.[57] These particular Alans, who an eyewitness describes as nomads continuously roaming about in tent carts, were most likely inhabitants of the steppes, not the Caucasian highlands.[58]

Discord within the Chaghadaid khanate, which became endemic in the fourteenth century, also generated waves of defections and migrations. One such episode is reported by Ibn Baṭṭūṭa, who relates that, following the overthrow of ʿAlā' al-Dīn Tamarshirin (r. 1331–1334), members of his family, courtiers, and "forty thousand" (i.e., a large number) of his adherents found refuge in the Delhi Sultanate.[59]

Yet another catalyst of population movement was the deepening struggles between the autonomous khanates that emerged after the division of the empire in 1260. In some cases, this involved the flight of military units. An early example of this is provided by the emergence of the Qara'unas or Negüderis. When fighting broke out in 1262 between Berke and Hülegü, some Iran-based units of the Golden Horde fled east and joined Negüder, a Jochid commander stationed in Khurasan. Thereafter, the Ilkhans pressured them into moving southeast to the region between Ghazna and India, where some ten thousand of these men soon became notorious freebooters whose activities as robbers and slavers are vividly portrayed by Marco Polo.[60]

While much concerning the history of the Qara'unas/Negüderis remains obscure, it seems fair to say that they "accreted" over time out of disparate elements—Mongols, Turks, Khaljis, Afghans, and Indian slaves—which formed around a nucleus of Jochid troops and commanders. The result was a loosely structured "refugee state" that functioned for decades as a buffer between the Ilkhanate and the Delhi Sultanate.[61]

Civilians were also set in motion by Chinggisid civil wars. In Inner Asia, the Uighurs—early sedentary adherents of Chinggis Khan—were increasingly exposed to such pressure in the late 1260s, when their homeland became a major front in the struggle between the Yuan rulers and their rivals in Central Asia, who were led by Qaidu (a descendent of Ögödei). As the conflict intensified, the Uighur court, which was loyal to Qubilai, abandoned Turfan and moved their seat of government to Qamil in Gansu sometime between 1270 and 1275. They then moved the capital farther east, to Yongchang, at around 1283. With the retreat of their ruling house, Uighurs departed their homeland in numbers and settled permanently in China. No figures are given, but the fact that the Yuan authorities repeatedly urged the Uighur government-in-exile to reassemble its widely dispersed and impoverished subjects leaves the strong impression that this decades-long migration was extensive.[62]

Movement of this kind was a recurrent, nearly permanent feature of the Chinggisid age. While hardly exclusive to periods of active campaigning, these transfers were perhaps most numerous and far-reaching during the initial phases of the Mongol conquests. As we have seen, the responses to this expansion ranged from resistance to negotiated surrender, orderly retreat, or panicked flight. The Mongols could not always predetermine the reaction, but on some occasions they intentionally sought to disperse populations for a variety of reasons: to create a no-man's-land or buffer zone around recent conquests; to expand pasture at the expense of cultivation; and to sow discord and confusion in the hopes of demoralizing the opposition.

To date, the resistance—the notable battles, sieges, and forced surrenders—has received the lion's share of attention. However, the time has come to subject the retreats, flights, and migrations of the defeated to more searching and comprehensive study. For this too was part of the Mongols' strategy for imperial expansion and consolidation, and the same can be said for their practice of replacing departed populations, our next topic.

Replacement

John of Plano Carpini, speaking of "Sakint," namely Iamkint or Yangikent on the lower Syr Darya (Jaxartes River), relates that although the population surrendered voluntarily and the city spared destruction, "many men were killed and others transported" and that the Tartars "filled [the city] with fresh inhabitants."[63] Briefly stated, this is a policy the Mongols followed throughout their domains, one already in evidence during Chinggis Khan's reign. Two of the earlier instances are reported by Li Zhichang, who traveled to Turkestan in 1221–1222. On the outward leg of his journey he encountered a colony of Chinese artisans at Chinqai's City, a granary and military base in western Mongolia, and on his return heard reports of large numbers of Chinese, mainly artisans, settled in Qianqianzhou, on the upper Yenisei, to ply their crafts.[64] The latter were only the first of several waves of forced Chinese immigration to southern Siberia; such, at any event, is the clear implication of Qubilai's decree of 1272 directing his officials "to send, *as before,* South Chinese peasants [*nanren baiming* 南人百名]," together with oxen and equipment, to the Kyrgyz land.[65] Moreover, the reference to "South Chinese peasants" suggests that populations of newly conquered lands—in this case, the territories of the Southern Song—were particularly vulnerable to long-distance deportation, as evidenced by Mongol practices in the eastern Islamic world.

When Li Zhichang reached Samarqand on December 3, 1221, he saw Chinese artisans "everywhere," and further on reports that since the region's population had dropped to a quarter of its preconquest level of one hundred thousand households, the locals were "not able to care for their fields and gardens by themselves and were forced to depend upon the [assistance] of Chinese, Kitans, Tanguts, and others."[66] Since the Mongols reached Samarqand in the spring of 1220, it is noteworthy that the East Asian "aid-workers" were in place and functioning within a year or so, for this indicates that the decision to rebuild was taken soon after the occupation or perhaps even before.[67] Whatever the timing, the newcomers apparently had some impact, for Yelü Chucai, the influential Kitan statesman and administrator who traveled in Central Asia from 1219 to 1225, describes Samarqand as a flourishing city with a varied and productive agriculture.[68]

The use of transported Chinese artisans and agriculturalists in Inner and Central Asia was common during the early decades of the empire.[69] In 1259, Chang De, an envoy of Möngke to Hülegü, came across a number of these settlements over the course of his travels. In northern Dzungaria, by the Ulungur (Longgu龍骨) River and Lake Qizilbash (Qizelibasi 乞則裏八寺), he saw "numerous Chinese growing wheat, barley, millet, and [other] grains." Further west, in the Ili River valley, he observes "many people" from Shaanxi living in (the unidentified) Tiemuer Chancha (鐵木兒忏察) and Almaliq, the principal city of the region. He also notes that "the Muslim

[Huihe 回紇] populace [there] has become mixed with the Chinese and over time their customs have gradually come to resemble those of the Middle Kingdom."[70] Such a cultural imprint supposes, of course, a significant Chinese presence in the area over multiple generations.

There was as well a noticeable Chinese presence in the Ilkhanate. In his agricultural manual, Rashīd al-Dīn relates that Chinese (*Khiṭāyān*) from North China were first settled in Marv, whereupon some of this population moved to Tabriz and Khoy (Khūy). No numbers are given, but Mustawfī says in 1340 that Khoy—a medium-size town in Azerbaijan—was still largely Chinese. All of this indicates that thousands of Chinese agriculturalists were relocated to Iran sometime in the thirteenth century, perhaps in the mid-1250s in conjunction with Möngke's plans to revitalize the area's rural economy.[71]

The conquest of Turkestan seems to have played a pivotal role in these resettlement programs. At any rate, there is no doubt that the Mongols began transporting newly subordinated Muslim communities to the east right after the first Chinese colonies were established in Central Asia. Writing in the 1260s, Juwaynī speaks in general of the large levy of Muslim artisans that were settled in the "farthest countries of the East" following the Mongol invasion of 1219–1223. More specifically, Khwarazmian artisans "were distributed and sent to the countries of the East" and that in his own day, "there are many locales in those climes that are cultivated and well peopled by its inhabitants."[72] While Rashīd al-Dīn's claim that the Mongols sent one hundred thousand Khwārazmian artisans "to the lands of the East" is overstated, thousands were indeed deported, an assertion supported by the Chinese records.[73] We know, for instance, that in 1223 there were "over a thousand artisans of the Western Region [Xiyu 西域]" under the control of a single Chinese official.[74] Additionally, the Western Region contributed some three hundred artisans to a colony in Hongzhou, to the west of Beijing.[75] Another colony of artisan-agriculturalists, which was located at Simali/Xinmalin, in the neighborhood of Kalgan, was founded during Ögödei's reign with three thousand households from Samarqand.[76]

Aside for the communities around Beijing, there were other Muslim settlements in western China. Jūzjānī, also writing in the 1260s, repeatedly refers to reports that reached India concerning the great size of the Islamic population in the "Further East," which is attributed to the Mongol elites' relocation of numerous captives (*asīr*) from Turkestan and Iran to the cities of North China (Tamghāj), particularly the Tangut (Tankūt) land, the region of the Ordos and the contemporary provinces of Gansu and Ningxia.[77] Moreover, since most served the Mongol court in some official capacity, the "Saracens" of "Cataia," in Rubruck's words, resided there "with alien status."[78]

Though less noticed, the Mongols also regularly transplanted Russian civilians to distant places, a practice that began during the opening stages of the conquest and persisted down to the fourteenth century.[79] For the most part, agriculturalists were moved into the steppe and there formed into colonies to perform various services for their Mongol masters. On Carpini's testimony, we know that the Tartars established "a certain town of Ruthenians [Russians]" somewhere "in the land of the Comans." Its population can be gauged from the fact that an imperial agent, a "*baskak,*" was in charge and that troops had to be sent to quell a disturbance there.[80] A decade later, another eyewitness, Rubruck, relates that Batu had founded "settlements" of Russians on the lower courses of the Don and Volga Rivers to operate ferry services for the benefit of traveling merchants and envoys.[81] More unexpectedly, he reports that many Russian families were sent "out into the wilds to tend the Tartars' livestock" and that his personal servants, left behind in Batu's camp, narrowly escaped a similar fate when their Mongol hosts began "asking them if they knew how to tend cattle and milk mares."[82] Though surprising, these assertions are supported by Chinese, European, and Mongol sources from the Ming and Qing periods, which indeed affirm that the Mongols made extensive use of sedentary peoples as shepherds.[83]

For a final, and illuminating, example of the empire's deportation practices, we turn to the relocation of "Germans" to Turkestan—a trek that began during the Mongols' invasion of Central Europe in 1241. In the course of these operations, Buri, a grandson of Chaghadai, had several encounters with the Saxons of Transylvania.[84] Famed for their mining skills, they were often brought into Central European and Balkan states as autonomous communities by local rulers in order to develop metallurgical industries.[85] Their well-deserved reputation soon attracted the Mongols' attention, and Buri returned to the steppe with a contingent of "German slaves." According to Rubruck, these prisoners—apparently accompanied by their families—were first sent to Talas/Taraz in Turkestan. After Buri's fall and execution, Batu and Möngke jointly decided to transfer them to the city of Fūlād (Persian for "steel") in the Ili River valley, where they mined gold and made weapons for their Mongol masters.[86]

This episode is instructive on several counts. It speaks to the impressive distances that people were transported, in this particular instance about 2,600 air miles (4,000 kilometers) from the Saxons' first home in Central Europe to their second home in Central Asia. It also sheds light on the Mongols' knowledge of, and desire for, the specialized skills of individual communities, even those located on the outer fringes of the empire. What is more, it reveals that some transported communities were transported more than once as prizes between competing Chinggisid lines.

While unusually well documented under the Mongols, population transfers were hardly unique to the period. Over the centuries, nomadic polities formed agricultural and artisanal colonies in or near the steppe as a means of securing goods from the sedentary world that they could not produce on their own.[87] In pursuit of these goals, nomads became, in Toynbee's apt phrase, "herders of human beings."[88] What distinguishes the Mongol case is the unprecedented scale, both in terms of the numbers of colonists and the distances involved. Their specific motives for doing so are best explored in a comparative framework.

The nomads' practice of herding sedentaries is an ancient one, frequently remarked in Greek sources, which relate that, following their invasion of the Near East, the Scythians transferred numerous conquered people to new territories. These sources also note that the Huns and Avars drove hundreds of thousands of Byzantines into the steppe.[89] Closer to the Mongols, the Kitan—founders of the Liao dynasty (907–1125), which controlled Manchuria, North China, and the eastern steppe—adopted similar policies. In the 920s, during the early days of their empire, the Kitan forcibly relocated hundreds of thousands of Chinese and Bohai soldiers, officials, agriculturalists, and artisans, most of whom were settled in and around Shangjing, their main capital in western Manchuria.[90] At the height of their power, in 1004, they transported some seven hundred Chinese and Bohai households to Zhenzhou—a military base in central Mongolia—to provision a cavalry garrison.[91] At about the same time, on the other end of the steppe, the Polovetsy (Q̱ipchaqs), though not organized into a state, regularly captured Russian town dwellers and agriculturalists, herding them into the steppe. Just as frequently, Russian princes mounted counterraids, bringing back throngs of Polovetsian cattle and slaves (*cheliad*).[92]

Such forced relocations continued into the post-Mongol era, most notably in Temür's efforts to repopulate and rebuild Samarqand, his capital, by means of extensive population transfers, which were ongoing and drew upon all his subject peoples: Turks, Arabs, Persians, Greeks, Armenians, and Indians. This project's scale is indicated by the regular patrols that were needed to prevent those so transported from escaping back to their homelands.[93]

The objectives behind these transfers are readily discernible and help us understand their varied functions and persistent use by imperial regimes, whatever their origin. Perhaps most commonly, empires establish colonies and garrisons to facilitate communication and improve security by placing loyal subjects in newly subjugated lands or strategic areas. On some occasions, such relocations are mainly punitive, serving as a means for breaking resistance, diluting political opposition, or isolating religious heterodoxy. On others, skilled and celebrated peoples are enticed to a royal court for the purpose of enhancing its grandeur and the ruler's majesty. Lastly, resettlement programs, especially those involving agriculturists and artisans, can have purely economic goals, most obviously to repopulate derelict provinces, improve production in the center, and increase the flow of revenue.

The assortment of motives in the Mongol case emerges from a court debate in 1231. This discussion arose, according to the Chinese records, when an official, a certain Kesi (or Kumusi) Buhua (Buqa), memorialized Ögödei requesting the transport of Chinese households to Turkestan (Xiyu 西域) to help mine and refine precious metals, sow fields, and plant grapes (*putao* 葡萄). The emperor agreed and ordered ten thousand households from the area north of Zhongdu/Beijing sent there. At this juncture, Yelü Chucai intervened, arguing that since those designated for removal had always been loyal subjects, the order should be rescinded. Better, he continued, to wait until Henan was subjugated and then dispatch ten thousand households from that region, a proposal that won Ögödei's approval.[94]

While there is no indication as to whether the Henan households were ever sent to Turkestan, the debate itself leads us to two important conclusions: recently conquered peoples, as previously suggested, were prime candidates for relocation; and the Mongols' practice of civilian resettlement was mainly directed toward economic goals. Furthermore, taking into account that the axis of their expansion was basically east to west, it can be argued that the Mongols generally brought East Asian colonists to the west to repair the damage caused by their own military operations, while European and Muslim colonists were taken east as human booty to produce specialty industrial and agricultural goods. Put differently, the Mongols sent East Asians to the west to increase the *quantity* of production and Westerners to the east to improve the *quality* of production.[95] All this, of course, was geared to Mongol tastes, preferences, and priorities.

Consequences

The population movements produced by the Mongols' expansion played out differently across the continent, but everywhere there were consequences. In attempting to measure these convergent if not always identical effects, I can only point out several issues that deserve more thorough investigation and offer a few provisional hypotheses that address the demographic, cultural, military-political, and ethnoreligious consequences.

Demography

Though shifts in population profiles of premodern societies are notoriously hard to chart, the demographic implications of population movements under the Mongols warrant our attention, at least for the better-documented zones of the empire. For Iran, Petrushevskii argued that between 1220 and 1340 there was a drastic fall in the total population, number of settlements, and concomitantly tax receipts, within the territories constituting the Ilkhanate.[96] More specific figures can be cited in the case of China. By Ho Ping-ti's reconstruction, the combined Song and Jin population on the eve of the Mongol invasions was around one hundred million, whereas by the early Ming period it was just over sixty million.[97]

The accuracy of these figures, as well as the reason behind this precipitous decline, is still an open question. To be sure, in the early years of the empire, Mongol methods of warfare—most notably the use of recently surrendered populations as "arrow fodder" in siege operations—resulted in heavy casualties, and their incessant demands on subjects provoked numerous rebellions that were brutally suppressed, thus further raising the body count.[98] But this does not account for the entire loss, as population transfers must also be taken into consideration. One particularly grim episode from the early fourteenth century is worth examining in detail, for it speaks to the question of the scale and human costs of such relocations.

The incident in question was precipitated by the intensification of power struggles within the Chaghadaid khanate. Starting in 1306, these conflicts triggered a steady flow of refugees from Turkestan into northern Iran. This movement involved civilians, contingents of Mongol troops, and descendants of several Chinggisid lines, including dissident Chaghadaid princes. Chief among these princes was Yasa'ur, who, after secret negotiations with Öljeitü, prepared a surprise defection.[99] In February of 1314, he suddenly crossed the Amu Darya into Ilkhanid territory with five *tümens*, nominally fifty thousand troopers and their families. Öljeitü granted his new subjects a station in the region of Balkh and Shuburghān, and Yasa'ur soon set about creating his own power base in Khurasan, a key element of which was the acquisition of additional civilian subjects from his former home territory in Turkestan. To this end, he launched a major attack to the north in late 1314, with the Ilkhanate's approval and support. Once the defending Chaghadaid forces were in retreat, Yasa'ur's troops plundered and despoiled the country from Tirmidh to Samarqand and took much of its population into captivity. Only some of the notables managed to find sanctuary in Khwārazm, while the remainder—peasants and the poor—were driven back to Khurasan.[100]

Yasa'ur's intention was to settle these unfortunates near the Murghab River for the purpose of revitalizing his territory's economy. However, before he could implement this project, the Chaghadaid forces regrouped and came in pursuit of their "rustled" subjects. The dissident prince turned to meet the enemy north of the Amu Darya, while ordering that his captives be sent still further south toward Herat. According to Sayfī (writing in Herat only five years after the event), due to this second drive, these "miserable, famished people, ill-clothed and on foot, passed into a barren waste [land] and nearly a hundred thousand individuals, women and men perished . . . in consequence of the cold."[101] Again, while exact numbers are hard to verify, there can be little doubt about the magnitude of this disaster. Without question, one can expect very high levels of mortality during any hurried or long-distance deportation, particularly those involving sedentary communities.

This brings up another, complicating factor in assessing this population loss—disease. Of course, the Black Death comes immediately to mind. This scourge began in eastern Inner Asia in the 1330s, reaching the Crimea in 1346 from whence it spread into the Mediterranean and Europe.[102] While this great pandemic, which apparently followed the trans-Eurasian trade routes, was a continental menace, the massive population movements so common in the Mongol era must have fostered serious outbreaks of infectious disease on the local and regional level. People in stressful flight or on forced marches, suffering from malnourishment and moving across cultural and ecological frontiers, as well as between different disease pools, were highly susceptible to and in all probability further spread a variety of ailments. In light of the above, any analysis of demographic decline in this period will have to take into account not only Mongol warfare, but the empire's population transfers, as the latter development provided an optimum social and biological matrix for the outbreak and transmission of infectious disease.

Cultural Transfer

Like disease, human skills are readily transmittable. Technology transfer or, more accurately, technician transfer, was another consequence of, and indeed a frequent motive for, many deportations. To cite two examples, Muslim weavers sent east in the 1220s taught their craft to the inhabitants of North China, and the Chinese artillerymen attached to Hülegü's forces brought gunpowder and other Chinese technologies to West Asia.[103] All told, in their search for talent, the Mongols showed a decided preference for individuals and communities possessing practical, often manual skills. In addition, it may fairly be said that these artillerymen, artisans, engineers, and artists were excellent agents of diffusion, as they were far more open to innovation and alien culture than scholars or ritual specialists committed to specific worldviews.[104]

In assessing this complex issue, one point should be borne in mind: modern nationalist preoccupation with the priority of invention seriously hampers our understanding of the nature of change and innovation, especially in the technological sphere. This is because the diffusion of skills is not just a matter of cultural change by simple addition. What is really important is that innovation often occurs when attempts are made to duplicate material culture in new environments or when technologists, suddenly removed to new surroundings, are set to work fashioning traditional products with new materials.[105] To date, we have hardly begun to address these processes in an in-depth or, of equal significance, in-breadth fashion. The Mongol period calls for both perspectives because the demic diffusion that was initiated by the empire's rise was unprecedented and unsurpassed in terms of its range and intensity until the global exchange of peoples and cultures in the post-Columbian era.

Military and Political Repercussions

One of the least appreciated legacies of Chinggisid expansion was the vast number of men and military formations that were mobilized to resist their victorious advance as well as the mass of defeated and dispersed armies left in their wake. Many of these disorganized and surrendered remnants were rapidly pressed into Mongol service. More specifically, these men were organized into new units to assist in further conquest and the garrisoning of newly subdued territories. Consequently, they were often transported far from their home ground and injected into foreign ethnic and cultural milieus. As soldiers of the empire, they were not only armed but privileged; for this reason, these men inevitably became embroiled in politics, either in competition with one another or with the indigenous populace. The Bekrin's deep involvement in the ethnic and communal clashes in Irbil is a case in point, as is the continuing role of the Oirats in late Ilkhanid politics. Those left behind in 1296, interchangeably described as a "tribe[s] [*qawm*]" or "arm[ies] [*lashkar*]," in the Persian sources, retained sufficient military power to become players and, for a brief while, kingmakers in the incessant struggles over the throne following Abū Saʿīd's death in 1335.[106]

Those defeated and defecting forces that managed to flee beyond the Mongols' reach regularly negotiated a new place for themselves in states bordering on the empire, usually as mercenaries. Like the Mongols' garrison units, they served in privileged military formations that enabled them to act as disruptive political elements. This is well illustrated by the Oirats' behavior after their defection to the Mamluks. Accustomed to exercising influence in disputed successions and embittered by their treatment, they staged a revolt in 1299 to topple al-Nāṣir Muḥammad (r. 1293–1294, 1298–1309, 1310–1341) and restore the Mongol Sultan Kitbugha (r. 1294–1296). In the event, the attempt failed and many Oirats were killed, thereby limiting their future participation in Mamluk politics.[107] By way of contrast, the Qipchaq migrations into the Balkans had far more profound and lasting effects. As Vásáry has convincingly argued, these immigrants were instrumental in fashioning new elites among the Bulgarian and Romanian upper classes. To wit, they founded new dynasties and provided hired soldiers to all the warring parties. The division and discord that ensued paved the way for the Ottoman conquest in the fourteenth century.[108]

But in considering the buildup of this expanded pool of military recruits the matter does not end here. One by-product of the steppe peoples' military operations— whether raids or campaigns of conquest—was the creation of large numbers of displaced persons and prisoners of war. The fate of such people was seldom pleasant. Some of them were retained by nomads as domestic slaves and servants, for which there is a rich and wholly native terminology in Turkic and Mongolian. As a consequence of the improvements they made to the extended communication and supply networks in the steppe, the Chinggisids were able to absorb more sedentary slaves than was usual in nomadic societies.[109] Still, there were limits and most prisoners were ransomed or sold as slaves.[110] Some, of course, remained within the empire; for example, a *waqf* deed from 1326 records the presence of a diverse group of slaves (*ghulāmān*)—Turks, Russians, Chinese, Persians, and Indians—engaged in field work in Bukhara.[111] The majority, however, was sent to international markets supplying slaves, especially for military purposes, to the sedentary world.

The institution of the slave soldier and, more generally, that of the warrior-bondsman, in which loyalty was to the person of the ruler rather than to the state, was well established in the Muslim world long before the Mongols.[112] While the origin of the *mamlūk/ghulām* system and the exact social-legal status of its personnel remain the subject of dispute, there is wide consensus that the primary recruiting ground for "slave soldiers" was the steppe and Inner Asia where, it deserves to be stressed, guard corps of warrior-bondsmen had very deep roots.[113]

The Mongols did much to extend and solidify these kinds of institutions. First, and most obviously, their conquests set in motion countless nomads toward the south and west, thus rapidly creating a much expanded pool of *mamlūks* that were eagerly purchased by sedentary states from North India to North Africa. The center of this trade, into the fifteenth century, was the Crimea, which supplied the Mediterranean world with domestic and military slaves of varied ethnic backgrounds—Slavs, Hungarians, North Caucasians, and steppe peoples, most conspicuously Qipchaqs.[114] The decided preference for the Qipchaqs in thirteenth-century Egypt is perhaps just another way of saying that there were large numbers of them available on the Chinggisid-era slave markets.[115] Second, and often overlooked in this regard, the Mongols raised their own royal guards units during the same period, especially in the east. Furthermore, the Yuan guards were traditionally foreigners, ethnically different from the indigenous population and the royal house. The more important of these Yuan units—the Alan, Qipchaq, Qangli, and Russian guards—were recruited from the same source upon which the Mamluks, the Delhi Sultanate, and the kingdoms of Hungary and the Balkans were dependent, that is, the territories of the Golden Horde.

Although the methods of recruitment differed—impressment in the Yuan, hired mercenaries in the Balkans, and slave soldiers in the Delhi Sultanate and Mamluk kingdom—their function was the same: they were the king's men, his retinue and guard. As such, they were involved in high politics and power struggles. In this way, the Qipchaqs, who did not form their own state in the steppe, were major power brokers in regimes across Eurasia during the Mongol period.[116] This was particularly true of Egypt, where they became a self-perpetuating elite and the dominant player in the state. The Qipchaq *mamlūks* in the Delhi Sultanate never enjoyed such power. In fact, it is most characteristic of the age that they had to share power with freeborn Muslim immigrants, Khalaj tribesmen, and later on Mongol defectors, all of whom were refugees generated by Chinggisid expansion and princely politics.[117]

One last military-political implication of the population movements of this era call for comment—their role in slowing down and halting Mongol expansion. To be sure, this was a complex phenomenon that cannot be reduced to a single factor; certainly ecological preferences and constraints, logistical and communications difficulties, and internal political divisions all came into play, but so did the flight of defeated armies and civilians, which had the long-term effect of increasing the human and military resources available to polities along the empire's periphery.

Such movements, quite naturally, gave rise to émigré politics that encouraged resolve and resistance. Persons capable of fleeing usually have means and connections and are accustomed to exercising a measure of influence at home, and tend therefore to be politically active abroad. Jūzjānī, a refugee in North India who was both an anti-Mongol publicist and an official of the Delhi Sultanate, personifies this brand of individual politics. However, collective efforts are also in evidence. Royal houses in exile can be extremely energetic in urging and organizing resistance against those who displaced them. This is exemplified by the fall of the Song. In 1279, when military collapse was eminent, the court, its leading officials, and many subjects escaped by sea to Champa and Annam. Once there, thousands of Chinese expatriates incited and participated in the resistance of these two states—both former clients of the Song—against the Yuan forces penetrating Southeast Asia in the 1280s, resistance that was at least temporarily effective.[118] Even more enduring, of course, was the resistance offered by the Egyptian Mamluks and the Delhi Sultanate, both of which welcomed anti-Mongol émigrés of all kinds.

Ethnic and Religious Transformations

Population movements occasioned by the Mongols' expansion initiated or facilitated fundamental shifts in the identities of subject peoples and the conquerors themselves. Since these were processes, not events, they had long gestation periods and are most dramatically manifested by the formation of new ethnic and religious collectivities, which only become fully visible in the aftermath of imperial disintegration. This was a multifaceted phenomenon that took a variety of forms, but all of them shared a common ingredient: the repeated disruption of established population patterns due to Mongol methods of conquest and rule.

This transformation was most pronounced in the steppe where some of the more visible pre-Chinggisid ethnicities, the Qipchaqs and Qanglis, seemingly vanished or, more accurately, were submerged, while new ones, such as the Noghais, Kazakhs, and Uzbeks, took their place. During this comprehensive reshuffling of steppe peoples, new structural features and patterns of ethnonyms surfaced as well.[119]

Similar far-reaching changes also occurred along the steppe's margins. The Oirats, originally a forest people, suddenly resurfaced in early Ming times as steppe nomads in Dzungaria. For the most part, details of their relocation remain obscure, but several contributing factors are readily identified. First, as noted, thousands of Oirats were permanently transferred to the west, thereby thinning their ranks on home ground. Second, those who remained in the east were soon caught up in the Toluid civil war over the accession of Qubilai; these Oirats backed Ariq Böke—the eventual loser—and suffered heavy casualties in fighting Qubilai's forces in Mongolia, so that their population was further diminished and dispersed.[120] These two events, which took place within a comparatively short period (1251–1264), help explain the Oirats' disappearance from southern Siberia, if not their later reconstitution in Jungharia.

Relocation was but one possible outcome; other peoples were "reconfigured." In North Caucasia, the Mongol invasions were particularly devastating for the Alans, who were "slaughtered" and "scattered" in the words of one source or "driven away" and "destroyed" according to another.[121] As a result of their dwindling numbers and consequent decrease in their ethnic territory, neighboring peoples—the Circassians and Abazas—moved in, replacing the weakened Alans in the Kuban and western lowlands.[122] Moreover, due to the increase of Qipchaq elements in the region after their flight from the Mongols, some groups of Alans underwent Turkicization, contributing major ethnic traits to the formation of the Qarachai-Balqar peoples.[123]

The preceding cases involve peoples with limited populations and close ties to the steppe world; under conditions associated with the rise and fall of a large nomadic empire, the aforementioned transformations are more or less expected. But what of the Mongol imprint on large-scale sedentary societies? We can explore this issue by comparing three case studies from Inner and East Asia.

The first treats the Tangut Xixia kingdom, one of the Mongols' earliest enemies. As is well known, in the century following their ultimate defeat in 1227, the Tanguts gradually disappeared from view. Part of the general population fled south where they were absorbed by the Tibetans and the remaining urban population was Sinicized, while some of the leadership was co-opted by the Chinggisids and Mongolized.[124] Lastly, the sizeable nomadic component of the Xixia kingdom was scattered or impressed for military service and later show up as "Tangut" lineages in the new Mongolian and Turkic ethnic formations of the post-Chinggisid era.[125]

What is of equal interest is that many peoples inhabiting the territory of the former Tangut kingdom, while becoming Chinese in speech, were also converting to Islam, a conversion attributable to the presence of the many Muslim colonies the Mongols established in the region. The steady growth of these communities is noted by Marco Polo, who tells us that while idolaters were still in the majority, there were many Muslims in all the cities and towns, some apparently organized into artisan colonies.[126] One of the reasons they flourished in their new home was that Ananda, Qubilai's grandson, who had princely jurisdiction over the Tangut land, had embraced Islam. With the help of Muslim officials and advisers, he actively propagated the faith in the region. These efforts apparently bore fruit, for Rashīd al-Dīn reports that, by the time of Temür Qaghan (r. 1296–1307), the major cities were predominantly Muslim, though the rural areas still practiced idolatry.[127] All these assertions as to the spread of Islam in the Gansu corridor are corroborated by the Chinese sources, which record that in 1272 there were sufficient numbers of younger males to create a "Xixia Muslim [*huihui* 回回] Army."[128]

The end product of this ethnic and religious transformation, which took centuries to complete, was the emergence of the Hui nationality in Gansu and Ningxia provinces, the core territory of the old Tangut kingdom.[129]

A similar identity shift took place in the Uighur territories, our second case study. One obvious difference is that the Uighur kingdom was an early and favored ally of the Mongols, whereas the Tanguts were an adversary. Nonetheless, forces unleashed by Chinggisid policies and politics brought about fundamental changes in the region. First of all, the Uighurs were heavily recruited and deployed throughout the empire as soldiers, administrators, and cultural specialists.[130] Later, as noted, civil war among the Mongols led to a new wave of out-migration, including the Uighur court, a development that further weakened the Uighurs' cultural and political influence on their home ground. Second, the Mongols introduced an Islamic presence into the region, establishing a Muslim artisanal colony at Besh Baliq (the Uighurs' summer capital) in the 1220s.[131] Over the next hundred years, this community clearly grew in size, for by the early fourteenth century, the long-dominant Buddhists felt threatened enough to persuade Changshi, the Chaghadaid khan (r. ca. 1335–1337), to desecrate mosques in Uighuristan.[132]

Although the Chinggisids had no interest in undermining their identity and every reason to preserve it, they nevertheless created conditions in which Islam spread while Uighur identity slowly eroded and was lost. The historian Muḥammad Ḥaydar, widely traveled in West and East Turkestan, who knew of the Uighurs through earlier Persian accounts of the Mongols, reports that in his day (1541) the name "Uighur is quite unknown" and no one "understood which country is meant."[133] While Turkic speech was retained, identities became localized, attached to various oases and cities—a situation that remained in force until the 1920s, when Turkestani intellectuals revived the ethnonym Uighur for political purposes.

Our last case, Nanzhao/Dali, an independent kingdom that was roughly coterminous with the later province of Yunnan, underwent simultaneous transformations. Before the Mongols, there were few Chinese in the region, but Qubilai's conquest of 1253 set in motion long-term changes in its ethnic composition. The first arrivals were soldiers, mainly Chinese conscripts who were discharged following the campaign. Several decades later, the Yuan court sent fifty thousand Chinese military colonists, together with their families, to the newly established province of Yunnan—a practice that was continued under the Ming and Qing dynasties. The principle architect of this transformation was the Bukharan Sayyid Ajall, who Qubilai appointed to oversee southern Sichuan and Yunnan in 1273. He proved to be an able and energetic administrator who effectively restored order, established stable governance, and improved the control over water supplies. All of these contributions encouraged additional Chinese immigration to these distant and still largely non-Han lands. At the same time, Ajall, his family, and associates managed to advance the cause of Islam, which already had a toehold in southwest China.[134] The result, over the next few centuries, was the spread of Islam and the steady buildup of Chinese population in the region, a development that also changed the definition of China.[135]

Conclusions

An analysis of the assembled data suggests a number of working hypotheses:

1. In pursuit of imperial goals and individual princely interests, the Chinggisids were indeed "herders of human beings."
2. The population movements in this era took a variety of forms—military deployments, the retreat of defeated armies, the migration of refugees, resettlement programs, political defections, and trafficking in slaves.
3. Individual movements numbered from tens to hundreds of thousands, and, taken together, they involved millions of people.
4. In variable combinations, the Mongols' policies of deployment, displacement, and replacement possessed a synergy that generated substantial changes in population distributions and the primary identity of communities at very different levels of complexity.
5. While some of the changes were intended, many were not. One of the most striking of the unforeseen consequences was Islam's steady and extensive penetration into Inner and East Asia.[136]

To sum up, none of the issues raised here can be resolved from afar or solely through a broad historical analysis. Each is a complicated problem that must be scrutinized in light of local conditions and sources—literary, archaeological, ethnographic, and linguistic.[137] But I do believe that for full comprehension, all must also be situated in a continental context, that of the many long-range and interlocking population movements inaugurated by the Chinggisids' imperial venture.

Notes

1. Bar Hebraeus, *The Chronography of Gregory Abu'l Faraj,* tr. E. A. W. Budge (London, 1932), vol. 1, p. 439. On this episode see R. Amitai-Preiss, *Mongols and Mamluks: The Mamluk-Īlkhānid Ilkhanid War, 1260–1281* (Cambridge, 1995), pp. 50–53.

2. *Yuanshi* (Beijing, 1978), ch. 15, pp. 321, 325; ch. 18, p. 398; and ch. 22, p. 485.

3. ʿAṭa-Malik Juwaynī, *Taʾrīkh-i Jahāngushā,* ed. M. M. Qazwīnī (London, 1912–1937), vol. 3, pp. 91–92, 107, 113, 120–121, 266; tr. J. A. Boyle, *History of the World Conqueror* (Cambridge, MA, 1958), vol. 2, pp. 608, 618, 622, 626–627, 716; Rashīd al-Dīn, *Jāmiʿ al-tawārīkh,* 2 vols., ed. B. Karīmī (Tehran, 1959), vol. 2, pp. 707, 709, 710, 715; and Bar Hebraeus, *Chronography,* pp. 419, 469.

4. *Histoire de la Géorgie,* pt. I, *Histoire ancienne, jusqu'en 1469 de JC,* tr. M. Brosset (St. Petersburg, 1850), pp. 557–558; and H. R. Roemer, "Jalayirids, Muzaffarids and Sarbadars," in *The Cambridge History of Iran,* vol. 6: *The Timurid and Safavid Periods,* ed. P. Jackson (Cambridge, 1986), p. 19.

5. Brosset, *Histoire,* p. 487; and Bar Hebraeus, *Chronography,* p. 353.

6. M. D. Poluboiarinov, *Russkie liudi v Zolotoi Orde* (Moscow, 1978), pp. 40–43.

7. Rashīd al-Dīn, ed. Karīmī, vol. 1, p. 409. For an overview see E. Bretschneider, *Medieval Researches from Eastern Asiatic Sources* (London, 1967), vol. 2, pp. 80–81; and H. Franke, "Europa in der ostasiatischen Geschichtesschreibung des 13. und 14. Jahrhunderts," *Saeculum,* 2 (1951), pp. 70–72.

8. *Yuanshi,* ch. 99, pp. 2529–2530; and Hsiao Ch'i-ch'ing, *The Military Establishment of the Yuan Dynasty* (Cambridge, MA, 1978), p. 100.

9. *Yuanshi,* ch. 34, pp. 758, 767.

10. Ibid., ch. 100, p. 2562. Military colonies—in theory, self-supporting military bases—were heavily used in the Yuan. See Foon Ming Liew, *Tuntian Farming of the Ming Dynasty (1368–1644)* (Hamburg, 1984), pp. 1–13.

11. *Yuanshi,* ch. 34, pp. 770–771.

12. Ibid., ch. 35, p. 782.

13. Ibid., ch. 138, p. 3337 and ch. 144, p. 3446; Yang Yu, *Beiträge zur Kulturgeschichte Chinas unter der Mongolenherrschaft: Das Shan-kü Sin-hua das Yang Yü,* tr. H. Franke (Wiesbaden, 1956), pp. 71–72; and E. I. Kychanov, *Ocherk istorii tangutskogo gosudarstva* (Moscow, 1968), pp. 325–326.

14. *Yuanshi,* ch. 35, p. 794; ch. 36, pp. 800, 805, 806.

15. Ibid., ch. 35, p. 790.

16. For information on these donors see L. Hambis, *Le chapitre CVIII du Yuan che* (Leiden, 1954), pp. 17–19, 55–58, 107–108, 160–162.

17. T. T. Allsen, "Mongols and North Caucasia," *Archivum Eurasiae Medii Aevi,* 8 (1987–1991), pp. 34–38.

18. Quan Heng, *Das Keng-shen wai-shih: Eine Quelle zur späten Mongolenzeit,* tr. H. Schulte-Uffeflage (Berlin, 1963), p. 63.

19. L. Hambis, "Note sur l'installation des Mongols dans la Boucle du Fleuve Jaune," in *Mongolian Studies,* ed. L. L. Ligeti (Amsterdam, 1970), p. 173; and H. Serruys, "The Mongols in China during the Hung-wu Period," *Melanges chinois et bouddhiques,* 11 (1959), pp. 49, 103–105, 201, 227.

20. *Yuanshi,* ch. 14, p. 288; ch. 28, p. 619; and ch. 99, p. 2524; and Hsiao, *Military Establishment,* pp. 99–100.

21. *Yuanshi,* ch. 4, pp. 70, 71; ch. 121, p. 2976; ch. 123, p. 3031; and ch. 134, p. 3256.

22. Ibid., ch. 99, p. 2528; ch. 123, p. 3039; ch. 134, p. 3263; and ch. 136, p. 3296; and Hsiao, *Military Establishment,* p. 99.

23. This term derives from the Turkic *qaya,* "crag" or "rockface." See V. M. Nadeliaev (ed.), *Drevnetiurskii Slovar* (Leningrad, 1969), p. 406.

24. Rashīd al-Dīn, *Jāmiʿ al-tawārīkh,* ed. ʿA.ʿA. ʿAlīzādah (Moscow, 1980), vol. 2, pt. 1, pp. 343–345.

25. Abū al-Qāsim Qāshānī, *Taʾrīkh-i Ūljāytū,* ed. M. Hambly (Tehran, 1969), pp. 113–115.

26. Bar Hebraeus, *Chronography,* pp. 485–487. For background see J. M. Fiey, *Chrétiens syriques sous les Mongols: (Il-khanat de Perse, XIIIe-XIVe s.)* (Louvain, 1975), pp. 53–55.

27. Besides the account found in Qāshānī (n. 30), see *The Monks of Kublai Khan,* tr. E. A. W. Budge (London, 1928), pp. 231, 261, 263–267, 285–286, 296–297, 301.

28. P. Pelliot, *Reserches sur les Chrétiens d'Asie Centrale et d'Extrême Orient* (Paris, 1973), pp. 32–33; and V. Minorsky, "Mongol Place-names in Mukri Kurdistan (Mongolica 4)," *Bulletin of the School of Oriental and African Studies,* 19/1 (1957), pp. 72–73.

29. Juwaynī, ed. Qazwīnī, vol. 3, pp. 92–93; tr. Boyle, vol. 2, p. 608. For details see T. T. Allsen, "The Circulation of Military Technology in the Mongolian Empire," in *Warfare in Inner Asian History (500–1800),* ed. N. Di Cosmo (Leiden, 2002), pp. 278–279.

30. For the graphic and contemporaneous account of Thomas of Spalato see *Der Mongolensturm: Berichte von Augenzeugen und Zeitgenossen, 1235–1250,* tr. H. Göckenjan and J. R. Sweeney (Vienna, 1985), pp. 254–259. For analysis see J. R. Sweeney, "'Spurred on by Fear of Death': Refugees and Displaced Populations during the Mongol Invasion of Hungary," in *Nomadic Diplomacy, Destruction and Religion from the Pacific to the Adriatic,* ed. W. Schlepp and M. Gervers, Toronto Studies in Central and Inner Asia, no. 1 (Toronto, 1994), pp. 34–62.

31. On the extent of their dispersal see the remarks of William of Rubruck, *The Mission of Friar William of Rubruck,* tr. P. Jackson and ed. P. Jackson and D. Morgan (London, 1990), pp. 70, 105–106, 113.

32. Muḥammad al-Nasawī, *Sīrat al-sulṭān Jalāl al-Dīn Mankubirtī,* ed. Ḥ. Ḥamdī (Cairo, 1953), p. 284.

33. *Armianskie istochniki o Mongolakh,* tr. A. G. Galstian (Moscow, 1962), p. 23; Kirakos Gandzaketsi, *Istoriia Armenii,* tr. L. A. Khanlarian (Moscow, 1976), pp. 139–140; R. W. Thompson (tr.), "The Historical Compilation of Vardan Arewelcʿi," *Dumbarton Oaks Papers,* 43 (1989), p. 213; and Ia. A. Fedorov and G. S. Fedorova, *Rannie Tiurki na Severnom Kavkaze* (Moscow, 1978), p. 257ff.

34. N. Berend, *At the Gates of Christendom: Jews, Muslims and 'Pagans' in Medieval Hungary, c. 1000–c. 1300* (Cambridge, 2001), pp. 70–73, 87–93; A. Pálóczi Horváth, "L'immigration et l'établissement des Comans en Hongrie," *Acta Orientalia Hungaricae,* 29 (1975), pp. 318, 326–328; A. Pálóczi Horváth, "Steppe Traditions and Cultural Assimilation of a Nomadic People: The Cumanians in Hungary in the 13th–14th Century," in *Archaeological Approaches to Cultural Identity,* ed. Stephen Shennan (London, 1989), pp. 291–302.

35. I. Vásáry, *Cumans and Tatars: Oriental Military in the Pre-Ottoman Balkans, 1185–1365* (Cambridge, 2005), pp. 63–68.

36. Rubruck, *Mission,* p. 70.

37. Brosset, *Histoire,* pp. 611–613, 633, 635–636, 638.

38. Nasawī, *Sīra,* pp. 94, 95, 111, 253, 292, 346; and P. Jackson, "Jalāl al-Dīn, the Mongols and the Khwarazmian Conquest of Panjāb and Sind," *Iran,* 28 (1990), pp. 45–54.

39. Nasawī, *Sīra,* p. 174; and C. Cahen, "Abdallaṭīf al-Baghdādī et les Khwārizmiens," in *Iran and Islam: In Memory of the Late Vladimir Minorsky,* ed. C. E. Bosworth (Edinburgh, 1971), pp. 157, 159.

40. S. Orbelian, *Histoire de la Sioune,* tr. M. Brosset (St. Petersburg, 1864), pp. 225–226; Brosset, *Histoire,* pp. 491–508, 514–515; G. V. Tsulia, "Dzhelal ad-Din v otsenke gruzinskoi letopisnoi traditsii," *Letopisi i khroniki 1980g.* (Moscow, 1981), pp. 112–128; Galstian, *Armianskie istochniki,* pp. 24 and 33–34; Kirakos, *Istoriia,* pp. 127, 149–153.

41. I. P. Petrushevskii, *Zemledelie i agrarnye otnosheniia v Iran XIII-XIV vekov* (Moscow, 1960), pp. 41–46; and J. M. Smith, Jr., "Mongol Nomadism and Middle Eastern Geography: Q̱ishlaqs and Tümens," in *The Mongol Empire and Its Legacy,* ed. R. Amitai-Preiss and D. O. Morgan (Leiden, 1999), pp. 39–56.

42. Jūzjānī, *Ṭabaqāt-i nāṣirī,* 2 vols., tr. H. G. Raverty (rpt. New Delhi, 1970), vol. 1, p. 299. Cf. the remarks of Rubruck, *Mission,* p. 262. On Jalāl al-Dīn's political failure see D. O. Morgan, "The Mongols and the Eastern Mediterranean," *Mediterranean Historical Review,* 4/1 (1989), p. 201; and A. G. C. Savvides, *Byzantium and the Near East: Its Relations with the Seljuk Sultanate of Rum, the Armenians of Cilicia and the Mongols, A.D. c.1192–1237* (Thessaloniki, Greece, 1981), pp. 177–182. For the impact of these and other refugees on Mamluk Syria see Amitai's chapter in this volume.

43. C. F. Petry, *The Civilian Elite of Cairo in the Later Middle Ages* (Princeton, 1981), pp. 161–164.

44. See J. Paul, "L'Invasion mongole comme 'révélateur' de la société iranienne," in *L'Iran face à la domination mongole,* ed. D. Aigle (Tehran, 1997), pp. 37–53.

45. See e.g., S. M. Ikram, *Muslim Civilization in India* (New York, 1964), pp. 41–42, 45, 114, 120–121, 124; and K. A. Nizami, "India's Cultural Relations with Central Asia during the Medieval Period," in *Central Asia: Movement of Peoples and Ideas from Times Prehistoric to Modern,* ed. A. Guha (New Delhi, 1970), pp. 162–163.

46. A. Wink, *Al-Hind: The Making of the Indo-Islamic World* (Leiden, 2002), vol. 2, pp. 190–194; P. Jackson, *The Delhi Sultanate: A Political and Military History* (Cambridge, 2003), pp. 34–43, 79–82.

47. Jūzjānī, *Tabaqāt-i nasīrī,* ed. W. Nassau Lees (Calcutta, 1864), pp. 144, 172, 281, 324–325.

48. Tuotuo, *Jinshi* (Beijing, 1975), ch. 107, p. 2355, and ch. 109, p. 2406.

49. P. J. Smith, "Family, Landsmann, and Status-Group Affinity in Refugee Mobility Strategies: The Mongol Invasions and the Diaspora of the Sichuanese Elite, 1230–1330," *Harvard Journal of Asiatic Studies,* 52/2 (1992), pp. 668–672.

50. *Polnoe sobranie russkikh letopisei,* II, *Ipat'evskaia letopis* (rpt. Moscow, 1998), pp. 842–843; and *The Hypatian Codex,* pt. 2, *The Galician-Volynian Chronicle,* tr. G. A. Perfecky (Munich, 1973), p. 75.

51. Nakamachi Nobutaka, "The Rank and Status of Military Refugees in the Mamluk Army: A Reconsideration of the Wafidiyah," *Mamluk Studies Review,* 10/1 (2006), pp. 55–81, esp. 57–60.

52. Brosset, *Histoire,* p. 601.

53. Bar Hebraeus, *Chronography,* p. 508; Rashīd al-Dīn, ed. Karīmī, vol. 2, p. 919; ed. ʿAlīzādah, vol. 2, pt. I, pp. 223, 228–229.

54. Abū al-Fidā', *The Memoirs of a Syrian Prince,* tr. P. M. Holt (Wiesbaden, 1983), p. 26, and see Amitai's chapter in this volume.

55. Abū Bakr al-Ahrī, *Ta'rīkh-i Shaikh Uwais: An Important Source for the History of Adharbaijān,* ed. and tr. H. B. Van Loon (Gravenhage, 1954), pp. 74, 173–174.

56. George Pachymérès, *Relations historiques,* tr. A. Failler and V. Laurent (Paris, 1984), vol. 2, p. 444.

57. A. E. Laiou, *Constantinople and the Latins: The Foreign Policy of Andronicus II, 1281–1326* (Cambridge, MA, 1972), pp. 89–90; and J. V. A. Fine, Jr., *The Late Medieval Balkans* (Ann Arbor, MI, 1987), pp. 227, 233, 285, n. 6.

58. R. Muntaner, *The Chronicle of Muntaner,* tr. Lady Goodenough (rpt. Nendeln, 1967), vol. 2, pp. 533–536.

59. Ibn Baṭṭūṭa, *The Travels of Ibn Baṭṭūṭa,* tr. H. A. R. Gibb (Cambridge, 1971), vol. 3, pp. 562, 563–564.

60. Marco Polo, *The Description of the World,* tr. A. C. Moule and P. Pelliot (London, 1938), vol. 1, pp. 121–122. See also Pelliot, *Notes on Marco Polo* (Paris, 1959), vol. 1, pp. 183–196.

61. J. Aubin, "L'Ethnogénèse des Qaraunas," *Turcica,* 1 (1969), pp. 65–94; Jackson, *Delhi Sultanate*, pp. 115–116, 119–122; and A. P. Martinez, "Some Notes on the Il-Xanid Army," *Archivum Eurasiae Medii Aevi,* 6 (1986–1988), pp. 218–242.

62. Allsen, "The Yuan Dynasty and the Uighurs of Turfan in the 13th Century," in *China among Equals: The Middle Kingdom and Its Neighbors, 10th–14th Centuries*, ed. M. Rossabi (Berkeley, 1983), pp. 253–258.

63. John of Plano Carpini, *The History of the Mongols, The Mongol Mission: Narratives and Letters of the Franciscan Missionaries in Mongolia and China in the Thirteenth and Fourteenth Centuries,* ed. C. Dawson (New York, 1955), p. 29; *The Vinland Map and the Tartar Relation,* ed. R. A. Skelton (New Haven, CT, 1995), p. 78; and Pelliot, *Recherches,* p. 40.

64. Li Zhichang, *Xi you ji,* in *Menggu shiliao sizhang,* ed. Wang Guowei (Taipei, 1975), pp. 284, 366–367; and Li Chih-chang, *The Travels of an Alchemist,* tr. A. Waley (London, 1963), pp. 72–73, 124.

65. *Yuanshi,* ch. 7, p. 141. My italics.

66. Li Zhichang, *Xi you ji,* p. 327; Li Chih-chang, *Travels,* p. 93.

67. On the conquest see F. Grenet and M. Isamiddinov, "La prise de Samarcand par Gengis-Khan," *L'Histoire,* 149 (1991), pp. 8–14.

68. I. de Rachewiltz (tr.), "The Hsi-yu lu by Yeh-lü Ch'u-ts'ai," *Monumenta Serica,* 21 (1962), pp. 21–22.

69. For an overview see H. Serruys, "Chinese in Southern Mongolia during the Sixteenth Century," *Monumenta Serica,* 18 (1959), pp. 3–10.

70. Shao Yuanping, *Yuanshi leibian* (Taipei, 1968), ch. 42, p. 51a; and Bretschneider, *Medieval Researches,* vol. 1, pp. 124–125, 126–127.

71. Rashīd al-Dīn, *Athār wa-aḥyā',* ed. M. Sutādah and I. Afshār (Tehran, 1989), p. 144; Ḥamdallāh Mustawfī Qazwīnī, *The Geographical Part of the Nuzhat al-Qulūb,* ed. G. Le Strange (London, 1915), p. 85; and Rashīd al-Dīn, ed. Karīmī, vol. 2, p. 687.

72. Juwaynī, ed. Qazwīnī, vol. 1, pp. 9, 101; tr. Boyle, vol. 1, pp. 13, 128.

73. Rashīd al-Dīn, ed. Karīmī, vol. 1, p. 373.

74. *Yuanshi,* ch. 153, p. 3609.

75. For documentation see T. T. Allsen, *Commodity and Exchange in the Mongol Empire: A Cultural History of Islamic Textiles* (Cambridge, 1997), pp. 43–45.

76. Rashīd al-Dīn, ed. Karīmī, vol. 1, p. 641; tr. Boyle p. 276; and Pelliot, "Une ville musulmans dans la Chine du Nord sous les Mongols," *Journal Asiatique,* 211 (1927), pp. 261–279.

77. Jūzjānī, ed. Lees, pp. 380–381, 383–384, 402; tr. Raverty, vol. 2, pp. 1106–1107, 1111, 1112, 1158].

78. Rubruck, *Mission,* p. 163.

79. As late as 1322, Mongolian officials took away many "Christians [Russians]" to the Horde; see *Polnoe sobranie russkikh letopisei,* III, *Novgorodskaia pervaia letopis* (rpt., Moscow, 2000), p. 339; and *The Chronicle of Novgorod,* tr. R. Michell and N. Forbes (rpt. New York, 1970), p. 122.

80. Carpini, *History,* p. 40.

81. Rubruck, *Mission,* pp. 108–109, 130.

82. Ibid., pp. 107, 256.

83. See H. Serruys, "Chinese in Southern Mongolia," pp. 27–29, 41, 78–80, 84; Matteo Ricci, *China in the Sixteenth Century: The Journals of Matthew Ricci, 1583–1610,* tr. L. J. Gallagher (New York, 1953), p. 513; H. Serruys, "A Question of Thievery," *Zentralasiatische Studien,* 10 (1976), pp. 296–298.

84. Rashīd al-Dīn, ed. ʿAlīzādah, vol. 2, pt. 1, pp. 164–165; tr. Boyle, p. 70; *The Secret History of the Mongols,* tr. de Rachewiltz (Leiden, 2004), vol. 1, par. 262, p. 194; vol. 2, p. 959; and Pelliot, *Notes sur l'histoire de la Horde d'Or* (Paris, 1949), p. 127 and n. 2.

85. See Fine, *Late Medieval Balkans,* pp. 141, 199–200, 282–284.

86. Rubruck, *Mission,* pp. 144–146, 226, 230–234, 245; and the commentary of Pelliot, *Recherches,* pp. 141–142.

87. For a discussion see A. M. Khazanov, *Nomads and the Outside World* (2nd ed. Madison, CT, 1994), pp. 225–226.

88. A. J. Toynbee, *A Study of History* (London, 1934–1954), vol. 2, pp. 317–319; vol. 3, p. 22.

89. Diodorus Siculus, *Library of History,* tr. C. H. Oldfather, Loeb Classical Library (Cambridge, MA, 2000), II.43.4–7; Procopius, *History of the Wars,* tr. H. B. Dewing, Loeb Classical Library (Cambridge, MA, 2001), II.iv.5–6.

90. Ho-dong Kim, "The Resettlement of the Pohai (or Palhae) Population in Liao in the 920's," *Journal of Turkic Studies,* 9 (1985), pp. 187–196; N. Standen, "What Nomads Want: Raids, Invasions and the Liao Conquest of 947," in *Mongols, Turks and Others: Nomads and the Sedentary World,* ed. R. Amitai and M. Biran (Leiden, 2005), pp. 155–156, 158–159; and K. Wittfogel and Feng Chia-sheng, *History of Chinese Society, Liao (907–1125)* (Philadelphia, 1949), pp. 54, 67, 142–143, 555–557.

91. N. N. Kradin et al., "Preliminary Results of the Investigation of Kitan Ancient Town Chintolgol Balgas in 2004," *Nomadic Studies Bulletin,* 10 (2005), pp. 72–80.

92. *Polnoe sobranie russkikh letopisei,* I, *Lavrent'evskaia letopis* (rpt. Moscow, 1997), pp. 224–225, 228, 277, 279; and *The Russian Primary Chronicle,* tr. S. Hazard Cross and O. P. Sherbowitz-Wetzor (Cambridge, MA, 1973), pp. 179, 181, 200, 202.

93. Ruy Gonzalez de Clavijo, *Embassy to Tamerlane,* tr. Guy Le Strange (London, 1928), pp. 202, 286, 288.

94. Su Tianjue (ed.), *Yuan wenlei* (Taipei, 1967), ch. 57, pp. 14a–b; *Yuanshi,* ch. 146, p. 3458.

95. The comparative framework and terminology used throughout this section follow those of Toynbee, *Study of History,* vol. 7, pp. 108–139.

96. Petrushevskii, *Zemledelie,* pp. 38–40, 92–101.

97. Ho Ping-ti, "An Estimate of the Total Population of Sung-Chin China," in *Études Song,* ed. F. Aubin (Paris, 1970), ser. 1, vol. 1, p. 52; and Ho Ping-ti, *Studies on the Population of China, 1368–1953* (Cambridge, MA, 1967), p. 258.

98. See the remarks of Carpini, *History,* pp. 36, 42, 45; and the analysis of J. M. Smith, "Demographic Considerations in Mongol Siege Warfare," *Archivum Ottomanicum,* 13 (1993–1994), pp. 329–334.

99. R. J. Kempiners, Jr., "Vassaf's *Tajziyat al-Amsar wa Tazjiyat al-A'sar* as a Source for the History of the Chaghadayid Khanate," *Journal of Asian History,* 22/1 (1988), pp. 178, 184–187.

100. Qāshānī, *Ta'rīkh-i Ūljāytū,* pp. 164, 213.

101. Sayf b. Muḥammad b. Ya'qūb al-Harawī, *Ta'rīkh-i nāmah-i Harāt,* ed. M. Siddiqi (Calcutta, 1944), pp. 643–644. A parallel passage can be found in Ḥāfiẓ-i Abrū, *Dhayl-i jāmi' al-tawārīkh-i rashīdī,* ed. Kh. Bayānī, "Salsalat-i intishārāt-i anjuman-i a'ṣār millī," no. 88 (Tehran, 1971), pp. 113, 114–115.

102. W. H. McNeill, *Plagues and Peoples* (Garden City, NY, 1976), pp. 132–175, 263–264; M. W. Dols, *The Black Death in the Middle East* (Princeton, 1977), pp. 35–68.

103. Allsen, "Circulation of Military Technology," pp. 272–284; Allsen, *Commodity and Exchange,* pp. 94–98.

104. On these themes see T. T. Allsen, *Technician Transfer in the Mongolian Empire,* Central Eurasian Studies Lectures 2 (Bloomington, IN, 2002), pp. 1–28.

105. Cf. A. Sherratt, "The Trans-Eurasian Exchange: The Prehistory of Chinese Relations with the West," in *Contact and Exchange in the Ancient World,* ed. V. Mair (Honolulu, 2006), pp. 35, 53.

106. Ahrī, *Ta'rīkh-i Shaikh Uwais,* pp. 63, 64–65, 80, 163, 164, 181; and Ḥāfiẓ-i Abrū, *Dhayl,* pp. 197, 200, 201, 204, 212. For analysis see C. Melville, *The Fall of Amir Chupan and the Decline of the Ilkhanate, 1327–37: A Decade of Discord in Mongol Iran,* Research Institute for Inner Asian Studies, no. 30 (Bloomington, IN, 1999), pp. 16–17, 33, 46–57; and P. Wing, "The Decline of the Ilkhanate and the Mamluk Sultanate's Eastern Frontier," *Mamluk Studies Review,* 11/2 (2007), pp. 78–88.

107. R. Irwin, *The Middle East in the Middle Ages: The Early Mamluk Sultanate* (London, 1986), p. 100.

108. Vásáry, *Cumans and Tatars,* pp. 166–167.

109. Cf. the observations of Carpini, *History,* pp. 38–39, 42; and Rubruck, *Mission,* p. 127.

110. On slavery in nomadic societies see A. M. Khazanov, *Sotsial'naia istoriia Skifov* (Moscow, 1975), pp. 133–148; and P. B. Golden, "The Terminology of Slavery and Servitude in Medieval Turkic," in *Studies in Central Asian History in Honor of Yuri Bregel,* ed. D. DeWeese (Bloomington, IN, 2001), pp. 27–56.

111. *Bukharskie dokumenty XIV veka,* ed. and tr. O. D. Chekhovich (Tashkent, 1965), pp. 108–109, 184.

112. D. Ayalon, "Preliminary Remarks on the Mamluk Military Institution in Islam," in *War, Technology and Society in the Middle East,* ed. V. J. Parry and M. E. Yapp (London, 1975), pp. 44–58.

113. For a survey of views see D. Ayalon, "The European-Asiatic Steppe: A Major Reservoir of Power for the Islamic World," in *Trudy dvadtsat piatogo mezhdunarodnogo kongressa vostokovedov* (Moscow, 1967), vol. 2, pp. 47–52; C. I. Beckwith, "Aspects of the Early History of the Central Asian Guard Corps in Islam," *Archivum Eurasiae Medii Aevi,* 4 (1984), pp. 29–43; and P. B. Golden, "Khazar Turkic Ghulams in Caliphal Service," *Journal asiatique,* 292/1–2 (2004), pp. 279–309.

114. See G. I. Bratianu, *Recherches sur le commerce génois dans la Mer Noire au XIII*[e] *siècle* (Paris, 1929), pp. 228–230; V. V. Badian and A. M. Chiperis, "Torgovlia Kaffy v XIII-XIV vv.," in *Feodal'naia Tavrika,* ed. S. I. Bibikov (Kiev, 1974), pp. 178–180, 187; I. Origo, "The Domestic Enemy: The Eastern Slaves in Tuscany in the Fourteenth and Fifteenth

Centuries," *Speculum,* 30 (1955), pp. 321–366; and the comprehensive study of L. Tardy, *Sklavenhandel in der Tartarei* (Szeged, 1983), p. 88ff.

115. A preference noted by al-ʿUmarī, *Das Mongolische Weltreich: al-ʿUmarīs Darstellung der mongolischen Reiche in seinem Werk Masālik al-abṣār fī 'l-mamālik al-amṣār,* ed. and tr. K. Lech (Wiesbaden, 1968), pp. 70, 138.

116. On these issues see Berend, *Gates of Christendom,* pp. 142–147, 171–183, 244–266; J. W. Dardess, *Conquerors and Confucians: Aspects of Political Change in Late Yuan China* (New York, 1973), p. 38ff.; and P. B. Golden, "The Qipchaqs of Medieval Eurasia: An Example of Stateless Adaptation in the Steppe," in *Rulers from the Steppe: State Formation on the Eurasian Periphery,* ed. G. Seaman (Los Angeles, 1991), pp. 132–157.

117. On the balance between these forces see P. Jackson, "The Mamluk Institution in Early Muslim India," *Journal of the Royal Asiatic Society* (1990), pp. 340–358.

118. Hok-lam Chan, "Chinese Refugees in Annam and Champa at the End of the Sung Dynasty," *Journal of Southeast Asian History,* 7/1 (1966), pp. 1–10.

119. For an overview see P. B. Golden, "'I will give the people unto thee': The Chinggisid Conquests and Their Aftermath in the Turkic World," *Journal of the Royal Asiatic Society,* 3rd ser., 10/1 (2000), pp. 21–41.

120. Rashīd al-Dīn, ed. Karīmī, vol. 1, p. 624; tr. Boyle, p. 256.

121. *Novgorodskaia pervaia letopis,* 264; *Chronicle of Novgorod,* p. 64; *Travels to Tana and Persia by Josafa Barbaro and Ambrogio Contarini,* ed. Lord Stanley of Alderley (London, 1873), p. 5; *Barbaro i Kontarini o Rossii,* tr. E. Ch. Skrzhinskaia (Leningrad, 1971), pp. 115, 137.

122. See Allsen, "Mongols and North Caucasia," pp. 34–35 and the literature cited therein.

123. Ia. A. Fedorov, *Istoricheskaia etnografiia Severnogo Kavkaza* (Moscow, 1982), pp. 100–104; P. B. Golden, *An Introduction to the History of the Turkic Peoples* (Wiesbaden, 1992), p. 391; and *Istoriia narodov Severnogo Kavkaza s drevneishikh vremen do kontsa XVIII v.,* ed. B. B. Piotrovskii (Moscow, 1988), pp. 237–238.

124. E. I. Kychanov, "Nekotorye suzhdeniia ob istoricheskikh sud'bakh Tangutov posle nashestviia Chingiskhana," *Kratkie soobshcheniia instituta narodov Azii,* 76 (1965), pp. 154–165.

125. T. I. Sultanov, *Kochevye plemena Priaral'ia v XV-XVII vv.* (Moscow, 1982), pp. 8, 15, 31, 42, 49; B. A. Akhmedov, *Gosudarstvo kochevykh Uzbekov* (Moscow, 1965), pp. 16, 46, 106.

126. Marco Polo, *Description of the World,* vol. 1, pp. 150–151, 156, 158, 178–179, 181, 182, 183.

127. Rashīd al-Dīn, ed. Karīmī, vol. 1, pp. 613, 646, 672–675; tr. Boyle, pp. 243, 283, 323–326.

128. *Yuanshi,* ch. 7, p. 137.

129. For the frontiers of the Xixia see *Zhongguo lishi ditu ji,* ed. Tan Qixiang, vol. 4: *Song, Liao, Jin de qi* (Shanghai, 1982), maps 36–37.

130. Allsen, "Uighurs of Turfan," pp. 265–267; A. A. Semenov, "Ocherk kul'turnoi roli Uigurov v mongol'skikh gosudarstvakh," in *Materialy po istorii i kul'ture uigurskogo naroda,* ed. G. S. Sadvakasov (Alma Ata, 1978), pp. 32–48.

131. Allsen, *Commodity and Exchange,* pp. 39–41.

132. Muʿīn al-Dīn Naṭanzī, *Muntakhab al-tawārīkh-i muʿīnī,* ed. J. Aubin (Tehran, 1957), p. 112.

133. Muhammad Haydar, *A History of the Moghuls of Central Asia,* tr. E. Denison Ross (rpt. New York, 1970), p. 360.

134. Ch'en Yuan, *Western and Central Asians in China under the Mongols,* tr. and ed. Ch'ien Hsing-hai and L. Carrington Goodrich (Los Angeles, 1966), pp. 57–60; P. Buell, "Saiyid Ajall," in *In the Service of the Khan: Eminent Personalities of the Early Mongol-Yuan Period (1200–1300),* ed. I. de Rachewiltz et al. (Wiesbaden, 1993), pp. 475–478; J. Herman, "The Mongol Conquest of Dali: The Failed Second Front," in *Warfare in Inner Asian History (500–1800),* ed. N. Di Cosmo (Leiden, 2002), pp. 307–314.

135. The movement of Chinese into Yunnan is carefully documented in J. Lee, "The Legacy of Immigration in Southwest China, 1250–1850," *Annales demographie historique* (1982), pp. 279–304, esp. pp. 285–289.

136. This phenomenon has been noted by a number of scholars, starting with Ricci, *China in the Sixteenth Century,* pp. 106, 324. Cf. Toynbee, *Study of History,* vol. 7, pp. 158–161; and A. M. Khazanov, "The Spread of World Religions in Medieval Nomadic Societies of the Eurasian Steppe," in *Nomadic Diplomacy, Destruction and Religion from the Pacific to the Adriatic,* ed. W. Schlepp and M. Gervers, Toronto Studies in Central and Inner Asia, no. 1 (Toronto, 1994), pp. 27–29.

137. For examples see J. Aubin, "Un Santon quhistani de l'époque timouride," *Revue des études islamiques,* 35 (1967), pp. 185–216, esp. pp. 195–196; R. Bulliet, "Medieval Nishapur: A Topographic and Demographic Reconstruction," *Studia Iranica,* 5/1 (1976), pp. 67–89, esp. pp. 69–70, 87–89; and T. Halasi-Kun, "Ottoman Data on Lesser Cumania," *Archivum Eurasiae Medii Aevi,* 4 (1984), pp. 92–124.

SEVEN

The Mongols and Nomadic Identity
The Case of the Kitans in China

Michal Biran

One of the salient aspects throughout the Eurasian steppes during and after the Mongol conquest was a major shift in ethnicity and identity. This chapter examines this phenomenon through the prism of the later history of the Kitans. My principal argument is that Mongol imperial policies played a crucial role in determining the direction of identity change among their mixed subject population,[1] and contributed to the Kitan assimilation in China more than "the cohesive force of the Chinese nation"[2] that often gets the credit for nomadic "sinicization."

The Mongols and the Ethnic Configuration of Eurasia

Peter Golden and Thomas T. Allsen have persuasively argued that the Mongol period basically reshaped the ethnic configuration of Eurasia. The crucial factors in this process were the devastation left in the wake of the initial Mongol drive; the formation of new ethnic and political taxonomies under the Mongol empire; the empire's policy of ruling via foreigner administrators; and the imperial disintegration, which forced many new collectivities to refashion their identities. These factors led to the uprooting of many hitherto well-established peoples (such as the Tanguts, the Uighurs, the Qipchaqs, and the Kitans) and to the emergence of new groupings, which form the basis of many contemporary Central Asian nations (e.g., the Uzbeks and Kazakhs). The majority of pre-Mongol steppe peoples lost their identity as ethnic groups. As a result, they were either reduced to clan or tribal units in the new collectivities that took shape in Mongol and post-Mongol Eurasia, or assimilated into the sedentary civilizations surrounding them.[3] Fascinating as it may be, this phenomenon has yet to attract a thorough investigation.[4] This study endeavors to shed light on this shift by tracing the fate of the Kitans both during and after the Mongol era.

The Kitans are indeed an illuminating case study for Eurasian identities. Throughout their pre-Mongol history, the Kitans displayed a unique ability to preserve their distinct identity. Additionally, their far-flung geographical dispersion on the eve of the Mongol invasion enables scholars to compare acculturation and identity change in different parts of the empire. Although the focus of this chapter is on the Kitans in China, it will occasionally draw insights from their counterparts in Iran.

The Kitans

The Kitans, a tribal confederation that originated in the Xianbei 鮮卑 and rose in the Mongolian-Manchurian borderland, near the Liao 遼 River, appear in historical sources from the fourth century CE onward. Falling within the orbit of both the nomadic states of Mongolia—most notably the Turk and Uighur realms—and the Chinese empire, particularly the Tang dynasty, the Kitans were consecutively subject to one or another of these polities from the sixth to ninth centuries. In the early tenth century, exploiting power vacuums in both China and Mongolia, Abaoji 阿保機 (r. 907–926) united the Kitan tribes, transformed himself into an emperor (as opposed to the loose, rotational leaders of the preimperial Kitans), and aspired to conquer both steppe and sown. In time, Abaoji founded the Liao 遼 dynasty, which ruled over Manchuria, Mongolia, and parts of north China for over two centuries (907–1125). His transition from tribal chieftain to emperor prompted substantial changes in the lifestyle and culture of the Kitan elite. However, befitting their Inner Asian character, they did not relinquish their native traditions, such as the Kitan language, shamanic rituals, origin myth, nomadic lifestyle, and elevated status of women. Instead, the Kitans added new layers to their heritage, thereby creating their own, nuanced imperial tradition. Within this framework, the royal clan adopted a surname, Yelü 耶律, and its members married exclusively women from the Xiao 蕭, a clan of Uighur origin (with its subclans of Shulü 述律 and Yaoli 姚里) that became the Liao consort clan. In parallel, the Kitans started embracing the Chinese imperial tradition, not least its trappings, including its reign titles, calendar, and the Chinese language, which they used alongside Kitan and Turkish. Other major changes were the invention of two Kitan scripts; intensive urbanization, which did not prevent the Kitans from maintaining their nomadic lifestyle (for example, the royal court's seasonal movements continued throughout the Liao dynasty); patronage of Buddhist institutions, for the purpose of enhancing the Kitans' own legitimacy; the modification of their burial customs; and the emergence of a unique and sophisticated material culture that revolved around gold. They also set up a dual administration, in which the southern branch was responsible for the sedentary population and the northern branch for the nomadic sector.

Moreover, it was during the Liao period that Chinggis Khan's forefathers migrated to Mongolia. Kitan rule in this realm, especially the unprecedented scope of urbanization and the strength of its garrisons, made a deep impression on the local nomads. In a similar vein, Kitan cities served as a platform for introducing Chinese and Kitan concepts to the Mongolian steppe. In consequence, the Mongolian word *Kitad* became the designation for north China. Moreover, the word *Cathay*—the term for China in medieval Europe as well as Western and Central Asia—derived from the ethnic affiliation (*Khitai*) of the Liao's rulers. Put differently, while preserving much of their pre-imperial traits (first and foremost the nomadic way of life) and cultivating their own imperial tradition, the Kitans were also able to portray themselves as no less Chinese than the Song both within and outside their realm.[5]

In the early twelfth century, with the fall of the Liao at the hands of the Jurchens (another wave of Manchurian invaders), most of the Kitans remained in north China under the rule of the Jurchen Jin 金 dynasty (1115–1234). However, a small group, estimated at 20,000 men, followed a Kitan prince, Yelü Dashi 耶律大石, to the west, where he swiftly established the Qara Khitai (i.e., the Liao Kitans) or Western Liao (Xi Liao 西遼) empire in Central Asia (1124–1218).[6]

The Jin Kitans reportedly numbered between 750,000 and 1.5 million men, and were treated as a separate ethnic group along with Chinese and other non-Jurchen people.[7] A handful of these Kitans, refusing to acknowledge Jin rule, moved to the forests of northern Manchuria, where they hunted for subsistence and yearned to revive the Liao.[8] That said, most of this populace placed themselves at the Jin's disposal, serving primarily as border guards.

The Kitans also played an important role in shaping the Jurchen polity, as some rose to senior positions in the Jin bureaucracy. Donning the hat of cultural agents, the Kitans introduced Chinese culture to the Jurchens. For instance, most Jurchen translations of Chinese works derived from Kitan renderings. Kitan fluency in Chinese, Mongol, and naturally their own language also qualified them for jobs as translators and emissaries.[9]

Be that as it may, relations between the Kitans and the Jurchen were not always peaceful, as Kitan rebellions were a common occurrence. The largest insurgency erupted during the reign of Jin monarch Hailing wang 海陵王 (r. 1150–1161). This confrontation was provoked by Hailing wang's forced conscription of Jin Kitan troops for his attack against the Song and by his 1161 decree calling for the liquidation of all male progeny of the Yelü clan and the Zhao 趙 (descendants of the Song royal house)—last-gasp measures aimed at neutralizing attempts to undermine his legitimacy. The rebels, though not well organized, even established their own dynasty before they were quelled by the new Jin emperor Shizong 金世宗 (r. 1161–1189). In the immediate aftermath of the failed "coup," many of the Kitan military units (*mengan mouke* 猛安謀克) were dismantled, and the troops were divided among various Jurchen units. While the regime allowed the Kitan herders to maintain their tribal divisions, the elite were ordered to change their surnames: Yelü became Yila 移剌 and Xiao became Shimo 石抹. The Jin also transferred more Kitans from the empire's northwestern frontier—one of the rebellion's strongholds—to the east, with the objective of negating the possibility that they would join forces with the Qara Khitai. In parallel, the regime consciously promoted Kitan assimilation by, say, encouraging them to marry Jurchens. These steps notwithstanding, Kitan mutinies recurred in 1177, 1183, and 1195. The insurrection of 1177 even entailed the proclamation of an independent Kitan state. Not only were all these revolts smashed, but the Jurchens subsequently carried out mass slaughters and population transfers to the east. These heavy-handed measures were accompanied by acculturation programs. In the early thirteenth century, for instance, the Jin passed several laws that were designed to abrogate the differences between Jurchen and non-Jurchen soldiers. However, these gestures were late in coming: by this time, the Kitans were well aware of the approaching Mongol storm, and many of them saw this as a golden opportunity to exact their revenge against the Jin.[10]

In the meantime, the Qara Khitai managed to build a powerful empire in Central Asia (ca. 1124 or 1131 to 1218). At its height, this polity stretched from the Oxus River in western Uzbekistan to the Altai Mountains in northeastern Xinjiang. Until 1175, the state's borders ran even further east into the Naiman and the Yenisei Kyrgyz on the fringes of western Mongolia. The population of this vast empire was heterogeneous. Besides the Kitans, who constituted but a small minority in their own domain, there were Turks (Uighurs included), Iranians, Mongols, and a few Han Chinese. While most of the populace was sedentary and Muslim, there was an appreciable nomadic component (led by the Kitans themselves) as well as flourishing Buddhist, Nestorian, and even Jewish communities.[11] The Qara Khitai's religious tolerance, their by and large indirect form of rule, their shrewd use of the Kitans' Chinese and nomadic cultural capital, and the relative prosperity and stability that they brought to Central Asia enabled the empire to govern this diverse land effectively, up to the rise of Chinggis Khan. While the original intention of the polity's above-mentioned founder, Yelü Dashi, was to restore the former boundaries of the Liao, the geopolitical situation dictated a steady westward advance, into the Muslim world. That said, the Qara Khitai continued to send spies and even small forces to the Jin border throughout the 1100s. Likewise, several Kitan rebels from North China tried to enter its territory and/or collaborate with the regime.[12] In fact, recent archaeological discoveries and philological research suggest that the Kitan character of the Qara Khitai was more pronounced than previously thought.[13]

Kitan Identity on the Eve of the Mongol Invasion

While political and geographical differences existed between the various Kitan groups, the Jin branch and the Qara Khitai shared more than a few discernible identity markers. To begin with, the Kitans in China and Central Asia were referred to and referred to themselves as Kitans or Qara Kitans (the Liao Kitans).[14] Moreover, they had a common origin myth: a man riding a white horse along the Muddy River and a woman traveling along the Huang River in a small cart drawn by a gray ox met at the confluence of these waterways by the Muye 木葉 Mountain. The two married and their eight sons became the forefathers of the eight original Kitan tribes. With the passage of time, the patriarch and matriarch were deemed to be incarnations of the god of heaven and goddess of earth. In deference to this myth, a white horse and gray ox were commonly sacrificed by Kitans before any important decision or enterprise, such as a pivotal military campaign.[15]

Another facet of this identity was the Kitan language and scripts. The Kitan language is defined as an Altaic, para-Mongolian tongue. While closer to Mongolian, it features significant Tungusic elements. The two Kitan scripts, which were created in the early 900s as part of the Liao dynasty's formation, are both Sinitic. Despite considerable progress on the small Kitan script in recent years (thanks mainly to the unearthing of tomb inscriptions), neither script has yet been fully deciphered.[16] Even in the heyday of the Liao dynasty, however, other scripts were also employed, with Chinese serving as the principal diplomatic and administrative language. Both the Qara Khitai and the Jin Kitans continued to use the Kitan scripts (in Jin China up to 1191, when it was banned), side by side with other languages and scripts: mainly Chinese and Jurchen under the Jin and Chinese, Persian, and Uighur among the Qara Khitai.[17]

The Kitans continued to wax nostalgic for the halcyon days of the Liao and its original center—the land of the pines and deserts (*songmo* 松漠) along the Liao River. These sentiments could easily arouse antagonism toward the Jurchens for having destroyed the Liao. Regardless of their location, Kitan members of the royal and consort clans retained their prestige, standing, selective connubial patterns (though they also took non-Kitan spouses), and distinct surnames. Furthermore, the royal clan upheld its nomadic social norms, including the high position of women in politics.[18] Another part of the Liao legacy that was preserved by the Kitans in China and Central Asia was their reverence for the Chinese imperial tradition. The extent of this dedication is hard to gauge, but the upper-class Jin Kitans and Qara Khitai were certainly familiar with Chinese trappings and exhibited a command of the language.[19]

The Jurchens were well aware of the affinity between the two Kitan groups. In fact, the fear that they would one day unite loomed large over the Jin's foreign and domestic policies.[20] While this threat never materialized, the existence of the independent Qara Khitai was apparently meaningful to the Kitans in the Jin. Kindling their hope to restore the Liao, it also buoyed their Kitan identity. For instance, upon accompanying Chinggis Khan to Central Asia in the 1220s, Yelü Chucai 耶律楚材, a Kitan from the Jin, collected every bit of information he could find about the Qara Khitai.[21]

On the eve of the Mongol conquest, the Kitans in China found themselves in a unique position. As Rashīd al-Dīn observed, the Kitans were "adjacent to the Mongol nomads, and their language, physiognomy and customs are quite similar."[22] Put differently, the two groups shared a resemblance in terms of their nomadic lifestyle, combat tactics, rituals, and language.[23] Another Kitan advantage was their expertise in the sedentary culture of China. This dual nomadic–Chinese identity made the Kitans extremely useful to the Mongols during their expansion. What is more, it would ultimately facilitate their assimilation into one of the two societies.

The Mongol Conquest of the Kitans

By dint of the Mongol conquests, the assorted Kitan groups all found themselves under the same authority. However, instead of leading to their unification, this turn of events scattered their communities throughout the Eurasian continent.

Both the Qara Khitai and the Jin Kitans were subsumed by the Mongol empire in the early thirteenth century, during the first stages of its expansion. Mongol assaults into Jin territories began in 1211. Within four years, they had entered the Jin capital of Zhongdu 中都 or Yanjing 燕京 (near modern Beijing), compelling the Jurchens to take flight southward to Kaifeng. However, Chinggis Khan soon turned his attention to the west. In 1218, his forces seized the Qara Khitai territory in what was a swift and uncharacteristically benign campaign, before proceeding into Central Asia. Although Chinggis Khan dispatched General Muqali (in 1217–1223) to reengage the Jin, this rather bloody affair was only completed in 1234 (by Ögödei, Chinggis Khan's son and heir). While a fair share of Kitans died in battle against the Mongols, most of them chose to switch over to the juggernaut at an early stage of the conquests.[24] By so doing, they averted the catastrophe that befell several of their contemporaries—the Tanguts, the Qipchaqs, and Khwārazmians included. More specifically, the Kitans became allies of the Mongols and heavily influenced the formation of the world empire.

The Database

Before exploring the ramifications of the Mongols' ascent on Kitan identity, a few words about the database that undergirded this study are in order. Yuan sources cite the names of over two hundred Kitans who were active in Mongol China. About half of these figures surface in the dynastic history, the *Yuanshi* 元史, whereas the remainder are scattered in, above all, Yuan literary collections (*wenji* 文集), epitaphs, and local gazetteers. A few prominent Kitans also turn up in Muslim sources, foremost among them records from the Ilkhanate. Some of these individuals are explicitly referred to as Kitans or "Liao people" (Liao ren 遼人), while others have been identified on the basis of their distinctive surnames: Yelü/Yila, Shimo/Shulü, and Xiao. Since the last is also a Chinese surname, if a Xiao is not specifically described as a Kitan or Liao, s/he was excluded from this survey.[25]

It bears noting that the information about many of these Kitans is limited to their name and occasionally their position or the odd biographical note (e.g., son of so and so, filial son, died young). For the more important figures, however, there are more detailed sources that allow us to track certain families over several generations.[26] In addition, the data is elite-biased. Since most of the rank-and-file Kitans lacked surnames, their identity has evidently passed under the radar. Although a few women appear in the sources, the list is male dominated. The Kitans in China practiced a wide range of professions (most exotically, a *fengshui* expert and a sculptor specializing in Buddhist images), yet most of the well-documented Kitans were military men.[27] Notable exceptions are Yelü Chucai (1189–1243), Chinggis Khan's astrologer and Ögödei's chief minister, and Yelü Youshang 耶律有尚 (d. 1320), a celebrated Confucian scholar.

Main Factors behind Identity Change

Over the next few pages, we will explore two developments that had a major impact on the Kitan identity: the loss of the Kitans' political frameworks and their geographical distribution. This will be followed by a discussion of the two main paths of Kitan assimilation, each of which roughly corresponds to its own period. The first phase is the absorption into the Mongol ranks, which was most salient in the conquests period, from the united Mongol empire period (1206–1260) to the fall of the Song (1279). During this time, the Kitans played a more active role in the Mongol army and administration, so that they feature more prominently in the relevant sources. Throughout the postconquest period (1279–1368), the main thrust of Kitan assimilation was in the Chinese realm. The primary impetus behind this shift was that the Mongols were now less dependent on the Kitans and thus less willing to accept them in their midst. Accordingly, the number of Kitans mentioned in the source material decreases significantly, but this drop-off might also stem in part from the nature of the documents rather than the processes under review.[28] In the pages to come, we will take stock of the main incentives behind identity change at each of these stages and the manifestations of this trend.

The Breakup of the Kitan Political Framework: The Rise and Fall of Yelü Liuge's State

Identity in China and, all the more so, on the steppe was largely political. For this reason, the mere existence of the Qara Khitai empire and the pining for the Liao significantly bolstered Kitan identity among the Jin Kitans. Soon after Chinggis Khan invaded the Jin, a Kitan commander established a short-lived Kitan state in Manchuria (1213–1233 or 1236), under Mongol dominion. The founder was Yelü Liuge 耶律 留哥 (1174–1220), a descendant of the Liao royal family who had served as a commander of a thousand in the Jin army. While heading an army totaling an estimated 100,000 Kitans, Liuge surrendered to the Mongols in 1212. That said, he was not the first Kitan who submitted to Chinggis Khan. Among the ruler's closest supporters were several other Kitan noblemen, some of whom had joined Temüjin even before he assumed the title Chinggis Khan. However, while the other Kitans joined the empire as individuals, Liuge came as a leader who aspired to build a Kitan state.[29] After defeating Jin troops with Mongol help in 1213, his followers (allegedly 600,000 men!) enthroned him as the king of Liao (*Liao wang* 遼王) in the Kitans' ancestral land of Liaodong. The new state was called "the Great Liao" (Da Liao 大遼), thereby restoring its namesake after more than a century of Jin rule. The recently enthroned monarch chose a reign title and conferred Chinese honorifics on his wife and several of his leading followers. Most importantly, these steps were reminiscent of those taken by Yelü Dashi upon establishing the Qara Khitai dynasty in 1124.[30] What is more, the Great Liao featured many of the aforementioned

Kitan identity markers, such as the tribal religion, the trappings of Chinese imperial tradition (reign titles, seals, etc.), the elite status of the Yelü clan, and the lofty standing of women. Last but not least, a considerable portion of the state's residents was Kitan.

Symbolism aside, the Great Liao failed to attract most of the Kitans or forge a sustainable political entity. One of the reasons for these shortcomings was the domestic instability that plagued the new Liao dynasty. After a series of victories against the Jin in 1215, elements within the polity's top brass demanded that Liuge promote himself from king to emperor, so as to assume an equal footing with Chinggis Khan and his Jin counterpart. When Liuge declined, on the grounds that this contradicted the terms of surrender with the Mongols (not to mention the true balance of power), they mutinied against him, enthroned his viceroy as emperor, and raided Korea.

The rebels viewed themselves as the Liao's true heirs. For example, they demanded that the Koreans submit to the newfangled entity. In so doing, they were harking back to the Kitans' dominion over Korea from the tenth to the twelfth centuries.[31] Correspondingly, Liuge hastened to ask for Chinggis Khan's help in this "civil war." As a token of his allegiance, he presented the emperor with his eldest son, Xuedu 薛闍, as a hostage. Only in 1219, with the assistance of Mongols, as well as Korean and Jurchen defectors, did Liuge finally manage to stamp out the insurrection of this "fake Liao state" (*wei Liao guo* 偽遼國). However, by then, he and his state had lost much of their power.[32] Following the victory, some of the rebellious Kitans were given to the Koreans in return for their military services, while others chose to stay on the peninsula. In addition, a considerable portion of the defeated troops—reportedly 50,000 Kitans—was divided among various Mongol units.

Liuge died soon after the triumph (1220), without having consolidated his realm. Centered in Guangning 廣寧 (part of modern-day Liaoning), the Great Liao continued to exist under the rule of his widow and then his son, Xuedu. Fighting alongside Ögödei in Korea between 1230 and 1237, Xuedu "liberated" over 6,000 Kitan households and brought them to Guangning. However, the successes of both father and son were not enough to avert the downfall of their state. Already in 1227, when Chinggis Khan sent Xuedu back to Manchuria to head his father's state, he instructed him to share the command of his armies with the khan's younger brother, Belgütei (Bolugutai, 孛魯古台). In 1233 or 1236, Ögödei formally abolished the Liao entity, adding the Guangning region to Belgütei's appanage. Nevertheless, Liuge's sons and grandsons continued to serve in the Mongol army and acquitted themselves well in battles against Korea, the Jin, and the Song. They continued to lead the Guangning troops and administer the region until 1269 when it was placed under the purview of Liaoyang, the Jin's eastern capital. Henceforth, there would be no other attempts to set up a Kitan state under Mongol rule.[33]

All the blame for the abolishment of the Great Liao cannot be placed entirely on Liuge's failure to secure an alliance with fellow Kitans, for the consolidation of Ögödei's holdings in north China also played an instrumental role. So long as the Jin war raged on, the Mongols tolerated the handful of kingdoms that were established in Manchuria by various Jin defectors, who had exploited the temporary power vacuum in the area since 1214. When the Jin finally succumbed in 1234, these states were no longer of any use to the Mongols, and Ögödei preferred to subsume Manchuria—a region that was partly suited for nomadism and close to Mongolia—under his direct rule. "The time of the petty kings," as Rashīd al-Dīn put it, "was over."[34] As a result, the Kitans in China no longer had a political framework to help them retain their identity. Moreover, the termination of both the Qara Khitai and the Jin (the Kitans' foil and arch rivals) also accelerated the decline of Kitan identity and encouraged them to throw in their lot with the Mongols.

At around the same time, the remnants of the Qara Khitai royal house were manipulating the upheavals that were instigated by the Mongol invasion on the other side of the steppe for their own benefit. More specifically, Baraq Ḥājib, a scion of the Qara Khitai royal house, founded a Kitan state in Kirmān (a province in southern Iran) in 1222. While also bearing the name Qara Khitai, this incarnation had limited political and territorial ambitions, as its monarchy was subject to both the Mongols and the Abbasid caliph. Located in a comparatively marginal area of the Mongol empire, outside the steppe belt and far from Mongolia, the area was moderately conducive to transhumance.[35] It existed as a vassal of the united Mongol empire and then the Ilkhanate until 1306, when the polity was dismantled either for neglecting to pay its dues to the Mongols or as part of Ilkhan Öljeitü's efforts to centralize his administration. While retaining fewer Kitan markers (the most prominent of which was the elevated status of women) and despite its rulers' conversion to Islam (a step that the Qara Khitai had eschewed in Central Asia), the mere existence of this state enabled the Kitans to hang on to their identity, if only in name. However, their "Kitanness" frayed in the immediate aftermath of the Qara Khitai's dissolution, which only reinforced their assimilatory mind-set.[36]

Geographical Dispersion: Population Movements and Their Impact

As demonstrated in Allsen's chapter in this volume, one of the distinguishing features of Mongol rule was the colossal population movements that were triggered by its armies' advance. In this respect, the Kitans were no exception. Due to their early incorporation into the Mongol ranks and their value as both nomadic soldiers and qualified administrators, Kitans were indeed dispatched across the Eurasian continent to serve the needs of the ever-expanding empire. However, even before their integration, Chinggis Khan's attacks against the Jin spawned Kitan refugees. Many escaped with the Jin court to Kaifeng in 1214, where they subsequently fought against the Mongols, and a few Kitans migrated to the lands of the Song.[37] With respect to those under the empire's rule, Chinggis and his successors transferred farmers to Central Asia with the objective of repopulating areas that were devastated by war. In addition, one of Chinggis Khan's earliest Kitan supporters, Yelü Ahai 耶律 阿海, was appointed governor of Transoxania, a position later held by his son.[38]

At any rate, the prime catalyst of Kitan relocation was military deployment. The Kitans indeed made substantial military and administrative contributions in the Jin campaigns (1211–1215, 1217–1223, and 1229–1234) as the Mongols took full advantage of their close familiarity with the terrain and its inhabitants.[39] Both as groups and individuals, they also took part in all the empire's other major battles: Korea in the 1210s–1230s, where some of the troops settled down following the mutiny against Liuge; Chinggis Khan's campaign in Central Asia (1220–1225); the Eastern European front during Ögödei's reign (1237–1241); the fighting in the Middle East under Hülegü during the 1250s; Möngke's battles in Sichuan (1258–1259); and Qubilai's conquest of the Dali kingdom (1253–1256) and the Song dynasty (1268–1279).[40]

Most of the Kitan-related information in the Chinese sources pertains to those who returned to China. However, it stands to reason that some fell on the battlefield and others remained in their new locations.[41] With respect to north China, while a substantial Kitan population indeed remained in Manchuria and Inner Mongolia, after 1215, the region of Yanjing (or Zhongdu, near present-day Beijing) was by and large administered by Kitans and became a central destination for ordinary Kitan migrants as well.[42] In general, the later distribution, especially after the sixteenth century, of tribal names and toponyms across Eurasia bearing the word *Khitai/Khatai* is reflective of the magnitude of Kitan dispersion, which probably included the descendants of the Qara Khitai.[43] In the thirteenth century, this Eurasia-wide movement considerably thinned the original Kitans' ranks.

The division of the Mongol empire into the four khanates engendered a formidable shift in the patterns of Kitan mobility, largely confining its purview to the Yuan's borders where it assumed a southward trajectory. While south China's flourishing economy might have influenced this turn of events, most recorded cases of migration were initiated by the Mongols, especially their military and administrative appointments. After the conquest of the Song, the empire returned the majority of its "ethnically" Mongol forces to the north, while garrisoning the new army (former Song units) and the Han army in the south. By this juncture, most of the Kitan troops were in the Han army, so that they were primarily serving in south and southwestern China.[44] Similarly, the lion's share of documented administrative appointments of Kitans after 1279 were in south China, particularly Huguang 湖廣, Yunnan 雲南, Sichuan 四川, Jiangnan 江南, Zhejiang 浙江, and Jiangxi 江西.[45] It is not uncommon to find several generations of one family spread out in various parts of China, with the last generation located in the south. For example, the family of the brothers Yelü Ahai and Tuhua originated in Inner Mongolia. Both men joined Temüjin in Mongolia before the Baljuna Covenant (1203) and took part in the early battles against the Jin in north China. Ahai accompanied Chinggis Khan to Central Asia and was assigned to administer Transoxania, where he died in approximately 1223. His son Miansige 綿思哥 inherited the post in Samarqand, but returned to China following the Ṭarabī rebellion (1238–1239) and then was appointed as *darughachi* (governor) of Zhongdu. In the meantime, one of his siblings became left prime minister of Liaodong, and another commanded the Kitan and Han army in Zhongdu. Miansige's son Maige 買哥 succeeded his father in Zhongdu; however, in 1258, he went to fight in Sichuan and was killed in action. Of his seven sons, only two left an imprint: Laoge 老哥 was a right prime minister, probably in the capital of Dadu (Beijing); Luma 驢馬, a *bitikchi* (scribe) in the guard, was stationed nearby. In 1288, Luma was sent to put down a revolt that was launched by Qadan (Hadan 哈丹 or Hadan tuolugan 哈丹禿魯干), a descendant of Chinggis Khan's brother who joined Nayan's rebellion in Manchuria. His post was inherited by one of his six sons. The other three sons for whom there is data were stationed to the south in Jiangxi, Huguang, and Zhejiang, respectively.[46]

Ahai's brother, Yelü Tuhua, was in the vanguard of both the first (1211–1214) and second (Muqali-led) waves of Mongol attacks on the Jin. His two sons resided in Shaanxi 陝西 during the 1230s and 1240s, where they filled military and administrative posts and sponsored Daoist activities. In the following decade, they took part in the campaigns against the Song in Sichuan. Apart from a grandson of a lesser wife who was sent to administer Weijinglu 衛輝路 in Henan 河南 during the early 1260s, the next generation of this family remained in Sichuan. Tuhua's grandsons continued to lock horns with the Song from 1260 to 1278 and some fell in action. His great-grandson Mangudai 忙古帶 (1250–1307) was born in Shaanxi, but migrated to Sichuan with his father before the age of ten. After proving himself in the battles of

Sichuan, Mangudai was transferred to Yunnan in the early 1280s. At this point in his career, he waged war against various minor kingdoms, invaded Vietnam, and put down local revolts. He died in 1307 while serving as both a general and left prime minister of Yunnan's mobile secretariat. Mengudai's two surviving sons (one of whom died young, leaving behind a pair of small children) also held positions in Yunnan. Reservations aside, some scholars consider Tuhua and his offspring to be the forefathers of the modern-day Yunnan Kitans.[47] From our standpoint, though, the crux of this narrative is that by the end of the 1200s, the fourth and fifth generations of this Inner Mongolian family were mostly settled in different parts of south China, and the same could be said for numerous other Kitan families.[48]

Paths of Identity Change

Mongolization

The abolition of the Kitan political framework and the people's geographic dispersion precipitated slippage in their ethnic identity. What is more, the empire's unprecedented success encouraged the Kitans, as well as many other groups, to identify with the victors and "become Mongols."[49] The above-mentioned similarities between the Kitans and Mongols in all that concerned language, physiognomy, and customs undoubtedly facilitated this process, as did the two groups' interaction in the military. This sense of unity comes across in the dialogue that was presumably held between Chinggis Khan and Yaoli Shi (姚里氏, i.e., "of the Yaoli clan," a subclan of the Xiao), Liuge's widow and successor.[50] Upon the emperor's return from Central Asia in 1225, Yaoli Shi, along with Liuge's younger sons, a grandson, and nephew, paid him a visit in the Tanguts' land. She asked Chinggis to accept her and Liuge's son, Shange 善哥, as a replacement for Liuge's eldest son, Xuedu—the above-mentioned hostage who was entrusted to him in 1216—so that the firstborn could succeed his father as head of the Liao state. Chinggis replied that

> Xuedu is already a Mongol. He followed us to the Western Regions; and when the Muslims surrounded the heir apparent in the city of Khwārazm,[51] Xuedu whisked him to safety with a thousand men, though he himself was wounded by a lance. He also fought with us against the Muslims in Bukhara and Samarqand and was struck by an arrow. Because he repeatedly rendered such services, he was given [the title] *Badoulu* [拔都魯 = Bagatur or Bahadur = Brave]. I cannot part with him; let Shange inherit his father's post instead.[52]

In sum, what makes one a Mongol, according to the great khan, is the bond between comrades-in-arms, excelling in warfare, and proven loyalty. Since most of the documented Kitans were soldiers, this path was readily available to them.

This dialogue also attests to Chinggis Khan's willingness to accept the Kitans into the Mongol ranks. The evidence strongly suggests that this path was open, above all, to those who had joined his army before the 1206 *quriltai* or during the Mongols' initial assaults against the Jin, where the Kitans' efforts were particularly valuable. Early defectors from the Jin were treated as *nökers* (companions, i.e., individuals who voluntarily detached themselves from their own clan to join the promising leader and become part of his tribe), and attained status and privileges that were on par with those of the Mongols.[53]

As a result, seniority in Mongol service, namely early capitulation to Chinggis Khan, became a valuable form of social capital for the Kitan elite families documented in the *Yuanshi,* in addition to high standing under the Liao or Jin, if there was any.[54] This sort of dedication, which was often the basis for a Kitan's appointment to hereditary posts, was also immensely appreciated by later Mongol khans, like Qubilai.[55]

The Mongol willingness to accept Kitans in their midst found expression in the bestowment of Mongolian names, nicknames, and titles on leading Kitan allies, although the conferring of Chinese titles was more prevalent even at the outset of the Mongols' expansion.[56] This in turn increased the popularity of Mongolian names among the Kitans, although quite a few Kitans bore both Mongolian and Chinese appellations in tandem.[57] While the conferred Mongolian names and titles appear mainly in the united empire period, the practice of taking Mongolian names lasted throughout the Yuan era and was also commonplace among non-Kitan segments of the Yuan polity, including its Chinese subjects. One reason for the popularity of adopting a Mongolian name was that it could help its possessor attain a job that was theoretically reserved for Mongols.[58]

There are also a few recorded cases of Mongols conferring Mongolian wives on their choice allies. These women often entered polygamous households. For instance, Chinggis Khan gave Yelü Ahai a Mongolian wife to compensate him for the Jin's detention of his original family after he crossed over to the Mongols.[59] Shimo Yexian, another early defector, had multiple spouses: a Mongolian, who was his principal wife; a Chinese woman from the Xiao 肖 clan (not the Kitan Xiao); and a member of the Kitan Yelü clan.[60] Yexian's son and one of his great-grandsons married Qonggirad Mongols.[61] Yelü Zhu 耶律鑄 (1221–1285), the son of Yelü Chucai, had six Mongolian wives (two from Chinggis' Kiyat clan), a Christian spouse (who might have been also a Mongol), and another of indeterminate ethnicity, though not a Kitan. Two of his sons also took Mongolian wives. Unlike Yexian and Ahai, Zhu eschewed the Kitan custom whereby royal Kitans marry women from the Xiao clan.[62]

All the above does not mean, however, that, at this stage, the Kitans were eager to shed their identity or neglect its Chinese component. However, Yelü Zhu embodies the nuances of "Kitanness" during his age. Besides his six Mongolian wives, Zhu was born in Chinggis Khan's camp in Central Asia, grew up in Ögödei's guard in Mongolia, won fame as a rider and archer, and possessed a Mongolian nickname (Tughus, i.e., peacock). Moreover, thanks to his close ties with the khan, he played an important role in selecting the location of the imperial capital, Qaraqorum. His Mongolian bona fides notwithstanding, when Zhu was sent by Möngke to collect land taxes from Yanjing, he issued the following request: "All my ancestors read Confucian books; Confucian scholars (*rusheng* 儒生) dwell on the Central Plain. [Therefore,] I would like to take along my son to Yan[jing] so he can study with a distinguished teacher."[63] Möngke duly granted Zhu his wish. Both father and son (the latter, Yelü Xiliang 耶律希亮, was born to a Mongol women and married a Jalayirid Mongol) enjoyed illustrious careers in the Yuan civil administration and wrote Chinese literary collections.[64] By virtue of such expertise in Chinese language and culture, Kitans served as intermediaries between the Mongols and the Chinese. Many were given administrative positions in China. What is more, quite a few Kitan figures are credited with talking their masters out of destroying Chinese cities.[65]

It stands to reason that those Kitans who consorted primarily with Mongols, be it their fellow soldiers in the invading armies or their associates in Manchuria and eastern Inner Mongolia (parts of which remained under Mongol rule after the Yuan collapse in 1368), gradually assimilated into Mongol society. A reference from Qubilai's time (1284) indeed notes that, unlike "ordinary" Kitans (and Jurchens), those "who were born in the northwest and do not speak Chinese" should be treated like Mongols.[66] The appearance of the surname Yelü in Monggoljin and Juu Uda (areas of Inner Mongolia near the Kitan homeland) indeed reinforces this argument.[67] Similarly, the language of the Dagurs (Daurs)—a Mongolian-speaking minority currently inhabiting northeast Inner Mongolia and Manchuria—resembles Kitan. According to the Dagurs' tradition, they are of Kitan descent and might indeed be the progeny of these same Mongolized Kitans.[68]

From Mongols to Chinese

Once the empire stabilized, and certainly after the conquests, the Mongols were less in need of the Kitans' above-mentioned services as soldiers and intermediaries, so that their willingness to accept the Kitans (and others) as full-fledged Mongols gradually declined. As a result, the Kitans turned to Chinese society as their target for assimilation. More than anything else, three Mongol policies are responsible for this development: their military reforms; the transfer of Kitans to South China; and, above all, the Kitans' classification as Hanren (Northern Chinese).

As discussed above, the army played a key role in identity change. While the military indeed constituted a melting pot that forged an imperial identity, especially for those Kitans in the Mongol guards or those scattered among different Mongol units, it concomitantly served as a framework for preserving the ancestral identity of those in Kitan units that remained intact or were commanded by fellow Kitans. In any event, within the framework of Chinggis Khan's reforms, military units replaced most tribal units as the lodestone of identity.[69] Quite a few of the early Kitan leaders of the anti-Jin insurgency joined the Mongols with their retainers, many of whom were probably Kitans. At least at the start, these figures continued to preside over their troops.[70] In fact, the modern-day Yunnan Kitans, a group consisting of approximately 150,000 people, claim to descend from the Kitan troops who arrived in the region under the command of Yelü Menggudai, Tuhua's grandson, in the 1280s.[71] Yuan sources also mention several units that featured a massive Kitan presence: naturally "the Kitan army" (Qidan jun 契丹軍), as Liuge's troops were sometimes called; the Black army (Hei jun 黑軍), a unit comprised of 12,000 "top soldiers," which was led by Shimo Yexian and his heirs; and the *Jiu* army (Jiu jun 糺軍, Mongolian Jüyin).[72] The literal meaning of *jiu* is "mixed" or "merged." Accordingly, the Jiu army consisted of a wide array of ethnicities (including Kitans, Jurchens, Tatars, Tanguts, and Ongguts). Living along and beyond the Jin frontier zone, they worked for the Jurchens as border patrol troops. In essence, the Jiu were comprised of several groups, which were primarily distinguished by their location along the border areas (e.g., the Jiu of the Northwest, etc.). Some of them, Kitans included, rebelled against the Jin as early as 1207, whereas others were incorporated into the Mongol army at various stages of the empire's conquest of the Jurchen realm.[73]

At any rate, these units were gradually disbanded. In addition, the lion's share of the Jiu army was dissolved and its troops were allocated to various Mongol units. For instance, upon defeating the "Juyin troops of the Qara Khidat and the Jurchen" in around 1214, Chinggis Khan divided them among his trusted allies Muqali and Bo'urchu.[74] A significant portion of Liuge's forces eventually underwent a similar process. As already noted, some fifty years later, his descendants would lose their command posts in the army of Guanning (where the Kitan army's troops had settled). Likewise, the

Black army was dispersed between 1295 and 1311, "for these were days of peace."[75]

In parallel, the standing of the Kitans' hereditary military leaders was compromised by the reforms of Ögödei and, above all, Qubilai. As the conquest of China proceeded, the number of non-Mongols, especially Chinese, in the imperial army swelled. Most of the Kitans were incorporated into the Han army, which Ögödei set up in the aftermath of his victory over the Jin. Nevertheless, some of the hereditary families still fought under the command of Mongol princes.[76] However, after putting down the rebellion of Li Tan (理談, a Chinese military leader who betrayed his new lords) in 1262, Qubilai introduced his above-mentioned reform: military and civilian power were separated; the relatives of officers were stripped of their military positions; authority over the conscription of troops and supplies was delegated away from the commanders; and the latter were placed under the direct supervision of imperial guards. In so doing, Qubilai substantially reduced the power of the non-Mongol hereditary lords, Kitans or otherwise.[77]

With the end of the conquest, the shared Mongol–Kitan military experience was significantly reduced. Following the defeat of the Song, the empire transferred its Mongol troops back to the north and stationed units of the Han army and the newly conquered army (Song troops) in the south. By then, most of the Kitans already belonged to the Han army, so that many were garrisoned in south China, especially Jiangnan, where they could not practice nomadism.[78] The steady decline of the Yuan army between the late thirteenth century and early to mid-fourteenth century further eroded the Kitan commanders' sway and diminished their contact with the Mongol brass. From Qubilai's time onward, the symbiosis between the Kitans and Mongols in the imperial army steadily gave way to a Kitan–Chinese bond.

The Mongols transferred not only military personnel to the south, but administrative officials as well. The only relatives that accompanied these officials to their new locations were their nuclear families, and these Kitans rarely came back north. Because south China was inhospitable to nomadism, most of these administrators (like their fellow Kitan soldiers) were forced to give up their nomadic way of life, which was a major facet of their Kitan identity. In addition, this trajectory ratcheted up their contacts with the Chinese, who vastly outnumbered all the other ethnic groups in the south. As demonstrated above, these policies also dispersed Kitan communities, thereby making it difficult for individuals to find a wife from the same background. Consequently, Kitan intermarriage with Han women skyrocketed toward the mid- to late Yuan period.[79]

A no less significant factor in the Kitans' absorption into Chinese society was their classification as Hanren. In the wake of the Song's elimination, the Yuan state divided its subject population into four classes: 1) Mongols; 2) people of various categories (Semuren 色目人); 3) northerners or northern Chinese (Hanren 漢人); and 4) southerners (Nanren 南人). The Kitans were classified as Hanren, together with the Jurchens, the Northern Chinese, and the tribes of Yunnan and Sichuan—all of which fell under the Mongol yoke before Qubilai assumed the helm in 1260. Most of the other steppe peoples, such as the Uighurs, Tanguts, Khwārazmians, and Qipchaqs, fell under the heading of Semuren—a more privileged class than that of the Kitan.[80] Put differently, the Kitans' official status was lower than that of the Mongols and Semuren. Although this division was not always clear-cut or rigorously enforced, many senior-level posts were now less accessible to Kitans.[81] The state's official hierarchy thus hindered their assimilation into the Mongols' ranks. In fact, from Qubilai's time onward, the number of Kitans that are mentioned in Yuan sources consistently drops.

On the other hand, the Kitans' acceptance into Chinese society was bolstered by their familiarity with the Chinese language and culture as well as the diversity of Mongol-ruled China. Furthermore, their integration was buoyed by their ability to retain Kitan age-old social norms, such as levirate marriages and the elevated status of military officers. Historically speaking, these norms were incompatible with Chinese traditions, but during the Yuan era they were partially countenanced thanks to Mongol influence.[82] Documented references to the Kitans as filial sons or chaste wives, that is, exemplary Confucians, also attest to their smooth assimilation into Chinese society.[83]

The most conspicuous sign of Kitan inroads into Chinese society was the adoption of local surnames. As opposed to their experience under the Jin, this transpired without any external pressure. Taking a Chinese family name was a shortcut to acceptance into Chinese ranks, for it negated the most glaring sign of otherness—a multisyllable surname.[84] In some instances, the name change had more to do with personal circumstances. For example, a Kitan surnamed Shimo was orphaned at the age of seven. Raised by a Chinese family, he took the name of his adoptive parents, Zheng 鄭.[85] More often than not, Chinese surnames were chosen with historical or phonetic considerations in mind. The most popular Chinese family name among Kitans was Liu 劉, on account of its vocal similarity to Yelü and its prestige as the surname of Han dynasty emperors. Other popular choices were Li 李 and Wang 王. While the former was the family name that Tang rulers had conferred upon the elites of their Kitan vassals, Wang literally means king or prince, so that it preserved the memory of the Kitans' royal ancestry. Most families with the name Xiao 萧 simply held on to this appellation, for it is also a Chinese surname. Some Xiao who had changed their name to Shimo or Shulü eventually reverted back to the original. In Yunnan, the name Yelü was usually changed to Alu 阿律; thereafter, it was pared down to A 阿, in deference to the first character in the name Abaoji, the founder of the Liao dynasty.[86] At the outset of this symbiosis, the Kitan and Chinese family names were often used simultaneously, but the latter eventually supplanted their antecedents.[87] From the standpoint of the present study, the most important trend is that, with the exception of the Yunnan case, the surnames that the Kitans adopted rendered them indistinguishable from the Chinese. In contrast, the Uighurs adopted rare Chinese characters, such as Xie 偰 or Lian 廉, as their Chinese surnames, which continued to serve as ethnic markers.[88] For the Kitans, though, the use of Chinese surnames was both a sign of assimilation and an incentive to continue along this path. It also meant that the Kitans became almost untraceable in late Yuan sources. In fact, Ming sources (1368–1644) treat Kitan identity as a past affiliation that was no longer in force.[89]

Two cases of Kitans who retained their ancestral identity until the end of the Yuan era promise to shed light on the multicultural identities of Yuan society. The first is Shimo Yisun 石抹宜孫 (d. 1359). His great-grandfather Shimo Yexian was one of the northern Manchurian Kitans who refused to acknowledge Jin rule and wasted no time in switching his allegiance to Chinggis Khan. Yisun inherited his father's Black army post as *Yanhai shang fu wanhu* 沿海上副万户 (the vice-commander of 10,000 of the coast), before being transferred to Chuzho 處州, Zhejiang. In addition to his military pedigree, Yisun was famous for his erudition in all that concerned Chinese culture. He evidently acquired this learning from his father, also known as a general and scholar, who was well versed in, among other things, classics, astronomy, and geography. Moreover, both father and son had a Chinese-style name (*zi* 字). The younger Shimo was a talented poet, prolific reader, and close friend of preeminent Confucian scholars, not least Song Lian 宋濂 and Liu Ji 劉基. Beginning in 1351, Yisun took an active and highly commended part in repulsing a litany of anti-Yuan insurrections in the Zhejiang and Jiangsu regions. Unlike his Confucian friends, he refused to desert the Yuan for the emergent Zhu Yuanzhang 朱元璋, who eventually founded the Ming dynasty. When Ming troops conquered Chuzhou in 1360, Yisun escaped to Fujian, where he sought to recruit an army with which to retake the city. Upon realizing that his efforts were in vain, the commander returned to Chuzhou where he was killed in defense of the Yuan cause. By virtue of his loyalty, Yisun was honored posthumously by none other than

Zhu Yuanzhang himself.[90] In sum, Shimo Yisun was a scholar-general who was proud of his Liao descent, expressed his allegiance to the Mongol cause both in Confucian terms and on the battlefield, and was well-versed in Chinese literary tradition.

These same characteristics also apply to our second example, the Kitan general and poet Shulü Jie 述律傑 (d. 1357), who went by a handful of other names: Shulü Duoerzi (述律朵兒只 or 鐸爾直), a Kitan surname that he used in concert with a Mongolian first name; Shulü Cundao 述律存道, Shulü Zundao 述律 遵道, or Shulü Congdao 述律從道, which feature his Chinese-style name (Cundao with the variants Zundao and Congdao) instead of his Chinese or Mongolian first names; and, mostly among Chinese scholars, as Xiao Cundao 肖存道, a purely Chinese name, or in his literary name (*hao* 號), Heye 鶴野). In any event, between 1332 and 1340, Jie uncharacteristically changed the family name Shimo back to Shulü, an act that bears witness to abiding feelings for his Kitan origins.

Shulü Jie was the grandson of Shimo Anzhi, another early backer of Chinggis Khan. The family moved to Sichuan during Möngke's reign, and Jie inherited his father's post as commander of 10,000 in Baoning 保寧, Sichuan. Falling under his jurisdiction was the city of Chengdu 成都, where he built his home with his Yelü wife, established an academy for classical learning, and assumed responsibility for the imperial examinations that were conducted therein. After years of suppressing rebellions and getting involved in the succession struggles that roiled the area's capital cities of Shaanxi, Sichuan, and Yunnan, he was dispatched to the Yunnan in 1340. There he served as commander in chief (*Yunnan duyuan shuai* 云南都元帥) and was subsequently delegated administrative duties as well. While coping with yet another mutiny in 1356 (this time in Shaanxi), Jie perished on the field of battle. Apart for his military career, the Kitan nobleman was a highly regarded poet who was well versed in Chinese literature. Lastly, Shulü Jie was on close terms with a wide array of distinguished Yuan scholars (e.g., Su Tianjue 蘇天爵, Yu Ji 虞集, and Huang Jin 黃晉), many of whom referred to him in their writing.[91]

While retaining some ancestral characteristics, the late Yuan Kitans were deeply assimilated into Chinese society and culture. Accordingly, the modern-day Yunnan Kitans, who claim to derive from their Yuan namesakes, are presently classified as Hanren in China, rather than a separate minority.[92]

Conclusion

In summation, the Kitans embraced cultural pluralism long before the rise of Chinggis Khan. Upon first encountering the Mongols, they exhibited a well-defined identity, with one leg in the Chinese world and another in the steppe nomadic realm. Imperial policies were the key factor behind the direction of Kitan assimilation. While some Kitans were pulled into the Mongols' ranks, most of those in China eventually immersed themselves in the local society. By dissolving the Kitans' state in Manchuria and their special military units; by dispersing Kitan troops in various Mongol military units throughout Eurasia and transferring their civilians all across China; and, last but not least, by classifying them as Hanren instead of Mongols or Semuren, the empire essentially pushed the Kitans into the bosom of the Chinese. However, it bears noting that this development was facilitated by the legitimacy of Kitan social norms due to the penetration of Mongolian customs into Yuan China. All told, these developments eclipsed the Kitans' ethnic identity and led to their full absorption into Chinese society.

On the other side of the steppe, most of these factors—the dissolution of a Kitan political framework, the collectivity's geographical dispersion, and the similarities between Kitan and Mongol social norms—also prompted assimilation into the surrounding sedentary population, as the Kitans were subsumed by the Turco-Iranian Muslims, a fate also shared by the Mongols in West Asia.[93] At any rate, the examples cited throughout this chapter demonstrate that the Mongols were indeed agents of cultural change in all that concerns Kitan identity.

Notes

This study was supported by the Israel Science Foundation (grant no. 818/03). I would also like to thank Yang Qiao and Andrei Gomulin for their research assistance.

1. For the role of the state in determining identity change in the Chinese context see, e.g., M. Elliot, *The Manchu Way: The Eight Banners and Ethnic Identity in Late Imperial China* (Stanford, 2001); D. M. Robinson, "The Ming Court and the Legacy of the Yuan Mongols," in *Culture, Courtiers and Competition: The Ming Court (1368–1644)*, ed. D. M. Robinson (Cambridge, MA, and London, 2008), pp. 365–421.

2. See, e.g., Qiu Shusen, "Lun Yuandai Zhongguo shaoshu minzu xin geju ji qi shehui yingxiang," paper given in the International conference on Mongol Yuan studies, Nanjing, 2002.

3. T. T. Allsen, "Ever Closer Encounters: The Appropriation of Culture and the Apportionment of Peoples in the Mongol Empire," *Journal of Early Modern History*, 1 (1997), pp. 2–23; P. B. Golden, "'I will give the people unto thee': The Chinggisid Conquests and their Aftermath in the Turkic World," *Journal of the Royal Asiatic Society*, 3rd ser., 3/10 (2000), pp. 21–41; and M. Biran, *Chinggis Khan* (Oxford, 2007), pp. 101–102.

4. For the fate of several leading Uighur families under the Yuan see M. Brose, *Subjects and Masters: Uyghurs in the Mongol Empire* (Bellingham, WA, 2007).

5. For an in-depth look at the Liao see, inter alia, V. Hansen and F. Louis (eds.), *Perspectives on the Liao* (New Haven, CT, 2010); K. A. Wittfogel and Feng Chia-sheng, *History of Chinese Society: Liao (907–1125)* (Philadelphia, 1949); D. Twitchett and K.-P. Tietze, "The Liao," in *The Cambridge History of China*, vol. 6: *Alien Regimes and Border States 907–1368*, ed. D. Twitchett and H. Franke (Cambridge, 1994), pp. 43–153; Shen Hsueh-man (ed.), *Gilded Splendor: Treasures of China's Liao Empire (907–1125)* (New York, 2006); N. Standen, "What Nomads Want: Raids, Invasions, and the Liao Conquest of 947," in *Mongols, Turks and Others: Eurasian Nomads and the Outside World,* ed. R. Amitai and M. Biran (Leiden, 2005), pp. 129–174; N. Standen, *Unbounded Loyalty: Frontier Crossings in Liao China* (Honolulu, 2007); Liu Pujiang, *Song mo zhi jian: Liao Jin Qidan Nüzhen shi yan jiu* (Beijing, 2008); and Liu Pujiang, *Liao Jin shi lun* (Shenyang, 1999). D. Kane expounds on the Kitan language in D. Kane, *The Kitan Language and Script* (Leiden, 2009).

6. For more on the Qara Khitai see M. Biran, *The Empire of the Qara Khitai in Eurasian History: Between China and the Islamic World* (Cambridge, 2005) and Wei Liangtao, *Kalahan wang chao shi, Xi Liao shi* (Beijing, 2010), pp. 204–383. For the Qara Khitai as meaning the Liao Kitans see D. Kane, "The Great Central Liao Kitan State," in *Perspectives on the Liao*, ed. V. Hansen and F. Louis (New Haven, CT, 2010), p. 7. Professor Kane convincingly suggests that the Mongolian term **hara-kida* was a derivative of the Kitan **xuri(s) kida(n)*—the Chinese equivalent for the Liao Kitans. Additionally, this was how the Kitans referred to themselves on the eve of the Jurchen conquest. Since "Qara/Khara" is the word for "black" in Mongolian and Turkic, the name was understood in both the Muslim world and Yuan China as meaning "the Black Kitans." Kane's interpretation implies that the Liao dynasty in China and Yelü Dashi's Central Asian polity went by the same name (both Rashīd al-Dīn and *The Secret History of the Mongols* indeed used the same appellation for both entities).

7. Su Pengyu, "Mengyuan shiqi Qidanren de qianyi yanjiu," *Anyang shifan xueyuan xuebao,* 1 (2010), p. 72. For more on the Jin Kitans see Liu Pujiang, "Liao chao wangguo zihou de Qidan yimin," *Yanjing xuebao,* 10 (2001), pp. 135–172; Chen Shu, "Da Liao wajie yihou de Qidan ren," *Liao Jin shi lunji,* 1 (1987), pp. 297–323; H. Franke, "The Forest People of Manchuria: Kitans and Jurchens," in *The Cambridge History of Early Inner Asia,* ed. D. Sinor (Cambridge, 1990), pp. 410–412; and S. Jagchid "Kitan Struggles against Jurchen Oppression—Nomadism versus Sinicization," in S. Jagchid, *Essays in Mongolian Studies* (Provo, UT, 1988), pp. 34–49.

8. Song Lian, *Yuanshi* (Beijing, 1976), ch. 149, p. 3512; ch. 149, p. 3529; ch. 150, p. 3541 (hereafter cited as *YS*); and Jagchid, "Kitan Struggles," p. 166.

9. J. Jahunhen, *Manchuria: An Ethnic History* (Helsinki, 1996), p. 140. Also see, inter alia, Tuotuo, *Jin shi* (Beijing, 1976), ch. 8, pp. 184–185; ch. 99, p. 2186; ch. 105, p. 2321 (hereafter cited as *JS*); and *YS,* ch. 150, p. 3548.

10. For instance see *JS,* ch. 132, p. 2825; ch. 133, pp. 2849–2851; *YS,* ch. 149, p. 3512; H. Franke, "The Chin Dynasty," in *The Cambridge History of China*, vol. 6, pp. 241, 243–244; Jagchid, "Kitan Struggle," pp. 38–43; He Junzhe et al., *Jin chao shi* (Beijing, 1992), pp. 266–273, 351–353; Chen Shu, "Da Liao wajie yihou," pp. 302–304; Liu Pujiang, "Qidan yimin," pp. 152–155; Feng Jiqin, "Jin Yuan shiqi Qidan ren xing ming yanjiu," *Heilongjiang minzu congkan,* 4 (1992), pp. 106–107. For the connection between the Kitan original names and their Jin variants see esp. Chen Lü, *An ya tang ji,* ed. Siku quanshu, ch. 6, p. 25.

11. For more on the Kitans in West Asia see Biran, *The Empire,* passim.

12. See the references in ns. 7 and 11 above.

13. Kane, "The Great Central Liao Kitan State," p. 7 (and see n. 6 above). For discussion on the archaeological remains see esp. V. P. Zaytsev, "Rukopisnaiia kniga bol'shogo kidan'skogo pis'ma iz kollektsii Instituta vostochnyx rukopisei RAN," *Pis'mennye Pamiatniki Vostoka,* 2/15 (Autumn–Winter 2011), pp. 130–150, or http://en.wikipedia.org/wiki/Nova_N_176 (accessed September 18, 2012); and Franz Gernet, "Maracanda/Samarkand, une métropole pré-mongole: Sources écrites et archéologie," *Annales. Histoire, Sciences Sociales,* 59/5–6 (September–December 2004), p. 1064.

14. This chapter follows in the footsteps of the subjective view on the formation of ethnic identity, which was expanded on by Barth in his introduction to F. Barth (ed.), *Ethnic Groups and Boundaries* (Boston, 1969), pp. 9–39. According to Smith, "Ethnic community is a named human population with shared ancestry myths, histories and cultures, having an association with a specific territory and a sense of solidarity." A. D. Smith, *The Ethnic Origin of Nations* (Oxford, 1986), p. 32.

15. For more on the Qara Khitai see Franke, "The Forest People," pp. 405–406; and Tuotuo, *Liaoshi* (Beijing, 1976), ch. 30, pp. 356, 357 (hereafter cited as *LS*). For more on the Jin Kitans see *YS,* ch. 149, p. 3512.

16. The Kitan language and scripts have attracted a great deal of scholarly research, especially on the part of Kane, *The Kitan Language,* passim; and Kane, "The Great Central Liao Kitan State," pp. 5–56. A large-scripted Kitan book was unearthed in Kyrgyzstan and recently published by V. Zaytsev, "Rukopisnaiia kniga," pp. 130–150.

17. Kane, *Kitan language,* pp. 3–4; Biran, *The Empire,* pp. 127–128.

18. Biran, *The Empire,* pp. 162–163; Hu Xiaopeng and Su Pengyu, "Mengyuan shiqi Qidan ren hunyi yanjiu," *Xibei shidaxue bao,* 46/6 (2009), pp. 44–48; and *YS,* ch. 149, p. 3152.

19. For the place of Chinese culture in the Kitan identity see, inter alia, Feng Jiqin et al., *Qidan zu wenhua shi* (Heilongjiang, 1994); and the references in n. 5 above.

20. For instance, when Qara Khitai spies were spotted in Jin border markets in 1177, the Jurchens closed the markets for three years and exiled the Kitans living in the area to the east. Moreover, they severed relations with the Tanguts for presumably allowing these spies to enter the Jin through their lands. See, inter alia, *JS,* ch. 50, p. 1114; ch. 134, pp. 2870–2871; R. Dunnell, "The Fall of the Xia Empire," in *Rulers from the Steppe,* ed. G. Seaman and D. Marks (Los Angeles, 1991), pp. 161–162; and Biran, *The Empire,* p. 57.

21. Yelü Chucai is discussed by I. De Rachewiltz, "Yeh-lü Ch'u-ts'ai, Yeh-lü Chu, Yeh-lü Hsi-liang," in *In the Service of the Khan: Eminent Personalities of the Early Mongol-Yuan Period,* ed. de Rachewiltz et al. (Wiesbaden, 1993), pp. 136–175.

22. Rashīd, ed. Karīmī, vol. 1, p. 321; and Rashīd, tr. Thackston, vol. 1, p. 214.

23. Rashīd al-Dīn's assertion as to the similarities between the Kitans and Mongols is backed by modern linguistics and other sources. See Biran, *The Empire,* pp. 143–145; and *YS,* ch. 149, p. 3151.

24. Allsen provides a fine description of these conquests in T. T. Allsen, "The Rise of the Mongolian Empire and Mongolian Rule in North China," in *The Cambridge History of China,* vol. 6, pp. 348–372.

25. Yao Jingan's index of the *Yuanshi* (*Yuanshi ren ming suoyin* [Beijing, 1982]) includes 34 Yelüs (p. 94), 20 Yila (p. 175), 35 Shimo (p. 57), and 30 Xiao (p. 282); and de Rachewiltz and May Wang's *Repertory of Proper Names in Yuan Literary Sources* (Taipei, 1988–1996) includes 87 Yelüs (vol. 3, pp. 2293–2298), 22 Xila (vol. 1, pp. 972–973), 37 Shimo (vol. 2, pp. 1679–1680), 1 Shulü (vol. 4, p. 567), and 551 Xiao (vol. 1, p. 744–764), only three of whom can be positively identified as Kitans or Liao (though more appear as

Kitans in the *YS*). Combined with those mentioned in the *Yuanshi* and subtracting those appearing in both indices along with those known by multiple names, our final tally is slightly over 200 names. This includes a few Kitans with other surnames (Wang, Liu, and Li—see below) or without one.

26. There is an abundance of information on the families of Yelü Chucai, Yelü Liuge 耶律 留哥, the brothers Yelü Tuhua 耶律禿花 and Yelü Ahai 耶律 阿海, Xila Nieer 移剌捏兒, Yelü Youshang 耶律有尚, Yelü Temo 耶律忒末, Shimo Yexian 石抹也先, Shimo Bodar 石抹孛迭兒, Shimo Anzhi 石抹按只, Shimo Mingan 石抹明安, Shimo Mingli 石抹明里, Shimo Gougou 石抹狗狗, Xiao Baizhu 蕭拜住, and Wang Xun 王珣.

27. Ma Mingda,"Yuan dai diaosujia gouchen," *Xibei minzu yanjiu,* 1 (1997), pp. 239–242; and Wang Deyi, *Yuan ren zhuanji ziliao suoyin* (Taipei, 1979–1982), p. 1980.

28. For Yuan sources on Toghon Temür's reign (1333–1368), including the limitations of the *Yuanshi* annals for this period, see Cang Xiuliang (ed.), *Zhongguo shixue mingzhu pingjie* (Jinan, 1990), vol. 2, pp. 223–245; Wang Shenrong, *Yuanshi tan yuan* (Changchun, 1991), pp. 1–283; and F. W. Mote, "A Note on Traditional Sources for Yuan History," in *The Cambridge History of China,* vol. 6, pp. 689–693.

29. Liuge is discussed in various works, such as the following: *YS,* ch. 1, pp. 16, 19, 20; ch. 149, pp. 3511–3514; *JS,* ch. 14, p. 314; ch. 102, p. 2245; ch. 103, pp. 2278, 2281; Rashīd, ed. Karīmī, vol. 1, pp. 327–328, and Rashīd, tr. Thackston, vol. 1, p. 221–222; Tu Ji, *Mengwuer shi ji* (Taipei, 1962), ch. 31, pp. 1–4; Ke Shaomin, *Xin Yuanshi* (Beijing, 1979), ch. 134, pp. 1–5; Yanai Watari, *Yuan dai jing lue Dongbei kao* (Taipei, 1963), pp. 76–90; Liu Pujiang, "Q̱idan yimin," pp. 158–160; H. D. Martin, *The Rise of Chinggis Khan and His Conquest of North China* (Baltimore, 1950), pp. 150–158, 195–203, 215–218, 236–237, 283–284; Jagchid, "Kitan Struggles," p. 180.

30. Liu Pujiang, "Q̱idan yimin," p. 159. Liuge's name and reign titles appear on four seals that were unearthed in Manchuria: three in Liaoning (during the 1910s and 1970s), and one in Heilongjiang (1984). All are dated to Tiantong 3 (天统, "heavenly rule," 1215), made of copper, and inscribed in Chinese. None of them contain any hint of submission to the Mongols. The *Yuanshi* calls Liuge's state "Liao" and its reign title Yuantong (元统, "original rule"); *YS,* ch. 149, p. 3512; Bayan, "Yelü Liuge zhi tiantong jinian," *Shehui kexue jikan,* 3 (1985), p. 92; and Xu Yucai, "Dandong diqu faxian Jinmo Yelü Liuge Da Liao zhengquan tong yin," *Wenwu,* 5 (1985). For more on the similar measures that were adopted by Yelü Dashi see *LS,* ch. 30, p. 357; and Biran, *The Empire,* p. 38.

31. Chŏng In-ji, *Gaoli shi (Koryŏsa)* (Seoul, 1990), vol. 1, ch. 22, p. 441.

32. According to the *YS,* Liuge commanded the force that defeated the Kitan rebels; *YS,* ch. 149, p. 3513; Yanai Watari (*Dongbei,* p. 79) casts doubt on this account, on the grounds that Liuge is not mentioned in the Korean sources (*Gaoli shi [Koryŏsa],* vol. 1, ch. 22, p. 441ff.; vol. 2, ch. 103, p. 261ff.).

33. See n. 29 above, esp. *YS,* ch. 149, pp. 3514–3515.

34. Rashīd, ed. Karīmī, p. 328, and Rashīd, tr. Thackston, p. 223.

35. For Kirman's topography, population, and economy see A. K. S. Lambton, "Kirmān," *Encyclopaedia of Islam,* 2nd ed. Online. http://referenceworks.brillonline.com/entries/encyclopaedia-of-islam-2/kirman-COM_0521 (accessed at the National Library of Israel, July 13, 2012).

36. For more on the Q̱ara Khitai in Kirman see Nāṣir al-Dīn Munshī Kirmānī, *Simṭ al-'ulā li'l-haḍra al-'ulyā,* ed. I. 'Abbās (Tehran, 1328/1949); Anonymous, *Ta'rīkh-i shāhī-i Q̱arā Khitā'iyyān,* ed. M. I. Būstānī Pārīzī (Tehran, 1976–1977); G. Lane, *Early Mongol Rule in Thirteenth Century Iran: A Persian Renaissance* (New York, 2003), pp. 102–122; and

Biran, "Kitan Migrations in Inner Asia 10th–14th Centuries," *Journal of Central Eurasian Studies,* 3 (2012), pp. 92–96.

37. Su Pengyu, "Mengyuan shiqi Qidanren de yanjiu" (MA thesis, Northwest Normal University, Laozhou, China, 2010), p. 11. Also see, inter alia, *YS,* ch. 149, p. 3522; ch. 150, p. 3559.

38. Li Zhichang, "*Changchun xi you ji,*" in *Menggu shiliao sizhong,* ed. Wang Guowei (Taipei, 1975), p. 327. The English version of this work is Li Chih-chang, *The Travels of an Alchemist,* tr. A. Waley (London, 1963), p. 93. Also see *YS,* ch. 150, pp. 3548–3549; and P. D. Buell, "Yeh-lü A-hai, Yeh-lü T'u-hua," in *In the Service of the Khan*, pp. 112–120.

39. Kitans guided the Mongol troops on their first incursions into the Jin. Following the Jurchens' capitulation, Kitans administered the Zhongdu conquest of 1215. Lastly, five out of Muqali's ten *tumen* commanders in the Jin campaign (1217–1223) were Kitans.

40. See *YS,* ch. 149, pp. 3512, 3515, 3522, 3532, 3533; ch. 150, p. 3548; ch. 151, p. 3577; ch. 154, pp. 3641–3642; ch. 166, p. 3907; and ch. 179, p. 4156.

41. Life paths of this sort are well documented for those who saw action in Sichuan, e.g., *YS,* ch. 149, p. 3522ff.; and ch. 154, pp. 3460–3462.

42. e.g., *YS,* ch. 153, p. 3610; and Su Pengyu, "Mengyuan shiqi Qidanren de yanjiu," p. 14.

43. Toponyms, including the name Khitai, exist/existed in the following settings: the lower Don region, near the Caspian sea, during the fourteenth century; the sixteenth century in the Ob region, western Siberia; modern-day Bashkiria on both sides of the Ural Mountains; the steppes of contemporary southern Moldavia, which were formerly inhabited by the Qipchaq tribes; and present-day Tajikistan. Tribes and clans bearing the name Kitan surface among the Uzbeks, Kazakhs, the Tatars of Crimea, Afghans, Kyrgyz, Nogais, and Bashkirs. See D. Sinor, "Western Information on the Kitans and Some Related Questions," *Journal of the American Oriental Society,* 115 (1995), pp. 262–269; Biran, *The Empire,* pp. 89–90. For the later dispersion of the Qara Khitai see ibid., 86–90; and Biran, "Kitan Migrations," 92–97. While certain Qara Khitai reached Mamluk Egypt, the Delhi Sultanate, and the Ilkhanate (not only Kirman), none merited a biography in the *Yuanshi.*

44. Hsiao Ch'i-ch'ing, *The Military Establishment of the Yuan Dynasty* (Cambridge, MA, 1978), p. 54.

45. See *YS,* ch. 23, p. 521; ch. 35, p. 790; ch. 149, p. 3537; ch. 150, p. 3542; ch. 154, p. 3640; ch. 166, p. 3906; ch. 179, p. 4156; ch. 183, p. 4209; ch. 188, p. 4270–4721, 4309; Yu Xilu (comp.), *Zhishun Zhenjiang zhi,* in *Song-Yuan difangzhi congkan* (Taipei, 1980), vol. 3, ch. 15, p. 2820; Zhang Xuan (comp.), *Zhizheng Jinling xinzhi,* in *Song-Yuan difangzhi congkan* (Taipei, 1980), vol. 6, pp. 5594, 5608; Su Pengyu, "Mengyuan shiqi Qidanren de yanjiu," pp. 18–23.

46. *YS,* ch. 150, pp. 3548–3551; and Tu Ji, *Mengwu'er shi ji,* in *Yuan shi er zhong* (Shanghai, 1989), vol. 2, ch. 49, pp. 375–380; also see Buell, "Yeh-lu A-hai," pp. 112–120.

47. Zhou Qingshu surveys the various stelae and Daoist inscriptions that pertain to Tuhua's family in Zhou Qingshu, "Yuan Huanzhou Yelü jiazu shishi huizheng yu Qidan ren de nanqian," *Mengyuan de lishi yu wenhua* (Taipei, 2001), vol. 2, pp. 501–540. Cf. Meng Zhidong, *Yunnan Qidan houyi yanjiu* (Beijing, 1995), pp. 56–64, who claims that Mangudai is an ancestor of the Yunnan Kitans. However, Meng's account of the family's chronology is highly problematic.

48. For instance, the families of Shimo Yexian, Shimo Anzhi, and see below.

49. This observation was made by Rashīd al-Dīn, who expounded on this thought: "Now [presumably the early fourteenth century] it has come about that the people of Khitai, Jurchen, Nankiyas [i.e., south China], Uighur, Qipchaq, Turkmen, Qarluq, Qalaj, and all the prisoners and the Tajik races that have been brought up among the Mongols are also called Mongols. All that assemblage takes pride in calling itself Mongol." Rashīd, ed. ʿAlīzādah, vol. 1, pp. 163–164; and Rashīd, tr. Thackston, vol. 1, p. 44 (also see Lane's chapter in this volume). Cf. the similar Kitanization process that the Chinese underwent during Liao rule; P. Crossley, "Outside In: Power, Identity and the Han Lineage of Jizhou," in *Perspectives on the Liao,* ed. V. Hansen and F. Louis (New Haven, CT, 2010), pp. 121–155.

50. Peng Daya and Xu Ting, *Heida shi lue,* in *Wang Guowei yishu* (Shanghai, 1983), vol. 13, p. 25a.

51. The *Yuanshi* text reads *Hemi* 合迷, which might be referring to Hami in Eastern Xinjiang. I am following Tu Ji, *Mengwuer shi ji* (Taipei, 1962), ch. 31, p. 294, who changed *Hemi* to *Heliqi* 合立盅, that is *Qurumchi*—the Mongolian name for Khwārazm. This version dovetails smoothly with the chronological and geographical context. For *Qurumchi* as Khwārazm see I. de Rachewiltz, tr. and annot., *The Secret History of the Mongols* (Leiden, 2004), vol. 2, p. 962.

52. *YS,* ch. 149, p. 3154. After Yaoli Shi explained that, unlike her son Shange, Xuedu was born to Yelü Liuge's principal wife and thus deserved the post, Chinggis Khan granted her request. Liuge's family members who accompanied Yaoli Shi on her visit remained in the Mongol army.

53. I. de Rachewiltz, "Personal and Personalities in North China in the Early Mongol Period," *Journal of the Economic and Social History of the Orient,* 9 (1966), pp. 88–144, esp. p. 129.

54. See, inter alia, *YS,* ch. 146, p. 3455; ch. 149, pp. 3511, 3529, 3532, 3534; ch. 150, pp. 3541, 3554, 3548; ch. 151, p. 3576; ch. 152, p. 3603; ch. 154, p. 3640; ch. 166, p. 3906; ch. 169, p. 3976; ch. 179, p. 4156; ch. 188, p. 4309; ch. 193, p. 4382; and Yu Ji, *Daoyuan xue gu lu,* ed. Wanyou wenku (Shanghai, 1937), ch. 10. Cf. *YS,* ch. 174, p. 4064. This source—the biography of the eminent Confucian Yelü Youshang—only mentions his family's relation to the Liao royal house.

55. A noteworthy example turns up in the biography of Shimo Mingli, a cook whose family had already joined the Mongols by Chinggis Khan's time and later served Tolui's household. Qubilai assigned Mingli to his heir apparent Zhenjin (真金 1243–1285). Sometime later, the khan asked his son to choose ten loyal servants who deserved a reward, and Mingli was among them. Qubilai remembered the chef and elevated him to a higher place on the list. Responding to doubts about this award, Qubilai said that "Mingli's grandfather Henu 曷魯 served Chinggis Khan, Tolui, and me and my brothers. Where were you people at that time?" *YS,* ch. 169, p. 3976. Also see Huang Jin, *Jinhua Huang xiansheng wenji,* Sibu conggan ed., ch. 27, p. 5bff. (hereafter cited as "Huang Jin").

56. For instance, Yelü Chucai was called Urtu Saqal, "long beard," by the Mongols; Wang Xun was dubbed Qara Yuanshuai 哈剌元帥, "the black general-in-chief" (the second word is Chinese) (*YS,* ch. 149, p. 3535); Yila Nieer merited the title Yeke Bitikchi, "grand scribe"; *YS,* ch. 149, p. 3529); both Yelü Xuedu and his brother Shange were promoted to *bagatur/bahadur* (*YS,* ch. 149, pp. 3514, 3515); and the Mongolian title of Yeke Noyan (也可那延 Yeke Nayan, "grand noble" or "grand commander") along with the Chinese titles Zongling 總領 and Taichuan 太傅 were conferred upon Yelü Tuhua (*YS,* ch. 149, p. 3532). Furthermore, every Kitan biography in the *Yuanshi* contains a wide range of Chinese titles that were imparted to Kitans.

57. e.g., Yelü Ahai named his elder son Mangutai 忙古台 [Mon: Mangghudai, "he who is Mongol"] (*YS*, ch. 150, p. 3548), and Mongolian names were popular in the families of Yelü Tuhua, Yelü Liuge, and Shimo Mingan (Mingan itself is a Mongolian name, meaning "a thousand"). As noted, it was common for the same person to have both a Mongolian and Chinese or Kitan names. For instance, Liuge's grandson Shouguonu 收國奴 took the name Shila 石剌 (i.e., Shira, Mongolian for "yellow"); Shimo Yexian was also known as Mangudai (Huang Jin, ch. 27, p. 5b); and Tuhua's descendants Tuomenda'er (Tumendar, a Mongol name) 禿满答兒 and Mangudai also went by the Chinese names of Yuntong 雲童 and Baojian 寶劍, respectively (Zhou Qingshu, "Yuan Huanzhou Yelü," pp. 528–532). Also see, inter alia, Feng Jiqin, "Qidan ren xing ming," p. 110; *YS*, ch. 101, p. 2995; ch. 179, pp. 4156–4157; ch. 197, p. 4446; ch. 200, p. 4492; Yu Xilu, *Zhishun Zhenjang zhi*, ch. 15, p. 2820; and Huang Jin, ch. 27, p. 5b.

58. E. Endicott-West, *Mongolian Rule in China: Local Administration in the Yuan Dynasty* (Cambridge, MA, 1989), pp. 82–83, 95; and H. Serruys, "Remains of Mongol Customs in China during the Early Ming Period," *Monumenta Serica*, 16 (1957), pp. 149–165.

59. *YS*, ch. 150, p. 3548.

60. Hu Zhihui, *Zi shan da quan ji* (Taipei, 1983), ch. 16, p. 4.

61. Huang Jin, ch. 27, pp. 7a–8a.

62. For an in-depth look at Yelü Zhu's life and wives see I. de Rachewiltz, "A Note on Yelü Zhu and His Family," in *Meng Yuan shiji minzushi lun ji: ji nian Weng Dujian xiansheng danchen yi bai zhou nian*, ed. Hao Shiyuan and Luo Xianyou (Beijing, 2006), pp. 269–281. Also see Hu Xiaopeng and Su Pengyu, "Mengyuan shiqi qidan ren hunyin yanjiu," pp. 44–48; and Su Pengyu, "Mengyuan shiqi Qidanren de yanjiu," pp. 48–49.

63. *YS*, ch. 180, p. 4159; and Yelü Zhu, *Shuangxi zuiyin ji*, Siku quanshu ed., esp. ch. 2, p. 7a.

64. See de Rachewiltz, "Yeh-lü Ch'u-ts'ai," pp. 172–175. Cf. Su Pengyu, "Mengyuan shiqi Qidanren de yanjiu," p. 52, who deems Yelü Chucai's family to be a paradigm of Kitan Mongolization.

65. e.g., *YS*, ch. 149, pp. 3529, 3548; and Huang Jin, ch. 27, p. 5b. The most celebrated example is that of Yelü Chucai, who supposedly persuaded Ögödei not to convert all of north China into pastureland.

66. *YS*, ch. 13, p. 268.

67. C. P. Atwood, *Encyclopedia of Mongolia and the Mongol Empire* (New York, 2004), p. 319.

68. For more on the Dagurs and their connection to the Qidan see, inter alia, Sun Jingji and Sun Hong, *Qidan minzu shi* (Guilin, 2009), pp. 267–270; Janhunen, *Manchuria*, pp. 144–148; Batubaoyin et al. (eds.), *Dawo'er zu yuan yu Qidan lun* (Beijing, 2011), passim. That said, the Dagurs are only portrayed as a distinct group in the seventeenth century, and their current status and identity has much to do with China's twentieth-century minority policies.

69. See Biran, *Chinggis Khan*, pp. 41–42.

70. e.g., Yelü Temu and his son defected to the Mongols in 1214, along with 30,000 men (*YS*, ch. 193, p. 4382); Shimo Axin, also known as Shimo Yexian, led 12,000 men over to the empire (ibid., ch. 152, p. 3603); Yila Nie'er joined Chinggis with over a hundred men (ibid., ch. 149, p. 3529); and Wang Xun surrendered on behalf of his 100,000 troops, though those troops, coming from Xun's prefecture, were not necessarily Kitans (ibid., ch. 149, p. 3534).

71. For more on the Yunnan Kitans see Meng Zidong, *Yunnan Qidan* (Beijing, 1995), passim. Some researchers cast doubt on their "Kitanness," noting that the lion's share of Menggudai's force was Chinese or, at best, mixed (Zhou Qingshu, "Yuan Huanzhou Yelü," pp. 536–540; Sun Jingji and Sun Hong, *Qidan minzu shi,* pp. 263–666). That said, it seems plausible that a group in a relatively secluded place like Yunnan, where some nomadism was possible and other Kitan commanders were stationed, would embrace their commander's identity and call themselves Kitans. Whether these same people, if they actually existed, were indeed the forefathers of the modern-day Yunnan Kitans is a different matter.

72. For data on the Kitan army see *YS,* ch. 98, pp. 2508, 2509; ch. 118, p. 2931; and ch. 149, pp. 3511, 3513; and Hsiao Ch'i-ch'ing, *Military Establishment,* pp. 74, 174. In any event, the *Yuanshi*'s terminology is rather ambiguous. For the Black army see Huang Jin, ch. 27, p. 5a; *YS,* ch. 152, p. 3603; ch. 150, p. 3542. There are several contradictory accounts regarding the provenance and composition of the Black army. Some believe that it was comprised of retainers, with whom Shimo Yexian defected to the Mongols. Others claim that it was a unit of elite soldiers who were recruited immediately following the Mongol conquest of Zhongdu in 1215 (Huang Jin, ch. 27, p. 5a). Lastly, there are scholars who contend that the army mainly consisted of the troops of Jin commander Zhang Jing, a defector who subsequently mutinied against his new lords. Jing's insurrection was put down in 1215 by Shimo Yexian (and other Kitans), who then appropriated the rebel troops (*YS,* ch. 150, p. 3541).

73. Cai Meibiao, "Jiu yu Jiujun zhi yanbian," *Yuanshi Luncong,* 2 (1983), pp. 1–22, esp. p. 13ff. He also discusses the various Jiu groups. Some of the Kitan commanders that switched over to the Mongols also belonged to this group.

74. Tr. de Rachewiltz, *The Secret History,* para. 248, vol. 1, p. 175; and para. 266, vol. 1, p. 198. Also see vol. 2, p. 893–894, 972.

75. Huang Jin, ch. 27, pp. 4b–5a.

76. For more on the Han army see esp. Sun Kekuan, *Menggu Han jun ji Han wenhua yanjiu* (Taipei, 1958).

77. e.g., Hsiao Ch'i-ch'ing, *Military Establishment,* pp. 12–14. Rossabi, among others, examines the rebellion of Li Tan, a Chinese commander in M. Rossabi, *Khubilai Khan* (Berkeley, 1988), pp. 62–67.

78. Su Pengyu, "Mengyuan shiqi Qidanren de yanjiu," p. 36, and the table therein; and Su Pengyu, "Meng-Yuan shiqi Qidan ren de qiaoyi," *Anyang Shifan Xueyuan Xuebao* 安陽師範學院學報, 1 (2010), p. 75.

79. Hu Xiaopeng and Su Pengyu, "Mengyuan shiqi Qidan ren hunyi yanjiu," pp. 44–48.

80. For discussion of the Yuan system see, inter alia, F. W. Mote, "Chinese Society under Mongol Rule," in *The Cambridge History of China,* vol. 6, pp. 616–664, esp. 627–635; Yanai Watari, *Yuan dai Meng Han Semu daiyu kao* (Taipei, 1963); and Meng Siming, *Yuandai shehui jiezhi zhidu* (Beijing, 1938). The most granular description of these categories turns up in the literary collection of Tao Zongyi (fl. 1360–1368), a southern Chinese who enumerates 72 names of Mongolian tribes or clans, 31 groups of Semuren, and 8 groups of Hanren, Kitans included. Tao Zongyi, *Chuo geng lu* (n.d. rpt. Taipei, 1987), "Shizu," pp. 24–28. Elliot delves into the meaning of Hanren in the northern dynasties; M. Elliot, "Hushuo: The Northern Other and the Naming of the Han Chinese," in *Critical Han Studies: The History, Representation and Identity of China's Majority,* ed. T. S. Mullaney et al. (Berkeley, 2012), pp. 173–190.

81. For a recent criticism of the perceived wisdom surrounding Yuan classification see Funada Yoshiyuki, "Semuren yu Yuan dai zhidu, shehui- Zhongxin tantao Menggu, Semu, Hanren, Nanren huafen de zhiwei," *Yuanshi luncong,* 9 (2004), pp. 162–174. Funada claims that the division was not initiated by the Mongols, but was the handiwork of their Chinese advisers. Moreover, he concludes that it was not tightly kept until the early fourteenth century. The most glaring example that he cites is from the Nanjing gazetteer of 1290 in which both Kitans and Mongols(!) are classified as Semu, another subdivision of northerners (Beiren 北人); the other subdivision of northerners is called Hanren (ibid., p. 174) and Zhang Xuan, *Zhizheng Jinling xinzhi* in *Sung-Yuan difangzhi congshu* (Taipei, 1980), vol. 6, pp. 5a–12b. Regardless of the system's provenance, it was clearly used by the Yuan administration from the 1320s onward. For example, the quotas for examination candidates were divided according to these classifications. Also see the references in n. 80 above.

Concerning senior-level posts, Qubilai, for instance, dismissed the Kitan, Jurchen, and Han *darughachi* (*daluhuazhi*, local commissioners) in 1268, but allowed the *semu* to keep their posts; *YS,* ch. 6, p. 118. Other incidents of this sort point to the fact that this rule was not always strictly observed. That said, it eventually had an impact on Kitan mobility, inter alia. Also see *YS,* ch. 21, p. 458; ch. 92, p. 2052; and Endicott-West, *Mongolian Rule,* pp. 79–83, 95, including the references therein.

82. Hu Zhiyu, *Zi shan da quan ji* (Taipei, 1983), ch. 16, p. 3. For discussion on the Kitans' leviratic customs see, inter alia, Wittfogel and Feng, *History of Chinese Society,* pp. 207, 211; and J. Holmgren, "Marriage, Kinship and Succession under the Ch'i-tan Rulers of the Liao Dynasty (907–1125)," *T'oung Pao,* 52 (1986), pp. 44–91. The levirate among the Mongols in Iran is documented, inter alia, in Rashīd, ed. ʿAlīzādah, vol. 3, pp. 96–98, and Rashīd, tr. Thackston, vol. 3, pp. 515–516 (the marriage arrangement of Abaqa Khan). For the complex denouement of leviratic marriage in Yuan China see, inter alia, Bettine Birge, "Levirate Marriage and the Revival of Widow Chastity in Yuan China," *Asia Major,* 3rd ser., 8/2 (1995), pp. 107–146. The Kirmanid Kitans also preserved the group's traditional marriage patterns. Both the dynasty's founder, Baraq Ḥājib, and his heir, Quṭb al-Dīn, adhered to leviratic custom, marrying the wives of their predecessors. The same can be said for the two Kirmanid queens, Terken Khatun and Padshāh Khatun. The latter also took two "infidel" husbands: Ilkhan Abaqa (r. 1265–1282) and then his son Gaikhatu (r. 1291–1294). Leviratic marriages are forbidden according to Islamic law, and women are prohibited from taking a husband from outside the faith. However, since these are Kitan and Mongol norms, the Kirmanid historians depicted both queens as exemplary Muslims. See Biran, "Kitan Migrations," pp. 94–95.

83. For example, *YS,* ch. 197, p. 4443, 4446; ch. 200, p. 4492; and Huang Jin, ch. 27, p. 7a.

84. P. Ebrey, "Surnames and Han Chinese Identity," in *Negotiating Ethnicities in China and Taiwan,* ed. M. J. Brown (Berkeley, 1995), pp. 11–36.

85. Su Tianjue, *Yuan wenlei* (Beijing, 1958), vol. 1, ch. 55; cited in Feng Jiqin, "Qidan ren xing ming," p. 109.

86. Feng Jiqin, "Qidan ren xing ming," pp. 106–110.

87. See the example of Shulü Jie 述律傑 below. A much earlier case involves Yelü Chucai, who in his literary collection refers to the same man as both Yila Zichun 移剌子春 and Liu Zichun 劉子春 (Yelü Chucai, *Zhan ran jushi wenji* [Beijing, 1986], ch. 2, p. 38, ch. 3, p. 48; ch. 10, p. 231; cited by Feng Jiqin, "Qidan ren xing ming," p. 108).

88. For more on the Uighurs see Brose, *Subjects and Masters,* esp. pp. 122–163.

89. See, e.g., Zhang Tingyu, *Ming shi* (Beijing, 1974), ch. 179, p. 4756; ch. 320, pp. 8279, 8280; ch. 328, p. 8504.

90. An account of Shimo Yisun turns up in the *YS*, ch. 188, pp. 4309–4311; also see J. W. Dardess, *Confucianism and Autocracy* (Berkeley, 1983), pp. 117, 124, 133.

91. For more on Shulü Jie see Fang Linggui, "Yuan Shulü Jie jiaoyou kaolüe," in *Mengyuan shi ji minzu shi lunji*, ed. Hao Shiyuan and Luo Xianyou (Beijing, 2006), pp. 242–268; Fang Linggui, "Yuan Shulü Jie Shiji Jikao," in *Yuanshi Congkao* (Beijing, 2004), pp. 247–274; and Chen Shisong, "Yuandai Qidan 'Shishu mingjiang' Shulü Jie shiji," *Ningxia shehui kexue*, 2 (1996), pp. 79, 80–86. There is no biography of Shulü Jie in the *Yuanshi*, but he does merit a few mentions therein. See, e.g., *YS*, ch. 44, p. 922; and ch. 183, p. 4209. The main sources on Shulü Jie are to be found in the writings of his associates, esp. Yu Ji, *Daoyuan*, ch. 10; Chen Lü, *An ya tang ji*, ch. 6; and the Yunnan gazetteer.

92. See Meng Zidong, *Yunnan Qidan*, passim; and n. 71 above.

93. For the Kitans in Western Asia see Biran, "Kitan Migrations," pp. 95–97.

EIGHT

Persian Notables and the Families Who Underpinned the Ilkhanate

George Lane

> Now it has come about that the people of the Khitāī, Jurchen, Nankiyas [South China], Uighur, Qipchaq, Turkoman, Qarluq, Qalaj, and all the prisoners and Tajik races that have been brought up among the Mongols, are also called Mongols. All the assemblage takes pride in calling itself Mongol.[1]

The picture often painted of the Mongols as an occupying force imposed on a subject people, ruling through a brutal military regime, is misleading, and for the most part essentially false. Though the initial decades following the bloody irruption of Chinggis Khan and his sons on Iran were marked by brutality, anarchy, and political chaos, once Möngke Qa'an had responded three decades later to the requests of the delegation "to build a bridge of justice"—that is, to extend full Chinggisid rule over western Asia—the resulting regime was one that was accepted, often popular, and was awake to the realities and aspirations of the people upon whom it rested.[2] Hülegü's entourage would have been familiar with "the rules of the cities," they would have been aware of the relationship between the welfare of their sedentary subjects and the prosperity of the state, and they ensured that their conquest was relatively nondestructive.

But the incorporation of the Iranian heartlands into the Chinggisid empire proper was not a one-sided decision. The notables of the various Iranian city-states had not been unaware of events and developments in the east. Westerners were not infrequent visitors to the increasingly opulent and cosmopolitan Mongol court. The accession of Möngke witnessed an acceleration of traffic to Qaraqorum of supplicants eager to assure their place in the new world order. Among those eager supplicants was an embassy from Qazwin, a city with strong links with the Chinggisid elite, which sought more than the usual requests for recognition, allegiance, and aid. The notables of Qazwin, and in particular members of the Iftikhār family, had long and close ties with the Chinggisid nobility, including one who enjoyed the position as tutor to the young Toluid princes.[3] This embassy from Qazwin, led by their chief *qāḍī* and including merchants, wished to capitalize on those links and finally "to bring Iran in from the cold" and have their land incorporated fully into the empire, with a royal prince appointed to replace the corrupt and heavy-handed military governor, Baiju Noyan. The elite of Qazwin would have been fully aware of the success and prosperity of fellow Muslims and Persian communities elsewhere in the empire. Both groups were well represented in the *keshig* (the royal bodyguard). The omnipresent *bitikchis* were generally recruited from non-Mongols, and Muslims swelled their ranks.[4] The likes of Sayyid ʿAjall ʿUmar al-Bukhārī, long before his elevation to governor of Dali, would have been an inspiration for those left in the anarchy of the Iranian plateau. That a "conspiracy" was afoot when the delegation traveled eastward is made plain by later developments.

ʿAṭā Malik Juwaynī recognized "God's secret intent" in sending the world the Mongols not only in the annihilation of the Ismāʿīlīs but in the rise of Möngke and the placing of the "keys to the lands of the world" in the "hands of the [Mongols'] power" (*dar dast-i qudrat*).[5] Juwaynī, having traveled east himself, was fully aware that Persians and Muslims were among those who exercised power on behalf of the Mongols. The hope was that the appointment of a royal prince who would establish his throne in Iran could be co-opted and integrated into the political and cultural elite of Iran. That this was the unspoken agenda and long-term plan is made plain by the appearance of Qāḍī Baydawī's "pocket history," the *Niẓām al-tawārīkh,* which hardly a decade after Hülegü Khan's establishment of his seat of government in Marāgha was already portraying the Ilkhanate as a legitimate, entrenched Iranian dynasty and lending the regime the weight of his considerable reputation and support.[6] The secondary aim of converting the Chinggisid leadership to Islam would not be realized for more than another four decades, but their gradual conversion to Persian culture was evident in the immersion of the Mongol elite grouped around the Ilkhan in the cultural landscape, as exemplified by the Mongol commander Suqunjaq.[7]

Juwaynī had begun the recording of his history of the Mongols at the urging of his companions at Möngke's court, and his imagery drew deep from within Iran's rich mythological and cultural heritage to adorn and dress his Mongol heroes. Juwaynī had begun a process that would culminate in the magnificent creation of the Mongol Demotte *Shāhnāma*. Möngke's court receptions invoke the verse of Firdawsī: Sorghaghtani Beki is praised with words from Mutannabī; local victories receive stanzas previously addressed to the glorious Caliph al-Muʿtaṣim Billāh; and only a *bayt* from the *Shāhnāmah* can capture the advance of Hülegü's mighty army.[8] Juwaynī was writing an unfolding history and he must have been fully aware of the weight his words might bear and the echo his images would chime. He was painting the Chinggisids not so much as they wished to be seen but more how he and the Persian elite might wish them to be.

Hülegü's assault on the Ismāʿīlīs' strongholds was widely welcomed and there was little sign of opposition to the devastating attack on Baghdad in which the Iranian local leaders were well represented.[9] The Iranians had assessed the potential and outcome of the establishment of a Chinggisid regime and they knew that they had little to lose but possibly a great deal to gain. The caliph had failed on all counts. He had neither unified the Muslim world nor confronted its enemies in the form of the Ismāʿīlīs and the Khwārazmian brigands. Their new ruler, Hülegü, had sought legitimacy from his subjects and had received a fatwa from the *ʿālim,* Ibn Ṭāwūs, stating a just infidel ruler to be preferable to an unjust Muslim sovereign.[10] If the Persian notables had dared to envisage a partnership, Hülegü did not destroy their optimism.

Hülegü was rapidly adopted by the notables of Iran as a "legitimate" sovereign in that his position as king was fully accepted and recognized and his new subjects were quick to realize that they were to enjoy a large degree of autonomy and joint rule. Even the *ʿulamāʾ* retained their positions of influence and prestige, and those high officials who partook in the Mongol administration never suffered rebuke or criticism from their compatriots. In the case of the Parwānah of Rūm, his own self-doubts were allayed and put to rest by the renowned Sufi poet and former leading member of the *ʿulamāʾ*, Jalāl al-Dīn Rūmī. "These works [on behalf of the Mongols] too are work done for God, since they are the means of procuring peace and security for Muslimdom."[11] Hülegü himself was quick to establish through a fatwa that "a just infidel is preferable to an unjust Muslim ruler" and encouraged those with ability, Muslim or otherwise, to seek the highest posts.[12]

Hülegü had already had some indirect experience of rule and administration in dealing with his lands in Tibet.[13] This Tibetan appanage was held by the Ilkhans following Hülegü's death until the last decades of the thirteenth century. It is recorded that the abbot of P'ag-mo-gru-pa continued to receive generous gifts from the Ilkhans in Iran until at least the rule of Arghun Khan. Hülegü appointed local representatives (*yul bsruns*) and military overseers and was well respected by the local people, who considered him a manifestation of a spiritual power, gNam-t'e. So successful was this situation deemed to be that Hülegü's appanage continued to function with its Ilkhanid ties, long after the appanages of other Mongol princes had been dissolved.[14] It would seem therefore a very canny and fortuitous choice made by the Qāḍī of Qazwin when he allegedly selected Hülegü to lead the expedition to the West. Even if the details of this anecdote remain dubious, the sentiment underpinning its narrative is revealing.[15]

Though the political and military elites were dominated by the Mongols, the role of Persian and other non-Mongol administrators was central and real power was devolved to local people. While the myth that the Mongols were unable to manage the day-to-day running of their administration has long been discredited, the reason that they devolved so much power to local people has often been misunderstood. Such figures as the bureaucrat and political survivor Arghun Aqa; the cultured Ghazan Khan; the warrior, businessman, and sophisticate Suqunjaq Noyan; and the "Renaissance Man" Bolad Aqa clearly illustrate the Mongols' ability to run governmental affairs, so the reason for placing so much administrative power with non-Mongols was likely to have had an element of choice rather than being unavoidable necessity. Though certainly deficient in enough manpower to run the entire bureaucracy, key positions were willingly entrusted to Iranian officials even where qualified Mongols were available.

It should be remembered that the first "Mongol" invasion, the Q̱ara Khitai offensive of the twelfth century, was generally accepted and sometimes even welcomed in the Islamic world, and the Q̱ara Khitai had no problem recruiting Muslims to their infidel administration. Ibn Maḥmūd Uzjandī, a Persian notable, "saw the rectitude of seeking connections with the Khitai," while ʿArūḍī Samarqandī observed that "[the Ghurkhan's] justice had no bounds, nor was there any limit to the effectiveness of his commands, and indeed, in these two things lies the essence of kingship."[16]

The decision to award non-Mongols positions of prestige and power was unlikely to have been seen in such divisive and partisan terms, since by the fourth and fifth decades of the thirteenth century the Mongols' *ordus* were no longer the preserve of solely Turco-Mongol tribes. The *ordus* had evolved into cosmopolitan and multicultural mobile cities. The sons and daughters of all the local rulers, makers, and breakers of the growing empire were "invited" to live as guests of the imperial family at their various *ordus* and cultural cross-fertilization would have been an inevitable product of such close proximity between captive and captor. The hostage sons of the Persian elite were educated and molded alongside the sons of the Chinggisid elite, the Chinese elite, the Armenian elite, and many other elites. The Chinggisid *ordus* fostered a whole generation of new leaders especially groomed and nurtured to take up the onerous task of running the vast empire they had all inherited. It is often overlooked that ʿAṭā Malik Juwaynī (1226–1283), the historian and governor of Baghdad under Hülegü, spent his childhood and early adolescence in Mongol camps. His father entered

Chinggisid service just after the fall of the Khwārazm-shāh and he traveled to the east in 1235–1236 when his son ʿAṭā Malik was just ten. Juwaynī became the epitome of Persian sophistication and learning and he cultivated the arrogance of the traditionalist toward the new elite of Uighur speakers. He obviously considered himself schooled in the manner and style of his illustrious forefathers, and yet it must be remembered that this refinery and sophistication was acquired during his formative years spent in the Chinggisid courts and *ordus* alongside the new growing elite of the expanding empire. His formidable and impressive education was instilled in him, presumably in company with other youngsters of his generation, from a multitude of backgrounds, in the camps of the Chinggisid lords and princes. It was from this vast pool of talent that the Chinggisids were able to select their administrators and the first criterion for choice was unlikely to have been ethnicity. The incident recorded by the Shirazi poet Saʿdī, of his chance encounter with the Juwaynī brothers and the pādishāh Abaqa, illustrates the familiarity and geniality that pervaded the relations between Mongols and Persians.[17] This intimacy, which had been developing during Juwaynī's childhood, had become entrenched by the time Abaqa had assumed the throne. ʿAṭā Malik, in his autobiographical account of his terrible tribulations toward the end of his life, is still able to describe the first two Chinggisid rulers of Iran in complimentary terms, "The methods and judgment of [his] father [Hülegü] were strengthened and he soothed the troubles of the world through his kindness and justice."[18] Though the military option was always available, the Chinggisids sought alternative ways to expand their borders and envelop more under their spreading umbrella. They had long had non-Mongol agents to advance their interests and to explore nonmilitary options. Seljuqid Rūm avoided widespread devastation and bloodshed through timely negotiations as early as 1236, during the reign of the Great Khan Ögödei. A certain merchant, Shams al-Dīn ʿUmar Qazwīnī, accompanied by two Mongols, was sent to the Seljuq sultan of Rūm, ʿAlāʾ al-Dīn Kayqubād (r. 1220–1237), to negotiate on the Mongols' behalf the Sultan's submission and payment of tribute.[19] Though he undoubtedly had his own financial interests at heart, this agent painted a rosy picture of life for those who cooperated with the Mongols. The family of the Rūmī historian Ibn Bībī had a similar background and career development as the Juwaynīs, though not on such a grand scale. The father, Majd al-Dīn Muḥammad, and mother, Bībī Munajjima, a celebrated astrologer, enjoyed positions of respect and influence at the Khwārazm-shāh's court, then in the administration of the Rūmī Seljuqid sultans, and, finally, due to the cross-generational patronage of the Juwaynī family, in the regime of the Seljuq Parwānah of Konya, whose loyalty lay with the Mongols.[20]

Muslims in particular benefited from their early cooperation with the Chinggisids. There are (mostly later) references to Sufis in the inner sanctums of the Chinggisid court from early in the movement westward. A certain Chishtī saint who was "not only present but in a position of authority [at the Mongol Court]" secured the release of a fellow Sufi after a few apt words in Chinggis Khan's ear. The Great Khan was moved to mercy when he heard that the father of the captive Sufi was a man of generosity toward not only his own people, but also to strangers, a practice of which Chinggis Khan approved.[21] The significance of such tales is firstly that they were believed and reported in the expectation of being believed and secondly in that they reflect a Muslim presence at and access to the royal courts. Subsequently, there was even a widespread Sufi belief, which gained currency in later centuries, that Muslim saints rode with and even led the Chinggisid forces in their initial invasion of the lands of the Khwārazm-shāh.[22]

The welcome the Uighurs, Kitans, and elements among the Khwārazmians gave the initial Mongol irruptions secured them a privileged position not only in the relentless Mongol war machine but in the subsequent empire building that followed. Within a few decades not only were Turanian Muslims being appointed to positions of power and prestige, but it was Persian rather than Uighur that had become the empire's lingua franca.[23] Even Persian cooking was found in the proffered cuisine of the Yuan royal courts following the exchange of agrarian produce encouraged at the highest levels of government.[24] The construction of the city walls and palaces of the new Chinggisid capital for the emergent Yuan empire was entrusted to a certain Ikhtiyār al-Dīn and his son Muḥammad-Shāh. The chronicler Ouyang Xuan (1274–1358) records that the two were high-ranking officials in the Ministry of Works whose Muslim ancestors hailed from the *Xiyu,* the "Western Regions."[25] Ikhtiyār al-Dīn was appointed director of the *Chadie'er* (*chador;* "tent") bureau and became chief architect-engineer for the construction of Qubilai's capital. "The services of [Yeheidie'er/Ikhtiyār al-Dīn] were highly appreciated," an inscription reports.[26] The *Yuanshi* records that Ikhtiyār al-Dīn (Yeheidie'er) was the architect responsible for the construction of the still magnificent Beihai island in Beijing, and in the section on punishments in the *Yuan dian zhang,* it is reported that this same supervising architect presented an account of a break-in to these private gardens by a drunk.[27] However, the *Yuanshi* omits the name of this Muslim from the Western Regions while recording the names of his Chinese colleagues, which suggests that the spirit of cosmopolitanism prevalent during the Yuan years did not extend into the Ming era. The entrepreneur ʿAlāʾ al-Dīn, a Persian, traveled to Quinsai (Hangzhou) after donating to the military funds of Qubilai Khan, and established a mosque and energized a community that thrives to this day. He left a grandson, the poet Ding Henian, whose verses are still enjoyed today. The tombstones of such illustrious names as Muḥammad b. Arslān al-Khānbāliqī, Maḥmūd b. Muḥammad b. Aḥmad al-Simnānī, Maḥmūd b. Muḥammad b. Jamāl al-Dīn Khurasānī, and ʿAlāʾ al-Dīn b. Shams al-Dīn al-Isfahānī, along with the descendants of Sayyid ʿAjall ʿUmar Bukhārī and members of the Banū Muḥammad Halibī, which are preserved in the city's 1281 mosque, attest to the status of the Persian community of Eastern China.[28] The first *darughachi* of Shanghai county, Sharaf al-Dīn (She-la-fu-ding), the son of a presumably Khwarazmian artisan, also buried in Hangzhou, enjoyed positions of authority over not only Chinese but Mongol subjects.[29]

When Hülegü sought people to help him run his new kingdom, there would have been available young men from Iran's leading families with whom he could have been acquainted either through reputation or personal contact to appoint to positions of power. Hülegü's love of intellectual stimulation and theological jousting might have been nurtured during youthful contact and observation of foreign envoys and hostage communities present in the royal *ordus* where he resided during his formative years. The members of these leading families would not have been viewed as strangers but more as allies and possibly even acquaintances and as much a part of the ruling establishment as their Mongol brothers. Integration had happened at the top long before it happened on the ground. The Qazwīnīs, the Juwaynīs, the Simnānīs, the Iftikhāriyāns, and the Karts had become as much a part of the Mongol empire's elite as were the Turco-Mongol tribes from the steppe. It was they who were to run the lands of Īrānzamīn that stretched from the Euphrates to the Oxus (Jayḥūn), or rather, "from the lands of the Arabs to the borders of Khojand," as the historian Bayḍāwī defined the Ilkhan Abaqa's territory.[30]

Whispers of intrigue would have snaked to all corners of Asia and beyond when Möngke Qa'an devised his long-term strategy to establish his immediate family at the heart of the empire. The leading sons of Persia would have identified with the Toluids' aspirations and their strategic view of the world would not have been one of Iranians against Turks, or even of Muslims against pagans, but more of Toluids against the "uncooked" Chaghadaids, and other possible rival Mongol claimants to the throne. Their "us" would have been the Toluids, and their "them" those who would oppose the Toluid aspirations. Mustawfī in his epic *Ẓafarnāmah* consistently describes the Ilkhans as Iranians while the Chaghadaids and Jochids remain Turanians.[31] The Persian elite would have more readily identified their interests as lying with the Toluid princes than the despised "Turks" of the Golden Horde. And when Hülegü would have been seeking loyal servants, he would have recognized these same Persian families as his natural allies. Loyalty was sought not only from those in the highest positions, the governors, maliks, and rulers of the provinces, but also in the very heart of the administrative machine. Officials, ministers, and leading bureaucrats all vied for influence and promotion and favor was granted for loyalty as well as for ability.

Alliances were sought and made when first the Mongol armies penetrated west and laid siege to the Khwārazm-shāh's crumbling defenses. The fragility of the Khwārazm-shāh's empire became apparent as not only did his generals and some governors switch their allegiance, but even Muḥammad II's mother, the infamous Terkan Khātūn, made overtures to the advancing Chinggis Khan. Nasawī, Jalāl al-Dīn Mingbarnī's secretary, reports Chinggis Khan's words thus:

> You well know that . . . my land is so rich in treasure that it is unnecessary to seek them elsewhere. If you will ease the way for merchants from both sides it will be for the good of all and to our mutual advantage.[32]

Shams al-Dīn Muḥammad Kart (r. 1245–1278), "a man of great sufficiency, cunning, and rashness," revered by his subjects, admired by his peers, befriended by the powerful, respected by his overlords, and praised by chroniclers and poets, is credited with founding the Kart dynasty of Herat and considered himself heir to the Ghurid throne and legacy.[33] Rukn al-Dīn Khaysārī, Shams al-Dīn Muḥammad's uncle and predecessor as leader of the Karts, had originally received a *yarligh* for the administration of Ghūr from Chinggis Khan in recognition of his prompt submission to the Mongols and for services subsequently rendered.[34] The intimate relationship between the Karts and the Chinggisid elite has however already been the subject of a detailed study.[35]

But it was not only local rulers who had established intimate and binding links with the Chinggisid establishment. The administration itself was a mix of Persian and Mongol, Turk and Tajik, at all levels and the intrigues and political machinations were making ethnic lines and identities effectively irrelevant. Qazwin became the key city with Mongol commanders after their initial bloody visit on October 7, 1220/617. This first visit was immortalized by Mustawfī, who recounted the haunting tale of his great grandfather of ninety-three, Amīn Naṣr, an eyewitness.[36] Subsequent visits were of a dramatically less confrontational character and cordial relations were soon established, first with Ögödei Qa'an and eventually with Möngke Qa'an, who appointed Iftikhār al-Dīn Muḥammad governor of Qazwin along with his brother Malik Imām al-Dīn Yaḥyā, an administrative position the brothers maintained for twenty-seven years.[37] Given the proximity of Alamut and the Ismāʿīlīs, Qazwin was in an exposed region. During the 1240s, when chaos and anarchy became too much for the citizens to bear, it was the Mongols to whom the city elders turned for help.

Like the Juwaynīs, their political rivals and fellow Persian bureaucrats, Qazwīnī notables and leading families played a central and pivotal role in the unfolding drama of Toluid fortunes in Iran. The family of the historian Mustawfī was particularly active in challenging the influence of the Juwaynīs. The rivalry between these two great families became bloody during the Mongol era and even though Ḥamdallāh b. Tāj al-Dīn Abī Bakr Mustawfī Qazwīnī, to give him his full name, was not personally involved, his sentiments are betrayed in his writing by his omission of the trials and tribulations of the historian ʿAṭā Malik ʿAlāʾ al-Dīn Juwaynī and his failure to detail his cousin's role in the death of Sharaf al-Dīn Hārūn Juwaynī, son of the *ṣāḥib dīwān,* Shams al-Dīn Juwaynī.

Mustawfī, as Ḥamdallāh is commonly called, was born in Qazwin in 1281. He lived, worked, and eventually died in Qazwin, though the date of his death is not known other than that it was no earlier than 1344. He entered government service from his early youth, following the tradition of his forefathers, and in the course of his work traveled extensively around the country. His work was concerned with the finances of Chinggisid Iran and the tax assessment of institutions and individuals; the experience he amassed from his visits to Tabriz, Isfahan, Shiraz, and Baghdad helped both his career, the coffers of the state, and his future geographical and historical literary works. In Baghdad he spent time as the assessor of estates (*taqdīr al-amwāl*). His most important position was administering the *tūmāns* of Qazwin, Zanjan, Abhar, and Turmin, where in 1314 he was appointed controller of finances.[38] Ḥamdallāh's first love was writing, and the writing of history in particular. He was an admirer of scholars and he reserved his greatest respect for the learned and the scholarly, and especially for the great statesman and respected academic Rashīd al-Dīn, whom Ḥamdallāh had the great fortune to have served. Despite having entered the Chinggisid administration of Iran as an accountant in his youth, he was eventually able to spend most of his time pursuing his major preoccupation, the composition of his chronicles and histories. At the conclusion of his verse history, the *Ẓafarnāmah,* he states that from the age of forty he had been able to devote himself fully to the pursuit of knowledge. "Since I reached the age of forty years, knowledge has become the ruler of the kingdom of my heart."[39] However, his years as an accountant obviously rewarded him financially if not spiritually, since evidence exists that he was a wealthy, propertied man. Though he would undoubtedly have inherited substantial real estate, his time in government service would have rewarded him with additional financial means. His name is mentioned in a land ledger for Qazwin and the city's environs associating him with parks and gardens, which highlights his well-known interest in horticulture, flora, and fauna.[40]

ʿAbd al-Ḥusayn Nawāʾī, the editor of Mustawfī's *Tārīkh-i Guzīdah*, refers to the properties and estates owned by the historian as mentioned in the local documents and archives but he provides no details or dates since unfortunately the ledgers (*ṭūmār*) are undated.[41] Nawāʾī cites the modern historian ʿAbbās Iqbāl for 1350 being the date of his death. His tomb remains standing today in the western area of Qazwin in the place of the cotton spinners, on the eastern side of the square between the Imāmzādah ʿAlī and Amīna Khātūn. Mustawfī appears to have remained aloof from the political intrigues which preoccupied most of those in positions of power and influence. Not so his cousins, whose machinations demonstrate the equal involvement of both Iranian and Turanian figures.

Khwāja Fakhr al-Dīn Muḥammad and Khwāja Saʿd al-Dīn Muẓaffar, both older than Mustawfī, served the eminent *noyan* Buqa, and later his brother, Aruq. Their names are usually associated with that of the Juwaynīs, with whom they were bitterly involved in rivalrous disputes. Khwāja Fakhr al-Dīn Muḥammad, if his younger cousin the historian is to be believed, led a successful and rewarding career first as the *ṣāḥib dīwān* to Prince Geikhatu in Rūm, and then later as a very competent administrator under Arghun Khan. Unfortunately such competence contrasted unfavorably with the chief vizier, Saʿd al-Dawla Yahūdī. The minister consequently spread slanderous rumors about the newly appointed adviser who, as a result, was arrested and executed. The historian Mustawfī's later account of his older cousin's fate is embellished with details not found in the contemporary source. He reports that Arghun sought detailed information on the state's finances from his vizier, Saʿd al-Dawla, who had explained that it would take him some time to compile and gather such data. However, upon hearing of the royal request, Fakhr al-Dīn, newly arrived from his successes in Rūm, was able to supply the Ilkhan with all the relevant figures and accounts. Saʿd al-Dawla was not amused, and, according to Mustawfī, he then sought out the king when in his cups and obtained permission to have the clever accountant killed.[42] Divine justice, maybe, for a man who had risen on the coattails of Shams al-Dīn Juwaynī and had then poisoned the mind of Buqa Chingsang against the great man in thanks.

> [Amīr ʿAlī Tamghachī], Fakhr al-Dīn Mustawfī, and Ḥusām al-Dīn Ḥājib, all of whom had been elevated by Ṣāḥib Shams al-Dīn's patronage, were so greedy for status that they plotted his downfall and said to Buqa, "So long

as the Ṣāḥib is alive you will not flourish. Once he gets power he will do to you what he did to Arghun Aqa and other amirs."[43]

Khwāja Sa'd al-Dīn Muẓaffar, another of Mustawfī's older cousins, accused Hārūn, the son of the renowned *ṣāḥib dīwān* Shams al-Dīn Juwaynī, of responsibility for a murder actually carried out by his commander, Aruq, who considered himself above the law. As a result of this slander the gifted, artistic Hārūn, who had married the daughter of the last 'Abbasid caliph, was executed.[44] These were court intrigues involving Mongol lords as much as Persian notables, and the backs that were stabbed and the fingers clutching the daggers were as likely to be Mongol as they were Persian. The blood spilled, the posts vacated, the reputations ruined, and offices occupied were not ordained or determined by race or even religion but more by the personal links in the chessboard of Ilkhanid court politics.

Another Qazwīnī family of notables with strong links to the Chinggisid elite were the Iftikhāriyāns.[45] They were well known to Mustawfī and he devotes space to the family in his chapter on Qazwīn's leading families in his *Tārīkh-i Guzīdah*.[46] The Iftikhāriyān claimed descent from the first caliph, Abū Bakr, which was the justification for their use of the *nisba* Bakrī, but their first concrete historical link is to the twelfth century when the "learned and pious" Iftikhār al-Dīn Muḥammad Bakrī studied under Ibn Yaḥyā Naysābūrī (d. 1155), a pupil of al-Ghazālī. The family gained political prominence, however, in the thirteenth century, and it was Iftikhār al-Dīn Muḥammad Bakrī's grandson, also Iftikhār al-Dīn Muḥammad, the son of Abū Naṣr, who forged the first links with the Chinggisid invaders. Iftikhār al-Dīn Muḥammad served as a tutor at the Great Khan Ögödei's court where he instructed the young Chinggisid princes, including the sons of Tolui, Möngke in particular.[47] This early service bore much fruit, and when the Toluids moved to establish their authority in southwestern Asia, their old friend was not forgotten. Mustawfī claims that prince Abaqa and his son Arghun, along with their amīrs and captains, spent eighteen days at the home of Malik Iftikhār al-Dīn Muḥammad. Qazwin became a favorite city with all the Ilkhans, who visited frequently, starting with Hülegü who enjoyed a warm bath in a "Muslim *ḥammām*."[48] As noted above, Möngke Qa'an appointed Iftikhār al-Dīn Muḥammad governor of Qazwin along with his brother Malik Imām al-Dīn Yaḥyā and they ruled over the city for twenty-seven years.[49]

It is noteworthy that it was the chief justice of Qazwin who allegedly traveled to Möngke Qa'an's court to petition the Great Khan to send Iran a king to bring justice, peace, and prosperity to their land. In Mustawfī's rather fanciful account, to Möngke's delight the Qāḍī chose Hülegü from among the assembled lords and grandees. In particular, Qāḍī Shams al-Dīn Aḥmad Makkī Qazwīnī requested that the Mongol army under Hülegü's command first rid the world of the Ismāʿīlī menace. Earlier in his account, Mustawfī records Möngke's personal misgivings and worries concerning the situation in the western provinces.[50] Ibn al-Ṭiqṭaqā also recounts some details of this story and claims that he heard an eyewitness account from Malik Imām al-Dīn Yaḥyā, Iftikhār's brother and joint governor of Qazwin, a fact that emphasizes Iftikhār's family connections with the Chinggisid elite. Mustawfī devotes a section of his *Selected History* to the Iftikhārīyāns and notes that Iftikhār al-Dīn Yaḥyā was a linguist skilled in written and spoken Turkish and Mongolian (*khaṭṭ wa-zabān-i turkī wa-mughūlī*) and that his work was highly regarded and considered authoritative by the Mongols. He eloquently translated the classic *Book of Kalila and Dimna* into Mongolian and the *Book of Sindbad* into Turkish, which suggests an intimate and ongoing acquaintance with both languages. With Möngke on the Chinggisid throne, Iftikhār al-Dīn Muḥammad in particular prospered and through him the city, which gained some fine buildings. However, Mustawfī fails to mention that Iftikhār's final two years were spent in disgrace and it is Rashīd al-Dīn who provides the details of the fifty toman—five hundred thousand (dinār?) bribe he paid to informants (*īghāqān*) to avoid an audit of the books. In 1280, after two years of destitution (*maflūk*), he died in an unnamed Mongol *ordu*.[51]

Though his brother had fallen from grace, Imām al-Dīn Yaḥyā not only continued as governor of Qazwin, but had the area under his jurisdiction expanded to include, first, the whole of ʿIrāq al-ʿAjam, from Tabriz to Yazd, and later ʿIrāq al-ʿArab, which included Baghdad. He outlived his other brothers and died around the beginning of 1301; he was succeeded by his son, another Iftikhār al-Dīn. His other brothers had been governors at various times of Māzandarān, Gurjistan (Georgia), Mosul, and Diyār Bakr.[52] Imām al-Dīn Yaḥyā was buried in a *madrasa* that he had founded in Darb Firāshā, east of Baghdad. He had built the *madrasa* for a respected Shāfiʿī cleric and this demonstrates that the Iftikhārīyān's close connections with the Chinggisids did not preclude close ties with the religious establishment.[53]

The fate of one of the Iftikārīyān brothers is further revealing of relationships within the circles of the elite and between Iranians and Turanians. In fact, as has been mentioned previously, the Ilkhanid establishment, Mongols, Turks, and Persians, Muslims and non-Muslims, often regarded themselves in the context of Western Asia as Iranians, while considering those north of the Oxus and the Caucasus as Turanians. Whether all the Mongol lords embraced this new identity is doubtful but that such a development was even conceivable is significant. Ghazan's plea for unity and compassion was still a generation away, but the seeds sown so long ago were taking firm roots.[54]

This Iftikhārīyān brother, Raḍī al-Dīn Bābā, had been governor of Diyār Bakr and then of Mosul. On ascending the throne in 1265, Abaqa had appointed him joint governor of Diyār Bakr with Jalāl al-Dīn Ṭarīr.[55] He was also a poet, as was his son, and their patrons included a wide range of important figures. The son's patrons included the Mongol generals Esen Qutlugh and Tuqman, as well as Öljeitü's two prime ministers, Rashīd al-Dīn and Sāwajī. The Mongol camp must have changed greatly from its early days on the steppe if its generals were now versed in, and patrons of, Persian poetry. Raḍī al-Dīn Bābā included Shams al-Dīn Juwaynī among his patrons, and the poet obviously felt confident enough in his friendship with this immensely powerful figure to send the *ṣāḥib dīwān* a rather cheeky and very sarcastic composition on the occasion of his dismissal from Diyār Bakr's governorship.[56] This verse contrasts strongly with his panegyrics quoted in Jājarmī's anthology.[57] But Raḍī al-Dīn Bābā's connections could not save him from the long arm of Chinggisid justice. As his sarcastic ode to the *ṣāḥib dīwān* shows, Raḍī al-Dīn felt humiliated by his ignominious dismissal from Diyār Bakr and his later replacement as governor of Mosul. He was determined upon revenge on both Masʿūd, a Christian who had replaced him as civil governor, and Ashmut, a Christian Mongol who had been appointed military governor (*shaḥna*), though Bar Hebraeus claims that Ashmut was, in fact, an Uighur.[58] The opportunity for revenge occurred two years later, after he was reinstated. Once again in office, Raḍī al-Dīn Bābā made accusations of financial impropriety against the two, saying Masʿūd was "destroying the country of Mawṣil and that he [Masʿūd] did not know how to rule." Raḍī al-Dīn strengthened his accusations with bribes, and after an inquiry the two, Masʿūd and Ashmut, were dismissed and the Qazwīnī was restored to his post. However, the story did not end there and in 1280 Masʿūd and Ashmut approached Abaqa demanding justice, and they produced evidence of the bribery that had undermined their case. After deliberating for a month, Abaqa's court found Raḍī al-Dīn Bābā guilty of corruption and he was duly executed and his head paraded around Mosul. The judges who had accepted bribes were also exposed and disgraced.[59] This case reveals that the courts actually functioned and made strenuous efforts to arrive at a just and open verdict. It also demonstrates that Persians could take Mongols to court and expect to receive a considered judgment.

The Mongol Ilkhans oversaw a period of Iranian history often referred to as a "Golden Age" by art and literary historians. Generally, this appellation is applied in relation to the literary arts, which flourished during the thirteenth and fourteenth centuries. Poetry, and Sufi poetry in particular, from this period has not been surpassed, or even equaled, and poets such as Jalāl al-Dīn Rūmī have achieved international eminence. Rūmī and other poets of the time were recognized and acclaimed during their own lifetimes, and the fact that their rich and powerful patrons had the time and money to indulge in such cultivated pastimes, rather than being forced to squander their wealth on weapons and armies, suggests that the *Pax Mongolica* had given birth to a culturally rich and sophisticated milieu. It is an indication of the influence of the Persian elite that Mongols also became patrons of these wordsmiths and, though generally averse to flattery and panegyrics, the Mongols slowly succumbed to this pervasive Persian vice. Though it has been suggested by such respected thinkers as Lewisohn, Arberry, Hamid Algar, and Manūchihr Murtaḍawī that the rise of mysticism and the growing popularity of the Sufi poet Ibn al-ʿArabī were reflective of the political instability and the barbarism of daily life under the Mongols, there is no evidence to support this assertion.[60] The popularity of Rūmī, Sufism, Zen Buddhism, and mysticism in California has not been blamed on the harshness and horror of life in the Golden State. In fact, the rise of interest in Sufism, and the indulgence in such soul-seeking and cultivated and refined occupations, suggests the opposite. The elite had the time, the money, and the inclination to indulge in the luxury of poetry readings, meditation, and the contemplation of the deeper meaning of life. They could afford the luxury of court poets and forgo the expense of a military buildup.

Members of the Persian elite could be found among the practitioners of Sufism and poetry, and the reaction of their families and their Mongol friends and associates is revealing. Fakhr al-Dīn ʿIrāqī (1213–1289) was born into a wealthy and influential family of religious scholars. However, while still a young man he became captivated by a passing group of Qalandars (antinomian wandering dervishes), and in particular a beautiful youth among them. He immediately left home and family and took to the road. After traveling throughout Iran, he ended up in India, where he met his future spiritual master. He returned to his home in the later 1250s, and in this his early life resembles that of another famous poet, Saʿdī of Shiraz. Both had left their homes during a period of instability and considerable danger and both returned once Hülegü had established the stability and security of the Ilkhanate. ʿIrāqī eventually settled in Konya, where he befriended the Tabriz-appointed overseer of Rūm, the Parwānah Muʿīn al-Dīn, who was also a friend of Rūmī. Though nominally a Qalandar who would shock his admirers with pronouncements such as, "Bring me wine for I have renounced renunciation, for all my vaunted self-righteousness seems to me but swagger and self-display," ʿIrāqī led a life of quiet luxury and great regard.[61] The parwānah sought his company on a daily basis and the poet remained honored and respected by all. Even after the parwānah's fall into disgrace, ʿIrāqī enjoyed the highest regard and even Shams al-Dīn Juwaynī, Abaqa's *ṣāḥib dīwān,* felt honored entertaining and supporting him.[62] In return, ʿIrāqī dedicated his *ʿUshshāqnāmah* to Shams al-Dīn, the Ilkhanid chief minister, illustrating the accessibility of the dīwān to Sufi influence and another path of commonality shared by Mongols and Persians.[63]

Another powerful aristocratic family of the time with a Sufi poet in their midst were the Simnānīs of western Khurasan.[64] Though the family was rich and powerful, it was a financially modest member of their clan that ensured the longevity and fame of their name. The Sufi and poet ʿAlāʾ al-Dawla al-Simnānī (1261–1336), who abandoned the luxury and indolence of the Ilkhanid court and broke off a long friendship with the immensely powerful Arghun Khan (r. 1284–1291) himself, embraced piety, asceticism, and mysticism rather than continue his life as a trained and influential courtier.[65] His family merits mention in Mustawfī's *Tārīkh-i Guzīdah,* where the Sufi poet is included in the section listing eminent shaykhs. Mustawfī mentions that Simnānī's father held a position of high ministerial rank.[66] Like the other prominent Khurasani family, the Juwaynīs, the Simnānīs were fully involved with the intrigues and machinations of the Ilkhanid court, where they had the ear of Arghun Khan for whom they had worked before his elevation to Ilkhan. The Simnānī family were descendants of local landowners (*mulūk*) around the village of Biyābānak, about fifteen kilometers west of Simnān, and their holdings were large enough for the father and uncle of the poet, Simnānī, to call themselves maliks. Prior to the arrival of the Chinggisids the family had found employment with the Khwārazm-shāh, and just like the Juwaynīs, had swapped allegiances seamlessly, though in the case of the Simnānīs, they ended up working for Arghun Khan, the Juwaynī brothers' nemesis.

The poet's mother's family were descended from reputable notables. Ḍiyāʾ al-Mulk Muḥammad b. Mawdūd, grandfather of the Sufi poet on his mother's side, served as military reviewer, first for the ill-fated ʿAlāʾ al-Dīn Muḥammad Khwārazm-shāh and then for his son Jalāl al-Dīn, before the "heroic" prince's dramatic escape across the Indus in ca. 1221.[67] Ḍiyāʾ al-Mulk's son Khwāja Rukn al-Dīn Ṣāʾin was a chief magistrate (*qāḍī jumlat al-mamālik*) until his execution in 1301 on the orders of Ghazan Khan, for "mischief making" (*khalal uftad*), along with various other officials.[68] Rukn al-Dīn Ṣāʾin was also a boon companion of the supposedly anti-Muslim Arghun.[69]

On the Sufi poet's paternal side, there were similar connections, with his great-grandfather Amīr Ḍiyāʾ al-Dīn Biyābānakī Simnānī being one of five vice-regents appointed by the Khwārazm-shāh in 1200.[70] Both his father and his paternal uncle entered Arghun Khan's service when the prince was ruler of Khurasan.

The uncle, Jalāl al-Dīn Mukhlaṣ Simnānī, who merits a page in Khwāndamīr's *Record of Ministers* and a chapter in Mustawfī's *Ẓafarnāmah*, fell from grace and was executed as a result of the machinations surrounding the appointment of the Jewish chief minister, Saʿd al-Dawla.[71] However, Jalāl al-Dīn's original appointment again casts doubt on the common assertion that Arghun Khan ran a markedly anti-Muslim administration and Mustawfī's account of this Sunni minister's downfall contains no suggestion that his religion played any role in his demise.

ʿAlāʾ al-Dawla Simnānī's closeness to Arghun Khan is evident from the poet's spiritual autobiography, where he records long, intimate conversations between the two about religion and the nature of God. When Arghun famously had the poet arrested after the now pious Simnānī had fled the royal court without permission, their conversation reflects their tempestuous and intimate relationship. "Until that time I was your servant. Now I recognize my own lord and I am no longer bound to you. I have no fear of you."[72] Arghun had ordered that a Buddhist monk be brought before him so that Simnānī and the monk could engage in religious debate. He commanded the monk to ask any question of Simnānī, and his answer to Arghun is revealing of the relationships which must have existed at the courts of that time. "'Question him!' The monk laughed and said, 'Since childhood he and I have been together. What could he know that I could question him about?'"[73] Persian nobles grew up alongside the Chinese and Chinggisid elite, sharing the same dreams and aspirations, ambitions, and opportunities. Simnānī reports the monk's words without contradiction, so it must be assumed they are accurate and that playtime in those young formative years was not segregated according to race or religion.

The debate between the Buddhist monk and Simnānī, the young Sufi, was held before an audience of great lords (*umarā-i buzurg*). Simnānī was convinced that with the help of his true God he could shame and ridicule his spiritual opponent and he detected in Arghun sympathy for his views. "I saw that my words had taken hold in Arghun's heart." After the debate the king led the Sufi outside to a small, quiet garden where they sat together so that, according to the poet's colorful account, Arghun could hear more of Simnānī's "welcome words."[74] Arghun revealed himself as being sympathetic to Islam and willing to listen to a friend but mainly he showed himself very reluctant to lose a very dear boon companion.

Simnānī uses Arghun's habit of forcing wine on him when he was fasting to reflect on and question the Islamic ruling on the permissibility of breaking the fast. He also uses the copious consumption of wine by the

Buddhist monk, apparently a companion of his since childhood, to pour scorn on the Buddhists. "You sit here, and in your belly there is nearly five *mann* (15 kilograms) of wine. In what manner are you a Buddhist?"[75]

Simnānī had followed the conventional upbringing of a young Persian noble of the times. He moved in elite circles without ethnic boundaries and it was in such circumstances that he entered into a close friendship with Prince Arghun at whose Khurasan-based court Simnānī's relatives were already employed. From the age of four until fifteen he studied under a local teacher, Ṣadr al-Dīn Akhfāsh, noteworthy for his vehement opposition to Sufism. Simnānī came into contact with Sufism only by chance, and very superficially, in his youth. He would have encountered Qalandars, who were often figures of fun and ridicule, and it is unlikely such figures would have impressed an ambitious young notable. However, it is worth noting that the largest landowner in Simnān, Sayyid Ibrāhīm, was a minor Sufi figure who later became a devotee of Simnānī.

ʿAlāʾ al-Dawla Simnānī joined Arghun's court at the age of fifteen and continued there until his sudden mystical conversion to the true path of Sufism. His first religious experience famously occurred on the battlefield while engaged in hostilities against ʿAlīnāq, a general representing Arghun's rival, Aḥmad Tegüder (r. 1282–1284).[76] He was twenty-four years old, and the deep mystical state that enveloped him lasted throughout the actual battle and into the next day as well, and affected him profoundly. However, it must be assumed that on that day he continued to perform effectively throughout the battle despite his ecstatic state of mind, since there is no mention of erratic behavior in accounts of this ultimately indecisive military encounter.

Simnānī continued to be welcome at Arghun's court despite his private misgivings about fighting Muslims on behalf of his pagan masters. For Simnānī, life was irrevocably changed and after this noetic experience he felt that his soul had now "turned away in disgust from the pleasures of this world and [he] became weary of the company of the Sultan."[77] Interestingly, a close spiritual adviser urged him to continue in the service of Arghun Khan, arguing that as many devout people as possible should seek service in the court and thereby bring their influence to bear on the Sultan. Simnānī remained with the Sultan for another year and a half, though he gave up alcohol and adopted a life of asceticism while at the court. Eventually he also abandoned his courtly and costly robes, hat, and belt and donned the coarse dress of the dervish, a symbolic act of renunciation.

From Simnānī's own writings it is known that he was well versed in the rational and the traditional sciences and the education open to all the offspring of the elite, Mongol, Turk, and Tajik, but by his own admission his education was deficient in theological training. He now devoted himself to the study of comparative religion and immersed himself in the principles of belief of the Indians, Persians, Arabs, Greeks, and Turks, as well as the Sunni schools and the various Islamic sects such as the Qalandars, the Nuṣayriyya, and the Ibn al-Iʿrābiyya [*sic*].[78] Lacking a spiritual guide, he acquired his knowledge from books, though it is not known if he had access to Naṣīr al-Dīn Ṭūsī's library in Marāgha. What is noteworthy, however, is that his education up to this time had been acquired in the Mongol *ordu* where he grew up along with his contemporaries, including Arghun, who is often considered a Mongol of the more traditional mold.

During the 1280s, Simnānī continued to have mystical experiences and his health declined because of the ascetic practices that were increasingly absorbing his time. Arghun had given him permission to return to Simnān and it was there, in October 1287, that he first encountered Akhī Sharaf al-Dīn al-Ḥanawayh, a disciple of Nūr al-Dīn al-Isfarāʾinī to whom Simnānī also attached himself. As a result of his acquaintance with al-Isfarāʾinī and his mystic exercises and practices through the latter's disciple Sharaf al-Dīn, Simnānī decided to divest himself of all his worldly wealth and possessions. After providing generously for his wife and son, he donated all his money to charity and *waqfs* and paid for the construction of the Khānagāh-i Sakkākiyya.[79] However, it is believed that he retained control over these funds and endowments and he did not leave himself destitute.

In 1288 Simnānī decided that he had to see his Sufi master al-Isfarāʾinī in person and set off on the journey from Simnān to Baghdad without first obtaining permission from the sultan, Arghun Khan. When the sultan heard of his departure, he immediately dispatched troops to waylay his friend and bring him back to Sharūyāz near Tabriz, from where Arghun was directing construction of the new capital, Sulṭāniyya. Arghun instructed his soldiers to use force if it should prove necessary. Simnānī was detained at the court for eighty days, where he was reprimanded for his behavior by his relatives and forced into theological debates with Buddhist monks for Arghun's entertainment. Simnānī defeated his theological opponents, and so pleased Arghun that the Sultan pleaded unsuccessfully for his friend to remain at court, even as a dervish dressed in Sufi robes. After Simnānī's departure his uncle, with Arghun's consent, dispatched another Sufi, Ḥājjī-i Āmulī, to stay close to the wayward poet and ensure that he did not go to Baghdad in search of his mentor al-Isfarā'inī.[80] The latter consoled Simnānī with a message of assurance that their spiritual communion could continue without physically meeting, and in the meantime he sent him a Sufi "coat of many colors" (*khirqa mulammaʿa*).[81] These episodes throw light on the nature of personal relationships at the highest levels of the Ilkhanid administration.

It was not a court where ethnic divisions were prevalent, and it was a court where lively debate and discussion were encouraged. The figure of Arghun, so often portrayed as cruel, intolerant, and bloodthirsty, is given a surprisingly human face. Arghun had finally given his friend permission to retire to his *khānagāh* in Simnan. However, Simnānī had promised the sultan that he would break all contact with the courtiers and the administration, "Never [again] will I associate with the people from the sultan's world" (*hargiz bih dīdan ahl-i dunyā az salāṭīn narawam*), a pledge he honored and referred to many years later, when he formally responded to Amīr Chūpān's request for an audience.[82]

It was not until September 1289 that Simnānī, journeying to Baghdad, met his spiritual master, who commanded him to make the *ḥajj* before returning to Simnan to attend to his dying mother. It is likely that the politically astute al-Isfarāʾinī decided that it would be safer for his disciple to be well out of the way while the political machinations in which the Simnānī family were deeply involved took their course. It was on his return to his hometown that Simnānī learnt of the execution of his father, implicated in intrigues supposedly involving the Mamluks. His uncle Khwāja Rukn al-Dīn Ṣā'in was executed by Ghazan in 1301 and the Ilkhanid court continued to discourage the relationship between Simnānī and al-Isfarāʾinī in Baghdad, though it was tolerated. Simnānī maintained a friendship with Ṣafī al-Dīn, eponymous founder of the Safawid Sufi order, who enjoyed the support and admiration of Ghazan Khan. Öljeitü, however, invited the poet to the inauguration of his own religious center, the Abwāb al-birr in Sulṭāniyya, but after the sultan's adoption of Shiʿism, to which Simnānī expressed his disapproval, relations soured.[83] During this period, Simnānī enjoyed the friendship of a major religious figure with strong links to the Mongol-led administration, Ṣadr al-Dīn Ibrāhīm Ḥamūya Juwaynī (1246–1322) of the Kubrawī order. Ṣadr al-Dīn is regarded as instrumental in the conversion to Islam of Ghazan Khan and the many notables, soldiers, and "obstinate polytheists" who followed his lead.[84] In 1272 he married the daughter of ʿAṭā Malik Juwaynī, governor of Baghdad. In fact, Simnānī's estrangement from the court did not adversely affect his relations with the *ʿulamāʾ*, who became progressively more important in the Ilkhanid administration as Islam became more entrenched and integrated among the Mongol elite. Another prominent figure, ʿAbd al-Razzāq al-Kāshānī, a leading exponent of the ideas of Ibn ʿArabī, was in close contact with Simnānī, the two exchanging correspondence on the ontological nature of God and the universe.

It was not until the enthroning of Abū Saʿīd that Simnānī was once again welcomed to the Ilkhanid court, and he harbored a particularly close relationship with the Amīr Chūpān, who is mentioned with affection and admiration in the *Chihil Majlis*.[85] His rehabilitation was so complete that Amīr Chūpān sought his intercession with Abū Saʿīd, with whom the amīr was on the point of war. Simnānī, referred to now as the *shaykh al-mashāyikh*, attempted to charm the sultan with Mongol expressions and his famed eloquence, but to no avail, and Chūpān went on to meet his fate.[86] He had been more successful when he interceded for Ghiyāth al-Dīn Kart in 1314/5 with Öljeitü.[87]

For Mustawfī, Arghun Khan's accession to the Ilkhanid throne in 1284 "made all hearts glad" and "the soot of calamity was wiped from the mirror of good fortune. From the garden of greatness, the weeds were cleared."[88] This praise is excessive even by mediaeval Persian standards of hyperbole. "The face of the earth was wearing brocade of golden Chinese weaving; the garden gleamed with the colour of the narcissus."[89] Arghun's appointment of a Mongol, Buqa, as his *chingsang* (loosely applied Chinese title for minister) and chief minister reinforces the sense of integration between Persian and Mongol, Tajik and Turanian, Muslim and non-Muslim at the Ilkhanid courts.[90] Unfortunately, Buqa's presentation by Khwāndamīr as Khwāja Shams al-Dīn Muḥammad Buqa must be considered a copyist's error, rather than evidence of Muslim leanings or sympathies on the part of this leading Chinggisid lord. Buqa's duplicity toward Shams al-Dīn Juwaynī had allowed him to assume the reins of administrative power over the Ilkhanid state.

Buqa and Aruq were the sons of Ögölai Qorchi of the Oyrat tribe, who had come to Iran with Hülegü. Both had been attendants of Abaqa Khan and Aruq had returned from a mission to the Qa'an with a *kök tamgha* (blue seal), on the strength of which he was appointed commander of all *shünchis* (provisioners). Buqa was a *tamghachi* and kept the store of pelts, in addition to being a top commander. However, Buqa, though he had served Arghun loyally and effectively for many years, met the fate so common among Ilkhanid courtiers. His intrigues involved other courtiers and commanders, both Iranian and Turanian, and it is apparent that ethnicity was no measure of the strength or degree of influence at court. Mustawfī speaks highly of this Mongol minister, though the fact that Buqa appointed the author's uncle, Fakhr al-Dīn, to the chancellery, might have colored his judgment and inspired his more excessive claims. According to the nephew, "Iran became like a brimming spring of cheer (*jū khurram*)" after his uncle took hold of the economic reins and when later, at Malik Jalāl al-Dīn Mukhlaṣ Simnānī's prompting, Fakhr al-Dīn was appointed to Anatolia, "Rūm [became] such that God was envious of it."[91] Mustawfī credits Buqa's initial successes to the work of his uncle. Fakhr al-Dīn survived his Mongol master, and Buqa's arrogance and greed finally reached the ears of Arghun, who ordered his onetime friend and confidant removed from office. Arghun had heeded the words of, among others, Sa'd al-Dawla b. Ṣafī al-Dīn Abharī (the Jewish minister already mentioned; see also below) and Ordu Qaya, who had backed up their tales of corruption by demonstrating how much tax could be delivered to the royal court if none was creamed off for the collectors.[92] Rather than accepting his dismissal and throwing himself on the generosity and goodwill of his king, Buqa allowed his anger to cloud his judgment and he began scheming and plotting against the throne. But his fate was unavoidable and the "Old Wolf of the World" (*kāī, pīr gurg [kurk] kuhn*)[93] was sentenced to death with the following instructions: "Take off his head and in vengeance, lay him open with the sword. Take his heart from his black body and drown his whole face in blood."[94]

Though in Buqa's case, the conspiracy against him was led by Mongol lords, Persian nobles were also involved at every level. Sa'd al-Dawla had the ear of the Ilkhan, and together with a Mongol administrator was able to collect solid evidence of corruption. Ḥusām al-Dīn Qazwīnī, acting as Buqa's deputy, was caught red-handed by *ayqaqs* (informants), returning from Fars province with a shortfall of one and a half million dinars. Amīr 'Alī Tamghachi, Buqa's governor of Tabriz, was relieved of his office to face charges of corruption.[95] Aruq was dismissed from office and in his place Arghun appointed Ordu Qaya as governor (*amārat*), Sharaf al-Dīn as malik, and Sa'd al-Dawla as overseer (*ashrāf*).[96] Among the leading supporters of Buqa who were executed following his failed attempt at bribing various commanders and princes were the following minor figures who were central to his rule: Amīr 'Alī Tamghachi, Ḥusām al-Dīn Qazwīnī, 'Imād al-Dīn Munajjim, Shim'ūn known as Rūm Qal'a, and Bahā' al-Dawla Abū al-Karam Naṣrānī.[97]

Brokenhearted, Arghun Khan appointed Malik Jalāl al-Dīn Mukhlaṣ Simnānī as his former boon companion's replacement. Mukhlaṣ was a Muslim and, like his predecessor, he quickly fell victim to the fatal attractions of the powerful office of the *ṣāḥib dīwān*. According to Mustawfī, the aging Darius of Simnān, as he sarcastically dubbed Jalāl al-Dīn Mukhlaṣ, had little confidence in his own abilities and it was this insecurity that was behind his recommendation to Arghun that the able and well-regarded Fakhr al-Dīn of the Qazwīnī political clan be entrusted with the governorship of Rūm under Prince Geikhatu:

> We must find a skilled man, and famous, to govern that pleasant land, for without a man who is incapable of evil action, misfortune will rapidly overtake the land of Rūm. We need a man who will show Geikhatu the right path and act as vizier in his presence.[98]

With his only real rival far away in Anatolia, Jalāl al-Dīn Mukhlaṣ enjoyed the trappings of his position without being able to meet the considerable demands of the job. "He was idle, negligent and confused by the affairs of the kingdom" and gossip, along with the endemic political intrigue of a Persian court, provided fertile soil for a shrewd and ambitious political adventurer to sow greedy seeds of discontent and paranoia. Khwāndamīr, writing two centuries later, blames the Jewish vizier Saʿd al-Dawla for bringing on his predecessor's ruin and also blames this minister with poisoning Arghun's mind against Muslims in general and feeding him ideas of his own divinity and powers of prophecy inherited from Chinggis Khan himself. Mustawfī blames Saʿd al-Dawla for bringing on the death of his uncle Fakhr al-Dīn Mustawfī, but not of direct responsibility for the demise of Jalāl al-Dīn Mukhlaṣ. Much has been made of Arghun's supposed dislike of Muslims, though there is little evidence of this, and the fate of Mukhlaṣ is heralded as evidence of this ill will. However, as far as Mustawfī was concerned, and he was close enough to the players and the events to have had personal insight, it was Jalāl al-Dīn Mukhlaṣ who had essentially engineered his own downfall.

Like the future minister Rashīd al-Dīn, Saʿd al-Dawla's medical background allowed him access to court circles and his diplomatic skills attracted attention in the highest echelons.[99] He became personal physician to Arghun Khan and the two developed a close friendship. When Arghun Khan was stricken with a fatal disease, Bar Hebraeus remarks on the "the great care he [Saʿd al-Dawla] endeavored in every possible way to heal him." As shown above, Saʿd al-Dawla had originally been sent to investigate accusations of malpractice against Aruq, a Mongol administrator appointed by his brother, Buqa, to oversee Iraq and Diyār Bakr. Saʿd al-Dawla b. Ṣafī al-Dīn Abharī reported back to Arghun that the province was in a state of disorder, rampant corruption, and poverty, and the sultan duly appointed him, in ca. 1287, *mushrif al-mamālik* (head of auditing). Aruq and Qutlugh Shāh, the governor of Baghdad, both lost their jobs. Saʿd al-Dawla became *ṣāḥib dīwān* in 1289. That he was an able administrator and that the country flourished for the first years of his rule is generally conceded in the sources. Also noted was the wide background of people appointed to high office under his rule including Mongols, Christians, Turks, Jews, and Shiʿi and Sunni Muslims. He appointed both relatives and high-ranking Mongols to positions of power. One brother, Fakhr al-Dawla, was appointed to rule Baghdad while another, Amīn al-Dawla, was appointed to Diyār Bakr. His cousin, Muḥazzib al-Dawla Abū Manṣūr Ṭabīb, became overseer of Tabriz. Ordu Qaya became his personal assistant, Joshi Noyan was made amīr of Shiraz and Quchan was appointed amīr of Tabriz. These three Mongols were named liegemen (*nūkār*) and had unrestricted access to the vizier. Sarban, the son of Suqunjaq Aqa, acted as the amīr and tax collector for the province of Fars.[100] He ruled with the help and support of his friend and long-time colleague, a Mongol, Ordu Qaya. However, for many he was too effective and efficient and the fact that "to the nobles of the camp he paid no heed, and he reduced the taking and giving of their hands, and he treated with contempt the principal Amîrs and directors of affairs" meant that he had powerful enemies among the Mongol elite, as well.[101] There is also consensus that his autocratic nature and blatant promotion of his often undeserving and incompetent family members ensured his ignominious downfall. What is interesting in the drama of his fall is the roll call of players who conspired in Saʿd al-Dawla's demise.

Saʿd al-Dawla had earned the enmity of at least two leading families, the Mustawfīs and the Simnānīs, because of his perceived role in the downfall of Fakhr al-Dīn Mustawfī in 1290 and of Jalāl al-Dīn Mukhlaṣ in 1289. In addition, powerful Mongol amīrs such as Tughan, who had long resented Saʿd al-Dawla's influence with the Ilkhan, joined the ranks of the conspirators against the vizier. The establishment, Persian and Mongol, were united and together they plotted the minister's downfall. A banquet was held at the home of the Mongol amīr Tugharjar, to which the minister and those surrounding him were treacherously invited. It was to be their last invitation anywhere. An Arabic *qaṣīda* celebrated the massacre and the consequent attack on the Jewish community of Baghdad. A few lines actually applaud the perfidy of Tugharjar, who instigated the murder of his guests in his own house, an act as inimical to Mongols as to Muslims:

> Tughachar prince, fulfilled with strength and zeal,
> Hath caused the pillars of their power to reel.
> His fleshing falchion on their flesh did feed
> And none would hold him guilty for the deed.[102]

Saʿd al-Dawla's friend and colleague, and close friend also of Suqunjaq's son, Sarban, the Mongol Ordu Qaya, and others close to the *ṣāḥib dīwān* were murdered at the same time, before the mob moved on to raid their victims' homes. This whole incident reveals the interwoven nature of the Persian and Mongol establishment. The elite were not drawn from one community and authority and influence were not determined by race. Saʿd al-Dawla, a Jew, had authority over both Mongols and Persians, and those who would oppose or depose him could not rely on their ethnicity to help them.

The Muẓaffarids were another family who had established links with the Chinggisids when Hülegü set off for Baghdad. They traced their ancestry back to the Arab invasions when they had settled in Khwāf, Khurasan. At the time of the first Mongol irruptions the family had moved to Yazd and entered the service of the Atabeg ʿAlāʾ al-Dawla. The atabeg had dispatched Abū Bakr b. al-Ḥājjī, the eldest son of the Muẓaffarid clan, along with three hundred horsemen to join Hülegü at the siege of Baghdad in 1258. After this, Abū Bakr was posted to the Egyptian frontier, where he was killed in battle with the Arabs, presumably at the battle at ʿAyn Jālūt. His brother Muḥammad succeeded him as a lieutenant to the Atabeg of Yazd. A third son, Manṣūr, settled in Maybūd near Yazd with his father, and it is from his issue that the family achieved fame and greatness.

Sharaf al-Dīn Muẓaffar ibn Manṣūr was the youngest of the sons and was entrusted with the governorship of his district, Maybūd, which he proceeded to carry out with gusto, reputedly clearing out the whole region of brigands. He eventually entered Mongol service under Arghun to whom he was presented. Under the Ilkhan Geikhatu he was sent with an army to Lūristān, where he was charged with defeating the rebel atabeg, Afrāsiyāb (himself son of the rebellious former atabeg of Yazd, Yūsuf Shāh), who had murdered Arghun's ambassadors. Muẓaffar succeeded in subduing Afrāsiyāb and coaxing him back into an alliance. In 1295 the new Ilkhan, Ghazan, recognized Muẓaffar's value, awarded him all the insignia of authority, and made him amīr of a thousand. On Öljeitü's accession, Muẓaffar was put in charge of security on the roads from Ardistān to Kirmānshāh and from Herat and Marw to Abarqūh and accompanied the sultan on his campaign to Gilān. Muẓaffar died in 1314, possibly poisoned by his enemies, who included the recently subdued rebellious Shabānkāraʾīs.

The rise of the thirteen-year-old Mubāriz al-Dīn Muḥammad to take over his father's various positions saw the Muẓaffarids established among the Ilkhanid elite. The intrigues at the courts of Öljeitü and Abū Saʿīd are well documented and the young Mubāriz al-Dīn, cruel, bloodthirsty, and treacherous while at the same time religiously conservative, cultured, and brave, fitted in well. Excelling himself in campaigns against the Sīstānīs, also known as the Nīkūdārīs (i.e., the Mongol Negüderis), and against the last of the atabegs of Yazd, Mubāriz al-Dīn had laid the groundwork for his descendants who eventually, after the collapse of the Ilkhanid regime following the death of Abū Saʿīd, assumed the governorship of Shīrāz.[103]

The developments at the central *ordu* and among the main movers and shakers of the Ilkhanid state were by no means atypical. At the provincial level integration and cultural fertilization was occurring at every level. The example of the Karts has already been examined, but even a cursory investigation of events in Kirmān or Yazd or Shīrāz reveals a similar situation.

The integration of the Qara Khitai of Kirmān into the cultural life of the Persian elite could serve almost as a dress rehearsal for the absorption of the Ilkhanid sophisticates into the Persian milieu of the later thirteenth century. Pādshāh Khātūn, a wife of the Ilkhan Abaqa, wrote verse to express her identity crisis, one minute hankering back in her dreams to a golden age in the saddle and on the steppe, the next enjoying the trappings of a Persian princess in her sumptuous palace.[104]

> Although I am the child of a mighty Sulṭān
> And the fruit of the garden that is the heart of the Turks,
> I laugh at fate and prosperity,
> But I cry at this endless exile.[105]

The formidable Terkan Khātūn, Pādshāh's mother, ruled Kirmān through its golden years and the twenty-six or so years she wielded power are universally recognized as the heyday of this southern province. The Qutlugh Khans, as these descendants of the Qara Khitai became known, exhibited the influence of the steppe in the leading role played by their women, but their court was decked in the trappings of Persian culture and tradition. Both mother and daughter felt at home in the central *ordu* in Azerbaijan where they both maintained their own courts, but at the same time Kirmān remained their base. Terkan Khātūn had no compunction in using her daughter's renowned beauty to entice Abaqa into marriage though such a union was forbidden under Islamic law. Though the anonymous *Tārīkh-i shāhī* claims she had misgivings and worries about the marriage, Waṣṣāf describes the Kirmānī queen as actively promoting her daughter's union with the Ilkhan.[106] It is generally agreed, however, that the marriage was strong and that Abaqa was very much taken with his new wife, his "rosebud" who "more than compensated for the other *khawātīn*."[107]

The title that Baraq Ḥājib, the founder of the Kirmān dynasty, carried had two forms of the honorary "Qutlugh" (fortunate). He had been named Qutlugh Khan by Chinggis Khan and Qutlugh Sulṭān by the caliph and his situation and the development of his dynasty illustrates well the mingling of the cultures of steppe and sown which Īrānzamīn was becoming.[108] The Qara Khitai had been welcomed when first they had appeared from the East and had adjusted to their adopted role of barrier against the threat to the Islamic world from the steppe.[109] After their demise, this much-diluted Turco-Mongol tribe had found partial resurrection in the south in the province of Kirmān. It is interesting that they clung to their steppe heritage with pride and made no attempt to submerge that identity within the brotherhood of Islam. Though practicing Muslims with a history of pious works, patronage, and support from the *'ulamā'*, they would not renounce their pre-Islamic past. Pādshāh Khātūn made a happy marriage with an infidel prince and relished her connections with the steppe. Pādshāh committed to verse her fantasies of a life in the saddle and on the steppe, but in her husband's *ordu* she was able to abandon the persona of the pious and delicate Muslim princess and embrace the role of the hardy Turanian wench fresh from the saddle, wielding the wine flagon ready to replenish the empty goblets of her lord and his table. Her mother had been fearful that the duties expected of her at her husband Abaqa's *ordu* might prove challenging for the "proud and well-bred," "dainty coquette," that the cultural clash of a sheltered aristocratic Persian upbringing and the reality of the Turanian dinner party might prove overwhelming for her sensitive princess. Terkan Khātūn's fears were quickly allayed, her "divine guardian angels brought forth words of comfort" and her daughter embraced her Turkish heritage.[110] A happy compromise was achieved and the Muslim historians remember both mother and daughter with respect and affection.

Writing in 1275, Nāṣir al-Dīn Bayḍāwī portrays the Ilkhanate as the natural successor state of the preceding Iranian dynasties. His sovereign was Abaqa Khan who was "willingly just and compassionate" and "greatly favored Muslims." Bayḍāwī claims that the esteemed Mongol Suqunjaq Aqa and the Persian sophisticate, Shams al-Dīn Juwaynī, occupied a pivotal role in Abaqa's court, which had become an "assembly of the sultans of Iran" (*imrūz dargāh-i aw salāṭīn īrā nrā anjamanī ast*).[111] The picture that emerges of the establishment of the Ilkhanate is not one of forceful and violent occupation and the aggressive suppression of the indigenous culture by an alien and predatory force. It is more the assimilation and integration of the new world order and the absorption of a conquering Persian-speaking ruling class. In this new world, Suqunjaq, the quintessential man of the sword and Chinggisid hero, is remembered for having prevented both the ill-treatment of the condemned and the molestation of his political rival's wife and child.[112] In his Marāgha residence, he spent money on the trappings of culture and refinement and established business dealings with Shams al-Dīn Juwaynī.[113] In Shiraz he cultivated the local *'ulamā'* and notables and earned a reputation for justice, astute judgment, and for being a bulwark against oppression and corruption.[114] The librarian, chronicler, and biographer Ibn al-Fuwaṭī recounts how the son of a close aide to the *noyan* "kept company with the learned men of the Uighurs and bakhshis, and learned from them how to write the Uighur script as well as their language."[115] Such proficiency in eastern languages was not always enough for the Ilkhanid *dīwān*, as the example of a certain Muẓaffar al-Dīn Qutlugh Beg b. Ibrāhīm, the court translator, suggests. As *al-amīr al-tarjumān* (Amīr Translator), he was required to transform "Turkic and Uighur and Persian into eloquent Arabic."[116] Suqunjaq's downfall was the result of the machinations of Persian courtiers, an example possibly of the equality existent in the "new world order" he had fought so hard to achieve.[117]

That a cleric of such stature as Bayḍāwī, a widely respected authority on jurisprudence, deemed it appropriate and desirable to legitimize and recognize this new world order and its manifestation in Iran underlines the readiness of the Persian elite to accept and integrate with the new Mongol-led court. The germ of the concept of Iran once again a player on the global stage must have accompanied the Qazwīnī embassy to Möngke Qa'an ca. 1251, and endorsement of the new status quo was contained in Bayḍāwī's "pocket-history."[118] The steppe had met the sown and they had formed a happy union. In the later years of the Ilkhanate in particular it was no longer possible to make a distinction between Mongol camps and Persian camps.[119] The two had intermingled so much that ethnic divisions had long ceased to be meaningful and loyalties did not run along racial lines. When ʿAlāʾ al-Dawla Simnānī passes judgment on those in command he derides the Mongol sultan for his Shiʿite leanings while praising the Mongol amīr Chūpān for his loyalty to the Sunni cause.[120] On a broader front, it can be argued the historians of the time often see the world and identify their place in it from a political perspective. They portray the world in which they and their masters are operating from the viewpoint of the Toluids and see the opposition as the forces loyal to the Jochids of the Qipchaq khanate and the Chaghadaids. Hence their belittling of the serious strife between Arigh Bökea and his older brother, Qubilai. The Yuan dynasty and the Ilkhanate represented the bold new face of the progressive, integrated Chinggisids whereas the reactionaries, remnants of the humiliated Ögödeids and Chaghadaids, saw in Arigh Böke their last chance of stemming the tide of reform and change that was sweeping the transformed Chinggisid empire.[121] Just as his brother Qubilai Khan was making the journey from steppe to sown in a united China, so Hülegü was treading a similar path in the west when he founded the Ilkhanate and successfully integrated his top commanders and their families with the leading families from Iran, many of whose youngsters grew up alongside the children of the Turco-Mongol elite. It was from these cosmopolitan *ordus* that a new elite with a broader vision and braver aspirations was to emerge.

Notes

1. Rashīd al-Dīn, *Jāmiʿ al-tawārīkh,* ed. M. Rawshān and M. Mūsawī (Tehran, 1994), p. 78; tr. W. A. Thackston, *Rashiduddin Fazlullah's Jami'u't-tawarikh: Compendium of Chronicles* (Cambridge, MA, 1998–1999), p. 44.

2. Ḥamdallāh Mustawfī, *Ẓafarnāmeh* (Tehran, 1999), p. 1168; tr. L. J. Ward, "*Ẓafarnāmeh* of Mustawfī" (PhD dissertation, University of Manchester, 1983), pp. 13–14. Mustawfī provides the most detailed depiction of the Qazwini delegation to Möngke where he records the delegation's request for a king to be appointed as a replacement of the very unpopular Baiju Noyan. [Editors' note: Möngke also had other reasons for continuing the expansion into southwest Asia; see e.g., T. T. Allsen, *Mongol Imperialism* (Berkeley, 1987), pp. 77–79].

3. Ḥamdallāh Mustawfī, *Tārīkh-i Guzīdah* (Tehran, 1983), p. 799.

4. See C. Melville, "The Survival of the Royal Mongol Household," in *Beyond the Legacy of Genghis Khan,* ed. L. Komaroff (Leiden, 2006), pp. 135–164.

5. Juwaynī, *Tārīkh-i jahāngushā,* ed. M. M. Qazwīnī (London, 1912–1937), vol. 3, p. 139; tr. J. A. Boyle, *Genghis Khan: The History of the World Conqueror* (Manchester, 1997), p. 638; G. Lane, "Whose Secret Intenṭ" in *Eurasian Influences on Yuan China,* ed. M. Rossabi (Singapore, 2013), pp. 1–40.

6. See C. Melville, "From Adam to Abaqa: Qâḍî Baidâwî's Rearrangement of History," *Studia Iranica,* 30 (2001), pp. 67–86; 36 (2007), pp. 7–64; ʿAbdallah Baydawi, *Nature, Man and God in Mediaeval Islam,* tr. and ed. E. Calverley and J. Pollock (Leiden, 2002).

7. Suqunjaq (Su'unchaq) was a Mongol general from the Suldus tribe who served as the governor of Shiraz in the 1270s and 1280s. More about him below, and see G. Lane, *Early Mongol Rule in Thirteenth Century Iran* (London, 2003), pp. 135–144.

8. Juwaynī, vol. 3, pp. 7, 60, 107; tr. Boyle, pp. 552, 589, 618.

9. J. M. Smith, Jr., "High Living and Heartbreak on the Road to Baghdad," in *Beyond the Legacy of Genghis Khan,* p. 130.

10. Ibn Ṭabāṭabā (Ibn al-Ṭiqṭaqā), *On the Systems of Government and the Moslem Dynasties,* tr. C. E. J. Whitting (London, 1990), p. 14; Muḥammad ʿAlī bin Ṭabāṭabā (Ibn al-Ṭiqṭaqā), *Tārīkh-i Fakhrī,* tr. M. W. Gulpāyigānī (Tehran, 1360/1981), pp. 18–19.

11. Jalāl al-Dīn Rūmī, *Kitāb fīhi mā fīh,* ed. Badīʿ al-Zamān Farūzānfar (Tehran, 1362/1983), pp. 11, 64; Jalāl al-Dīn Rūmī, *Discourses of Rumi,* tr. A. J. Arberry (Richmond, Surrey, 1994), pp. 23, 75.

12. Ibn Ṭabāṭabā, tr. Whitting, p. 14; Ibn Ṭabāṭabā (Ibn Ṭiqṭaqā), tr. Gulpāygānī, pp. 18–19.

13. E. Sperling, "Hülegü and Tibet," *Acta Orientalia,* 44 (1990), pp. 145–157.

14. L. Petech, *Central Tibet and the Mongols* (Rome, 1990), pp. 11, 88–90. Cf. T. T. Allsen, "Sharing out the Empire: Apportioned Lands under the Mongols," in *Nomads in the Sedentary World,* ed. A. M. Khazanov and A. Wink (Richmond, Surrey, 2001), pp. 172–190.

15. Mustawfī, *Ẓafarnāmah,* p. 1168; tr. Ward, pp. 13–14.

16. ʿAwfī, *Lubāb al-albāb,* ed. M. ʿAbbās (Tehran, 1361/1982), vol. 1, p. 244; Niẓāmī-i ʿArūdī Samarqandī, *Chahār maqāla,* ed. M. Muʿīnī (Tehran, 1377/1998), p. 38; tr. E. G. Browne, *The Chahár Maqála—"Four Discourses"* (London, 1978), p. 39.

17. Saʿdī, *Kulliyat-i Saʿdī,* ed. M. A. Farūghī (Tehran, 1368/1989), pp. 1181–1182.

18. ʿAṭā Malik Juwaynī, *Tasliyat al-ikhwān,* ed. A. Māhyār (Tehran, 1361/1982), p. 61.

19. Ibn Bībī, *Akhbār-i Salājiqah-i Rūm,* ed. M. Mashkūr (Tehran, 1971), pp. 202–205.

20. See C. Melville, "The Early Persian Historiography of Anatolia," in *History and Historiography of Post-Mongol Central Asia and the Middle East: Studies in Honor of John E. Woods,* ed. J. Pfeiffer and S. A. Quinn, with the assistance of E. Tucker (Wiesbaden, 2006), pp. 137–140.

21. Amīr Ḥasan Sizjī, *Nizam ad-Din Awliya's Morals for the Heart,* tr. Bruce Lawrence (New York, 1992), pp. 99–100; Amīr Ḥasan Sizjī, *Fawā'id al-fu'ād,* ed. M. L. Malik (Lahore, 1966), p. 28.

22. Dawlatshāh, *Tadhkirat al-shu'arā',* ed. E. G. Browne (London, 1901; rpt. Tehran, 1382/2003), pp. 134–135; see D. DeWeese, "Stuck in the Throat of Chingīz Khan," in *History and Historiography of Post-Mongol Central Asia and the Middle East,* pp. 23–60.

23. D. O. Morgan, "Persian as a *lingua franca* in the Mongol Empire," in *Literacy in the Persianate World: Writing and the Social Order,* ed. B. Spooner and W. L. Hanaway (Philadelphia, 2012), pp. 160–171.

24. See P. Buell, *A Soup for the Qan* (London, 2000), pp. 67–80; T. T. Allsen, *Culture and Conquest in Mongol Eurasia* (Cambridge, 2001), pp. 127–140.

25. Ch'en Yüan, *Western and Central Asians in China under the Mongols,* Monumenta Serica Monograph Series XV (Nettetal, 1989). During the Yuan dynasty (and in Chinese terminology in general), lands from Xinjiang to Europe were included in the term "Western Regions."

26. Ouyang Xuan, *Guizhai ji,* ch. 9, cited in Ch'en Yüan, *Western and Central Asians,* pp. 219–220.

27. Cited in Ch'en Yüan, *Western and Central Asians,* pp. 224–225.

28. G. Lane, "Phoenix Mosque of Hangzhou," *Encyclopaedia Iranica,* http://www.iranicaonline.org/articles/phoenix-mosque (accessed March 31, 2014).

29. Guo Xiaohang, "Yuan dai shouren Shanghhai xian daluhuazhi Shelafuding kaoshi," *Shilin,* 4 (2007), pp. 185–188.

30. Nāṣir al-Dīn Bayḍāwī, *Niẓām al-tawārīkh,* ed. Mir Hāshim Muḥaddith (Tehran, 1381/2002), p. 3.

31. Mustawfī, *Ẓafarnāmah,* e.g., pp. 217, 241, 242, 494, 502, etc.

32. Shihāb al-Dīn Muḥammad b. Aḥmad, Nasawī, *Sīrat Jalāl al-Dīn Mīnkubirnī* [*sic*], ed. M. Mīnuvī (Tehran, 1986), p. 49. [Editors' note: This book was originally written in Arabic in the thirteenth century and translated to Persian in the early fourteenth century; for the name Mingbarnī see P. Jackson, *The Delhi Sultanate: A Political and Military History* (Cambridge, 1999), p. 32, n. 44.]

33. Rashīd al-Dīn, *Jāmi' al-tawārīkh,* p. 1105.

34. See L. G. Potter, "The Kart Dynasty of Herat" (PhD dissertation, Columbia University, 1992), pp. 35–36.

35. Lane, *Early Mongol Rule,* pp. 152–176.

36. Mustawfī, *Ẓafarnāmah,* pp. 1024–1025; tr. in E. G. Browne, *Literary History of Persia* (Cambridge, 1920), vol. 3, pp. 96–98.

37. Mustawfī, *Tārīkh-i guzīdah,* p. 797.

38. Ibid., p. 9.

39. Mustawfī, *Ẓafarnāmah,* p. 1472: *chū sālim miyāmad biḥud chihil, khirad gasht shāhanshah malak-i dil;* tr. Ward, p. 671.

40. Mustawfī, *Tārīkh-i guzīdah,* intro., p. 10.

41. Ibid.

42. Mustawfī, *Ẓafarnāmah,* pp. 178–181, tr. Ward, pp. 331–334.

43. Rashīd al-Dīn, p. 1157; tr. Thackston, p. 564.

44. Rashīd al-Dīn, p. 1163; tr. Thackston, p. 566.

45. See F. de Blois, "Iftikhāriyān of Qazvin," in *Iran and Iranian Studies: Essays in Honour of Iraj Afshar*, ed. Kambiz Eslami (Princeton, 1998), pp. 13–23.

46. Mustawfī, *Tārīkh-i guzīdah,* pp. 798–800.

47. Ibid., p. 799.

48. Ibid., p. 793.

49. Ibid., p. 797.

50. Ibid., pp. 588–589; Mustawfī, *Ẓafarnāmah,* pp. 1168, 1129; tr. Ward, pp. 10–14; also Ḥamdullah Mustawfī, *Zafarnāmah,* vol. 8 (Qisma Sultāniyyah), ed. Nāhid Zakkari (Tehran, 1389/2011), p. 164.

51. Rashīd al-Dīn, tr. Thackston, p. 540.

52. Mustawfī, *Tārīkh-i guzīdah,* p. 800.

53. Pseudo-Ibn al-Fuwaṭī, *al-Ḥawādith al-Jāmiʿa,* tr. ʿAbd Āl Muḥammad Āyatī (Tehran, 2002), p. 304; Pseudo-Ibn al-Fuwaṭī, *al-Ḥawādith al-Jāmiʿa* (Baghdad, 1932), p. 478; Ṣafadī, *Nakt al-himyān fī nukat al-ʿumyān* (Cairo, 1911), p. 204; cited in F. de Blois, "The Iftikhāriyān of Qazvin," p. 16.

54. Rashīd al-Dīn, pp. 1304, 1443; tr. Thackston, pp. 652, 714.

55. Rashīd al-Dīn, p. 1061; tr. Thackston, p. 518.

56. Mustawfī, *Tārīkh-i guzīdah,* pp. 733.

57. Al-Jājarmī, *Mūnis al-aḥrār,* ed. M. ibn Badr (Tehran, 1958), pp. 506–508, 761–764.

58. Bar Hebraeus, *The Chronography of Gregory Abu'l Faraj,* tr. E. Wallis Budge (Oxford, 1932; rpt. Piscataway, NJ, 2003), p. 456.

59. Ibid., pp. 459–460, 462.

60. See Lane, *Early Mongol Rule,* pp. 229–230.

61. W. Chittick and P. Wilson, *Fakhruddin ʿIraqi: Divine Flashes* (New York, 1982), p. 36.

62. For the contemporary biography see A. Arberry (ed. and tr.), *ʿUshshāqnāma: The Songs of Lovers* (London, 1939).

63. Fakhr al-Dīn ʿIrāqī, *Majmūʿat āṣār,* ed. N. M. Khazāʾī (Tehran, 1372/1993), p. 387; see also intro., p. 25, n. 47.

64. See J. J. Elias, *The Throne Carrier of God* (Albany, NY, 1995).

65. Khwāndamīr, *Ḥabīb al-siyar* (Tehran, 1353/1974–1975), p. 220; tr. Thackston (Cambridge MA, 1994), p. 125.

66. Mustawfī, *Tārīkh-i guzīdah,* pp. 675–676.

67. Khwāndamir, *Ḥabīb al-siyar,* vol. 3, p. 208, tr. Thackston, vol. 3, p. 119.

68. Khwāndamir, *Dastūr al-wuzarāʾ* (Tehran, 1938), pp. 323–324; Faṣīḥ Khwāfī, *Mujmal-i Faṣīḥī* (Mashad, 1960), vol. 2, p. 382; Mustawfī, *Tārīkh-i guzīdah,* p. 605.

69.ʿAlāʾ al-Dawla Simnānī, *Chihil majlis,* ed. Amīr Iqbāl Sīstānī (Tehran, 2000), p. 166.

70. Faṣīḥ Khwāfī, *Mujmal al-Faṣīḥī,* vol. 2, pp. 276–277.

71. Khwāndamir, *Dastūr al-wuzarāʾ*, p. 295; Mustawfī, *Ẓafarnāmah,* pp. 1319–1320; tr. Ward, pp. 329–330.

72. Simnānī, *Chihil majlis,* p. 132.

73. Ibid., p. 132.

74. Ibid., p. 133.

75. Ibid., p. 132.

76. See Faṣīḥ Khwāfī, *Mujmal-i Faṣīḥī,* vol. 2, p. 353.

77. Elias, *The Throne Carrier of God,* p. 19.

78. Ibid., p. 21. The identity of the Ibn al-I'rābiyya remains unknown.

79. Cited in ibid., p. 25.

80. Simnānī, *Chihil majlis,* pp. 131–134, 167–168.

81. Faṣīḥ Khwāfī, *Mujmal-i Faṣīḥī,* vol. 2, p. 360.

82. Simnānī, *Chihil majlis,* p. 130.

83. Faṣīḥ Khwāfī, *Mujmal-i Faṣīḥī,* vol. 3, p. 14; Simnānī, *Chihil majlis,* p. 130.

84. Khwāndamīr, *Ḥabīb al-siyar,* p. 144, tr. Thackston, p. 81; Yaḥyā b. 'Abd al-Laṭīf Qazwīnī, *Kitāb Lubb al-tawārīkh* (Tehran, 1363/1984), p. 238; Faṣīḥ Khwāfī, *Mujmal-i Faṣīḥī,* vol. 2, p. 371; Dawlatshāh, *Tadhkirat al-shu'arā',* p. 214; see C. Melville, "Pādshāh-i Islām: The Conversion of Sultan Maḥmūd Ghāzān Khān," *Pembroke Papers,* 1 (1990), pp. 159–177.

85. Simnānī, *Chihil majlis,* pp. 130, 138, 139ff.

86. Mustawfī, *Ẓafarnāmah,* tr. Ward, p. 661; Ḥāfiẓ-i Abrū, *Dhayl Jāmi' al-Tawārīkh al-Rashīdī* (Tehran, 1350/1971), pp. 174–175.

87. Faṣīḥ Khwāfī, *Mujmal-i Faṣīḥī,* vol. 3, pp. 23, 24.

88. Mustawfī, *Ẓafarnāmah,* tr. Ward, pp. 312–313.

89. Ibid., p. 311.

90. Khwāndamīr, *Dastūr al-wuzarā',* p. 295.

91. Mustawfī, *Ẓafarnāmah,* p. 1312; Ward, p. 314 (my translation, slightly different from Ward's).

92. Khwāndamīr, *Ḥabīb al-siyar,* p. 128; tr. Thackston, p. 72.

93. Mustawfī, *Ẓafarnāmah,* p. 1318; tr. Ward, p. 326.

94. Mustawfī, *Ẓafarnāmah,* p. 1318; tr. Ward, p. 327.

95. Rashīd al-Dīn, p. 1168; tr. Thackston, p. 569.

96. Rashīd al-Dīn, p. 1167; tr. Thackston, p. 568.

97. Rashīd al-Dīn, p. 1171; tr. Thackston, p. 570.

98. Mustawfī, *Ẓafarnāmah,* p. 1319; tr. Ward, p. 329.

99. See W. Fischel, *Jews in the Economic and Political Life of Mediaeval Islam* (London, 1937), pp. 90–117.

100. Rashīd al-Dīn, p. 1175; tr. Thackston, p. 572.

101. Bar Hebraeus, tr. Budge, p. 490.

102. Zayn al-Dīn 'Alī b. Sa'īd, quoted in Browne, *Literary History of Persia,* vol. 3, p. 36.

103. See Maḥmūd Kutubī, *Tārīkh Āl Muẓaffar,* ed. 'Abd al-Ḥusayn Nawā'ī (Tehran, 1335/1956), pp. 3–4. For the Muẓaffarids see H. R. Roemer, "Jalayirids, Muzaffarids and Sarbadars," in *The Cambridge History of Iran,* ed., P. Jackson, vol. 6, *The Timurid and Safavid Periods* (Cambridge, 1986), pp. 11–16.

104. See Lane, *Early Mongol Rule,* p. 110.

105. Naṣīr al-Dīn Munshī Kirmānī, *Simṭ al-'ulā* (Tehran, 1362/1983), p. 70; Anonymous, *Ta'rīkh-i shāhī-i Qarā Khitā'iyyān* (Tehran, 1355/1976), intro., p. 61; Shabānkāra'ī, *Majma' al-ansāb* (Tehran, 1363/1984), p. 201.

106. *Tārīkh-i shāhī,* p. 139.

107. Waṣṣāf, *Tārīkh-i Waṣṣāf* (Bombay, 1269/1852–1853; rpt. Tehran, 1338 S./1959–1960), p. 291; 'Abd al-Moḥammad Āyatī, *Taḥrīr-i-Tārīkh-i-Waśśāf* (Tehran, 1372/1993), p. 165.

108. Waṣṣāf, p. 287; Āyatī, pp.162–163; Juwaynī, vol. 2, p. 214; tr. Boyle, vol. 1, p. 479.

109. See M. Biran, *The Empire of the Qara Khitai in Eurasian History* (Cambridge, 2005), pp. 45–59.

110. *Tārīkh-i shāhī,* p. 139; Lane, *Early Mongol Rule,* pp. 109–11.

111. *Niẓām al-Tawārīkh,* pp. 132–133; see Melville, "From Adam to Abaqa," pp. 67–86.

112. Rashīd al-Dīn, pp. 1128, 1146; tr. Thackston, pp. 550, 559.

113. J. Aubin, *Émirs mongols et vizirs persans dans les remous de l'acculturation,* "Studia Iranica," Cahier 15 (Paris, 1995), p. 23.

114. Waṣṣāf, pp. 204–205; Āyatī, pp. 116–117.

115. Cited in D. DeWeese, "Cultural Transmission and Exchange in the Mongol Empire: Notes from the Biographical Dictionary of Ibn al-Fuwaṭī," in *Beyond the Legacy of Genghis Khan,* p. 25.

116. Cited in ibid., p. 24.

117. Waṣṣāf, pp. 205–206; Āyatī, pp. 117–118; Lane, *Early Mongol Rule,* pp. 135–140.

118. C. Melville, "From Adam to Abaqa (Part II)," pp. 17, 58–63.

119. Jennifer Jay makes an interesting comparison with the situation in China as the Yüan administration slowly became established. See J. Jay, *A Change in Dynasties: Loyalism in Thirteenth-Century China* (Bellingham, WA, 1991).

120. Simnānī, *Chihil majlis,* p. 130.

121. [Editors' note: cf. M. Biran, *Qaidu and the Rise of the Independent Mongol State in Central Asia* (Richmond, Surrey, 1997), pp. 107–112, esp. 111–112; R. Amitai, *Holy War and Rapprochement: Studies in the Relations between the Mamluk Sultanate and the Mongol Ilkhanate (1260–1335)* (Turnhout, 2013), ch. 4.]

NINE

The Mongol Empire and Its Impact on the Arts of China

Morris Rossabi

Ever since the landmark 1968 exhibition at the Cleveland Museum of Art on "Chinese Art under the Mongols," historians and art historians have recognized that the era of the Mongol empire was not devoid of artistic and cultural merit.[1] It was clear that the stereotyped image of the Mongols as barbaric plunderers needed to be recast. Research, which has continued apace, has further altered this earlier perception. A joint Metropolitan Museum of Art and Cleveland Museum of Art exhibit on Chinese and Central Asian textiles, which derived in part from the Mongol era, focused on the mutual diffusion of Central Asian, Chinese, Iranian, Tibetan, and Indian motifs throughout the Mongol domains.[2] A show on the Yuan dynasty at the National Palace Museum in Taipei attested to the remarkable efflorescence of Chinese art during the century of Mongol rule, and the joint Metropolitan Museum of Art and Los Angeles County Museum of Art exhibition entitled "The Legacy of Genghis Khan" revealed the ever-widening cultural significance of the Mongol empire by drawing on examples of Chinese, Iranian, Russian, Central Asian, and Arab art.[3] All four of these exhibitions, as well as the research of individual scholars, have yielded irrefutable evidence of the vitality and creativity of the arts in the Mongol era.[4]

However, one question arises: What role did the Mongols themselves play in these artistic developments? Some art historians, while acknowledging the achievements of the thirteenth and fourteenth centuries, provide only backhanded compliments to the Mongols. For example, a specialist who described the Yuan advances in Chinese porcelain, writes that the "Mongols' greatest contribution [was] that for the most part they remained aloof, neither apparently imposing standards, nor making exacting demands in terms of form or style."[5] Another writer on Chinese porcelains of the Mongol era referred to the Mongols as a "singularly uncultivated race" and asserted that "there are few signs of their having exercised much constructive influence on the arts during their stay in China."[6] This and other similar observations emphasized the negative impact of the Mongols in what the author perceived to be a remarkable era of innovations in design and form in Chinese porcelain. Sherman Lee and Wai-kam Ho attributed the advances in painting to Chinese who were unwilling to serve the Mongols. Abandoning public life and thus avoiding the government service to which they would have gravitated in a Chinese dynasty, some of these educated Chinese became recluses. Living in retirement, a few returned to the traditional Confucian lifestyle, part of which entailed, at a minimum, dabbling in painting.[7] This interpretation once again minimized Mongol influence and credited them only with a peripheral impact on the arts.

To be sure, the Mongols themselves were generally not the artists or artisans. They were not the potters who produced the Chinese blue-and-white porcelains; they were not the calligraphers whose writings adorned the Iranian illustrated manuscripts; they were not the weavers who fashioned the Central Asian textiles; and they were not the metal workers who created both the decorative and functional gold objects produced in the Russian domains. Their nomadic lifestyle, prior to their conquests, did not lend itself to the development of an artisan class, nor did frequent migrations provide opportunities to carry some of the heavy equipment required by craftsmen. These artifacts cannot therefore be classified as Mongol art. They are rightly considered to be examples of Chinese, Central Asian, Russian, or Iranian art.

This chapter deals with specific arts and artists to determine the extent of Mongol influence, in particular, on Chinese art. It will thus appear to be merely a list, though it will also highlight the differing roles the Mongols played in fostering arts and culture. Moreover, even a simple catalog may result in greater understanding of the Mongol influence on the arts. At the very least, it will yield data needed to assess the Mongol contribution or lack thereof.

Chinese Porcelains

Chinese porcelains attracted the Mongols, partly because they recognized their value in trade. Yet, "porcelain, much as it may have been admired, was not always the subject of such extensive comment as scholars today might hope for."[8] Chinese sources about foreign commerce in porcelains are scarce.

Similarly, contemporaneous writings on Mongol-era porcelains are overly general and yield few details on foreign influence on Chinese designs or shapes or vice versa. Analysis of such links must be based upon visual, not textual, evidence.[9]

The most obvious innovation was the use of cobalt blue, imported from West and Central Asia, on Yuan porcelains. West Asian potters had, for some centuries, employed cobalt to decorate pottery, and, via the Mongols, the Chinese learned of the practice. By the fourteenth century (and perhaps even earlier), the Chinese produced blue-and-white porcelains, with some meant for trade with West Asia. The Topkapi collection in Istanbul has forty blue-and-white porcelains deriving from the fourteenth century, and the Ardabil Shrine in Iran houses thirty-two of them, some of which are of Yuan origin.[10] Both collections consist principally of Ming (1368–1644) porcelains, the era of greatest production, as well as greatest expansion of trade with West Asia, in blue-and-white wares. Nonetheless, the blue-and-white porcelains and the commerce in them doubtless originated in the Yuan.

Admittedly, Chinese ceramics reached West Asia and North Africa even before the Mongol invasions. The excavations in Fustat in Old Cairo confirm a tenth-century date for shards and intact Chinese celadons. By the twelfth century, Longquan 龍泉 (a site in the modern province of Zhejiang 浙江) celadons were the most abundant imports, arriving via the Red Sea to Egypt.[11] Excavations in the old port city of Siraf (now the modern village of Taheri on the Iranian coast of the Persian Gulf) have uncovered Chinese jars, lamp holders, pots, plates, bowls, and ewers that predate the Yuan. Earthenware of red, pink, and pale green colors, along with Longquan celadons, have been found and attest to a lively commerce even before the Song dynasty. Some of the wares have the names of the owners in Arabic or brief phrases from the Qur'an. Yet these pre-Mongol era ceramics scarcely betray foreign influence or specific accommodations to foreign tastes.

The Mongol era witnessed such changes. With a Mongol commissioner supervising the important site at Jingdezhen 景德鎮, the center of blue-and-white porcelain production, a Mongol role seems to be indisputable. A Mongol commissioner of 8A (or perhaps 9A) rank, with help from an assistant commissioner, managed the Fuliang Porcelain Office (fuliang ciju 浮梁磁局), which was founded in 1278, within a year of Mongol conquest and occupation of the region.[12] Moreover, West Asian pottery has not been found in China and certainly not in the porcelain centers.[13] Neither did numerous Chinese potters travel to West Asia. It thus seems likely that the Mongols, who traveled in their domains, alerted Chinese potters to West Asian tastes, providing them with information about the shapes and decorative motifs that would appeal to potential customers from these distant lands.

The Chinese porcelains exported to West Asia doubtless catered to this clientele. Jingdezhen and other sites produced massive plates, jars, dishes, and vases designed for this market.[14] West Asian peoples characteristically placed their food on large plates, from which each diner ate. Dishes of more than one foot in diameter were extremely rare in the history of Chinese ceramics of the Tang and Song dynasties. Mongols probably instructed the Chinese to produce such massive dishes in order to satisfy the West Asian market. By the early Ming dynasty (1368–1644), Chinese potters had adopted additional Islamic shapes, including tankards, the so-called moon flash, and several types of ewers, and the Chinese court traded some of these objects to West Asia.[15]

The Mongols would have also informed the Chinese potters that their clients in Iran and the Arab world were sophisticated and demanded porcelains of exceptional quality. The wares sent to West Asia were thus superior to the export porcelain shipped to Southeast Asia. According to a leading specialist on Yuan porcelain, of the wares dispatched to West Asia, "the best [were] of superlative quality and in greater quantity" and "we find export celadons and blue and white wares especially attaining standards in terms of quality and splendour of decoration that have rarely been surpassed except under strictly directed imperial patronage and in other periods."[16] She attributed this striking development to foreign merchants, but surely much of the credit should go to the Mongol managers of porcelain production and to the Mongols who had been in West Asia and returned to China.

The Mongol supervisors and the Chinese potters recognized the West Asian preference for decoration. The Song emphasis on refinement, introspection, and purity did not suit the more flamboyant West Asian clients. Chinese painters could now experiment with more elaborate motifs for this market. However, they used their own artistic vocabulary and did not, for the most part, incorporate Islamic motifs. They depicted plants, including flowers and fruits, dragons, mandarin ducks, cranes, phoenixes, cloud collars, and waves, all of which resonated with traditional Chinese symbolism and culture.[17] West Asian artists would themselves adopt some of these Chinese motifs in tiles, pottery, and illustrated manuscripts.

These Mongol influences challenge the assertion that the Mongols' major contribution was simply not to interfere with the Chinese ceramicists' creativity. Instead, the Mongols were actively involved as superintendents of the major porcelain center, as intermediaries between Chinese potters and West Asian consumers, and conveyors of information to Chinese potters about shapes and decorations that would appeal to the Islamic world. They did not intend to foster innovations, creativity, and diffusion of motifs and shapes from China to West Asia. Their principal motivation appears to have been profit, for they recognized how lucrative the commerce in porcelains could be. Yet profit prompted them to be keenly aware of the West Asian market for Chinese porcelains and to assist Chinese potters to cater to the demands of Islamic consumers.

Chinese Paintings and Textiles

The traditional attribution for the efflorescence of Chinese painting under Mongol rule also requires emendation. According to a leading specialist, "the Mongols' Eurasian commitments, their nomadic origin, their cult of virility and movement . . . largely eliminated any possibilities of a direct and significant contribution to Chinese art."[18] The Mongols' initial abolition of the civil service examination system, "which blocked the scholar's only access to government service," and its reestablishment in a limited way in 1315 undermined the possibility of official careers.[19] Chinese who earlier sought highly valued government positions no longer had that option. Denied such social mobility into the scholar-official or governing classes, they turned to other professions, including medicine, science, and, most important in this connection, painting. Painters who took this route were professionals and diverged from the Song dynasty ideal of amateur scholar-painters.

Others who became painters, specifically in South China, resolutely refused any collaboration with their Mongol overlords. They were, in particular, unwilling to serve the Mongols in any official capacity, and some scholar-officials, such as Wen Tianxiang 文天祥 (1236–1283), even sought to overthrow China's new rulers.[20] Some members of this traditional elite, thwarted by the abolition of the civil service examinations, turned to such practical pursuits as medicine for employment. A few, frustrated by what they perceived to be a barbarous period in Chinese history or disenchanted by the stiff taxes and persecution reputedly characterizing the Mongol era, turned away and became recluses (*yinshi* 隱士). Others continued to resist the Mongols, albeit nonviolently. These so-called leftover subjects (*yimin* 遺民) also dropped out of public life and sought to express their opposition to Mongol rule through covert criticism.[21]

Painting offered an acceptable Confucian outlet for some and a means of affirming their antipathy toward "barbarian" control for others. The

Mongols would have liked to recruit some of these talented men but were rebuffed. Zheng Sixiao 鄭思肖 (1241–1318) was perhaps the painter who was most implacably hostile to the Mongols.[22] He and like-minded painters used their paintings for indirect criticism of the foreign rulers. The Mongols clearly had no influence on their work and indeed suspected that some were so loyal to the Southern Song dynasty that they would seek to overthrow Mongol rule. Thus a few of the painters, who either lived in or moved principally to South China, reaffirmed the Song amateur-painter ideal.

However, the Mongols had considerable influence on the professional painters of North China. The Mongol court, based in Daidu, was, according to the latest study of Yuan dynasty painting, "an important center for art collection and production."[23] It was a major source of patronage for some of the most illustrious Yuan dynasty painters. Mongol support for Zhao Mengfu 趙孟頫 (1254–1322), the greatest artist of the Yuan, is well known. The court appointed him to the Ministry of War and eventually rewarded him with the presidency of the Hanlin Academy 翰林院, the most prestigious scholarly organization in the country. His bureaucratic responsibilities were limited, affording him leisure time to pursue his real career as a painter-calligrapher. He performed his tasks admirably, helping to eliminate abuses in the postal station system and pleading with Qubilai Khan to reduce taxes on areas devastated by natural disasters. Yet he had abundant opportunities to devote himself to his art.[24] Li Kan 李衎 (ca. 1245–1320), a renowned painter of bamboo, became the Minister of Personnel.[25] Other painters received appointments in the Ministry of Works and the Censorate, among other government bodies.

The Mongol court offered remarkable patronage to these painters, granting them employment that allowed considerable free time to paint or to produce fine calligraphy. Several, including Liu Guandao 劉貫道 (whose depiction of Qubilai Khan on a hunt is one of the better-known Yuan dynasty paintings), even became court painters. For the most part, however, the Mongols recruited these talented painters into government. Qubilai Khan and Tugh Temür, the Wenzong emperor (文宗 1328–1329 and 1329–1333) were ardent recruiters, but the reign of Ayurbarwada, or Renzong (仁宗 1312–1320), witnessed the height of court patronage. One tangible outcome of such support was formal portraits of Qubilai, Wuzong 武宗, Renzong, Wenzong, and other emperors as well as of fifteen empresses.[26] Another result was the Wenzong emperor's founding of the Pavilion of the Star of Literature (Kuizhangge 奎章閣), where connoisseurs met to collect and appreciate calligraphy and eventually painting.[27]

Still another Mongol influence was in the depiction of subjects. Animals, in particular horses, often served as motifs in paintings. The painters knew the Mongols' fondness for animals and catered to their patrons' tastes. It is no accident that one of Zhao Mengfu's most famous works is the *Sheep and Goat* in the Freer Gallery of Art collection.[28] Zhao sought, in part, to appeal to the Mongols. His numerous depictions of horses gained him devotees among the Mongol elite, though, perhaps unbeknownst to his patrons, he used horses to symbolize ideas and values with which the Mongols were unfamiliar. Part of his motivation was his effort to imitate, pay homage to, and perhaps surpass, the Tang dynasty paintings of horses.[29] Another of his objectives was to use great horses as symbols of outstanding officials, including himself. Depictions of horses as elegant and dignified manifested the idealization of the noble and martial spirit.[30] Ren Renfa 任仁發 (1254–1327), another painter of horses, also reputedly used horses for symbolic purposes. One of his horse paintings, for example, supposedly offers "a quiet tribute to the blessings of good government."[31] Zhao Mengfu's own son Zhao Yong 趙雍 (1289–1360) and grandson Zhao Lin 趙麟, who both served as government officials, followed their brilliant forebear into careers or sidelines as painters and continued to use horses as symbols of good governance.[32] The paintings naturally had great visual appeal because of the beauty and power of the horses, another element that made them attractive to the Mongols and prompted them to offer patronage.[33]

Greater opportunities for women also played a role in Chinese painting. Because of the vital roles women played in the Mongol pastoral economy, women had considerable social, economic, and political leverage.[34] Mongol women had more rights than females in other East (or West) Asian civilizations of that time, and the power and prestige of several elite women, such as Chinggis Khan's mother, Höelün, and wife Börte, and Qubilai Khan's mother, Sorghaghtani Beki, and wife Chabi, attest to their significance. Greater opportunities for women in political and social life spilled over into the arts. When the Mongols occupied China, a few elite women artists capitalized on the conquerors' more liberal attitudes to come to the fore with their work. Guan Daosheng 管道昇 (1262–1319), Zhao Mengfu's wife, was the most revered of these painters, and thirty-three works attributed to her have been preserved in such major collections as the Osaka Municipal Museum, the Yale University Art Gallery, the Freer Gallery of Art, the Metropolitan Museum of Art, the Museum of Fine Arts in Boston, and the Fogg Art Museum.[35] In a lengthier description of her career, I wrote: "Kuan Tao-sheng [Guan Daosheng] would probably have produced her fine calligraphy and paintings under any conditions, yet Mongol rule in China, with its relatively greater opportunities for women, may have encouraged her to pursue her artistic career and facilitated acceptance of her work . . .

Kuan's is certainly a case where the Mongol rulers patronized and, on occasion, subsidized her and her husband's artistic career."[36] Zhao Mengfu's daughter, Zhao Youxi 趙由皙, also benefited from such Mongol support because she, too, was a painter and calligrapher whose works the Renzong emperor favored.[37]

The Mongols' attitudes toward women, among other factors, played a role in the renaissance of Chinese textiles. The higher status of women contributed to a greater appreciation of female artisans, and, in the Chinese tradition, weaving was women's work. The exhibition "When Silk Was Gold," mounted at the Cleveland Museum of Art and the Metropolitan Museum of Art, attests to the results of this higher status—an astonishing collection of silks with Chinese designs such as the dragon and phoenix mingled with Iranian and Central Asian motifs such as felines and falcons.[38] The so-called cloths of gold (*nasīj*) were designed to cater to the Mongol elite. Because Chinese and Central Asian weavers knew of the Mongols' fondness for gold, they used gold thread for the clothing, banners, Buddhist *mandalas,* and *ger* decorations they produced.[39] The identification of gold and imperial authority reaffirmed their preference for such textiles.[40]

In addition, the Mongols themselves took steps to foster the development of luxury textiles. More than one-half of the agencies the Mongols founded in the Ministry of Works supervised the production of textiles.[41] As Paul Pelliot first noted, the Mongols also forcibly moved communities of weavers from Central Asia and Iran where they introduced Islamic motifs into Chinese textiles.[42] Finally, the Mongols' interest in Buddhism, particularly the Tibetan variety, prompted them to commission banners and mandalas such as the spectacular *Yamantaka Mandala with Imperial Portraits,* now found at the Metropolitan Museum of Art.[43] This *kesi* 刻絲 (silk tapestry with cut design), which was heavily influenced by Tibetan Buddhism, not only depicts a variety of Buddhist figures and Tibetan adepts but also the Wenzong emperor and his older brother the Mingzong 明宗 emperor and their respective wives. Such commissions indicated both the Mongols' fondness for elaborate textiles as well as patronage for their creation.

The Mongols' appreciation of Chinese art led them to preserve and collect Chinese paintings and other works of art, which had an impact on artistic diffusion. When Qubilai Khan's troops occupied Hangzhou, the Southern Song capital, they saved the Imperial Palace collection of painting and transported much of it to Daidu. Qubilai himself preserved this collection, but his great-granddaughter Sengge Ragi added to it. Unlike her great-grandfather, she had been reared in the capital of China, not in the steppelands of Mongolia, and was thus more Sinicized and more receptive to Chinese culture.[44] She herself favored works that portrayed Buddhist figures, birds, animals, and flowers and ensured that such older paintings be preserved and obtained paintings with similar motifs. Her nephew, the Wenzong emperor, one of the most Sinicized of the Mongol rulers, was also an avid collector and preserver of Southern Song paintings. Without these rulers, the Imperial Palace collection could have been damaged and some works lost. Artistic diffusion could have been impeded.[45] The producers of Iranian illustrated manuscripts would not have had access to the Chinese motifs from which they borrowed. The arrival of Chinese textiles and pattern books in the Mongol Ilkhanate provided models of Chinese motifs and designs to Iranian craftsmen and artists. Textiles would have been easy to transport along the Silk Roads to Iran.

The Mongols not only enriched Chinese textiles by facilitating the inclusion of West Asian motifs and designs into the silks produced in China but also recruited other foreign craftsmen and artists to work for them in the Middle Kingdom. The various projects they undertook (construction of a summer capital in Shangdu 上都, building of a new capital in Daidu, funding the erection of Buddhist statues and the painting of Buddhist murals, etc.) necessitated employment of numerous artisans and painters, some of whom were non-Chinese. Even before they occupied South China, they had recruited foreign craftsmen, including the renowned Frenchman Guillaume Boucher.[46] Central Asians, Tibetans, Persians, Indians, Nepalese, and Koreans arrived in China at the behest of the Mongols. Like the international coterie of advisers and officials at the Mongol court, an international group of craftsmen served the Mongols in China.

Anige 阿尼哥 (1245–1306), a talented Nepalese craftsman, architect, and painter, was perhaps the most renowned such foreigner. Introduced to the Mongols by the Tibetan Buddhist 'Phags-pa Lama (1235–1280), he quickly impressed Qubilai Khan and his wife Chabi with his manifold skills. He was one of about eighty Nepalese craftsmen brought by the 'Phags-pa Lama in 1260 to build a stupa for the Sa-skya Pandita (1182–1251), the fourth patriarch of the Sa-skya sect. Only fifteen years old at the time, Anige was already an accomplished sculptor in the Himalayan Buddhist tradition. 'Phags-pa recognized his talent and sent him to Kaiping 開平, Qubilai Khan's summer residence later renamed Shangdu ("Xanadu"). Qubilai "tested [his] skill by asking him to repair a bronze statue that had been judged as damaged 'beyond repair' by all the other court artists."[47] Anige performed so brilliantly that Qubilai insisted that he remain at court. Chabi, whom 'Phags-pa had apparently initiated into the practices of Tantric Buddhism, found a kindred spirit in the Himalayan Buddhist artisan and artist.

With support from the Great Khan and his wife, Anige set about incorporating Himalayan Buddhist art into China. Court commissions resulted in his construction of the Da Shengshou Wan'ansi 大聖壽萬安寺 and the Da Huguo Renwangsi 大護國仁王寺, two Buddhist temples in the new capital city of Daidu. Neither has survived, but the "White Stupa" he constructed, fifty-one meters in height, remains as an important site in Beijing.[48] These structures, as well as other Buddhist temples he built, reflect the influence of Himalayan Buddhist art, with its depiction of Tantric deities. In addition, however, he built a Confucian school, with statues of Confucius and some of his disciples, for Qubilai, and a Daoist temple, with images of Daoist adepts, for Temür, Qubilai's grandson who succeeded him as the Yuan emperor. He also received commissions to fashion an armillary sphere and other astronomical instruments, a sign of his ability in a wide variety of media. As a reward for his outstanding achievements, Qubilai appointed him the first Supervisor-in-Chief of All Classes of Artisans, a position that permitted him to recruit talented jade carvers, goldsmiths, weavers, and potters from China and other regions in Asia to foster a great period in the decorative arts. All of these crafts benefited from his assiduous support.

Beyond acknowledging his skills as an administrator, sculptor, and architect, a Chinese art historian has recently argued that Anige painted the famous portraits of Qubilai and Chabi found in the National Palace Museum in Taipei. Based on a detailed analysis of the paintings, he concludes that they reflect the traditions of the Himalayan Buddhist depictions of the human figure and that they undeniably resemble the techniques and styles of Anige's sculptural and textile images.[49] Whether or not his conclusions are valid, it still seems evident that Anige's principal contributions were in the realms of religious art. Moreover, the Mongol emperors were integral to this kind of art. As the same art historian wrote, "The patterns of religious art at the court were to a large extent shaped by the Yuan rulers' religious practices."[50]

Conclusion

In short, these findings challenge the conventional wisdom that the Mongols merely had a passive role in the efflorescence of Yuan art and in the diffusion of motifs. Their contributions did not consist simply of permitting artists and craftsmen to pursue their crafts of their own volition. First, because the Mongols were consumers of some of the products, artists, and craftsmen needed to cater to their tastes, which without a doubt influenced the subjects (e.g., horses) and types of artworks. Second, the Mongols' control over much of Asia and their movement of artisans from one region of their empire to another resulted in considerable diffusion of motifs and technologies. Aware of foreigners' tastes, they also provided guidance to craftsmen who wished to trade their objects with the outside world. Moreover, for example, Anige, a foreign craftsman, helped to introduce Himalayan Buddhist art into China. Third, the Yuan government offered tax exemptions and freedom from corvée labor for artisans and established numerous official agencies for the promotion of crafts. Fourth, it offered official appointments for artists and craftsmen in order to support their work. Fifth, the Mongols preserved the objects that were produced—in part, through the Imperial Palace collection. Sixth, Mongol women played a significant role as consumers of artworks as well as in their protection and preservation.

Notes

1. S. Lee and Wai-kam Ho, *Chinese Art under the Mongols: The Yuan Dynasty (1279–1368)* (Cleveland, 1968). In 1955, the British Museum had organized an exhibition entitled "The Arts of the Mongol Period," which started the process of reevaluation. See J. Ayers, "Some Chinese Wares of the Yüan Period," *Transactions of the Oriental Ceramic Society, 1954–1955,* 29 (1957), p. 69.

2. A. Wardwell and J. Watt, with an essay by M. Rossabi, *When Silk Was Gold* (New York, 1997).

3. L. Komaroff and S. Carboni (eds.), *The Legacy of Genghis Khan: Courtly Art and Culture in Western Asia, 1256–1353* (New York, 2002).

4. The Metropolitan Museum's exhibition "The World of Khubilai Khan: Chinese Art in the Yuan Dynasty" took place after this chapter was completed. See James C. Y. Watt (ed.), *The World of Khubilai Khan Chinese Art in the Yuan Dynasty* (New York, 2010). See also Morgan's chapter in this volume.

5. M. Medley, *Yuan Porcelain and Stoneware* (New York, 1974), p. 1.

6. Ayers, "Some Chinese Wares," p. 70.

7. Lee and Ho, *Chinese Art,* pp. 89–95.

8. J. A. Pope, *Chinese Porcelains from the Ardebil Shrine* (Washington, DC, 1956), p. 20.

9. Useful sources in such visual inspections include Ye Peilan, *Yuandi ciqi* (Beijing, 1998); Nakazawa Fujio, *Chūgoku no toji: Gen Min no seika,* vol. 8 (Tokyo, 1995); *Yuan and Ming Blue and White Wares from Jiangxi* (Hong Kong, 2002); and *Jingdezhen Wares: The Yuan Evolution* (Hong Kong, 1984).

10. Pope, *Chinese Porcelains,* p. 59; a preliminary study of the Topkapi collection may be found in J. A. Pope, *Fourteenth-Century Blue-and-White: A Group of Chinese Porcelains in the Topkapu Sarayi Müzesi, Istanbul* (Washington, DC, 1952), which counted thirty-one blue-and-white porcelains. A more comprehensive study (R. Krahl, *Chinese Ceramics in the Topkapi Saray Museum, Istanbul* [London, 1986], vol. 1, p. 3) found forty blue-and-white porcelains.

11. G. T. Scanlon, "Egypt and China: Trade and Imitation," in *Islam and the Trade of Asia,* ed. D. S. Richards (Philadelphia, 1970), p. 88; the Topkapi collection has 406 Longquan celadons. All are photographed in the Krahl book.

12. D. M. Farquhar, *The Government of China under Mongol Rule* (Stuttgart, 1990), p. 84. It is surprising that only one government office was established to take charge of the

porcelain industry while dozens were created for textile production. Possible explanations may be that more textiles were produced in a wider variety of materials and the textile industry was more widely dispersed.

13. Pope, *Chinese Porcelains,* p. 44.

14. For Chinese efforts to cater to Islamic tastes in the Ming see K. Aga-Oglu, "Blue-and-White Porcelain Plates Made for Moslem Patrons," *Far Eastern Ceramic Bulletin,* 3/3 (1951), pp. 12–16.

15. Pope, *Chinese Porcelains,* pp. 86–88, offers precise descriptions of these shapes.

16. Medley, *Yuan Porcelain,* pp. 5–6.

17. For a listing of these designs see Pope, *Fourteenth-Century,* pp. 33–48; Krahl offers photographs of each of the Yuan dynasty porcelains.

18. Lee and Ho, *Chinese Art,* p. 3.

19. Ibid., p. 76.

20. For a study of this important official see W. Brown, *Wen T'ien-hsiang* (San Francisco, 1986).

21. Lee and Ho, *Chinese Art,* p. 91; J. Cahill, *Hills beyond a River: Chinese Painting of the Yüan Dynasty, 1279–1368* (New York, 1976), pp. 15–16.

22. For more on Zheng see F. W. Mote, "Confucian Eremitism in the Yüan Period," in *The Confucian Persuasion,* ed. A. F. Wright (Stanford, 1960), pp. 234–236; *Sung Biographies: Painters,* ed. H. Franke (Wiesbaden, 1976), pp. 15–22; and Harvard Yenching Sinological Index Series, *Combined Indices to Thirty Collections of Liao, Chin, and Yuan Biographies* (rpt. San Francisco, 1974), p. 206c. On another so-called loyalist painter see J. Jay, "The Life and Loyalism of Chou Mi (1232–1298) and His Circle of Friends," *Papers on Far Eastern History,* 28 (1983), pp. 49–105.

23. M. Weidner, "Painting and Patronage at the Mongol Court of China, 1260–1368" (PhD dissertation, University of California at Berkeley, 1982), p. 1.

24. The sources on Zhao are voluminous, some of which are cited in my brief consideration of his work in *Khubilai Khan: His Life and Times* (Berkeley, 1988), pp. 166–168 and 265–266. Additional sources would include Song Lian et al., *Yuanshi* (Beijing, 1976), 172, pp. 4018–4023; R. Vinograd, "Some Landscapes Related to the Blue-and-Green Manner from the Early Yüan Period," *Artibus Asiae,* 41 (1979), pp. 106–124; R. Vinograd, "*River Village*—The Pleasures of Fishing and Chao Meng-fu's Li-Kuo Style Landscapes," *Artibus Asiae,* 40 (1978), pp. 124–134; Li Lin-ts'an, "Human Figures as a Chronological Standard for Dating Chinese Landscape Paintings," *National Palace Museum Bulletin,* 14/3 (July–August, 1979), pp. 2–14; Chiang I-han, "A Calligraphic Handscroll by Chao Meng-fu (1254–1322)," *National Palace Museum Bulletin,* 10/3 (July–August, 1975), pp. 1–10; Li Chu-tsing, "The Freer Sheep and Goat and Chao Meng-fu's Horse Paintings," *Artibus Asiae,* 30/4 (1968), pp. 279–326; Li Chu-tsing, *The Autumn Colors on the Ch'iao and Hua Mountain: A Landscape by Chao Meng-fu* (Ascona, 1965); Chen Gaohua, *Yuandai huajiashike* (Shanghai, 1980), pp. 30–99; and Wen Fong, "Images of the Mind," in *Images of the Mind,* ed. Wen Fong (Princeton, 1984), pp. 94–102. For a comprehensive study of Zhao and his art see Shane McCausland, *Zhao Mengfu: Calligraphy and Painting for Khubilai's China* (Hong Kong, 2011).

25. Li served in numerous areas—as keeper of ritual objects, as a tax administrator, and as ambassador to Annam. See Chang Kuan-pin, "Li K'an and a Revival of Bamboo Painting in the Style of Wen Tung," *National Palace Museum Bulletin,* 13/5 (November–December, 1978), pp. 2–6.

26. Weidner, "Painting," p. 57. Two recent doctoral dissertations reveal the importance of the Mongol period in art. See L. Akbarnia, "Khita'i: Cultural Memory and the

Creation of a Mongol Visual Idiom in Iran and Central Asia" (PhD dissertation, Harvard University, 2007); and Y. Kadoi, "Aspects of Iranian Art under the Mongols: Chinoiserie Reappraised" (PhD dissertation, University of Edinburgh, 2004), published as *Islamic Chinoiserie: The Art of Mongol Iran* (Edinburgh, 2009). A. Weitz, "Art and Politics at the Mongol Court of China: Tugh Temur's Collection of Chinese Painting," *Artibus Asiae*, 64/2 (2004), pp. 243–280, suggests that the Yuan emperors deliberately patronized the Kuizhangge's studies of painting in order to incorporate Mongols into a Chinese context, serving as a means of legitimation.

27. On Wenzong's literary and artistic interests see Kanda Kiichirō, "Gendai no Bunshū no fūryū ni tsuite," in *Haneda hakushi shōju kinen tōyōshi ronsō* (Kyoto, 1950), pp. 477–488.

28. See the detailed analysis of this work in Li Chu-tsing, "The Freer Sheep and Goat," pp. 279–326; McCausland, *Zhao Mengfu*, 145–148.

29. See, e.g., his assertion that "I am proud of this painting, which is not inferior to any T'ang master's workshop" (translated in Chang Yüan-chien, "Jen Ch'i Tu and the Horse and Figure Painting of Chao Meng-fu," *National Palace Museum Bulletin*, 17/3–4 [July–October, 1982], p. 2).

30. Chang, "Jen Ch'i Tu," pp. 9–10.

31. R. Harrist, *Power and Virtue: The Horse in Chinese Art* (New York, 1997), p. 29.

32. J. Silbergeld, "In Praise of Government: Chao Yung's Painting, Noble Steeds, and Late Yüan Politics," *Artibus Asiae*, 46/3 (1985), p. 159.

33. Li Chu-tsing, "Grooms and Horses by Three Members of the Chao Family," in *Words and Images: Chinese Poetry, Calligraphy, and Painting*, ed. A. Murck and Wen Fong (New York, 1991), pp. 206–209.

34. M. Rossabi, "Khubilai Khan and the Women in His Family," in *Studia Sino-Mongolica: Festschrift für Herbert Franke*, ed. W. Bauer (Wiesbaden, 1979), pp. 153–157.

35. For a list see M. Weidner et al., *Views from Jade Terrace: Chinese Women Artists, 1300–1912* (Indianapolis, 1988), pp. 179–180 and 294–295.

36. M. Rossabi, "Kuan Tao-sheng: Woman Artist in Yuan China," *Bulletin of Sung Yuan Studies*, 21 (1989), p. 83.

37. Jiang Yihan, "Zhaoshi yimen hezha yanjiu," *Gugong Jikan*, 11/4 (1977), pp. 23–32.

38. Wardwell and Watt, *When Silk Was Gold*.

39. See ibid., pp. 142–163, for depictions of a number of such textiles.

40. H. Serruys, "Mongol *Altan* 'Gold' = 'Imperial,'" *Monumenta Serica*, 21 (1962), pp. 360–364. For a thorough description of the importance of textile and of gold to the Mongols see T. T. Allsen, *Commodity and Exchange in the Mongol Empire: A Cultural History of Islamic Textiles* (Cambridge, 1997), esp. pp. 11–26, 60–70.

41. Farquhar, *Government of China*, pp. 200–214.

42. P. Pelliot, "Une ville musulmane dans la Chine du Nord sous les Mongols," *Journal Asiatique*, 211 (1927), pp. 261–279; see also T. Allsen, *Commodity and Exchange*, pp. 39–45.

43. Watt and Wardwell, *When Silk Was Gold*, pp. 95–99.

44. On her see Fu Shen, "Nücang jia huangzi dachang gongzhu: Yuandai huangshi shuhua shoucang shilue," *Gugong Jikan*, 1/3 (1978), pp. 25–51.

45. On their efforts see M. Weidner, "Yüan Dynasty Court Collections of Chinese Paintings," *Central and Inner Asian Studies*, 2 (1988), pp. 10–22.

46. See the fine study by L. Olschki, *Guillaume Boucher: A French Artist at the Court of the Khans* (Baltimore, 1946).

47. Jing Anning, "The Portraits of Khubilai Khan and Chabi by Anige (1245–1306), a Nepali Artist at the Yuan Court," *Artibus Asiae,* 52/1–2 (1994), p. 45.

48. H. Franke, "Consecration of the 'White Stūpa' in 1279," *Asia Major,* 3rd ser., 7/1 (1994), pp. 155–181.

49. Jing Anning, "Portraits," pp. 71–77.

50. Ibid., p. 56.

TEN

The Impact of the Mongols on the History of Syria
Politics, Society, and Culture

Reuven Amitai

My intention in this chapter is to show that Eurasian nomads could have a significant impact on societies that were not ruled by them at all or only in a transitory manner. The test for this hypothesis will be Syria from 1260 CE onward.[1] In the first sixty years of the thirteenth century, the country was mostly ruled by Ayyūbid princes generally based within it, and then by the Mamluk sultans (until 1516) whose capital was Cairo. Until 1291 there was also a shrinking Frankish presence on much of the coast. Twice the Mongols occupied most of the country for a few months, in 1260 and 1300, and several other times Mongol forces campaigned in it, but permanent control of the country remained beyond their grasp. Yet, as I will try to show in this chapter, the Mongols had a profound effect on the political, social, and cultural history of Syria, with many implications felt long after the Mongols had disappeared as a significant political and military factor in the region.

On the whole, the subject of Syria under the early Mamluks—and thus resisting the Mongols—has never received the systematic attention that it deserves. While aspects of Mamluk rule of the country have been studied, as well as social institutions and the civilian population, there has been little comprehensive treatment in the scholarly literature of this region for the first decades of Mamluk rule, let alone the full quarter millennium of their control over the country.[2] I offer here some preliminary thoughts on what to my mind is an important topic in both Mamluk and Mongol studies, as well as a significant topic in the examination of regional, and perhaps even world history.

The focus of this chapter is not the many Mongol campaigns in Syria and the Mamluk countermeasures, nor the diplomatic and ideological aspects of this sixty some years' conflict. These matters have been explored and discussed in several modern studies, starting perhaps with the third volume of A. C. M. D'Ohsson's *Histoire des Mongols.*[3] Bertold Spuler's *Die Mongolen in Iran* was a more systematic review of these subjects, and even more so the long article by John A. Boyle in the fifth volume of *The Cambridge History of Iran.*[4] There were subsequent important studies by Peter Jackson, John M. Smith, Jr., David Morgan, Timothy May, and most recently Anne Broadbridge; I have also devoted a large portion of my own work to this subject.[5] My researches have led me to think that Hülegü's campaign of 1260 into Syria was part of an ongoing campaign of Mongol world conquest, motivated to a large degree by a belief in an imperialist Tengri-inspired ideology.[6] Based on a reconstruction of the sophisticated administrative system that the Mongols established in Syria in 1260, there is no doubt that the Mongols intended to stay in the country and use it as a base for further expansion, particularly to Egypt.[7] Hülegü's own truculent statements to Quṭuz, as expressed in a letter from late spring 1260 in very sophisticated Arabic—composed by no less than Naṣīr al-Dīn Ṭūsī—leave no doubt as to his plans vis-à-vis Egypt.[8]

The subsequent campaigns into the country—be they the big invasions of 1280, 1281, 1299, 1300, 1303, or the many smaller raids over the years—were in my opinion also partially motivated by this traditional imperialist ideology, although other factors came into play too: the desire to revenge ʿAyn Jālūt and previous defeats; the wish to weaken, if not eradicate, a dangerous enemy with aspirations for regional hegemony, an enemy that was fighting in the name of a descendent of the ʿAbbāsid caliphs; the hope for booty, and even the revenues of newly conquered lands; and, probably, the need perhaps to keep the generals and their troops busy at times. I have suggested that the Mamluks in general and Syria in particular loomed large in the eyes of the Ilkhans and their entourage, although it was not necessarily their major concern most of the time.[9] I confess that not all have agreed with this view of a long-term Ilkhanid fixation on Syria; that is, that it was often for them a foremost part of their foreign policy and military strategy.[10] One point in favor of my assessment is the ongoing Mongol *démarche* toward the Franks in Europe. The Ilkhans dispatched some fifteen diplomatic missions to the papacy and various Frankish leaders in the first fifty years of their rule.[11] The main goal of these embassies was to garner support for a joint campaign against the Mamluks: What would have been the point, had the Mongols not themselves seen this as a foremost strategic goal?

Yet, whatever the exact Ilkhanid motivation, there is no denying the magnitude of their invasions of Syria. Hülegü entered the country with as many as a hundred thousand troops, although after a few months perhaps only 10 percent were still there, meeting their demise at ʿAyn Jālūt. In 1281, it is possible that the army led by Mengü Temür, brother of Abaqa, numbered some eighty thousand horsemen, and Ghazan's army almost twenty years later was perhaps not much smaller.[12] These large armies had to deal with serious logistical challenges, mainly the finding of adequate pasturage and water, problems accentuated with the end of winter, and the rainy season. This is a topic well covered by John Mason Smith, Jr., as well as David Morgan, and I have also discussed the matter at some length.[13] This is not, however, our concern here, yet I suspect that the last word has not been said on this logistical question.

Usually the Mongol campaigns and raids in Syria were thrown back by the Mamluks, although not without considerable efforts. Twice, in 1260 and 1300, the Mongols occupied much of the country, albeit for just a few months each time. For the inhabitants of Syria and the Mamluk elite, both local and in Cairo, the threat of Mongol invasions and raids was a very real one. The combination of invasions, occupation, and threats might well have had an impact on the course of Syrian history: it is with this possible influence that I deal in this chapter.

The impact of the Mongols on Syria before the crucial year of 1260 seems to have been fairly minimal, although toward the end of the 1250s increasing attention was drawn to the ever-closer menace. The Mongols based in Azerbaijan or Anatolia had occasionally launched raids into the country in the 1240s and 1250s, mainly via the Jazīra, but these seem to have been of minimal consequence.[14] There is evidence that the Ayyūbid princes of Aleppo, Damascus, Karak, and elsewhere were in contact with the nearby Mongol governors, and some sent envoys to them or even to the Great Khan's court in Mongolia to make some form of submission. However, one does not get the impression that until the conquest of Baghdad in early 1258, the political elite of the country was unduly concerned with these new conquerors. Had Hülegü's campaign never materialized, or had he been satisfied with taking up residence in Azerbaijan, even after the taking of Baghdad, the impact on Syrian history—both short- and long-term—would have been minimal beyond the influx of some refugees.

However, as we know, things turned out differently. After desultory negotiations between Hülegü and al-Malik al-Nāṣir Yūsuf, Ayyūbid ruler of Aleppo and Damascus, the Mongols under their ruler invaded Syria at the very beginning of 1260. Aleppo was soon taken, then northern Syria and the central cities of the country—most importantly Damascus; Mongol raiders reached as far south as Gaza and there was skirmishing with the Franks along the coast.[15] The resulting collapse of Ayyūbid rule over most of the country can surely be seen as the first real impact of the Mongols on the country. While some minor princes from this family survived the year by first submitting to the Mongols and then to the triumphant Mamluks, the Ayyūbids never regained their power in a meaningful way, and all but disappeared by the end of the first third of the fourteenth century.[16] The Mongols thus unwittingly paved the way for the rise of Mamluk rule in Syria, certainly one important aspect of their long-term impact on the course of history in the region.

I have mentioned that the Mongols quickly established a fairly complicated administrative system in conquered Syria, at least as far south as the environs of the Golan Heights. Led by Kitbuqa, the Mongol commander in the region after Hülegü's withdrawal from the country (and earlier, the commander of the advance force that took Damascus and the surrounding country), the new bureaucracy was composed of local, mostly Muslim, officials: Persians, Central Asians, and even the occasional Mongol. While this edifice is impressive for its complexity and the quickness of its establishment, it seems to have left little imprint on local consciousness or institutions.[17] About the only thing of lasting value that I can think of is a "Mongol" coin, of which several exemplars exist, struck in Hama in 658 AH/1260 CE. The text is in Arabic, but the message is purely Mongolian.[18] This, too, left no impact on the numismatic usage of the country, which reverted to earlier norms—modified by evolving Mamluk practice—after the expelling of the Mongols.

Yet, there are several areas where this half-year stay of the Mongols left an imprint on the country. Firstly, there was widespread destruction of fortifications, be they in urban or rural settings. The conquest of Aleppo was accompanied by much devastation, not only of the city wall and the citadel, but of much of the city itself. The citadels of Damascus and Baalbek were partially destroyed, as were castles in the countryside, such as al-Ṣubayba and ʿAjlūn. All of this destruction necessitated reconstruction afterward, although in the case of Aleppo it was only in the 1290s that serious restoration work on the fortifications was begun.[19]

Secondly, there was the impact on the non-Muslim communities and their relationship with the Muslim population. In Damascus, the local Christian population had briefly enjoyed the disestablishment of Islam as the state religion, perhaps too much. The relatively ostentatious displays of Christian ritual, tacitly permitted if not actively abetted by some of the Christian Mongols (first and foremost Kitbuqa) and their officials, were a great affront to the Muslims. The public displays of Christian piety, along with the loud ringing of the wooden chimes to call to prayer, the drinking of wine and sprinkling it on Muslims—this was not just the practice of religious freedom, but a deliberate provocation of Muslim sensibilities, under the apparent aegis of the relatively tolerant, and perhaps even pro-Christian, Mongols. For the Muslims this was a humiliation that they could hardly abide, and on September 4, 1260, with the arrival to Damascus of news of the Mamluk victory at ʿAyn Jālūt, they responded with a veritable pogrom against the various Christian communities; in fact, some of this spilled over to riots against the Jews, but these were curtailed when it was remembered that the latter had kept a low profile during the Mongol occupation.[20] The brief flurry of public and flamboyant Christian behavior under Mongol patronage appears to have affected Muslim-*dhimmī* relations in Damascus and perhaps elsewhere in Syria and the Malmuk Sultanate as a whole for some time. I will be returning to this matter below. I do want to emphasize now that when one looks at the identity of local pro-Mongol Quislings in 1260, Christians do not stand out, but rather Muslims.[21] Perhaps there was a later perception among Muslims that the local Arabic-speaking Christians were a kind of fifth column working in favor of the Mongols, as suggested by some scholars.[22] The evidence for this, however, is far from conclusive, and to the best of my knowledge is derived mainly from the polemical anti-*dhimmī* text by Ghāzī b. al-Wāsiṭī, which should best be taken with a large grain of salt.[23]

Another effect of the short Mongol conquest of 1260 on the population of Syria was providing an intimacy with the Mongol threat itself. The impression that one gets from reading the contemporary Syrian sources such as Ibn Wāṣil or Abū Shāma—written in more or less real time—is that with all of the shock of the taking of Baghdad in 1258, the threat presented by the Mongols before 1260 to Syria was still rather abstract.[24] In 1260, however, the danger that the Mongols embodied was brought home: their invasion of northern Syria was both destructive and bloody, Aleppo and nearby Ḥārim being the prime examples. Elsewhere, citadels were taken after some sharp fighting, such as in Baalbek and Damascus (the latter after a rebellion led by Ayyūbid officers). Mongol raiders swept through Palestine and Trans-Jordan, gathering much booty, including livestock. The Mongol troops that remained in the country after Hülegü's withdrawal spread out to find pasturage for their horses, and there is no reason to think that they always distinguished between pastureland and farmland. Additional taxes and other demands were imposed on the urban population at least, and a new and strange ruling group was now in charge with little in common with most of the inhabitants.[25] Certainly the "weirdness" of the Mongols, speaking an unfathomable language (although many "Mongols" probably spoke forms of Turkish, which would have been familiar to the Mamluks and to Syrian elites) and preceded and accompanied by their reputation for ferociousness, now firmly in charge, must have created a sense of dislocation among Syrians from different strata. True, in September 1260 the Mongols and their minions were thrown out, and in the aftermath of ʿAyn Jālūt some of the myth of the invincible Mongols was surely destroyed. However, the Mongols were now something very tangible that was still to be feared. In the future, the threat of a returning Mongol army to Syria would be much more palpable—even if mixed with rumor and myth—and continued to influence the population of the country, be it on the Mamluk ruling class, the civilian elite, the urban masses, the nomads, and probably even the rural majority. This fear—strengthened and refined by the events of 1260—does much to explain the policies and actions of the Mamluks and their subjects in the subsequent decades. I might add that at least among the upper echelons of the Mamluk army and state in Egypt and the civilian elite there, the apprehensions toward the Mongols in the post-1260 period are also clearly seen, although perhaps not quite as immediately and blatantly as with their Syrian peers.

This brings us to another matter that begins in 1260 (and perhaps before), and continues to play a role afterward. I am referring to migration motivated by Mongol advances and conquests, or out of fear of such occurrences. I am not dealing here with one of the many instances in which the Mongols deliberately moved groups of peoples for their own needs, sometimes across long distances, which has been so well analyzed by T. Allsen.[26] The phenomenon of refugees fleeing from the Mongols has been discussed for a particular area and in a general sense by J. R. Sweeney, C. Kaplonski, and now by Allsen.[27] The phenomenon of refugees to, in, and from Syria, has not—as far as I can tell—received any systematic treatment by modern scholars, although en passant comments have been made in studies.

I do not get the impression that the Mongols moved large numbers of civilian or military prisoners out of the country either in 1260 or in subsequent campaigns. There are some notable exceptions to this (the imprisoned Baḥrī Mamluks in Aleppo in 1260; and Damascus residents of Palestinian origin in 1299), but I do not think that this made any significant demographic change in the long run.[28] What does seem to have had an effect on the demographic and social fabric of the country was the movement of refugees. This took place in waves: the first would have been the influx of people from both Iraq and the Jazīra in the aftermath of events of 1258 and 1259; the long Mongol siege of Mayyāfāriqīn (now Silvan in southeastern Turkey), ending in the spring of 1260, is an example of an incident surely leading to spontaneous emigration out of the Jazīra into Syria.[29] A second wave of refugees would have left north Syria at the end of 1259 and the beginning of 1260, heading for the south and finding at least temporary refuge in the cities and towns of the region, but perhaps also in rural areas. Finally, there would have been the movement of people out of Syria to Egypt. This would have surely included individuals and groups from beyond the Euphrates who had first looked for refuge in Syria, as well as north Syrians, who had initially fled to the south. Those fleeing to Egypt in the spring of 1260 included all swaths of the population: Ayyūbid scions, important bureaucrats and *ʿulamāʾ* (scholars), officers and soldiers, nomads (including Kurds and Turcomen, and perhaps even Bedouin), and common people. Among the more important personalities were al-Manṣūr Muḥammad, Ayyūbid prince of Hama, and the official and writer Ibn Shaddād al-Ḥalabī.[30] How many of all of these immigrants and refugees (i.e., those fleeing just in front of the Mongols or in the direct aftermath of their conquest) stayed in the place of refuge and how many eventually went back when things quieted down is unclear, but at the very least all of this movement of people led to confusion and difficult circumstances for both the migrants and the hosts. This was another factor in the general sense of uncertainty and displacement that characterized 1260 in both Syria and Egypt, making it difficult for the authorities to keep control and to adopt an effective strategy vis-à-vis the Mongol invaders.

In the following years, with reports of impending Mongol campaigns to the country (not that all of these reports turned out to be true), the above-described phenomena of northern Syrians moving south repeated itself.[31] However, in all subsequent cases, fewer people seemed to have been involved, and the impact on the general political, demographic, and social situation appears to have been less decisive.

After 1260, there also was a continuation of immigration from the "East" over the Euphrates into Syria (and perhaps, ultimately, beyond). This border, along with that to the north with Anatolia (including Cilicia), was far from hermetically sealed, even when warfare was at its height. There appears always to have been a steady trickle of merchants, scholars, deserters, and even spies plying their way between Syria and Ilkhanid-controlled territory.[32] Immigrants could also make the trek, not necessarily with ease, but with effort and, with a little luck, with success. The impression that I get is that besides the occasional Mamluk deserter fleeing eastward, most of this movement was to the west into Syria. We first have a fairly substantial number of military and political refugees out of Iraq, the Jazīra, and Anatolia. For the early years of the Mamluk-Mongol war this was a veritable stream at times, including political figures (such as ʿAbbāsid scions and the surviving sons of Badr al-Dīn Luʾluʾ, ruler of Mosul), Mamluk-like officers and troops from various places—Baghdad and Seljuq Anatolia can be noted—Kurds, Turcomen, and many thousands of disgruntled Mongols.[33] All of these were referred to by the Mamluk writers as *wāfidiyya* or *mustaʾminūn*, "those seeking refuge." There is still some debate among specialists about the nature of these waves of military immigrants, particularly Mongols, and their impact on and integration into Mamluk society, both in Syria and Egypt. My own view today represents perhaps a middle position between that of David Ayalon and that of Nakamachi Nobutaka: the Mongol and other *wāfidī* officers rarely if ever got to the top of the political and military hierarchy, but the *wāfidī* troops played a not insignificant role in the emerging army of the Mamluk Sultanate, even if the vast majority of them were integrated into units of secondary importance.[34] Certainly, the growth of the nomadic population in Syria, not the least along the Palestinian coast, had a long-term, secondary effect on the demographic, social, economic, and settlement history of the country (more about this below). The Mongols thus unwittingly contributed to the strengthening of the army that was organizing to meet any invasion from them. This, of course, is certainly a discernable impact on Syrian (and Egyptian history).

But that is not all: there was also a continual seepage of civilian immigrants across the Euphrates into Syria. It is impossible to estimate their number, relative or absolute, but here and there we have some indication of the nature of this movement. Thus, in 1271, a Mamluk raiding party under the governor of Damascus, Taybars al-Wazīrī, reached Ḥarrān, today in southeastern Turkey. The sources note that already a good portion of the population had left the city, some to elsewhere in the Jazira and some to Syria. Among those who immigrated to Syria at the end of the 1260s was the Banū Taymiyya clan, whose most famous son was be Taqī al-Dīn Aḥmad ibn Taymiyya (d. 1328), the renowned Ḥanbalī scholar and public figure. Emmanuel Sivan, who has studied the impact of Ibn Taymiyya's views on modern Islamist ideology, has suggested this scholar's extreme and strident views can at least be partially explained by the traumas of his youth: the harsh treatment of his city and family by the Mongols and the subsequent need to immigrate to Syria.[35] I am not sure that we are able to suggest such a psychological profile of this great scholar, but there is no doubt that he was engaged with the Mongols on a number of levels. This included leading the civilian population of Damascus during the short Mongol occupation of Damascus in 1300 and composing fatwas—probably later—to show that the Mongols' conversion to Islam was not a true one and therefore they could still be fought as infidels.[36] Yet, without going as far as Professor Sivan, I find it notable that the most towering intellectual opponent of the Mongols, let alone the one that stood up to them at times in Damascus (while knowing when to compromise), was an individual who had been driven out of his hometown by them. This, too, is an aspect of the impact of the Mongols on Syria, and for me it remains the most outstanding example of the role of refugees from the across the Euphrates into Syria. On the other hand, we might mention the exact opposite of Ibn Taymiyya among these refugees in terms of world outlook: Muḥammad ibn Dāniyāl (d. 1310), the eye doctor, courtier, bon vivant, poet, and playwright. Hailing from Mosul, he fled to Cairo in the aftermath of the Mongol takeover in the early 1260s. Ibn Dāniyāl's dissolute lifestyle and satirical approach to life in general (as expressed in his writings) strike an interesting counterbalance to Ibn Taymiyya's severe attitudes, and show another way that the refugee experience might impact on the developments of a creative personality.[37]

We can look at other developments in Syria that began in 1260, and continued through the next few decades. One is the situation on the frontier with the Mongols. In order to understand the Mamluk-controlled, that is, Syrian, side of the frontier, it is useful to compare it to its Mongol counterpart, meaning the western Jazīra. According to Rashīd al-Dīn, much was devastated and depopulated.[38] This must have been the result of a combination of the initial invasion, the continual border warfare in the region, the presence of a large number of Mongols in the area, and perhaps also heavy-handed administration. The situation across the Euphrates was somewhat different: the Arabic sources, primarily the geographical-historical work *al-Aʿlāq al-khaṭīra* by Ibn Shaddād al-Ḥalabī, describe some areas in northern and northeastern Syria that were occupied, even thriving, while others were abandoned, or at least in a sorry state.[39] Here, the role of the Mamluk authorities was probably directly responsible for a relatively positive situation: the efforts to keep some select fortifications ready and garrisoned, regular patrols in the area, the pacification of the nomads—be they Bedouin or Turcomen—and the willingness to meet even a rumor of an impending Mongol campaign with a strong Mamluk force paid off in the long run with regard to the overall prosperity and demographic stability in wide swaths of north and northeastern Syria. A less determined effort on the part of the Mamluks would probably have resulted in a situation similar to that on the other side of the Euphrates.[40] The Mongols "compelled"—so to speak—the Mamluks to react in a certain way to preserve their rule in Syria, and this too can be counted among their influences on the country and its rulers.

Part of the determined drive to keep the Mongols out of Syria was an ongoing and fairly intensive program in rebuilding fortifications. It is well known that the Mamluks had a selective policy of the repair and construction of forts. On the whole, those on the seacoast that were captured from the Franks were at least partially destroyed and abandoned. Many captured from the Franks inland were repaired, expanded, and garrisoned—Safad and Crac des Chevaliers (Ḥisn al-Akrād) come to mind—as were others that the Mamluks took control of after 1260. Most spectacular of this last class and also very strategically important were the frontier fortresses of al-Raḥba and al-Bīra, along with others in the frontier area to the north such as ʿAyn Tāb. In order to bring word of a Mongol invasion in real time to the center of the country, rapid communication systems were instituted (or perhaps continued, expanded, and institutionalized): a network of bonfires and the pigeon-post to the major cities of Syria, where the horse-relays (*barīd*) could take over. The refortification of Syria under the early Mamluks can only be understood within the framework of the war with the Mongols and the goal to prepare the country as best as possible for a potential attack from their direction.[41] This also explains to a certain degree the efforts expended on certain inland fortresses whose strategic importance is perhaps not obvious at first glance—such as al-Ṣubayba in the Golan Heights and Karak in Trans-Jordan. I would suggest that they were intended to provide refuge for Mamluk soldiers and islands of potential resistance in the occurrence of the worst case scenario: the reconquest of Syria by the Mongols. In fact, this is exactly what happened in 1299–1300, and Baybars al-Manṣūrī—commander and historian—subsequently remarks with some satisfaction that in spite of the defeat of the Mamluk army at Wādī al-Khaznadār and the embarrassing retreat to Egypt, not one castle in Syria was lost to the Mongols before they withdrew in mid-spring.[42]

It is difficult to gauge the extent of long-term damage that subsequent Mongol invasions and raids inflicted on the country. We can assume that the damage to pasture and farm lands caused by the movement of large cavalry-based armies and their need to find food was temporary, and within a year or so forgotten. Some cities—not the least Aleppo, which was taken again more than once—were damaged to a degree, but there is no indication that the trauma of 1260 was repeated; in any event, as I mentioned above, it was only in the 1290s that the fortifications of the city began to be repaired in earnest. On the whole, in subsequent campaigns, many of the urban centers of central Syria were bypassed. The occupation of Damascus in 1300 resulted in what appears to have been substantial destruction to the citadel and its environs (as well as the suburb of Ṣāliḥiyya), but there is no reason to think that these damages were not repaired within a few years.[43] Here, at least, the impact of the Mongols was not extensive, although perhaps the fear of what the Mongols might destroy in future campaigns remained a real one.

Having looked at the ways that the Mongols influenced developments in the realm of demography, settlement, and landscape in a general way in Syria from 1260 onward, I would like now to concentrate briefly on three ways that the Mongols directly impacted on the nature of political rule in the country. Firstly, as alluded to above, the Mongols basically eliminated the Ayyūbid hegemony over most of Syria. For almost a decade the nascent Mamluk regime in Egypt had been in conflict with the Syrian Ayyūbids, under the leadership of al-Nāṣir Yūsuf, but the sides had battled each other to a standstill. There is no reason to suspect that this situation was going to change much, if at all, in the foreseeable future. Without the arrival of the Mongols, it does not seem an irrational assumption that the new Mamluk regime, which had yet to show the military prowess for which it would subsequently become noted under Baybars (in order to meet the Mongol challenge), would have broken out of the confines of Egypt. At the same time, there is no reason to seriously suggest that the authority established by al-Nāṣir Yūsuf over Aleppo and Damascus, and his supremacy vis-à-vis the other Ayyūbid princes, would have been challenged in a serious way by his kinsmen or others (including the Franks). It took the Mongol muscle to dislodge al-Nāṣir Yūsuf and the Ayyūbids from most of Syria; ironically, it was the Mamluks who were to enjoy the fruits of this development. We have here the fruition of a process that began in the mid-ninth century, from the time of the Ṭūlunids (868–905), where any independent ruler of Egypt would do what he could to gain control over Syria, not the least as a bulwark toward dangers from the east. Certainly, the Mamluk control of Syria—occasioned by the Mongol conquest, and then directed against them—can be seen as the ultimate expression of this long-term strategic trend.

Secondly, as a result of this new Mamluk sovereignty, Syria was now firmly under the control of a relatively centralized state based in Cairo.[44] This is not the place to examine the full implications of this quarter of a millennium of generally direct management from Egypt, but it is clear that the era of political disintegration (and frequent infighting) that characterized the Ayyūbid period was over.[45] How a comparatively robust local cultural and intellectual life fared under the new Turkish rulers from Egypt is an interesting question that has yet to receive serious attention. I attempt some preliminary thoughts on the matter below.

Thirdly, there is the Syrian expression of a sultanate-wide development: the strengthening of the Mamluk military machine to meet the danger of an impending Mongol invasion. In the early 1260s, the Mamluk leadership—based in Egypt, but spending a large amount of time in Syria—was convinced that another campaign from the Ilkhanate was sure to come, and made efforts to prepare the army and related matters accordingly. This includes what appears to be the doubling of the regular army, including that in Syria, financed in part by the addition of new lands (not the least those captured from the Franks) and the more efficient administrative system facilitated by a regime led by officers. As I have pointed out above, the Syrian auxiliary forces increased dramatically in size and quality, due, inter alia, to immigration from Mongol-controlled territory. As I have also noted, fortifications and communications were repaired, improved, and maintained. Transportation was enhanced by the building of bridges, at least in Palestine: these would facilitate the movement of troops over seasonal riverbeds during the winter, the season that the Mongols chose to launch their campaigns.[46] Another aspect of this resolute policy is the dramatic expansion and institutionalization of a foreign espionage system, a topic I have discussed at length in the past.[47] The relevance here is that the jumping-off point for this whole network of agents, couriers, and raiders was north and northeastern Syria, particularly the frontier fortresses that I have noted previously.

In short, the Mongols indirectly contributed to the increasing militarization of Syria, with economic, social, political, and even cultural implications. I will just mention in a few words three long-term repercussions of the Mamluk control of Syria, going beyond the time of their rule, thus bringing home some of the indirect effects of the Mongols on the development on the country.

The first is something that I have described above: the influx of nomads of various kinds to Syria as refugees from the Mongols, and the further impact on life in the country. Some of these—and the Shahrazūrī Kurds come to mind—arrived in the years before 1260, some probably that year, and many—Turcomen and Mongols in particular—in the aftermath of that decisive time. As I have noted, this was not just a matter of being pushed out by Hülegü and his successors, or fleeing before the Mongol danger—real or perceived—but also the warm reception accorded to them by Baybars and his cohorts, and their integration into the Mamluk army. Many of these refugees were settled along the Syrian coast, and particularly in Palestine. Thus Kurds were permitted to set up their abode near Gaza; the Turcomen were given lands in various places on the coast; and the Oirat Mongols who came in the mid-1290s settled near ʿAthlīt, south of Haifa. When I say "settled" it should be clear that I am not suggesting that these nomads became sedentary, at least in the short run. Rather, they were permitted to practice a form of nomadic pastoralism, although—at least initially—within certain geographic limitations, mostly in territories recently taken from the Franks. This provided a cheap and efficient military presence in the area, without necessitating the allocation of expensive regular Mamluk troopers. The downside was that over time these populations—who were generally known as Turcomen, *tarākima* in Arabic, until the early twentieth century, even though they were almost completely Arabized—made a notable contribution to the gradual depopulation of the regular sedentary population in these areas, and disrupted traditional landholding and settlement patterns.[48]

A second long-term influence of the Mongols in Syria contributed indirectly to the gradual but final eradication of the Frankish presence in the Levant. This is partly apparent from my previous discussion: if the Mamluks had not taken Syria in the aftermath of the Mongol invasion of the country, obviously they would not have had much direct contact with the Franks of the Levant, and little opportunity to confront them militarily. Secondly, the whole jihadi ethos which was cultivated under Baybars and his successors, or perhaps I could say, briefly by the unfortunate Quṭuz and his successors, which first developed in the struggle with the Mongols, certainly contributed to this newfound militancy vis-à-vis the Franks. Certainly, no Ayyūbid prince had referred to himself as *mubīd al-faranj wa'l-tatar,* "annihilator of Franks and Mongols," as did Baybars and some of the sultans after him.[49] Thirdly, as I have suggested over the years, the perception by the Mamluk leadership that the Ilkhans were negotiating with the Franks in Outremer and Europe also may have played a role. The Mamluk fear that they would have to fight either a joint Mongol-Frankish army, or two separate armies at the same time, was a real one, and this appears to be one reason why they applied themselves systematically to taking apart the Frankish entity in Syria.[50]

Finally, there may be a completely unexpected consequence of the Mongol invasion of 1260, and the resulting Mamluk incorporation of Syria into their state. Recent research has begun to show that it was during the period of Mamluk rule that we have the decisive Islamization of much of Palestine. Here I am citing the research of my colleagues Ronnie Ellenblum and Nimrod Luz.[51] This ties in well with what we know about Mamluk Egypt, which also saw a significant reduction of the Coptic population, both in absolute and relative terms.[52] What was it about the Mamluk period that proved so conducive to religious change? Important scholars such as Claude Cahen and Eliyahu Ashtor have given this matter some attention, and spoke, inter alia, of the increasing militancy of the ruling Mamluks, the *'ulamā',* and the wider urban population.[53] This seems reasonable as far as it goes, although I could note two reservations. Often, it was the Mamluks who were a force for relative moderation toward the *dhimmī* population and tried to moderate and control the masses, often led by religious personalities of different stripes.[54] Secondly, beyond this general militancy—which was influenced by and expressed in the war with the Mongols (as well as the Franks and Armenians)—little explanation is offered for how this actually contributed to the mechanism of religious change.

I will offer two partial reasons that contributed to this development. The first is that under the Mamluks, religious patronage was increased toward the *ʿulamāʾ* and *ṣūfīs* (mystics), which are not two mutually exclusive categories. This process too demands a more serious and detailed discussion, but here it will suffice to say that trends of religious patronage that began more than a century earlier in Syria under the Zengids (which themselves had both local and Seljuq antecedents) appear to have reached a higher degree under the Mamluks.[55] This included the building and endowment of religious institutions, most importantly the *madrasa,* or religious college, which employed and churned out religious scholars. So the number of "professional" religious men increased, and this probably contributed in a significant way to the more militant Muslim ambience toward non-Muslims throughout the Sulanate.[56]

I would like to make another suggestion, for a development that we can discern under the early Mamluks: the growth of a "muscular" Sufism, at times supported and abetted by the Mamluk establishment. Recently, Tamer al-Leithy has written about the activities of *ṣūfīs* in Upper Egypt, particularly in Qūṣ, where they were engaged in the destruction of churches and other actions discomforting to the local Christians. These were not necessarily with the approval, even tacit, of the political establishment.[57] However, in Syria, or at least in Palestine, this approval—implicit or otherwise—from the authorities was certainly found at times. Thus, the *ṣūfī* personality Khidr al-Mihrānī, the spiritual mentor of Sultan Baybars, attacked the Georgian monastery of the Valley of the Cross in Jerusalem with impunity, killing the abbot, and turning it into a *khānqāh* (*ṣūfī* hospice).[58] It is difficult to see how this was done without official support, even if it was expressed in the turning of a blind eye. In the mid-fourteenth century, a *ṣūfī* shaykh of the Banū Wafāʾ family moved into the village of Sharafāt to the south of Jerusalem, and within a few years had driven out the Christian inhabitants.[59] The source, Mujīr al-Dīn al-Ḫanbalī's history of Jerusalem and Hebron, tells this story in detail, including the direct patronage from senior Mamluk officer that this shaykh enjoyed.[60] My guess is that these two stories were repeated in Mamluk Palestine, as I hope will be revealed by future research. It would seem thus that life was made at times very difficult for local Christians, compelling them to move or to convert. Along with these *ṣūfī* ruffians, we should note that the Mamluks were contributing to the changing landscape of the region: it was more Muslim, filled with minarets, shaykhs' tombs, and other Muslim holy spots.[61] The Mamluks thus contributed in more than one way to creating a more Islamic ambience.

Let us remember, were it not for the Mongols there is a good chance that the Mamluks would have not have taken over the country, and the Ayyūbid status quo might well have continued: the modus vivendi with the Franks could well have kept up and perhaps also the local Christian communities would have managed on as before. I know that we are admonished not to let our counterfactual fantasies get the better of us, but perhaps a moderate dose of this line of thinking might help us to emphasize the great changes that were inaugurated when the Mamluks took over Syria, a direct—if unplanned—consequence of the activities of the Mongols in Syria in 1260.

There is another area that needs to be explored: What was the direct impact of Mongol rule in nearby countries (Iraq, the Jazīra, Azerbaijan, and Anatolia) on cultural life in Syria? In other words, did the cultural and scientific effervescence that took place under the Mongol aegis, developments about which we are increasingly aware in recent years, somehow have an impact on parallel activities in the Mamluk Sultanate, particularly Syria, which was close by?[62] This does not seem impossible, since—as I noted before—the frontier between the Mamluk Sultanate and the Ilkhanate was far from a closed one, and scholars, inter alia, made their way across the border in both directions, in spite of the ongoing war (including, at times, incessant fighting in the frontier region). Scholars from Mongol-controlled territory could have come for short- or long-term visits to Syria (and Egypt), or even immigrated, and thus could have influenced their colleagues there. One notable example is the famous jurist, physician, and astronomer Quṭb al-Dīn Maḥmūd b. Masʿūd Shīrāzī, who arrived in the sultanate as an official envoy of the Ilkhan Aḥmad Tegüder in 1282, and took advantage of his stay—mostly in Cairo—for scholarly contacts. How this may have influenced scholars in Egypt and Syria remains unclear, although he was surely able to collect material for his own work.[63] Other visitors are the many scholars and officials from the Ilkhanate who traveled or moved to the sultanate in the early decades of the fourteenth century, especially after the peace treaty of 1323. This movement westward appears to have gained strength as a result of the confused state in the realm of the Ilkhanate after Abū Saʿīd's death in 1335. Such knowledgeable immigrants (or refugees) are noted as sources by Ibn Faḍl Allāh al-ʿUmarī in his section on the Mongols in the encyclopedia *Masālik al-abṣār*.[64] It would appear that at least a little of the intellectual and scholarly activity in the Ilkhanate indeed somehow bubbled over and impacted on the sultanate, especially Syria (and we can also suppose vice versa), but the exact mechanism for this process is yet unclear, let alone the degree of real influence. Further study of this matter will surely bring to our attention more examples of "visiting scholars" from Mongol-controlled territory and perhaps reveal the extent of cultural and scientific influence from that direction.

At this time, we must therefore be satisfied to speak only of the indirect consequence of the coming of the Mongols to the region and their impact on the cultural life of Syria (and by extension Egypt), a matter that has been touched on above: refugee scholars from the east, on the one hand, and increased patronage from the ruling class, on the other hand, which together with a long-established local scholarly tradition, led to certain flowering of scholarship and cultural life in Syria in the late thirteenth century and early fourteenth century primarily concentrated in Damascus, but also discernable in Aleppo and many of the smaller cities of the country. This is a topic that demands a comprehensive investigation, but we might just note the following fields and practitioners: historiography (al-Dhahabī, al-Yūnīnī, al-Birzālī and al-Jazarī), biographical dictionaries and belles lettres (al-Ṣafadī), scientific geography and cosmography (Abū al-Fidā', also a historian, and al- Dimashqī), administrative manuals and encyclopedias (Ibn Faḍl Allāh al-ʿUmarī), and religious studies (of whom Ibn Taymiyya is perhaps the most outstanding figure, but far from alone).[65] Damascus, for sure, had a vibrant intellectual and scholarly scene. Might we allow ourselves to see the contribution of the Mongols, albeit in an indirect fashion, to this development? It is interesting to note that almost all the figures that are noted here have something of substance and interest to say about the Mongols. It is clear how high the Mongols figured in the consciousness of Syrian (and Egyptian) scholars, and how these took advantage of this knowledge to write about them extensively in their works.[66] Under Mamluk guidance and protection, intellectual and scholarly life thrived and developed, certainly early in their regime. Ultimately and in a roundabout way, the Mongols contributed here too.

In other words, without the campaign of Hülegü to southwest Asia in the late 1250s, culminating in the invasion of Syria and the defeat at ʿAyn Jālūt in 1260, the possibility of a Mamluk conquest of Syria would have been unlikely, and thus the history of the region would probably have been very different. We have seen the impact on politics and administration (centralization, militarization), demography (immigration, mobility, and the influx of nomads), as well as certain aspects of religious and general culture (an emphasis on jihad, Islamization, changing landscape). Contacts with the Mongols perhaps brought wider cultural horizons, a phenomenon not only limited to Syria or even the sultanate. The course of a quarter of a millennium's history in Syria was therefore set by events that began years before on the other side of Asia. This was not exactly the world of the Mongols, but it was decisively influenced by it. Thus, in Syria too, in a generally indirect way, the Mongols were agents of change, cultural and otherwise.

Notes

Some of the research for this study was conducted within the framework of the Center of Excellence "The Formation of Muslim Society in Palestine/Eretz Israel," funded by the Israel Science Foundation (ISF no. 1676/09). An earlier version was presented at the Burdick-Vary Symposium "The Mongol World Empire and Its World," held at the University of Wisconsin–Madison on April 9–10, 2010, and sponsored by the Institute for the Research in the Humanities there; I am grateful to David Morgan for inviting me to that meeting. I decided not to use my lecture from the 2006 conference which serves as the basis of this volume, as my paper there was subsequently partially superseded by the article by Kate Raphael, "Mongol Siege Warfare on the Banks of the Euphrates and the Question of Gunpowder (1260–1312)," *Journal of the Royal Asiatic Society,* 3rd ser., 19/3 (2009), pp. 355–370.

1. In the Mamluk period, Syria (Ar. *bilād al-shām*) was the territory of Greater Syria, including therefore the modern states of Syria (but not east of the Euphrates), Lebanon, Jordan, Israel, and the Palestinian Authority.

2. For a short survey of the history of Syria under the Mamluks see H. Lammens and C. E. Bosworth, "al-Shām," *Encyclopaedia of Islam,* 2nd ed. (Leiden, 1954–2005), vol. 9, 268–269. For an idea of the extent of the research literature on the history of the country in this period see the *Mamluk Online Bibliography,* http://mamluk.lib.uchicago.edu/index.html, s.v. "Syria" (accessed April 7, 2014).

3. The Hague, 1834 (4 vols.), reprinted Tientsin, China, 1940.

4. 4th ed., Leiden, 1985; "Dynastic and Political History of the Īl-Khāns," in *The Cambridge History of Iran,* ed. J. A. Boyle (Cambridge, 1968), vol. 5, pp. 303–428.

5. Peter Jackson, "The Crisis in the Holy Land in 1260," *English Historical Review,* 95 (1980), pp. 481–513; Peter Jackson, *The Mongols and the West, 1221–1410* (Harrow, UK, 2005), chs. 5 and 7; John M. Smith, Jr., "ʿAyn Jālūt: Mamluk Success or Mongol Failure," *Harvard Journal Asiatic Studies,* 44 (1984), pp. 307–345; David Morgan, "The Mongols in Syria, 1260–1300," in *Crusade and Settlement: Papers Read at the First Conference of the Society for the Study of the Crusades and the Latin East and Presented to R.C. Smail,* ed. P. Edbury (Cardiff, 1985), pp. 231–235; David Morgan, "The Mongols and the Eastern Mediterranean," in *Latins and Greeks in the Eastern Mediterranean after 1204,* ed. B. Arbel et al. (London, 1989), pp. 198–211 [= *Mediterranean Studies Review,* 4/1 (June 1989)]; Timothy May, "The Mongol Presence and Impact in the Lands of the Eastern Mediterranean," in *Crusades, Condottieri, and Cannon: Medieval Warfare in Societies around the Mediterranean,* ed. D. J. Kagay and L. J. Andrew Villalon (Leiden, 2003), pp. 133–156; Anne Broadbridge, *Kingship and Ideology in the Islamic and Mongol Worlds* (Cambridge, 2008); R. Amitai, *Mongols and Mamluks: The Mamluk-Īlkhānid War, 1260–1281* (Cambridge, 1995); and the papers collected in the third section of R. Amitai, *The Mongols in the Islamic Lands: Studies in the History of the Ilkhanate* (Aldershot, UK, 2007).

6. "Mongol Imperial Ideology and the Ilkhanid War against the Mamluks," in *The Mongol Empire and Its Legacy,* ed. R. Amitai-Preiss and D. Morgan (Leiden, 1999), pp. 57–72 (reprinted in Amitai, *The Mongols in the Islamic Lands*).

7. R. Amitai, "Mongol Provincial Administration: Syria in 1260 as a Case-Study," in *In Laudem Hierosolymitani: Studies in Crusades and Medieval Culture in Honour of Benjamin Z. Kedar,* ed. I. Shagrir et al. (Aldershot, UK, 2007), pp. 117–143.

8. On this letter see Amitai-Preiss, *Mongols and Mamluks,* p. 36 and n. 64; W. Brinner, "Some Ayyūbid and Mamlūk Documents from Non-archival Sources," *Israel Oriental Studies,* 2 (1972), pp. 117–143; D. Aigle, "Les correspondances adressées par Hülegü au prince ayyoubide de Syrie, al-Malik al-Nāṣir Yūsuf. La construction d'un modèle," in *Pensée grecque et sagesse d'Orient. Hommages à Michel Tardieu,* ed. M.-A. Moezzi et al. (Turnhout, 2009), pp. 1–21.

9. Amitai-Preiss, *Mongols and Mamluks,* ch. 10.

10. Cf. Morgan, "The Mongols and the Eastern Mediterranean."

11. J. A. Boyle, "The Il-Khans of Persia and the Christian West," *History Today,* 23/8 (1973), pp. 554–563 (reprinted in J. A. Boyle, *The Mongol World Empire 1206–1370* [London, 1977]); J. Richard, "The Mongols and the Franks," *Journal of Asian History,* 3 (1969), pp. 45–57 (reprinted in J. Richard, *Orient and Occident au Moyen Age: contacts et relations (XIIe–XVe siècles)* [London, 1976]); Jackson, *The Mongols and the West,* ch. 7.

12. For the size of these armies and the campaigns in general see Amitai-Preiss, *Mamluks and Mongols,* chs. 2 and 8; R. Amitai, "Whither the Ilkhanid Army? Ghazan's First Campaign into Syria (1299–1300)," in *Warfare in Inner Asian History,* ed. N. Di Cosmo (Leiden, 2002), pp. 221–264 (reprinted in Amitai, *The Mongols in the Islamic Lands*).

13. See J. M. Smith, Jr., "ʿAyn Jālūt: Mamluk Success or Mongol Failure," cited in n. 7 above, and J. M. Smith, Jr., "Nomads on Ponies vs. Slaves on Horses," *Journal of the American Oriental Society,* 118 (1998), pp. 54–62; Morgan, "The Mongols in Syria" (see also the discussion in Jackson, *The Mongols and the West,* pp. 178–179); Amitai, *Mongols and Mamluks,* ch. 10; R. Amitai, "The Logistics of the Mongol-Mamlūk War, with Special Reference to the Battle of Wādī al-Khaznadār, 1299 C.E," in *Logistics of War in the Age of the Crusades,* ed. J. H. Pryor (Aldershot, UK, 2006), pp. 25–42. I do not go as far as both Smith and Morgan in attributing such a decisive role to the logistical difficulties the Mongols may have encountered in Syria.

14. Northern Mesopotamia, today divided between northern Iraq, northeast Syria, and southeastern Turkey.

15. Jackson, "Crisis in the Holy Land," pp. 490–507; R. Amitai, "Mongol Raids into Palestine (A.D. 1260 and 1300)," *Journal of the Royal Asiatic Society,* (1987), pp. 236–255 (reprinted in Amitai, *The Mongols in the Islamic Lands*).

16. On the fate of the Ayyūbids under the Mamluks see R. Irwin, *The Middle East in the Middle Ages: The Early Mamluk Sultanate 1250–1382* (London, 1986), pp. 45–46.

17. Amitai, "Mongol Provincial Administration."

18. The text on the obverse reads: "The most splendid / Möngke Q̱aghan / and by his good fortune, / the conqueror of the world / his brother Hülegü, / may their grandeur be augmented." See S. Heidemann, *Das Aleppiner Kalifat (AD 1261): vom Ende des Kalifates in Bagdad über Aleppo zu den Restaurationen in Kairo* (Leiden, 1994), pp. 243, 285; N. Amitai-Preiss and R. Amitai-Preiss, "Two Notes on the Protocol on Hülegü's Coinage," *Israel Numismatic Journal,* 10 (1988–1989), p. 125.

19. Amitai-Preiss, *Mongols and Mamluks,* pp. 26, 32–33, 204; K. Raphael, *Muslim Fortresses in the Levant: Between Crusaders and Mongols* (London, 2010), pp. 93–94, 103, 121–122.

20. This particular aspect of the Mongol occupation of 1260 and its implications for Muslim–Christian relations in Damascus and the sultanate as a whole has yet to be studied in any depth. For brief discussions see R. S. Humphreys, *From Saladin to the Mongols: The Ayyubids of Damascus, 1193–1260* (Albany, NY, 1977), p. 359; Amitai, *Mongols and Mamluks,* pp. 31, 45–46 (in n. 124 there is a list of Arabic sources that report on Christian behavior under the Mongols, and the post-ʿAyn Jālūt Muslim response). See particularly the text by Ghāzī b. al-Wāsiṭī that was edited and translated by R. Gottheil, "An Answer to the Dhimmis," *Journal of the American Oriental Society,* 41 (1921), pp. 407–410 (tr. 445–450), but this account is clearly colored by its anti-Christian polemical nature.

21. The most prominent being Zayn al-Dīn al-Ḥāfiẓī; Amitai, "Mongol Provincial Administration," pp. 130–131.

22. See E. Ashtor, "Mamluks," *Encyclopaedia Judaica* (1st ed., Jerusalem, 1971–1972), vol. 11, 834; N. Levtzion, "Conversion to Islam in Syria and Palestine and the Survival of Christian Communities," in *Conversion and Continuity: Indigenous Christian Communities in Islamic Lands, Eighth to Eighteenth Centuries,* ed. M. Gervers and R. J. Bikhazi (Toronto, 1990), p. 300.

23. Gottheil, "An Answer to the Dhimmis," pp. 410, 410–412 (tr. 450, 452); Ghāzī b. al-Wāsiṭī accuses Christians of spying for the Mongols: in the first passage, it is the Christian official (and historian) al-Makīn ibn al-ʿAmīd, and in the second, they were local Christians, Georgians, and Armenians living in and around the Monastery of the Cross near Jerusalem.

24. For the experience of these two authors during the late 1250s and 1260 and how this influenced their historical writing see K. Hirschler, *Medieval Arabic Historiography: Authors as Actors* (London, 2006).

25. See the Jackson and Amitai works cited in n. 15 above; also Humphreys, *From Saladin to the Mongols,* pp. 348–358; Amitai-Preiss, *Mongols and Mamluks,* pp. 26–35.

26. T. T. Allsen, *Commodity and Exchange in the Mongol Empire: A Cultural History of Islamic Textiles* (Cambridge, 1997), particularly ch. 3.

27. J. R. Sweeney, "'Spurred on by the Fear of Death': Refugees and Displaced Populations during the Mongol Invasion of Hungary," in *Nomadic Diplomacy, Destruction and Religion from the Pacific to the Adriatic,* ed. M. Gervers and W. Schlepp, Toronto Studies in Central and Inner Asia, No.1 (Toronto, 1994), pp. 34–62; C. Kaplonski, "The Mongolian Impact on Eurasia: A Reassessment," in *The Role of Migration in the History of the Eurasian Steppe: Sedentary Civilization vs. "Barbarian" and Nomad,* ed. A. Bell-Fialkoff (New York, 2000), pp. 256–257; see also Allsen's chapter in this volume.

28. Shihāb al-Dīn Aḥmad b. ʿAbd al-Wahhāb al-Nuwayrī, *Nihāyat al-arab fī funūn al-adab* (Cairo, 1346/1923–1418/1997), vol. 27, p. 388; Shams al-Dīn Muḥammad b. Aḥmad al-Dhahabī, *Taʾrīkh al-islām wa-wafayāt al-mashāhīr waʾl-aʿlām* (Beirut, 1401/1981–1424/2004), vol. 70 (691–700), p. 426. This information is from the obituary of ʿAlī b. al-Shaykh Shams al-Dīn ʿAbd al-Raḥmān ibn Qudāma al-Muqaddasī, who went off to rescue his kinsmen in Mongol captivity, most probably in the aftermath of the occupation of Damascus in 1300. I have to correct my statement in my 1987 article ("Mongol Raids into Palestine"), where I suggested that these were Jerusalemites. Rather, these *maqādisa* were the descendents of refugees from the Nablus region in the mid-twelfth century (and thus, by extension, from the wider Jerusalem region), who settled in the Damas-

cus area, particularly in what was to become the suburb of Ṣāliḥyya. See E. Sivan, "Refugiés syro-palestiniens au temps des croisades," *Revue des isalmiques études,* 35 (1967), pp. 135–147.

29. For this siege see my recent article "*Im Westen nichts Neues?* Re-examining Hülegü's Offensive into the Jazīra and Northern Syria in Light of Recent Research," in *Historicizing the "Beyond": The Mongolian Invasion as a New Dimension of Violence?,* ed. F. Krämer et al. (Heidelberg, 2011), pp. 83–96.

30. Humphreys, *From Saladin to the Mongols,* pp. 352–353; C. Cahen, *La syrie du nord à l'époque des croisades et la principauté franque d'Antioche* (Paris, 1940), p. 75.

31. Thus in 680/1281 (in the events that led to the battle of Wādī al-Khaznadār), there were rumors of an impending Mongol invasion, leading the people of Aleppo to flee to Central Syria until "it was empty of its inhabitants" (Taqī al-Dīn Aḥmad b. ʿAlī al-Maqrīzī, *Kitāb al-sulūk li-maʿrifat al-duwal wa'l-mulūk* [Cairo, 1934–1973], vol. 1, p. 691). In 699/1299, with news of Ghazan's approach, rumors were flying and "people arrived [in Damascus] one after another struck in fear (or in flight)." (ibid., vol. 1, p. 885) See also Ibn Taghrī Birdī, *al-Nujūm al-zāhira fī mulūk miṣr wa'l-qāhira* (Cairo, 1348–1392/1929–1970), vol. 8, p. 131; al-Yūnīnī, in Li Guo (ed. and tr.), *Early Mamluk Syrian Historiography: al-Yūnīnī's Dhayl Mir'āt al-zamān* (Leiden, 1998), vol. 1, p. 176 (translation), vol. 2, p. 206 (Arabic text); al-Nuwayrī, *Nihāyat al-arab fī funūn al-adab,* vol. 31, p. 413 (I am grateful to Dr. Amir Mazor for these last-mentioned references). In 702/1302, just before another Mongol offensive, "people arrived in Damascus from Aleppo and Hama out of fright of the Mongols. The people of Damascus prepared to flee, and they were all but ready to go out," but did not leave due to clear orders to stay put (Maqrīzī, *Sulūk,* vol. 1, p. 930). In 1261, the people of north Syria supposedly fled to Aleppo at the news of the impending Mongol invasion; Bar Hebraeus, *The Chronography of Bar Hebraeus Gregory Abû'l-Faraj,* tr. E. A. W. Budge (London, 1922; rpt. Amsterdam, 1976), p. 439 (he speaks of "all the inhabitants of Syria," but it is clear that this only refers to the north of the country, and certainly not "all" were involved).

32. This is surveyed briefly in Amitai-Preiss, *Mongols and Mamluks,* ch. 9.

33. For ʿAbbasid scions see P. M. Holt, "Some Observations of the ʿAbbasid Caliphate of Cairo," *Bulletin of the School of Oriental and African Studies,* 47 (1984), pp. 501–507; and Heidemann, *Das Aleppiner Kalifat,* esp. chs. 3–4; for the surviving sons of Badr al-Dīn Lu'lu' see D. Patton, *Badr al-Dīn Lu'lu': Atabeg of Mosul, 1211–1259* (Seattle, 1991), pp. 70–78; for Mamluk-like officers see Ibn Shaddād al-Ḥalabī, *Ta'rīkh al-malik al-ẓāhir (Die Geschichte des Sultan Baibars),* ed. A. Ḥuṭayṭ (Wiesbaden, 1983), pp. 330–331, 337. Ibn Shaddād al-Ḥalabī notes that some three thousand military refugees fled from Baghdad to the sultanate during Baybars's reign. For a general discussion on these and the Seljuq military refugees see Amitai-Preiss, *Mongols and Mamluks,* pp. 109–110, 149–150, 165–166. For Kurds and Turcomen see Ibn Shaddād al-Ḥalabī, *Ta'rīkh,* p. 335, who notes that forty thousand(!) Turcomen households fled to Syria under Baybars. See Amitai-Preiss, *Mongols and Mamluks,* pp. 69–71, for a further discussion of the Turcomen and Kurds during the early Mamluk Sultanate. For later developments under the Mamluks see B. Kellner-Heinkele, "The Turkomans and *Bilād aš-Šām* in the Mamluk Period," in *Land Tenure and Social Transformation in the Middle East,* ed. T. Khalidi (Beirut, 1984), pp. 169–180.

34. D. Ayalon, "The Wafidiya in the Mamluk Kingdom," *Islamic Culture,* 25 (1951), pp. 91–104 (reprinted in D. Ayalon, *Studies on the Mamlūks of Egypt (1250–1517)* [London, 1977]); Nakamachi Nobutaka, "The Rank and Status of Military Refugees in the Mamluk Army: A Reconsideration of the *Wāfidīya,*" *Mamluk Studies Review,* 10/1 (2006), pp. 55–81.

35. E. Sivan, *The Radicals of Islam: Medieval Theology and Modern Politics* (2nd rev. ed., New Haven, CT, 1990), pp. 96–97.

36. R. Amitai, "The Mongol Occupation of Damascus in 1300: A Study of Mamluk Loyalties," in *The Mamluks in Egyptian and Syrian Politics and Society,* ed. A. Levanoni and M. Winter (Leiden, 2004), pp. 21–41; D. Aigle, "The Mongol Invasions of Bilād al-Shām by Ghāzān Khān and Ibn Taymīya's Three 'Anti-Mongol' Fatwas," *Mamluk Studies Review,* 11/2 (2007), pp. 89–120; T. Raff, *Remarks on an Anti-Mongol Fatwa by Ibn Taimiya* (Leiden, 1973).

37. See now Li Guo, *The Performing Arts in Medieval Islam: Shadow Play and Popular Poetry in Ibn Dāniyāl's Mamluk Cairo* (Leiden, 2012).

38. Rashīd al-Dīn Abū al-Khayr Faḍl Allāh al-Hamadānī, *Jāmiʿ al-tawārīkh,* ed. B. Karīmī (Tehran, 1338/1959), vol. 2, p. 1104; translation in W. M. Thackston, *Rashiduddin Fazlullah's Jamiʿu't-tawarikh: Compendium of Chronicles. A History of the Mongols* (Cambridge, MA, 1998–1999), vol. 3, p. 756.

39. ʿIzz al-Dīn Muḥammad b. ʿAlī ibn Shaddād al-Ḥalabī, *al-Aʿlaq al-khaṭīra fī dhikr umarā' al-shām wa'l-jazīra,* partial ed. [North Syria exclusive of Aleppo] by A. M. Eddé in "La description de la Syrie du Nord de ʿIzz al-Dīn ibn Šaddād," *Bulletin des Etudes Orientales,* pp. 32–33 (1981–1982), pp. 294, 394, 373–375, 396, 397; see the further discussion in Amitai-Preiss, *Mongols and Mamluks,* pp. 202–205.

40. "Northern Syria between the Mongols and Mamluks: Political Boundary, Military Frontier and Ethnic Affinity," in *Frontiers in Question: Eurasian Borderlands c. 700–1700,* ed. N. Standen and D. Power (London, 1999), pp. 128–152 (reprinted in Amitai, *The Mongols in the Islamic Lands*).

41. On fortifications see the new and comprehensive book by Kate S. Raphael, *Muslim Fortresses in the Levant: Between Crusaders and Mongols* (Abington, UK, 2011). Some preliminary thoughts on the matter were presented in Amitai-Preiss, *Mongols and Mamluks,* pp. 76–77; see ibid., pp. 74–75, for a discussion of communications.

42. Baybars al-Manṣūrī, *Zubdat al-fikra fī ta'rīkh al-hijra,* ed. D. S. Richards (Beirut, 1998), p. 345; on p. 333 we learn that Ghāzān called on the commanders of the fortresses to surrender, but this order was not heeded.

43. Baybars, *Zubda,* p. 333; see also the discussion in Amitai, "The Mongol Occupation of Damascus."

44. Cf. the words of Robert Irwin: "It was because of the persistence of the Mongol threat and the dependence of Syria on Egypt that Muslim Syria was effectively united with Egypt in a way that it had not been since the time of Saladin" (Irwin, *The Middle East in the Middle Ages,* p. 47). On the nature of Mamluk rule in Syria, and the general dominance of Egypt over Syria see D. Ayalon, "Egypt as a Dominant Factor in Syria and Palestine during the Islamic Period," in *Egypt and Palestine: A Millennium of Association (868–1948),* ed. A. Cohen and G. Baer (Jerusalem, 1984), pp. 17–47 (reprinted in D. Ayalon, *Outsiders in the Lands of Islam: Mamluks, Mongols and Eunuchs* [London, 1988]).

45. I should note, however, that Mamluk Syria was not devoid of fighting among the members of the military-political elite, sometimes due to conflicts with the sultan in Egypt and at other times due to local struggles among the Mamluks. This phenomenon is found from 1260 onward, but seems to have gotten worse over two and a half centuries of Mamluk rule in the country.

46. The season (late fall–early winter) when Mongol campaigns were launched is brought home by Smith, "ʿAyn Jālūt."

47. R. Amitai, "Mamluk Espionage among Mongols and Franks," *Asian and African Studies* (Haifa), 22 (1988), pp. 173–181; Amitai-Preiss, *Mongols and Mamluks,* pp. 139–152.

48. See D. Kushnir, "The Turcomans in Palestine during the Ottoman Period," *International Journal of Turkish Studies,* 11/1–2 (2005), pp. 81–94; T. Ashkenazi, *Les Turkmênes en Palestine* (Tel Aviv, 1930), in Hebrew (this latter work is a short pamphlet of some 16 pp.).

49. E. Combe et al. (eds.), *Répertoire chronologique de l'épigraphie arabe* (Cairo, 1943), vol. 12, pp. 141–142 (no. 4612, Nabī Mūsā, 668/1269–1270); p. 193 (no. 4690, Damascus, 673/1274–1275); p. 195 (no. 4692, Damascus, 673/1274–1275); pp. 226–227 (no. 4738, Damascus, 676/1277–1278). Cf. pp. 128–129 (no. 4593, Homs, 666/1267–1268): *mubīd al-faranj wa'l-arman wa'l-tatar,* i.e., "the annihilator of the Franks, Armenians, and Mongols."

50. R. Amitai-Preiss, "Mamluk Perceptions of the Mongol-Frankish Rapprochement," *Mediterranean Historical Review,* 7 (1992), pp. 50–65 (reprinted in Amitai, *The Mongols in the Islamic Lands*). In this vein, Robert Irwin (*The Middle East in the Middle Ages,* p. 47) writes: "Similarly, it was the persistence of the Mongol threat which spurred Baybars and his successors to eliminate the remnants of the Crusader principalities."

51. R. Ellenblum, "Settlement and Society Formation in Crusader Palestine," in *The Archaeology of Society in the Holy Land,* ed. Thomas Evan Levy (Leicester, 1995), pp. 502–511. Ellenblum shows that large swaths of rural Palestine remained Christian in the first centuries after the Muslim conquest of the country, up to the Crusader conquest. It was unlikely that this situation changed under Frankish rule. The corollary is that the decisive Islamization of the country took place in the post-Crusader era, i.e., the Ayyūbid and, more importantly, the Mamluk periods. N. Luz, "Aspects of Islamization of Space and Society in Mamluk Jerusalem and Its Hinterland," *Mamluk Studies Review,* 6 (2002), pp. 133–154. Cf. Levtzion, "Conversion to Islam in Syria and Palestine."

52. D. P. Little, "Coptic Conversion to Islam under the Baḥrī Mamlūks, 692–755/1293–1354," *Bulletin of the School of Oriental and African Studies,* 39 (1976), pp. 552–569 (reprinted in D. P. Little, *History and Historiography of the Mamlūks* [London, 1986]).

53. C. Cahen, "Dhimma," *Encyclopaedia of Islam,* vol. 2, 230; E. Ashtor, "Mamluks," *Encyclopedia Judaica,* vol. 11, 834–835.

54. See Little, "Coptic Conversion"; D. P. Little, "Religion under the Mamluks," *The Muslim World,* 73 (1983), pp. 165–181 (reprinted in D. P. Little, *History and Historiography of the Mamlūks* [London, 1986]); N. Luz, "The Public Sphere in Mamluk Jerusalem," *Hamizraḥ Heḥadash,* 46 (2004), pp. 127–144 (in Hebrew) for an example of how the Mamluk authorities attempted to restrain local religious figures in late fifteenth-century Jerusalem (1473–1474).

55. This matter is discussed at some length in the final chapter of R. Amitai, *Holy War and Rapprochement: Studies in the Relations between the Mamluk Sultanate and the Mongol Ilkhanate (1260–1335)* (Turnhout, 2013). There is a rich scholarly discussion of this important subject. See, e.g., I. M. Lapidus, *Muslim Cities in the Later Middle Ages* (Cambridge, MA, 1967), esp. chs. 3–4; R. S. Humphreys, "A Cultural Elite: The Role and Status of the *'Ulamā'* in Islamic Society," in R. S. Humphreys, *Islamic History: A Framework for Inquiry,* 2nd ed. (Princeton, 1991), pp. 187–208; J. Berkey, *The Formation of Islam: Religion and Society in the Near East, 600–1800* (Cambridge, 2003), pp. 224–230 and passim.

56. C. Cahen, *L'Islam des origines au début de l'Empire ottoman* (Paris, 1995), has the following relevant pithy comments: "La liaison entre l'aristocratie militaire étrangère et la

population civil autochtone est assurée par les «savants» à la fois porte-parole du people et garants du régime qui multiplie à leur benefice les waqfs . . . Le régime, défini par le hanbalite Ibn Taymiyya comme une association entre le soldat et le «cleric», accentue l'intoléance envers les minoritaires, voire les étrangers" (pp. 370–371).

57. T. el-Leithy, "Sufis, Copts and the Politics of Piety: Moral Regulation in Fourteenth-Century Upper Egypt," in *Le développement du soufisme en Égypte à l'époque mamelouke,* ed. R. J. A. McGregor and A. Sabra, published as *Cahiers des Annales islamologiques, 27* (2006), pp. 75–119.

58. P. M. Holt, "An Early Source on Shaykh Khaḍir al-Mihrānī," *Bulletin of the School of Oriental and African Studies,* 46 (1983), pp. 33–39; C. Müller and J. Pahlitzsch, "Sultan Baybars I and the Georgians in the Light of New Documents Related to the Monastery of the Holy Cross in Jerusalem," *Arabica,* 51/3 (2004), pp. 258–290.

59. Luz, "Aspects of Islamization," pp. 145–146, 148–149.

60. Mujīr al-Dīn, *al-Uns al-jalīl bi-ta'rīkh al-quds wa'l-khalīl* (Amman, 1973), vol. 2, pp. 147–148, cited by Luz, "Aspects of Islamization," p. 148, n. 60.

61. Luz, "Aspects of Islamization," p. 135; Y. Frenkel, "Baybars and the Sacred Geography of Bilad al-Sham: A Chapter in the Islamization of Syria's Landscape," *Jerusalem Studies in Arabic and Islam,* 25 (2001), pp. 153–170.

62. This matter is discussed by T. T. Allsen, *Culture and Conquest in Mongol Eurasia* (Cambridge, 2001), who looks at it from the larger view of all of Mongol-controlled Asia, and G. Lane, *Early Mongol Rule in Thirteenth-Century Iran: A Persian Renaissance* (London, 2003), who concentrates on the Ilkhanate. Currently a number of scholars are looking into this subject from different perspectives: Michal Biran, Leigh Chipman, and Sabine Schmitdke.

63. E. Weidemann, "Ḳuṭb al-Dīn Shīrāzī," *Encyclopaedia of Islam,* vol. 5, 547. For the Ilkhanid diplomatic mission in which he participated see Broadbridge, *Kingship and Ideology,* pp. 39–40 (who, however, does not mention Shīrāzī per se). I am grateful to Leigh Chipman for first bringing to my attention the role of Shīrāzī in possible exchange between scholars from the two states.

64. These are listed in the introduction to the excellent edition and translation: K. Lech, *Das Mongolische Weltreich: al-ʿUmarīs Darstellung der mongolischen Reiche in seinem Werk Masālik al-abṣār fī 'l-mamālik al-amṣār* (Wiesbaden, 1968), pp. 29–41.

65. Historiography: D. P. Little, "Historiography of the Ayyūbid and Mamlūk Epochs," in *The Cambridge History of Egypt,* vol. 1: *Islamic Egypt, 640–1517,* ed. C. Petry (Cambridge, 1998), pp. 427–430. Biographical dictionaries and belles lettres: D. P. Little, "Al-Ṣafadī as Biographer of His Contemporaries," in D. P. Little, *Essays on Islamic Civilization Presented to Niyazi Berkes* (Leiden, 1976), pp. 190–210 (reprinted in D. P. Little, *History and Historiography of the Mamlūks* [London, 1986]). Scientific geography and cosmography: see the introductory remarks in P. M. Holt (tr. and ed.), *The Memoirs of a Syrian Prince: Abu'l-Fidā', Sultan of Ḥamāh (672–732/1273–1331)* (Wiesbaden, 1983), pp. 8–10. It is worth noting in the context of this chapter that Abū al-Fidā' Ismāʿīl was born in Damascus in late 1273, because his family—the Ayyūbid rulers of Hamah (albeit under Mamluk control)—had fled from their city due to rumors of a Mongol invasion. D. M. Dunlop, "al-Dimashqī," *Encyclopaedia of Islam,* vol. 2, 291. Administrative manuals and encyclopedias: see the biographical remarks in the introduction of Lech, *Das Mongolische Weltreich,* pp. 13–14. Religious studies: some idea of the vigorous scholarly life in the religious sciences is found in N. A. Ziadeh, *Urban Life in Syria under the Early Mamluks* (Beirut, 1953), pp. 169–178. For the complex social, economic, and political life of religious scholars that accompa-

nied their intellectual activity see M. Chamberlain, *Knowledge and Social Practice in Medieval Damascus, 1190–1350* (Cambridge, 1994).

66. On what the Mamluk sources (Syrian and Egyptian) have to teach us about the Mongols see the comments in R. Amitai-Preiss, "Arabic Sources for the History of the Mongol Empire," in *The Proceedings of the Sixth International Congress of Mongolists* (Ulaanbaatar, August 11–15, 1992), published in *Mongolica,* 5 [20] (1994), pp. 99–105; R. Amitai, "Al-Nuwayrī as a Historian of the Mongols," in *Historiography of Islamic Egypt (c.950–1800),* ed. H. Kennedy (Leiden, 2001), pp. 25–26; R. Amitai, "An Arabic Biographical Notice of Kitbughā, the Mongol General Defeated at ᶜAyn Jālūt," *Jerusalem Studies in Arabic and Islam,* 33 (2007), p. 220, n. 3.

ELEVEN

The Tatar Factor in the Formation of Muscovy's Political Culture

István Vásáry

Continuity and disruption have always been crucial questions in historical research, and Russian history is no exception to this rule. The Tatar, or Mongol, invasion of Russia in the 1240s and the ensuing two and a half centuries of foreign rule—called the "Tatar yoke" by later Russian historiographers—fundamentally changed the Russian principalities.[1] In a gradual consolidation process, the grand prince of Moscow united nearly all Russian principalities and lands around his office by the second half of the fifteenth century, and all forms of Tatar overlordship had been terminated by 1480 (or, according to some historians, by 1502). The emerging Russian state, often referred to as Muscovy or Muscovite Russia, vastly differed from the Russian principalities of pre-Mongol times, as it was a strong, centralized state with a developed autocracy and sophisticated bureaucracy. The genesis of Russian autocracy and bureaucracy has persistently intrigued historians of Russia. Since both apparatuses emerged in the immediate aftermath of the protracted Tatar yoke, the time has come to lift the veil on the Mongols' role in the development of Moscow and Russian institutions. The "Tatar question" in Russian history has evoked the most diverse—at times diametrically opposed—views, both among scholars and the general public. Beginning with the Russian ecclesiastical annalists of the thirteenth century and ending with modern Soviet historians, the discourse on this topic has more often than not been accompanied by emotions, sometimes even of a passionate nature. The 250-year submission of the Russian principalities to Tatar rule is an undeniable fact, and this prolonged historical experience could not have transpired without leaving its mark on Russian life. The contacts between the two nations, cultures, and worldviews were bound to have affected the economy, society, and culture of both parties involved in many and manifold ways.

The first, extended period of Russian–Tatar contacts, which is traditionally labeled the "Tatar yoke," ended in 1480 or 1502, whereas the second phase lasted from approximately 1480/1502 to 1552 and 1556 (the dates of the Russian conquest of Kazan and Astrakhan, respectively)—a period marking the final coalescence of Muscovy.[2] Our primary concern in this chapter is the first, formative phase of this story.

After the long centuries of Tatar rule, the Russians wanted to forget their humiliation, and this perspective has generally been in the ascendancy ever since. In consequence, the Tatars' role has either been negated or minimized, and everything that has been ascribed to them is conspicuously negative. The Mongols have become scapegoats who are occasionally held responsible for all the cul-de-sacs of Russian history, even in periods that followed the Tatar yoke. Blaming the Mongols for all the shortcomings of Russia's historical development is as ridiculous as imputing all the aberrations of nineteenth-century capitalism to the sixteenth-century Reformation. Nevertheless, this outlook was shared by giants of Russian culture like Chaadaev, Pushkin, and Karamzin. Even modern Soviet and Russian historiography could not emancipate itself from the traditional image of the "barbarian enemy."[3] What is more, Western historians of Russia have also failed to notice that the Tatars have been viewed almost exclusively from the Russian angle. Likewise, it has generally been forgotten that, unlike, say, the Assyrians whose history belongs only to the past, the Tatars are not an extinct nation, as different member groups (Kazan Tatars, Mishers, Noghays, and Crimean Tatars) submitted to Russian rule and are now citizens in various parts of the Russian commonwealth. Russian airs of superiority toward the "barbarian" Tatars were further aggravated by Western misbeliefs, the epitome of which could be a bon mot from Napoleon's time (perhaps even coined by the French emperor himself): "Scratch a Russian, and find a Tatar!"[4] The implications of this revealing aphorism of self-complacent European haughtiness can be condensed into four points: the Europeans are good; the Russians are bad; the Tatars and other Orientals are the worst; and the Tatars are responsible for all the Russians' faults. Needless to say, such simplifications and prejudices are inadmissible and unpardonable for historians.

These preliminary remarks are not a digression from the proposed theme, but illustrate that the question of the Tatar factor in the formation of Muscovy's political culture is densely interwoven with ideological elements. Although I do not pretend to be free of preconceptions (is there any historian who can make such a claim?), at the very least scholars must endeavor to be as objective as possible. To begin with, it is incumbent upon me to clarify the two basic concepts of this chapter: *factor* and *political culture*. Instead of the term "factor" I could have readily used "influence" or "impact," as many researchers have indeed done. However, this course would have been anathema for a historian that who aspires to seal off all channels of "outside influence." By employing the term "factor," I wish to emphasize that the question that begs asking is not whether the Tatars influenced Russian policy or not. The 250-year submission of the Russian principalities to Mongol rule is a hard fact. One may deny or minimize the *significance* or *weight* of these contacts for one side or the other, but the *fact* itself must be reckoned with. Within this framework, the connotation of the term "factor" is both narrower and broader than that of "influence." Narrower in the sense that it does not speak of effects (in contrast to influence), and broader in that its presence is beyond doubt (unlike that of influence). In so doing, I am toeing the line of this volume, *Nomads as Agents of Cultural Change:* as Eurasian nomads, the Mongols indeed fomented cultural change in Russia between the thirteenth and fifteenth centuries, especially in the field of political culture. By "political culture" (to return to the second pillar of this chapter's title), I mean the institutions and practices of state administration and the ways of thinking about or the mentality toward the political sphere.[5] In the pages that follow, I will scrutinize some concrete examples in the field of political culture and try to grasp the Tatar factor, if any, in their emergence and development. Given the space constraints, this will constitute a mere cursory glance at a theme that indeed merits a comprehensive reassessment, despite the excellent monographs by Charles J. Halperin and Donald Ostrowski, respectively.[6]

Before delving into the problems of Russian political culture during the Tatar period, a few words on the origins of the Mongol empire's political and administrative institutions and practices are in order. Alongside the nomadic, indigenous steppe traditions, the main source of inspiration for all the nomadic empires of Inner Asia has always been China and its institutions. This also applies to the Tatars, with the slight difference that some of the Chinese influences reached the Mongols through the mediation of the Qara Khitai. In this respect, David Morgan judiciously views the Mongol empire as "a successor state, on a much grander scale, to the Qara Khitai empire."[7] More specifically, after subjugating the Qara Khitai empire in 1218, the Mongols adopted elements of its administrative structure, which was a strange amalgam of autochthonous nomadic (Kitan and Turkic), Chinese, and Muslim features.[8]

In the mid-thirteenth century, the Russian principalities were militarily crushed and subdued by the Mongol empire. The principal task of the Tatars in all their conquered territories was to organize the administration and tax-collecting apparatuses. As Thomas Allsen observes in his excellent book on Mongol imperialism, the Mongols demanded the following from the local elites: 1) the personal appearance of the local ruler at the khan's court; 2) recognition of the Mongol governors; 3) hostages; 4) provisions for the Mongol army; 5) support for the troops; 6) extending the post-relay system (*yam*); 7) a census of the population; and 8) collecting taxes.[9] Plainly put, the Mongols were interested in three things from their newly conquered lands: political loyalty to the khan (1, 2, 3), military submission (4, 5), and regular taxation (6, 7, 8). Because of the Tatars' demands, the military and administrative structures of the Russian principalities could not remain as they were. Keeping in contact with the Tatar authorities and meeting the empire's military and fiscal objectives required new structures and institutions. At the outset, the Tatars imposed their own apparatuses and methods on the Russians, but the latter soon began to adapt them. In the process of this centuries-long adaptation, some of the practices were accepted, modified, and integrated into the Russian system, while others were discarded. Furthermore, some of the customs left an intellectual mark on the Russian way of life.

The main symbol of imperial power in the conquered Russian lands during the thirteenth century was the Tatar governor, namely the *basqaq*. In the fourteenth century, another term, *darugha,* seems to have displaced *basqaq*.[10] The etymological background of these terms has been fully elucidated, and there is a unanimous consensus that they both derive from the verb "to press" (Turkic: *bas-* and Mongolian: *daru-*). It appears as though the Turkic *basqaq* served as the basis for its Mongolian loan translation *darugha*. In an earlier work, I sought to clarify the process of where, when, and how the system of *basqaqs* came into being.[11] I have reached the conclusion that its birthplace was eleventh-century Transoxania, under the reign of the Qarakhanids. *Basqaqs* were apparently chief officials of territorial and/or administrative units. Thereafter, the Seljuqs took control of this institution. The original connotation of *basqaq* was "governor, director," and the Seljuqs equated it with the Persian term *shiḥna*. The Qara Khitai also inherited the term from the Qarakhanids and used it until the Mongol conquest. In turn, the Mongols wrested it from the Qara Khitai. This, then, is another telling example of how the Qara Khitai acted as conduit for the Chinese, nomadic (Turkic and Mongolian), and Islamic influences on the Mongols.[12]

Though *darugha* was a Mongol loan translation of Turkic *basqaq* and both signified the same function, the purview of these dignitaries evolved in various directions in different parts and periods of the Mongol empire. Since the emphasis of this article is on the Golden Horde, a detailed map of the distribution and usage of these terms between the thirteenth and fifteenth century in the Mongol empire and its successor states is beyond our scope. That said, I cannot refrain from a critique of Ostrowski's theory on these two concepts. In attempting to categorize their usage systematically, Ostrowski has concluded that the *darughachi* (the Mongol form used in Yuan China) was equivalent to the Chinese *taishou* (civilian governor), whereas the *basqaq* was akin to the *duwei* (military governor).[13] Moreover, he claims that the Mongols' putative embracement of the Chinese two-pronged administration is tied to the Kitan Yelü Chucai, the chief administrator of the early Mongol empire in China. Ostrowski even drew up a comparative table of what he believes to be the Mongols' corresponding military and civilian governors throughout their lands. His erudition notwithstanding, Ostrowski has failed to convince me of the basic correctness of his theory. The facts are more complicated and contradictory, so that it is hard to accept this sort of coerced systematization. The duties and competences of senior officials were never divided so rigidly in premodern Eurasian nomadic societies. What is more, civilian and military functions were often handled by the same authority. Consequently, it seems somewhat far-fetched to argue that the *basqaq* was a military governor and the *darugha* was his civilian counterpart. That said, Ostrowski makes a couple of sharp observations that call attention to the possibility that the Mongols drew on the Chinese dual administrative system.

Suffice it to say that the Mongols did not use the Turkic term *basqaq*, only its Mongol translation: *darugha(chi)*. According to the *Secret History of the Mongols*, Ögödei appointed *darughachis* to govern the towns that were conquered during the western campaign.[14] Moreover, in Yuan China, where Mongol tradition was strong and well documented in the Chinese sources, only *darughachis* were known as Mongol functionaries.[15] On the other hand, the term *basqaq* only surfaces in Ilkhanid Iran and the Golden Horde, where Turks and Turkic languages played key roles.[16]

In the Golden Horde and the Russian principalities that were subjected to the Tatar polity, the system of *basqaqs* (Russian: *baskachestvo*) administered the taxpaying populace. Taking censuses, collecting taxes, and maintaining a line of communication with the central power were the chief tasks of these early governors, who were assigned to territorial units as well as to cities. During the first half of the fourteenth century, the system underwent far-reaching changes, as the *basqaqs* disappeared from Russia, first from the northeast and then from all the principalities. The main reason for this development was that the Russian princes themselves assumed the *basqaqs'* responsibilities. In other words, they now served as the agents or governors of the Tatar khan. Another probable factor behind the demise of the *basqaqs* was the popular uprisings against these despised officials.[17] Exploiting the psychological effects of these movements, the Russian princes convinced their Tatar overlords that, as totally reliable subjects of the khan, they could do a better job collecting taxes than the *basqaqs*. In parallel, the control over Russian affairs shifted directly to the capital of Saray, the home of various *darughas* who were charged with supervising the Russian principalities. It appears as though the term *basqaq* fell out of use by the mid-1300s, whereas *darugha* spread across the territories of the Golden Horde between the fourteenth and fifteenth centuries.[18] There are several accounts of *darughas* orchestrating Russian affairs from Saray. For example, in 1432 Prince Iurii Dmitrievich went to the Golden Horde and was received by one Min-Bulat, the *darugha* of Moscow (*doroga Moskovskoi Min'bulat*).[19] In all likelihood, Min-Bulat was a high-ranking official in charge of supervising Muscovite affairs, particularly matters of finance and taxation. It stands to reason that the *darugha* of Moscow had counterparts with the same authority over other subjected Russian territories, such as Tver' and Riazan'. In the fourteenth century, however, other Russian territorial *darughas* must have gradually disappeared, as the responsibility of collecting and presenting the taxes from all the Golden Horde's Russian principalities was transferred to the grand prince of Moscow.

The Russian annals describe Grand Prince Dmitrii Donskoi's campaign against the Bulgars in 1376. The Bulgarian princes, Asan and Mahmet, surrendered to the Russians, who installed a *darugha* and *tamozhnik* (customs official) in the town of Bolgary.[20] Put differently, the Russians availed themselves of the same administrative positions that informed the Tatar state apparatus. After the conquest of Kazan, the Russian sovereign imposed a *darugha* on the Siberian khan Yadigar.[21] Here too, an indigenous office was maintained by the Russians. These cases thus attest to the fact that the Russians did not touch the local systems of administration.

In accepting the duties of gathering the tribute and taxes on behalf of the Tatars, Muscovite princes had to conform to the centralized imperial system of tax collection. That said, the princes tended to use their own Russian terminology. For instance, the grand prince appointed *namestniki* and *volosteli* as heads of the *uezdy* and *volosti*, respectively. By the end of the fourteenth century, Muscovy apparently had fifteen *namestniki* and about a hundred *volosteli*. These dignitaries were remunerated through *kormlenie* (feeding); that is, they were allotted a portion of the taxes that they collected. This transformation of Muscovite political institutions must have been initiated between 1330 and 1350, during the reigns of Ivan Kalita (1325–1340) and Semen the Proud (1341–1353)—the first Muscovite princes to bear the title of "Grand Prince of Vladimir" and "Suzdal." Ivan and Semen were frequent guests in Saray, as they paid a combined total of twelve visits to the Tatar capital. As Ostrowski accurately notes, owing to their new duties as tax collectors, the Russian princes were essentially compelled to adopt the Mongols' administrative structures.[22]

While most of the era's Tatar terms, such as *basqaq* and *darugha,* faded away from the Russian lexicon and were replaced by Russian technical terms, some of them persevered and became integrated into the language. For instance, the *put'* system of fourteenth- to fifteenth-century medieval Russia was inspired by the *darugha* system. Overseen by a boyar, the *put'* (literally: road)—an administrative-territorial unit in the household of the grand prince—was not only a structural borrowing. As I have argued elsewhere, the name *put'* itself was a strangely misunderstood loan translation of the Tatar term *darugha.*[23] Similarly, as in the rest of the empire, the Mongols undoubtedly incorporated the *yam*—a sophisticated postal system, which was originally based upon Chinese patterns, in their Russian territories.[24] In the fourteenth century, the Russians took over the function of maintaining the entire Tatar postal service, while preserving the name *yam.* A special tax, also called *yam,* was exacted to maintain this service, and the official in charge of the postal levies was called *jamshchik.*[25] From the fourteenth to the fifteenth century, the *iamskaia gon'ba* (postal service) was well known and in operation throughout Muscovite Russia.[26]

It is no accident that the Tatar regime, which facilitated and promoted commerce and thus the exchange of goods and ideas, was quite instrumental in the development of the circulation of Russian money and coinage in general. Therefore, it comes as no surprise that the *den'ga* (plural *den'gi*), the name of an Old Russian monetary unit (the word for "money" in modern Russian), and the *altyn,* the name of an Old Russian coin worth six *den'gas,* come from the Tatar *tenke/denge* and *altïn,* respectively.[27] Fourteenth- and fifteenth-century Russian coins were markedly influenced by Islamic coinage.[28] Minting coins has always been a symbol of sovereignty, both in the West and the East. For instance, *sikka* (coinage) and *khuṭba* (homage to the ruler during the Friday prayer) were outward signs of Muslim rule. In light of the above, the striking fact that there was no Russian coinage for over a hundred years after the Tatar conquest is understandable. Minting was only revived between 1360 and 1380, during the reign of Grand Prince Dmitrii Donskoi, who did everything in his power to bolster the renascent sense of Russian statehood. However, the new Russian coins bore evident signs of subordination to the Golden Horde. The use of Arabic inscriptions on Russian coins—albeit in what was occasionally a distorted, imitative form—and the added emphasis on inscriptions rather than figures testify to a constant and durable Tatar influence.[29]

Russian coinage between 1360 and 1480 is an extremely interesting phenomenon in its own right, as it reflects a historical paradox. The emergent

Grand Principality of Moscow gave voice to its aspirations for sovereignty by minting its own coins with the name of the Russian grand prince. That said, the ongoing submission to the Tatars had to be admitted by placing the Tatar khan's name on the reverse side. After the "stand on the Ugra" in 1480, the symbolic turning point in Russian–Tatar contacts, Ivan III replaced the Tatar khan's name on the reverse of his coins with his own name, which was engraved in Arabic characters as "Iban."[30] Over the past two decades, several important hoards have turned up in Russia, prompting a serious reassessment of our knowledge in the field of Tatar and Russian numismatics. We can expect many comparable findings in the future.

Direct or indirect Tatar influences can also be detected in various facets of the Muscovite administrative system during the fourteenth and fifteenth centuries. Given the constraints of time and space, a few random examples will suffice. Since taxation was the core issue of Tatar rule in the subjugated lands, it is only natural that the basic Mongol tax, the *tamga* (a sort of VAT), found its way into the medieval Russian principalities. Though later this tax and its Tatar term would slowly fall out of use in Russia, the modern terms *tamozhnia* (customs' office) and *tamozhennik* (customs' officer) constitute firm evidence of the long Tatar presence in Russia.[31]

Tax exemptions conferred by the Tatar khans as a special sign of privilege were well known throughout the Mongol empire. The favored person was termed a *darkhan* in Mongolian and *tarkhan* in Turkic.[32] This standing was also granted to institutions, most notably the Taoist monks in Yuan China and the Russian Church. Six of the *darkhan* charters to the church dating from between 1267 and 1379 have been preserved in both an abridged (fifteenth century) and extended (sixteenth century) version. As per these documents, the khan or his wife endowed or renewed fiscal immunity to different Russian metropolitans and the entire Russian Church.[33] These documents, which are referred to as *tarkhannye iarlyki* (or *gramoty*) in the Russian literature, reveal a wide array of Tatar taxes that were imposed on the "nonfavored" populace. The *tarkhan* exemptions of the Russian Church—a possible remnant of the Tatar yoke—were maintained throughout the early Muscovite period. It was only with the promulgation of the Sudebnik 1550 goda (Law Code of 1550) and the Sobornoe ulozhenie 1584 goda (Synodal Code of 1584) that these privileges were abolished.[34] Upon the integration of the Bashkirs into Russia after 1552, the institution of *tarkhan* was not only maintained, but a special privileged class of Bashkir *tarkhans,* who loyally served the Russian tsar in military and civilian posts, came into being. In the 1730s, there were 773 such *tarkhans* registered in Bashkiria, but only 366 in the 1760s.[35] This institution finally lost its significance in the mid-nineteenth century when some of the Bashkir *tarkhans* became Russian noblemen, while most of the others slid to the rank of commoners.

In the field of jurisprudence, the Tatar impact is presumably negligible. The Tatars' legal system was originally based on the *Yasa*, Chinggis Khan's code, though also drawing heavily on the Turco-Mongol customary law.[36] From the 1300s onward, the majority of the Mongols in the Golden Horde as well as Ilkhanid Iran embraced Islam, and subsequently adhered to both Islamic law (*sharīʿa*) and the *Yasa*. Yet none of these ideological and legal systems managed to enthrall the Russians, who must have viewed them with contempt. Nevertheless, a few Mongol juridical practices apparently did leave their mark on the Russian lexicon.[37] In a number of articles, Horace W. Dewey and, intermittently, Ann Kleimola have demonstrated that at least two medieval Russian legal customs can be partly connected to the Tatars.[38] One of them is the practice of collective suretyship, which is called *poruka* in Russian. This form of liability affected all members of a community in matters of fiscal obligation, forced labor, and transgression. In other words, every member of a commune could be forced to pay the tributes and taxes that were levied on the entire community, to execute corvée labor, and be held responsible for the iniquities and crimes perpetrated by any "associate." The first forms of collective suretyship (*krugovaia poruka* in Russian) clearly date back to pre-Mongol, Kievan Russia, as the earliest known occurrence of the word *poruka* appears in the Smolensk-German trade treaty of 1229.[39] While in Western Europe the institution of collective suretyship receded and lost its significance during the thirteenth century, in the Russian lands it was revised and expanded during the period of Tatar dominion (the thirteenth to fifteenth centuries). Over the two centuries of Muscovite Russia (sixteenth to seventeenth centuries), there was an unprecedented spike in this arrangement: "in the end a great web of *poruka* lay over the land."[40] One may safely assume that, while the Mongol conquerors did not introduce collective suretyship to Russia, the expansive use of its different forms by the Tatar administration and military contributed to its survival and strengthening therein. As was often the case, the Tatar model promoted, buttressed, or simply underscored certain features of native Russian institutions. One of the more tantalizing novelties of suretyship in Muscovite Russia was the extension of "old communal suretyship in criminal and fiscal matters to another sphere—political 'loyalty.'" Though somewhat of a stretch, the argument can thus be made that "all loyal Russians were obliged to be political informers."[41] One of the more far-reaching consequences of political suretyship was the gradual loss, from the fifteenth century onward, of the boyars' age-old right to free departure. In Muscovy, this reached the point where if a boyar left the grand prince to serve another prince, he was regarded as a traitor and treated accordingly.[42]

Attempting to coerce tardy debtors into honoring their financial obligations by means of punishment seems to be another practice bearing Mongol traces. This juridical-punitive process was called *pravezh* (from the verb *pravit'* "to right"), and can roughly be translated as "collection/exaction (of debt)." When the authorities resorted to *pravezh* (*stavit' na pravezh*), a constable (*pristav*) would beat the debtor on the shins with a cudgel on a daily basis. From the sixteenth to the seventeenth century, this institution played a key role in the juridical life of Muscovite Russia. It was finally abolished in 1718, only to be replaced by forced labor. Though different forms of ignominious penalties, such as pillory, were well known and practiced throughout the Middle Ages, *pravezh* (not least the beating on the shins) was largely unheard of in territories west of China. Therefore, it may very well have reached Russia through the mediation of the Tatars.[43]

A third instance of a possible Tatar influence on Russian jurisprudence was the institution of *kabala*—bondage or debt-slavery. *Kabala* could be regarded as the next legal step, should the *pravezh* fail to yield results. People who could not pay off their debts (by themselves or through guarantors) were obliged to sell themselves into bondage. Since the details of this arrangement were laid down in a written contract known as a *kabala*, the indentured servants were called *kabal'nye kholopy/liudi* (contract bondsmen/people) and the institution itself was known as *kabal'noe kholopstvo* (contract serfdom). While the first appearance of this institution in Muscovy can be traced to the fifteenth century, it flourished over the next two centuries, reaching its peak in the 1500s. In the following century, contract serfdom became intermingled with complete serfdom. However, both institutions were abolished by edicts of Peter the Great between 1718 and 1723.[44]

Kabala, the Russian term for document, "title-deed, (sale) contract," evidently derives from the Tatar language, but its original source is Arabic.[45] P. Petrov noted that the Arabic *qabāla*, which was later borrowed by the Persian and Turkic languages, originally had the broad meaning of "contract or agreement (especially for hire, lease, etc.)." By the thirteenth century, though, its primary meaning in most areas of the Muslim world was "deed of purchase," often used in connection with real estate. This connotation, together with the broader meaning of "contract," is still in use today. In all likelihood, the Arabic word penetrated the Russian language, via the Tatars, as early as the 1300s, with the basic connotation of "contract, agreement."[46] Since the use of the term *kabala* in medieval Russia was exclusively limited to debt transactions (among them the institution of debt-slavery, which evolved under this name during the fifteenth century) and given the absence of these connotations in the Muslim world, this legal institution must have been an indigenous Russian development.[47] The different forms of *kabala* bondages and contracts (*zaemnaia raspiska, zakladnaia kabala, rostovaia kabala, sluzhilaia kabala, zazhilaia kabala,* and *verchaia kabala*) are indeed unique Russian institutions with no direct equivalents in the Muslim world.[48] This case exemplifies the fact that there need not be a direct correlation between the name of a political or social institution and its development. Put differently, the foreign appellation of an institution is not necessarily indicative of a foreign origin. On the other hand, the presence of an indigenous name does not automatically imply that the institution is autochthonous. As we have already seen, suretyship and exaction of debt had Russian names (*poruka* and *pravezh*), but a great deal of Tatar sway could be detected in both cases.

Last but not least, it is impossible to completely grasp the formation of those same princely and grand princely chancelleries that issued those documents that enabled us to reconstruct the social and administrative changes in the fourteenth and fifteenth centuries without an understanding of their Tatar superiors. The Russians indeed possessed their own Slavic literacy and traditions that long predated the Mongol empire and they retained most of their Slavic terminology, some elements of which derived from Greek (e.g., *d'iak, pod'iachii, pisets* for "secretary, scribe" and *gramota* for "diploma, document"). However, the new role that the princely chancelleries assumed under Mongol rule demanded knowledge of the ways and means of the Tatar chancelleries. In fact, there is strong evidence that, as late as the fifteenth century, some of the Russian *d'iaki* (scribe-secretaries) knew Turkic and the Uighur alphabet.[49] On the back of a few Russian grand princely documents from the mid-fifteenth century, inter alia, are short notes that were written with Uighur letters.[50] In all likelihood, these are the unofficial addenda of Russian scribes, one of whom even calls himself "Andirey bitigchi," namely d'iak Andrei or Andrew the scribe. These documents thus clearly attest to the fact that some of the grand princely scribes were familiar with the Turkic-Uighur script as late as the mid-1400s.[51]

Insofar as the technical jargon of the Russian chancelleries under the Tatar yoke is concerned, there are only a few Russian borrowings from the suzerain. The most important loan word is *iarlyk,* the Tatar khan's decree. To this day, it denotes the official diploma of an Oriental sovereign.[52] Another example is a loan translation from Tatar: the Russian *chelom bit'* (to apply for or petition). The original meaning of this word is "to beat (the ground with) the forehead," which is a rendering of the Tatar-Turkic *baš ur* "to beat (the ground with) the head." Accordingly, from the sixteenth century onward, the Russian word for the act of an official petition became *chelobit'e* and the written document itself was called *chelobitnaia*.[53] Finally, Russian chancellery clerks must have been well acquainted with the so-called *baysa*s, or tablets of authority, which were important cachets of the khan's envoys. The Mongol-Turkic *baysa*—both the word and object—is a derivative of the Chinese *paizi*. According to the *Kazanskii letopisets,* in 1476, Aḥmad Khan's emissaries appeared before the Grand Prince Ivan III in Moscow to demand the tribute that was due for the past few years, but the grand prince vehemently refused to comply. What is more, he spat on the khan's symbol, threw the tablet on the ground, and stamped on it.[54] Instead of *paizi,* this Russian source employs the term *basma*—a Russian borrowing from Turkic.[55] While probably known, the word *baisa,* along with the object, fell out of use in Russia as soon as Tatar power waned.

With these sundry examples of the Tatar impact on the practices and institutions of early Muscovy behind us, let us now turn our attention to the Muscovite political mentality, which permeated the entire society. The institutional changes in Muscovy between 1320 and 1480 were indeed substantial, but are no less compelling than the new political ideas that the Tatars ushered in. Notwithstanding the considerable attention it has received from historians, Muscovite political thought merits a new monographic evaluation. For the time being, we will highlight one basic aspect of this intricate topic by answering the following two questions: Who was considered the legitimate sovereign of the Russian lands between 1240 and 1480—the Russian grand prince, the Tatar khan, or both? What was the basis for political legitimacy in Muscovite Russia?

Since Russia's entry into the Christian ecumene by dint of St. Vladimir's baptism, the Byzantine emperor, the *basileus,* was deemed to be the legitimate sovereign of the whole Christian empire. While Kievan Rus' and later the Russian principalities were governed de facto by the grand prince and the princes, spiritual leadership was in the hands of the Byzantine emperor. Inasmuch as the grand prince behaved as a veritable sovereign with all the imperial trappings of rulership (e.g., regalia, coinage, and liturgical homage), this modicum of ideological incongruity vis-à-vis the *basileus* caused no tension in the Russian mind because all this occurred within the Christian fold. However, the situation was fundamentally altered with Russian submission to the Tatars. Before Mongol rule, the Russian grand prince and the princes merely had to acknowledge the Byzantine emperor's spiritual ascendancy, but now they found themselves under the jurisdiction of an emperor, the Tatar khan, who truly called the shots; for without his consent, the Russian grand prince had no power. In other words, the investiture of the Russian grand princely throne was subject to the approval of the Mongol ruler. The Russians seem to have fully understood the new state of affairs, as they began to refer to the Tatar khan as *tsar* ("emperor"), a title hitherto reserved for the universal Christian ruler—the *basileus* of the Byzantine empire. The shift from *basileus* to *khan* was first noticed and analyzed by Michael Cherniavsky, in his masterly essay "*Khan* or *Basileus:* An Aspect of Russian Mediaeval Political Theory."[56] Anyhow, this turn of events was a serious breach of the status quo: instead of the "ideal" Byzantine emperor, a Christian ruler who lived far enough away to refrain from interfering all that much in Russian affairs, now they had to contend with a "real" emperor who curtailed the grand princes' rights to the privileges of dominion: regalia, coinage, and liturgical homage. As for the first component, the imperial status of the khan was always expressed in contemporaneous Russian miniatures by the Tatar khan donning a crown, whereas the grand prince was represented in his cap. Secondly, as discussed above, practically no independent Russian coinage was minted between 1240 and 1360. The third point is rather odd. In pre-Tatar times, some diptychs continued to be produced with the names of the sovereigns. However, the grand princes' names appeared in lieu of the Byzantine emperor. During the thirteenth and fourteenth centuries, all the rulers were left out of the liturgical and service books, the khan included. This peculiar situation can best be explained by what Halperin dubs the "ideology of silence."[57] The imperial edicts that were issued to the Russian metropolitans expressly state that the Russian clergy was obliged to pray regularly for the khans of the Golden Horde, in return for the Russian Church's fiscal immunity. The omission of the Tatar ruler's name from the diptychs clearly shows that, whereas the Christian clergy had no choice but to openly pray for the "pagan" sovereign, they were reluctant to write down his name in the liturgy book itself.

In reality, then, the Russians were ruled by the Tatar *tsar,* in whose name the grand prince governed his lands. Even after the fall of Constantinople and the Byzantine empire in 1453, the Russian grand prince did not immediately become *tsar,* namely the successor of the Byzantine *basileus,* for the Russians still had a sovereign in the person of the Tatar khan. What is more, following the official abrogation of submission to the Mongols, the Muscovite grand princes eschewed the formal adoption of this honorific. That said, the first step in that direction was obviously taken that same year by Ivan III, upon releasing coins that substituted the Tatar khan's name with that of his own.[58] It was only in 1547 that the grand prince's grandson and second successor, Ivan IV, was crowned *tsar,* thereby allowing the latter to launch his campaigns for the final annexation of the Kazan and Astrakhan polities, in 1552 and 1556, as a worthy opponent of the Mongol *tsars* of Kazan and Astrakhan.

In sum, Muscovy's digestion of the Tatar political culture lasted for almost three hundred years. During this time, the figure of the Tatar khan supplanted the image of the Byzantine emperor. Despite medieval Russia's Christian and Byzantine cultural roots, even the independent Muscovite grand prince followed in the footsteps of his onetime Tatar suzerain. In a bow to political reality, the "Tsar of All Russia" became a successor to the khans of the Golden Horde, as Ivan IV and his progeny's imperial titles contained, inter alia, the honorific "Tsar of Kazan and Astrakhan."[59] As the Russian empire was consolidating its power thanks to the annexation of Kazan and Astrakhan, Russian clergymen began to build up the polity's ideological foundations by embracing the theory of a "Third Rome." But this is a story for another day.

Notes

Part of a larger research project, this chapter was made possible by the financial support of the Hungarian Scientific Research Foundation (OTKA, project no. 49704).

1. For more on the "Tatar yoke" and the simplistic views of history that stem from this phrase see C. J. Halperin, *The Tatar Yoke* (Columbus, OH, 1986), pp. 15–18.

2. Most historians aver that the so-called stand on the Ugra River in 1480 spelled the end of direct Tatar rule over Russia, while others opine that the final nail in the coffin was inflicted on the Great Horde by Mengli-Girey, the Crimean khan, in 1502. For more on these two events see I. M. Kudriavtsev, "'Ugorshchina v pamiatnikakh drevnerusskoi literatury (Letopis'nye povesti o nashestvii Akhmata i ikh literaturnaia istoriia," *Issledovaniia i materialy po drevnerusskoi literature,* 1 (Moscow, 1961), pp. 23–67; G. E. Orchard, "The Stand on the Ugra," *New Review,* 5/1 (1965), pp. 34–43; V. D. Nazarov, "Konets zolotoordynskogo iga," *Voprosy istorii,* 10 (1980), pp. 104–120; V. V. Kargalov, *Konets ordynskogo iga* (Moscow, 1980); L. J. D. Collins, "On the Alleged 'Destruction' of the Great Horde in 1502," in *Manzikert to Lepanto: The Byzantine World and the Turks 1071–1571,* ed. A. Bryer and M. Ursinus (Amsterdam, 1991), pp. 361–399.

3. C. J. Halperin, "Medieval Myopia and the Mongol Period of Russian History," *Russian History,* 5 (1978), pp. 188–191; C. J. Halperin, "Soviet Historiography on Russia and the Mongols," *Russian Review,* 41 (1982), pp. 306–322.

4. B. Evans, *Dictionary of Quotations* (New York, 1968), p. 602; I. Grudzinska Gross, *The Scar of Revolution: Custine, Tocqueville, and the Romantic Imagination* (Berkeley, 1991), pp. 53–59.

5. For a similar definition of political culture, especially as a kind of mentality, see E. L. Keenan, "Muscovite Political Folkways," *The Russian Review,* 45 (1986), pp. 115–116, n. 1.

6. C. J. Halperin, *Russia and the Golden Horde: The Mongol Impact on Medieval Russian History* (Bloomington, IN, 1985); D. Ostrowski, *Muscovy and the Mongols: Cross-Cultural Influences on the Steppe Frontier, 1304–1589* (Cambridge, 1998). Earlier scholarship on this

theme has been completely superseded by Halperin's and Ostrowski's monographs. Examples of the prior works include, among others, A. M. Sakharov, "Les Mongols et la civilisation russe," *Contributions à l'histoire russe (Cahiers d'histoire mondiale)* (Neuchâtel, 1958), pp. 77–97; B. B. Szczesniak, "A Note on the Character of the Tatar Impact upon the Russian State and Church," *Etudes Slaves et Est-Européennes,* 17 (1972), pp. 92–98; P. H. Silfen, *The Influence of the Mongols on Russia: A Dimensional History* (Hicksville, NY, 1974).

7. D. Morgan, *The Mongols* (Oxford, 1986), p. 50. But cf. M. Biran, *The Empire of the Qara Khitai in Eurasian History: Between China and the Islamic World* (Cambridge, 2005), pp. 202–206.

8. For a nice recent monograph on the Qara Khitai see Biran, *The Empire.*

9. T. T. Allsen, *Mongol Imperialism: The Policies of the Grand Khan Möngke in China, Russia, and the Islamic Lands, 1251–1259* (Berkeley, 1987), p. 114.

10. For more on these terms see I. I. Sreznevskii, *Materialy dlia slovaria drevnerusskogo iazyka po pis'mennym pamiatnikam,* 3 vols. (St. Petersburg, 1893–1903), vol. 1, pp. 43, 706; M. Fasmer, *Ėtimologicheskii slovar' russkogo iazyka,* 4 vols. (Moscow, 1986–1987), vol. 1, pp. 131, 484; E. N. Shipova, *Slovar' tiurkizmov v russkom iazyke* (Alma-Ata, 1976), pp. 64, 118.

11. I. Vásáry, "The Origin of the Institution of Basqaqs," *Acta Orientalia Hungarica,* 32 (1978), pp. 201–206. Semenov's attempt to prove—on the basis of Old Russian hagiographic texts pertaining to St. Pafnutii of Borovsk—that the word and institution of *basqaqs* were of Cuman origin and taken over by the Tatars from the Cumans cannot help but come up short (A. A. Semenov, "K voprosu o zolotoordynskom termine 'baskak,'" *Izvestiia Akademii nauk SSSR* [*Otdelenie literaturty i iazyka*], 6/2 [1947], pp. 143–146).

12. Biran, *The Empire,* pp. 93–201 (Pt. II: Aspects of Cultural and Institutional History). For the *basqaq* see pp. 120–123.

13. Ostrowski, *Muscovy and the Mongols,* pp. 37–43; D. Ostrowski, "The Tamma and the Dual Administrative Structure of the Mongol Empire," *Bulletin of the School of Oriental and African Studies,* 61 (1998), pp. 63–74.

14. "Spoiling and making the people of the cities having at their head Asud, Sesüd, Bolar, Mankerman, and Kiwa, placing *daruγačin* and *tammačin,* they returned" (*The Secret History of the Mongols,* tr. F. W. Cleaves [Cambridge, MA, 1982], p. 215 [(§274]). For an interpretation of this passage see I. de Rachewiltz (tr. and ed.), *The Secret History of the Mongols: A Mongolian Epic Chronicle of the Thirteenth Century* (Leiden, 2004), p. 1009.

15. See, e.g., I. de Rachewiltz et al. (ed.), *In the Service of the Khan: Eminent Personalities of the Early Mongol-Yüan Period (1200–1300)* (Wiesbaden, 1993), p. 769. In this book, the *darughachi* is translated as "resident commissioner."

16. G. Herrmann, *Persische Urkunden der Mongolenzeit* (Wiesbaden, 2004), pp. 75–76; B. Spuler, *Die Goldene Horde: Die Mongolen in Rußland 1223–1502* (Wiesbaden, 1965), pp. 333–340; A. Iu. Iakubovskii and B. D. Grekov, *Zolotaia Orda i ego padenie* (Moscow, 1950), pp. 131–132.

17. For a discussion on these uprisings against the *basqaqs* see A. A. Zimin, "Narodnye dvizheniia 20-kh godov XIV veka i likvidatsiia sistemy baskachestva v Severo-vostochnoi Rusi," *Izvestiia Akademii nauk SSSR (Seriia istorii i filosofii),* 9/2 (1952), pp. 61–65.

18. For *darugha* in the Golden Horde see I. Vásáry, "The Golden Horde Term Daruġa and its Survival in Russia," *Acta Orientalia Hungarica,* 30 (1976), pp. 187–197.

19. *Polnoe sobranie russkikh letopisei,* VIII, p. 96 (*Voskresenskaia letopis'*) and XII, p. 15 (*Nikonovskaia letopis'*). For a discussion on the accounts of this visit in the Russian sources see Vásáry, "The Golden Horde," p. 191.

20. *Polnoe sobranie russkikh letopisei,* VIII, p. 25 (*Voskresenskaia letopis'*). For the corresponding accounts in other Russian annals see Vásáry, "The Golden Horde," p. 191, n. 26.

21. Vásáry, "The Golden Horde," p. 192.

22. Ostrowski, *Muscovy and the Mongols,* p. 44.

23. Vásáry, "The Golden Horde," pp. 193–196.

24. P. Olbricht, *Das Postwesen in China unter der Mongolenherrschaft im 13. und 14. Jahrhundert* (Wiesbaden, 1954); A. Silverstein, *Postal Systems in the Pre-Modern Islamic World* (Cambridge, 2007), pp. 143–164.

25. For Russian *iam* and *iamshchik* see Sreznevskii, *Materialy,* vol. 3, pp. 1658, 1659; Fasmer, *Ėtimologicheskii slovar',* vol. 4, pp. 555, 557; Shipova, *Slovar' tiurkizmov,* pp. 436–437.

26. I. A. Gurliand, *Iamskaia gon'ba v Moskovskom gosudarstve do kontsa XVII veka* (Iaroslavl', 1900); G. Alef, "The Origin and Early Development of the Muscovite Postal Service," *Jahrbücher für Geschichte Osteuropas,* 15 (1967), pp. 1–15 (rpt. in G. Alef, *Rulers and Nobles in Fifteenth-Century Muscovy* [London, 1983]).

27. For Russian *den'ga/den'gi* and *altyn* see Sreznevskii, *Materialy,* vol. 1, p. 18, 652; Fasmer, *Ėtimologicheskii slovar',* vol. 1, pp. 72–73, 449; Shipova, *Slovar' tiurkizmov,* pp. 30–31, 119.

28. See G. Alef, "The Political Significance of the Inscriptions on the Muscovite Coinage in the Reign of Vasilii II," *Speculum,* 35 (1959), pp. 1–19 (rpt. Alef, *Rulers and Nobles*).

29. The majority of Russian coin hordes from between 1380 and 1480 have been discovered in the territory of the Riazan' and Moscow Principalities; see the comments and excellent photographs at *ZENO.RU—Oriental Coins Database,* http://www.zeno.ru/showgallery.php?cat=2690 (accessed August 6, 2007). That said, limited amounts of coins were also minted and issued by other Russian towns, in their capacity as the center of principalities. In Riazan', most coins derived from the Golden Horde were countermarked by either Cyrillic letters or the *tamgha* of Riazan' (V. L. Ianin and S. A. Ianina, "Nachal'nyi period riazanskoi monetnoi chekanki," in *Numizmaticheskii sbornik, Gosudarstvennyi Istoricheskii muzei* [Moscow, 1955], pt. 1, pp. 109–123). What is more, the obverse of several coins that were minted in Moscow featured the Christian symbol of a mounted figure spearing a dragon, while Arabic-letter imitations were engraved on the reverse. These Russo-Tatar silver *den'gas* were quite common in the fifteenth century.

30. One of the coins is on display at *ZENO.RU—Oriental Coins Database,* http://www.zeno.ru/showphoto.php?photo=20226&cat=5598 (accessed August 6, 2007); M. Cherniavsky, "Khan or Basileus: An Aspect of Russian Mediaeval Political Theory," *Journal of the History of Ideas,* 20 (1959), p. 470.

31. For Old Russian *tamga,* as well as Russian *tamozhnia* and *tamozhennik,* see Sreznevskii, *Materialy,* vol. 3, pp. 924, 925; Fasmer, *Ėtimologicheskii slovar',* vol. 4, p. 18; Shipova, *Slovar' tiurkizmov,* pp. 305–307.

32. For *tarkhan/darkhan* in the Turco-Mongol world see G. Doerfer, *Türkische und mongolische Elemente im Neupersischen* (Wiesbaden, 1965), vol. 2, pp. 460–474.

33. On the publication of these documents see *Pamiatniki russkogo prava* (Moscow, 1955), vol. 3, pp. 364–491; for a detailed analysis see A. P. Grigor'ev, *Sbornik khanskikh iarlykov russkim mitropolitam* (St. Petersburg, 2004).

34. B. D. Grekov (ed.), *Sudebniki XV–XVI vekov* (Moscow, 1952), pp. 153 (art. 43), 223–232; I. I. Smirnov, "Sudebnik 1550 goda," *Istoricheskie zapiski,* 24 (1947), pp. 322–330;

V. Petrov, "Sobornoe ulozhenie 1584 goda ob otmene tarkhanov," in *Sbornik statei po russkoi istorii posviashchennykh S.F. Platonovu* (St. Petersburg, 1922), pp. 191–201.

35. On the history of Bashkir *tarkhanstvo* see V. V. Vel'iaminov-Zernov, "Istochniki dlia izucheniia tarkhanstva, zhalovannogo bashkiram russkimi gosudariami," *Zapiski Akademii nauk* (St. Petersburg), 4 (1864), supplement No. 6, pp. 1–48.

36. There is an extensive literature on the Mongol *Yasa*. For some of the most important items see G. Vernadsky, "The Scope and Contents of Chingis Khan's Yasa," *HJAS*, 3 (1938), pp. 337–360; D. Ayalon, "The Great Yāsa of Chingiz Khān: A Re-examination," *Studia Islamica*, 33 (1971), pp. 97–140 [A]; 34 (1971), pp. 151–180 [B]; 36 (1972), pp. 113–158 [C1]; 38 (1973), pp. 107–156 [C2]; D. Morgan, "The 'Great Yāsā of Chingiz Khān' and Mongol Law in the Īlkhānate," *Bulletin of the School of Oriental and African Studies*, 49 (1986), pp. 163–176; I. de Rachewiltz, "Some Reflections on Činggis Qan's ǰasaγ," *East Asian History*, 6 (December 1993), pp. 91–103; Morgan, "The Great *Yasa* of Chinggis Khan Revisited," in *Mongols, Turks, and Others: Eurasian Nomads and the Sedentary World*, ed. R. Amitai and M. Biran (Leiden, 2005), pp. 291–308.

37. Even V. A. Riasanovsky—a staunch opponent and denier of Mongol influence on Russian politics, law, and culture—admits that they did have some impact on Russian law, though only of a secondary nature (V. A. Riasanovsky, "The Influence of Ancient Mongol Culture and Law on Russian Culture and Law," *Chinese Social and Political Science Review*, 20 [1936–1937], p. 530). Moreover, he points to the Tatars' indirect sway on the increase in the severity of punishments in administrative and criminal cases (V. A. Riasanovsky, *Fundamental Principles of Mongol Law* [Bloomington, IN, 1965], p. 278).

38. H. W. Dewey, "Russia's Debt to the Mongols in Suretyship and Collective Responsibility," *Comparative Studies in Society and History*, 30 (1988), pp. 249–270; H. W. Dewey and A. M. Kleimola, "Suretyship and Collective Responsibility in Pre-Petrine Russia," *Jahrbücher für Geschichte Osteuropas*, 18 (1970), pp. 337–354; H. W. Dewey, "Political Poruka in Muscovite Rus'," *Russian Review*, 46 (1987), pp. 117–133; H. W. Dewey and A. M. Kleimola, "From the Kinship Group to Every Man His Brother's Keeper: Collective Responsibility in Pre-Petrine Russia," *Jahrbücher für Geschichte Osteuropas*, 30 (1982), pp. 3213–3235; H. W. Dewey and A. M. Kleimola, "Coercion by Righter (Pravezh) in Old Russian Administration," *Canadian-American Slavic Studies*, 9 (1975), pp. 156–167; H. W. Dewey and A. M. Kleimola, "Russian Collective Consciousness: The Kievan Roots," *Slavonic and East European Review*, 62 (1982), pp. 181–182.

39. R. I. Avanesov (ed.), *Smolenskie gramoty XIII–XIV vekov* (Moscow, 1963), p. 21.

40. Dewey and Kleimola, "Suretyship," p. 343. From the end of the fifteenth century onward, the written forms of suretyship appeared, spread, and became common in Muscovite Russia. These surety bonds, which are termed *poruchnye zapisi* in Russian, provide a valuable insight into the everyday legal life of Muscovite Russia. For an overview of the historical development of suretyship in Old Russian law and the classification of different types of suretyships see M. Szeftel, "The History of Suretyship in Old Russian Law," *Recueils de la Société Jean Bodin pour l'histoire comparative des institutions*, 29 (1971), pp. 841–866.

41. Dewey and Kleimola, "Suretyship," p. 348. For a good description of political *poruka* also see Dewey, "Russia's Debt to the Mongols," pp. 265–267.

42. For more on this development see G. Alef, "The Crisis of the Muscovite Aristocracy: A Factor in the Growth of Monarchical Power," *Forschungen zur osteuropäischen Geschichte*, 15 (1970), pp. 15–58 (rpt. in Alef, *Rulers and Nobles*).

43. Dewey and Kleimola, "Coercion by Righter."

44. Much has been written on this key legal institution of Muscovite Russia. See V. I. Sergeevich, *Drevnosti russkogo prava,* vol. 1: *Territoriia i naselenie* (St. Petersburg, 1909), pp. 159–176; V. Egorov, "Kabal'nye den'gi v kontse XVI veka," *Zhurnal Ministerstva narodnogo prosveshcheniia,* 28 (1910), pp. 49–65; V. M. Paneiakh, *Kabal'noe kholopstvo na Rusi v XVI veke* (Leningrad, 1967); V. M. Paneiakh, *Kholopstvo v XVI—nachale XVII veka* (Leningrad, 1975). Paneiakh's monographs include a detailed bibliography of all the previous scholarship.

45. Petrov, "O termine kabala," pp. 113–114; Sreznevskii, *Materialy,* vol. 1, p. 1169; Fasmer, *Etimologicheskii slovar',* vol. 2, p. 148; Shipova, *Slovar' tiurkizmov,* pp. 145–146. Beginning with Sergeevich (*Drevnosti,* vol. 1, p. 159), Russian historians have often noted that the word *kabala* has Arabic origins, but none of them have elaborated on this topic.

46. Petrov, "O termine kabala," p. 114.

47. Conversely, G. Vernadsky saw direct parallels of Russian *kabala* in Uighur juridical documents from the Mongol period; G. Vernadsky, "A propos des origines du servage de 'kabala' dans le droit russe," *Revue historique du droit français et étranger,* 4th ser. 14 (1935), pp. 360–367.

48. *Zaemnaia raspiska* was a simple "loan receipt." *Zakladnaia kabala* was a "mortgage bond." *Rostovaia kabala* was a contract that stipulated fixed interest rates on a loan that was to be paid in money or agrarian products. *Sluzhilaia kabala* was one of the most prevalent forms of this sort of bondage. According to this arrangement, the debtor paid off the interest of his loan by working in the creditor's household. In a *zazhilaia kabala,* the debtor obliged himself to a lifetime of bondage in the service of the creditor. Lastly, *verchaia kabala* was a document given to the surety by the debtor in the event that the latter could not pay. It secured the surety's demand of the debtor if a lawsuit became inevitable.

49. For the Uighur-lettered Turkic language that was used in the chancelleries of the Tatar states see A. P. Grigor'ev, "Oficial'nyi iazyk Zolotoj Ordy XIII–XIV vv.," in *Tiurkologicheskii Sbornik* 1977 (Moscow, 1981), pp. 81–89; I. Vásáry, "Bemerkungen zum uigurischen Schrifttum in der Goldenen Horde und bei den Timuriden," *Ural-altaische Jahrbücher,* Neue Folge, 7 (1987), pp. 115–126.

50. D. A. Obolenskii, kn. "Vostochnye podpisi na starinnykh russkikh gramotakh," *Izvestiia Imperatorskogo russkogo arkheologicheskogo obshchestva,* 2 (1861), pp. 22–24; A. A. Bobrovnikov, "O mongol'skikh podpisiakh na russkikh aktakh," *Izvestiia Imperatorskogo Russkogo Arkheologicheskogo obshchestva,* 3 (1861), pp. 19–29.

51. For the text and more details about these notes see I. Vásáry, *Az Arany Horda kancelláriája* (Budapest, 1987), p. 73.

52. Sreznevskii, *Materialy,* vol. 3, pp. 1660–1662; Fasmer, *Ėtimologicheskii slovar',* vol. 4, p. 561; Shipova, *Slovar' tiurkizmov,* pp. 438–439.

53. P. B. Golden, "Turkic Calques in Medieval Eastern Slavic," *Journal of Turkic Studies,* 8 (1984), p. 109. For *chelom biti* and *chelobitie* in Old Russian texts see Sreznevskii, *Materialy,* vol. 3, pp. 1488–1490.

54. *Polnoe sobranie russkikh letopisei,* XIX, p. 200.

55. Inostrantsev was the first to draw a correlation between *basma* and the definition of *baysa;* K. A. Inostrantsev, "K voprosu o 'basme,'" *Zapiski Vostochnogo otdeleniia imperatorskogo russkogo arkheologicheskogo obshchestva,* 18 (1907–1908), pp. 175–179. A handful of scholars have judiciously concurred with his view: A. N. Samoilovich, "O 'paiza'—'baiza' v Dzhuchievom uluse," *Izvestiia Akademii nauk,* 6th ser. 20 (1926), p. 1120; A. A. Spicyn, "Tatarskie baisy," *Izvestiia arkhivnoi kommissii,* 29 (1929), pp. 131–132; N. Ts. Münküyev, "A New Mongolian P'ai-tzŭ from Simferopol," *Acta Orientalia Hungarica,* 31 (1977), p. 199.

For a discussion on the relationship between the terms *baysa* and *basma* in Russian see Vásáry, *Az Arany Horda kancelláriája,* pp. 64–66.

56. Cherniavsky, "Khan or Basileus," pp. 459–476.

57. Halperin, *Russia and the Golden Horde,* pp. 61–74.

58. See n. 31 above.

59. It was, above all, Jaroslaw Pelenski who emphasized the significance of the capture of Kazan and Astrakhan in the establishment of the new Russian imperial ideology; see J. Pelenski, "State and Society in Muscovite Russia and the Mongol-Turkic System in the Sixteenth Century," *Forschungen zur osteuropäischen Geschichte,* 27 (1980), p. 166.

TWELVE

Mongol Historiography since 1985
The Rise of Cultural History

David Morgan

In a Festschrift essay in which he discussed and celebrated the scholarly achievement of my undergraduate tutor at Oxford, the late Patrick Wormald commented that "In the last decade, James Campbell has turned, as most top-notch historians eventually do, to the historiography of his subject."[1] While, unlike Campbell and indeed Wormald, I have no claim to be regarded as a top-notch historian, I too have turned to look at the historiography of my own subject: the Mongol empire. This is for a very specific reason. Twenty years ago I published a general book on the subject, which ought by now to have been superseded.[2] However, since in 2005 it was reprinted for the twenty-first time, it would seem that it has not. Apparently it is still the first book that many people read on the subject (though, as I remarked in the introduction, it is my earnest hope that it will not invariably also be the last). This has made me a little uneasy. What I tried to do in the book was to provide a conspectus of where the subject was in the mid-1980s. The publishers from time to time suggested that I should revise it for a second edition; but this I was reluctant to do, in that I saw the book as a kind of period piece. The study of the Mongol empire has made enormous strides in the past two decades, arguably more significantly than in any comparable period. It seemed to me that the book was in a number of respects so outdated, and hence perhaps misleading, that what it needed was not so much revision as a complete rewriting, preferably by someone else. However, eventually I saw a possible way forward, following the example of Peter Brown, who in 2000 published a second edition of his famous 1967 biography, *Augustine of Hippo,* in which he left the original text untouched but added two new chapters, one on new evidence, the other on new directions. We do not, I think, have sufficient new Mongol evidence for it to require its own chapter, but new directions we have in abundance.

So I have written a new chapter, "The Mongol Empire since 1985," and my book appeared with that addition and various other changes, such as a supplementary bibliography, in 2007. My contribution to this volume is a series of reflections, based to some extent on the new chapter, in which I shall pay particular attention to what seems to me to be the most conspicuous recent development, what I have called "the rise of cultural history."

When, at the age of fourteen, I read my first book on the Mongol empire—Michael Prawdin's *The Mongol Empire: Its Rise and Legacy,* first published in English translation in 1940—the conventional image of the Mongols was not a flattering one. True, there were military historians and theorists who saw much of interest in the phenomenon of the Mongol conquests. The most notable of these was perhaps Sir Basil Liddell Hart, an early apostle of tank warfare whose ideas are often said to have been a great deal more influential in Nazi Germany, in connection with *Panzer* warfare and the idea of the *Blitzkrieg,* than they were in his native England. Hart wrote about Chinggis Khan and Sübe'etei in his *Great Captains Unveiled* of 1928. He seems to have regarded the Mongol tactical approach in their campaigns, from which he thought a good deal could usefully be learnt, as the thirteenth-century equivalent of tank warfare. This is symptomatic of how the Mongols were seen: they were at best little more than a military phenomenon. What they had done was to fight—with remarkable, indeed almost unparalleled success—and conquer. That was about it; there was little constructive to be seen. Indeed, apart from the extraordinary extent of their conquests, what the Mongols were most remembered for was brutality and vandalism: they had killed vast numbers of people and had destroyed enormous tracts of land and numerous great cities. In common parlance, the most widely used phrase (and this has still not disappeared) that involved the Mongols was as a way of stigmatizing a political opponent by describing him (or her, in the case of Mrs. Thatcher) as being "to the right of Genghis Khan."

This is certainly unfair to the right, if not to Chinggis: in terms of massacres, though both right and left made their contributions, the left was undoubtedly well ahead during the twentieth century. But is it unjust to attribute massacre and destruction to the Mongols? That it is, is now widely argued by their apologists. The argument tends to go along the lines of suggesting that while no doubt a good many people were killed during the Mongol campaigns, there was nothing unusual about this, and the Mongols were no worse, indeed possibly better, than their contemporaries in that respect. Jack Weatherford, a writer for whom the Mongols can do little wrong, does not deny the massacres, but argues (and there is something in this) that the Mongols should at least be given the credit for only killing, and not previously torturing, their victims, unlike some of their enemies and other contemporary powers. "By comparison," he writes, "with the terrifying acts of civilized armies of the era, the Mongols did not inspire fear by the ferocity or cruelty of their acts so much as by the speed and efficiency with which they conquered and their seemingly total disdain for the lives of the rich and powerful."[3]

Let us take a look at a contrary view. Hugh Kennedy, a distinguished historian, usually of early Islamic history, published a book in a series on military history, in which he dealt with nomad warfare: Huns, Arabs, Turks, Mongols, and Vikings (what the Vikings were doing in the book was not altogether clear—"nomads of the seas," perhaps?—or they may have been included at the insistence of the publisher).[4] Kennedy will have nothing to do with the notion that the Mongols have been sadly misunderstood and maligned: "Revisionist historians have questioned the extent of Mongol ferocity and destructiveness, suggesting that such accounts are largely rhetoric and hyperbole. However, the weight of contemporary evidence is very strong and it is backed up by the archaeology."[5] In my opinion this is right. In *The Mongols*—and for once I still agree with myself—I argued that the contemporary evidence was indeed telling. It was not that one should believe that a thirteenth-century historian was providing us with a reliable statistic when he told us, for example, that 2,400,000 people were killed by the Mongols when they took Herat. What is significant is that such figures were quoted at all: they are evidence of shock, of the fact that the Mongol conquests were something quite unprecedented. To argue that "medieval chroniclers always exaggerate" will not do. Persian chroniclers who write about the Seljuk invasions of the eleventh century do not quote figures for massacres (or indeed for the size of invading nomad armies) that are remotely comparable with those to be found in the Mongol-period sources. Later writers, many of whom were employed by Mongol governments, tell much the same story. No one attempts to "tone down" the horrors of the initial Mongol invasions. It is of course worth bearing in mind that it would hardly have occurred to the Mongols themselves that there was anything at all discreditable about their campaigns and massacres. It was, after all, the will of Tenggeri. I suspect that they would have found their modern apologists something of a puzzle, even an embarrassment.

In 1977 I attended a conference in Oxford on the Islamic world after the Mongol conquests. It was on this occasion that I first ventured to try out my notoriously heretical views on the "Great *Yasa* of Chinggis Khan." During the conference I heard Professor Joseph Fletcher of Harvard give what struck me as a remarkable paper. I took no notes, and forgot about it. Or did

I? Fletcher died, still in his forties, in 1984. Two years later, a memorial issue of the *Harvard Journal of Asiatic Studies* included a previously unpublished paper of his, "The Mongols: Ecological and Social Perspectives."[6] This was based on his Oxford paper. It was published more or less simultaneously with my *The Mongols:* and it contains virtually every good idea that is to be found in my book. There are two possible explanations for this, of which the less probable, by rather a substantial margin, is that we were two geniuses, working on parallel lines. Reviewing the later volume, edited by Beatrice Manz, which reprinted Fletcher's articles, I expressed the opinion that this essay "may . . . be said simply to be in many ways the best single discussion of the Mongol imperial phenomenon ever written."[7] I see no reason to change that view.

One of Fletcher's ideas that I did not steal for my book—perhaps he added it after the Oxford occasion—is his explanation of "Why did the Mongols wreak so much destruction?" We may note, first of all, that Fletcher had no doubt that they *did* wreak a great deal of destruction: "They came as an avalanche, a cyclone, massacred large numbers of people, and did such destruction that the effect of their mayhem is arguably still perceptible."[8] But he has an explanation that tries to makes sense of this. He declines to resort to the kind of nonexplanation offered by J. J. Saunders, for whom the Mongols suffered from some "blind unreasoning fear and hatred of urban civilisation."[9] What he does is to contrast the earlier advent of the Turks in the Islamic world with that of the Mongols. Why did the Turks cause so much less damage? According to Fletcher, because they took their time in arriving, and were able to adapt gradually to the very different conditions that they found in their new home: "the Mongols simply came too fast. Unlike the Turks, they entered the desert habitat suddenly, en masse, in centrally-planned campaigns . . . There was no time for them to acculturate themselves to the desert habitat; so they carried with them . . . attitudes nurtured in the East Asian steppe: disdain for peasants, who like the animals that the Mongols herded, lived directly off what grew from the soil . . . With the steppe extortion pattern in mind, the Mongols did violence and used terror, reinforced by their ideology of universal dominion, to induce their victims to surrender peaceably."[10]

This seems to me to make a great deal of sense. And of course the implication is that these attitudes were not likely to last. The Mongols, Fletcher says, "came to understand settled society no less quickly than had the Turks," but the inescapable fact is that "by that time the Mongolian juggernaut had done its dreadful work."[11] Still, what follows, if we accept something like Fletcher's explanation, is that we would expect Mongol rule, once established, to be very different from Mongol conquest, and that is the conceptual step that the authors of the older literature rarely seemed to take: once a brutal barbarian, they tended to assume, always a brutal barbarian.

There is, however, one honorable exception to this generalization. Art historians, especially those who study the Islamic world, have, from their perspective, long taken a very different view of the nature and significance of the Mongol period. This tradition goes back at least as far as 1931, when a celebrated Exhibition of Persian Art was held at Burlington House in London.[12] A permanent result of the exhibition was a volume, which included a catalogue of the Persian miniatures that had been exhibited, but much more too, published in 1933.[13] For our purposes, the crucial figure was Basil Gray, who was then a young scholar who had just succeeded to what had been Arthur Waley's post at the British Museum. He wrote the early chapters of the book, including chapter 2, "The Early Persian Style and Fourteenth Century Changes," which examines the Mongol period and its aftermath. Gray long remained a formative and influential figure who by no means confined his interests to Persian art, but what he published in that field was of great importance, even though, it is said, he accomplished it without knowing any Persian at all.[14] He lived until 1989, dying in office as president of the British Institute of Persian Studies. I often encountered him in that context, as I was myself for many years a member of the Institute's Governing Council.[15]

Gray does not seem at first to take an especially benevolent view of the Mongols themselves and their contribution: "Terrific as were the destructions wrought by the Mongols . . . and permanent as was the resulting impoverishment of Persia, it is evident that they caused no break in culture," but, he adds, this was "partly because they brought nothing to take its place."[16] Yet he goes on to praise "the enlightened patronage . . . of the later Ilkhans, which made the period from 1267 to 1335 one of the most fruitful in the history of Persian literature," and he makes a similar point about Mongol rule in China.[17] He argues that earlier rulers in Persia had also behaved destructively, and he concludes that "As far as possible the Mongol conquerors spared the lives of scholars and craftsmen, and they brought a strong central government, which is the first requisite of civilization. Probably the chaos that succeeded the break-up of the Mongol power in Persia in 1335 was actually more disastrous than the invasions had been"—this last, a very dubious proposition indeed, in my opinion.[18] In parenthesis, it is interesting to note that the most recent detailed examination of at any rate the first period of Ilkhanid rule, George Lane's *Early Mongol Rule in Thirteenth-Century Iran: A Persian Renaissance,* takes a very similar view to Gray's of the Mongol rulers as patrons, as the book's subtitle indicates.[19] It is possible to argue that Lane has an overgenerous tendency to give the Ilkhanid regime the benefit of every possible doubt, as Charles Melville seems to be suggesting in his very fair and balanced review in the *Bulletin of the School of Oriental and African Studies*.[20] Yet Lane's evidence, however one may think it should be interpreted, is undeniably there, and it cannot simply be wished away. But the main burden of Gray's chapter, and of course the reason why Gray was able to take, for his day, an unusually nuanced view of the Mongol impact, was his lengthy and trailblazing discussion of the art, especially the miniature painting, of the Mongol period, full as it was of rich new developments, not least the incorporation of elements from Chinese art—something which could hardly have happened but for the Mongols' forcible unification of most of Asia. The question arises: Was this perception of the Mongol impact Gray's own original insight? Not entirely, it would seem. For example, F. R. Martin's *The Miniature Painting and Painters of Persia, India and Turkey,* which was published as long ago as 1912, discusses the innovations of the Mongol period and especially the East Asian influence that was facilitated by the establishment of Mongol hegemony.[21] On the other hand, there is no sign of any similar perspective in a book published not long before the book to which Gray contributed, A. U. Pope's *Introduction to Persian Art*—and Pope was not only the most celebrated historian of Persian art of his generation, but is described on the title page of his book as "Director of the International Exhibition of Persian Art, London, 1931."[22] It would appear that Gray can be given the credit for precipitating a more positive assessment of Mongol influence into the forefront of scholarly consciousness, even if his ideas were not entirely original. Later, of course, some historians had begun to take this on board, at least up to a point.[23]

If we leap forward seventy years from 1931, we arrive at another exhibition, which for Mongol empire studies was certainly no less significant than the Burlington House exhibition. This was "The Legacy of Genghis Khan: Courtly Art and Culture in Western Asia 1256–1353," shown at the Metropolitan Museum of Art in New York and the Los Angeles County Museum of Art, in 2002/3. That was, so far as I am aware, incomparably the finest exhibition of art and artifacts of the Mongol period ever collected together and shown. The catalogue is itself a publication of rare magnificence.[24] As well as the catalogue and a wealth of color plates, it contains a series of excellent articles, not only by art specialists of the stature of Sheila Blair, Robert Hillenbrand, and Linda Komaroff, but also valuable studies by two leading historians, Morris Rossabi and Charles Melville. The exhibition and the volume demonstrate how far we have come since Gray wrote his pioneering assessment. But what is interesting is that, in general terms, progress has been in very much the directions that Gray would have expected and liked. There is a particularly strong emphasis on the importance of cross-cultural contacts. To quote a typical example from the articles in the catalogue, here is how Komaroff begins her essay on "The Transmission and Dissemination of a New Visual Language": "Ilkhanid artists created a new visual language in response to the demands of their patrons, whose aspirations and tastes were shaped not only by their encounter with the urban, Islamic culture of Iran but also by contact with the highly sophisticated civilization of China."[25] Overall, as I remark in the new chapter in *The Mongols,* "It would hardly have been possible to walk attentively around the great exhibition, or even to read through the catalogue, and to come away thinking that the Mongol era was solely about killing and devastation."[26]

The exhibition's time in Los Angeles was made the occasion for a three-day symposium, "Beyond the Legacy of Genghis Khan," at which I had the privilege of being one of the participants. Again, the symposium showed how fruitful such proceedings can be when historians and art historians are actually prepared to talk, and listen, to each other. As one example, Oliver Watson, in an aside which was fairly peripheral to his main argument, provided strong supporting evidence, from the pottery record, that Alexander Morton is right in arguing that Rashīd al-Dīn's *Letters* are spurious. A volume containing twenty-four of the papers, edited by Komaroff, was published in 2006.[27] Again, the importance and fertility of cultural transmission across the length and breadth of Mongol-dominated Asia is a constant theme of the papers.

It will be seen, then, that I take a very positive view of what the art historians have taught us: they have been, in general, right during a long period in which historians, not to mention the general public, have often been wrong. However, before I disappear entirely beneath sackcloth and ashes, let me enter one caveat. It does seem to me that, occasionally, art historians of the Mongol period allow their justified enthusiasm to carry them rather further than the evidence would suggest is defensible. An example from some years ago is Oleg Grabar and Sheila Blair's book, *Epic Images and Contemporary History,* a study of the illustrations in the astonishing manuscript that the art-historical thought police now require us to call, not the "Demotte," but the "Great Mongol" *Shāhnāmah.*[28] This is an immensely valuable attempt to assemble in as complete a form as possible, and to discuss, the illustrations in the book that, the authors write, is the "earliest surviving masterpiece of Persian painting." Where my reservations come in is when the authors attempt to show that the illustrations have a subtext; that is, that they contain direct and pointed references to actual events in late Ilkhanid Iran; and when they argue that the manuscript's patron must have been the vizier Ghiyāth al-Dīn, son of the great Rashīd al-Dīn.[29] Now my difficulty with this—and I say it with reluctance: there are few if any Islamic art historians for whom I have greater respect than Grabar and Blair—is not that what they say is implausible. It might very well be right. But there is no actual hard evidence whatever to support their contention. As I said in my review of the book, "The whole argument is a succession of suppositions, any of which might be right but all of which may equally well be completely wrong."

As is well known, the Grabar and Blair approach has subsequently been taken very much further, by Abolala Soudavar, in a virtual monograph that evolved out of a presentation at a conference in Oxford.[30] To quote Robert Hillenbrand's summary, in his *The Legacy of Genghis Khan* article on "The Arts of the Book in Ilkhanid Iran," Soudavar suggested that "the Great Mongol *Shahnama* . . . is nothing less than a daring attempt to reconfigure the *Shahnama* as a chronicle of the royal Mongol house. By this reckoning, every episode chosen to be depicted . . . was selected because it also served to present some event in recent Mongol history and this brought Firdausi's text right up to contemporary Iran." Hillenbrand adds, as well he might, that this theory "has not won universal acceptance." He contends, however, that "Soudavar . . . has been able to propose a sequence of remarkably exact correlations between episodes in Firdausi's epic and Mongol history," and he cannot believe that this is all coincidence.[31] A contributor to a volume I was recently reviewing remarked, I fear all too accurately, that "If one thing is certain in scholarship it's that we usually find what we are looking for."[32] Well, like the more modest proposals of Grabar and Blair, Soudavar's argument might be right; but then again it might not. And I can see no way, in the present state of the evidence, of determining this, one way or the other. Hillenbrand certainly knows a great deal more history than I, or most other historians, know art history; but I remain a little puzzled that he and others should be so ready to accept a theory which, however fascinating and indeed attractive it may be, is so singularly lacking in tangible support.

Let me now turn to the writing of history, my own discipline. If asked to name the three most outstanding books on the history of the Mongol empire published during the last few years, I would nominate Thomas Allsen's *Culture and Conquest in Mongol Eurasia,* Igor de Rachewiltz's *The Secret History of the Mongols: A Mongolian Epic Chronicle of the Thirteenth Century,* and Peter Jackson's *The Mongols and the West 1221–1410.*[33] I refrain from nominating Michal Biran's *The Empire of the Qara Khitai in Eurasian History: Between China and the Islamic World* only because it is not, strictly speaking, a book about the Mongol empire, though its implications for and relevance to Mongol studies are far-reaching.[34] It is Allsen's book that illustrates most clearly, from a historian's point of view, the developments that I have discussed in connection with Mongol-period art history. Although Jackson's remarkable book, which throws a flood of new light on its subject, inevitably has strong cultural overtones (and see especially, for example, his chapters on "Images of the Enemy" and "Traders and Adventurers"), it is not a book whose general focus could be described as cultural. Most of de Rachewiltz's magnificent book is a commentary on the *Secret History* (the translation of the text takes up only 218 of the book's more than 1,400 pages). In reviewing the book, I expressed the view that the commentary constituted "by far the fullest and best-informed collection of material on the prehistory and early history of the Mongol Empire I have ever encountered."[35] And of course, inevitably, a very large part of what de Rachewiltz has unearthed for us could properly be described as "cultural."

But Allsen's *Culture and Conquest* is cultural history par excellence. Drawing on earlier scholarship, his own and others', but also putting the evidence together in a way that is startlingly innovative, he discusses "Political-Economic Relations," "Intermediaries" like Marco Polo, Bolad Aqa, and Rashīd al-Dīn, and—perhaps most strikingly of all—"Cultural Exchange" in the fields of historiography, geography and cartography, agriculture, cuisine, medicine, and printing. We may note that he does not discuss art: evidence that cultural transmission, however important it may have been in that area, was very far indeed from being confined to it.

Discussing the book in an article published in 2004, I suggested that "Allsen is able to break so much new ground because he is equally familiar with the Persian and the Chinese sources, and is therefore able to use them to shed light on each other."[36] When I began to study the Mongol empire, as I wrote in *The Mongols,* it was fairly usual for the historian "to choose his end of Asia, west or east, and to base his work on the sources in one of the two major languages—Persian and Chinese."[37] As I was probably, at that early stage, suffering from the quite widespread delusion that Persian is a comparatively easy language, and being myself "linguistically challenged," I took the coward's way out and learnt Persian; which did, however, result in the inestimable benefit, for me, of acquiring a very great scholar, the late Professor Ann Lambton, both as Persian teacher and, subsequently, as my research supervisor. Even then there had been, of course, exceptions to the "Persian or Chinese" rule. The most obvious is Paul Pelliot, who may have held the record for the number of languages in which he was at home: certainly his record for posthumous publication (he is still publishing; and he died in 1945) is unlikely to be equaled. Joe Fletcher would admit, slightly guiltily, to having learnt fifteen languages. At the end of an article published in 2000, which covers some of the same ground as this paper, but is far more comprehensive, Peter Jackson remarked, I have no doubt correctly, that a satisfactory successor to my *The Mongols* would need to have as its author a scholar who had far more extensive linguistic skills than I have—someone in that respect, that is to say, in the Allsen mold.[38] And it is likely to be vastly more cultural in its concerns and emphasis than my book was—or at any rate it ought to be. We can already see signs of this in publications intended for a wide readership. The most recent Mongol book to reach me while I was writing the original version of this chapter was George Lane's *Daily Life in the Mongol Empire*.[39] My immediate thought was that such a book could hardly have been written thirty years ago. Then I recalled that I have on my shelves Charles Commeaux's *La vie quotidienne chez les Mongols de la conquête (XIIIe siècle),* which was published in 1972.[40] But that is, by today's standards, a fairly thin run-through, by an author who had also written histories of China, India, Turkey, and Japan. I do not recall ever seeing a reference to it in anyone's footnotes. Even a brief glance at Lane's book shows how much richer the field now is.

In his 1955 inaugural lecture as the first Professor of Medieval and Renaissance Literature at Cambridge, C. S. Lewis (who at that point in his life was rather younger than I am now) chose to depict himself as a kind of anachronism or survival, "Old Western Man," and in conclusion, said, "Speaking not only for myself but for all other Old Western Men, I would say, use your specimens while you can. There are not going to be many more dinosaurs."[41] Admittedly, people are still, in ever-increasing numbers, reading the works of Lewis (though not predominantly his literary criticism), more than forty years after his death; so his books are some distance from the extinction he perhaps anticipated. Still, in terms of the historiography of the Mongol empire, it might be said that, although Tom Allsen and I are not all that far apart in age (and I am a little the younger of us), it is I who represent Old Central Asian Man, and he the future. Will anyone still be reading my *The Mongols* in forty years' time? I very much hope not, as that, like claims that a book is "definitive," would be evidence that the field of study was dead.[42] (I admit, though, that I do have hopes for the longevity of the version of William of Rubruck's travel account that Peter Jackson and I produced for the Hakluyt Society: after all, the society's previous version, by W. W. Rockhill, survived for ninety years.[43]) I am not, now, going to learn Chinese (my point being not so much that life is too short, as that I am at the wrong end of it). But my next book, which will be a study of Ilkhanid Iran, will undoubtedly be a great deal more cultural in its approach than would or could have been the case, but for the remarkable developments in scholarship that have been the subject of this chapter.

Notes

1. P. Wormald, "James Campbell as Historian," in *The Medieval State: Essays Presented to James Campbell,* ed. J. R. Maddicott and D. M. Palliser (London, 2000), p. xx.

2. D. Morgan, *The Mongols* (Oxford, 1986; 2nd ed., 2007).

3. J. Weatherford, *Genghis Khan and the Making of the Modern World* (New York, 2004), p. 116.

4. H. Kennedy, *Mongols, Huns and Vikings: Nomads at War* (London, 2002).

5. Ibid., p. 138.

6. *Harvard Journal of Asiatic Studies,* 46 (1986), pp. 11–50; reprinted in J. Fletcher, *Studies on Chinese and Islamic Inner Asia,* ed. B. F. Manz (Aldershot, 1995).

7. *Journal of the Royal Asiatic Society,* 3rd ser., 6/1 (1996), p. 148.

8. Fletcher, "The Mongols," pp. 39–40.

9. Ibid., p. 43; quoted from J. J. Saunders, "The Nomad as Empire-Builder: A Comparison of the Arab and Mongol Conquests," in his *Muslims and Mongols,* ed. G. W. Rice (Christchurch, NZ, 1977), p. 48.

10. Fletcher, "The Mongols," p. 42.

11. Ibid.

12. On this see B. W. Robinson, "The Burlington House Exhibition of 1931: A Milestone in Islamic Art History," in *Discovering Islamic Art: Scholars, Collectors and Collections,* ed. S. Vernoit (London, 2000), pp. 147–155. The young Robinson himself "paid numerous visits" to the exhibition, which "sealed his destiny, for it pointed the way to his future as a scholar" (R. Hillenbrand, "Basil W. Robinson 1912–2005," *Iran,* 44 [2006], p. v).

13. L. Binyon et al., *Persian Miniature Painting* (London, 1933; rpt. New York, 1971). I cite the reprint.

14. See e.g., from later in Gray's career, his *Persian Painting* (Geneva, 1961) and later reprints.

15. Nor have I forgotten the courtesy with which he treated me at our first meeting, when he was a member of the committee that in 1973 interviewed me for a BIPS Fellowship: the most terrifying interview I have ever endured (the other members of the committee were Professors A. K. S. Lambton and R. C. Zaehner, Sir Max Mallowan, and Sir Mortimer Wheeler). On Gray see R. Pinder-Wilson, "Basil Gray 1904–1989," *Proceedings of the British Academy,* 105 (2000), pp. 439–457, and, more briefly, in *Iran,* 27 (1989), pp. v–vi.

16. Binyon et. al., *Persian Miniature Painting,* p. 29.

17. Ibid., pp. 29–30.

18. Ibid., p. 30.

19. London, 2003.

20. *Bulletin of the School of Oriental and African Studies,* 67/2 (2004), pp. 238–240.

21. I owe this reference to the late Alexander Morton.

22. A. U. Pope, *An Introduction to Persian Art since the Seventh Century A.D.* (London, 1930).

23. Even Morgan (*The Mongols,* 1st ed., p. 195) makes a brief comment about Chinese influence on Persian miniature painting.

24. L. Komaroff and S. Carboni (eds.), *The Legacy of Genghis Khan: Courtly Art and Culture in Western Asia* (New York, 2002).

25. Ibid., p. 169.

26. Morgan, *The Mongols,* 2nd ed., p. 206.

27. L. Komaroff (ed.), *Beyond the Legacy of Genghis Khan* (Leiden, 2006).

28. Chicago, 1980.

29. See my review in the *Bulletin of the School of Oriental and African Studies,* 65/2 (1982), pp. 364–365.

30. "The Saga of Abu-Sa'id Bahador Khan: The Abu-Sa'idname," in *The Court of the Il-khans, 1290–1340,* ed. J. Raby and T. Fitzherbert (Oxford, 1996), pp. 95–218.

31. R. Hillenbrand, "The Arts of the Book in Ilkhanid Iran," in *The Legacy of Genghis Khan*, p. 158.

32. S. Pollock, "The Transformation of Culture-power in Indo-Europe, 1000–1300," in *Eurasian Transformations, Tenth to Thirteenth Centuries: Crystallizations, Divergences, Renaissances,* ed. J. P. Arnason and B. Wittrock (Leiden, 2004), p. 247.

33. T. T. Allsen, *Culture and Conquest in Mongol Eurasia* (Cambridge, 2001); I. de Rachewiltz (ed., tr., and comp.), *The Secret History of the Mongols: A Mongolian Epic Chronicle of the Thirteenth Century,* 2 vols. (Leiden, 2004); Peter Jackson, *The Mongols and the West 1221–1410* (Harlow, UK, 2005).

34. Cambridge, 2005.

35. *Bulletin of the School Oriental and African Schools,* 67/3 (2004), p. 412.

36. "The Mongols in Iran: A Reappraisal," *Iran,* 42 (2004), p. 134.

37. Morgan, *The Mongols,* 1st ed., p. 6.

38. P. Jackson, "The State of Research: The Mongol Empire 1986–1999," *Journal of Medieval History,* 26/2 (2000), p. 210.

39. Westport, CT, 2006.

40. Paris, 1972.

41. C. S. Lewis, "*De Descriptione Temporum,*" in his *Selected Literary Essays,* ed. W. Hooper (Cambridge, 1969), p. 14.

42. Cf. Morgan, "The Mongols in Iran: A Reappraisal," pp. 131–132.

43. *The Mission of Friar William of Rubruck: His Journey to the Court of the Great Khan Möngke 1253–1255,* tr. P. Jackson, ed. P. Jackson with D. Morgan (London, 1990).

Bibliography

Abū al-Fidā'. *The Memoirs of a Syrian Prince: Abu'l Fidā', Sultan of Ḥamāh (672–732/1237–1330).* Tr. and ed. P. M. Holt. Wiesbaden, 1983.

Aga-Oglu, Kramer. "Blue-and-White Porcelain Plates Made for Muslim Patrons." *Far Eastern Ceramic Bulletin,* 3/3 (1951), pp. 12–16.

al-Aharī, Abū Bakr Quṭbī. *Ta'rīkh-i Shaikh Uwais: An Important Source for the History of Adharbaiján.* Ed. and tr. H. B. Van Loon. Gravenhage, 1954.

Aigle, Denise. "The Mongol Invasions of Bilād al-Shām by Ghāzān Khān and Ibn Taymīya's Three 'Anti-Mongol' Fatwas." *Mamluk Studies Review,* 11/2 (2007), pp. 89–120.

———. "Les correspondances adressées par Hülegü au prince ayyoubide de Syrie, al-Malik al-Nāṣir Yūsuf. La construction d'un modèle." In *Pensée grecque et sagesse d'Orient. Hommages à Michel Tardieu,* ed. M.-A. Moezzi, J.-D. Dubois, C. Jullien, and F. Jullien. Turnhout, 2010, pp. 1–21.

Akbarnia, Ladan. "Khita'i: Cultural Memory and the Creation of a Mongol Visual Idiom in Iran and Central Asia." PhD dissertation, Harvard University, 2007.

Akhmedov, Buri Ahmedovich. *Gosudarstvo kochevykh uzbekov* [The State of the Nomadic Uzbeks]. Moscow, 1965.

Alderley, Lord Stanley of, ed. *Travels to Tana and Persia by Josafa Barbaro and Ambrogio Contarini.* London, 1873.

Alef, Gustave. "The Political Significance of the Inscriptions on the Muscovite Coinage in the Reign of Vasilii II." *Speculum,* 35 (1959), pp. 1–19. (Reprinted in G. Alef, *Rulers and Nobles in Fifteenth-Century Muscovy.* London, 1983.)

———. "The Origin and Early Development of the Muscovite Postal Service." *Jahrbücher für Geschichte Osteuropas,* 15 (1967), pp. 1–15. (Reprinted in G. Alef, *Rulers and Nobles in Fifteenth-Century Muscovy.* London, 1983.)

———. "The Crisis of the Muscovite Aristocracy: A Factor in the Growth of Monarchical Power." *Forschungen zur osteuropäischen Geschichte,* 15 (1970), pp. 15–58. (Reprinted in G. Alef, *Rulers and Nobles in Fifteenth-Century Muscovy.* London, 1983.)

Alekseev, Andrei Yu. *Khronografiia evropeiskoi Skifii* [The Chronography of European Scythia]. St. Petersburg, 2003.

Alekseev, Andrei Yu., N. K. Kachalova, and S. P. Tokhtas'ev. *Kimmeriitsy: etnokul'turnaia prinadlezhnost'* [The Cimmerians—Their Ethno-Cultural Affiliation]. St. Petersburg, 1993.

Allard, Francis. "*The Archaeology of Dian: Trends and Tradition.*"*Antiquity,* 73 (279), pp. 77–85.

Allard, Francis, Diimaajav Erdenebaatar, Natsagyn Batbold, and Bryan Miller. "A Xiongnu Cemetery Found in Mongolia." *Antiquity,* 76 (2002), pp. 637–638.

Allsen, Thomas T. "The Yuan Dynasty and the Uighurs of Turfan in the 13th Century." In *The Middle Kingdom and Its Neighbors, 10th–14th Centuries,* ed. M. Rossabi. Berkeley, 1983, pp. 243–280.

———. *Mongol Imperialism: The Policies of the Grand Khan Möngke in China, Russia, and the Islamic Lands, 1251–1259.* Berkeley, 1987.

———. "Mongols and North Caucasia." *Archivum Eurasiae Medii Aevi,* 7 (1987–1991), pp. 5–40.

———. "The Rise of the Mongolian Empire and Mongolian Rule in North China." In *The Cambridge History of China,* vol. 6: *Alien Regimes and Border States 907–1368,* ed. H. Franke and D. Twitchett. Cambridge, 1994, pp. 321–413.

———. "Spiritual Geography and Political Legitimacy in the Eastern Steppe." In *Ideology and the Early State,* ed. H. Claessen and J. Oosten. Leiden, 1996, pp. 116–135.

———. *Commodity and Exchange in the Mongol Empire: A Cultural History of Islamic Textiles.* Cambridge, 1997.

———. "'Ever Closer Encounters': The Appropriation of Culture and the Apportionment of Peoples in the Mongol Empire." *Journal of Early Modern History,* 1 (1997), pp. 2–23.

———. *Culture and Conquest in Mongol Eurasia.* Cambridge, 2001.

———. "Sharing out the Empire: Apportioned Lands under the Mongols." In *Nomads in the Sedentary World,* ed. A. M. Khazanov and A. Wink. Richmond, Surrey, 2001, pp. 172–190.

———. *Technician Transfer in the Mongol Empire.* Eurasian Studies Lectures, 2. Bloomington, IN, 2002.

———. "The Circulation of Military Technology in the Mongolian Empire." In *Warfare in Inner Asian History 500–1800,* ed. N. Di Cosmo. Leiden, 2007, pp. 265–293.

———. "Mongols as Vectors for Cultural Transmission." In *The Cambridge History of Inner Asia,* vol. 2: *The Chinggisid Age,* ed. N. Di Cosmo, A. J. Frank, and P. B. Golden. Cambridge, 2009, pp. 135–154.

Amartuvshin, Chunag, and William Honeychurch. *Survey and Bioarchaeology of Southern Mongolia: The Baga Gazaryn Chuluu Project.* Ulaanbaatar, 2009.

———. *Dundgobi aimagt hiisen arkheologiin sudalgaa: Baga Gazaryn Chuluu* [Archaeological Research in the Middle Gobi: Baga Gazaryn Chuluu]. Ulaanbaatar, 2010.

Amartuvshin, Chunag, and P. Khatanbaatar. "Khunnu bulshny sudalgaa [Research on the Xiongnu Burials]." In *Dundgobi aimagt hiisen arkheologiin sudalgaa: Baga Gazryn Chuluu,* ed. C. Amartuvshin and W. Honeychurch. Ulaanbaatar, 2010, pp. 202–296.

Amitai, Reuven. "Mongol Raids into Palestine (A.D. 1260 and 1300)." *Journal of the Royal Asiatic Society,* 119/2 (1987), pp. 236–255. (Reprinted in R. Amitai, *The Mongols in the Islamic Lands.* Aldershot, UK, 2007.)

———. "Mamluk Espionage among Mongols and Franks." *Asian and African Studies* (Haifa), 22 (1988), pp. 173–181.

———. "Mongol Imperial Ideology and the Ilkhanid War against the Mamluks." In *The Mongol Empire and Its Legacy,* ed. R. Amitai-Preiss and D. Morgan. Leiden, 1999, pp. 57–72. (Reprinted in R. Amitai, *The Mongols in the Islamic Lands.* Aldershot, UK, 2007.)

———. "Al-Nuwayri as a Historian of the Mongols." In *Historiography of Islamic Egypt (c.950–1800),* ed. Hugh Kennedy. Leiden, 2001, pp. 23–36. (Reprinted in R. Amitai, *The Mongols in the Islamic Lands.* Aldershot, UK, 2007.)

———. "Whither the Ilkhanid Army? Ghazan's First Campaign into Syria (1299–1300)." In *Warfare in Inner Asian History*, ed. N. Di Cosmo. Leiden 2002, pp. 221–264. (Reprinted in R. Amitai, *The Mongols in the Islamic Lands*. Aldershot, UK, 2007.)

———. "The Mongol Occupation of Damascus in 1300: A Study of Mamluk Loyalties." In *The Mamluks in Egyptian and Syrian Politics and Society*, ed. A. Levanoni and M. Winter. Leiden, 2004, pp. 21–41.

———. "The Logistics of the Mongol-Mamlūk War, with Special Reference to the Battle of Wādī al-Khaznadār, 1299 C.E." In *Logistics of War in the Age of the Crusades*, ed. J. H. Pryor. Aldershot, UK, 2006, pp. 25–42.

———. "An Arabic Biographical Notice of Kitbughā, the Mongol General Defeated at ᶜAyn Jālūt." *Jerusalem Studies in Arabic and Islam*, 33 (2007), pp. 219–234.

———. "Mongol Provincial Administration: Syria in 1260 as a Case-Study." In *In Laudem Hierosolymitani: Studies in Crusades and Medieval Culture in Honour of Benjamin Z. Kedar*, ed. I. Shagrir, R. Ellenblum, and J. Riley-Smith. Aldershot, UK, 2007, pp. 117–143.

———. *The Mongols in the Islamic Lands: Studies in the History of the Ilkhanate*. Aldershot, UK, 2007.

———. "*Im Westen Nichts Neues?* Re-examining Hülegü's Offensive into the Jazīra and Northern Syria in Light of Recent Research." In *Historicizing the "Beyond"—The Mongolian Invasion as a New Dimension of Violence?*, ed. F. Krämer, K. Schmidt, and J. Singer. Heidelberg, 2011, pp. 83–96.

———. *Holy War and Rapprochement: Studies in the Relations between the Mamluk Sultanate and the Mongol Ilkhanate (1260–1335)*. Turnhout, 2013.

———. "Hülegü and His Wise Men: Topos or Reality?" In *Tabriz under Mongol and Timurid Rule. Studies in the Cultural and Intellectual History of an Islamicate City (13th—15th Centuries)*, ed. J. Pfeiffer. Leiden, 2014, pp. 15–34.

Amitai, Reuven, and Michal Biran. "Introduction." In *Mongols, Turks and Others: Eurasian Nomads and the Sedentary World*, ed. R. Amitai and M. Biran. Leiden, 2005, pp. 1–14.

———, eds. *Mongols, Turks and Others: Eurasian Nomads and the Sedentary World*. Leiden, 2005.

Amitai-Preiss, Nitzan, and Reuven Amitai-Preiss. "Two Notes on the Protocol on Hülegü's Coinage." *Israel Numismatic Journal*, 10 (1988–1989), pp. 117–128.

Amitai-Preiss, Reuven. "Mamluk Perceptions of the Mongol-Frankish Rapprochement." *Mediterranean Historical Review*, 7 (1992), pp. 50–65. (Reprinted in R. Amitai, *The Mongols in the Islamic Lands*. Aldershot, UK, 2007.)

———. "Arabic Sources for the History of the Mongol Empire." In *The Proceedings of the Sixth International Congress of Mongolists* (Ulaan Baatar, August 11–15, 1992), published in *Mongolica*, 5 [20] (1994), pp. 99–105.

———. *Mongols and Mamluks: The Mamluk-Īlkhānid War, 1260–1281*. Cambridge, 1995.

———. "Northern Syria between the Mongols and Mamluks: Political Boundary, Military Frontier and Ethnic Affinity." In *Frontiers in Question: Eurasian Borderlands c. 700–1700*, ed. N. Standen and D. Power. London, 1999, pp. 128–152. (Reprinted in R. Amitai, *The Mongols in the Islamic Lands*. Aldershot, UK, 2007.)

Anderson, Benedict. *Imagined Communities*. 2nd ed. London, 1991.

Anderson, David, and Christopher Gillam. "Paleoindian Colonization of the Americas: Implications from an Examination of Physiography, Demography, and Artifact Distribution." *American Antiquity*, 65/1 (2000), pp. 43–66.

André, Guilhem. "Une tombe princière Xiongnu à Gol Mod, Mongolie (campagnes de fouilles 2000–2001)." *Artibus Asiae,* 57 (2002), pp. 194–205.
Andronicos, Manolis. "The Royal Tombs of Philip II." *Archaeology,* 31/4 (1978), pp. 33–41.
Anonymous. *Ta'rīkh-i shāhī-i Qarā Khitā'iyyān,* ed. M. I. Būstānī Pārīzī. Tehran, 1355/1976.
Anthony, David. "The Opening of the Eurasian Steppes at 2000 BC." In *The Bronze Age and Early Iron Age Peoples of Eastern Central Asia,* ed. V. Mair. Philadelphia, 1998, pp. 94–113.
Anthony, David W., and N. B. Vinogradov. "Birth of the Chariot." *Archaeology, 48* (1995), pp. 36–41.
Ashkenazi, Tovia. *Les Turkmênes en Palestine.* Tel Aviv, 1930.
Ashtor, Eliyahu. "Mamluks." *Encyclopaedia Judaica,* 1st ed. Jerusalem, 1971–1972, vol. 11, pp. 834–835.
Atalay, Besim. *Divanü lugat-it-turk Dizini. Endeks* [Index to the Compendium of the Dialects of the Turks]. Ankara, 1943.
Atwood, Christopher P. *Encyclopedia of Mongolia and the Mongol Empire.* New York, 2004.
Aubin, Jean. "Un santon quhistani de l'epoque timouride." *Revue des études islamiques,* 35 (1967), pp. 185–216.
———. "L'Ethnogénèse des Qaraunas." *Studia Turcica,* 1 (1969), pp. 65–94.
———. *Emirs, mongols et viziers Persans dans les remous de l'acculturation.* Studia Iranica, Cahier 15. Paris, 1995.
Avanesov, Ruben Ivanovich, ed. *Smolenskie gramoty XIII–XIV vekov* [Smolensk Chronicles of the 13th–14th Centuries]. Moscow, 1963.
ʿAwfī, Muḥammad. *Lubāb al-albāb.* Ed. Muḥammad ʿAbbās. Tehran, 1361/1982. 2 vols.
Ayalon, David. "The Wafidiya in the Mamluk Kingdom." *Islamic Culture,* 25 (1951), pp. 91–104. (Reprinted in D. Ayalon, *Studies on the Mamlūks of Egypt [1250–1517],* London, 1977.)
———. "The European-Asiatic Steppe: A Major Reservoir for Power in the Islamic World." In *Trudy dvadtsat piatogo mezhdunarodnogo kongressa vostokovedov,* vol. 2. Moscow, 1967, pp. 47–52. (Reprinted in D. Ayalon, *The Mamlūk Military Society,* London, 1979.)
———. "The Great Yāsa of Chingiz Khān: A Re-examination." *Studia Islamica,* 33 (1971), pp. 97–140 [A]; 34 (1971), pp. 151–180 [B]; 36 (1972), pp.113–158 [C1]; 38 (1973), pp. 107–156 [C2]. (Reprinted in D. Ayalon, *Outsiders in the Lands of Islam,* London, 1979.)
———. "Preliminary Remarks on the *Mamluk* Military Institution in Islam." In *War, Technology and Society in the Middle East,* ed. V. J. Parry and M. E. Yapp. London, 1975, pp. 44–58. (Reprinted in D. Ayalon, *The Mamlūk Military Society,* London, 1979.)
———. "Egypt as a Dominant Factor in Syria and Palestine during the Islamic Period." In *Egypt and Palestine: A Millennium of Association (868–1948),* ed. A. Cohen and G. Baer. Jerusalem, 1984, pp. 17–47. (Reprinted in D. Ayalon, *Outsiders in the Lands of Islam: Mamluks, Mongols and Eunuchs,* London, 1988).
Āyatī, ʿAbd al-Muḥammad, *Taḥrīr-i tārīkh-i waṣṣāf.* Tehran, 1372/1993.
Ayers, John. "Some Chinese Wares of the Yüan Period." *Transactions of the Oriental Ceramic Society, 1954–1955,* 29 (1957), pp. 69–86.
Badian, V. V. and A. M. Chiperis. "Torgovlia Kaffy v XIII–XIV vv. [The Trade in Kaffa in the 13th–14th Centuries.]" In *Feodal'naia Tavrika* [Feudal Tavrika], ed. S. N. Bibikov. Kiev, 1974, pp. 174–189.

Bagley, Robert W. "Shang Archaeology." In *The Cambridge History of Ancient China,* ed. Michael Loewe and Edward L. Shaughnessy. Cambridge, 1999, pp. 545–586.

Balabanlilar, Lisa. *Imperial Identity in the Mughal Empire: Memory and Dynastic Politics in Early Modern South and Central Asia.* London, 2012.

Ban Gu 班固, comp. *Hanshu* 漢書 [The Official History of the Former Han]. In the collected edition of the Twenty-Four Histories (*Ershisi shi* 二十四史), vol. 2. Beijing, 1997.

Bar Hebraeus. *The Chronography of Gregory Abu'l Faraj.* Tr. Ernest A. Wallis Budge. London, 1932; rpt. Piscataway, NJ, 2003.

Barbieri-Low, Anthony J. "Wheeled Vehicles in the Chinese Bronze Age (c. 2000–741 B.C)." *Sino-Platonic Papers,* 99 (2000), pp. 1–99.

Barfield, Thomas. "The Xiongnu Imperial Confederacy: Organization and Foreign Policy." *Journal of Asian Studies,* 41 (1981), pp. 30–36.

———. "The Shadow Empires: Imperial State Formation along the Chinese-Nomad Frontier." In *Empires: Perspectives from Archaeology and History,* ed. S. E. Alcock, T. N. D'Altroy, K. D. Morrison, and C. M. Sinopol. Cambridge, 2001, pp. 10–41.

———. "Steppe Empires, China, and the Silk Route: Nomads as a Force in International Trade and Politics." In *Nomads in the Sedentary World,* ed. A. M. Khazanov and A. Wink. London, 2001, pp. 234–249.

Barth, Fredrik, ed. *Ethnic Groups and Boundaries.* Boston, 1969.

Baştuğ, Sharon. "Tribe, Confederation and State among Altaic Nomads of the Asian Steppes." In *Rethinking Central Asia,* ed. K. Ertürk. Reading, 1999, pp. 77–110.

Batbold, Natsagyn, B. Jargalan, and M. Tsengel. *Khovd, Bayan-Ulgii aimagt ajillasan kheeriin shinjilgeenii angiin tailan* [Field Research Report on Work Conducted in Khovd and Bayan-Olgii Aimags]. Ulaanbaatar, 2008.

Batsaikhan, Zagd. *Khunnu: arkheologi, ugsaatny zui, tuukh* [The Xiongnu: Archaeology, Ethnography, and History]. Ulaanbaatar, 2003.

Batubaoyin 巴圖寶音, Meng Zhidong 孟誌東, and Du Xinghua 杜興華, eds. *Dawo'er zu yuan yu Qidan lun* 達斡爾族源於契丹論 [On the Dagur's Origin and the Kitans]. Beijing, 2011.

Bauer, Wolfgang, ed. *Studia Sino-Mongolica: Festschrift für Herbert Franke.* Wiesbaden, 1979.

Bayan 伯顏. "Yelü Liuge zhi tiantong jinian 耶律留哥之天統紀年[The Chronological Record of Yelü Liuge's Reign Title, Tiantong]." *Shehui kexue jikan* 社會科學輯刊, 3 (1985), p. 92.

Bayarsaikhan, D. *Mongolian Sculpture.* Ulaanbaatar, 1989.

Baybars al-Manṣūrī. *Zubdat al-fikra fī taʾrīkh al-hijra.* Ed. Donald S. Richards. Beirut, 1998.

Bayḍawī, Nāṣir al-Dīn ʿAbdallāh. *Nature, Man and God in Medieval Islam.* Tr. and ed. Edwin Calverley and James Pollock. Leiden, 2002.

———. *Niẓām al-tawārīkh.* Ed. Mir Hāshim Muḥaddath. Tehran, 1381/2002.

Beck, Horace. *The Beads from Taxila.* Delhi, 1941.

Beckwith, Christopher I. *The Tibetan Empire in Central Asia.* New Jersey, 1987.

———. "Aspects of the Early History of the Central Asian Guard Corps in Islam." *Archivum Eurasiae Medii Aevi,* 4 (1989), pp. 29–43.

———. "The Chinese Names of the Tibetans, Tabghach, and Turks." *Archivum Eurasiae Medii Aevi,* 14 (2005), pp. 5–20.

———. *Empires of the Silk Road: A History of Central Asia from the Bronze Age to the Present.* Princeton, 2009.

Benjamin, Craig. "Hungry for Han Goods: Zhang Qian and the Origins of the Silk Roads." In *History and Society in Central and Inner Asia,* ed. M. Gervers, U. E. Bulag, and G. Long. Toronto, 2007, pp. 3–29.

Berend, Nora. *At the Gates of Christendom: Jews, Muslims and 'Pagans' in Medieval Hungary, c. 1000–c. 1300.* Cambridge, 2001.

Berkey, Jonathan. *The Formation of Islam: Religion and Society in the Near East, 600–1800.* Cambridge, 2003.

Bernard, Paul. "The Greek Kingdoms of Central Asia." In *History of Civilization of Central Asia: The Development of Sedentary and Nomadic Civilizations 700 B.C. to A.D. 250,* ed. J. Harmatta. Paris, 1994, pp. 99–129.

Binyon, Laurence, J. V. S. Wilkinson, and Basil Gray. *Persian Miniature Painting.* London, 1933; rpt. New York, 1971.

Biran, Michal. "The Mongol Transformation: From the Steppe to Eurasian Empire." *Medieval Encounters,* 10/1–3 (2004), pp. 338–361.

———. *The Empire of the Qara Khitai in Eurasian History: Between China and the Islamic World.* Cambridge, 2005.

———. *Chinggis Khan: The Makers of the Islamic World.* Oxford, 2007.

———. "Kitan Migrations in Inner Asia 10th–14th Centuries." *Journal of Central Eurasian Studies,* 3 (2012), pp. 85–108.

———. "The Mongols and the Inter-Civilizational Exchange." In *The Cambridge History of the World,* vol. 5, ed. B. Z. Kedar and M. Wiesner-Hanks. Cambridge, forthcoming.

Birge, Bettine. "Levirate Marriage and the Revival of Widow Chastity in Yuan China." *Asia Major,* 3rd ser., 8 (1995), pp. 107–146.

———. *Women, Property and Confucian Reaction in Sung and Yuan China 960–1368.* Cambridge, 2002.

Blanton, Richard, Gary Feinman, Stephen Kowalewski, and Peter Peregrine. "A Dual-Processual Theory for the Evolution of Mesoamerican Civilization." *Current Anthropology,* 37/1 (1996), pp. 1–14.

de Blois, Francois. "The Iftikhāriyān of Qazvin." In *Iran and Iranian Studies: Essays in Honour of Iraj Afshar,* ed. Kambiz Eslami. Princeton, 1998, pp. 13–23.

Bobrov, V. V., A. S. Vasyutin, and S. A. Vasyutin. "The Onset of the Hunnu Period in the Sayano-Altai." *Archaeology, Ethnology and Anthropology of Eurasia,* 9/1 (2002), pp. 123–130.

Bobrovnikov, Andrei Andreevich. "O mongol'skikh podpisiakh na russkikh aktakh [On the Mongol Signatures on Russian Acts]." *Izvestiia Imperatorskogo Russkogo Arkheologicheskogo obshchestva,* 3 (1861), pp. 19–29.

Bogdanov, E. S. and I. Y. Sljusarenko. "Egyptian Faience Amulets from Gorny Altai." *Archaeology, Ethnology and Anthropology of Eurasia,* 32/4 (2007), pp. 77–80.

Bokovenko, N. A. "Scythians in Siberia." In *Nomads of the Euroasian Steppe in the Early Iron Age,* ed. J. Davis-Kimbal, V. B. Bashilov, and L. T. Yablonsky. Berkeley, 1995, pp. 253–314.

———. "The Origins of Horse Riding and the Development of Ancient Central Asian Nomadic Harness." In *Kurgans, Ritual Sites, and Settlements: Eurasian Bronze and Iron Age,* ed. Jeannine Davis-Kimbal, Eileen M. Murphy, Ludmila Koryakova, and Leonid T. Yablonksy. Oxford, 2000, pp. 304–310.

Bokovenko, N. A., and Iu. A. Zadneprovskii. "Rannie Kochevniki Vostochnogo Kazakhstana" [The Early Nomads of Eastern Kazakhstan]. In *Stepnaia Polosa Aziatskoi*

Chasti SSSR v Skifo-sarmatskoe Vremia [The Steppe Zone of the Asiatic Region of the USSR during the Scythian-Sarmatian Period], ed. N. G. Gorbunova. Moscow, 1992, pp. 140–148.

Boyle, John A. "The Mongol Commanders in Afghanistan and India." *Islamic Studies,* 2 (1963), pp. 235–247.

———. "Dynastic and Political History of the Īl-Khāns." In *The Cambridge History of Iran,* vol. 5., ed. John A. Boyle. Cambridge, 1968, pp. 303–428.

———. "The Il-Khans of Persia and the Christian West." *History Today,* 23/8 (1973), pp. 554–563. (Reprinted in J. A. Boyle, *The Mongol World Empire 1206–1370,* London, 1977.)

Brashinskii, I. B., *Grecheskii keramicheskii import na Nizhnem Donu v V-III vv. do n.e.* [Greek Ceramic Imports to the Area of the Lower Don in the 5th–3rd Centuries BCE]. Leningrad, 1981.

Bratianu, George I. *Recherches sur le commerce génois dans la Mer Noire au XIIIe siècle.* Paris, 1929.

Bretschneider, Emil. *Medieval Researches from Eastern Asiatic Sources.* London, 1967. 2 vols.

Brinner, William. "Some Ayyūbid and Mamlūk Documents from Non-archival Sources." *Israel Oriental Studies,* 2 (1972), pp. 117–143.

Broadbridge, Anne F. *Kingship and Ideology in the Islamic and Mongol Worlds.* Cambridge, 2008.

Brose, Michael C. *Subjects and Masters: Uyghurs in the Mongol Empire.* Bellingham, WA, 2007.

Brosseder, Ursula. "Fremde Frauen in Ivolga?" In *Scripta Praehistorica in Honorem Biba Teržan,* ed. M. Blečić. Ljubljana, 2007, pp. 883–893.

———. "Khunnugiin ueiinkhen, tednii gadaad khariltsaa [The Xiongnu and Their Foreign Relations]." In *Mongolie, les Xiongnu de l'Arkhangai,* ed. J.-P. Desroches and G. André. Ulaanbaatar, 2007, pp. 85–87.

———. "Xiongnu Terrace Tombs and their Interpretation as Elite Burials." In *Current Archaeological Research in Mongolia: Proceedings of the August 2007 Archaeological Symposium in Ulaanbaatar, Mongolia,* ed. J. Bemmann, H. Parzinger, E. Pohl, and D. Tseveendorj. Bonn, 2009, pp. 247–280.

———. "Belt Plaques as an Indicator of East–West Relations in the Eurasian Steppe at the Turn of the Millennia." In *Xiongnu Archaeology: Multidisciplinary Perspectives of the First Steppe Empire in Inner Asia,* ed. U. Brosseder and B. Miller. Bonn, 2011, pp. 349–424.

Brosset, Marie, tr. *Histoire de la Géorgie.* Pt. 1: *Histoire ancienne, jusqu'en 1469 de JC.* St. Petersburg, 1850.

Brown, Peter. *Augustine of Hippo.* London, 1967; 2nd ed., 2000.

Brown, William. *Wen T'ien-hsiang.* San Francisco, 1986.

Browne, Edward G. *A Literary History of Persia,* vol. 3. Cambridge, 1920.

Brumfield, Elizabeth, and Timothy Earle, eds. *Specialization, Exchange, and Complex Societies.* Cambridge, 1987.

Budge, Ernest A. W., tr. *The Monks of Kublai Khan.* London, 1928.

Buell, Paul. "Sino-Khitan Administration in Mongol Bukhara." *Journal of Asian History,* 13 (1979), pp. 121–151.

———. "Saiyid Ajall." In *In the Service of the Khan: Eminent Personalities of the Early Mongol-Yuan Period (1200–1300),* ed. I. de Rachewiltz, Hok-Lam Chan, Ch'i-Ch'ing Hsiao, and Peter W. Geier. Wiesbaden, 1993, pp. 466–479.

———. "Yeh-lü A-hai, Yeh-lü T'u-hua." In *In the Service of the Khan: Eminent Personalities of the Early Mongol-Yuan Period,* ed. I. de Rachewiltz, Hok-Lam Chan, Ch'i-Ch'ing Hsiao, and Peter W. Geier. Wiesbaden, 1993, pp. 112–122.

Buell, Paul, and Eugene Anderson. *A Soup for the Qan.* London, 2000.

Bulliet, Richard. "Medieval Nishapur: A Topographic and Demographic Reconstruction." *Studia Iranica,* 5/1 (1976), pp. 67–89.

Bunker, Emma, Katheryn Linduff, and Wu En, eds. *Ancient Bronzes of the Eastern Eurasian Steppes from the Arthur M. Sackler Collections.* New York, 1997.

Cahen, Claude. *La syrie du nord à l'époque des croisades et la principauté franque d'Antioche.* Paris, 1940.

———. "Dhimma." *Encyclopaedia of Islam,* 2nd ed. Leiden, 1954–2005, vol. 2, pp. 234–237.

———. "ʿAbdallaṭīf al-Baghdādī et les Khwārizmiens." In *Iran and Islam: In Memory of the Late Vladimir Minorsky,* ed. Clifford E. Bosworth. Edinburgh, 1971, pp. 149–166.

———. *L'Islam des origines au début de l'empire Ottoman.* Paris, 1995.

Cahill, James. *Hills beyond a River: Chinese Painting of the Yüan Dynasty, 1279–1368.* New York, 1976.

Cai, Meibiao 蔡美彪. "Jiu yu Jiujun zhi yanbian 乣與乣軍之演變 [The Transformations of the Jiu and the Jiu Army]." *Yuanshi Luncong* 元史論叢, 2 (1983), pp. 1–22.

Cang, Xiuliang 倉修良, ed. *Zhongguo shixue mingzhu pingjie* 中國史學名著評介 [Review of Famous Works of Chinese Historiography]. Jinan, 1990. 3 vols.

Chamberlain, Michael. *Knowledge and Social Practice in Medieval Damascus, 1190–1350.* Cambridge, 1994.

Chan, Hok-lam. "Chinese Refugees in Annam and Champa at the End of the Sung Dynasty." *Journal of Southeast Asian History,* 7/2 (1966), pp. 1–10.

Chang, Chun-shu. *The Rise of the Chinese Empire: Nation, State, and Imperialism in Early China, ca. 1600 B.C.–A.D. 8.* Ann Arbor, MI, 2007.

Chang, E., Ywangbo Ch., and Yoon S. "Archaeological Research on Xiognu Tombs of Duurlig Nars, Mongolia." In *Xiongnu: The First Empire of the Steppes,* ed. E. Chang. Seoul, 2007, pp. 214–231.

Chang, Kuan-pin. "Li K'an and a Revival of Bamboo Painting in the Style of Wen Kung." *National Palace Museum Bulletin,* 13/5 (November–December, 1978), pp. 2–6.

Chang, Kwang-chih. *The Archaeology of Ancient China,* 4th ed. New Haven, CT, 1986.

Chang, Yüan-chien. "Jen Ch'i Tu and the Horse and Figure Painting of Chao Meng-fu." *National Palace Museum Bulletin,* 17/3–4 (July–October, 1982), pp. 2–12.

Chavannes, Edouard. *Documents sur les Tou-Kiue (Turcs) Occidentaux.* Paris, 1903–1941.

Chekhovich, Olga D., tr. *Bukharskie dokumenty XIV veka* [Documents of Bukhara from the 14th Century]. Tashkent, 1965.

Chen, Gaohua 陳高華. *Yuandai huajia shike* 元代畫家史料 [Historical Sources on Yuan Dynasty's Artists]. Shanghai, 1980.

Chen, Lü 陳旅. *An ya tang ji* 安雅堂集 [Chen Lü's Literary Collection]. Siku quanshu ed.

Chen, Shisong 陳世鬆. "Yuandai Qidan 'Shishu mingjiang' Shulü Jie shiji 元代契丹詩書名將述律傑事輯 [Summary of the Life of Shulü Jie, a Famous Kitan Poet and Writer of the Yuan Dynasty]." *Ningxia shehui kexue* 寧夏社會科學, 2 (1996), pp. 80–86, 79.

Chen, Shu 陳述. "Da Liao wajie yihou de Qidan ren 大遼瓦解以後的契丹人 [The Kitans after the Dissolution of the Great Liao]." *Liao Jin shi lunji* 遼金史論集, 1 (1987), pp. 297–323.

Ch'en, Yuan. *Western and Central Asians in China under the Mongols.* Tr. and ed. Ch'ien Hsinghai and L. Carrington Goodrich. Los Angeles, 1966.

Cheng, Te-k'un. "Some New Discoveries in Prehistoric and Shang China." In *Ancient China: Studies in Early Civilization*, ed. D. T. Roy and Tsuen-hsuin Tsien. Hong Kong, 1978, pp. 1–12.

Cherepnin, L. V., ed. *Pamiatniki russkogo prava*. Vyp. 3, *Pamiatniki prava perioda obrasovaniia Russkogo tsentralizovannogo gosudartsva: XIV–XV vv.* [Monuments of Russian Law: Third Release, Monuments of the Law of the Formative Period of Russian Centralized State: The 14th–15th Centuries]. Moscow, 1955.

Cherniavsky, Michael. "Khan or Basileus: An Aspect of Russian Mediaeval Political Theory." *Journal of the History of Ideas*, 20 (1959), pp. 459–476. (Reprinted in M. Cherniavsky, ed., *The Structure of Russian History*, New York, 1970, pp. 65–79.)

Chernykh, Evgeny N. *Ancient Metallurgy in the USSR: The Early Metal Age*. Cambridge, 1992.

Chernykh, Evgeny, Evgeny V. Kuz'minykh, and L. B. Orlovskaia. "Ancient Metallurgy of Northeast Asia from the Urals to the Saiano-Altai." In *Metallurgy in Ancient Eastern Eurasia from the Urals to the Yellow River*, ed. K. M. Linduff. Lewiston, NY, 2004, pp. 15–36.

Chiang I-han. "A Calligraphic Handscroll by Chao Meng-fu (1254–1322)." *National Palace Museum Bulletin*, 10/3 (July–August, 1975), pp. 1–10.

Chikisheva, T. A., N. V. Polosmak, and P. V. Volkov. "Dental Remains from Mound 20 at Noin Ula, Mongolia." *Archaeology Ethnology & Anthropology of Eurasia*, 37 (2009), pp. 145–151.

Chikisheva, T. A., and D. V. Pozdnyakov. "Physical Anthropology of the Gorny Altai Populations in the Hunno-Sarmatian Period." *Archaeology, Ethnology and Anthropology of Eurasia*, 3/3 (2000), pp. 116–131.

Chittick, William, and Peter Wilson. *Fakhruddin 'Iraqi: Divine Flashes*. New York, 1982.

Chochorowskii, Jan. "Die Frage der skythischen Expansion auf das Gebiet des Karpatenbeckens." *Acta Archaeologica Carpathica*, 15 (1975), pp. 5–30.

———. "Die Rolle der Vekeryug-Kultur (VK) im skythische Einflüsse." *Mitteleuropa. Praehistorische Zeitschrift*, 60 (1985), pp. 230–271.

———. *Ekspansja Kimmeryjska na Tereny Evropy Srodkowej* [The Khimmerian Expansion into Central Europe]. Krakow, 1993.

———. "Skifskie nabegi na territorii Srednei Evropy [Scythian Invasions to Central Europe]." *Rossiiskaia Arkheologiia*, 4 (1994), pp. 49–64.

Chŏng, In-ji 鄭麟趾. *Gaoli shi (Koryŏsa)* 高麗史 [History of Korea]. Seoul, 1990.

Christian, David. "Inner Eurasia as a Unit of World History." *Journal of World History*, 5 (1994), pp. 173–211.

———. "Silk Roads or Steppe Roads? The Silk Roads in World History." *Journal of World History*, 11/1 (2000), pp. 1–26.

Chugunov, Konstantin, Hermann Parzinger, and Anatoly Nagler. "Arzhan 2: la tombe d'un prince scythe en Sibérie du Sud. Rapport préliminaire des fouilles russo-allemandes de 2000–2002." *Arts Asiatiques*, 59 (2004), pp. 5–29.

Ciarla, Roberto. "Rethinking Yuanlongpo: The Case for Technological Links between the Lingnan (PRC) and Central Thailand in the Bronze Age." *East and West*, 57 (2007), pp. 305–330.

Clauson, Gerard. *An Etymological Dictionary of Pre-Thirteenth-Century Turkish*. London, 1972.

Clavijo, Ruy Gonzalez de. *Embassy to Tamerlane, 1403–1406*. Tr. Guy Le Strange. London, 1928.

Cleaves, Francis Woodman. "The Sino-Mongolian Inscription in Memory of Chang Ying-rui." *Harvard Journal of Asiatic Studies,* 13 (1950), pp. 1–131.
———, tr. *The Secret History of the Mongols.* Cambridge, MA, 1982.
Collins, Leslie J. D. "On the Alleged 'Destruction' of the Great Horde in 1502." In *Manzikert to Lepanto: The Byzantine World and the Turks 1071–1571* (special issue of *Byzantinische Forschungen*), ed. A. Bryer and M. Ursinus. Amsterdam, 1991, pp. 361–399.
Combe, Etienne, Jean Sauvaget, and Gaston Wiet, eds. *Répertoire chronologique de l'épigraphie arabe,* vol. 12. Cairo, 1943.
Commeaux, Charles. *La vie quotidienne chez les Mongols de la conquête (XIIIe siècle).* Paris, 1972.
Crawford, Gary W. "East Asian Plant Domestication." In *Archaeology of Asia,* ed. M. T. Stark. Malden, MA, 2006, pp. 77–95.
Cross, Samuel Hazard, and Olgerd P. Sherbowitz-Wetzor, tr. *The Russian Primary Chronicle.* Cambridge, MA, 1973.
Crossley, Pamela Kyle. *A Translucent Mirror: History and Identity in Qing Imperial Ideology.* Berkeley, 1999.
———. "Outside In: Power, Identity and the Han Lineage of Jizhou." In *Perspectives on the Liao,* ed. V. Hansen and F. Louis. New Haven, CT, 2010, pp. 121–155.
Crowe, Yolanda. "Late Thirteenth-Century Persian Tilework and Chinese Textiles." *Bulletin of the Asia Institute,* 5 (1991), pp. 153–161.
Danilov, Sergei V., and Natal'ia V. Tsydenova. "Ceramic Roof Tiles from Terelzhiin Dorvolzhin." In *Xiongnu Archaeology: Multidisciplinary Persepctives of the First Steppe Empire in Inner Asia,* ed. U. Brosseder and B. Miller. Bonn, 2011, pp. 341–348.
Dankoff, Robert, and James Kelly, trs. *Compendium of the Turkic Dialects (Dīwān lughāt al-Turk),* by Maḥmūd al-Kāshgharī. Cambridge, MA, 1982. 3 vols.
Dardess, John W. *Conquerors and Confucians: Aspects of Political Change in Late Yuan China.* New York, 1973.
———. *Confucianism and Autocracy.* Berkeley, 1983.
Davydova, Antonina V. *Ivolginskii arkheologicheskii kompleks: Ivolginskoe gorodishche* [Ivolga Archaeological Complex: The Ivolga Fortified Settlement]. St. Petersburg, 1995.
———. *Ivolginskii arkheologicheskii kompleks: Ivolginskii mogil'nik* [Ivolga Archaeological Complex: The Ivolga Cemetery]. St. Petersburg, 1996.
Debaine-Francfort, Corinne. "Archéologie du Xinjiang des origines aux Han: IIème partie." *Paleorient,* 15/1 (1989), pp. 183–213.
DeWeese, Devin. "Cultural Transmission and Exchange in the Mongol Empire: Notes from the Biographical Dictionary of Ibn al-Fuwaṭī." In *Beyond the Legacy of Genghis Khan,* ed. L. Komaroff. Leiden, 2006, pp. 11–29.
———. "Stuck in the Throat of Chingīz Khan: Envisioning the Mongol Conquests in Some Sufi Accounts from the 14th to 17th Centuries." In *History and Historiography of Post-Mongol Central Asia and the Middle East: Studies in Honor of John E, Woods,* ed. J. Pfeiffer and S.A. Quinn. Wiesbaden, 2006, pp. 23–60.
Dewey, Horace W. "Political *Poruka* in Muscovite Rus'." *Russian Review,* 46 (1987), pp. 117–133.
———. "Russia's Debt to the Mongols in Suretyship and Collective Responsibility." *Comparative Studies in Society and History,* 30 (1988), pp. 249–270.
Dewey, Horace W., and Ann M. Kleimola. "Suretyship and Collective Responsibility in Pre-Petrine Russia." *Jahrbücher für Geschichte Osteuropas,* 18 (1970), pp. 337–354.

———. "Coercion by Righter (*Pravezh*) in Old Russian Administration." *Canadian-American Slavic Studies,* 9 (1975), pp. 156–167.

———. "From the Kinship Group to Every Man His Brother's Keeper: Collective Responsibility in Pre-Petrine Russia." *Jahrbücher für Geschichte Osteuropas,* 30 (1982), pp. 321–335.

———. "Russian Collective Consciousness: The Kievan Roots." *Slavonic and East European Review,* 62 (1982), pp. 181–182.

al-Dhahabī, Shams al-Dīn Muḥammad b. Aḥmad. *Taʾrīkh al-islām wa-wafayāt al-mashāhīr waʾl-aʿlām.* Beirut, 1401/1981–1424/2004.

Di Cosmo, Nicola. "Ancient Inner Asian Nomads: Their Economic Basis and Its Significance in Chinese History." *Journal of Asian Studies,* 53/4 (1994), pp. 1092–1126.

———. "State Formation and Periodization in Inner Asian History." *Journal of World History,* 10 (1999), pp. 1–40.

———. *Ancient China and Its Enemies: The Rise of Nomadic Power in East Asian History.* Cambridge, 2002.

Diakonoff, Igor M. "Cimmerians." *Acta Iranica,* 21 (1981), pp. 103–140.

———. "Kimmeriitsy i skify na Blizhnem Vostoke [Cimmerians and Scythians in the Near East]." *Rossiiskaia Arkheologiia,* 1 (1994), pp. 108–116.

Dietz, Ute Luise. "Horseback Riding: Man's Access to Speed?" In *Prehistoric Steppe Adaptation and the Horse,* ed. M. Levine, C. Renfrew, and K. Boyle. Cambridge, 2003, pp. 189–199.

Diodorus Siculus. *Library of History.* Tr. C. H. Oldfather. Cambridge, MA, 2000.

Dobrovits, Mihaly. "The Thirty Tribes of the Turks." *Acta Orientalia Hungarica,* 57 (2004), pp. 257–262.

Doerfer, Gerhard. *Türkische und mongolische Elemente im Neupersischen.* Wiesbaden, 1963–1975. 4 vols.

D'Ohsson, Abraham C. M. *Histoire des Mongols.* The Hague, 1834–1835. 4 vols.; rpt. Tientsin, China, 1940.

Dols, Michael W. *The Black Death in the Middle East.* Princeton, 1977.

Dorjsuren, Ts. "Kharaagiin Noyon Uuland 1954 ond arkheologiin shinjilgee khiisen tukhai" [On the 1954 Archaeological Research at Kharaa Noyon Uul]. *Shinjlekh ukhaan setguu,* 4 (1954), pp. 33–42.

———. *Umard Khunnu* [The Northern Khunnu]. Ulaanbaatar, 1961.

Drompp, Michael. "Imperial State Formation in Inner Asia: The Early Turkic Empires (6th to 9th Centuries)." *Acta Orientalia Academiae Scientiarum Hungaricae,* 58/1 (2005), pp. 101–111.

———. "The Lone Wolf in Inner Asia." *Journal of the American Oriental Society,* 131 (2011), pp. 515–526.

Du, You 杜佑. *Tongdian* 通典 [Comprehensive Institutions]. Beijing, 1988.

Dubin, Lois. *The History of Beads from 30,000 BC to the Present.* London, 2009.

Duman, L. I. "Rasseleniie nekitajskikh plemen vo vnutrennikh rajonakh Kitaiia i ikh sotsial'noe ustrojstvo v III–IV vv. n.e [Dispersion of Non-Chinese Tribes in the Inner Areas of China and Their Social Organization in the 3rd–4th Centuries CE]." In *Kitaj: Istoriia, Kultura i Istoriografiia,* ed. N. Z. Munkuev. Moscow, 1977, pp. 40–61.

Dunlop, Douglas M. "Al-Dimashḳī, Shams al-Dīn Abū ʿAbd Allāh." *Encyclopaedia of Islam,* 2nd ed. Leiden, 1954–2005, vol. 2, p. 291.

Dunnell, Ruth. "The Fall of the Xia Empire: Sino-Steppe Relations in the Late 12th–Early 13th Century." In *Rulers from the Steppe,* ed. G. Seaman and D. Marks. Los Angeles, 1991, pp. 158–180.

Dussubieux, Laure, and Bernard Gratuze. "Nature et origine des objets en verre retrouvés à Begram (Afghanistan) et à Bara (Pakistan)." In *De l'Indus à l'Oxus. Archéologie de l'Asie Centrale,* ed. O. Bopearachchi, C. Landes, and C. Sachs. Lattes, 2003, pp. 315–323.

Eaton, Michael D., D. L. Evans, D. R. Hodgson, and R. J. Rose. "Effect of Treadmill Incline and Speed on Metabolic Rate during Exercise in Thoroughbred Horses." *Journal of Applied Physiology,* 79 (1995), pp. 951–957.

Ebrey, Patricia. "Surnames and Han Chinese Identity." In *Negotiating Ethnicities in China and Taiwan,* ed. M. J. Brown. Berkeley, 1995, pp. 11–36.

Ecsedy, Hilda. "Tribe and Tribal Society in the 6th Century Turk Empire." *Acta Orientalia Hungarica,* 25 (1972), pp. 245–262.

———. "A Contribution to the History of Karluks in the T'ang Period." *Acta Orientalia Hungaricae,* 34 (1980), pp. 23–37.

Egorov, V. "Kabal'nye den'gi v kontse XVI veka [The Kabala Payments in the End of the 16th Century]." *Zhurnal Ministerstva narodnogo prosveshcheniia,* 28 (1910), pp. 49–65.

Elias, Jamal J. *The Throne Carrier of God.* New York, 1995.

Ellenblum, Ronnie. "Settlement and Society Formation in Crusader Palestine." In *The Archaeology of Society in the Holy Land,* ed. T. E. Levy. Leicester, 1995, pp. 502–511.

Elliot, Mark C. *The Manchu Way: The Eight Banners and Ethnic Identity in Late Imperial China.* Stanford, 2001.

———. "Hushuo: The Northern Other and the Naming of the Han Chinese." In *Critical Han Studies: The History, Representation and Identity of China's Majority,* ed. T. S. Mullaney, James Leibold, Stephane Gros, and Eric Vanden Bussche. Berkeley, 2012, pp. 173–190.

Endicott-West, Elizabeth. *Mongolian Rule in China: Local Administration in the Yüan Dynasty.* Cambridge, MA, 1989.

Enoki, Kazuo. "On the Relationship between the Shih-chi, Bk. 123 and the Han-shu, Bks. 61 and 96." *Memoirs of the Research Departement of Toyo Bunko,* 41 (1983), pp. 1–31.

Erdenebaatar, Diimaazhav, Ch. Erööl-Erdene, N. Batbold, A. Frantsis, and B. Miller. "Umard Khunnugiin yazguurtny bulshny sudalgaa [Research on the Noble Graves of the Northern Khunnu]." *Tuukhiin Sudlal,* 33 (2002), pp. 20–28.

Erdenebaatar, Diimaazhav, T. O. Iderkhangai, B. Galbadrakh, E. Minzhiddorzh, and S. Orgilbaiar. "Excavations of Satellite Burial 30, Tomb 1 Complex, Gol Mod 2 Necropolis." In *Xiongnu Archaeology: Multidisciplinary Persepctives of the First Steppe Empire in Inner Asia,* ed. U. Brosseder and B. Miller. Bonn, 2011, pp. 303–314.

Evans, Bergen. *Dictionary of Quotations.* New York, 1968.

von Falkenhausen, Lothar. "The Regionalist Paradigm in Chinese Archaeology." In *Nationalism, Politics, and the Practice of Archaeology,* ed. Philip L. Kohl and Clare Fawcett. Cambridge, 1995, pp. 198–217.

———. "Some Reflections on Sanxingdui." In *Regional Culture, Religion and Arts before the Seventh Century: Papers from the Third International Conference on Sinology.* Taipei, 2002, pp. 59–97.

———. "The External Connections of Sanxingdui." *Journal of East Asian Archaeology,* 5 (2003), pp. 191–245.

Fan, Ye 範曄, comp. *Hou Hanshu* 後漢書 (The Official History of the Later Han). In the collected edition of the Twenty-Four Histories (*Ershisi shi* 二十四史), vol 3. Beijing, 1997.

Fang, Linggui 方齡貴. "Yuan Shulü Jie shiji jikao 元述律傑事跡輯考 [Research on the Deadsof Shulü Jie of the Yuan]." *Yuanshi Congkao* 元史叢考, 2004, pp. 247–274.

———. "Yuan Shulü Jie jiaoyou kaolüe 元述律傑交游考略 [Research on the Associations of Shulü Jie of the Yuan]." In *Mengyuanshi ji Minzushi Lunji* 蒙元史暨民族史論 集, ed. Hao Shiyuan 郝時遠 and Luo Xianyou 羅賢佑. Beijing, 2006, pp. 242–268.

Fang, Xuanling et al., eds. 房玄齡等. *Jinshu* 晉書 [The Official History of the Jin]. In the collected edition of the Twenty-Four Histories [*Ershisi shi* 二十四史], vol. 4. Beijing, 1997.

Farquhar, David. *The Government of China under Mongolian Rule: A Reference Guide.* Stuttgart, 1990.

Fasmer, M. *Ėtimologicheskii slovar' russkogo iazyka,* I–IV [Etymological Dictionary of the Russian Language, vols. 1–4]. 2nd, stereotyped ed. Moscow, 1986–1987.

Fedorov, Ia. A. *Istoricheskaia etnografiia Severnogo Kavkaza* [Historical Ethnography of the Northern Caucasus]. Moscow, 1982.

Fedorov, Ia. A., and G. S. Fedorova. *Rannie tiurki na Severnom Kavkaze* [The Early Turks in the Northern Caucasus]. Moscow, 1978.

Feng Jiqin 馮繼欽. "Jin Yuan shiqi Qidan ren xing ming yanjiu 金元時期契丹人姓名研究 [Study of the Names That the Kitans Adopted in Jin and Yuan Periods]." *Heilongjiang minzu congkan* 黑龍江民族叢刊, 4 (1992), pp. 106–110.

———. "Cong zhanji he guanzhi kan Qidan ren zai Mengyuan shiqi de fenbu 從戰跡和官職看契丹人在蒙元時期的分布 [On the Distribution of the Kitans according to Their Records in War and Their Official Positions]." *Beifang Wenwu* 北方文物, 42 (1995), pp. 64–70.

Feng Jiqin 馮繼欽, et al. *Qidan zu wenhua shi* 契丹族文化史 [A Cultural History of the Kitan Ethnicity]. Heilongjiang, 1994.

Fiey, Jean M. *Chrétiens syriaques sous les mongols (Il-khanat de Perse, XIIIe–XIVe).* Louvain, 1975.

Fine, John V. A., Jr. *The Late Medieval Balkans.* Ann Arbor, MI, 1987.

Fischel, Walter. *Jews in the Economic and Political Life of Mediaeval Islam.* London, 1937.

Fiskesjö, Magnus, and Chen Xingcan. *China before China: Johan Gunnar Andersson, Ding Wenjiang and the Discovery of China's Prehistory.* Stockholm Museum of Eastern Antiquities, 2004.

Fitzgerald-Huber, Louisa. "Qijia and Erlitou: The Question of Contacts with Distant Cultures." *Early China,* 20 (1995), pp. 17–68.

Flad, Rowan K. "Divination and Power: A Multiregional View of the Development of Oracle Bone Divination in Early China." *Current Anthropology,* 49 (2008), pp. 403–437.

Fletcher, Joseph. "The Mongols: Ecological and Social Perspectives." *Harvard Journal of Asiatic Studies,* 46 (1986), pp. 11–50.

———. *Studies on Chinese and Islamic Inner Asia.* Ed. B. F. Manz. Aldershot, UK, 1995.

Fong, Wen. "Images of the Mind." In *Images of the Mind,* ed. Wen Fong. Princeton, 1984, pp. 94–102.

Foon, Ming L. *Tuntian Farming of the Ming Dynasty (1368–1644).* Hamburg, 1984.

Frachetti, Michael. *Pastoralist Landscapes and Social Interaction in Bronze Age Eurasia.* Berkeley, 2008.

Frank, Andre Gunder. *The Centrality of Central Asia.* Amsterdam, 1992.

Franke, Herbert. "Europa in der ostasiatischen Geschichtsschreibung des 13. und 14. Jahrhunderts." *Saeculum,* 2 (1951), pp. 65–75.

———. ed. *Sung Biographies: Painters.* Wiesbaden, 1976.

———. "The Role of the State as Structural Element in Polytechnic Societies." In *Foundations and Limits of State Power in China,* ed. S. R. Schram. London, 1987, pp. 87–112.

———. "The Forest People of Manchuria: Kitans and Jurchens." In *The Cambridge History of Early Inner Asia,* ed. D. Sinor. Cambridge, 1990, pp. 400–423.

———. "The Chin Dynasty." In *The Cambridge History of China,* vol. 6, ed. H. Franke and D. Twitchett. Cambridge, 1994, pp. 215–320.

———. "Consecration of the 'White Stūpa' in 1279." *Asia Major,* 3rd ser., 7/1 (1994), pp. 155–181.

Frenkel, Yehoshua. "Baybars and the Sacred Geography of Bilad al-Sham: A Chapter in the Islamization of Syria's Landscape." *Jerusalem Studies in Arabic and Islam,* 25 (2001), pp. 153–170.

Fu Shen 傅申. "Nücang jia huangzi dazhang gongzhu: Yuandai huangshi shuhua shoucang shilue 女藏家皇姊大長公主—元代皇室書畫收藏史略 [The Collection of the Princess Sengge Ragi: A Short History of the Painting and Calligraphy Collections of the Yuan Imperial Family]." *Gugong Jikan* 故宮季刊, 1/3 (1978), pp. 25–51.

Funada, Yoshiyuki 舩田善之. "Semuren yu Yuan dai zhidu, shehui- Zhongxin tantao Menggu, Semu, Hanren, Nanren huafen de zhiwei 色目人與元代制度、社會—重新探討蒙古、色目、漢人、南人劃分的位置 [The Semu People and the System of Society in the Yuan: Re-examining the Classification of the Mongols, Semu, Hanren, and Nanren]." *Yuanshi luncong* 元史論叢, 9 (2004), pp. 162–174.

Galibin, V. A. "Osobennosti sostava stekliannykh bus ivolginskogo mogil'nika khunnu [Characteristics of the Composition of Glass Beads from the Ivolga Cemetery of the Xiongnu]." In *Drevnee Zabaikal'e i ego kul'turnye sviazi* [Ancient Trans-Baikal and Its Cultural Connections], ed. P. B. Konovalov. Novosibirsk, 1985, pp. 46–50.

Galstian, A. G., tr. *Armianskie istochniki o mongolakh* [Armenian Historians on the Mongols]. Moscow, 1962.

Gandzaketsi, Kirakos. *Istoriia Armenii* [History of Armenia]. Tr. L. A. Khanlarian. Moscow, 1976.

Gernet, Franz. "Maracanda/Samarkand, une métropole pré-mongole: Sources écrites et archéologie." *Annales. Histoire, Sciences Sociales,* 59/5–6 (September–December, 2004), pp. 1043–1064.

Giele, Enno. "Evidence for the Xiongnu in Chinese Wooden Documents from the Han Period." In *Xiongnu Archaeology: Multidisciplinary Perspectives of the First Steppe Empire in Inner Asia,* ed. Ursula Brosseder and Byran Miller. Bonn, 2011, pp. 49–76.

Giles, Herbert A. *A Chinese-English Dictionary.* New York, 1964.

Giraud, René. *L'empire des Turcs celestes.* Paris, 1960.

———. *Göktürk İmparatorluğu. İlteriş, Kapgan ve Bilge Hükümdarlıkları (680–734)* [The Empire of the Göktürk: The Reigns of İlteriş, Kapgan, and Bilge (680–734)]. Istanbul, 1999.

Göckenjan, Hansgerd, and James R. Sweeny, tr. *Der Mongolensturm: Berichte von Augenzeugen und Zeitgenossen, 1235–1250.* Vienna, 1985.
Golden, Peter. B. "The Migrations of the Oguz." *Archivum Ottomanicum,* 4 (1972), pp. 45–84.
———. "Imperial Ideology and the Sources of Political Unity amongst the Pre-Cinggisid Nomads of Western Eurasia." *Archivum Eurasiae Medii Aevi,* 2 (1982), pp. 37–76.
———. "Turkic Calques in Medieval Eastern Slavic." *Journal of Turkic Studies,* 8 (*Turks, Hungarians and Kipchaks. A Festschrift in Honor of Tibor Halasi-Kun*). Cambridge, MA, 1984), pp. 103–111.
———. "The Qipchaqs of Medieval Eurasia: An Example of Stateless Adaption in the Steppe." In *Rulers from the Steppe: State Formation on the Eurasian Periphery,* ed. G. Seaman. Los Angeles, 1991, pp. 132–157.
———. *An Introduction to the History of the Turkic Peoples.* Wiesbaden, 1992.
———. "'I will give the people unto thee': The Chinggisid Conquests and Their Aftermath in the Turkic World." *Journal of the Royal Asiatic Society,* 3rd ser., 10/1 (2000), pp. 21–41.
———. *Ethnicity and State Formation in Pre-Činggisid Turkic Eurasia.* The Central Eurasian Studies Lecture. Bloomington, IN, 2001.
———. "The Terminology of Slavery and Servitude in Medieval Turkic." In *Studies in Central Asian History in Honor of Yuri Bregel,* ed. D. DeWeese. Bloomington, IN, 2001, pp. 27–56.
———. "Khazar Turkic Ghulams in Caliphal Service." *Journal Asiatique,* 292 (2004), pp. 279–309.
———. "Irano-Turcica: The Khazar Sacral Kingship Revisited." *Acta Orientalia Hungaricae,* 60 (2007), pp. 161–194.
Good, Irene. "On the Question of Silk in Pre-Han Eurasia." *Antiquity,* 69/266 (1995), pp. 959–968.
Good, Irene, J. Mark Kenoyer, and Richard H. Meadow. "New Evidence for Early Silk in the Indus Civilization." *Archaeometry,* 50/3 (2009), pp. 457–466.
Gorbunova, Nataliya G. "Traditional Movements of Nomadic Pastoralists and the Role of Seasonal Migrations in the Formation of Ancient Trade Routes in Central Asia." *Silk Road Art and Archaeology,* 3 (1993/1994), pp. 1–10.
Gottheil, Richard. "An Answer to the Dhimmis." *Journal of the American Oriental Society,* 41 (1921), pp. 383–457.
Grabar, Oleg, and Sheila Blair. *Epic Images and Contemporary History.* Chicago, 1980.
Grantovskii, E. A., Pogrebova, M. N. and D. S Raevskii. "Kimmeriitsy na Blizhnem Vostoke [Cimmerians in the Middle East]." *Vestnik drevnei istorii,* 4 (1996), pp. 69–85.
Gray, Basil. *Persian Painting.* Geneva, 1961.
Grekov, B. D., ed. *Sudebniki XV–XVI vekov* [Law Codes (*Sudebniks*) of the 15th–16th Centuries]. Moscow, 1952.
Grenet, Franz, and Muhammedjan Isamiddinov. "La prise de Samarcande par Gengis-Khan." *L'Histoire,* 149 (1991), pp. 8–14.
Grigor'ev, A. P. "Oficial'nyi iazyk Zolotoi Ordy XIII–XIV vv. [The Official Language of the Golden Horde in the 13th–14th Centuries]." In *Tiurkologicheskii Sbornik,* 1977 (Moscow, 1981), pp. 81–89.
———. *Sbornik khanskikh iarlykov russkim mitropolitom* [Collection of the Khan's *Yarliks* Given to the Russian Metropolitans]. St. Petersburg, 2004.

Grudzinska Gross, Irena. *The Scar of Revolution: Custine, Tocqueville, and the Romantic Imagination.* Berkeley, 1991.

Guliaev, V. I., and E. N. Savchenko. "K voprosu o roli zolota v pogrebal'nom ritual skifov [On the Role of Gold in the Burial Ritual of the Scythians]." In *Evraziiskie drevnosti,* ed. A. I. Melyukova, M. G. Moshkova, and V. A. Bashilov. Moscow, 1999, pp. 151–157.

Gumilev, Lev. N. *Drevnie tiurki* [The Ancient Turks]. Moscow, 1967.

———. *Eski Türkler* [The Ancient Turks]. Istanbul, 1999.

Guo, Baojun 郭宝钧. *Yinzhou cheqi yanjiu* 殷周车器研究 [Research on Shang and Zhou Chariot Equipment]. Beijing, 1998.

Guo, Dashun. "Northern Type Bronze Artifacts Unearthed in the Liaoning Region, and Related Issues." In *The Archaeology of Northeast China,* ed. S. M. Nelson. London, 1995, pp. 182–205.

Guo, Li. *Early Mamluk Syrian Historiography: al-Yūnīnī's Dhayl Mir'āt al-zamān.* Leiden, 1998. 2 vols.

———. *The Performing Arts in Medieval Islam: Shadow Play and Popular Poetry in Ibn Dāniyāl's Mamluk Cairo.* Leiden, 2012.

Guo, Xiaohang 郭曉航. "Yuan dai shouren Shanghhai xian Daluhuazhi Shelafuding kaoshi 元代首任"上海縣达魯花赤"舍剌甫丁考釋 [The Study and Interpretation of the First Shanghai Da- lu- hua- chi She- la- fu- ding in the Yuan Dynasty]." *Shi Lin* 史林 *Historical Review,* 4 (2007), pp. 185–188.

Gurliand, Ilya A. *Iamskaia gon'ba v Moskovskom gosudarstve do kontsa XVII veka* [The Imperial Russian Post-horse Relay System in the Moscovite State up to the End of the 18th Century]. Yaaroslav, 1900.

Haenisch, Erich. *Wörterbuch zu Manghol un Niuca Tobca'an (Yuan-ch'ao pi-shi). Geheime Geschichte der Mongolen.* Wiesbaden, 1962.

Ḥāfiẓ-i Abrū. *Dhayl jāmiʿ al-tawārīkh-i rashīdī.* Ed. Khānbābā Bayānī. Tehran, 1350/1971.

Hahn, Istvan. "Foreign Trade and Foreign Policy in Archaic Greece." In *Trade and Famine in Classical Antiquity,* ed. P. Garnsey and C. R. Whittaker. Cambridge, 1983, pp. 30–36.

Halasi-Kun, Tibor. "Ottoman Data on Lesser Cumania." *Archivum Eurasiae Medii Aevi,* 4 (1984), pp. 92–124.

Hall, Mark, and Sergei Minyaev. "Chemical Analyses of Xiongnu Pottery: A Preliminary Study of Exchange and Trade on the Inner Asian Steppes." *Journal of Archaeological Science,* 29 (2002), pp. 135–144.

Hall, Mark E. "Towards an Absolute Chronology of the Iron Age of Inner Asia." *Antiquity,* 71 (1997), pp. 863–874.

Halperin, Charles J. "Medieval Myopia and the Mongol Period of Russian History." *Russian History,* 5 (1978), pp. 188–191.

———. "Soviet Historiography on Russia and the Mongols." *Russian Review,* 41 (1982), pp. 306–322.

———. "Russia in the Mongol Empire in Comparative Perspective," *Harvard Journal of Asiatic Studies,* 43 (1983), pp. 239–261.

———. *Russia and the Golden Horde: The Mongol Impact on Medieval Russian History.* Bloomington, IN, 1985.

———. *The Tatar Yoke.* Columbus, OH, 1986.

Hambis, Louis, tr. *Le chapitre CVIII du Yuan Che.* Leiden, 1954.

———. “Note sur l’installation des Mongols dans la Boucle du Fleuve Jaune.” In *Mongolian Studies,* ed. L. Ligeti. Amsterdam, 1970, pp. 167–179.
Hansen, Valery, and Francis Louis, eds. *Perspectives on the Liao.* New Haven, CT, 2010.
al-Harawī, Sayf b. Muḥammad b. Yaʿqūb. *Taʾrīkh-nāmah-i harāt.* Ed. M. Ṣiddiqi. Calcutta, 1944.
———. *Pīrāstah-i tārīkh-nāmah-i harāt.* Ed. M. A. Fakrat. Tehran, 1381/2002.
Harrist, Robert. *Power and Virtue: The Horse in Chinese Art.* New York, 1997.
Harvard Yenching Sinological Index Series. *Combined Indices to Thirty Collections of Liao, Chin, and Yuan Biographies.* Cambridge, MA, 1940; rpt. San Francisco, 1974.
Ḥaydar, Mīrzā Muḥammad. *A History of the Moghuls of Central Asia.* Tr. E. Denison Ross. London, 1898; rpt. New York, 1970.
He, Junzhe 何俊哲 et al. *Jin chao shi* 金朝史 [History of the Jin Dynasty]. Beijing, 1992.
Heidemann, Stephan. *Das Aleppiner Kalifat (AD 1261): vom Ende des Kalifates in Bagdad über Aleppo zu den Restaurationen in Kairo.* Leiden, 1994.
Heissig, Walther. *The Religions of Mongolia.* Berkeley, 1980.
Hemphill, Brian, and J. P. Mallory. “Horse-Mounted Invaders from the Russo-Kazakh Steppe or Agricultural Colonists from Western Central Asia? A Craniometric Investigation of the Bronze Age Settlement of Xinjiang.” *American Journal of Physical Anthropology,* 124 (2004), pp. 199–222.
Henthorn, W. E. *Korea: The Mongol Invasions.* Leiden, 1963.
Herman, John. “The Mongol Conquest of Dali: The Failed Second Front.” In *Warfare in Inner Asian History (500–1800),* ed. N. Di Cosmo. Leiden, 2002, pp. 295–334.
Herrmann, Gottfried. *Persische Urkunden der Mongolenzeit.* Documenta Iranica et Islamica, 2. Wiesbaden, 2004.
Higham, Charles. *The Bronze Age of Southeast Asia.* Cambridge, 1996.
Hillenbrand, Robert. “The Arts of the Book in Ilkhanid Iran.” In *The Legacy of Genghis Khan,* ed. L. Komaroff and S. Carboni. New York, 2002, pp. 134–167.
———. “Basil Robinson, 1912–2005.” *Iran,* 44 (2006), p. v.
Hirotoshi, Shimo. “The Qaraunas in the Historical Materials of the Ilkhanate.” *Memoirs of the Research Department of Toyo Bunko,* 35 (1977), pp. 131–181.
Hirschler, Konrad. *Medieval Arabic Historiography: Authors as Actors.* London, 2006.
Ho, Ping-ti. *Studies on the Population of China, 1368–1953.* Cambridge, MA, 1967.
———. “An Estimate of the Total Population of Sung-Chin China.” In *Études Song,* ed. F. Aubin. Paris, 1970, pp. 33–53.
Höh, M. von der, N. Jaspert, and J. R. Oesterle. “Court, Brokers and Brokerages in the Medieval Mediterranean.” In *Cultural Brokers at Mediterranean Courts in the Middle Ages,* ed. M. von der Höh, N. Jaspert, and J. R. Oesterle. Paderborn, 2012, pp. 9–32.
Höllmann, Thomas. *Die Seidenstraße.* Munich, 2004.
Holmgren, Jennifer. “Marriage, Kinship and Succession under the Ch’i-tan Rulers of the Liao Dynasty.” *T’oung Pao,* 72 (1986), pp. 44–91.
Holotová-Szinek, Juliana. “Preliminary Research on the Spatial Organization of the Xiongnu Territories in Mongolia.” In *Xiongnu Archaeology: Multidisciplinary Perspectives of the First Steppe Empire in Inner Asia,* ed. U. Brosseder and B. Miller. Bonn, 2011, pp. 425–440.
Holt, Peter M. “An Early Source on Shaykh Khaḍir al-Mihrānī.” *Bulletin of the School of Oriental and African Studies,* 46 (1983), pp. 33–39.
———. “Some Observations of the ʿAbbasid Caliphate of Cairo.” *Bulletin of the School of Oriental and African Studies,* 47 (1984), pp. 501–507.

Honey, David. *Stripping off Felt and Fur: An Essay on Nomadic Sinification.* Papers on Inner Asia, 21. Bloomington, IN, 1992.

Honeychurch, William. "Inner Asian Warriors and Khans: A Regional Spatial Analysis of Nomadic Political Organization and Interaction." PhD dissertation, University of Michigan, 2004.

———. "Xiongnu Settlement in Mongolian Archaeology." Paper presented at the International Conference on Xiongnu Archaeology. Ulaanbaatar, Mongolia, October 16–18, 2008.

———. "Thinking Political Communities: Social Stratification among Ancient Nomads of Mongolia." In *The Anthropological Study of Class and Consciousness,* ed. P. Durrenberger. Boulder, CO, 2012, pp. 29–63.

———. "The Nomad as State Builder: Historical Theory and Material Evidence from Mongolia." *Journal of World Prehistory,* 26 (2013), pp. 283–321.

———. *Inner Asia and the Spatial Politics of Empire,* forthcoming.

Honeychurch, William, and Chunag Amartuvshin. "States on Horseback: The Rise of Inner Asian Confederations and Empires." In *Archaeology of Asia,* ed. M. T. Stark. Malden, MA, 2006, pp. 255–278.

———. "Hinterlands, Urban Centers, and Mobile Settings: The 'New' Old World Archaeology from the Eurasian Steppe." *Asian Perspectives,* 46/1 (2007), pp. 36–64.

———. "Timescapes from the Past: An Archaeogeography of Mongolia." In *Mapping Mongolia: Situating Mongolia in the World from Geologic Time to the Present,* ed. P. Sabloff. Philadelphia, 2011, pp. 195–219.

Honeychurch, William, Albert Nelson, and Chunag Amartuvshin. "Death and Social Process among the Ancient Xiongnu of Mongolia." In *Xiongnu: The First Empire of the Steppes,* ed. Eunjeong Chang. Seoul, 2007, pp. 134–153.

Hoyt, Donald F., and C. Richard Taylor. "Gait and the Energetics of Locomotion in Horses." *Nature,* 292 (1981), pp. 239–240.

Hsiao, Ch'i-ch'ing. *The Military Establishment of the Yuan Dynasty.* Cambridge, MA, 1978.

Hu, Xiaopeng 鬍小鵬, and Su Pengyu 蘇鵬宇. "Mengyuan shiqi Qidan ren hunyin yanjiu 蒙元時期契丹人婚姻研究 [On the Marriage of the Kitans in the Yuan Dynasty]." *Xibei shidaxue bao* 西北師大學報, 46/6 (2009), pp. 44–48.

Hu, Zhihui 胡祇遹. *Zi shan da quan ji* 紫山大全集 [Hu Zhiyu's Literary Collection]. Taipei, 1983.

Huang, Jin 黃晉. *Jinhua Huang xiansheng wenji* 金華黃先生文集 [Huang Jin's Literary Collection]. Ed. Sibu conggan.

Hucker, Charles O. *A Dictionary of Official Titles in Imperial China.* Taipei, 1985.

Hulsewe, Anthony. "The Problem of the Authenticity of Shi-chi ch. 123, the Memoir on Ta-Yiian." *T'oung Pao,* 61/1–3 (1975), pp. 83–132.

Humphreys, R. Stephen. *From Saladin to the Mongols: The Ayyubids of Damascus, 1193–1260.* Albany, NY, 1977.

———. "A Cultural Elite: The Role and Status of the *'Ulamā'* in Islamic Society." In R. S. Humphreys, *Islamic History: A Framework for Inquiry,* 2nd ed. Princeton, 1991, pp. 187–208.

Iakubovskii, Aleksander Iu., and Boris D. Grekov. *Zolotaia Orda i eë padenie* [The Golden Horde and Its Fall]. Moscow, 1950.

Ianin, V. L., and S. A. Ianina. “Nachal'nyi period riazanskoi monetnoi chekanki [The Early Period of Coinage in Ryazan‘].” In *Numizmaticheskii sbornik, Gosudarstvennyi Istoricheskii muzei,* pt. I. Moscow, 1955, pp. 109–123.
Ibn al-Fuwaṭī (Pseudo), ʿAbd al-Razzāq b. Aḥmad. *al-Ḥawādith al-jāmiʿa waʾl-tajārib al-nāfiʿa fī al-miʾa al-sābiʿa.* Ed. Muḥammad Riḍā al-Shabībī and Muṣṭafā Jawād. Baghdad, 1932.
———. *al-Ḥawādith al-jāmiʿa.* Tr. ʿAbd al-Muḥammad Āyatī. Tehran, 2002.
Ibn al-Ṭiqṭaqā, Muḥammad b. ʿAlī. *Taʾrīkh-i fakhrī.* Tr. Muḥammad Waḥīd Gulpayigānī. Tehran, 1360/1981–1982; partially translated by C. E. J. Whitting, *On the Systems of Government and the Moslem Dynasties.* London, 1947; rpt. London, 1990.
Ibn Baṭṭūṭa. *The Travels of Ibn Battuta,* vol. 3. Tr. Sir Hamilton Gibb. Cambridge, 1971.
Ibn Bībī. *al-Awāmir al-ʿalāʾiyya fī al-umūr al-ʿalāʾiyya.* Ed. Adnan Sadik Erzi. Ankara, 1956. Vol. 1 of the printed text, ed. N. Lugal and S. A. Erzi. Ankara, 1957.
———. “Saljūq-nāmah-i ibn bībī.” In M. Makhkour, *Akhbār-i Salājiqah-i Rūm.* Tehran, 1971.
Ibn Shaddād al-Ḥalabī, ʿIzz al-Dīn Muḥammad b. ʿAlī. *Al-Aʿlaq al-khaṭīra fī dhikr umarāʾ al-shām waʾl-jazīra.* Partial ed. [North Syria Exclusive of Aleppo] by A.M. Eddé, in “La description de la Syrie du Nord de ʿIzz al-Dīn ibn Šaddād.” *Bulletin des Etudes Orientales,* 32–33 (1981–1982), pp. 265–402.
———. *Taʾrīkh al-malik al-ẓāhir (Die Geschichte des Sultan Baibars).* Ed. Aḥmad Ḥuṭayṭ. Wiesbaden, 1983.
Ibn Taghrī Birdī, Abū al-Maḥāsin Yūsuf. *al-Nujūm al-zāhira fī mulūk miṣr waʾl-qāhira.* Cairo, 1348–1392/1929–1970.
Ikram, S. M. *Muslim Civilization in India.* New York, 1964.
Il’inskaia, Varvara A., and Aleksey I. Terenozhkin. *Skifiia VII–VIII vv* [Scythia in the 7th–8th Centuries]. Kiev, 1983.
İnalcık, Halil. “The Question of the Emergence of the Ottoman State.” *International Journal of Turkish Studies,* 1 (1981–1982), pp. 71–79.
———. “Osmanlı Beyliğinin Kurucusu Osman Bey” [“Osman Bey, the Founder of the Ottoman Principality”], *Belleten,* 71 (2007), pp. 479–537.
Indrisano, Gregory. “Subsistence, Environmental Fluctuation and Social Change: A Case Study in South Central Inner Mongolia.” PhD dissertation, University of Pittsburgh, 2006.
Inostrantsev, Konstantin A. “K voprosu o ‘basmè’ [About the “Basma”].” *Zapiski Vostochnogo otdeleniia imperatorskogo russkogo arkheologicheskogo obshchestva,* 18 (1907–1908), pp. 172–179.
ʿIrāqī, Fakhr al-Dīn. *ʿUshshāqnāma, The Songs of Lovers.* Ed. and tr. Arthur Arberry. London, 1939.
———. *Majmūʿa-i āṣār.* Ed. N. M. Khazāʾī. Tehran, 1372/1993.
Irwin, Robert. *The Middle East in the Middle Ages: The Early Mamluk Sultanate.* London, 1986.
Ishjamts, N. “Nomads in Eastern Central Asia.” In *History of Civilization of Central Asia: The Development of Sedentary and Nomadic Civilizations. 700 B.C. to A.D. 250,* ed. J. Harmatta. Paris, 1994, pp. 151–169.
Ivantchik, Askold I. *Kimmeriitsy* [The Cimmerians]. Moscow, 1996.
———. “The Current State of the Cimmerian Problem.” *Ancient Civilizations,* 7/3–4 (2001), pp. 307–339.

———. "Early Eurasian Nomads and the Civilizations of the Ancient Near East (Eight–Seventh Centuries BCE). " In *Mongols, Turks and Others: Eurasian Nomads and the Outside World,* ed. R. Amitai and M. Biran. Leiden, 2005, pp. 103–127.

Jackson, Peter. "The Crisis in the Holy Land in 1260." *English Historical Review,* 95 (1980), pp. 481–513.

———. "Jalal al-Din, the Mongols, and the Khwarazmian Conquest of Panjab and Sind." *Iran,* 28 (1990), pp. 45–54.

———. "The Mamluk Institution in Early Muslim India." *Journal of the Royal Asiatic Society,* 122/2 (1990), pp. 340–358.

———. "The State of Research: The Mongol Empire 1986–1999." *Journal of Medieval History,* 26/2 (2000), pp. 189–210.

———. *The Delhi Sultanate: A Political and Military History.* Cambridge, 2003.

———. *The Mongols and the West, 1221–1410.* Harlow, UK, 2005.

Jackson, Peter, and David Morgan, ed. and tr. *The Mission of Friar William of Rubruck: His Journey to the Court of the Great Khan Möngke 1253–1255.* London, 1990.

Jacobson-Tepfer, Esther. "The Emergence of Cultures of Mobility in the Altai Mountains of Mongolia: Evidence from the Intersection of Rock Art and Paleoenvironment." In *The Archaeology of Mobility: Old World and New World Nomadism,* ed. H. Barnard and W. Wendrich. Los Angeles, 2008, pp. 200–229.

Jacobson-Tepfer, Esther, James E. Meacham, and Gary Tepfer. *Archaeology and Landscape in the Mongolian Altai: An Atlas.* Redlands, CA, 2010.

Jagchid, Sechin, and Van Jay Symons. *Peace, War, and Trade along the Great Wall.* Bloomington, IN, 1989.

al-Jājarmī, Muḥammad b. Badr. *Mūnis al-aḥrār,* vol. 1. Tehran, 1958; vol. 2, Tehran, 1971.

Janhunen, Juha. *Manchuria: An Ethnic History.* Helsinki, 1996.

Jay, Jennifer. "The Life and Loyalism of Chou Mi (1232–1298) and His Circle of Friends." *Papers on Far Eastern History,* 28 (1983), pp. 49–105.

———. *A Change in Dynasties: Loyalism in Thirteenth-Century China.* Bellingham, WA, 1991.

Jiang Yihan 姜一涵. "Zhaoshi yimen hezha yanjiu 趙氏一門合札研究 [A Study of the Collected Writings of One Family of the Zhao Clan]." *Gugong Jikan* 故宮季刊, 11/4 (1977), pp. 23–50.

———. Jiangxi Provincial Museum and Chinese University of Hong Kong. *Yuan and Ming Blue and White Wares from Jiangxi.* Hong Kong, 2002.

Jing, Anning. "The Portraits of Khubilai Khan and Chabi by Anige (1245–1306), a Nepali Artist at the Yuan Court." *Artibus Asiae,* 52/1–2 (1994), pp. 40–86.

al-Juwaynī, ʿAṭā-Malik. *Taʾrīkh-i Jahāngushā.* Ed. Mīrzā Muḥammad Qazwīnī. London, 1912–1937. 3 vols.

———. *The History of the World Conqueror.* Tr. John A. Boyle. Cambridge, MA, 1958. 2 vols. Reprinted as *Genghis Khan: The History of the World Conqueror,* tr. J. A. Boyle. Manchester, 1997.

———. *Tasliyat al-ikhwān.* Ed. A. Māhyār. Tehran, 1361/1982.

Jūzjānī. *Ṭabaqāt-i Nāṣirī.* Ed. W. Nassau Lees. Calcutta, 1864.

———. *Ṭabaḳāt-i-Nāṣirī: A General History of the Muhammadan Dynasties of Asia, including Hindustan; from A.H. 194 (810 A.D.) to A.H. 658 (1260 A.D.) and the Irruption of the Infidel Mughals into Islam*, 2 vols. Tr. H. G. Raverty. London, 1881–1899; rpt. New Delhi, 1970. 2 vols.

Kadoi, Yuka. "Aspects of Iranian Art under the Mongols: Chinoiserie Reappraised." PhD dissertation, University of Edinburgh, 2004.

———. *Islamic Chinoiserie: The Art of Mongol Iran.* Edinburgh Studies in Islamic Art. Edinburgh, 2010.

Kanda Kiichirō 神田喜一郎. "Gendai no Bunshū no fūryū nit suite 元代の文宗の風流に就いて [About the Frivolous Behavior (*fengliu*) of Yuan Wenzong]." In *Haneda hakushi shōju kinen tōyōshi ronsō* 羽田博士頌壽記念東洋史論叢, 羽田博士還暦記念會編 [Studies in Honour of Tōru Haneda on the Occasion of His Sixtieth Birthday]. Kyoto, 1950.

Kane, Daniel. *The Kitan Language and Script.* Leiden, 2009.

———. "The Great Central Liao Kitan State." In *Perspectives on the Liao,* ed. V. Hansen and F. Louis. New Haven, CT, 2010, pp. 5–11.

Kaplonski, Christopher. "The Mongolian Impact on Eurasia: A Reassessment." In *The Role of Migration in the History of the Eurasian Steppe: Sedentary Civilization vs. "Barbarian" and Nomad,* ed. A. Bell-Fialkoff. New York, 2000, pp. 256–257.

Kargalov, Vadim V. *Konets ordynskogo iga* [The End of the Horde's Yoke]. Moscow, 1980.

Ke, Shaomin 柯劭忞. *Xin Yuanshi* 新元史 [The New Official History of the Yuan]. Beijing, 1979.

Keenan, Edward L. "Muscovite Political Folkways." *Russian Review,* 45 (1986), pp. 115–181.

Kellner-Heinkele, Barbara. "The Turkomans and *Bilād aš-Šām* in the Mamluk Period." In *Land Tenure and Social Transformation in the Middle East,* ed. Tarif Khalidi. Beirut, 1984, pp. 169–180.

Kempiners, Russell G., Jr. "Vassaf's *Tajziyat al-Amsar wa Tazjiyat al-A'sar* as a Source for the History of the Chaghadayid Khanate." *Journal of Asian History,* 22/2 (1988), pp. 160–187.

Kennedy, Hugh. *Mongols, Huns and Vikings: Nomads at War.* London, 2002.

Khatanbaatar, P., B. Jargal, W. Honeychurch, and Ch. Amartuvshin. "Khunnugiin bulshnaas ilersen khar' garaltai oldvoruud [Artifacts of Foreign Origin Discovered in a Khunnu Burial]." *Arkheologiin Sudlal,* 4/24 (2007), pp. 305–322.

Khazanov, Anatoly M. *Ocherki voennogo dela sarmatov* [Essays on the Samatian Military Affairs]. Moscow, 1971; 2nd rev. ed., St. Petersburg, 2007.

———. "Legenda o proiskhozdenii skifov (Herodotus, IV, 5–6) [The Legend about the Origin of the Scythians in Herodotus, IV, 5–6]." In *Skifskii mir,* ed. A. Terenozhkin. Kiev, 1975, pp. 74–93.

———. *Sotsial'naia istoriia skifov* [A Social History of the Scythians]. Moscow, 1975.

———. *Zoloto skifov* [The Scythian Gold]. Moscow, 1975.

———. "The Early State among the Scythians." In *The Early State,* ed. H. J. M. Claessen and P. Skalnik. The Hague, 1978, pp. 77–92.

———. "Les scythes et la civilization antique: problèmes des contacts." *Dialogues d'histoire ancienne,* 7 (1982), pp. 7–51.

———. *Nomads and the Outside World.* 2nd ed. Madison, WI, 1994.

———. "The Spread of World Religions in Medieval Nomadic Societies of the Eurasian Steppes." In *Nomadic Diplomacy, Destruction and Religion from the Pacific to the Adriatic,* ed. W. Schlepp and M. Gervers. Toronto Studies in Central and Inner Asia, 1. Toronto, 1994, pp. 11–33.

———. "Nomads in the History of the Sedentary World." In *Nomads in the Sedentary World,* ed. A. M. Khazanov and A. Wink. London, 2001, pp. 1–23.

———. "Nomads of the Eurasian Steppes in Historical Retrospective." In *Nomadic Pathways in Social Evolution,* ed. N. N. Kradin, D. M. Bondarenko, and T. J. Barfield. Moscow, 2003, pp. 25–49.

Khudyakov, Yuri S. "Problems of the Genesis of Culture of the Hunnic Period in the Altai Mountains." *Ancient Civilizations from Scythia to Siberia,* 3/2–3 (1996), pp. 329–346.

———. "Armaments of Nomads of the Altai Mountains (First Half of the 1st Millennium AD)." *Acta Orientalia,* 58/2 (2005), pp. 117–133.

———. "Vliianie Khunnskoi kul'tury na drevnikh kochevnikov yujnoi Sibiri [The Influence of Hun Culture on the Ancient Nomads of Southern Siberia]." *Arkheologiin Sudlal,* 31 (2011), pp. 148–160.

Khwāfī, Faṣīḥī. *Mujmal-i Faṣīḥī,* vol. 2. Ed. Maḥmūd Farrukhī. Mashhad, 1960.

Khwāndamir, Ghiyāth al-Dīn. *Dastūr al-wuzarā'.* Ed. Sa'īd Nafīsī. Tehran, 1317/1938–1939.

———. *Tārīkh-i ḥabīb al-siyar fī akhbār-i afrād-i bashar.* Ed. Muḥammad Dabīr Siyāqī. Tehran, 1353/1974–1975.

———. *Habibu's-Siyar. Tome Three: The Reign of the Mongol and the Turk.* Tr. W. M. Thackston. Cambridge, MA, 1994.

Kidd, Fiona. "The Ferghana Valley and Its Neighbours during the Han Period (206 BC–223 AD)." In *Social Orders and Social Landscapes,* ed. L. M. Popova, C. W. Hartley, and A. T. Smith. Newcastle, 2007, pp. 359–375.

Kim, Ho-dong. "The Resettlement of the Pohai (or Palhae) in Liao in the 920s." *Journal of Turkic Studies,* 9 (1985), pp. 187–196.

Kirmānī, Nāṣir al-Dīn Munshī. *Simṭ al-'ulā li'l-ḥaḍra al-'ulyā.* Ed. 'A. Iqbāl. Tehran, 1328/1949; 1362/1983.

Komaroff, Linda, ed. *Beyond the Legacy of Genghis Khan.* Leiden, 2006.

Komaroff, Linda, and Stefano Carboni, eds. *The Legacy of Genghis Khan: Courtly Art and Culture in Western Asia, 1256–1353.* New York, 2002.

Konovalov, Prokopy B. *Khunnu v Zabaikal'e* [The Khunnu of Trans-Baikal]. Ulan-Ude, 1976.

Koryakova, Ludmila, and Andrej Epimakhov. *The Urals and Western Siberia in the Bronze and Iron Ages.* Cambridge, 2007.

Koshelenko, Gennady A., and Viktor N. Pilipko. "Parthia." In *History of Civilization of Central Asia: The Development of Sedentary and Nomadic Civilizations 700 B.C. to A.D. 250,* ed. J. Harmatta. Paris, 1994, pp. 131–149.

Kossak, Georg. "Von den Anfängen des Skytho-Iranischen Tierstiels." In *Bayerische Akademie der Wissenschaften. Philosophisch-Historishe Klasse Abhandlungen.* Neue Folge, Heft 98. Munich, 1987, pp. 24–86.

Kradin, Nikolay N. "Structure of Power in Nomadic Empires of Inner Asia: An Anthropological Approach." In *Hierarchy and Power in the History of Civilizations: Ancient and Medieval Cultures,* ed. L. E. Grinin, D. M.Beliaev, and A.V. Korotayev. Moscow, 2008, pp. 98–124.

Kradin, Nikolay N., et al. "Preliminary Results of the Investigation of [the] Kitan Ancient Town Chintolgoi Balqas in 2004." *Nomadic Studies Bulletin,* 10 (2005), pp. 72–80.

Krahl, Regina. *Chinese Ceramics in the Topkapi Sarayi Museum, Istanbul.* London, 1986. 3 vols.

Kudriavtsev, I. M. "Ugorshchina v pamiatnikakh drevnerusskoi literatury (Letopis'nye povesti o nashestvii Akhmata i ikh literaturnaia istoriia) [Ugorschina in the Old Russian Literary Monuments (Chronicle Reports about the Invasion of Akhmat and

Their Literary History)].” In *Issledovaniia i materialy po drevnerusskoi literature,* vol. 1. Moscow, 1961, pp. 23–67.

Kürsat-Ahlers, Elçin. “The Role and Contents of Ideology in the Early Nomadic Empires of the Eurasian Steppes.” In *Ideology and the Formation of Early States,* ed. H. Claessen and J. Osten. Leiden, 1996, pp. 137–152.

Kushnir, David. “The Turcomans in Palestine during the Ottoman Period.” *International Journal of Turkish Studies,* 11/1–2 (2005), pp. 81–94.

Kutubī, Maḥmūd. *Tārīkh Āl-Muẓaffar.* Ed. ʿAbd al-Ḥusayn Nawāʾī. Tehran, 1335/1956.

Kuzmin, N. Yu. “Prospects for Correlating Radiocarbon and Archaeological Chronologies of the Scythian and Hunno-Sarmatian Age Burials in the Sayan-Altai Region.” *Archaeology, Ethnology and Anthropology of Eurasia,* 35/3 (2008), pp. 77–87.

Kuzmina, Elena E. “Cultural Connections of the Tarim Basin People and Pastoralists of the Asian Steppes in the Bronze Age.” In *The Bronze Age and Early Iron Age Peoples of Eastern Central Asia,* ed. V. H. Mair. Philadelphia, 1998, pp. 63–93.

———. “The Eurasian Steppes: The Transition from Early Urbanism to Nomadism.” In *Kurgans, Ritual, Sites, and Settlements: Eurasian Bronze and Iron Age,* ed. Jeannine Davis-Kimbal, Eileen M. Murphy, Ludmila Koryakova, and Leonid T. Yablonksy. Oxford, 2000, pp. 118–125.

———. *The Prehistory of the Silk Road.* Philadelphia, 2008.

Kuznetsov, Vladimir D. “Nekotorye problemy torgovli v Severnom Prichernomor'e v arkhaicheskii period [A Few Commercial Problems in the Northern Black Sea in the Archaic Period].” *Vestnik drevnei istorii,* 1 (2000), pp. 16–40.

Kuznetsova, Tatyana M. *Etiudy po skifskoi istorii* [Sketches of Scythian History]. Moscow, 1991.

Kychanov, Evgeny I. “Nekotorye suzhdeniia ob istoricheskikh sud'bakh Tangutov posle nashestviia Chingis Khana [On the Historical Destiny of the Tanguts after the Invasion of Chingghis Khan].” *Kratkie soobshcheniia instituta Azii,* 76 (1965), pp. 154–165.

———. *Ocherk istorii tangutskogo gosudarstva* [Outline of the History of Tangut State]. Moscow, 1968.

Laing, Ellen. “Recent Finds of Western-Related Glassware, Textiles, and Metalwork in Central Asia and China.” *Bulletin of the Asia Institute,* 9 (1995), pp. 1–18.

Laiou, Angeliki E. *Constantinople and the Latins: The Foreign Policy of Andronicus II, 1281–1326.* Cambridge, MA, 1972.

Lambton, Ann K. S. “Kirmān.” *Encyclopaedia of Islam,* 2nd ed. Online. http://reference works.brillonline.com/entries/encyclopaedia-of-islam-2/kirman-COM_0521 (accessed via the National Library of Israel, July 13, 2012).

Lammens, Henri, and C. Edmund Bosworth. “al-Shām.” *Encyclopaedia of Islam,* 2nd ed. Leiden, 1954–2005, vol. 9, pp. 268–269.

Lane, George. “Arghun Aqa: Mongol Bureaucrat.” *Iranian Studies,* 32/4 (1999), pp. 459–482.

———. *Early Mongol Rule in Thirteenth-Century Iran: A Persian Renaissance.* New York, 2003.

———. *Daily Life in the Mongol Empire.* Westport, CT, 2006.

———. “Phoenix Mosque of Hangzhou.” *Encyclopædia Iranica.* Online. http://www.irani caonline.org/articles/zarinaia (accessed August 16, 2012).

———. “Whose Secret Intent?” In *Eurasian Influences on Yuan China,* ed. Morris Rossabi. Singapore, 2013, pp. 1–40.

Lanfranchi, Giovanni B. *I Cimmeri. Emergenza delle élites militari iraniche nel Vicino Oriento (VIII-VII sec. a.C.).* Padua, 1990.
Lankton, James. *A Bead Timeline,* vol. 1: *Prehistory to 1200 CE.* Washington, DC, 2003.
———. "Gold-Glass Beads in Hellenistic Rhodes and Contemporary Java: Technological Challenges and Choices." Paper presented at the 18th Congress of AIHV on the History of Glass. Thessaloniki, Greece, September 21–25, 2009.
Lankton, James, and Bernard Gratuze. "Glass and Faience Beads and Pendants from Xiongnu Sites in Mongolia: Chemical Analysis and Preliminary Interpretation." LA-ICP-MS Analysis report for submission to Yale University, forthcoming.
Lapidus, Ira M. *Muslim Cities in the Later Middle Ages.* 1st ed. Cambridge, MA, 1967.
Lattimore, Owen. *Inner Asian Frontiers of China.* Oxford, 1940; rpt Boston, 1962.
———. *Studies in Frontier History.* Paris, 1962.
———. "Herdsmen, Farmers, and Urban Culture." In *Pastoral Production and Society,* ed. L'Equipe écologie et anthropologie des sociétés pastorales. Cambridge, 1979, pp. 479–490.
Lech, Klaus. *See* al-ʿUmarī.
Lee, James. "The Legacy of Immigration in Southwest China, 1250–1850." *Annales demographie historique* (1982), pp. 279–304.
Lee, Sherman, and Wai-kam Ho. *Chinese Art under the Mongols: The Yuan Dynasty (1279–1368).* Cleveland, OH, 1968.
Legrand, Sophie. "Karasuk Metallurgy: Technological Development and Regional Influence." In *Metallurgy in Ancient Eastern Eurasia from the Urals to the Yellow River,* ed. K. M. Linduff. Lewiston, NY, 2004, pp. 139–156.
———. "Sorting Out Men and Women in the Karasuk Culture." In *Are All Warriors Male? Gender Roles in the Euroasian Steppe,* ed. K. M. Linduff and K. S. Rubinson. Lanham, MD, 2008, pp. 153–174.
El-Leithy, Tamer. "Sufis, Copts and the Politics of Piety: Moral Regulation in Fourteenth-Century Upper Egypt." In *Le développement du soufisme en Égypte à l'époque mamelouke,* ed. R. J. A. McGregor and A. Sabra. Published as *Cahiers des Annales islamologiques,* 27 (2006), pp. 75–119.
Leslie, Donald D., and Kenneth H. J. Gardiner. "Chinese Knowledge of Western Asia during the Han." *T'oung Pao,* 68 (1982), pp. 254–307.
Leus, Pavel M. "New Finds from the Xiongnu Period in Central Tuva: Preliminary Communication." In *Xiongnu Archaeology: Multidisciplinary Perspectives of the First Steppe Empire in Inner Asia,* ed. U. Brosseder and B. Miller. Bonn, 2011, pp. 515–536.
Levtzion, Nehemia. "Conversion to Islam in Syria and Palestine and the Survival of Christian Communities." In *Conversion and Continuity: Indigenous Christian Communities in Islamic Lands, Eighth to Eighteenth Centuries,* ed. M. Gervers and R. J. Bikhazi. Toronto, 1990, pp. 289–311.
Lewis, Archibald. *Nomads and Crusades 1000–1368.* Bloomington, IN, 1988.
Lewis, Bernard. "The Mongols, the Turks and Muslim Polity." In Bernard Lewis, *Islam in History: Ideas, People and Events in the Middle East.* 2nd ed., Chicago, 1993, pp. 179–198.
Lewis, Clive S. "De Description Temporum." In Clive S. Lewis, *Selected Literary Essays,* ed. Walter Hooper. Cambridge, 1969, pp. 1–14.
Li, Chih-chang. *See* Li Zhichang.
Li, Chu-tsing. *The Autumn Colors on the Ch'iao and Hua Mountain: A Landscape by Chao Meng-fu.* Ascona, 1965.

———. "The Freer Sheep and Goat and Chao Meng-fu's Horse Paintings." *Artibus Asiae,* 30/4 (1968), pp. 279–326.
———. "Grooms and Horses by Three Members of the Chao Family." In *Words and Images: Chinese Poetry, Calligraphy, and Painting,* ed. A. Murck and Wen Fong. New York, 1991, pp. 206–209.
Li, Lin-ts'an. "Human Figures as a Chronological Standard for Dating Chinese Landscape Paintings." *National Palace Museum Bulletin,* 14/3 (July–August, 1979), pp. 2–14.
Li, Shuicheng. "The Interaction between Northwest China and Central Asia during the 2nd Millennium BC: An Archaeological Perspective." In *Ancient Interactions: East and West in Eurasia,* ed. K. Boyle, C. Renfrew, and M. Levine. Cambridge, 2002, pp. 171–182.
———. "Ancient Interactions in Eurasia and Northwest China: Revisiting J.G. Andersson's Legacy." *Bulletin of the Museum of Far Eastern Antiquities,* 75 (2003), pp. 9–30.
Li, Xian, et al. 李賢等, comps. *Da Ming yitongzhi* 大明一统志 [Comprehensive Gazetteer of the Great Ming]. Taipei, 1965. 10 vols.
Li, Yung-ti. "On the Function of Cowries in Shang and Western Zhou China." *Journal of East Asian Archaeology,* 5 (2003), pp. 1–26.
Li, Zhichang 李志常. *Xi you ji* 西遊記 [Journey to the West]. In *Menggu shiliao sizhang* 蒙古史料四種 [Four Types of Mongolian Historical Sources], ed. Wang Guowei 王國維. Taipei, 1975.
Li, Zichang (Li, Chih-chang). *The Travels of an Alchemist.* Tr. Arthur Waley. London, 1963.
Liaoning bowuguan 遼寧博物館 [Liaoning Museum]. *Liaohe Wengmin Zhan: Wenwu Jicui* 遼河文明展文物集萃 [Exhibition of Cultural Relics from the Civilization of the Liao River Valley]. Shenyang, 2006.
Liaonning daxue lishixi kaogu yanjiushi 遼寧大學歷史系考古研究室 [Archaeological Research Room of the Historical Department of Liaoning University] and Tieling shi bowuguan 鐵嶺市博物館 [Museum of Tieling City]. "Liaoning faku xian wanliu yizhi fajue 遼寧法庫縣灣柳遺址發掘 [Excavations at the Wanliu Site, Faku County, Liaoning]." *Kaogu,* 考古 12 (1989), pp. 1076–1086.
Liddell Hart, Basil. *Great Captains Unveiled.* Boston, 1928; rpt. New York, 1967.
Lin Yun. "A Reexamination of the Relationship between Bronzes of the Shang Culture and of the Northern Zone." In *Studies of Shang Archaeology,* ed. Kwang-chih Chang. New Haven, CT, 1986, pp. 237–273.
———. "Zai lun guajiang gou 再論掛韁鉤 [Reconsideration of Hooks for Hanging on Reins]." In *Lin Yun xueshu wenji* 林沄學術文集, ed. Lin Yun. Beijing, 1998, pp. 302–310.
Lindner, Rudi Paul. "What Was a Nomadic Tribe." *Comparative Studies in Society and History,* 24 (1982), pp. 689–711.
———. *Nomads and Ottomans in Medieval Anatolia.* Bloomington, IN, 1983.
Linduff, Katheryn M. "An Archaeological Overview." In *Ancient Bronzes of the Eastern Eurasian Steppes from the Arthur M. Sackler Collections,* ed. E. C. Bunker. New York, 1997, pp. 18–98.
———. "The Emergence and Demise of Bronze-Producing Cultures outside the Central Plain of China." In *The Bronze Age and Early Iron Age Peoples of Eastern Central Asia,* ed. V. H. Mair. Philadelphia, 1998, pp. 619–643.

———. "A Walk on the Wild Side: Late Shang Appropriation of Horses in China." In *Prehistoric Steppe Adaptation and the Horse,* ed. M. Levine, C. Renfrew, and K. Boyle. Oxford, 2003, pp. 139–162.

———. "The Gender of Luxury and Power among the Xiongnu in Eastern Eurasia." In *Are All Warriors Male? Gender Roles on the Ancient Eurasian Steppe,* ed. K. M. Linduff and K. S. Rubinson. Lanham, MD, 2008, pp. 175–212.

Little, Donald P. "Al-Ṣafadī as Biographer of His Contemporaries." In *Essays on Islamic Civilization Presented to Niyazi Berkes,* ed. D. P. Little. Leiden, 1976, pp. 190–210. (Reprinted in D. P. Little, *History and Historiography of the Mamlūks.* London, 1986.)

———. "Coptic Conversion to Islam under the Baḥrī Mamlūks, 692–755/1293–1354." *Bulletin of the School of Oriental and African Studies,* 39 (1976), pp. 552–569. (Reprinted in D. P. Little, *History and Historiography of the Mamlūks.* London, 1986.)

———. "Religion under the Mamluks." *The Muslim World,* 73 (1983), pp. 165–181. (Reprinted in D. P. Little, *History and Historiography of the Mamlūks.* London, 1986.)

———. "Historiography of the Ayyūbid and Mamlūk Epochs." In *The Cambridge History of Egypt,* vol. 1: *Islamic Egypt, 640–1517.* Ed. C. F. Petry. Cambridge, 1998, pp. 412–444.

Litvinskii, Boris A. "'Zolotye liudi' v drevnikh pogrebeniiakh Tsentral'noi Azii (opyt istolkovaniia v svete istorii religii) ["Golden People" in the Ancient Burials of the Central Asia (An Attempt at Explanation in the Light of the History of Religion)]." *Sovetskaia etnografiia,* 4 (1982), pp. 34–43.

Liu, Bing 劉冰. *Chifeng bowuguan wenwu dianzang* 赤峰博物館文物典藏 [Cultural Relics of the Chifeng Museum]. Hohhot, 2007.

Liu, Li. *The Chinese Neolithic: Trajectories to Early States.* Cambridge, 2004.

Liu, Mau-Tsai. *Die Chinesischen Nachrichten zur Geschichte der Ost-Türken (Tu-Küe).* Wiesbaden, 1958. 2 vols.

Liu, Pujiang 劉浦江. *Liao Jin shi lun* 遼金史論 [Historical Studies on the Liao and the Jin]. Shenyang, 1999.

———. "Liao chao wangguo zihou de Qidan yimin 遼朝王國自候的契丹移民 [Kitan Descendants in the Post-Liao Period]." *Yanjing xuebao* 燕京學報, 10 (2001), pp. 135–172.

———. *Song mo zhi jian: Liao Jin Qidan Nüzhen shi yanjiu* 鬆漠之間: 遼金契丹女真史研究 [The Land of the Pines and Forests: Studies on the Kitans and Jurchens, the Liao, and the Jin]. Beijing, 2008.

Liu, Xinru. "Migration and Settlement of the Yuezhi-Kushan: Interaction and Interdependence of Nomadic and Sedentary Societies." *Journal of World History,* 12/2 (2001), pp. 261–292.

Liu, Xu 劉昫, ed. *Jiu Tangshu* 舊唐書 [Old History of the Tang]. Beijing, 1995.

Louis, François. "Han Lacquerware and the Wine Cups of Noin Ula." *The Silk Road,* 4/2 (2006–2007), pp. 48–53.

Lu, Enguo. "The Podboy Burials Found in Xinjiang and the Remains of the Yuezhi." *Circle of Inner Asian Art Newsletter,* 15 (2002), pp. 21–22.

Lubo-Lesnichenko, Yevgenii. "External Relations of Central Asia According to Material from Pazyryk and Noin-ula." In *The Chinese and Their Northern Neighbors (ca. 1000 BC–ca. 2nd Century AD),* vol. 2., ed. K. M. Linduff. Pittsburgh, 1991, pp. 1–33.

Luz, Nimrod. "Aspects of Islamization of Space and Society in Mamluk Jerusalem and Its Hinterland." *Mamluk Studies Review,* 6 (2002), pp. 133–154.

———. "The Public Sphere in Mamluk Jerusalem." *Hamizraḥ Heḥadash,* 46 (2004), pp. 127–144 (in Hebrew).
Ma, Yong, and Sung Yutang. "The Western Regions under the Hsiung-nu and Han." In *History of Civilization of Central Asia: The Development of Sedentary and Nomadic Civilizations 700 B.C. to A.D. 250,* ed. J. Harmatta. Paris, 1994, pp. 227–246.
Ma Mingda 馬明達. "Yuan dai diaosujia gouchen 元代雕塑家鉤沉 [A Survey of the Sculptors in the Yuan Dynasty]." *Xibei minzu yanjiu* 西北民族研究, 1 (1997), pp. 239–242.
Makhortykh, Sergey B. "Kimmeriitsy i Drevnii Vostok [The Cimmerians and the Ancient East]." *Vestnik drevnei istorii,* 2 (1998), pp. 95–104.
———. *Kul'turnye kontakty naseleniia Severnogo Prichernomor'ia i Tsentral'noi Evropy v kimmeriiskuiu epokhu* [Cultural Contacts of the Population of the Northern Black Sea and Central Europe in the Cimmerian Period]. Kiev, 2003.
Mallory, James P., and Victor H. Mair. *The Tarim Mummies: Ancient China and the Mystery of the Earliest Peoples from the West.* New York, 2000.
Mandel'shtam, A. M. "Rannie kochevniki skifskogo perioda na territorii Tuvy [Early Nomads of the Scythian Period on the Territory of Tuva]." In *Stepnaia polosa Aziatskoi chasti SSSR v skifo-sarmatskoe vremia* [The Steppe Zone of the Asiatic Region of the USSR during the Scythian-Sarmatian Period], ed. N. G. Gorbunova. Moscow, 1992, pp. 178–196.
Mandel'shtam, A. M., and E. U. Stambul'nik. "Gunno-sarmatskii period na territorii Tuvy [Hun-Sarmatian Period in the Territory of Tuva]." In *Stepnaia polosa Aziatskoi chasti SSSR v skifo-sarmatskoe vremia* [The Steppe Zone of the Asiatic Region of the USSR during the Scythian-Sarmatian Period], ed. N. G. Gorbunova. Moscow, 1992, pp. 196–205.
Manz, Beatrice F. "Mongol History Rewritten and Relived." *Revue des mondes musulmans et de la méditerranée,* 89–90 (2000), pp. 129–149.
al-Maqrīzī, Taqī al-Dīn Aḥmad b. ʿAlī. *Kitāb al-sulūk li-maʿrifat al-duwal waʾl-mulūk.* Cairo, 1934–1973.
Martin, Fredrik R. *The Miniature Painting and Painters of Persia, India and Turkey from the 8th to the 18th Century.* London, 1912.
Martin, Henry D. *The Rise of Chingis Khan and His Conquest of North China.* Baltimore, 1950.
Martinez, Arsenio P. "Some Notes on the Il-Xanid Army." *Archivum Eurasiae Medii Aevi,* 6 (1986–1988), pp. 218–242.
May, Timothy M. "The Mongol Presence and Impact in the Lands of the Eastern Mediterranean." In *Crusades, Condottieri, and Cannon: Medieval Warfare in Societies around the Mediterranean,* ed. D. J. Kagay and L. J. A. Villalon. Leiden, 2003, pp. 133–156.
McCausland, Shane. *Zhao Mengfu: Caligraphy and Painting for Khubilai's China.* Hong Kong, 2011.
McChesney, Robert D. *Central Asia: Foundations of Change.* Princeton, 1996.
McNeill, W. H. *The Rise of the West.* Chicago, 1963.
———. *Plagues and Peoples.* Garden City, NY, 1976.
Medley, Margaret. *Yuan Porcelain and Stoneware.* New York, 1974.
Mei, Jianjun. *Copper and Bronze Metallurgy in Late Prehistoric Xinjiang: Its Cultural Context and Relationship with Neighboring Regions.* Oxford, 2000.

———. "Qijia and Seima-Turbino: The Question of Early Contacts between Northwest China and the Eurasian Steppe." *Bulletin of the Museum of Far Eastern Antiquities,* 75 (2003), pp. 31–54.

Mei, Jianjun, and C. Shell. "Copper and Bronze Metallurgy in Late Prehistoric Xinjiang." In *The Bronze Age and Early Iron Age Peoples of Eastern Central Asia,* ed. V. H. Mair. Philadelphia, 1998, pp. 581–603.

Melville, Charles. "Pādshāh-i Islām: The Conversion of Sultan Maḥmūd Ghāzān Khān." *Pembroke Papers,* 1 (1990), pp. 159–177.

———. *The Fall of Amir Chupan and the Decline of the Ilkhanate, 1327–37: A Decade of Discord in Mongol Iran.* Research Institute for Inner Asian Studies' Papers on Inner Asia, 30. Bloomington, IN, 1999.

———. "From Adam to Abaqa: Qadi Baidawi's Rearrangement of History." *Studia Iranica,* 30 (2001), pp. 67–86.

———. "Review of George Lane, 'Early Mongol Rule in Thirteenth-Century Iran: A Persian Renaissance.'" *Bulletin of the School of Oriental and African Studies,* 67/2 (2004), pp. 238–240.

———. "The Early Persian Historiography of Anatolia." In *History and Historiography of Post-Mongol Central Asia and the Middle East: Studies in Honor of John E. Woods,* ed. J. Pfeiffer and S. A. Quinn. Wiesbaden, 2006, pp. 135–166.

———. "The Survival of the Royal Mongol Household." In *Beyond the Legacy of Genghis Khan,* ed. L. Komaroff. Leiden, 2006, pp. 135–164.

Melyukova, A. I. "Scythians of Southeastern Europe." In *Nomads of the Eurasian Steppes in the Early Iron Age,* ed. J. Davis-Kimball, V. B. Bashilov, and L. T. Yablonsky. Berkeley, 1995, pp. 27–61.

Meng, Siming 蒙思明. *Yuandai shehui jiezhi zhidu* 元代社會階級制度 [The Class System in Yuan Society]. Beijing, 1938.

Meng, Zhidong 孟誌東. *Yunnan Qidan houyi yanjiu* 雲南契丹後裔研究 [Research on the Descendants of the Yunnan Kitans]. Beijing, 1995.

Metzner-Nebelsick, Carola. "Early Iron Age Pastoral Nomadism in the Great Hungarian Plain—Migration or Assimilation? The Thraco-Cimmerian Problem Revisited." In *Kurgans, Ritual Sites, and Settlements: Eurasian Bronze and Iron Age,* ed. Jeannine Davis-Kimbal, Eileen M. Murphy, Ludmila Koryakova, and Leonid T. Yablonksy. Oxford, 2000, pp. 160–184.

Michell, Robert and Nevill Forbes, tr. *The Chronicle of Novgorod.* London, 1914, rpt. New York, 1970.

Miller, Bryan K. "Khovd Archaeology: Archival Research and Field Survey Expedition." Online. http://www.mongoliacenter.org/fellowship/reports/Bryan.Miller.pdf (accessed June 1, 2006).

———. "Permutations of Peripheries in the Xiongnu Empire." In *Xiongnu Archaeology: Multidisciplinary Perspectives of the First Steppe Empire in Inner Asia,* ed. U. Brosseder and B. Miller. Bonn, 2011, pp. 559–578.

Miller, Bryan, F. Allard, D. Erdenebaatar, and C. Leeryan. "A Xiongnu Tomb Complex: Excavations at Gol Mod 2 Cemetery, Mongolia." *Mongolian Journal of Anthropology, Archaeology, and Ethnology,* 2 (2006), pp. 1–21.

Miller, Bryan, J. Bayarsaikhan, Ts. Egiimaa, and C. Lee. "Xiongnu Elite Tomb Complexes in the Mongolian Altai: Results of the Mongol-American Hovd Archaeology Project, 2007." *The Silk Road,* 5/2 (2008), pp. 27–35.

Minetti, A. E., L. P. Ardigò, E. Reinach, and F. Saibene. "The Relationship between Mechanical Work and Energy Expenditure of Locomotion in Horses." *Journal of Experimental Biology,* 202 (1999), pp. 2329–2338.

Miniaev, Sergei. "K probleme proiskhozhdeniia siunnu [The Problem of the Origins of the Xiongnu]." *Information Bulletin of the Association for the Study of the Cultures of Central Asia,* 9 (1985), pp. 70–78.

Miniaev, Sergei, and Lidiia Sakharovskaia. "Soprovoditel'nye zakhoroheniia 'tsarskogo' kompleksa No. 7v mogil'nike Tsaram [Accompanying Burials of Royal Complex No. 7 at the Tsaram Cemetery]." *Arkheologicheskie Vesti,* 9 (2002), pp. 86–118.

———. "Elitnyi kompleks zakhoronenii Siunnu v padi Tsaram [An Elite Burial Complex of the Xiongnu in the Tsaram Basin]." *Rossiiskaia Arkheologiia,* 1 (2007), pp. 194–210.

———. "Investigation of a Xiongnu Royal Complex in the Tsaram Valley: The Inventory of Barrow No. 7 and the Chronology of the Site." *The Silk Road,* 4/1 (2007), pp. 44–56.

Minorsky, Vladimir. "Mongol Place-names in Mukri Kurdistan (Mongolica 4)." *Bulletin of the School of Oriental and African Studies,* 19/1 (1957), pp. 58–81.

Mission archéologique française en Mongolie. *Mongolie: le premier empire des steppes.* Arles, 2003.

Molodin, Viacheslav I., and Kang In-Uk. "The Yarhoto Site (Turfan Depression, China) in the Context of the Hunnu Problem." *Archaeology, Ethnology, and Anthropology of Eurasia,* 3 (2000), pp. 89–99.

Momiyama, Akira. "Zhang Qian's Zaokong (Trailblazing): Discovery of the Western Regions (Xiyu)." In *Opening Up the Silk Road: The Han and the Eurasian World, Silk Roads Nara International Symposium (2005 Nara-shi, Japan).* Nara, 2007, pp. 17–22.

Mongolian National Museum of History and National Museum of Korea. *Mongolyn Morin Tolgoi khunnu ueiin bulsh* [The Xiongnu Period Burials of Morin Tolgoi, Mongolia]. Ulaanbaatar, 2001.

Morgan, David O. "Review of Oleg Grabar and Sheila Blair, 'Epic Images and Contemporary History: The Illustrations of the Great Mongol Shahnama.'" *Bulletin of the School of Oriental and African Studies,* 45/2 (1982), pp. 364–365.

———. "The Mongols in Syria, 1260–1300." In *Crusade and Settlement: Papers Read at the First Conference of the Society for the Study of the Crusades and the Latin East and Presented to R.C. Smail,* ed. P. Edbury. Cardiff, 1985, pp. 231–235.

———. "The 'Great Yāsā of Chingiz Khān' and Mongol Law in the Īlkhānate." *Bulletin of the School of Oriental and African Studies,* 49 (1986), pp. 163–176.

———. *The Mongols.* Oxford, 1986.

———. *Medieval Persia.* London, 1988.

———. "The Mongols and the Eastern Mediterranean." *Mediterranean Historical Review,* 4/1 (1989), 198–211.

———. "Review of Joseph F. Fletcher, and Beatrice Forbes Manz, 'Studies on Chinese and Islamic Inner Asia.'" *Journal of the Royal Asiatic Society,* 3rd ser., 6/1 (1996), pp. 147–148.

———. "The Mongols in Iran: A Reappraisal." *Iran,* 42 (2004), pp. 131–136.

———. "Review of Igor de Rachewiltz, 'The Secret History of the Mongols: A Mongolian Epic Chronicle of the Thirteenth Century. Translated with a Historical and Philological Commentary.'" *Bulletin of the School of Oriental and African Studies,* 67/3 (2004), pp. 410–412.

———. "The Great *Yasa* of Chinggis Khan revisited." In *Mongols, Turks, and Others: Eurasian Nomads and the Sedentary World,* ed. R. Amitai and M. Biran. Leiden, 2005, pp. 291–308.
———. *The Mongols,* 2nd ed. Oxford, 2007.
———. "Persian as a *Lingua Franca* in the Mongol Empire." In *Literacy in the Persianate World: Writing and the Social Order,* ed. B. Spooner and W. L. Hanaway. Philadelphia, 2012, pp. 160–171.
Mote, Frederick W. "Confucian Eremitism in the Yüan Period." In *The Confucian Persuasion,* ed. A. F. Wright. Stanford, 1960, pp. 202–240.
———. "Chinese Society under Mongol Rule." In *The Cambridge History of China,* vol. 6: *Alien Regimes and Border States 907–1368,* ed. H. Franke and D. Twitchett. Cambridge, 1994, pp. 616–664.
———. "A Note on Traditional Sources for Yuan History." In *The Cambridge History of China,* vol. 6: *Alien Regimes and Border States 907–1368,* ed. H. Franke and D. Twitchett. Cambridge, 1994, pp. 689–693.
Mozolevskii, B. M. *Tovsta Mogila* [Tovstva's Grave]. Kiev, 1979.
Müller, Christian, and Johannes Pahlitzsch. "Sultan Baybars I and the Georgians: In the Light of New Documents Related to the Monastery of the Holy Cross in Jerusalem." *Arabica,* 51/3 (2004), pp. 258–290.
Münküyev, N. Ts. "A New Mongolian *P'ai-tzŭ* from Simferopol." *Acta Orientalia Hungarica,* 31 (1977), pp. 185–215.
Muntaner, R. *The Chronicle of Muntaner,* vol. 2. Tr. Lady Goodenough. London, 1920–1921; rpt. Nendeln, 1967.
Murck, Alfred, and Wen Fong, ed. *Words and Images: Chinese Poetry, Calligraphy, and Painting.* New York, 1991.
Murzin, V. Yu. *Proiskhozhdenie skifov: osnovnye etapy formirovaniia skifskogo etnosa* [The Origin of the Scythians: Main Stages in the Formation of the Scythian Ethnic Identity]. Kiev, 1990.
Mustawfī, Ḥamdallāh Qazwīnī. *Tārīkh-i guzīdah.* Tehran, 1983.
———. "*Ẓafarnāmeh* of Mustawfī." Tr. L. J. Ward. PhD dissertation, University of Manchester, 1983.
———. *Ẓafarnāmah.* Tehran, 1999.
———. *Ẓafarnāmah,* vol. 8 ed. N. Zakkari. Tehran, 1389/2011.
Nadeliaev, V. M., ed. *Drevnetiurskii Slovar* [Dictionary of Old Russian]. Leningrad, 1969.
Nakamachi, Nobutaka. "The Rank and Status of Military Refugees in the Mamluk Army: A Reconsideration of the *Wāfidīyah.*" *Mamluk Studies Review,* 10/1 (2006), pp. 55–81.
Nakazawa, Fujio 中沢富士 et al. *Chūgoku no toji: 8 Gen Min no seika.* 中国の陶磁. 第8巻, 元·明の青花 [Chinese Porcelain, vol. 8: The Blue Flowers of Yuan and Ming]. Tokyo, 1995.
al-Nasāwī, Muḥammad. *Sīrat al-Sulṭān Jalāl al-Dīn Mankubirtī.* Ed. Ḥāfiẓ Ḥamdī. Cairo, 1953.
———. *Sīrat Jalāl al-Dīn Mīnkobarnī.* Ed. Mujtaba Mīnuwī. Tehran, 1986.
Naṭanzī, Mu'īn al-Dīn. *Muntakhab al-tawārīkh al-mu'īnī.* Ed. Jean Aubin. Tehran, 1337/1957.
Navaan, D. *Khunnugiin ov soyol: arkheologiin sudalgaany material* [Khunnu Cultural Heritage: Archaeological Research Material]. Ulaanbaatar, 1999.
Nazarov, Vladislav D. "Konets zolotoordynskogo iga [The End of the Golden Horde's Yoke]." *Voprosy istorii,* 10 (1980), pp. 104–120.

Nelson, Albert, Chunag Amartuvshin, and William Honeychurch. "A Gobi Mortuary Site through Time: Bioarchaeology at Baga Mongol, Baga Gazaryn Chuluu." In *Current Archaeological Research in Mongolia: Proceedings of the August 2007 Archaeological Symposium in Ulaanbaatar, Mongolia,* ed. J. Bemmann, H. Parzinger, E. Pohl, and D. Tseveendorj. Bonn, 2009, pp. 565–578.

Nelson, Albert, William Honeychurch, and Chunag Amartuvshin. "Caught in the Act: Understanding Xiongnu Site Formation Processes at Baga Gazaryn Chuluu, Mongolia." In *Xiongnu Archaeology: Multidisciplinary Perspectives of the First Steppe Empire in Inner Asia,* ed. U. Brosseder and B. Miller. Bonn, 2011, pp. 213–228.

Nikephorus, Patriach of Constantinople. *Short History.* Tr. Cyril Mango. Washington, DC, 1990.

Ningcheng xian wenhuaguan 寧城縣文化館 [Ningchen County Cultural Relics Bureau]. "Ningcheng Xian xin faxian de Xiajiadian shangceng wenhua muzang ji qi xiangguan yiwu de yanjiu 寧城縣新發現的夏家店上層文化墓葬及其相關遺物的研究 [Research on Upper Xinjiang Graves Newly Discovered in Ningcheng County and Related Artifacts]." *Wenwu ziliao congkan* 文物資料叢刊, 9 (1985), pp. 23–58.

Nizami, Khaliq A. "India's Cultural Relations with Central Asia during the Medieval Period." In *Central Asia: Movement of People and Ideas from Times Prehistoric to Modern,* ed. A. Guha. New Delhi, 1970, pp. 157–166.

Noonan, Thomas S. "The Grain Trade of the Northern Black Sea in Antiquity." *American Journal of Philology,* 94/3 (1973), pp. 231–242.

al-Nuwayrī, Shihāb al-Dīn Aḥmad b. ʿAbd al-Wahhāb. *Nihāyat al-arab fī funūn al-adab.* Cairo, 1346/1923–1418/1997.

Oates, Joan. "A Note on the Early Evidence for Horse and the Riding of Equids in Western Asia." In *Prehistoric Steppe Adaptation and the Horse,* ed. M. Levine, C. Renfrew, and K. Boyle. Cambridge, 2003, pp. 115–125.

Obolenskii, kn. D. A. "Vostochnye podpisi na starinnykh russkikh gramotakh [Eastern Signatures of Ancient Russian Documents]." *Izvestiia Imperatorskogo russkogo arkheologicheskogo obshchestva,* 2 (1861), pp. 22–24.

Odani, Nakao. "Nomadic Tribes on the Silk Road: Da Yuezhi and Xiongnu." In *Opening Up the Silk Road: The Han and the Eurasian world, Silk Roads Nara International Symposium (2005 Nara-shi, Japan).* Nara, 2007, pp. 51–61.

Olbricht, Peter. *Das Postwesen in China unter der Mongolenherrschaft im 13. und 14. Jahrhundert.* Wiesbaden, 1954.

Ol'khovskii, Vladislav S. *Pogrebal'no-pominal'naia obriadnost' naseleniia stepnoi Skifii (VII–VIII vv. do n.e.)* [Rituals of Burial and Commemoration of the Population of Scythia in the 7th–8th centuries BCE]. Moscow, 1991.

———. *Skifskaia triada. Materially i issledovaniia po arkheologii Rossii* [Scythian Triad: Sources and Studies of Russian Archaeology]. Moscow, 1997.

Olschki, Leonardo. *Guillaume Boucher: A French Artist at the Court of the Khans.* Baltimore, 1946.

Onaiko, Nadezhda A. *Antichnyi import v Pridneprov'e i Pobuzh'e v VII–V vv. do n.e.* [Ancient Import Trade along the Dneiper and Southern Bug rivers in the 7th–5th centuries BCE]. Moscow, 1966.

Onat, Ayşe, Sema Orsoy, and Konualp Ercilasun. *Han Hanedanlığı Tarihi. Hsiung-nu (Hun) Monografisi* [The History of the Han Dynasty. A Monograph on the Hsiung-nu (Huns)]. Ankara, 2004.

Orbelian, Stephannos. *Histoire de la Sioune.* Tr. M. Brosset. St. Petersburg, 1864.

Orchard, George E. "The Stand on the Ugra." *New Review,* 5/1 (1965), pp. 34–43.
Oriental Society of Hong Kong and the Fung Ping Shan Museum, *The Jingdezhen Wares: The Yuan Evolution.* Hong Kong, 1984.
Origo, Iris. "The Domestic Enemy: The Eastern Slaves in Tuscany in the Fourteenth and Fifteenth Centuries." *Speculum,* 30 (1955), pp. 321–366.
Ostrowski, Donald. *Muscovy and the Mongols: Cross-cultural Influences on the Steppe Frontier, 1304–1589.* Cambridge, 1998.
———. "The *Tamma* and the Dual Administrative Structure of the Mongol Empire." *Bulletin of the School of Oriental and African Studies,* 61 (1998), pp. 63–74.
Outram, Alan et al. "The Earliest Horse Harnessing and Milking." *Science,* 323 (2009), pp. 1332–1335.
Pachymérès, Georges. *Relations historiques,* vol. 2. Tr. A. Failler and V. Laurent. Paris, 1984.
Pálóczi Horváth, A. "L'immigration et l'éstablissement des Comans en Hongrie." *Acta Orientalia Academiae Scientarum Hungaricae,* 29 (1975), pp. 313–333.
———. "Steppe Traditions and Cultural Assimilation of a Nomadic People: The Cumanians in Hungary in the 13th–14th Century." In *Archaeological Approaches to Cultural Identity,* ed. S. Shennan. London, 1989, pp. 291–302.
Paneiakh, Viktor M. *Kabal'noe kholopstvo na Rusi v XVI veke* [Kabala Slavery in Sixteenth-Century Russia]. Leningrad, 1967.
———. *Kholopstvo v XVI—nachale XVII veka* [Slaves in the Sixteenth and Early Seventeenth Centuries]. Leningrad, 1975.
Parzinger, Hermann (Partsinger, German). "Stepnye kochevniki na vostoke Tsentral'noi Evropy. Nakhodki i pamiatniki v svete sravnitel'noi arkheologii [Steppe Nomads in the East of Central Europe. Findings and Monuments in the Light of Comparative Archaeology]." *Vestnik drevnei istorii,* 2 (1998), pp. 104–115.
———. *Die frühen völker Eurasiens: Vom Neolithikum bis zum mittelalter.* Munich, 2006.
———. "The 'Silk Roads' Concept Reconsidered: About Transfers, Transportation and Transcontinental Interactions in Prehistory." *The Silk Road,* 5/2 (2008), pp. 7–15.
Patton, Douglas. *Badr al-Dīn Lu'lu': Atabeg of Mosul, 1211–1259.* Seattle, 1991.
Paul, Jürgen. "L'Invasion mongole comme 'révélateur' de la société Iranienne." In *L'Iran face à la domination Mongole,* ed. D. Aigle. Tehran, 1997, pp. 37–53.
Pelenski, Jaroslaw. "State and Society in Muscovite Russia and the Mongol-Turkic System in the Sixteenth Century." *Forschungen zur osteuropäischen Geschichte,* 27 (1980), pp. 156–167.
Pelliot, Paul. "Une ville musulmane dans la Chine du Nord sous les Mongols." *Journal Asiatique,* 211 (1927), pp. 261–279.
———. *Notes sur l'histoire de la Horde d'Or.* Paris, 1949.
———. *Notes on Marco Polo,* vol. 1. Paris, 1959.
———. *Recherches sur les chrétiens d'Asie Centrale et d'Extrême Orient.* Paris, 1973.
Peng, Ke. "The Andronovo Bronze Artifacts Discovered in Toquztara County in Ili, Xinjiang." In *The Bronze Age and Early Iron Age Peoples of Eastern Central Asia,* ed. V. H. Mair. Philadelphia, 1998, pp. 573–580.
Peng, Ke, and Yanshi Zhu. "New Research on the Origins of Cowries Used in Ancient China." *Sino-Platonic Papers,* 68 (1995), pp. 1–21.
Peng Daya 彭大雅 and Xu Ting 徐霆. "Heida shi lue 黑韃事略 [Summary of the Records of the Black Tatars]." In *Wang Guowei yishu* 王國維遺書. Shanghai, 1983.

Perevodchikova, Elena V. *Lazyk zverinykh obrazov: Ocherki iskusstva evraziiskikh stepei skifkoi epokhi* [The Language of Bestial Images: Studies on the Art of the Eurasian Steppes in the Scythian Period]. Moscow, 1994.

Perfecky, George A., tr. *The Hypatian Codex,* pt. II: *The Galician-Volnian Chronicle.* Munich, 1973.

Petech, Luciano. *Central Tibet and the Mongols.* Rome, 1990.

Petrenko, Vladimira G. "K voprosu o khronologii ranneskifdkikh kurganov Tsentral'nogo Predkavkaz'ia [On the Chronology of the Early Scythian Burial Mounds of Central North Caucasus]." In *Problemy skifo-sarmatskoi arkheologii,* ed. A. I. Melyukova. Moscow, 1990, pp. 60–81.

———. "Scythian Culture in North Caucasus." In *Nomads of the Eurasian Steppes in the Early Iron Age,* ed. J. Davis-Kimball, V. B. Bashilov, and L. T. Yablonsky. Berkeley, 1995, pp. 2–25.

Petrov, P. I. "K voprosu o termine *kabala* [On the Term "kabala"]." *Narody Azii i Afriki,* 1 (1965), pp. 113–115.

Petrov, V. "Sobornoe ulozhenie 1584 goda ob otmene tarkhanov [Law Codes of the Year 1584 Concerning the Cancellation of *Tarkhans*]." In *Sbornik statei po russkoi istorii posviashchennykh S. F. Platonovu.* St. Petersburg, 1922, pp. 191–201.

Petrushevskii, Ilya P. *Zemledele i agrarnye otnosheniia v Iran XIII–XIV vekov* [Agriculture and Agrarian Relations in Iran, 13th–14th centuries]. Moscow, 1960.

Petry, Carl F. *The Civilian Elite of Cairo in the Later Middle Ages.* Princeton, 1981.

Pfeiffer, Judith, and Sholeh Quinn, eds. *History and Historiography of Post-Mongol Central Asia and the Middle East.* Wiesbaden, 2006.

Pinder-Wilson, Ralph. "Basil Gray 1904–1989." *Iran,* 27 (1989), pp. v–vi.

———. "Basil Gray 1904–1989." *Proceedings of the British Academy,* 105 (2000), pp. 439–457.

Pines, Yuri. "Beasts or Humans: Pre-Imperial Origins of the 'Sino-Barbarian' Dichotomy." In *Mongols, Turks and Others: Eurasian Nomads and the Outside World,* ed. R. Amitai and M. Biran. Leiden, 2005, pp. 59–102.

Piotrovskii, Boris B., ed. *Istoriia narodov Severnogo Kavkaza s drevneishikh vremen do kontsa XVIII v* [History of the People of the Northern Caucasus from Ancient Times to the End of the 18th Century]. Moscow, 1988.

Plano Carpini, John of. *The History of the Mongols.* In *The Mongol Mission,* ed. Christopher Dawson. New York, 1955.

Polin, Sergei V. *Ot Skifii k Sarmatii* [From Scythia to Sarmatia]. Kiev, 1992.

Pollock, Sheldon. "The Transformation of Culture-Power in Indo-Europe, 1000–1300." In *Eurasian Transformations, Tenth to Thirteenth Centuries: Crystallizations, Divergences, Renaissances,* ed. J. P. Arnason and B. Wittrock. Leiden, 2004, pp. 247–278.

Polnoe sobranie russkikh letopiseĭ, vol. 1: *Lavrent'evskaia letopis* [Full Collection of the Russian Chronicles, vol. 1: Lavrent'ev Chronicle]. Leningrad, 1926; rpt. Moscow, 1997.

Polnoe sobranie russkikh letopiseĭ, vol. 2: *Ipat'evskaia letopis* [Full Collection of the Russian Chronicles, vol. 2: Ipat'evski Chronicle]. Leningrad, 1927; rpt. Moscow, 1998.

Polnoe sobranie russkikh letopiseĭ, vol. 3: *Novgorogskaia pervaia letopis' starshego i mladshego izvodov* [Full Collection of the Russian Chronicles, vol. 3: The First Novgorod Chronicle of the Elder and Younger *izvods*]. Leningrad, 1928; rpt. Moscow, 2000.

Polo, Marco. *The Description of the World,* vol. 1. Tr. A. C. Moule and Paul Pelliot. London, 1938.

Polo'mak, Natal'ya V. "Nekotorye analogii pogrebeniiam v mogil'nike u derevni Daodunzhei i problema proiskhozhdeniia siunnuskoi kul'tury [Some Analogies to Burials from the Cemetery near Daodun'tszy Village and the Problem of the Origin of the Xiongnu Culture]." In *Kitai v epokhu drevnosti* [China in Ancient Times], ed. V. E. Larichev. Novosibirsk, 1990, pp. 101–107.

Polos'mak, Natal'ya V., E. S. Bogdanov, D. Tseveendorj, and N. Erdene-Ochir. "The Burial Construction of Noin Ula Mound 20, Mongolia." *Archaeology, Ethnology, and Anthropology of Eurasia,* 34/2 (2008), pp. 77–87.

Poluboiarinova, Marina D. *Russkie liudi v Zolotoi Orde* [Russian People in the Golden Horde]. Moscow, 1978.

Poo, Mu-chou. *Enemies of Civilization: Attitudes toward Foreigners in Ancient Mesopotamia, Egypt and China.* Albany, NY, 2005.

Pope, Arthur Upham. *An Introduction to Persian Art since the Seventh Century A.D.* London, 1930.

Pope, John A. *Fourteenth-Century Blue-and-White: A Group of Chinese Porcelains in the Topkapu Saray Müzesi, Istanbul.* Washington, DC, 1952.

———. *Chinese Porcelains from the Ardebil Shrine.* Washington, DC, 1956.

Potter, Lawrence G. "The Kart Dynasty of Herat." PhD dissertation, Columbia University, New York, 1992.

Pousaz, Nicole, Denis Ramseyer, and Turbat Tsagaan. "Mission archéologique helvético-mongole à Boroo Gol, Mongolie: campagne de fouilles." *SLSA Jahresbericht,* 2007, pp. 219–232.

Prawdin, Michael. *The Mongol Empire: Its Rise and Legacy.* Tr. Eden and Cedar Paul. London, 1940.

Procopius. *History of the Wars.* Tr. H. B. Dewing. Cambridge, MA, 2001.

Pshenitsyna, Maria N. "Tesinskii etap [The Tesinskii Stage]." In *Stepnaia polosa Aziatskoi chasti SSSR v skifo-sarmatskoe vremia* [The Steppe Zone of the Asiatic Region of the USSR during the Scythian-Sarmatian Period], ed. N. G. Gorbunova. Moscow, 1992, pp. 224–235.

Pulleyblank, Edwin G. "A Sogdian Colony in Inner Mongolia." *T'oung Pao,* 41 (1952), pp. 317–356.

———. *The Background of the Rebellion of An Lu-shan.* London, 1955.

———. "Some Remarks on the Toquzoghuz Problem." *Ural-Altaische Jahrbücher,* 28 (1956), pp. 35–42.

———. *Lexicon of Reconstructed Pronunciation in Early Middle Chinese Late Middle and Early Mandarin.* Vancouver, 1991.

Purcell, David, and Kimberly Spurr. "Archaeological Investigations of Xiongnu Sites in the Tamir River Valley: Results of the 2005 Joint American-Mongolian Expedition to Tamiryn Ulaan Khoshuu, Ogii nuur, Arkhangai aimag, Mongolia." *The Silk Road,* 4/1 (2006), pp. 20–32.

al-Qāshānī, Abū al-Qāsim. *Taʾrīkh-i uljaytū.* Ed. M. Hambly. Tehran, 1969.

Qazwīnī, Ḥamdallāh Mustawfī. *The Geographical Part of the Nuzhat al-Qulūb.* Ed. Guy Le Strange. London, 1915.

Qazwīnī, Yaḥyā ibn ʿAbd al-Laṭīf. *Kitāb lubb al-tawārīkh.* Tehran 1363/1984.

Qiu Shusen 邱树森. "Lun Yuan dai Zhongguo shaoshu minzu xin geju ji qi shehui yingxiang 論元代中國少數民族 新格局及其社會影響 [On the New Pattern of National Minorities and Its Impact on Yuan Society]." Paper given at the International Conference on Mongol Yuan Studies. Nanjing, 2002.

Quan, Heng. *Das Keng-shen wai-shih: eine Quelle zur späten Mongolenzeit.* Tr. Helmut Schulte-Ufflage. Berlin, 1963.

Rachewiltz, Igor de, tr. "The *Hsi-yu lu* by Yeh-lü Ch'u-ts'ai." *Monumenta Serica,* 21 (1962), pp. 1–128.

———. "Personal and Personalities in North China in the Early Mongol Period." *Journal of the Economic and Social History of the Orient,* 9 (1966), pp. 88–144.

———. "Turks in China under the Mongols: A Preliminary Investigation of Turco-Mongol Relations in the 13th and 14th Centuries." In *China among Equals,* ed. M. Rossabi. Berkeley, 1983, pp. 281–312.

———. "Some Reflections on Činggis Qan's *jasaγ.*" *East Asian History,* 6 (December 1993), pp. 91–103.

———. "Yeh-lü Ch'u-ts'ai, Yeh-lü Chu, Yeh-lü Hsi-liang." In *In the Service of the Khan,* ed. I. de Rachewiltz, Hok-Lam Chan, Ch'i-Ch'ing Hsiao, and Peter W. Geier. Wiesbaden, 1993, pp. 136–175.

———., ed. and tr. *The Secret History of the Mongols: A Mongolian Epic Chronicle of the Thirteenth Century.* Leiden, 2004. 2 vols.

———. "A Note on Yelü Zhu 耶律鑄 and His Family." In *Meng Yuan shiji minzushi lunji: ji nian Weng Dujian xiansheng danchen yi bai zhou nian* 蒙元史暨民族史論集: 紀念翁獨健先生誕辰一百周年 [Festschrift on the History of the Mongol-Yuan Period and Ethnohistory: In Commemoration of the Centenary of the Birth of Professor Weng Dujian], ed. Hao Shiyuan 郝時遠 and Luo Xianyou 羅賢佑. Beijing, 2006, pp. 269–281.

Rachewiltz, Igor de, Hok-Lam Chan, Ch'i-Ch'ing Hsiao, and Peter W. Geier, eds. *In the Service of the Khan. Eminent Personalities of the Early Mongol-Yüan Period (1200–1300).* Wiesbaden, 1993.

Rachewiltz, Igor de, and Wang, May. *Repertory of Proper Names in Yuan Literary Sources.* Taipei, 1988–1996. 4 vols.

Raff, Thomas. *Remarks on an Anti-Mongol Fatwa by Ibn Taimiya.* Privately printed pamphlet. Leiden, 1973.

Raphael, Kate. "Mongol Siege Warfare on the Banks of the Euphrates and the Question of Gunpowder (1260–1312)." *Journal of the Royal Asiatic Society,* 3rd ser., 19/3 (2009), pp. 355–370.

———. *Muslim Fortresses in the Levant: Between Crusaders and Mongols.* London, 2011.

Raschke, Manfred. "New Studies in Roman Commerce with the East." In *Aufstieg und Niedergang der römischen Welt im Spiegel der neueren Forschung II,* 9/2 (1978), pp. 604–1361.

Rashīd al-Dīn, Abū al-Khayr Faḍl Allāh al-Hamadānī. *The Successors of Genghis Kahn.* Tr. J. A. Boyle. New York, 1971.

———. *Jāmiʿ al-tawārīkh,* vol. 2, pt. I. Ed. ʿA.ʿA. ʿAlīzādah. Moscow, 1980.

———. *Athār wa Aḥyāʾ.* Ed. Manuchihr Sutuda and Iraj Afshar. Tehran, 1989.

———. *Jāmiʿ al-tawārīkh.* Ed. B. Karīmī. Tehran, 1338/1959; Ed. M. Rawshan and M. Mūsawī. Tehran, 1994.

———. *Rashiduddin Fazlullah's Jamiʿu't-tawarikh: Compendium of Chronicles. A History of the Mongols.* Tr. Wheeler M. Thackston. Cambridge, MA, 1998–1999. 3 vols.

Ratchnevsky, Paul. "Zum Asudruck T'ouhsia in der Mongolenzeit." In *Collectana Mongolica. Festschrift für Professor Dr. Rintchen zum 60. Geburtstag,* ed. W. Heissig. Wiesbaden, 1966, pp. 173–191.

———. *Genghis Khan.* London, 1993.

Rawson, Jessica. "Carnelian Beads, Animal Figures and Exotic Vessels: Traces of Contacts between the Chinese States and Inner Asia, ca. 1000–650 BC." *Eurasia Antiqua*, 14 (2008), pp. 1–43. Reprinted in *Archäologie in China, vol. 1: Bridging Eurasia*, ed. M. Wagner and W. Wei. Mainz, 2010, pp. 1–42.

Ren, Shinan 任式楠. "Zhongguo shiqian chengzhi kaocha 中國史前城址考察 [Survey of Prehistoric Walled Sites in Chinese History]." *Kaogu* 考古, 1 (1998), pp. 1–16.

Renfrew, Colin, and John Cherry, eds. *Peer Polity Interactions and Socio-Political Change.* Cambridge, 1986.

Riasanovsky, Valentin A. "The Influence of Ancient Mongol Culture and Law on Russian Culture and Law." *Chinese Social and Political Science Review,* 20 (1936–1937), pp. 499–530.

———. *Fundamental Principles of Mongol Law.* Bloomington, IN, 1965.

Riboud, Krishna. "A Comparative Study of Two Similar Han Documents: Polychrome Figured Silks from Lou-lan and Ilmovaja Pad." *Bulletin de Liaison du Centre international d'étude des textiles anciens (Lyon),* 28 (1968), pp. 26–61.

Ricaut, François, C. Keyser-Tracqui, J. Bourgeois, E. Crubezy, and B. Ludes. "Genetic Analysis of a Scytho-Siberian Skeleton and Its Implications for Ancient Central Asian Migrations." *Human Biology,* 76/1 (2004), pp. 109–125.

Ricci, Matteo. *China in the Sixteenth Century: The Journals of Matthew Ricci, 1587–1610.* Tr. L. J. Gallagher. New York, 1953.

Richard, Jean. "The Mongols and the Franks." *Journal of Asian History,* 3 (1969), pp. 45–57. (Reprinted in J. Richard, *Orient and Occident au Moyen Age: contacts et relations (XIIe–XVe siècles*). London, 1976.)

Richards, Donald S., ed. *Islam and the Trade of Asia.* Philadelphia, 1970.

Richter, Gisela. "Silk in Greece." *American Journal of Archaeology,* 33/1 (1929), pp. 27–33.

Robinson, Basil W. "The Burlington House Exhibition of 1931: A Milestone in Islamic Art History." In *Discovering Islamic Art: Scholars, Collectors and Collections,* ed. S. Vernoit. London, 2000, pp. 147–155.

Robinson, David M. *Culture, Courtiers and Competition: The Ming Court (1368–1644).* Cambridge, MA, 2008.

———. "The Ming Court and the Legacy of the Yuan Mongols." In *Culture, Courtiers and Competition: The Ming Court (1368–1644),* ed. D. M. Robinson. Cambridge, MA, 2008, pp. 365–421.

Roemer, Hans R. "Jalayirids, Muzaffarids and Sarbadars." In *The Cambridge History of Iran,* vol. 6: *The Timurid and Safavid Periods,* ed. P. Jackson. Cambridge, 1986, pp. 1–41.

Rogers, Daniel J. "The Contingencies of State Formation in Eastern Inner Asia." *Asian Perspectives,* 46/2 (2007), pp. 249–274.

———. "Inner Asian States and Empires: Theories, Data, and Synthesis." *Journal of Archaeological Research,* 20 (2012), pp. 205–256.

Rossabi, Morris. "Khubilai Khan and the Women in His Family." In *Studia Sino-Mongolica: Festschrift für Herbert Franke,* ed. W. Bauer. Wiesbaden, 1979, pp. 153–157.

———. *Khubilai Khan: His Life and Times.* Berkeley, 1988.

———. "Kuan Tao-sheng: Woman Artist in Yuan China." *Bulletin of Sung Yuan Studies,* 21 (1989), pp. 67–84.

Rubinson, Karen. "Mirrors on the Fringe: Some Notes." *Source,* 4/2–3 (1985), pp. 48–50.

———. "A Reconsideration of Pazyryk." In *Foundations of Empire: Archaeology and Art of the Eurasian Steppes,* ed. G. Seaman. Los Angeles, 1992, pp. 68–76.

Rubruck, William of. *The Mission of Friar William of Rubruck.* Tr. Peter Jackson and ed. David O. Morgan. London, 1990.
Rudenko, Sergei I. *Kul'tura khunnov i Noinulinskie kurgany* [Khunnu Culture and the Kurgans of Noin Ula]. Moscow, 1962.
Rūmī, Jalāl al-Dīn. *Kitāb fīhi mā fīhi.* Ed. Badīʿ al-Zamān Farūzānfar. Tehran, 1362/1983.
———. *Discourses of Rumi.* Tr. A. J. Arberry. Richmond, 1994.
Rybatzki, Volker. *Die Toñuquq-Inschrift.* Szeged, 1997.
Saʿdī. *Kulliyat-i Saʿdī.* Ed. M. A. Farūghī. Tehran, 1368/1989.
al-Ṣafadī, Ṣalāḥ al-Dīn Khalīl b. Aybak. *Nakt al-himyān fī nukat al-ʿumyān.* Ed. Aḥmad Zakī. Cairo, 1911.
Sakharov, Anatoly M. "Les Mongols et la civilisation Russe." In *Contributions à l'histoire russe (Cahiers d'histoire mondiale).* Neuchâtel, 1958, pp. 77–97.
Salmony, Alfred. "Archaeological Background of Textile Production in the Soviet Russian Territory." *The Bulletin of the Needle and Bobbin Club,* 26/2 (1942), pp. 3–14.
Salzman, Philip. *Pastoralists: Equality, Hierarchy, and the State.* Boulder, CO, 2004.
Samarqandī, ʿArūdī. *Chahār maqāla.* Tr. E. G. Browne. London, 1978.
———. *Chahār maqāla.* Ed. M. Muʿīnī. Tehran, 1377/1998.
Samarqandī, Dawlatshāh b. ʿAlāʾ al-Dawla. *Tadhkirat al-shuʿarāʾ.* Ed. E. G. Browne. London, 1901; rpt. Tehran, 1382/2003.
Samoilovich, Aleksandr N. "O 'paiza'—'baiza' v Dzhuchievom uluse [About "Paiza"—"Baize" in the Ulus of Juchi]." *Izvestiia Akademii nauk,* 20/6 (1926), pp. 1107–1120.
Saunders, John J. "The Nomad as Empire-Builder: A Comparison of the Arab and Mongol Conquests." In J. J. Saunders, *Muslims and Mongols: Essays on Medieval Asia,* ed. G. W. Rice. Christchurch, NZ, 1977, pp. 36–66.
Savinov, D. G. "Gunno-sarmatskoye vremya" [Hunno-Sarmatian Period]. In *Drevnie kul'tury Bertekskoi doliny* [Ancient Cultures of the Bertek Valley], ed. V. I. Molodin. Novosibirsk, 1994, pp. 144–146.
Savvides, Alexes G. C. *Byzantium and the Near East: Its Relations with the Seljuk Sultanate of Rum, the Armenians of Cilicia and the Mongols, A.D. c.1192–1237.* Thessaloniki, Greece, 1981.
Scanlon, George T. "Egypt and China: Trade and Imitation." In *Islam and the Trade of Asia,* ed. D. S. Richards. Philadelphia, 1970, pp. 81–96.
Schortman, Edward M., and Patricia A. Urban. "The Place of Interaction Studies in Archaeological Thought." In *Resources, Power and Interaction,* ed. E. M. Schortman and P. A. Urban. New York, 1992, pp. 3–15.
Sechin, Jagchid. "Kitan Struggles against Jurchen Opression—Nomadism versus Sinicization." In Jagchid Sechin, *Essays in Mongolian Studies.* Provo, UT, 1988, pp. 34–49.
Sela, Ron. *Ritual and Authority in Central Asia: The Khan's Inauguration Ceremony.* Papers on Inner Asia, 37. Bloomington, IN, 2003.
Semenov, Aleksandr A. "K voprosu o zolotoordynskom termine 'baskak' [On the the Term "baskak" in the Golden Horde]." *Izvestiia Akademii nauk SSSR (Otdelenie literaturty i iazyka),* 6/2 (1947), pp. 127–147.
———. "Ocherki kul'turnoi roli Uigurov v Mongolskikh gosudarstvakh [Outline of the Cultural Role of the Uygurs in the the Mongol states]." In *Materialy po istorii i kul'ture Uigurskogo naroda,* ed. G. S. Sadvakasov. Alm Ata, 1978, pp. 32–48.
Semenov, Vladimir A. *Suglug-Khem i Khaiyrakan: mogilniki skifskogo vremeni v Tsentralnotuvinskoi kotlovine* [Suglug-Khem and Khaiyrakan: Burials of the Scythian Period in the Central Tuvan Basin]. St. Petersburg, 2003.

Senga, Toru. "The Toquz Oghuz Problem and the Origins of the Khazars." *Journal of Asian History,* 24/1 (1990), pp. 57–69.
Sergeevich, Vasili I. *Drevnosti russkogo prava.* V. I: *Territoriia i naselenie* [Antiquities of Russian Law, vol. 1: Territory and Population], 3rd. ed. St. Petersburg, 1909.
Serruys, Henry. "Remains of Mongol Customs in China during the Early Ming Period." *Monumenta Serica,* 16 (1957), pp. 137–190.
———. "Chinese in Southern Mongolia during the Sixteenth Century." *Monumenta Serica,* 18 (1959), pp. 1–95.
———. "The Mongols in China during the Hung-wu Period." *Melanges chinois et bouddhique,* 11 (1959), pp. 2–328.
———. "Mongol *Altan* 'Gold' = 'Imperial.'" *Monumenta Serica,* 21 (1962), pp. 357–378.
———. "A Question of Thievery." *Zentralasiatische studien,* 10 (1978), pp. 287–309.
Sertkaya, Osman Fikri. *Göktürk tarihinin Meseleleri* [Problems in the History of the Göktürk]. Ankara, 1995.
Shabānkāraʾī, Muḥammad b. ʿAlī b. Muḥammad. *Majmaʿ al-ansāb.* Tehran, 1363/1984.
Shao, Wangping. "The Formation of Civilization: The Interaction Sphere of the Longshan Period." In *The Formation of Chinese Civilization: An Archaeological Perspective,* ed. S. Allan. New Haven, CT, 2005, pp. 85–123.
Shao, Yuanping 邵遠平. *Yuanshi liebien* 元史類編 [Thematical Compilations concerning the *Yuanshi*]. Taipei, 1968.
Shaughnessy, Edward L. "Historical Perspectives on the Introduction of the Chariot into China." *Harvard Journal of Asiatic Studies,* 48 (1988), pp. 189–237.
———. "Historical Geography and the Extent of the Earliest Chinese Kingdoms." *Asia Major,* 2 (1989), pp. 1–22.
Shelach, Gideon. "The Qiang and the Question of Human Sacrifice in the Late Shang Period." *Asian Perspectives,* 35 (1995), pp. 1–26.
———. *Leadership Strategies, Economic Activity and Interregional Interaction: Social Complexity in Northeast China.* New York, 1999.
———. "Early Pastoral Societies in Northeast China: Local Change and Interregional Interaction during c. 1100–600 BC." In *Mongol, Turks and Others: Eurasia and the Outside World,* ed. R. Amitai and M. Biran. Leiden, 2005, pp. 15–58.
———. *Prehistoric Societies on the Northern Frontiers of China: Archaeological Perspectives on Identity Formation and Economic Change during the First Millennium BCE.* Approaches to Anthropological Archaeology Series. London, 2009.
Shen, Hsueh-man, ed. *Gilded Splendor: Treasures of China's Liao Empire (907–1125).* New York, 2006.
Sheng, Angela. "Textiles from the Silk Road: Intercultural Exchanges among Nomads, Traders, and Agriculturalists." *Expedition,* 52 (2010), pp. 33–43.
Sher, Yakov A. "On the Sources of the Scythic Animal Style." *Arctic Anthropology,* 25/2 (1988), pp. 47–60.
Sherkova, Tatyana A. *Egipet i Kushanskoe tsarstvo* [Egypt and the Kushan Kingdom]. Moscow, 1991.
Sherratt, Andrew. "The Horse and the Wheel: The Dialectics of Change in the Circum-Pontic Regions and Adjacent Areas, 4500–1500 BC." In *Prehistoric Steppe Adaptation and the Horse,* ed. M. Levine, C. Renfrew, and K. Boyle. Cambridge, 2003, pp. 233–268.
———. "The Trans-Eurasian Exchange: The Prehistory of Chinese Relations with the West." In *Contact and Exchange in the Ancient World,* ed. V. Mair. Honolulu, 2006, pp. 30–61.

Shipova, Ekaterina N. *Slovar'* tiurkizmov v Russkom iazyke [The Dictionary of the Turkish Adoptions into the Russian Language]. Alma-Ata, 1976.
Sijzī, Amīr Ḥassan. *Fawāʾid al-fuʾād.* Ed. M. L. Malik. Lahore, 1966.
———. *Nizam ad-Din Awliya's Morals for the Heart.* Tr. Bruce Lawrence. New York, 1992.
Silbergeld, Jerome. "In Praise of Government: Chao Yung's Painting Noble Steeds, and Late Yüan Politics." *Artibus Asiae,* 46/3 (1985), pp. 159–202.
Silfen, Paul H. *The Influence of the Mongols on Russia: A Dimensional History.* New York, 1974.
Silverstein, Adam. *Postal Systems in the Pre-Modern Islamic World.* Cambridge, 2007.
Simnānī, ʿAlāʾ al-Dawla. *Chihil Majlis.* Ed. Amīr Iqbāl Sīstānī. Tehran, 1379/2000–2001.
Sinor, Denis. "The Establishment and the Dissolution of the Türk Empire." In *The Cambridge History of Inner Asia,* ed. D. Sinor. Cambridge, 1990, pp. 285–316.
———. "Western Information on the Kitans and Some Related Questions." *Journal of the American Oriental Society,* 115 (1995), pp. 262–269.
Sivan, Emanuel. "Refugiés Syro-Palestiniens au temps des croisades." *Revue des études islamiques,* 35 (1967), pp. 135–147.
———. *The Radicals of Islam: Medieval Theology and Modern Politics.* 2nd rev. ed. New Haven, CT, 1990.
Skelton, Raleigh A., ed. *The Vinland Map and the Tartar Relation.* New Haven, CT, 1995.
Skrzhinskaia, Elena Ch., tr. *Barbaro i Kontarini o Rossii* [Barbaro and Kontarini on Russia]. Leningrad, 1971.
Smirnov, Iakov I. "Sudebnik 1550 goda [Law Code of the Year 1550]." *Istoricheskie zapiski,* 24 (1947), pp. 267–352.
Smith, Anthony. *The Ethnic Origin of Nations.* Oxford, 1986.
Smith, John M., Jr. "ʿAyn Jālūt: Mamluk Success or Mongol Failure." *Harvard Journal of Asiatic Studies,* 44 (1984), pp. 307–345.
———. "Demographic Considerations in Mongol Siege Warfare." *Archivum Ottomanicum,* 13 (1993–1994), pp. 329–334.
———. "Nomads on Ponies vs. Slaves on Horses." *Journal of the American Oriental Society,* 118 (1998), pp. 54–62.
———. "Mongol Nomadism and Middle Eastern Geography: Qishlaqs and Tümen." In *The Mongol Empire and Its Legacy,* ed. R. Amitai-Preiss and D. O. Morgan. Leiden, 1999, pp. 34–56.
———. "High Living and Heartbreak on the Road to Baghdad." In *Beyond the Legacy of Genghis Khan,* ed. L. Komaroff. Leiden, 2006, pp. 111–134.
Smith, Paul J. "Family, *Landsmann,* and Status-Group Affinity in Refugee Mobility Strategies: The Mongol Invasions and the Diaspora of Sichuanese Elites, 1230–1330." *Harvard Journal of Asiatic Studies,* 52/2 (1992), pp. 655–708.
Sneath, David. "Introduction—Imperial Statecraft: Arts of Power on the Steppe." In *Imperial Statecraft: Political Forms and Techniques of Governance in Inner Asia, Sixth-Twentieth Centuries,* ed. D. Sneath. Bellingham, WA, 2006, pp. 1–22.
———. *The Headless State: Aristocratic Orders, Kinship Societ, and the Misrepresentation of Nomadic Inner Asia.* New York, 2007.
Song, Lian 宋濂, comp. *Yuanshi* 元史 [The Official History of the Yuan]. Beijing, 1976. Also in the collected edition of the Twenty-Four Histories [*Erhshisi shi* 二十四史], vol. 18. Beijing, 1997.
Soudavar, Abolala. "The Saga of Abu-Saʿid Bahador Khan: The Abu-saʿidname." In *The Court of the Il-khans 1290–1340,* ed. J. Raby and T. Fitzherbert. Oxford, 1996, pp. 95–218.

Sperling, Elliot. "Hülegü and Tibet." *Acta Orientalia Hungaricae,* 44 (1990), pp. 145–157.

Spicyn, A. A. "Tatarskie baisy [Tatar Paizas]." *Izvestiia arkhivnoi kommissii,* 29 (1929), pp. 130–141.

Spuler, Bertold. *Die Goldene Horde: Die Mongolen in Rußland 1223–1502.* 2nd ed. Wiesbaden, 1965; 1st ed. Leipzig, 1943.

———. *Die Mongolen in Iran: Verwaltung und kultur der Ilchanzeit. 1220–1350.* 4th ed. Leiden, 1985.

Sreznevskii, Izmail I. *Materialy dlia slovaria drevnerusskogo iazyka po pis'mennym pamiatnikam* [Sources for the Old Russian Dictionary Based on Written Literary Monuments], vols. 1–3. St. Petersburg, 1893–1903; Dopolneniia [Supplement]: St. Petersburg, 1912.

Standen, Naomi. "What Nomads Want: Raids, Invasions and the Liao Conquest of 947." In *Mongols, Turks and Others: Eurasian Nomads and the Sedentary World,* ed. R. Amitai and M. Biran. Leiden, 2005, pp. 129–174.

———. *Unbounded Loyalty: Frontier Crossings in Liao China.* Honolulu, 2007.

Stark, Sören. "On Oq Bodun, the Western Türk Qağanate and the Ashina Clan." *Archivum Eurasiae Medii Aevi,* 15 (2006–2007), pp. 159–171.

———. *Die Alttürkenzeit in Mittel-und Zentralasian.* Wiesbaden, 2008.

Staviskii, Boris J. "Central Asian Mesopotamia and the Roman World: Evidence of Contacts." In *In the Land of the Gryphons: Papers on Central Asian Archaeology in Antiquity,* ed. A. Invernizzi. Florence, 1995, pp. 191–202.

Su, Pengyu 蘇鵬宇. "Mengyuan shiqi qidanren de qianyi yanjiu 蒙元時期契丹人的遷移研究 [Research on the Migration of the Kitans during the Yuan Period]." *Anyang Shifan Xueyuan Xuebao* 安陽師範學院學報, 1 (2010), pp. 72–76.

———. "Mengyuan shiqi qidanren de yanjiu 蒙元時期契丹人研究 [Studies on the Kitans during the Yuan Period]." MA thesis, Northwest Normal University Institute of Culture and History, Lanzhou, China, 2010.

Su, Tianjue 蘇天爵. *Yuan wenlei* 元文類 [Categorized Literature from the Yuan Period]. Taipei, 1967.

Sultanov, Tursun I. *Kochevye plemena Priaral'ia v XV–XVII vv* [The Nomadic Tribes South of the Aral in the 15th–17th Centuries]. Moscow, 1982.

Sun Jingji 孫進己 and Sun Hong 孫泓. *Qidan minzu shi* 契丹民族史 [A History of the Kitan Nationality]. Guilin, 2009.

Sun Kekuan 孫克寬. *Menggu Han jun ji Han wenhua yanjiu* 蒙古漢軍及漢文化研究 [Study of the Mongolian Han Army and Han Culture]. Taipei, 1958.

Sweeney, J. R. "'Spurred on by Fear of Death': Refugees and Displaced Populations during the Mongol Invasion of Hungary." In *Nomadic Diplomacy, Destruction and Religion from the Pacific to the Adriatic,* ed. W. Schlepp and M. Gervers. Toronto, 1994, pp. 34–62.

Szczesniak, Boleslaw B. "A Note on the Character of the Tatar Impact upon the Russian State and Church." *Etudes Slaves et Est-Européennes,* 17 (1972), pp. 92–98.

Szeftel, Morris. "The History of Suretyship in Old Russian Law." *Recueils de la Société Jean Bodin pour l'histoire comparative des institutions,* 29 (1971), pp. 841–866.

Tal'ko-Gryntsevich, Iulian D. *Materialy k paleoetnologii Zabaikal'ia* [Materials on the Paleoethnology of the Trans-Baikal]. St. Petersburg, 1999.

Tan, Qixiang 譚其驤, ed. *Zhongguo lishi ditu ji* 中國歷史地圖集 [Atlas of Chinese History], vol. 6: *Song, Liao, Jin.* Shanghai, 1982.

Tao Zongyi 陶宗儀. *Chuo geng lu* 輟耕錄 [Tao Zongyi's Literary Collection]. n.d.; rpt. Taipei, 1987.
Tardy, Lajos. *Sklavenhandel in der Tartarei.* Szeged, 1983.
Tekin, Talat. *A Grammar of Orkhon Turkic.* Bloomington, IN, 1968.
———. *Orhon Yazıtları* [The Orhon Inscriptions]. Istanbul, 1995.
Teng, Ssu-yü. *Family Instructions for the Yen Clan: Yen-shih chia-hsün.* Leiden, 1968.
Terenozhkin, Aleksei I. *Kimmeriitsy* [The Cimmerians]. Kiev, 1976.
Thompson, Robert W., tr. "The Historical Compilation of Vardan Arewelc'i." *Dumbarton Oaks Papers,* 43 (1989), pp. 125–226.
Tignor, Robert et al. *Worlds Together, World Apart: A History of the World from the Beginning of Humankind to the Present.* 3rd ed. New York, 2011.
Tishkin Sergei V. "Characteristic Burials of the Xiongnu Period at Ialoman-II in the Altai." In *Xiongnu Archaeology: Multidisciplinary Persepctives of the First Steppe Empire in Inner Asia,* ed. U. Brosseder and B. Miller. Bonn, 2011, pp. 539–558.
Togan, Isenbike. "Cycles of Retribalization and the Role of the State." A research proposal submitted to the Fairbank Center for East Asian Research, Harvard University, 1987.
———. *Flexibility and Limitation in Steppe Formations.* Leiden, 1998.
———. "Altınordu Çözülürken Kırım'a Giden Yol [The Road Leading to Crimea at the Dissolution of the Golden Horde]." In *Türk-Rus İlişkilerinde Dün Bugün Sempozyumu. Ankara 12–14 Aralılk 1992.* Ankara, 1999, pp. 39–64.
———. "Alternative Passageways to Modern Nationhood: Patterns of Power-sharing and Concentration of Power in Central Asia and the Near East." In *Beijing Forum. Evolution of Civilizations: Historical Experiences in the Modern Times of the East and the West. Collection of Papers and Abstracts,* vol. 2. Beijing, 2006, pp. 516–545.
———. "7. ve 8. Yüzyıllarda Çin ve Türk Resmi Tarih Anlayışına Farklı Yaklaşımlar [Approaches to Chinese and Early Türk Official Historiography in the 7th–8th Centuries]." *Akademi Forumu,* 54. Ankara, 2008.
———. "Boy devlet İlişkileri ve "*Buluo*" (*Bölük*) meselesi [Tribe-State Relations and the Problem of *buluo* (*bölük*)]." In *Halil İnalcık armağanı* [Festschrift in Honour of Halil İnalcık], vol. 1. Ankara, 2009, pp. 43–86.
———. "Court Historiography in T'ang China: Assigning a Place to History and Historians at the Palace." In *Royal Courts in Dynastic States and Empires: A Global Perspective,* ed. J. Duindam, T. Artan, and M. Kunt. Leiden, 2011, pp. 171–198.
Togan, Isenbike, Gülnar Kara, and Cahide Baysal. *Eski Tang Tarihi (Chiu Tang-shu) 194a Türkler Bölümü* [The Turkic Tribes according to the History of the Ancient Turks in the *Jiu Tang shu* 194a]. Ankara, 2006.
Tokhtas'ev, Sergej. "Die Kimmerier in den antiken Überlieferung." *Hyperboreus,* 2/1 (1996), pp. 1–46.
Torbat, Tsagaan. *Khunnugiin jiriin irgediin bulsh* [The Xiongnu Burials of Common People]. Ulaanbaatar, 2004.
Torbat, Tsagaan, Chunag Amartuvshin, and Ulambayar Erdenebat. *Egiin Golyn sav nutag dakh' arkheologiin dursgaluud* [Archaeological Monuments of Egiin Gol Valley]. Ulaanbaatar, 2003.
Torbat, Tsagaan, D. Batsukh, T. Batbayar, N. Bayarkhuu, Kh. Jordana, and P. Giscard. "Baga Turgenii gol-VI Pazyrykiin ueiin tsogtsolboryn arkheologi, paleoantropologiin sudalgaa [Archaeology and Paleoanthropological Research at a Pazyryk Period

Complex, the Baga Tureg river-VI site]." *Arkheologiin Sudlal,* 4/24 (2007), pp. 188–215.
Torbat, Tsagaan, D. Bayar, D. Tseveendorj, N. Bayarkhuu, T. Iderkhangai, and P. Giscard. *Mongol Altain Arkheologiin Dursgaluud—I Bayan Oglii Aimag* [The Archaeological Findings in the Mongol Altai-I., Bayan-Ulgii Province]. Ulaanbaatar, 2009.
Toynbee, Arnold J. *A Study of History.* London, 1934–1954. 10 vols.
Trever, Kamila C. *Excavations in Northern Mongolia.* Leningrad, 1932.
Tseveendorj, D., N. Erdene-Ochir, N. V. Polos'mak, and E. S. Bogdanov. "Noyon Uulyn Khunnugiin yazguurtny bulshny 2006, 2009 ony arkeologiin maltlaga sudalgaany ur dungees [The Findings of the Archaeological Research and Excavations of the Khunnu Noble Graves in Noyon-Uul—2006, 2009]." *Arkheologiin Sudlal,* 29 (2010), pp. 255–273.
Tseveendorj, D., N. Polosmak, N. Batbold, N. Erdene-Ochir, and M. Tsengel. "Noyon Uuliin Khunnugiin yazguurtnii 20-r bulsh sudalgaa [Research of the Khunnu Noble Grave No. 20 in Noyon-Uul—An Archaeological Study]." *Arkheologiin Sudlal,* 4/24 (2007), pp. 288–304.
Tseveendorj, Damdinsurenjin. "Novye dannye po arkheologii khunnu [New Data on the Archaeology of the Khunnu]." In *Drevnie kultury Mongolii* [The Ancient Cultures of Mongolia], ed. R. S. Vasil'evskii. Novosibirsk, 1985, pp. 51–87.
Tsulia, G. V. "Dzhelal ad-Din v otsenke gruzinskoi letopisnoi traditsii [Jalal al-Din according to the Evaluation of the Georgian Chronical Tradition]." In *Letopisi i khroniki 1980g.*, ed. B.A. Rybakov. Moscow, 1981, pp. 112–128.
Tu Ji 屠寄. *Mengwuer shi ji* 蒙兀兒史記 [Historical records of the Mongols]. Taipei, 1962; in *Yuan shi er zhong* 元史二種 (Shanghai, 1989), vol. 2.
Tuotuo 脫脫. *Liao shi* 遼史 [The Official History of the Liao]. Beijing, 1974. 5 vols.
———. *Jin shi* 金史 [The Official History of the Jin]. Beijing, 1975. 8 vols.
Twitchett, Denis. "Introduction." In *The Cambridge History of China,* vol. 3: *Sui and Tang China, 589–906, Part 1,* ed. Denis Twitchett. Cambridge, 1979, pp. 1–47.
———. *The Writing of Official History under the Tang.* Cambridge, 1992.
Twitchett, Denis, and Klaus-Peter Tietze. "The Liao." In *The Cambridge History of China,* vol. 6: *Alien Regimes and Border States 907–1368,* ed. H. Franke and D. Twitchett. Cambridge, 1994, pp. 43–153.
al-ʿUlaymī, Mujīr al-Dīn Abū al-Yumn ʿAbd al-Raḥmān b. Muḥammad. *Al-Uns al-jalīl bi-taʾrīkh al-quds waʾ l-khalīl.* Amman, 1973. 2 vols.
al-ʿUmarī, Aḥmad b. Yaḥyā b. Faḍlāllah. *Das Mongolische Weltreich: al-ʿUmarī's Darstellung der mongolischen Reiche in seinem Werk Masālik al-abṣār fī al-mamālik al-amṣār,* ed. and tr. Klaus Lech. Wiesbaden, 1968.
Underhill, Anne P. *Craft Production and Social Change in Northern China.* New York, 2002.
UNESCO. *The Silk Roads Project: Integral Study of the Silk Roads—Roads of Dialogue, 1988–1997 UNESCO Report.* Paris, 2008.
Vadetskaya, El'ga B. *Tashtykskaia epokha v drevnei istorii Sibiri* [The Tashtyk Era in the Ancient History of Siberia]. St. Peterburg, 1999.
Vaissière, Étienne de la. *Sogdian Traders: A History.* Boston, 2005.
Vásáry, Istvan. "The Golden Horde Term *daruğa* and Its Survival in Russia." *Acta Orientalia Hungarica,* 30 (1976), pp. 187–197.
———. "The Origin of the Institution of *Basqaqs*." *Acta Orientalia Hungarica,* 32 (1978), pp. 201–206.

———. *Az Arany Horda kancelláriája* [Chancellery of the Golden Horde]. Kőrösi Csoma Társaság, Budapest, 1987.
———. "Bemerkungen zum uigurischen Schrifttum in der Goldenen Horde und bei den Timuriden." *Ural-altaische Jahrbücher,* Neue Folge 7 (1987), pp. 115–126.
———. *Cumans and Tatars: Oriental Military in the Pre-Ottoman Balkans.* Cambridge, 2005.
Vel'iaminov-Zernov, Vladimir V. "Istochniki dlia izucheniia tarkhanstva, zhalovannogo bashkiram russkimi gosudariami [Sources for the Study of the Tarkhan Status, Given by the Russian Tsars to the Bashkirs]." Supplement to *Zapiski Akademii Nauk* (St. Petersburg), 4/6 (1864), pp. 1–48.
Vernadsky, George. "A propos des origines du servage de 'kabala' dans le droit russe." *Revue historique du droit français et étranger,* 4/14 (1935), pp. 360–367.
———. "The Scope and Contents of Chingis Khan's *yasa.*" *Harvard Journal of Asiatic Studies,* 3 (1938), pp. 337–360.
———. *The Mongols and Russia* (in idem, *A History of Russia,* vol. 3). New Haven, CT. 1953. Russian translation: G. V. Vernadskii, *Mongoly i Rus'.* Moscow, 1997.
Vinograd, Richard. "River Village: The Pleasures of Fishing and Chao Meng-fu's Li-Kuo Style Landscapes." *Artibus Asiae,* 40 (1978), pp. 124–134.
———. "Some Landscapes Related to the Blue-and-Green Manner from the Early Yüan Period." *Artibus Asiae,* 41 (1979), pp. 106–124.
Vinogradov, Yu. G. *Politicheskaia istoriia Ol'viiskogo polisa VII–I do n.e* [Political History of the City of Olbia in the 7th–1st centuries BCE]. Moscow, 1989.
Volkov, Vitaly V. "Early Nomads of Mongolia." In *Nomads of the Eurasian Steppe in the Early Iron Age,* ed. J. Davis-Kimball, V. B. Bashilov, and L. T. Yablonsky. Berkeley, 1995, pp. 319–333.
Voskresensky, A. A., and N. P. Tikhonov. "Technical Study of Textiles from the Burial Mounds of Noin-Ula." *Bulletin of the Needle and Bobbin Club,* 20, 1/2 (1936), pp. 3–73.
Vysotskaia, Tatiana N. *Neapol'—stolitsa gosudarstva pozdnikh skifov* [Naples: The Capital of the Later Scythian State]. Kiev, 1979.
Wang, Pu 王溥, comp. *Tang Huiyao* 唐會要 [Institutional History of Tang]. Beijing, 1981.
Wang, Shenrong 王慎榮, ed. *Yuanshi tanyuan* 元史探元 [The Sources of the *Yuan shi*]. Changchun, 1991.
Wang Deyi 王德毅 et al. *Yuan ren zhuanji ziliao suoyin* 元人傳記資料索引 [Index of Biographical Materials on Yuan Figures]. Taipei, 1979–1982. 5 vols.
Wang Jianxin. "Xiongnu and Yuezhi in the Eastern Tianshan Mountians." Paper presented at the International Conference on Xiongnu Archaeology. Ulaanbaatar, Mongolia, October 16–18, 2008.
Wang Li 王力. *Hanyu yuyin shi* 漢語語音史 [History of Chinese Pronunciation]. Beijing, 1985.
Wardwell, Anne, and James C. Y. Watt, with an essay by M. Rossabi. *When Silk Was Gold.* New York, 1997.
Watson, Burton. *Records of the Grand Historian of China: Han Dynasty II.* New York, 1993.
Watt, James C. Y., ed. *The World of Khubilai Khan: Chinese Art in the Yuan Dynasty.* New York, 2010.
Waṣṣāf, Shihāb al-Dīn. *Tārīkh-i Waṣṣāf.* Tehran, 1959.
———. *Taḥrīr-i tārīkh-i waṣṣāf.* Ed. ʿAbd Āl Muḥammad Āyatī. Tehran, 1993.
Weatherford, Jack. *Genghis Khan and the Making of the Modern World.* New York, 2004.

Wei, Liangtao 魏良弢. *Kalahan wang chao shi, Xi Liao shi* 喀喇汗王朝史, 西遼史 [A History of the Qarakhanids and the Western Liao]. Beijing, 2010.
Wei, Shou 魏收, comp. *Weishu* 魏書 [The Official History of the Wei]. In the collected edition of the Twenty-Four Histories (*Ershisi shi* 二十四史), vol. 5. Beijing, 1997.
Wei, Zheng 魏徵, comp. *Suishu* 隋書 [The Official History of the Sui]. In the collected edition of the Twenty-Four Histories (*Erhshisi shi* 二十四史), vol.7. Beijing, 1997.
Weidemann, Eilhard. "Ḳuṭb al-Dīn Shīrāzī." *Encyclopaedia of Islam,* 2nd ed. Leiden, 1954–2005, vol. 5, p. 547.
Weidner, Marsha. "Painting and Patronage at the Mongol Court of China, 1260–1368." PhD dissertation, University of California at Berkeley, 1982.
———. "Yüan Dynasty Court Collections of Chinese Paintings." *Central and Inner Asian Studies,* 2 (1988), pp. 10–22.
Weidner, Marsha, Ellen Johnston Laing, Irving Yucheng Lo, Christina Chu, and James Robinson. *Views from Jade Terrace: Chinese Women Artists, 1300–1912.* Indianapolis, 1988.
Weitz, Ankeney. "Art and Politics at the Mongol Court of China: Tugh Temur's Collection of Chinese Painting." *Artibus Asiae,* 64/2 (2004), pp. 243–280.
Wheatley, David, and Mark Gillings. *Spatial Technology and Archaeology: The Archaeological Applications of GIS.* London, 2002.
Whitehouse, David. *Roman Glass in the Corning Museum of Glass,* vol. 2. Corning, NY, 2001.
Whitley, Thomas G., and Lacey Hicks. "A Geographic Information Systems (GIS) Approach to Understanding Potential Prehistoric and Historic Travel Corridors." *Southeastern Archaeology,* 22/1 (2003), pp. 76–90.
Wickler, S. J., D. F. Hoyt, E. A. Cogger, and M. H. Hirschbein. "Preferred Speed and Cost of Transport: The Effect of Incline." *Journal of Experimental Biology,* 203 (2000), pp. 2195–2200.
Wilkinson, Endymion. *Chinese History: A Manual Revised and Enlarged.* Cambridge, 2000.
Williams, James. "The Tahilt Region: A Preliminary Archaeological Survey of the Tahilt Surroundings to Contextualize the Tahilt Cemeteries." *The Silk Road,* 5/2 (2008), pp. 42–47.
Wing, Patrick. "The Decline of the Ilkhanate and the Mamluk Sultanate's Eastern Frontier." *Mamluk Studies Review,* 11/2 (2007), pp. 77–88.
Wink, Andre. *Al-Hind: The Making of the Indo-Islamic World,* vol. 2. Leiden, 2002.
Wittfogel, Karl A., and Feng Chia-sheng. *History of Chinese Society, Liao (907–1125).* Philadelphia, 1949.
Wood, Frances. *The Silk Road: Two Thousand Years in the Heart of Asia.* Berkeley, 2002.
Wormald, Patrick. "James Campbell as Historian." In *The Medieval State, Essays Presented to James Campbell,* ed. J. R. Maddicott and D. M. Palliser. London, 2000, pp. xiii–xxii.
Wright, Arthur F., ed. *The Confucian Persuasion.* Stanford, 1960.
Wu, En 烏恩. "Yin zhi Zhouchu de beifang qingtongqi 殷至周初的北方青銅器 [Northern Bronzes from Yin to the Early Zhou]." *Kaogu Xuebao* 考古學報, 2 (1985), pp. 135–156.
———. "Lüelun Ouya caoyuan zaoqi youmu yishu zhong de juanqu dongwu xingxiang 略論歐亞草原早期游牧藝術中的卷曲動物形象 [On the Curved Animal Figure in the Art of Early Nomadic Tribes in the Eurasian Steppe]." *Kaogu* 考古, 11 (2002), pp. 60–68.

———. "Lun Zhongguo beifang zaoqi youmu ren qingong daishi de qiyuan 論中國北方早期游牧人情銅帶飾的起源 [On the Origins of Bronze Belt Hooks among the Nomadic People of North China]." *Wenwu* 文物, 6 (2002), pp. 68–77.
———. "Ouya dalu caoyuan zaoqi youmu wenhua de jidian sikao 歐亞大陸草原早期游牧文化的幾點思考 [Some Ideas on Early Nomadic Culture in the Eurasian Steppe]." *Kaogu Xuebao* 考古學報, 4 (2002), pp. 437–470.
———. *Beifang caoyuan kaoguxue wenhua bijiao yanjiu* 北方草原考古學文化比較研究 [A Comparative Study of Archaeological Cultures from the Northern Steppe]. Beijing, 2008.
Wu, Yugui 吳玉貴. *Tujue hanguo yu Sui Tang guanxi shi yanjiu* 突厥汗國與隋唐關係史研究 [Research on the Relations between the Turkic States and the Sui and Tang Dynasties]. Beijing, 1998.
Xia, Zhengnong 夏征 農, ed. *Cihai* 辭海 [Cihai Dictionary]. Shanghai, 1999.
Xinjiang Institute of Cultural Relics and Archaeology and the Research Center of Cultural Heritage and Archaeology, Northwest China. "The 2006–2007 Excavation on the Dongheigou Site in Barkol County, Xinjiang." *Kaogu* 考古, 1 (2009), pp. 3–27.
Xu, Yucai 許玉材. "Dandong diqu faxian Jinmo Yelü Liuge Da Liao zhengquan tong yin 丹東地區發現金末耶律留哥大遼政權銅印 [A Copper Seal of Yelü Liuge's Great Liao Regime from the End of Jin Dynasty, Found in Dandong Region]." *Wenwu* 文物5 (1985).
Yadin, Yigael. *The Art of Warfare in Biblical Lands: In the Light of Archaeological Study.* Jerusalem, 1963.
Yamada, Nubuo. "The Formation of the Hsiung-nu Nomadic State." *Acta Orientalia,* 36 (1982), pp. 575–582.
Yanai, Watari 箭内亙. *Yuan dai jing lue Dongbei kao* 元代經略東北考 [On Manchuria in the Yuan Dynasty]. Taipei, 1963.
———. *Yuan dai Meng Han Semu daiyu kao* 元代蒙漢色目待遇考 [The Status of the Mongol, Han and Semu populations in the Yuan dynasty]. Taipei, 1963.
Yang, Bin. "Horses, Silver, and Cowries: Yunnan in Global Perspective." *Journal of World History,* 15/3 (2004), pp. 281–322.
Yang, Jianhua 楊建華. "Yanshan nan bei Shang Zhou zhi ji qingtongqi yicun de fenqun yanjiu 燕山南北商周之際青銅器遺存的分群研究 [Classification of Bronze Objects Dated to the Shang-Zhou Transition Period from the Area North and South of the Yan Mountas]." *Kaogu Xuebao* 考古學報, 2 (2002), pp. 157–174.
Yang, Yu. *Beiträge zur kulturgeschichte China unter des Mongolenherrschaft: Das Shan-kü Sinhua das Yang Yü.* Tr. H. Franke. Wiesbaden, 1956.
Yao, Jing'an 姚景安. *Yuanshi ren ming suoyin* 元史人名索引 [Index of the Proper Names in the *Yuanshi*]. Beijing, 1982.
Yao, Sui 姚燧. *Mu'an ji* 牧庵集 [Yao Sui's Literary Collection]. Sibu Congkan ed.
Ye Peilan 葉佩蘭. *Yuandai ciqi* 元代瓷器 [Yuan Porcelain]. Beijing, 1998.
Yelü, Zhu 耶律鑄. *Shuangxi zuiyin ji* 雙溪醉隱集 [Yelü Zhu's Literary Collection]. Siku quanshu ed.
Yelü Chucai 耶律楚材. *Zhan ran jushi wenji* 湛然局士文集 [Yelü Chucai's Literary Collection]. Beijing, 1986.
Yerool-Erdene, Chimiddorj. "Khunnugiin yazguurtny orshuulgyn dursgalyn sudalgaa." PhD dissertation, National University of Mongolia, 2010.
Yu, Ji 虞集. *Daoyuan xue gu lu* 道園學古錄 [Yu Ji's Literary Collection]. Ed. Wanyou wenku. Shanghai, 1937.

Yu, Xilu 俞希魯, comp. *Zhishun Zhenjiang zhi* 至順鎮江志 [Gazetteer of Zhenjiang in the Zhishun period]. In *Song-Yuan difangzhi congkan* 宋元地方志叢書 [Collection of Song and Yuan Gazetteers], vol. 3. Taipei, 1980.

Yü, Ying-shih. *Trade and Expansion in Han China: A Study in the Structure of Sino-Barbarian Economic Relations*. Berkeley, 1967.

———. "The Hsiung-nu." In *The Cambridge History of Early Inner Asia*, ed. D. Sinor. Cambridge, 1990, pp. 118–149.

Yun, Hyeung-Won. "The' Xiongnu Tombs at Khudgiin Tolgoi in Mongolia." In *Current Archaeological Research in Mongolia: Proceedings of the August 2007 Archaeological Symposium in Ulaanbaatar, Mongolia*, ed. J. Bemmann, H. Parzinger, E. Pohl, and D. Tseveendorj. Bonn, 2009, pp. 281–299.

Zadneprovskii, Iu. A. "Rannie kochevniki Semirech'ia i Tian'-Shania [Early Nomads of Semrich'e and Tian Shan]." In *Stepnaia polosa Aziatskoi chasti SSSR v skifo-sarmatskoe vremia* [The Steppe Zone of the Asiatic Region of the USSR during the Scythian-Sarmatian Period], ed. N. G. Gorbunova. Moscow, 1992, pp. 73–87.

Zaitsev, Yuvenaly P. "Skilur and His Kingdom (New Discoveries and New Questions)." *Ancient Civilizations*, 7, 3–4 (2001), pp. 239–271.

Zaytsev, Viacheslav P. "Rukopisnaia kniga bolshogo kidanskogo nis'ma is kollektsii Instituta vostochnych rukopiseĭ RAN [A Manuscript Codex in the Kitan Large Script from the Collection of the Institute of Oriental Manuscripts, Russian Academy of Sciences]." *Pismennye pamiatniki Vostoka*, 2/15 (2011), pp. 130–150.

ZENO.RU—Oriental Coins Database. Online. http://www.zeno.ru/showgallery.php?cat=2690.

Zhang Qiyun 張其昀et al., eds. *Zhongwen Da Cidian* 中文大辭典 [Big Dictionary of Chinese Language]. Taipei, 1962–1968. 40 vols.

Zhang, Tingyu, comp. 張廷玉. *Ming shi* 明史 [The Official History of the Ming]. Beijing, 1974. 20 vols.

Zhang, Xuan 張鉉, comp. "Zhizheng Jinling xinzhi 至正金陵新志 [Gazetteer of Nanjing in the Zhizheng Period]." In *Song-Yuan difangzhi congshu* 宋元地方志叢書 [Collection of the Gazetteers of the Song and Yuan Dynasties], vol. 6. Taipei, 1980.

Zhangjiakou shi wenwu shiye guanlisuo 張家口市文物事業管理所 [Zhangjuakou City Institute for the Administration of Field Work and Cultural Relics]. "Hebei Xuanhua Xiang Xiaobaiyang mudi fajue baogao 河北宣化縣小白楊墓地發掘報 [Report on the Excavations at the Xiaobaiyang Cemetery, Xuanhua County, Hebei]." *Wenwu* 文物, 5 (1987), pp. 41–51.

Zhongguo shehui kexueyuan kaogu yanjiusuo 中國社會科學院考古研究所 [Institute of Archaeology, Chinese Academy of Social Sciences]. *Yinxu Fuhao mu* 殷墟婦好墓 [The Fuhao Grave of Yinxu]. Beijing, 1980.

———. *Dadianzi: Xiajiadian xiaceng wenhua yizhi yu mudi fajue baogao* 一大甸子夏家店下層文化遺址與墓地發掘報告 [Dadianzi: Excavations of a Domestic Site and Cemetery of the Lower Xiajiadian Period]. Beijing, 1996.

———. *Anyang Yinxu Huanyuanzhuang dongdi Shangdai muzhang*安阳殷墟花园庄东地商代墓葬 [Shang Period Graves from the Eastern Area of Huanyuanzhuang, Yinxu, Anyang]. Beijing, 2002.

Zhou, Qingshu 周清澍. "Yuan Huanzhou Yelü Jiazu Shishi Huizheng yu Qidanren de Nanqian 元桓州耶律家族史事彙證與契丹人的南遷 [Study on the Historical Records on the Yelü Family of Huanzhou and the Migration of the Kitans to the South]." In *Mengyuan de lishi yu wenhua II*, 蒙元的歷史於文化 （下）[The History and Culture of the Yuan Mongols, Part II]. Taipei, 2001, vol. 2, pp. 501–540.

Zhou Mi. *Records of Clouds and Mist Passing Before One's Eyes.* Tr. Ankeney Weitz. Leiden, 2002.

Ziadeh, Nicola A. *Urban Life in Syria under the Early Mamluks.* Beirut, 1953.

Zimin, Aleksandr A. "Narodnye dvizheniia 20-kh godov XIV veka i likvidatsiia sistemy baskachestva v Severo-vostochnoi Rusi [Population Movements of the 1320s and the Cancellation of the *baskachestvo* in Northeastern Rus]." *Izvestiia Akademii nauk SSSR (Seriia istorii i filosofii),* 9/2 (1952), pp. 61–65.

Contributors

Thomas T. Allsen specializes in the role of steppe peoples in Eurasian cultural exchange. His latest book is *The Royal Hunt in Eurasian History* (University of Pennsylvania Press, 2006).

Reuven Amitai is Eliyahu Elath Professor for Muslim History at the Hebrew University of Jerusalem. He is the author of *Mongols and Mamluks: The Mamluk-Ilkhanid War, 1260–1281* (Cambridge University Press, 1995); *The Mongols in the Islamic Lands: Studies in the History of the Ilkhanate* (Ashgate, 2007); *Holy War and Rapprochement: Studies in the Relations between the Mamluk Sultanate and the Mongol Ilkhanate* (Brepols, 2013), and has coedited several volumes of collected studies.

Michal Biran is the Max and Sophie Mydans Foundation Professor in the Humanities at the Hebrew University of Jerusalem, and a historian of Inner Asia. Her books include *Qaidu and the Rise of the Independent Mongol State in Central Asia* (Curzon, 1997); *The Empire of the Qara Khitai in Eurasian History: Between China and the Islamic World* (Cambridge University Press, 2005, 2008); and *Chinggis Khan* (OneWorld Publications, 2007).

William Honeychurch is an anthropologist at Yale University and specializes in the archaeology of Inner Asia, complex societies, and interregional interaction. He has worked in Mongolia since 1991 and focuses on nomadic states and empires. His field projects in the Mongolian Gobi and forest steppe have emphasized regional survey, seasonal campsite excavation, and mortuary archaeology to better understand the foundations of pastoral nomadic organization and politics.

Anatoly M. Khazanov, FBA, is Ernest Gellner Professor of Anthropology at the University of Wisconsin–Madison. He is an author of about two hundred articles and six monographs, including *The Social History of the*

Scythians (Nauka, 1975) and *Nomads and the Outside World* (2nd ed., University of Wisconsin Press, 1994).

George Lane has been based at SOAS, the University of London, since being awarded his PhD in 2001. His first book, *Early Mongol Rule in 13th Century Iran,* appeared in 2003 followed by *Genghis Khan and Mongol Rule* (Routledge, 2004) and *Daily Life in the Mongol Empire* (Greenwood Press, 2006). He is currently preparing two books for publication, *The Mongols* and *The Persian Community of Mediaeval Hangzhou.*

David Morgan is Emeritus Professor of History and Religious Studies at the University of Wisconsin–Madison. His books include *The Mongols* (2nd ed., Blackwell, 2007). He is joint editor of *The New Cambridge History of Islam,* vol. 3 (Cambridge University Press, 2010).

Morris Rossabi teaches Chinese and Mongolian history at the City University of New York and Columbia University. Author of *Khubilai Khan* (University of California Press, 1988); *Voyager from Xanadu* (Kodansha America, 1992); *Modern Mongolia* (University of California Press, 2005); *The Mongols: A Very Short Introduction* (Oxford University Press, 2012); *A History of China* (Blackwell, 2013), and other books and articles, he has collaborated on exhibitions at the Metropolitan Museum of Art, Cleveland Museum of Art, and the Asian Art Museum.

Gideon Shelach-Lavi is the Louis Freiberg Professor of East Asian Studies at the Hebrew University of Jerusalem. Since 1995 he has been conducting archaeological fieldwork in Northeast China and is currently heading the Fuxin Regional Archaeological Project, in Liaoning province. Among his recent books are: *Prehistoric Societies on the Northern Frontiers of China: Archaeological Perspectives on Identity Formation and Economic Change during the First Millennium BCE* (Equinox, 2009); *Chifeng International Collaborative Archaeological Project* (coauthor, University of Pittsburgh Press, 2011); and *The Birth of Empire: The State of Qin Revisited* (coeditor, University of California Press, 2013).

İsenbike Togan is professor of Inner Asian Studies and Chinese History at Boğaziçi University and an honorary member of the Turkish Academy of Sciences. She specializes in tribe state relations, historiography, Sufism, and women in the early modern period, and is the author of *Flexibility and Limitation in Steppe Formations: The Kerait Khanate and Chinggis Khan* (Brill, 1998), as well as various articles on the above subjects. She is also the translator of the chapter on the Early Türk in the *Jiu Tangshu* into Turkish (*Eski Tang Tarihi*. Ankara: Türk Tarih Kurumu Yayınları, 2006).

István Vásáry is professor of Turkic and Central Asian Studies at the ELTE University of Budapest and corresponding member of the Hungarian Academy of Sciences. He is author of *The Golden Horde* (Kossuth, 1986), *Chancellery of the Golden Horde* (Korosi Csoma Tarsasag, 1987), *A History of Ancient Inner Asia* (Balassi Kiadó, 2003) (all three in Hungarian); *Cumans and Tatars: Oriental Military in the Pre-Ottoman Balkans, 1185–1365* (Cambridge University Press, 2005); *Turks, Tatars and Russians in the 13th–16th Centuries* (Ashgate, 2007); and more than 170 articles published in international and Hungarian periodicals.

Index

Entries are alphabetized word-by-word following the style used in the Bibliography. Page numbers in boldface type refer to illustrations.

Hülegü (Ilkhan), 120, 123, 128, 130, 136, 162, 182–186, 188, 192–193, 195, 201, 204–205, 208, 229–232, 239, 243
Hungary, Hungarians, 124–125, 139
Huns, 133, 273

Ialoman, 66
iarlyk, 262
Ibn al-ʿArabī, 200
Ibn al-Fuwaṭī, 207
Ibn al-Ṭiqṭaqā, 193
Ibn Bībī, 186
Ibn Dāniyāl, 236
Ibn Faḍl Allāh al-ʿUmarī, 242
Ibn Maḥmūd Uzjandī, 185
Ibn Shaddād al-Ḥalabī, 234, 236
Ibn Ṭāwūs, 184
Ibn Taymiyya, 235–236, 243
Ibn Wasil, 232
identity, 5, 6, 7, 24, 122, 142, 143, 152, 159, 193, 206, 207; change, 6, 158–159, 164–168; indigenous, 5; Kitan, 156, 158, 161, 152–172 *passim;* nomadic, 5, 152, 157; shift, 142
Iftikhāriyāns, Iftikhār al-Dīn Muḥammad, 188, 189, 192–193
Ikhtiyār al-Dīn, 187
Ilkhans, 125, 128, 184, 188, 192, 194, 229, 240; Ilkhanate, 7, 129, 131, 135, 158, 161, 176n.43, 182–183, 195, 205–208, 222, 238, 242, 244n.5. *See also* according to individual Ilkhans
Imām al-Dīn Yaḥyā, 189, 192–193. *See also* Iftikhāriyāns, Iftikhār al-Dīn Muḥammad
imperial portraits, 221
India, 6, 31n.54, 51, 75, 125–126, 128, 131, 138–139, 195, 276, 280; Indians, 42, 133, 138, 199, 222
Indus Valley, 75
Inner Asia, 2, 5–6, 8, 33, 45n.5, 50, 52–53, 55, 75, 88–89, 108, 111n.30, 129, 136, 138, 153, 254
Inner Mongolia, 16, 21, 52, 56, 59, 61, 162–164, 166
interaction, interregional, 26, 60, 77; intersocietal, 10, 13
Iran, 4–8, 109n.5, 120, 125–128, 131, 135, 153, 161, 180n.82, 182–209, 216, 221–222, 229, 231, 256, 260, 275–280; art, 8; clients of Chinese pottery, 217; conquest of, 182–183; Mongols in, 5, 7, 180n.82, 182–209; notables of, 184–188, 195, 207–208. *See also* elite, Iranian; Ilkhans
Iraq, 233, 234, 242
Islam, 3, 7, 37, 111n.30, 127, 141–143, 161, 183, 197, 20, 207, 231, 235, 260
Islamization, 240, 243, 249n.51; conversion to, 161, 200, 235
Ismāʿīlīs, 183–184, 190

Jackson, Peter, 229, 278–280
Jalāl al-Dīn Mingbarnī, Khwārazm Shāh, 189
al-Jazarī, 243
Jazira, 230, 233, 234, 235, 236, 242
Jerusalem, 241, 246n.28
Jews, 203, 232; Jewish, 155, 197, 202–204
Jiangnan, 163, 168
Jiangxi, 163
jihād, 240, 243
Jin dynasty r. 265–419, 99; r. 1115–1234, 122, 127, 135, 154–169
Jin Shizong, 155
Jingdezhen, 216–217
Jinshu, 99
Jiu Tangshu, 89, 91–93, 98, 101–108
Jochids, 188, 208. *See also* Golden Horde
Jurchens, 121, 154–157, 166–167, 169, 174n.20, 176n.39
Juwaynī(s), 186, 188, 190–191, 196
Juwaynī, ʿAṭā Malik, 183, 185–186, 190, 200
Juwaynī, Majd al-Dīn Muḥammad, 186
Juwaynī, Ṣadr al-Dīn Ibrāhīm Ḥamūya, 200
Juwaynī, Shams al-Dīn, 190–192, 194, 196, 201, 207

kabala, 261–262
kaghan. *See* qa'an, qaghan
Kaifeng, 157, 162
Kamenskoe, 40
Kaplonski, C., 233
Karak, 230, 237
Karasuk, 16–17, 21, 29n.33
Karts, 188–189, 205; Ghiyāth al-Dīn Kart, 201; Rukn al-Dīn Khaysārī Kart, 189; Shams al-Dīn Muḥammad Kart, 189
Kazakhs, 140, 152, 176n.43
Kazakhstan, 15, 16, 52, 55, 59, 70, 72, 74, 120
Kazan, 264, 265; Russian conquest of, 253, 257, 270n.59
Kennedy, Hugh, 273
kesi (silk tapestry with cut design), 221
Khalaj, 139
Khalkha Mongols, 89
al-Khānbāliqī, Muḥammad ibn Arslān, 188
khaqan. *See* qa'an
Khazar, 38
Khidr al-Mihrānī, 241

Khitans. *See* Kitan(s)
Khoy/Khūy, 131
Khurasan, 125, 127, 128, 135, 196–198, 205
Khwāndamīr, 201, 203
Khwārazm/Khwārazmian: artisans, 131, 188; brigands, 184; state, 124, 126, 135, 158, 164, 169, 177n.51, 187
Khwārazm-shāh, 125, 186, 187, 189, 196. *See also* ʿAlāʾ al-Dīn Muḥammad Khwārazm-shāh; Jalāl al-Dīn Mingbarnī, Khwārazm Shāh
Kiev, 41
kinship groups: *bod* (Turkic), 90, 101–106, 116nn.101, 104, 107; *boy* (Turkish), 102, 103, 106, 109n.10, 113n.50, 116n.107; *bu* (Chinese), 90, 91, 94–97, 99–102, 105–107, 111n.33, 112n.38, 113nn.50, 67, 114n.69; *omogh, obogh* (Mongolian), 97; *Stämme*, 89, 105, 115n.87, 117; *xing* (Chinese), 90; *zu* (Chinese), 90. *See also* non-kinship groups
Kirmān, 161, 176n.43, 205–206
Kitan(s), 38, 133, 152–172, 187, 254, 256; artisans, 130; assimilation, 159, 167–172; conquest of, 157; in China, 7, 152–172 *passim*; in Iran, 161, 172; language; 153, 156; names, 158; rule, 154, 155; script, 153, 156. *See also* China, Kitans in; elite, Kitan; identity, Kitan
Kitbuqa, 231
Komaroff, Linda, 276–277
Koreans/Korea, 121, 160, 162, 222
Kurds, 123, 234, 239
kurgan(s), 35, 39, 43
Kyrgyz, 103, 105, 120, 130, 155

lacquerware, 57, 60–66, 69, 73, 74
LA-ICP-MS, 71
Lambton, A.K.S., 279
Lane, George, 5, 276
Lee, Sherman, 215
legitimation, legitimacy, 4–6, 72, 76, 95, 153, 155, 172, 184, 208, 226n.26, 263
el-Leithy, Tamer, 241
Levant, 240
levirate marriages, 169, 180n.82
Lewis, C. S., 280
Li Kan, 219
Li Tan, 168, 179n.77
Liao dynasty, 4, 102, 133, 153–156, 159–160, 164, 170; legacy, 157; terminology, 95, 96
Liao River, 153, 156
Liddell Hart, Sir Basil, 272
lifestyle, nomadic, 10, 33, 37, 153, 157, 215; sedentary, 13
Liji, 11
Liu Guandao, 219
Liu Ji, 170
logistics, 230
long-distance contacts, 13, 15, 25, 55, 74
Longquan, 216, 224n.11
Los Angeles County Museum of Art, 214, 276
luo (small settlements), 91, 95, 99–101, 113nn.50, 67, 114n.69
Luz, N. 240

Macedonia, 43, 125
madrasa, 241
Maeotae, 35
Mamluk Sultanate (1250–1517), 6, 7, 126, 127, 139, 176n.43, 228, 228–251; in ʿAyn Jālūt, 232; elite, 230–233, 240; establishment, 241; Mamluk-Mongol war, 234; politics, 138; rule, 231, 236–239, 243; society, 235. *See also* Syria, under the Mamluks
Manchuria, 4, 56, 121, 133, 153–154, 159–162, 166, 172
al-Manṣūr Muḥammad, 234
manuscripts, illustrated, 215, 217, 222
Manz, Beatrice, 274
Maodun, 56
material culture, 14, 59, 60, 69, 72–73, 76–77, 137; nomadic, 4, 33, 153
May, T., 229
Mayyafariqin, 233
Medians, 35
Mediterranean, 7, 39, 42, 44, 64, 66–71, 75, 128, 136, 139
Melville, Charles, 276
Mengü Temür (Ilkhanid Prince), 230
Metropolitan Museum of Art, 214, 220–221, 276
Middle East, 162. *See also* Near East
migration, 33, 37, 76, 96, 119, 215; caused by Mongols, 129, 130, 142, 143, 163, 233; Great Migration of Peoples, 44; Kitan, 163, 176n.43; Muslims', 126; Qiphchaq, 124–126, 128, 138
military colonies, 122, 144n.10
Ming dynasty (1368–1644), 6, 122, 132, 135, 140, 142, 187, 216–217; sources, 170
Ministry of Works, 187, 219, 221
Minusinsk Basin, 21, 29n.33, 73
mobility 54, 74, 94, 126; impact on demography, 243; patterns of, 5, 52, 162; social, 218
Modun/Modu. *See* Maodun
Möngke, 122, 130–132, 162, 166, 171, 182, 183, 188, 189, 192–193, 208, 209n.2

Polo, Marco, 128, 141, 279
Polovetsy. *See* Qipchaq
Pontic Steppes, 36, 46n.21
Pope, A. U., 276
porcelain, Chinese, 214–218
poruka, 260, 262, 268n.41. See also *pravezh*
postal relay service, 6, 219, 258
postal system, 237. See also *barīd*
pravezh, 261, 262. See also *poruka*
Prawdin, Michael, 272
prestige goods, 54, 71, 73–74, 76–77
put', 258
Puzi county, 99

qa'an, 6, 189, 192, 201; Great Khan, 6, 165, 186, 187, 192, 223, 230; kaghan, 6; qaghan, 6, 98, 102–107, 110n.25, 115n.90. *See also* Qaghans, Turkic
Qadan, Hadan, 163
Qaghans, Turkic: Bilge Qaghan, 107, 108; Derish Qaghan, 101n.25; Elig Qaghan, 98, 102, 106, 107; death (636), 105; İlteriš Qaghan, 104; Ishbara Qaghan, 98; Kapgan Qaghan, 104; Shibi Qaghan, 98; submission to China (630), 105; Tuli Qaghan, 106
Qalandar(s), 195, 198, 199
Qanglis, 122, 123, 126, 140; Qangli Guard, 139
Qara Khitai, 154–161, 162, 173n.6, 174n.20, 176n.43, 185, 206, 254, 255, 266n.8, 278. *See also* Western Liao dynasty
Qara Khitai of Kirmān, 161, 162, 205, 206. *See also* Padshāh Khātūn; Qutlugh Khans; Terkan Khātūn
Qara'unas/Negüderis, 128, 129, 205
Qarachai-Balqars, 141
Qaraqorum, 120, 166, 182
Qarluq, 177n.49, 182
qayachi, 123
Qazwin, 182–193
Qazwīnī(s), 188, 194, 202, 208, 209n.2; notables, 190, 192
Qi county, 99
Qijia culture, 26
Qing dynasty, 121, 132, 142; political culture, 6
Qipchaq, 121–128, 133, 139–141, 152, 158, 169, 182; khanate, 208; migration, 138; tribes, 3, 176n.43; Qipchaq Guard, 121, 122
Qonggirad, 96, 112n.43, 163, 165
Qubilai Khan, 122–123, 140–142, 162, 165–169, 177n.55, 180n.81, 187, 208, 219–223
Quinsai. *See* Hangzhou (Quinsai)
Qus, 241
Quṭb al-Dīn Maḥmūd ibn Mas'ūd Shīrāzī, 242
Qutlugh Khans, 194, 203, 206. *See also* Qara Khitai of Kirmān
Qutuz, 229, 240

Raḍī al-Dīn Bābā, 194
al-Raḥba, 237
Rashīd al-Dīn, 131, 141, 157, 161, 173n.6, 174n.23, 177n.49, 190–194, 203, 236, 277, 279
recluses in Yuan, 215, 218
redistribution, 3
refugees, 124, 127, 135, 139, 143, 146n.41, 162, 230, 233–236, 239, 242, 246n.28, 247n.33
religion, 41, 192, 197, 199; nomads attitude toward, 3–5; transmission of, 50; tribal, 160; world, 37. *See also* Buddhism; Christian, Christians; Islam; Shamans
Ren Renfa, 220
ribbon mosaic, 68–69
Rome, Roman(s), 66; artifacts, 67–70; connections with China, 7; elite, 138; Roman Empire, 94; "Third Rome" theory, 265; trade, 64
Rossabi, Morris, 5, 7, 276
Rubruck, William of, 125, 132, 145n.31, 280
Rukn al-Dīn Ṣā'in, 189, 196, 200
Rūmī, Jalāl al-Dīn, 184, 195
Rus principalities, 252, 254–259, 263, 267n.29, 127
Russian, 252, 257, 260; art, 215; expedition, 60; historiography, 253; Russian Guard, 121, 139; -Tartar contacts, 252, 258–259, 263; traders and trade, 42. *See also* China, Russians in; Quipchaq, Qipchaq Guard; Qanglis, Qangli Guard

Sa'd al-Dawla Yahūdī, 191, 197, 202–204
Sa'd al-Dīn Muẓaffar, 191, 192
Sa'dī, 186, 195
Ṣadr al-Dīn Akhfāsh, 198
Safad, 236
Safawids, 4, 200
Ṣāliḥiyya (suburb of Damascus), 237
Samarqand, 57, 130–135, 163, 164
Sanxingdui, 25, 28n.17, 31n.54
Sa-skya Pandita, 222
satyr, 64, 65, **66**
Saunders, J. J., 274
Sāwajī, 194
Saxons, 132
Sayyid 'Ajall 'Umar al-Bukhārī, 183, 188
Scythian animal style, 41. *See also* animal style